PENGUIN BOOKS

The Letters of Evelyn Waugh

Evelyn Waugh was born in Hampstead in 1903, second son of the late
Arthur Waugh, publisher and literary critic, and brother of Alec Waugh,
the popular novelist. He was educated at Lancing and Hertford College,
Oxford, where he read Modern History. In 1927 he published his first
work, a life of Dante Gabriel Rossetti, and in 1928 his first novel, *Decline
and Fall,* which was soon followed by *Vile Bodies* (1930), *Black Mischief*
(1932), *A Handful of Dust* (1934), and *Scoop* (1938). During these years he
travelled extensively in most parts of Europe, the Near East, Africa, and
tropical America. In 1939 he was commissioned in the Royal Marines
and later transferred to the Royal Horse Guards, serving in the Middle
East and in Yugoslavia. In 1942 he published *Put Out More Flags* and then
in 1945 *Brideshead Revisited. When the Going was Good* and *The Loved One*
were followed by *Helena* (1950), his historical novel, *Men at Arms,* which
came out in 1952, is the first volume in a trilogy of war memoirs, and won
the James Tait Black Prize; the other volumes, *Officers and Gentlemen* and
Unconditional Surrender, were published in 1955 and 1961. Evelyn Waugh
was received into the Roman Catholic Church in 1930, and his earlier
biography of the Elizabethan Jesuit martyr, *Edmund Campion,* was
awarded the Hawthornden Prize in 1936. In 1959 he published the official
Life of Ronald Knox. He was married and had six children. From 1937
onwards he and his family lived in the West Country. He died in 1966.

Mark Amory, who is still a close friend of Evelyn Waugh's family, is a
well-known author and journalist. His biography of Lord Dunsany
appeared in 1972.

The Letters of Evelyn Waugh

Edited by Mark Amory

Penguin Books

Penguin Books Ltd, Harmondsworth, Middlesex, England
Penguin Books, 625 Madison Avenue, New York, New York 10022, U.S.A.
Penguin Books Australia Ltd, Ringwood, Victoria, Australia
Penguin Books Canada Ltd, 2801 John Street, Markham, Ontario, Canada L3R 1B4
Penguin Books (N.Z.) Ltd, 182-190 Wairau Road, Auckland 10, New Zealand

First published in Great Britain by Weidenfeld & Nicolson Ltd 1980
First published in the United States of America by Ticknor & Fields 1980
Published in Penguin Books 1982

Made and printed in Great Britain by
Hazell, Watson & Viney Ltd, Aylesbury, Bucks
Set in Ehrhardt

Contents

Preface

The art of writing letters has been pronounced dead as often as the novel and with more reason. So perhaps Evelyn Waugh will turn out – through a combination of talent, temperament and circumstance – to have been one of its last great practitioners. The telephone is rightly seen as the main enemy; the collected private recordings of eminent figures may soon be with us. Waugh was born late enough (1903) for his contemporaries to prefer that instrument, but he never cared for it himself and had a sufficiently fierce character to prevent others from so approaching him. If someone rang up about a matter of interest, he was asked to write. This attitude was sustained right up to Waugh's death in 1966.

Letters require leisure for composition, something to impart and a sympathetic reader; Waugh's life of intense but interrupted social activity provided all three, though not immediately. Almost nothing survives from his childhood, and from Oxford he wrote only to a few school friends. In the 1920s, except when in exile as a schoolmaster, he saw people often enough not to write. However, after his marriage in 1928 and its breakdown in 1929 he travelled virtually every year, creating ideal writing conditions of adventure, boredom and idleness. During the war he wrote almost exclusively to Laura Herbert, his second wife, revealing their relationship in a light that, if not precisely new, seems to me to have been often underemphasized and misunderstood. Their family life in the country, interspersed with 'raids' on London, again put the necessary distance between him and his correspondents while at the same time supplying material. Nancy Mitford's removal to Paris gave him the perfect recipient – an intimate, witty friend, totally removed from, but interested in, every detail of life in London. He wrote more and funnier letters in the 1950s than in any other decade.

Other factors increase the flow and the imbalance. Waugh maintained a continuous dialogue with A.D. Peters, his agent, and later with John MacDougall, his publisher. After he became famous, his letters were more likely to be kept. Naturally the proportion of destruction and loss increases with time, and World War II is a watershed, not so much because of destruction by bombs as because people moved and were careless of the trunk in the attic. Finally, Waugh died young himself; most of his contemporaries survived him and so retained papers that might have been thrown away at their own death. Of those that predeceased Waugh the most difficult to track down were Roman Catholic priests and homosexuals, due to the lack of obvious heirs.

I think Waugh foresaw that his letters would be collected, whereas I do not think that he foresaw the publication of his diaries. He asks Nancy Mitford to destroy something unkind he has written, saying, 'I believe you keep my letters', with no hint of reproach or trepidation. He certainly kept hers and most other personal ones in brown envelopes with the names of the writers on the outside, and constant notes to himself to preserve only interesting letters in future. When he hears that universities are willing to pay good money for this stock, he expresses relief that there is another bulwark against poverty in old age, though he never sold anything and appears disapproving when he thinks Cyril Connolly may be doing so. But, if he was aware that the world might some day see what he wrote for private reading, no hint of piety or self-consciousness, let alone fine writing, results.

When I inquired if his handwriting was hard to read, as I had noticed that a word here and there in the diaries had proved indecipherable, I was reassured: 'No, no, you see he wrote his letters in the morning, when he was sober. He wrote his diary at night when he was drunk.' However unfair this may be as a description of Waugh's evening condition, it does reflect a difference in tone. A diarist, after all, is writing for himself a record or reminder, and self-indulgence is natural, almost necessary. Letters are to please or inform. Waugh scarcely mentions politics, and writing is discussed only with a select number of other novelists, in particular Henry Green, Anthony Powell and Graham Greene; even then he is more likely to comment on their books than on his own. Religion is frequently brought up and with several of his close friends at some moment seriously urged upon them. John Betjeman receives the most sustained barrage of argument, but Waugh speaks of prayer or death to Ann Fleming, Lady Diana Cooper, Nancy Mitford and the Countess of Avon among others. But the bulk of the letters are designed to amuse; even business notes have jokes thrown in. I do not see it as part of an editor's job to assess how seriously a remark is intended and, indeed, with Waugh it seems to me an impossible task. His familiar gift of acute observation elegantly and precisely described is allied to a love of exaggeration that frequently takes off into fantasy. Here let me issue a warning that I fear will be ignored: Waugh enlarges and distorts more than I could teach myself to expect. Somewhere there is usually a molehill from which he fashions his mountain of embellishment and I am easier in my mind when I have discovered it. For example, if he says that Peter Quennell has collapsed from sexual excess and it transpires that in fact Quennell had a hangover that morning, I am confident the whole truth is known. I do see it as part of an editor's job to correct errors of fact and sometimes I have done so. This is emphatically not meant to imply that, where there is no comment, Waugh is necessarily entirely accurate. Silence may mean ignorance, not consent, or sometimes that laborious explanation would smother a harmless joke.

Inevitably a portrait of Waugh emerges. He has already been the subject of a volume of autobiography, a biography, the diaries, a collection of essays, and several critical studies and television programmes, as well as countless reviews and profiles. More are to follow. I shall not add comment on Waugh's character except to say that in my opinion this version shows him to his best advantage so far. In selecting 840 letters from perhaps 4,500, I have chosen what I found interesting or funny. I have made no attempt to suppress anything that reflected unfavourably on Waugh or anyone else, nor to show him in a sympathetic light. When Waugh is generous with money, it is included because it is an unfamiliar aspect; on the other hand, several instances of the trouble he took reading and commenting on the manuscripts of unknown writers have been left out as repetitious.

This is not a biography, so there is no attempt to cover everything. If important events in Waugh's life are mentioned in dull letters, those letters have been omitted. (There is a special case when a routine business note is included because it was written in the midst of his Gilbert Pinfold hallucination. The letter is not particularly interesting, but the fact that he could write it *is*.) There is no attempt at balance – either in reflecting the number of letters he wrote in any period or the people to whom he wrote them. If there are two accounts of the same event, the more enjoyable version wins. This has meant that some people are constantly elbowed aside. Letters to his mother, for example, are several times supplanted by livelier, more detailed accounts to his friends. Quirks of taste intrude. Perhaps others are less interested than I in suggested titles and abortive projects. Laura Waugh wrote few letters, so those to the children at school are by Evelyn. Is the resulting picture of family life made more vivid by acquaintance with the children? Over a thousand letters to A.D. Peters have been rejected; do the remainder convey the relationship? A large problem has been the recent publication of Waugh's diaries. The subject matter inevitably overlaps, though less than I at first feared; when he is writing most letters, he tends to skimp his diary. Broadly, schooldays are thoroughly covered there, almost unmentioned here; by 1948 the diaries were seven-eighths over, whereas a great number of the best letters were yet to come. Nevertheless, much appears in both. I have taken the view that this is no reason to leave something out – and then not quite stuck to my decision. In some cases where a letter adds nothing at all to the already published version and is not of major importance, I have let that sway me.

The lawyer pointed out over 150 potentially libellous passages. It is impossible to say precisely how many of these were cut for that reason alone; my estimate is around 50. I have cut one story that was false, but possibly not libellous. Deciding what would cause unacceptable pain or embarrassment can only be a matter of personal judgement, but I have taken the harsh view that the feelings of children must be largely ignored; they must learn to live with the behaviour of their parents. Two bargains were struck: so one expulsion from school and one rumoured passion remain unmentioned. In spite of all this, the overwhelming majority of cuts have been made to avoid repetition and such trivial topics as which train to catch.

The technicalities of presentation largely follow convention. Every intrusion into the text by me is enclosed in square brackets [ ], except for 'Postcard' and excisions which are only marked with the simple . . . , as Waugh himself uses this form rarely. His spelling is poor and has been silently corrected, except where he draws attention to it or where a name is immediately corrected in a footnote. Punctuation has also been silently supplied where necessary, but mannerisms, such as a full stop instead of a question mark and the eccentric use of hyphens and capital letters, have been retained. Dates are usually on the right in the original and vary in style. They have been shifted to the left and made uniform. Postscripts, often at the head of a letter when there was no room, have been placed at the end. When there was a postmark, I have assumed that the letter was written the day it was posted, unless there is evidence to the contrary. My troubles with dating are visible in a scattering of question marks against the day, month or sometimes even year about which I am not confident. In the few cases where Waugh typed, this is noted, as it also is when I have not seen the original or a photocopy. Letters to newspapers and magazines remain as they appeared. Footnotes are not aimed at the expert but at a younger generation, possibly of foreigners; where page numbers are given, they refer to the first British edition. Very few have been deemed so celebrated as to need no comment; silence is once again more likely to imply ignorance. I have tried to supply dates, occupation, the connection with Waugh (if unexplained) and a phrase of description from him or one of his circle if it seems helpful. Not all marriages are mentioned; there are more of women than of men, not because I think their sex good for nothing else, but because the change of name is essential for identification.

I should like to thank the Waugh family, often personified by Auberon Waugh, for help and support of every kind and for rarely suggesting discretion. Otherwise I am grateful in varying degrees to everyone who answered my letters; if that sounds grudging I must stress that I am *extremely* grateful to many of them and disappointed only by a tiny handful. It seems right and perhaps useful to mention all those who were kind enough to send me letters, even though some have naturally had to be omitted: Father Charles Acton for letters to Lady Acton; Sir Harold Acton; Professor Robin Anderson; Katharine Asquith; The Countess of Avon; the late Earl Baldwin of Bewdley; John Barr; Patricia Cowan for letters to Mother Bede; Eva Reichman for letters to Sir Max Beerbohm; Lady Betjeman; The Countess of Birkenhead for letters to the late Lord Birkenhead; Madame Jacques Bisch (Edith de Born); John Sparrow for letters to himself and to Sir Maurice Bowra; Bruce Hunter for letters to Lord Bradwell; Neville Braybrooke; Mother Bridget of St Mary's Convent, Ascot, for letters to herself, Mother Ignatius and Mother Mercedes; William F. Buckley, Junior; Noel Burditt; Robin Campbell; Lady Campbell-Orde; Father Philip Caraman; Dudley Carew; Lord David Cecil; Edwin Chapman-Andrews; Winston Churchill for letters to Randolph Churchill; Marjorie Somers Cocks for letters to John Somers Cocks; Deirdre Levi for letters to Cyril Connolly; Bruce Cooper; Lady Diana Cooper; Anthony Curtis; Diana Cuthbert; Basil Davidson; The Duchess of Devonshire for letters to herself and to Nancy Mitford; Lord and Lady Donaldson; Paul Doyle; John Duggan for letters to Alfred Duggan; Richard Eurich; Daphne Fielding; Gabriel Fielding; Margaret FitzHerbert; Colonel Brian Franks; Anne Fremantle; Roger Fulford; Thomas Gadd; Milton Gendel for letters to Judy Montagu; Sir Ian Gilmour; Graham Greene; Sir Rupert Hart-Davis; Veronica Gosling for letters to Robert Henriques; Harman Grisewood; Jonathan Guinness; Agnes Holmes; Patrick Hunter; Lady Hutchinson; Reginald Jennings; John Jolliffe; František Jungwirth; Susan Kennaway for letters to James Kennaway; Terence Kilmartin; Richard Kingzett of

Thomas Agnew & Sons; Ludovic Kennedy; the late Lord Kinross; Penelope Fitzgerald for a letter to E.V.Knox; Lady Pansy Lamb; Angela Laycock for letters to herself and Brigadier Laycock; James Leasor; Magnus Linklater for letters to Eric Linklater; Mary Wall of Little, Brown & Company for letters to Mr Kanon; The Countess of Longford; Peter Lunn; Lady Mary Lygon; Father P.MacCaffrey; Anne H.McCormick for a postcard to Thomas Merton; May MacDougall for letters to John MacDougall; Ian A.McKee of Methuen; Ruth McQuillan; Sir Philip Magnus-Allcroft; Olivia Manning; Frank Martin; Tom Maschler; Lady Mosley; Sir Arthur Norrington; Michael Oakley; Sonia Orwell for letters to George Orwell; John Osborne for a letter to John Betjeman; The Earl of Oxford and Asquith for letters to himself and Raymond Asquith; Gaston Palewski; The Reverend Peter Phillips; David Pryce-Jones; Daphne Pollen for letters to herself and to Arthur Pollen; Anthony Powell; J.F.Powers; Cyril Ray; Dame Flora Robson; Lady Sibell Rowley; Joan Saunders; Edward Sheehan; Muriel Spark; James Stern; Reynolds Stone; Warren Pollock for a letter to Peter Stucley; Walter Taplin; Dr R.E.S.Tanner; A.J.P.Taylor; Crispin Tickell; the late Lady Walston; Elizabeth Wansborough; Magdalen Goffin for letters to Father Aelred Watkin; Alec Waugh; Auberon Waugh; Harriet Waugh; Dom Hubert van Zeller; Mrs Weston Vernon for letters to P.G.Wodehouse; Vincent Whelan; Angus Wilson; Douglas Woodruff for letters to himself and to Mia Woodruff; Sebastian Yorke for letters to Henry Yorke.

Many others searched diligently but unsuccessfully; again it was a small proportion who could not be bothered to look in the attic. Among those who had no letters but gave me their time and knowledge were: Lady Agnew; John Albert; David Astor; Sir Alfred Ayer; the Earl Baldwin; Neil Balfour; Mrs M.J.Baylis; Sybille Bedford; Lord Blake; Lord Boothby; Viscountess Boyd; Viscountess Boyne; Alan Brien; Tom Burns; Christopher Chamberlin; Lady Mary Clive; Peter Coate; Catherine Corbett; Virginia Crawley; Andrew Croft; Teresa Cuthbertson; Bill and Annie Davis; Professor Robert Murray Davis; Lord Derwent; Paul Doyle; Lady Mary Dunn; Thomas Dunne; Jeremy Elwes; Peter Elwes; Lavinia Fleming; Gerrardine Fletcher; J.H.Flynn; Alastair Forbes; Sir John Foster; Viscountess Gage; Donat Gallagher; Barbara Ghika; Val Gielgud; Sir Alexander Glen; Lawrence Gowing; Alastair Graham; Major-General F.E.C.Graham; Bridget Grant; Basil Handford; Amanda Harling; Sir Roy Harrod; Lady Hartwell; Arabella Heathcoat-Amory; Robert Heber-Percy; Otto Herschen; Sir John Heygate; Peter Hiley; Heywood Hill; Anthony Hobson; Luned Jacobs; Dom Philip Jebb; Charlotte Joll; Hugh Kay, Jesuit Information Officer; Maurice Keen; Geoffrey Keating; Robert Kee; John Kennedy; Charles Kidd; Irving Kristol; Sir Thomas Lea; Mona Leith; Lady Amabel Lindsay; John Longe; Lady Dorothy Lygon; Geoffrey Lynch; Norman Mailer; Jean Miles; Raymond Mortimer; Lord Moyne; Sir Godfrey Nicholson; Nigel Nicolson; the Duke of Norfolk; Viscount Norwich; Major Murrough O'Brien; John Onslow; Peter Quennell; Isabel Quigley; Lord Rennel; John Robson; Anthony Shadforth; Professor Norman Sherry; Stephen Spender; Sir Anthony Stormer; Martin Stannard; Margaret Stephens; David Stirling; Irene Stirling; David Sylvester; Chloë Teacher; Jessica

Treuhaft; Philip Toynbee; Hugo Vickers; Palmer B.Wald; Lord Walston; Oscar Wood; Peregrine Worsthorne; Gerald Yorke; John Yorke.

Among the institutions that lent me letters or gave me information the University of Texas was easily the largest contributor with 1,416 items written by Waugh. The others are: Beinecke Library, Yale, for a letter to Edmund Wilson; Henry W. and Albert A.Berg Collection, New York Public Library, Astor, Lenox and Tilden Foundations; Bodleian Library, Oxford; Mugar Memorial Library of Boston University; Brandeis University for a letter to Joseph Heller; Written Archive Section of the British Broadcasting Corporation; University of Calgary for a letter to Mrs Ambrose Dudley; University of Southern California; Jacques Barzun Papers, Rare Book and Manuscript Library, Columbia University; Library and Records Department of the Foreign Office; London Library; Mills Memorial Library of McMaster University; Merton College, Oxford, for a letter to Sir Max Beerbohm; Merton Legacy Trust for a postcard to Thomas Merton; National Library of Scotland for letters to Ruth McQuillan; Tate Gallery; Time-Life News Service; University of Tulsa; information service of the United States Embassy, London; University College, London for letters to George Orwell and Dr Comfort; C.G.Petter and Joan Ryan of University of Victoria for letters to Sir John Betjeman; *Vogue* Information Service; and Walker Art Gallery. Where there is a very small amount of material I have mentioned it to limit optimistic applications.

Similarly among those who have been kind enough to allow me to quote material that is not my copyright, the literary executors of Nancy Mitford, her sisters Lady Mosley and the Duchess of Devonshire, are pre-eminent. I am also grateful to Sir John and Lady Betjeman, Lady Diana Cooper, Ann Fleming, Graham Greene, Lady Pansy Lamb, Anthony Powell, John Wain; and the literary executors of Katharine Asquith, Cyril Connolly, Thomas Merton and Henry Yorke.

Finally it is invidious, but I think desirable, to name those to whom I am most deeply indebted. Sir Harold Acton, Graham Greene, and the Earl of Oxford have written many long detailed letters; Ann Fleming and Lady Mary Lygon have submitted themselves to lengthy and repeated interrogation. I have raided the books on Waugh edited by Michael Davie, Donat Gallagher and David Pryce-Jones, and questioned them as well. Frances Donaldson's *Portrait of a Country Neighbour*, John St John's *To the War with Waugh* and Dudley Carew's *A Fragment of Friendship* illuminate different periods of Waugh's life. Christopher Sykes has suffered all these things. Much diligent research was done by Sarah Anderson. The back cover drawing was brought to my attention by John Saumarez-Smith. Alan Bell and David Bogie made many invaluable suggestions. Geoffrey Naylor prepared the index and contributed much useful information. Alex MacCormick was very helpful as the House editor. My mother Gaenor Amory spent endless hours checking each word of the typescript against the originals, filing, typing and deep in Debrett. Lady Dorothy Lygon, Anthony Powell, and Margaret Waugh read the manuscript and pointed out errors and improvements. My gratitude is theirs; any remaining mistakes are, of course, mine.

MARK AMORY

Chronological Table

1903   28 October. Born at 11 Hillfield Road, Hampstead.

1907   The Waugh family move to North End Road, Hampstead.

1910–
1917   Heath Mount, a local day school.

1917–
1921   Lancing College, Sussex.

1922–
1924   Hertford College, Oxford.

1925   Schoolmaster in Wales. Attempts suicide.

1926   Schoolmaster in Aston Clinton, Berkshire.
The Balance, A Yarn of the Good Old Days of Broad Trousers and High-Necked Jumpers, a short story published in *Georgian Stories*.

1927   Schoolmaster at Notting Hill, London.
Journalist on *Daily Express*.
Engaged to Evelyn Gardner.

1928   *Rossetti, His Life and Works*.
Marriage.
Decline and Fall, An Illustrated Novelette.

1929   Evelyn Gardner leaves Waugh.

1930   Divorce.
Vile Bodies.
Labels, A Mediterranean Journal (in USA, *A Bachelor Abroad*).
Conversion to Roman Catholicism.
Ethiopia – Zanzibar.

1931   *Remote People*.
East and Central Africa.
First visit to the Lygon family at Madresfield.

1932   *Black Mischief*.
British Guiana and Brazil.

1933   Return in May.
Meeting with Laura Herbert in Italy.

1934   Morocco.
Ninety-Two Days, The Account of a Tropical Journey through British Guiana and Port of Brazil.
Spitzbergen.
A Handful of Dust.

1935   Reporting Italian-Abyssinian war for *Daily Mail*.
       Edmund Campion: Jesuit and Martyr.
       Jerusalem.

1936   Annulment of his marriage confirmed.
       Rome – Abyssinia.
       Waugh in Abyssinia.
       Mr Loveday's Little Outing (short stories).

1937   Marriage to Laura Herbert.
       Move to Piers Court, Stinchcombe, Gloucestershire.

1938   Teresa born.
       Scoop, A Novel about Journalists.
       Hungary.
       Mexico.

1939   *Robbery under The Law: The Mexican Object-Lesson*.
       Auberon born.
       Royal Marines.

1940   Dakar expedition.
       Transfer to Commandos, Scotland.
       Mary born and died.

1941   The Battle of Crete.
       Return to Royal Marines and to Britain.

1942   *Put Out More Flags*.
       Margaret born.
       Work Suspended, two chapters of an unfinished novel.
       With Commandos in Scotland and Dorset.

1943   Death of Arthur Waugh.
       Resignation from Commandos.
       Granted leave to write.

1944   Yugoslavia with Randolph Churchill and 37th British Military Mission to the
       partisans.
       Harriet born.

1945   *Brideshead Revisited: The Sacred and Profane Memories of Captain Charles Ryder*.
       Demobilized. Piers Court.

1946   *When the Going Was Good*.
       Nuremberg.
       Spain.
       James born.
       Ireland.
       United States including Hollywood.

1947   *Scott-King's Modern Europe*.
       Wine in Peace and War.
       Ireland – Norway – Sweden – Denmark.

1948   *The Loved One: An Anglo-American Tragedy*.
       United States.

1949   Return in April.
1950   Italy.
       Septimus born.
       Helena.
1951   Near East.
1952   Sicily.
       The Holy Places.
       Men at Arms.
       Goa.
1953   Return in February.
       Love Among the Ruins: A Romance of the Near Future.
1954   Voyage to Ceylon and breakdown.
       Tactical Exercise (stories printed in the United States only).
       Jamaica.
       Death of Catherine Waugh.
1955   *Officers and Gentlemen*.
1956   Move to Combe Florey, Taunton, Somerset.
1957   *The Ordeal of Gilbert Pinfold*.
1958   Rhodesia.
1959   Return in April.
       The Life of the Right Reverend Ronald Knox.
1960   *Tourist in Africa*.
1961   *Unconditional Surrender* (in USA, *The End of the Battle*).
       British Guiana.
1962   Return in February.
1963   *Basil Seal Rides Again, or The Rake's Regress*.
1964   *A Little Learning* (autobiography).
1966   *Sword of Honour*, the war trilogy revised and published in one volume.
       10 April, dies at Combe Florey.

1 Education
1903-1924

J.C.R.   HERTFORD COLLEGE,

OXFORD.

Tuesday.

Dear Carew,

I liked your letter
well. You may convey my
surrender to Pollock and
Dick Harris. There are
things more worth defending
at Oxford. You and your
friends belong to Lancing &
the past, you know, and itt
always a mistake to try &
keep up with the past. Thank
You for reminding me.
        I thought the verses
very good. particularly the

To Dudley Carew, 1922

Introduction

Evelyn Arthur St John Waugh was born on 28 October 1903. While emphasizing that he doubted its relevance, Waugh devoted the first chapter of his
autobiography to heredity. His forebears came from the lowlands of Scotland,
where they farmed. In 1782 Alexander Waugh came south and made a name for
himself as a Nonconformist preacher. His son was also a clergyman but joined the
Church of England and his grandson, Waugh's grandfather, was a doctor – a solid
line of educated men. Waugh's father, also called Arthur, went to Sherborne and
New College, Oxford, before becoming a literary figure of a similarly reliable kind,
working in almost every available manner. He wrote verse, essays, biographies and
an autobiography; he reviewed books for the *Daily Telegraph;* he edited the
Nonesuch Dickens; he read manuscripts for publishers and, as Managing Director
of Chapman & Hall from 1902, he published them.

In 1893 Arthur Waugh had married Catherine Raban, who also came from a
family whose men engaged in the professions, though in this case mainly as soldiers,
lawyers and civil servants. In 1898 Alec was born, five years before his brother;
there were no other children. In 1907 Arthur Waugh moved to a new house in
Hampstead (it still stands but was reallocated to Golders Green before 1922), and
stayed there for twenty-six years. So Evelyn's childhood memories centre on
Underhill, as the house was called.

They were happy memories. The age gap and the fact that Alec was in the First
World War made a barrier between the two brothers. Evelyn has said, and Alec
accepted, that they were more like nephew and uncle than brothers; but a friendly
nephew and uncle, and so they remained. Arthur Waugh preferred Alec, who
shared his enthusiasm for cricket, his easy-going sociability, and even contrived to
adapt his father's role of unpretentious literary man to the twentieth century.
Catherine Waugh preferred Evelyn, so that he would later write: 'At the height of
the day's pleasure his [Arthur's] key would turn in the front door and his voice
would rise from the hall: "Kay, Kay, where's my wife?" and that was the end of my
mother's company for the evening.'[1] It is agreed that she had a strong character, but
a more detailed portrait never emerges. Her letters over the years to Evelyn are
affectionate but too conventional to be revealing.

From 1910 to 1917 Evelyn went daily to Heath Mount, a preparatory school of
about sixty boys, half of whom boarded. From May 1917 to 1921 he went to
Lancing, chosen because he was a pious boy at the time and the school was 'designed
originally to inculcate High churchmanship'.[2] Out of the ninety-seven boys in

Waugh's house at Lancing, twenty-two were the sons of clergymen. He did not go to Sherborne as his father and brother had done because Alec, who was asked to leave, had caused a furore by writing *The Loom of Youth*, a novel which dealt with homosexuality at public schools and became a controversial best-seller.

Waugh's life at Lancing began in misery. The indulged thirteen-year-old who had never lived away from home was shocked to find that people did not like him. 'Scholarship, skill in athletics and good looks made regimentation possible to bear and opened the door to popularity. Now Evelyn in those days was clever but not a scholarship-boy, courageous but no games-player, pleasant-featured but not good-looking.'[3] Gradually things improved. He formed a circle of friends which included Hugh, later Lord, Molson, Tom Driberg, later Lord Bradwell, and Dudley Carew. He became president of the Debating Society and editor of the school magazine.

His biographer reckons that in the summer of 1921 'He was nevertheless profoundly unhappy .... During the Easter holidays Evelyn's feeling for his father changed. He fancied that he saw through him and had discovered that the man he had loved and respected was a hollow sham. ... Soon after the psychological blow of losing faith in his father he received another; he lost his religious faith.'[4] Waugh himself is brisk with his own adolescent melancholy and cynicism.

He was constantly bored, and when on 15 July the news came that he had won a scholarship to Hertford College, Oxford, 'I was eager to go and my father was showing his habitual impatience to get a task finished; in this case my education'.[5] So he went up to Oxford in January, which was unusual. Hertford was a 'respectable but rather dreary' college. He began quietly, but meeting Terence Greenidge, and through him the members of the Hypocrites Club, changed all that. Soon many of his friends were Etonians, many were flamboyantly homosexual, many were spending and drinking as if there were no tomorrow. It was a brave new world, far from grey Hampstead, and he elected to remain in it.

There are few letters from Lancing, but the diary provides a detailed account. There is no Oxford diary (it was destroyed by Waugh) so the letters are the only written contemporary source. They leave out more than they reveal. The dates are a matter of guess-work, sometimes supported by replies. It has been stressed that Waugh considered himself an artist and only turned to writing when he had failed there. Nevertheless his interest in writing, particularly in technique, is strong at school and only gradually yields to other interests. This impression may have been reinforced by the fact that his letters were largely to an aspiring writer and those about writing have tended to be selected.

[1] Evelyn Waugh, *A Little Learning*, p.63.
[2] *A Little Learning*, p.96.
[3] Roger Fulford, 'At Lancing', *Evelyn Waugh and his World*, 1973.
[4] Christopher Sykes, *Evelyn Waugh*, 1975, pp.31–2.
[5] *A Little Learning*, p.103.

To Alec Waugh[1]   Underhill,
[May 1914]   North End Road,
                                                  Hampstead, N.W.
Dear Alec

I am so glad to hear you've got your firsts. Congratulations. I am just doing (?) a
piece of continuous prose, so I have not got much time

                                                  Ever Yours
                                                  Evelyn

[1] Alec Waugh (1898–   ). Evelyn's elder and only brother had received his first XI cricket colours.
See Appendix of Names.

To Catherine Waugh   [Lancing.]
[6 December 1920]

Darling Mother,
    I have just heard from father about your illness.[1] I can't say how sorry I am. The
whole day seems different. We are having the concert this afternoon and I am
hoping to see Barbara[2] but it all seems meaningless now.
    It was awfully kind of you to keep it from me until now. I do wish I was able to
come and see you, dear. It does seem so far away. Do get well quickly – I shall be
back in ten days now.

                                                  Your very loving,
                                                  Evelyn

[1] Catherine Waugh (died 1954) had had an operation in October. See Appendix of Names.
[2] Barbara Jacobs, daughter of W.W. Jacobs, author of The Monkey's Paw and many comic stories for
which he was paid more than any other English writer of the time except Rudyard Kipling. Barbara was
married to Alec Waugh from 1919 to 1921.

To Dudley Carew[1]   [Heads House,
[January 1921]   Lancing College,
                                                  Sussex.]

My dear Carew,
    I like the idea immensely. The whole conception of Jimmie and his rising out of

the rut for a moment only to slip back again and the ever delightful cynicism that contentment is the only failure is well brought out. But as it stands now it is too frail a scaffolding to support the theme (I'm afraid I'm mixing a metaphor but I want to be sincere rather than technically unimpeachable). I can see it rather degenerating into long conversations and descriptions of the weather. That was all right just to fix Jimmie but it wont do for 10,000 words.

Why not make more of Rodney? The idea of his deliberately adopting Jimmie's natural attitude is subtle.

Try and bring home thoughts by actions and incidents. Don't make everything said. This is the inestimable value of the Cinema to novelists (don't scoff at this as a cheap epigram it is really very true). Make things happen.

What part does Jimmie's Cambridge friend play in the show. Whatever the temptation, for God's sake don't bring characters on simply to draw their characters and make them talk. Fit them into a design. You dont put teapots into a water lily design because you can draw tea pots well. That is – I don't.

It is a damn good idea. Don't spoil it out of slackness or perversity but do MAKE THINGS HAPPEN. Have a murder in every chapter if you like but do do something. GO TO THE CINEMA and risk the headache.

This all seems bloody patronising and I find it, on reading it through, almost unreadable.

Evelyn

P.S. Keep this and reproduce it in a collotype facsimile in the biography.

---

[1] Dudley Carew (1903–   ). Journalist; Waugh's first literary admirer. See Appendix of Names.

To Arthur Waugh[1]   Heads House,
13 June [1921]   Lancing College,
                                                       Sussex.

Dear Father,

I've got the Scarlyn[2], all right. It was put up yesterday. It hardly seemed worth wiring as it wouldn't go before tomorrow. I am a little cheered. Of course it is no testimony to my brain – there was no serious competition – but I think it shows a certain capacity for work.

Do you know at all, what Meynell[3] is doing with *Conversion*[4]? I hope he understands that if he is printing it I can't sell copies here. I wish you could make this clear to him. It's awfully kind of him but I don't think he quite sees my position. Of course it would be delightful to have copies to give away.

Is there any merit in these verses? They are a bit sentimental I am afraid. I don't think the first verse is bad, is it?

I have written to Herberts farm asking for their terms. What ought I to pay? I fear Ferndown[?] would be too civilised and full of distractions. If we wanted that sort of thing it would be cheaper and more comfortable to go to the Molsons'[5] house in Lincolnshire they offered us.

Didn't you suggest that Carew should stay with us to watch cricket? How would it be if he stayed the week before I go down to Fulford[6]. He may be staying there at the same time as I.

I am beginning to read a little philosophy. It is rather interesting me. I am going to start on Bergson soon. Dobson[7], who lives in the fourth dimension is guiding me.

The play comes off on Friday and Sunday. Enclosed one of the Invitations. Some were on handmade paper for J.F.[8] and the elect.

                                                       Your loving
                                                       Son

[1] Arthur Waugh (1866–1943). Waugh's father. Managing Director of Chapman & Hall. See Appendix of Names.

[2] The Scarlyn Literature Prize.

[3] Probably Sir Francis Meynell (1891–1975). Creator of the Nonesuch Press, at this time working in Burns & Oates of which his father was managing director. Knighted in 1946. 'I like you Meynell,' said Bertrand Russell, 'because in spite of your spats there is much of the guttersnipe in you.' Ronald W.Clark, *Bertrand Russell*.

[4] *Conversion*, The Tragedy of Youth in three burlesques by Evelyn Waugh. Act I. School, as maiden aunts think it is. Act II. School, as modern authors say it is. Act III. School, as we all know it is. The play was performed with success, Waugh appearing as compère, but was not published and has not survived.

[5] Hugh Molson (1903–   ). Barrister, Conservative MP for over twenty years, Minister of Works 1957–9. Created Lord Molson 1961. Known as 'Hot-lunch'. 'A nice-natured youth with fish-like gills and a pompous manner of speaking.' A.L.Rowse, *A Cornishman at Oxford*, 1965.

[6] Roger Fulford (1902–   ). Historian. President of the Liberal Party 1964–5. Arrived in the same house as Waugh at Lancing on the same day and so sat next to him to eat, learn and pray: 'propinquity makes companionship'. Later they became friends.

[7] Claud Dobson (born 1902). Took a science scholarship to Lincoln College, Oxford.

[8] John Ferguson Roxburgh (1888–1954). Sixth-form master at Lancing 1911–23, headmaster of Stowe 1923–49.

To Dudley Carew   145, North End Road,
[January 1922]   Golders Green N.W.11.

Dear Carey,

I hope you had a cheery Christmas. I am pretty full of beans as I have been
allowed to go up to Hertford[1] next term. Oxford ought to be wonderful. Come up
for a scholarship next term and have a bust with me. I leave my bitterest curse upon
Lancing. Take care of the Magazine – it needs it also of the debating Society and
tell P.F.[2] to get on with selling *The Times, Punches* and assorted rubbish in the
librarians room. I don't know if we shall be able to fix up a week this holidays after
all. We have a long succession of guests and domestic crises.

On Friday we are having a dinner party for Barbara's twenty-first birthday.
Among others Sheila Kaye Smith[3] is coming. I look forward to meeting her. I have
been to several shows *Will Shakespeare*[4], Guignol and *The Sign on the Door*[5].
After the Guignol one always feels one is watching creditable amateurs. They are
supremely good. No acting in London to touch them or playwriting neither.

                                                        Yours
                                                        Evelyn

Seen John Onslow[6] this holidays?
Why the Hell haven't you written

    [1] Waugh had chosen Hertford because he was not confident of winning a scholarship to New College,
his father's preference, and because the Hertford scholarship was worth the most – £100 a year.
    [2] Philip Machin followed Waugh to Hertford. He became a private schoolmaster at St Ronan's near
Worthing and a social worker.
    [3] Sheila Kaye Smith (died 1956). Popular novelist, who according to Beverley Nichols in *Twenty-five*
called to mind 'bobbed hair, black eyebrows and a cottage on the Sussex Downs'.
    [4] By Clemence Dane.
    [5] By Channing Pollock, with Gladys Cooper.
    [6] John Onslow went to Sandhurst and became a major. He scarcely remembered Waugh.

To Dudley Carew   Hertford College,
[Early 1922]   Oxford.

Dear Carey,

... Of myself, I have not much to record. I am very shy and a little lonely still but
gradually settling down. I feel I am going to be immoderately happy. I wish I could find
some congenial friends. I have at present met a gloomy scholar from some grammar
school who talked nothing, some aristocratic New College men who talked winter
sports and motor cars and a vociferous Carthusian who talked filth.

Hertford seems a better College than I had supposed – there are a lot of cheery
souls besides the Lancing set. There is far too much religion in this University

though and not enough brains. I have little news except that I have spent an appalling amount of money. Write and tell me the Lancing scandal if you are not engaged next Brigaders[1].

> Yours
> Evelyn

[1] Brigaded Divinity, the top divisions taken together by the headmaster.

To Dudley Carew
[Early 1922]

JCR,
Hertford College,
Oxford.

Dear Carey,
Did you yourself honestly think your last letter adequate. If you did our correspondence ceases.
Love to Onslow, Pollock and Croft[1]

> Yours
> Evelyn

[1] Colonel N.A.C.Croft (1906–   ). Spent five years in the Arctic, about which he has written. First commandant of the Metropolitan Police Cadet Corps.

To Dudley Carew
[Early 1922]

[Hertford College,
Oxford.]

My dear Carey,
Our letters crossed. The one I received this morning was a little less unsatisfactory.
'I am very grateful indeed to the Debating Society for the vote of thanks. I cannot but feel that in my term of presidency I fell far short of the services of my predecessors and of my present successor; but I am sure that I can at least compete with them in the gratitude and good-will I bear the House.'
(Colonial papers please copy.) You can read that if you think necessary but its pretty pompous, isn't it?
I am glad you are finding Longe[1] a good fellow. I found that out last summer and forgot it again last term. Stick to Jonslow [John Onslow] he alone may be able to keep you wicked. Don't you go and get made a house captain you're a pretty good ass but you're better than that. Bully Lux[2] and for gods sake be unpleasant to Woodard[3]. *Sic itur ad astra.*
I don't feel that I can tell you all about Oxford yet. Largely because I haven't myself got it into full perspective. All I can say is that it is immensely beautiful and immensely different from anything I have seen written about it except perhaps

'Know you her secret none can utter'

I haven't got my friends into anything like an ordered sequence yet. Most of them are very clever but earnest. Others are fools and charming. I am not yet the centre of any group but on the fringes of many. I spend most of my time with Mallowan[4] and his New College friends.

I am learning to ride a bicycle – rather pleasurable and absurdly easy.

Yesterday my tutor said to me 'Damn you you're a scholar. If you can't show industry I at least have some right to expect intelligence!' I had just translated *Eramus* as Erasmus and it was too much for his scholarly manners.

I have been trying to do a poem for the Newdigate Prize. Pretty bloody rot. The only line I've written so far I like at all is

– – – – –'Till cold and grey

The mountains shivered and disgorged the day'.

I spoke at the Union, not over well, the other week. Still it seems to have made a fairly good impression. They made me 'tell' at the last debate. A job which necessitates sitting until half past eleven in tails, a white waistcoat and a draught to be followed by second-rate port, whiskey and sandwiches with the officers. The other teller was an Earl of something, wouldn't Bevan[5] have loved it. He seemed quite a pleasant soul – self-assured but one can't help that with a coronet.

There is an O.L. dinner tonight.

By the way speaking of O.L.s, what do people say of me now I have left. I am vain enough to be interested in knowing. I can't think they waste much charity.

Best wishes to P.F., Pollock and Onslow and all that set.

Yours
Evelyn

P.S. G.B.S. is rather second rate.

P.P.S. If you read my acknowledgement of the L.C.D.S.'s courtesy read note on colonial papers at your own discretion. It seems pompous without.

[1] John Longe became Governor of the Upper Nile in the Sudan.

[2] The Reverend Harry Lucas, senior history master.

[3] Woodard, a parson, had been Waugh's form master. Grandson of the founder of Lancing.

[4] Max Mallowan (1904–78). Married to Agatha Christie. Professor of Western Asiatic Archaeology, University of London, 1947–62. Knighted 1968.

[5] Emlyn Bevan (1903–72). Worked in Barclays Bank of which he was Vice-Chairman 1962–8. Referred to as 'Buttocks' in *A Little Learning*, p. 131.

To Tom Driberg[1]
13 February [1922]

Hertford College,
Oxford.

Dear Driberg,

Your letter this morning was just what an hungering O.L. wishes to receive. I heard from Carew and Longe and they told me nothing. Thank you so much.

(a) A man once lent his country house to a young couple for their 'honey-moon'.

'There is only one stipulation I would make,' he said, 'and that is – do be careful of the breakfast service – it's eighteenth-century Spode and has been in the family for years. I wouldn't have anything happen to it for worlds.'

The bridegroom promised and the young couple drove off.

A few weeks later the two men met. 'Well, my boy, I hope you found the cottage quite comfortable?'

'My dear fellow, I hardly know how to face you. We enjoyed ourselves immensely but – but – the whole breakfast service is broken!'

'Good God! how did that happen?'

'Well, you see, it was like this. On the first evening we went out into the garden under the moon and, feeling very sentimental I tried to pick her a rose. Doing this I stuck a thorn into my finger. It wasn't anything but it bled a little and Mary was rather concerned.

'Next morning we were going to have breakfast in bed and the butler was just bringing it in on a tray when my wife leant over and said

"How is your poor prick this morning dear?" And the butler dropped the tray.'

(b) What wines will Princess Mary and Lascelles[2] drink on their wedding night? She will open her 24 year old port and he will indulge in cider (in side her).

I'm afraid that was rather vulgar. But to more present matters.

I am enjoying life here very well. I do no work and never go to Chapel. As I am too bad to play soccer for Hertford I have joined a local hockey club with Southwell which is quite a joke. There is a pleasant old world violence about the game which appeals to me strongly.

Yesterday I heard Inge[3] preach at the University Church. Very witty and scholarly. Just what one wants at Oxford. Oxford is not yet quite itself but the aged war-worn hero type is beginning to go down. It ought to be right again by the time you come up. I am well pleased with Hertford. At first I thought I could not be happy outside New College but there are really an extremely pleasant set of men here. The buildings are pretty beastly.

I went to a wine with Hill[4] last night. He got pretty tight. I was cheery. The others more or less sober. I managed to drink $\frac{3}{4}$ of a bottle of Madeira, a glass of port and two tumblers of cider. It was very pleasant. My memories are vague but I distinctly remember standing in the quad and trying to quote Newbolts 'There's a breathless hush in the close tonight' to Molson[5]. I don't feel the least ill after it.

Love to Jacko[6]

Yours E.A.St J.W.

[1] Tom Driberg (1905–76). Journalist and Labour MP. Created Lord Bradwell 1975. See Appendix of Names.

[2] Henry Lascelles, sixth Earl of Harewood, married Princess Mary, daughter of George V, on 28 February 1922.

[3] Dean Inge (1860–1954). 'The Gloomy Dean' had been a tutor at Hertford 1889–1904 and was Dean of St Paul's 1911–34.

[4] James Hill (1902–   ) became Professor of English at the Muslim University of Aligarh in India.

[5] Not yet up at Oxford, but being coached for the New College scholarship examination.

[6] Jack Driberg (1888–1946). Anthropologist. Brother of Tom.

To Dudley Carew   Coll. Hert. Oxon.
[March 1922]

From the city of spires to the place of steps, greeting! Well well I suppose I must forgive you Carey. And I shall not be in the Philippines really. I am going to Skagarak to stay with the Maharajah of Bagdepaul with the little button on top. I am told his grand Vizier has very good taste in coffee.

. . . Of myself I can say little because I am too happy. One can pour out wrath and tears for pages but content is, at least to me, a more secret and inexplicable thing. Leave it as it is. Life is good and Oxford is all that one dreams.

For yourself. Now that you are again in my hands I must take thought. It is a grave responsibility & also I feel a prig now giving advice. My former counsels of imperfection were largely wanton taunts.

Well I am learning this that one can't fit peoples characters about. Each one is a design and must be completed its own way. The great and only mistake in design is that it becomes conventional (in passing – a wider outlook has given me a far larger realisation of Crease's[1] designs. I am convinced now that that man is a great artist. Before I hung my admiration on his character & did not understand his work fully. It is really great Carey. I am now convinced of that).

Well, you were made to be charming so keep on being charming but be honest and reserved too. Be as profligate as you like but dont be a pimp – don't be mean. Don't be selfconscious. Don't be too efficient or romantic. Do things because you want to whatever others say but don't do things because others tell you not to.

You force me to be a Polonius at eighteen. Well for Christs sake don't be a Laertes.

There is one thing more. I don't want the Waugh spirit to go on at Lancing even if it could. It rose pretty suddenly – except in the house in healthy Bolshevism I did[n't?] really influence Lancing for more than a term – let it die too. I felt you wanted that to happen by the tone of the last Magazine. Well I want that to happen, too. Let me see the next editorial unconventional but let it have the Carey touch not mine. Let Woodard & people think 'Well his influence has proved as superficial as his nasty character'. We know & one or two others. Let it rest at that. By the way you never told me if you wrote the Fishing Review did you? It was very nice – always excepting that awful sentence near the beginning. Thats the sort of spirit to keep up. If anyone thinks fit to defend me don't print it. But I can't think that they will, I imagine I am pretty well disliked now – as good God I deserved to be. I am changing pretty hard and I think for the better but I am not changing in my interest for Lancing & all of you.

                                               Yours
                                               Evelyn

[1] Francis Crease, calligrapher and an important influence. He lived four miles from Lancing and Waugh used to walk over for tea and instruction. Publications include *Thirty-four Decorative Designs*, with a preface by Waugh, 1927.

To Tom Driberg   Underhill,
Saturday [May? 1922]   145 North End Road,
                                                            N.W.11.

Dear Driberg,

After Oxford London, and particularly Suburbia, is quite indescribably dreary
and your letter came as a welcome interruption to the long backchat of the literary
cliques. There are rumours that the *Times Literary Supplement* is going to cease,
that Catherine Mansfield[1] is not going to die after all, that J.C.Squire[2] has taken
seriously to drink at last. No news I am afraid to match your ribald chronicle. It is
sad to think of Bond propagating his species.[3] He should be allowed to die out. O for
a Celibacy of the priesthood to avoid this multiplying of parsons.

I enjoyed last term immeasurably and left Oxford with regret and a pocket book
full of unpaid bills. I did no work & do not propose to do any next term so I am
trying to learn a little during the vac. I have schools at the end of next term. Between
whiles I read *Alice in Wonderland*. It is an excellent book I think.

Alec has a new novel coming out in a week or two called *The Lonely Unicorn* –
very grey & analytical.

How is the man Roxburgh? I had a letter from him recently – very insolent. His
sarcasm does not carry from Lancing to Oxford with advantage and his brain seems
rather inconsiderable when one is daily taught by dons of real education. Sorry
Carey is going to the dogs. Still it's better than falling in with the Dick Harris[4]
crowd.

I have just purchased the Riccardi Press *Shropshire Lad* – did I tell you I had got
their Rupert Brooke.

Did you see poor old Preters[5] failed in the scholarship exam again? I am sorry.
He ought to have got something.

Love to Lancing. I was staying quite near it last week – Ditchling – and thought of
coming over but was afraid I should not be welcome – I always hated O.L.s.

                                                            Yours
                                                            Evelyn Waugh

[1] Katherine Mansfield died in January 1923.

[2] J.C.Squire (1884–1958). Literary editor of the *New Statesman*, chief critic of the *Observer*, founder
and editor of the *London Mercury* 1919–34, a middlebrow literary power. He wrote about fifty books, now
out of print. Knighted in 1933.

[3] The wife of the school clergyman was pregnant.

[4] Dick Harris was Waugh's first house tutor. 'Such vestiges of happiness as I enjoyed during my first
term were entirely due to Dick Harris': *A Little Learning*, p. 108. He took over from his brother as
headmaster of St Ronan's.

[5] Hugh Molson was known as Preters because, when asked during his first term whether he was
interested in politics, he replied, 'Preternaturally so.' He was accepted at New College and became
President of the Union before taking a first in Law.

To Tom Driberg   Coll. Hert. Oxon.
[1922]

Dear Driberg,

I am so sorry that I have been so long writing to thank you for your letter. I hope the merry round goes on at Lancing. If you see Flynn [1] and if it is not too much of a trial to speak to him could you tell him that I consider it a most unfriendly act that he came to Oxford and didnt look me up.

I have written to J.F. and P.F. but neither have the manners to answer. I have come to the conclusion that J.F. is thoroughly second-rate.

Life here is very beautiful. Mayonnaise and punts and cider cup all day long. One loses all ambition to be an intellectual. I am reduced to writing light verse for the *Isis* and taking politics seriously. I made a very bad speech again at the Union last night. I dont know why it is I can never think clearly in that House. Did I show you that jolly Buckland 'In Memoriam' I found in the School library? I have made an essay out of it which I am hoping the Oxford fortnightly will print.

Do let me most seriously advise you to take to drink. There is nothing like the aesthetic pleasure of being drunk and if you do it in the right way you can avoid being ill next day. That is the greatest thing Oxford has to teach.

I have acquired the Riccardi Press *Shropshire Lad* and had it bound in quarter black Levant and $\frac{3}{4}$ parchment. It looks very well. Also the Florence Press Keats and the Vale Press *Cymbeline*. Preters was here for a couple of days. We made him beautifully drunk.

There is a jolly Problem Club run by some men at Balliol. Their last competition was to receive the offer of the queerest job. A friend of mine – a tall thin man – won the prize with the offer of being fat man in a Circus. He advertised 'Labourer weighing 38 stone would be glad to get light employment.'

The second prize went to the man who was offered the post of secretary to the Metropolitan of Constantinople to help him write a history of Coptic Christianity.

If it were not for the menace of Schools at the end of term life would be almost perfect. I am having to start work which I find agrees with me not at all. Never mind – where there is alcohol there is hope.

I have been elected secretary of the Fox – the Hertford debating Society an onerous but not honorific post.

Please give my love to anyone at Lancing who may remember me. Are you aiding P.F. in his scheme for making the magazine entirely official. I dont think its a bad thing. How is that bloody man Woodard. I hate him more and more with the lapse of time.

Good luck to the Blessed Virgin Mary
E.A.S.J.Waugh

[1] John Flynn (1903–   ). Followed Waugh to Hertford. Schoolmaster, then Colonial Administrator 1928–49.

To Dudley Carew   Coll. Hert. Oxon.
[31 May 1922]

My Dear Carey,

. . . I hope Heinemanns comes off now that the old man [1] is dead I should think it
will be a happy life there. Perhaps you will be able to act as ambassador with my first
book – many years ahead.

And what shall I tell you of local interests and Oxford intelligence, who are
standing with the world open. Only that I am still content to lead my solitary and
quiet life here. I have enough friends to keep me from being lonely and not enough
to bother me. I do a little work and dream a lot. I have exactly threepence in my
pocket and my cheques are worth only the twopenny stamp on them – but one
muddles along.

Eights week is just over. It was rather a bore. We had a College Ball which turned
the whole place upside down for a week end, exasperated the Scouts and ruined the
cooking. Our boat has floundered about in the third division with indifferent
success. New College are head of the river again & will all be blind tonight – all that
is except my friend Beadle who is serious minded.

I went the other day to coffee with some men in BNC [Brasenose College] to hear
an American revivalist of great transatlantic fame. I thought he was dangerously
near converting me to righteousness but like Pharoah, I steeled my heart. There
were a queer lot there – Pretty typical of Oxford. A logical & fierce conventionalist
from Worcester, a delightful Indian with great wondering faun eyes full of
superstition and simplicity from BNC, a well bred Roman Catholic and a few deep-
thinking, pipe-sucking Christians.

I spoke at the Union again the other night but not with success. I just can't go
down in that House. I get very nervous and find in the *Isis* 'Mr Waugh appeared
unaware of his audience'. My God.

I had a delightful adventure the other day. I went out for a long and solitary walk,
as is my custom, accompanied only with my big stick. In an obscure village miles
away I met a white dog and – as is also my custom – I addressed it with courtesy. It
seemed disposed to be friendly and made advances. Suddenly it saw my stick, gave a
great shout, leapt back about a yard with all its legs spread about, and began barking
furiously. A virago of a woman darted out of the cottage and said 'If you 'it that dog
with that stick again, I'll fetch my husband'. It was no good trying to explain. There
was not a witness and the dog was evidently bent on ruining my reputation so off I
had to go leaving another person unjustly incensed with me. Well, well.

I have begun writing for the local press a little. I have also been elected secretary
of the Hertford debating Society – the Fox. It is not an honour I coveted much but I
can only take a compliment.

I don't know if you have heard from ——. He is at the moment engaged in an
adultery with the wife of the parson he is living with. He is most amusing about it
all. The woman seems most erotic – he is also an Anglo-Catholic. I hear no news
from Lancing. Tell me anything of interest you hear. Are you going down there at
all.

What are you going to call your Verses 'Pearls for Swine' or 'Clover for Cows' or something like that?

Sorry [for] this long & illegible letter

Yours
Evelyn

¹ William Heinemann died in 1920.

To Dudley Carew   Oxford Carlton Club.

My poor Carey,

. . . I am sorry too that you are ill. What are you going to do? Of course no one in our class need ever starve because he can always go as a prep school master not a pleasant job but all roads lead to Sodom. I come down on the ninth. We must meet and discuss Nigeria or Zambesiland or Nicaragua. My life here has been extremely precarious 'unstable equilibrium' vide lux. At present I am keeping my balance but I may crash[?] any moment. We will then combine and run a Sadist brothel at Wigan.

Til then your very sympathetic friend
Evelyn

To Dudley Carew   Hertford College.
[1924]

Dear Carey

Give me your leave.

My dull brain was wrought with things forgotten. I have been living very intensely the last three weeks. For the last fortnight I have been nearly insane. I am a little saner now. My diary for the period is destroyed. I may perhaps one day in a later time tell you some of the things that have happened. It will make strange reading in the biography.

Apart from my own tragedy I have nothing to say. I am greatly interested in your novel.

I am speaking a paper at the Union on Thursday.

I want to go down for good but I cannot explain and my parents are obdurate.

Yours
· Evelyn Waugh

To Dudley Carew   Hertford College.
[1924]

Dear Carey,

    . . . As to Oxford & myself. I cannot yet explain all the things that are about me. St John has been eating wild honey in the wilderness. I do not yet know how things are going to end. They are nearing some sort of finality. One day I will tell you things to surprise you and sell an edition of the biography if faithfully recorded.

                                        Meanwhile
                                        Your friend
                                        Evelyn

2 Early Twenties
1924-1929

145, North End Road, N.W.11.

Speedwell 2022.

Dear Patrick

Thank you so much for
the advertisement. As soon
as I see any hope from my
window in the Slough of Despond I
will let you know.

As a matter of fact I
think there will probably be an
elopement quite soon.

Yours

Evelyn

To Patrick Kinross, 20 February 1928

Introduction

The last chapter of Waugh's autobiography begins with the day he left Oxford. It is entitled 'In Which Our Hero's Fortunes Fall Very Low'. He had been awarded a bad third, though as he had arrived late he had not completed the residence requirements and did not trouble to do so. Nor had he any idea of what he wanted to be.

Waugh tried many occupations in the next five years. The one with which he most persisted – teaching – was the one he least considered a career. He went to art school and decided that he was no draughtsman. He tried printing and was disappointed; hoped to become Charles Scott-Moncrieff's secretary but was not required; thought briefly of being a parson; wrote a novel and was told that it was no good; failed to complete another; was a journalist for only five weeks on the *Daily Express* and never had a line printed; applied for a 'fantastic job about toothbrushes'; and enrolled in the carpentry department of the Central School of Arts and Crafts in Southampton Row.

Chapman & Hall had not been doing well either and his father, who had no private income, could ill afford to keep him. In any case Waugh had seen a brighter world and only returned to the comforts of Hampstead when he had to. His new friends, however, were not always available. Alastair Graham went to Africa and later to Greece. Meanwhile, as Waugh describes in *A Little Learning*: 'I had in fact fallen in love with an entire family and rather as Mr E.M.Forster describes in *Howards End* had focussed the sentiment upon the only appropriate member, an eighteen-year-old daughter . . . . Olivia Plunket Greene was self-conscious, given to intense enthusiasms, a little crazy, truth-loving and in the end, holy.' Her brothers he had met at Oxford. David, the younger, was 'six foot seven inches tall, a languid dandy devoted to all that was fashionable'. Richard, the eldest, was 'more piratical in appearance, sometimes wearing earrings, a good man with a boat, a heavy smoker of dark strong tobacco, tinged, as were his siblings, with melancholy . . . .' Their mother, Gwen, niece of the theologian Baron von Hügel, 'lived with her children, on terms of serene equality', and also became a close friend.

So, between visits to Oxford and drinking a lot in London, Waugh became a schoolmaster, for two terms in Wales, five terms at Aston Clinton. 'I was from the first an obvious dud'[1] is his own verdict; but he was, at least to start with, a better master at a better school than readers of *Decline and Fall* might imagine. The boys appreciated his tolerance, were struck by his clothes and forgave his ineptitude at games.

In 1928 everything seemed to come right. Waugh had so far produced almost nothing but a long story for *The Balance*, published by his brother Alec, and an essay, *The Pre-Raphaelite Brotherhood*, privately printed by Alastair Graham. Now he brought out *Rossetti* in June and *Decline and Fall* in September. The first was a *succès d'estime*, the second a best-seller as well. Overnight Evelyn Waugh became a name that could be exploited in journalism.

In between he married Evelyn Gardner, daughter of Lady Burghclere (her father was dead). Waugh had written in his diary in April 1927, 'Met such a nice girl called Evelyn Gardiner'. He proposed in December and the wedding was in June (Harold Acton was best man). They were both twenty-four but she had been engaged several times before and her mother understandably opposed the match. Though She-Evelyn, as she came to be called by some, had been sharing a flat in Ebury Street with Pansy Pakenham, sister of the sixth Lord Longford, whom Waugh had known at Oxford, she was not a member of his own set. Dudley Carew describes her as simple, 'with a small up-turned nose and an engaging ingenuous manner'.[2] Nancy Mitford, who shared their house in Islington after they were married, said they were like two little boys.

She-Evelyn was ill in the autumn and in the new year they decided to go on a Mediterranean cruise. Far from being restored, at Haifa she needed a nurse and when they reached Port Said she had contracted pneumonia and her condition was critical. She recovered. Back in London Waugh had started *Vile Bodies* and would often go to stay in a country pub to write for the whole week. On 9 July he received her letter saying that she had fallen in love with John Heygate, a friend of both of them, and that they had become lovers. There was a reconciliation and she promised never to see him again. Within the month she met him at a party and they were photographed together. On 1 August Waugh returned to Canonbury Square to find it deserted. The next morning he received a letter from his wife saying that she was with Heygate. His first instinct was to file a petition for divorce; he was persuaded not to, but by 3 September found that for him it was the only course. He only met his wife once again, when she was to appear before an ecclesiastical court that was deciding on the annulment of the marriage.

Some friends see the breakdown of his marriage as a watershed in Waugh's life and found him more bitter and capricious afterwards. Certainly he was miserable, humiliated and inconsolable for a time.

There are few letters of this period. None to the Plunket Greenes survives, though certainly many were written; none to his wife, who 'cannot remember his writing me any'. Waugh kept letters of condolence from Harold Acton, Henry Yorke and Henry Lamb.

[1] *A Little Learning*, p. 222.
[2] *The World of Evelyn Waugh*, p. 42.

To Dudley Carew   Barford House[1],
[August 1924]   Warwick.

Dear Carey,
Here is an excellent cover for your book.[2] I am sorry that I have been such an unconscionable time in preparing it. Tell your publisher to send me proofs before he uses it and on no account to print it upon a glazed paper.

I like four or five guineas for a cover design but have been known to take three if accompanied by a promise of more employment. You might ask him to let me have a cheque as soon as he can...

                                             Yours
                                             Evelyn

[1] Barford House, the home of Alastair Graham (1904–   ). Described under the name Hamish Lennox in *A Little Learning* as 'the friend of my heart', which he remained for several years. He left Oxford to study architecture and to travel. Joined the Diplomatic Service 1928–33 and later became a recluse in Wales. Sebastian Flyte in *Brideshead Revisited* is partly based on memories of this friendship.
[2] Dudley Carew, *The Next Corner*, 1924. The cover was rejected.

To Harold Acton[1]   145 North End Road, N.W.11.
[December 1924]

Dear Harold,
Here is a photograph of myself. I do not think that it is very good but they offered to do it free so I let them, being poor.

I was sad that I saw so little of you when I was in Oxford. It seemed impossible ever to find you alone. There is so much that we might have discussed.

I have practically decided that it is impossible to draw in London between tube journeys and telephone calls and am seriously considering going to live in Sussex with a man called James Guthrie[2] who has a printing press where he is making books from copper plates – an enterprise which has not been seriously attempted since Peter's Blake.

I am almost sure that you would dismiss him as 'arty' but quite sure that you would be wrong because he is doing quite sincerely what all the 'arty' people are pretending to do.[3]

Audrey's[4] party the other night was fairly amusing. There was a meeting between 'Tasha'[5] and her husband[6] and also between Julia Strachey[7] and her father[8]. At the end when all the drink had been drunk and the band was tired out and there was no one left but a few poor drunks like Frank Dobson[9] & that monster Lady Duff Twisden[10] – have you met her? – there suddenly arrived uninvited about a hundred of your friends – David Green[11], Bryan Guinness[12], Rosse[13], Waters-Welch[14] and others. Brian Howard[15] was charming but the rest very, very silly. It was the first time I had talked to Rosse at all. I did not like him very much tho I tried to be nice to him because he was a friend of yours.

He said 'And who are all these curious people?' I said that they were my friends. 'Indeed. How extraordinary, and tell me is there anyone here anyone has ever heard of?'

I may be old-fashioned but it did not seem to me the way in which most noblemen I have met talked.

I went to the Laurencin Exhibition[16] but was much more enchanted by Woods'[17] Flowers Painting. It is quite stereoscopic. One literally had to go within a few inches of them to be convinced that they were painted on a flat surface and not modelled in wax. It really was uncanny and infinitely disagreeable. Did not Leonardo say, 'He should be deemed the greatest artist who can most make his figures to stand out from the surface on which they are painted'?

I lunched a little while back with the parents of that Charles James[18]. His mother said that she was a close friend of your mother's in Chicago.

I see announcements of Longford's marriage with Christine[19]. I am sure you must have been right in thinking her 'gravid'. Mary Somerville had formed the same impression.

I am engrossed in the *Discourses* of Sir Joshua Reynolds – also in entirely rewriting my bad book.

Love
Evelyn

[1] Harold Acton (1904–). Aesthete and author. See Appendix of Names.

[2] James Guthrie owned and ran the Pear Tree Press from 1899. On 18 December Waugh visited the Guthrie family but found that they used photographic methods. He decided against living there immediately and never worked for Guthrie, but kept in touch with him.

[3] Acton had written of Waugh's woodcuts the year before: 'At last you have escaped from the influence of that nice old maid [Francis Crease] who taught you illumination and whose drawings I have at the same time admired and deplored. At last you are the modern you were always intended to be.'

[4] Audrey Lucas, daughter of the author E.V.Lucas. In April 1925 Waugh felt 'largely responsible' when she became engaged to Harold Scott.

[5] Natasha Mamontoff was the first of Val Gielgud's five wives, 1921–5.

[6] Val Gielgud (1900–). Appointed BBC dramatic director 1929 and prolific author, mainly of thrillers.

[7] Julia Strachey (1901–). Novelist. Married 1927–37 to Stephen Tomlin and 1952–67 to Lawrence Gowing. Publications: *Cheerful Weather for the Wedding*, 1932, *The Man on the Pier*, 1951, retitled *An Integrated Man*, 1978.

[8] Oliver Strachey, brother of Lytton.

[9] Frank Dobson (1888–1963). Professor of Sculpture, Royal College of Art until 1953. His head of Osbert Sitwell is in the Tate Gallery. He painted the original curtain for *Façade*.

[10] Duff Smurthwaite (1896–1938), married 1917–26 to Sir Roger Twysden: 'a tall dark slant-eyed Englishwoman of thirty with a storied past and a notable capacity for drink and a string of admirers'. Carlos Baker, *Hemingway*. Model for Lady Brett Ashley in Hemingway's *The Sun Also Rises*.

[11] Probably David Plunket Greene (1904–41). Immensely tall brother of Olivia and so a member of the family with which Waugh had fallen in love. He drowned himself in the lake at Shearwater.

[12] Bryan Guinness (1905–   ). Married to Diana Mitford 1929–34, and to Elisabeth Nelson in 1936. Succeeded as Lord Moyne in 1944. His many publications include poetry, plays and autobiography.

[13] Michael, Earl of Rosse (1906–79). Roy Harrod wrote that at Oxford, 'Pink and very youthful, he sat there mainly listening'. Marie-Jacqueline Lancaster (ed.), *Brian Howard, Portrait of a Failure*, 1968. Married in 1935 Anne Messel, and so stepfather to the Earl of Snowdon.

[14] Arthur Waters Welch, nicknamed Lulu, a rich debonair member of the Hypocrites Club. Died 1934.

[15] Brian Howard (1905–58). Poet and impresario of the arts at Eton and Oxford. A flamboyant homosexual, he retained his 'outrageous' style with dwindling effect. An early anti-Fascist, he joined the RAF in the war. Committed suicide when his lover was killed in an accident. The model for Ambrose Silk in *Put Out More Flags*, he contributed a few characteristics to Anthony Blanche in *Brideshead Revisited*.

[16] Marie Laurencin (1886–1956), painter.

[17] William T. Woods.

[18] His father was in the British Army, his mother in Chicago society. Charles James himself was a dress-maker and designer of hats, in whose talent Cecil Beaton believed.

[19] Edward, Earl of Longford (1902–61) married Christine Trew in 1925. They had no children and he was succeeded by his brother Frank.

To Catherine Waugh
[January 1925]

[Arnold House,
Llanddulas,
Denbighshire.
North Wales.]

My Dear Mother

Thank you for your letter which arrived this morning. Last night a telegram was telephoned up & taken by Banks[1]. 'On, Waugh, On' from Hugh Lygon[2] & John Sutro[3].

There is a sea here & a railway & a quarry which periodically startles me with the most terrific cannonades. There are three pitch pine stair cases, the floors are covered with very highly polished linoleum. The house is on a hill with the perplexing result that one goes in at one door, climbs two stories & then on looking out of a window finds that one is on the ground floor again.

There is one sad thing. After all our trouble & expense I find that I shall not be required to wear either football or gym shoes. Do you think the shop would change them for some brown crepe soled shoes? If they will I[shall] send them back.

So far I have had nothing to do except preside at a sausage tea and say grace for it. It is the most curiously run school that ever I heard of. No time tables nor syllabuses nor nothing. Banks just wanders into the common room & says 'There are some boys in that class room. I think they are the first or perhaps the fourth. Will someone go & teach them Maths or Latin or something' and someone goes & I go on making a wood engraving. Perhaps things will be more highly organised later in the term.

Mrs Banks is not nearly as nice as you or Lady Plunket[4]. In fact I am inclined to dislike her. There is a partner's son, a man called Chaplin[5] who is definitely agreeable. He used to share rooms with Jim Hill at Teddy Hall; he adores Flecker; a man called Gordon who is dull & wears rimless pince-nez, a new tall man called Watson who has been a master in Egypt & Stowe & such places; & a horror, new & short, called Dean with a blue chin, black teeth, bad cold, & slight cockney accent.

The boys are given cream in their tea & heaps to eat & those I have seen look quite decent. We ate a good but teetotal dinner last night.

I will write again soon.

E

[1] Headmaster of Arnold House. Inexplicably referred to as Vanhomrigh in *A Little Learning*.

[2] Hugh Lygon (1904–36). Second son of Earl Beauchamp and a close Oxford friend, he was president of the Hypocrites Club when Waugh was elected. His circumstances and appearance contribute to Sebastian Flyte in *Brideshead Revisited*.

[3] John Sutro (1904–). Oxford and lifelong friend. He revived *The Cherwell* for which Waugh wrote on the Union; 'guide, philosopher and friend to all my generation, a consummate actor, mimic, improviser, journalist, vocalist, pianist and gastronomist'. Harold Acton, *Memoirs of an Aesthete*.

[4] Nickname for Gwen Plunket Greene, mother of Olivia.

[5] Nephew of Mr Banks.

To Harold Acton   Arnold House,
[February 1925]   Llanddulas,
                                               Denbighshire,
                                               North Wales.

Dear Harold,

I have meant to write to you a hundred times during the last three weeks but at all hours of the day I have been busied with teaching and beating and supervising footballings until when at last after dinner when all the animals were caged up and I at last had some peace, I have been too sad & too weary to write anything.

You have probably heard that I found it impossible to afford living in London any longer and have come here as a master. It is not really, I suppose, a bad school as schools go but it is a sorry waste of time & energy. I do not think that I am good at teaching – at any rate I have not succeeded so far in getting any idea into anyone's head. The only bright moments in the day are the times when posts are given out. Please write to me and tell me all about everyone at Oxford and particularly about yourself. Is the new book of Poems[1] published yet?

Alastair was coming here to see me this week end and I had been looking forward to it immensely – yesterday a wire arrived saying that he could not come after all. That was disappointing.

Here is a copy of a wood engraving I cut for Olivia². Do you like it at all? I want to write a book about Silenus³ but shall never have time.

Love
Evelyn

Write to me

¹ Harold Acton, *An Indian Ass*, 1925.

² Olivia Plunket Greene (1907–55). Waugh's love for her was at its height but she was never in love with him. A Roman Catholic, she became a Marxist as well, and lived in a cottage on the Longleat estate with her mother. She drank a lot and became eccentric, sending Waugh long ill-written letters about politics and religion. She never married.

³ Never written. Waugh gave the name to the architect in *Decline and Fall*.

To Harold Acton
[18 February 1925]

[Arnold House,
Llanddulas,
Denbighshire,
North Wales.]

Dear Harold,

An Indian Ass, which I had been eagerly awaiting arrived two days ago. You must think that I have, with all else, left my manners & friendship behind that I have taken so long to thank you for it. But indeed you cannot imagine what a time I am having. There is a woeful imposition called 'a week on duty' which has at last fallen to my turn. It means that from eight in the morning until eight at night one has literally no minute to spare in which to read a post card or visit a *cabinet*. From eight at night until ten I sit with a blue pencil correcting history essays. Last night a boy had written 'at this time it was reported that James II gave birth to a son but others supposed that it was conveyed to his bed in a hot water bottle'.

Now at last I have stolen two minutes in which to tell you how much I loved & love the book and how much I appreciate your sending them to me. Most of them I had heard before and they brought back many memories of a life infinitely remote. I still like the lament for Adonis by far the best and next to the 'Trépak' & 'Hilarity' – of the new ones I like the 'Prodigal Son' best.

I do not think Duckworth have produced it particularly well, do you? I prefer the plain cloth to the Gibbings paper but where was Peters drawing of the Ass? By the way how amusing about Peter¹ & Gosse². I hope he likes Silvia³ – she is so much the most amusing of the family tho' her painting is horrid – all iron bedsteads & Sickert. I must say I think the old man is tiresome.

I want to write a story about Silenus – very English & sentimental – A Falstaff forever babbling o' green fields – but shall never have time.

I got very very drunk all alone a little time back and was sick among some gooseberry bushes. I also found a hairdresser in a tiny town called Rhyl who collected Austin Spare's drawings and was writing a book about Cabbalism. I am growing a moustache & learning to smoke a pipe and ride a horse and am altogether quite becoming a man.

> My love to you,
> De profundis
> E

I leave here on April 2nd. Is there any chance of seeing you in London.

¹ Peter Quennell (1905–   ). Writer. In 1925 already a published poet and aspiring man of letters. Editor of the *Cornhill Magazine* 1944–51, *History Today* 1955–79.
² Sir Edmund Gosse (1849–1928). Established man of letters. Librarian to the House of Lords 1904–14; and from the age of seventy until his death chief reviewer for the *Sunday Times*. He had pronounced of Quennell, 'I have not met so poetical a poet since Swinburne.' A cousin and friend of Arthur Waugh.
³ Sylvia Gosse (1881–1968). Painter, daughter of Sir Edmund.

To Henry Yorke[1]   [Salisbury.]
Postcard [1926]

I have just finished reading *Blindness*. At the risk of appearing officious, I am impelled to write to you and tell you how very much I like it. It is extraordinary to me that anyone of our generation could have written so fine a book – and at Oxford of all places. I am seldom there now but, if I am, may I look you up?

¹ Henry Yorke (1905–75). Novelist under the pseudonym Henry Green. *Blindness,* his first book, had been started while he was at school. See Appendix of Names.

To Anthony Powell[1]   Barford House,
[October 1927]   Warwick.

Dear Tony
    Thanks for your letter. I am coming to London for a few days on Saturday. Would it be a good thing, perhaps, to call on Duckworth on Monday. I have one other chapter and am getting near the end now. Has that typist sent the second instalment?
    The pleasures of the countryside go on merrily, evictions, tremendous litigations about farmers shooting peoples' dogs, and scandal about the wicked Lord Warwick[2] who no one will know except Mrs Holden[3], because he is so full of drink

and drugs and sleeps with his secretary. This is a joke I am telling everyone because I think it is so funny, We were at the Holdens the other day and Mrs H. asked how Inez was and I said rather ill last time I saw her and living on Cachets de Faivre. Mrs H. 'I don't think I know the Faivres'.

Harvest Thanksgiving in the church. I help decorate the font but the rector's wife thinks my arrangement of pumpkins a little *suggestive* and changes it secretly.

We went to Kelmscott[4] the other day. I thought Miss Morris[5] a most detestable woman. I did put in some poisonous things about the mother.[6]

E

[1] Anthony Powell (1905–). Novelist. He was an editor at Duckworth, which had commissioned a biography of Rossetti from Waugh. See Appendix of Names.

[2] Sixth Earl of Warwick (1882–1928).

[3] Mrs Holden, an Edwardian beauty, was the mother of Inez Holden whom Waugh had got to know and like during his brief stay on the *Daily Express*. She also wrote novels including *Born Old; Died Young*, 1932.

[4] Kelmscott Manor House, bought by William Morris in 1871.

[5] May Morris (1862–1938), William Morris's daughter.

[6] The comments about Jane Morris in Waugh's *Rossetti* are not poisonous.

TO HAROLD ACTON   145 North End Road, N.W.11.
[January? 1928]

Dear Harold,

. . . Thank you ever so much for the copy of *Five Saints*[1] which reached me this morning. I have been reading them again with the utmost delight & admiration & with pride at the dedication. I hope it is selling well. I saw Peter's[2] review in the *New Statesman* but no others. I hear no reassuring news about Holden.

What attitude are you taking up about Brian & Robert's[3] book. I want so much to discuss this with you.

Can you one day soon come to tea with me & Evelyn[4] and Pansy Pakenham[5] at their lodgings in Sloane Square? I have told them so much about you & they are anxious to meet you.

Peter seems well & better.

I spend most of my day in an Institute of Surgery with a leg in an electric oven. *Rossetti* will be out soon. The novel does not get on.[6] I should so much value your opinion on whether I am to finish it.

Best love
Evelyn

[1] Harold Acton, *Five Saints and an Appendix* (poems), 1927.

[2] Presumably Peter Quennell, though the review is anonymous.

[3] Brian Howard and Robert Byron (1905–41). The latter was a writer, described as 'a shade portly, very fair, with a pale plump 18th century face and a revolving ruminant eye' in *Brian Howard*. Waugh subsequently fell out with his noisy Oxford friend over his anti-Catholicism. A Byzantine expert, Byron's most admired book is *The Road to Oxiana*, 1928. Howard and Byron planned a symposium to be

called 'Value' to which Waugh was to contribute a drawing of God consisting entirely of abstract form 'yet in some measure coherent and having perhaps some slight relation to the revelation of St John the divine'. (Letter by Howard.) Nothing appeared.

⁴ Evelyn Gardner (1903–   ). Married to Waugh 1928–30, to Sir John Heygate 1930–36 and to Ronald Nightingale in 1937.

⁵ Lady Pansy Pakenham (1904–   ). Married 1928–60 to Henry Lamb, the painter. Sister of Frank, and Violet, who married Anthony Powell. She wrote many serious letters to Waugh but his to her have been lost.

⁶ *Decline and Fall*, 1928.

TO PATRICK BALFOUR¹   145 North End Road, N.W.11.
[20 February 1928]

Dear Patrick

Thank you so much for the advertisement. As soon as I see any hope from my window in the Slough of Despond I will let you know.

As a matter of fact I think there will probably be an elopement quite soon.

Yours
Evelyn

¹ Patrick Balfour (1904–76). Writer. Succeeded as Lord Kinross 1939. At this time a gossip-columnist. See Appendix of Names.

TO ANTHONY POWELL   [The Barley Mow,
[7 April 1928]   Nr Wimborne,
                                              Dorset.]

Dear Tony

Thank you so much for your letter & the advance copy of *Rossetti*. I hope my other letter did not sound impatient – you know how temperamental we men of letters are. I [think] the books appearance admirable, dont you? Cover, wrapper, paper illustrations all excellent. I see a misprint or two that escaped me but they are purely literal & I dont think worth an errata slip. I suppose that the presentation copies wont go out until publication. You might keep an eye on the packers and see that they do not confuse the cards I sent Tom¹. There were seven inscribed 'with love' to go to the first list, one 'with kind regards' to Lady Burghclere² and a 'Geoffrey & Alathea³ with kind regards' for Geoffrey Fry. It might be a bore if they got mixed. If you can spare one I should rather like *Artwork*⁴ to have a review copy. I met the editor and he said he would give it a good notice. I have written to Sieveking⁵ about broadcasting. I think he is the man to approach.

I see the good custom growing of publishing single short stories at 2/6 or a shilling. Is there any chance of your doing this in your pamphlet series? I am thinking out a story about a religious maniac being murdered by a tramp. Called 'Advent.'

I hope the novel will be finished in a week. I will send it to you as soon as it is typed & then want to revise it very thoroughly and enlarge it a bit. I think at present it shows signs of being too short. How do these novelists make their books so long. I'm sure one could write any novel in the world on two post cards. Do you like 'Untoward Incidents'[6] as a title.

How glad I am we dropped 'Last born of Eve' now I see clown Mégroz's[7] absurd title. I am sure reviewers would have jumped at it.

Will you by any chance be at the Gamble-Carew[8] alliance at Exeter? The Sutros asked me to a Synagogue. I wish I could go.

By the way how many have you printed of *R*?

Lots of love to all at Henrietta Street from me & Evelyn.

E.W.

This is such a nice pub. Why dont you come to Wimborne for a week end?

[1] Tom Balston, a director of Duckworth.

[2] Waugh's future mother-in-law.

[3] Alathea Gardner (1893–1968). Evelyn's sister, Waugh's future sister-in-law. In 1915 she had married Geoffrey Fry (1888–1960) who was private secretary to Stanley Baldwin 1923–39, and created a baronet in 1937.

[4] *Artwork International*, founded 1927.

[5] Lance Sieveking (1896–1972). Joined the BBC in 1924. Produced the first television play.

[6] In another letter to Powell, Waugh explained: 'The phrase, you remember, was used by the Duke of Wellington in commenting on the destruction of the Turkish Fleet in time of peace at Navarino. It seems to set the right tone of mildly censorious detachment.'

[7] R.L. Mégroz (1891–1968). Journalist. Published in 1928 *Dante Gabriel Rossetti, the Poet of Heaven in Earth*.

[8] Dudley Carew married Anthea Gamble, daughter of the Dean of Exeter.

To Harold Acton   10 Hill St., Poole.
[27 April 1928]

Thank you so much for your letter. I am glad *Rossetti* reached you tho' I was unable to inscribe it as I should have liked. As you know I am not proud of the book. I think it has some eloquent phrases but there are few pages I can read without a shiver at some place or other. I have finished the novel. I think it is quite amusing. I am at work doing illustrations for it. May I dedicate it to you.[1] I am at present staying with Henry Lamb[2] who is painting my portrait & delivering illuminating discourses to me on Cézanne. E & I return to London in a few weeks & look forward greatly to seeing you again.

Love
E

[1] He did so.

[2] Henry Lamb (1902–60). His portrait of Waugh was exhibited in 1929.

To the Editor of the Times Literary Supplement
17 May 1928

D. G. ROSSETTI

Sir, – In this week's *Literary Supplement* I notice with gratitude the prominence given to my Life of Rossetti. Clearly it would be frivolous for a critic with pretensions even as modest as my own to genuine aesthetic standards to attempt to bandy opinions with a reviewer who considers that Rossetti's drawings 'refine on' those of Ingres; but I hope you will allow me space in which to call attention to three points in which your article appears to misrepresent me.

Your reviewer refers to me throughout as 'Miss Waugh.' My Christian name, I know, is occasionally regarded by people of limited social experience as belonging exclusively to one or other sex; but it is unnecessary to go further into my book than the paragraph charitably placed inside the wrapper for the guidance of unleisured critics, to find my name with its correct prefix of 'Mr.' Surely some such investigation might in merest courtesy have been taken before your reviewer tumbled into print with such phrases as 'a Miss of the Sixties.' In the second place, she, or he, writes 'the "squalid" Rossetti,' the inference of the inverted commas being that the phrase is my own; it is not. In the third place, there is nowhere in my book or in any of my other writings any statement or suggestion that could possibly imply, to an intelligent reader, that I prefer 'Morris's interminable, flaccid "grinds" to the best constructed narratives in English verse.'

Your obedient servant,
EVELYN ARTHUR ST JOHN WAUGH

To Harold Acton
[August 1928]

17a Canonbury Square,
Islington N1.

Dear Harold,

Thank you so much for your most kind letter about *Decline and Fall*. I am glad to think it amused you a little. Anyway I enjoyed writing it which is more than I can say about Rossetti or about Wesley with whom I am now travailing. As recreation I am beginning a detective story full of murder & mystery.[1]

Do please come & see us as soon as ever you can. A 19 bus from the corner of Theobalds Road, opposite the L.C.C. school where I learned carpentry will take you to us in about ten minutes. If you ask the conductor to tell you when you reach Compton Terrace, & then walk up Canonbury Lane you will find our dilapidated Regency Square.[2]

Do ring up and propose yourself for dinner one evening soon. We have very little furniture at present but I am anxious to show you what we have & to have your advice about decorations.

We await *Humdrum*[3] eagerly. When will it be out?

Yours affectionately,
Evelyn

[1] No fragment of either project survives.

[2] The Waughs, who, since their marriage, had been living in Harold Acton's flat or at Underhill, had taken a long lease in this then cheap district.

[3] Novel by Harold Acton, 1928.

To Harold Acton
[October 1928]

Oare House,
Marlborough.

Dear Harold,

I am so sorry not to have written before. The last three weeks have been very distracting with Evelyn in bed and my flat in possession of nurses & doctors. We have got away at last and we are staying in my brother in laws house[1] in the downs near Marlborough in great peace & luxury.

I do hope *Humdrum* is doing well. I think I shall be able to review it for the *Observer*. I was so sorry not to do it in *Vogue* but my article was written weeks ago, before it appeared.

We may be going to stay with Robert [Byron] at Savernake for a week when we leave here.

Meanwhile I have done no work of any kind. I hope to be able to do some here.

Before I left London I went to see Chirico's[2] *Vogue* covers & the Maillol[3] exhibition. I was disappointed by the wood engravings but transported by the sculpture. His first works I had seen except in photographs. I was also transported by *Orlando*[4] tho' I regretted the slight Clive Bell self consciousness – the references to the fact of the book she is writing being a book.

I did not 'cotton on' to Raymond Mortimer[5], I am afraid, but I like Reggie Turner[6] very much indeed.

Love
Evelyn

[1] Oare House, belonging to Geoffrey Fry.

[2] Georgio de Chirico (1888–1978). Italian painter linked with the Surrealists.

[3] Aristide Maillol (1861–1944). Sculptor.

[4] By Virginia Woolf, 1929.

[5] Raymond Mortimer (1895–1980). Literary critic.

[6] Reggie Turner (1869–1938) Journalist and wit. Loyal friend to Oscar Wilde.

To A.D.Peters[1]   17a Canonbury Square.

Dear Peters

I wondered who was responsible for my summons to *Vogue*. Thank you so much. The sum of five guineas was mentioned rather vaguely – I do not know whether this was for the article or for each thousand words. It would be nice to think the latter. Alas there was some vagueness as to whether this was a single commission or a more or less regular post[?]. Could you find out about this.

Yes I shall be pleased to write 'Wyndham Lewis stuff' or any other kind of 'stuff' that anyone will buy. Do you think any paper would like an illustrated, humorous London letter – like the 'Letters of Eve' in the good days of Fish.

I would also write an humorous serial called 'Grand Young man' dealing with the arrival in London of a young, handsome & incredibly wealthy marquess hitherto brought up in seclusion and the attempts made by various social, religious, political bodies & ambitious mothers to get hold of him.

I would also write a detective serial about the murder of an author rather like Alec Waugh.

I have both these stories fairly clear in my mind.[2]

Please fix up anything that will earn me anything – even cricket criticism or mothers welfare notes.

Yours
Evelyn Waugh

[1] Augustus Detlof Peters (1892–1973). Waugh's literary agent and friend for the rest of his life. Often referred to as 'Pete' or 'Peter'. See Appendix of Names.
[2] Neither of them appeared.

To W.N.Roughead[1]   17a Canonbury Square.

Dear Roughhead,

I have tonight sent off the last of the *Passing Show*[2] articles to Connery Chappel & will let you have them as soon as they come back typed.

Could you get the *Express* to take an article on the Youngest Generation's view of Religion? – very serious & Churchy. I see they are doing a series of the sort. It seems to me that it would be so nice if we could persuade them that I personify the English youth movement.

Has anything become of that little sketch called 'Loyalties'. It seems to me it might conceivably do for one of the weeklies – *New Statesman* & *Nation*.

Did the *Strand* like 'Consequences'?

Yours
Evelyn Waugh

Decline & *Fall* seems to be a best seller. That ought to make journalism easier, oughtn't it. But I find humorous articles an awful strain.

[1] W.N.Roughead (1905–75). Worked at A.D.Peters. See Appendix of Names.
[2] A magazine 'devoted to the brighter side of life' which ran 1915–39.

To Harold Acton   Union Club,
[February or March 1929]   Port Said. [1]

Dear Harold,

I should have written before but I have been so worried about Evelyn & with cabling bulletins to all our relatives that I have not written a letter since we started. You have probably heard how ill she has been. Double pneumonia critically ill for a fortnight.

At last she is out of danger. Meanwhile of course our trip is broken, we shall be here for a month, & all my work at a standstill. I hope now things are easier to start on a new novel.

In spite of all reports this is an intolerably dull town. Two expensive & very dirty hotels, one brothel, a cinema & this awful club where the shipping-office clerks try to create an Ethel M. Dell garrison life by drinking endless 'gin & tonic' & talking about 'the old country' & 'pukka sahibs'.

Apart from everything else this illness has been frightfully expensive, so that we shall not be able to do any more travelling unless perhaps we go to Cyprus for a fortnight while Evelyn recuperates. Do write to me & tell me about all you are doing

                                        Love
                                        Evelyn

I have sent off some cigarettes to you said to be aphrodisiac.

[1] The Waughs had set out on a Mediterranean cruise, intended as a belated honeymoon.

To Arthur Waugh   Union Club,
[March 1929]   Port Said.

Dear Chapman[1],

I am so sorry to hear of Mrs Pawley[?]'s death. Who will take care of that little girl?

I gather my letters have been delayed because I keep writing although it is hard to find anything to say.

Evelyn goes out for a short drive most days & is making good progress. We have had to give up the idea of Cyprus because everyone warns us that there are no hotels on the island fit for an invalid, but are going South instead to Helwan or Heliopolis or Luxor – wherever in fact I can persuade an hotel to give me advantageous terms in return for commendation in my book.

I dined at the Consulate the other evening. You can imagine what it was like when I say that after dinner the consuls wife led the women guests from the room with [the] words 'goodbye darling men. Keep your naughtiest stories for us'.

Alastair [2] has given us another £50 so we can just struggle along for another week or two. I hope to get some money out of the insurance company too. We nearly gave up Evelyn's policy at Christmas, so in some things we have been lucky.

I am so sorry to hear that you are so hard up. I hope you have not been gambling. I played Boule at the Casino here the other night in the hope of making our fortunes but without success.

I wonder when you are taking your holiday & where. We shall be coming back through France in the middle of May & might join you.

Yes, I think I can promise a novel[3] for the autumn and a very good one too.

I went to a Circus the other evening. About half way through a terrific fight broke out. Police whistles, truncheons, dust, tears, stones, fists everything except fire arms. The Arab next to me spoke English so I asked what the fight was about. He looked blank and said that there had been no fight as far as he knew. I pointed to the seething crowd at our feet. 'Oh that,' he said 'That is only the police'.

I am so glad you like Alan[4]. He is very pugnacious but I think he is kind if treated kindly. Taglioni does make nice food doesnt he?

The food here is pretty bad but excellent bread & vegetables. Everything except cigarettes very expensive. The very best Egyptian cigarettes cost about 5/- a hundred. I wish I could send some back but you would have to pay so much duty.

There are 3 good bookshops but none of them sell *Decline & Fall*. There is a cinema and a dance every Saturday. I went last Saturday with the consuls harlot wife. She opened her mouth and invited me to throw sugar into it.

Evelyns doctor is really very nice indeed.

The notices of Lambs exhibition seem rather tepid.[5]

Love
E

[1] Arthur Waugh was so nicknamed. He had become Chairman of Chapman & Hall in 1925.

[2] Alastair Graham, who was living in Athens, came to Port Said for a few days.

[3] *Vile Bodies* was published in 1930, but Waugh had not started writing. Duckworth had rejected *Decline and Fall* on the grounds of indecency. Waugh submitted it to Chapman & Hall in his father's absence and it was swiftly accepted. They published all his novels, but Duckworth continued to bring out his travel books. Anthony Powell considers that the split might not have taken place had not Gerald Duckworth, who was connected to Evelyn Gardner, involved himself.

[4] Probably Alan Hillgarth, author of *The Princess and The Perjurer*, 1924.

[5] Henry Yorke had written: 'Lamb is having his show and there is a portrait of you, not one of his best things, hanging on the walls of the Leicester Galleries. You look highly suspicious of everything in it. But there was a drawing of Evelyn which was frightfully good.'

TO HAROLD ACTON
Easter Day [1 April] 1929

Mena House Hotel,
Pyramids,
Cairo.

Dear Harold,

Evelyn & I came here on Thursday. I was glad to leave Port Said with all its associations of illness. This is a hotel just under the Pyramids some miles out of Cairo. Very enormous & hideously expensive but sunny & I think a good place for Evelyn's recuperation. There is a huge garden full of garish flowers & improbable insects – all rather like the final scene of a Paris review. The people range from exquisitely amusing Australian trippers with sun helmets & fly whisks to Cairo demi-mondaines in picture frocks – one with a pet monkey in silver harness which sits & fleas its rump on the terrace.

I spend most of my day in the bathing pool. There is a magnificent negro swimming instructor who recalls the rare atmosphere of Bourdon Street. The Sphinx is a complete fraud – a shapeless lump of masonry about as enigmatic as Romney Somers[1] but the Tutankhamen discoveries are real works of art – of exquisite grace – just as fine as anything which has survived of Athenian Art. I have tried to get photographs of some of the most lovely things but none are published. Instead I sent you some pornographica from Port Said. I hope that they were not confiscated in the post. I hope too that they did not make you pay any duty on the cigarettes. I paid it here, but I rather doubted the honesty of the tobacconist.

All the papers I open are full of photographs of your party at Lancaster Gate. It did not cause a twinge of homesickness in either of us but we do wish you were here with us to see the museum & laugh at the people in the hotel.

We leave here on the 12th & go to Malta where I hear there are fine churches & then to Constantinople for alas only two days. Then via Ragusa to Venice for another two days. It will just give me time I suppose to see some pictures. I wish it were for longer. Do please send us advice as to what to see in Venice in so short a time. Remember I know nothing of Venetian painting except from what I have seen in London & the Louvre. Where are the best Mantegnas or are they in Florence? I scarcely saw anything of Naples as I was so worried about Evelyn and so pestered by pimps whenever I set foot on the shore. But we are visiting Naples again on the way home. I suppose that there is no hope of your being in Florence in the middle of May?

Alastair visited us for two days at Port Said – a characteristic excursion.

Please give our love to all our friends. We both look forward so much to seeing you again.

Love
Evelyn

[1] An Oxford contemporary, who kept up a gallant façade even when losing all his money on horses. At one time kept a fish and chip shop, later a regular major in the R.A.S.C.

To HENRY YORKE   M Tokatliyan Oteli,
[4 May 1929]   Pera, Rue Istiklal,
                                 Istanbul

Dear Henry,

Well I must say that I *do* think it most extraordinary to be called 'Diggy'[1], (but I once knew a young man called Geoffrey Biddulph who had very eccentric habits as he had spent most of his life in James Joyce's Dublin; he had a sister called Hermione who lived in sin with a genealogist who kept pet squirrels. However all this is neither here nor there.) Evelyn and I are thrilled about your engagement. You must be married *at once* very obtrusively – a fashionable wedding is worth a four column review in the *Times Literary Supplement* to a novelist. It was a great sorrow to me that circumstances deprived us of a real wedding. I have a great many ideas about them. May I come and stage manage yours. No Florentine maids or picture hats, I can tell you.

We are also enormously looking forward to reading your novel[2] & it is maddening that I shall have to wait so long to see it. I think it is hopeless trying to send it out. There is a bottle of hair wash from Dellaz which has been following me round the Mediterranean since the end of February & meanwhile I am rapidly becoming bald.

I cant remember when I wrote last but I think it was a long time ago. From Egypt we went to Malta, some horribly picturesque streets – cobbles & steps & even '*native costume*' but the fortifications were clean and sensible looking and some remarkable baroque churches. Then we got onto the *Stella Polaris* again & have thrown ourselves into the social life of a 'pleasure cruise'. I am a member of the Sports Committee which is very serious indeed and Evelyn had to organise a fancy dress dance. I have a great rival for leadership of the bright young people in a stout Belgian. Today he appeared on deck in a Royal Yacht Squadron cap so I know when I am beaten.

All the sailors on the ship took to seamanship late in life. The Captain was a bank manager until a few years ago, the Purser the editor of a humorous Norwegian weekly, and the First engineer taught dancing. It seems very easy to be a captain because whenever there is any navigation to be done they hire a special pilot.

At Constantinople, we went to luncheon at the Embassy ten minutes after they had all sat down. When I recovered consciousness I found myself completely surrounded by Sitwells while H.E. the Ambassador with gallantry & tact of the corps diplomatique was making extensive & accurate quotations from *Decline & Fall* to a woman next to him, having been told by a secretary that one of his guests had written it, & thinking it was her.

We had fun at Athens with Mark[3] & Alastair [Graham]. Their new hobby is to talk Greek with a cockney accent so it is all very much like home from home.

Mark very sweet & skittish feeling relieved of the burden of keeping up appearances & having terrific affairs in an atmosphere of garlic & Charlie Chaplin moustaches.

When you are married will your father make you head of all his factories and will you still be poor. Do come and live in Islington. Will Diggy like me and Evelyn?

Sachy Sitwell[4] met a German on the boat who said 'Ah you English know how to do your guesswork. The red face tells me you like champagne, eh?'

> Love from us both,
> Evelyn.

---

[1] Adelaide Biddulph (1901–   ). Henry Yorke had written, 'To give you some more personal news I'm getting married. A girl with the strange name of Diggy Adelaide Biddulph. She hides a stupendous intellect behind an enormous capacity for idleness and an appearance of innocuousness.'

[2] *Living*, 1929.

[3] Mark Ogilvie-Grant (1905–69). Cousin of the Countess of Seafield and close friend of Nancy

JUNE 1929 35

Mitford, in whose *Pigeon Pie* he appears as 'The Wonderful Old Songster of Kew Green'. He lived in Athens after the war. Skilful imitator of, for instance, Clara Butt singing 'Land of Hope and Glory'.
    [4] Sacheverell Sitwell (1897–   ). Writer. Succeeded his brother Osbert as baronet 1969.

To Henry Yorke   145 North End Road, N.W.11.
[June 1929]

Dear Henry,

I have just got back and read *Living*. Someone told me, Harold I think, that it has not been getting very good notices. Has it been done in *Life and Letters* yet, do you know, because I want very much to say in print how enormously I admire it.

I really think that besides being a delightful book, it is an *important* one. I admire so much the way you have written it – like those aluminium ribbons one stamps out in railway stations on penny in the slot machines. The absence of all that awful thing they call 'word pictures', the way in which no appearances are described. The telegraphic narrative which might have been all wrong if you had used a present tense and is so perfectly right in the past. Indeed I don't see how else you could have made a framework for the dialogue which is magnificent. You seem to have invented an entirely new language, doing for Birmingham born people what Singe [*sic*] did with Irish – making an artistic form out of a dialect so that every word is startling. In fact I would have liked *all* the purpler patches eliminated – but that I know from experience is the thing one cannot bear to be told. It reminded me just a little of Opal Whitely's *Diary*[1].

I liked the rich people parts less than the poor and envied you the way in which you just stopped writing about them any more – though I thought the Tom Tyler incidents brilliant 'but it is quite true to say that there was nothing dirty in all this' and 'Dropping suddenly to be intimate' page 147. (I'm not sure that isn't the best sentence in the book.) and 'goodness she did like it' p. 155. Another sentence I loved was 'He spoke like he was sorry Lil was as she was'.

But I mustn't start copying out all the book because I expect that after writing it and reading it how many times in proof you know most of it well.

The thing I *envied* most was the way you managed the plot which is oddly enough almost exactly the way Firbank managed his.

I thought the incident of the courtesan and old Mr Dupret had more in it than you made.

I liked the way Bert wanted to go to the lavatory in the train – in fact the various ways they talked to each other about lavatories all through.

Evelyn is well again and is going to Canonbury Square to live in my flat with Nancy Mitford[2] while I write a book in a pub.

I hear Robert [Byron] has beaten us all by going to India in an aeroplane which is the sort of success which I call tangible.

A bald Norwegian with one eye fell in love with Evelyn so we spent all the last ten days eating caviar and drinking too much champagne.

We found bills of over £200 waiting for us and each overdrawn at our banks so I must write a lot quickly. I would rather fly to India. *The Birth Control Review* of New York have asked me for an article!

Do go and see Evelyn & Nancy – they would love it. When will you be married, where?

Love
Evelyn

¹ *The Diary of Opal Whiteley*, 1920, written by a whimsical child of six or seven.

² Nancy Mitford (1904–73). Novelist and biographer, and close friend of Waugh's. See Appendix of Names.

[Written on Bristol Hotel, Cairo, paper]

To Henry Yorke
[20 July 1929]

Abingdon Arms,
Beckley,
Oxford.

Dear Henry,

I was relieved to get your letter because once when I wrote a book a young man called Carew whom I had always liked wrote to tell me how good he thought my book was and I was so disgusted by his letter that I never could speak to him again without acute embarrassment and I thought perhaps my letter had had that effect on you well I am glad it hasn't.

I have written 25,000 words of a novel in ten days. It is rather like P. G. Wodehouse all about bright young people. I hope it will be finished by the end of the month & then I shall just have time to write another book before your party.

By the way would you like a seventeenth (or eighteenth I'm not sure) century water colour of the Prodigal Son which I bought in Malta for a wedding present or are you against 'antiques' & would rather have a labour saving device for the kitchen?

Nancy Mitford came & drove us to Savernake on Sunday & I formed a clear impression that she & Robert are secretly married or is that my novelists imagination?

In the evenings I sit with the famous in the kitchen drinking beer. I like so much the way they don't mind not talking. Rich people always get shy when there's a silence or else they start thinking but in this public house they will all sit mute for five or ten minutes and then just go on talking at exactly the place they left off. Were they like that at Birmingham. By the way *did* you say what the papers said you said about being jolly good pals with the boys at the works & all that? (I didn't know about Ld. Rosebery and was rather impressed.)

Do go and see Evelyn & Nancy. I've just sent them some caviar so you could eat that.

Are you going to Bryan & Diana's¹ party. I might go up for it if I thought there would be anyone who wouldn't be too much like the characters in my new book.

I know what you mean about purple patches. My new book is black with them –
but then I live by my pen as they say and you don't.

Yours
Evelyn

My distinguished sentiments to your young lady. I hope she's still firm about
Talkies

[1] Diana Mitford (1910–   ). Married 1929–34 to Bryan Guinness. See Appendix of Names.

TO HAROLD ACTON
Tuesday [July 1929]

The Abingdon Arms,
Beckley,
Oxford.

Dear Harold,

It is sad that we never meet now. How are you? I was in London yesterday & the
day before but they told me that you were away or I would have come to call. I see
your name often in the papers, reported as appearing at parties. I nearly came up
again today for Bryan's party but I feel so chained to this novel. I am sure you will
disapprove of it. It is a welter of sex and snobbery written simply in the hope of
selling some copies. Then if it is [at] all a success I want to try and write something
more serious. I have done half of it and hope to get it finished in another three
weeks.

It is very peaceful here, completely uninterrupted. I bought a copy of a magazine
in Oxford because I saw your name on the cover and found that poem I particularly
like about the bath.

I went to see Peter Quennell who seems still to be beset with quarrels – this time
with Sachie. Why is it I wonder that people who write books seem incapable of
sanity in their personal relations (except, I hope, us).

Do, if you ever have a spare minute between the Prince of Wales and Emerald
Lady Cunard[1], go and see Evelyn & Nancy in Islington. They would so much like it.

I long to see more of the Medici book[2] and to hear your criticisms of my
novelette.

I hope you are not really angry with me for admiring Henry's book.

Love
Evelyn

[1] Maud Burke (1872–1948). The hostess of her time. Married Sir Bache Cunard in 1895. Called
herself Emerald from 1926. 'I thought I had never seen a more amusing-looking little parakeet in her
pastel-coloured plumage'. *Cecil Beaton's Diaries 1948–55*, 1973.

[2] Harold Acton's *The Last of the Medici* was privately printed in 1930, published in 1932.

To Catherine and Arthur Waugh   The Ridgeway,
[August? 1929]   Shere,
                                                  Guildford.

Dear Mother & Father,
    I asked Alec to tell you the sad & to me radically shocking news that Evelyn has
gone to live with a man called Heygate[1]. I am accordingly filing a petition for
divorce[2].
    I am afraid that this will be a blow to you but I assure you not nearly as severe a
blow as it is to me.
    I am staying here with Lady Vita Russell[3] on my way to Bryan & Diana Guinness
in Sussex. I shall be in London on Wednesday or Thursday. My plans are vague
about the flat etc.
    May I come & live with you sometimes?

                                                  Love
                                                  Evelyn

Evelyns defection was preceded by no kind of quarrel or estrangement[4]. So far as I
knew we were both serenely happy. It must be some hereditary *tic*[5]. Poor Baroness.

    [1] John Heygate (1903–76). Writer. Succeeded as baronet 1940. See Appendix of Names.
    [2] He was persuaded not to until 3 September.
    [3] Lady Victoria Leveson-Gower married in 1896 Harold Russell, nephew of the Duke of Bedford. His
sister Elizabeth married Richard Plunket Greene.
    [4] On 9 July Evelyn had sent Waugh a letter declaring that she was in love with, and the lover of,
Heygate. There had been a reconciliation. Waugh had left London on 26 July and returned on 1 August
to find the house deserted. The next day he received a letter explaining that she had left him. She went to
Venice to stay with an aunt.
    [5] Two of Evelyn Gardner's sisters had been divorced.

To Harold Acton   The Ridgeway,
4 August 1929   Shere,
                                                  Guildford.

A note to tell you what you may have already heard. That Evelyn has been pleased
to make a cuckold of me with Heygate & that I have filed a petition for divorce.

                                                  E.W.

To Harold Acton   Barford House,
[September? 1929]   Warwick.

My Dear Harold
    No. Evelyn's defection was preceded by no sort of quarrel or estrangement.[1]
    Certainly the fact that she should have chosen a ramshackle oaf like Heygate adds

a little to my distress but my reasons for divorce are simply that I cannot live with anyone who is avowedly in love with someone else.

Everyone is talking so much nonsense on all sides of me about my affairs, that my wits reel. Evelyn's family & mine join in asking me to 'forgive' her whatever that may mean.

I am escaping to Ireland for a weeks motor racing in the hope of finding an honourable grave.

I have absolutely no plans for the future. Evelyn is to live on at Canonbury. Naturally I have done no work at all for two months.

I did not know it was possible to be so miserable & live but I am told that this is a common experience.

Love
E

[1] Acton had written on 5 August: 'Are you so very male in your sense of possession? I am somewhat astounded by all the philandering I see around me. Or is it the fact of its being Heygate? Or is it due to quarrels and boredom?'

To A. D. Peters
[September? 1929]

Knockmaroon,
Castleknock,
Co. Dublin.

Could you please find out how long they want this article[1] to be (the subject of which seems mildly comical in my present circumstances) and what they will pay. I dont know at all my next move but letters will be forwarded from 145 North End Road, N.W.11 so will you write there.

E.W.

[1] The *Daily Mail* published his article 'Let the Marriage Ceremony Mean Something' on 8 October.

To Henry Yorke
[September 1929]

The Royal George,
Appledore,
N. Devon.

Dear Henry,

I put off going abroad and came here to make a last effort at finishing my novel. It has been infinitely difficult and is certainly the last time I shall try to make a book about sophisticated people. It all seems to shrivel up & rot internally and I am relying on a sort of cumulative futility for any effect it may have. All the characters are gossip writers. As soon as I have enough pages covered to call it a book I shall join Bryan & Diana [Guinness] in Paris.

Do you & Dig share my admiration for Diana? She seems to me the one encouraging figure in this generation – particularly now she is pregnant – a great germinating vat of potentiality like the vats I saw at their brewery.

I suppose it would be absurd to suggest you coming here for a week end? It is a very long journey and not very comfortable when you get here but it is lonely and there is very interesting bathing if either of you like that full of unexpected cross currents. I can't remember how much I told you in my letter about the details of my divorce – but I expect you know all about it now.

I had a harrowing time with my relatives & Evelyns. The only parents to take a sensible line were the basement boy[Heygate]'s who stopped his allowance, cut him out of their wills and said they never wanted to see him again.

There is some odd hereditary *tic* in all those Gardner girls – I think it is an intellectual failing more than anything else. My horror and detestation of the basement boy are unqualified. There is practically no part of one that is not injured when a thing like this happens but naturally vanity is one of the things one is most generally conscious of – or so I find.

Can you suggest anything for me to do after Christmas for six months or so – preferably remunerative but that is not important – but essentially remote & unliterary? I might go and dig in Lord Redesdale's bogus gold mine [1] if he would let me. Or there is a man called Spearman [2] who says I can hunt whales. Do think of something?

                                                            Evelyn

P.S. If you hear any amusing opinions about my divorce do tell me. Particularly from the older generation. The Gardner line is that I am very 'unforgiving'.
P.P.S. It is extraordinary how homosexual people however kind & intelligent simply dont understand at all what one feels in this kind of case.

[1] Lord Redesdale, father of Nancy and Diana among other Mitfords, had a real though unremunerative gold mine in Canada.

[2] Sir Alexander Spearman (1901–   ). At Hertford with Waugh. Conservative MP 1941–66. He has no recollection of whales.

TO A. D. PETERS   Beckley,
[1929]   Oxon.

Dear Peters
    ... If *Harper's Bazaar* wont print *Vile Bodies* I'm afraid no one will, will they? Perhaps I could carve it up into short stories?

                                                Yours
                                                Evelyn Waugh

To HENRY YORKE   17A Canonbury Square.
[December? 1929]

Dear Henry,
   You must not think from this address that I have gone to stay with the Heygates.
I am living at Thame at Mr Fothergill's & expect to be here off and on until
Christmas. Why do not you & Dig come for a week end (as my guests of course.) It
would be such fun. Bryan & Diana have just left. It is really quite comfortable.
   I am so delighted to hear of your creating a scene at a night club with the
Heygates. I have decided that I have gone on for too long in that fog of
sentimentality & I am going to stop hiding away from everyone. I was getting into a
sort of Charlie Chaplinish Pagliacci attitude to myself as the man with a tragedy in
his life and a tender smile for children. So all that must stop and one conclusion I am
coming to is that I do not like Evelyn & that really Heygate is about her cup of tea.
   That novel about Vile Bodies is being printed off and I will send a copy as soon as
I get them dreading your verdict very much because now when anyone says they
liked *Decline & Fall* I think oh how bored they will be by *Vile Bodies*.
   I see Hamish [1] & Maurice [2] & I saw Harold [Acton] yesterday.
   I am afraid this is all about myself. What I really set out to do was to ask after Digs
tonsils. I do hope everything was completely successful. Did you go to the Brighton
Pageant. Alex Waugh was Nelson which I think is very funny.
   I envy you the Metropole.

                                            Love to you both,
                                            Evelyn

   [1] Hamish St Clair-Erskine (1909–73). 'An elegant and amiable young social butterfly'. Harold Acton,
Nancy Mitford. A major in the Coldstream Guards, he was wounded, taken prisoner, escaped and
awarded the MC in the war. Loved by Nancy Mitford.
   [2] Maurice Bowra (1898–1971). Warden of Wadham College, Oxford, from 1938. Knighted in 1951.
See Appendix of Names.

To HENRY AND ADELAIDE YORKE   12 Rue de Poitiers,
[1929]   Paris VIIeme.

Dear Henry and Dig,
   I am afraid that I am getting rather involved with things in Paris – a Russian
woman is painting my portrait who works with a flat iron & a curry comb & things
like that & there is a woman called Jump who I have to take about & I can't afford a
ticket home so that with one thing & another I must give up our Oxford expedition.
Nancy would adore to join you if Dig would act as chaperone – would that be a bore.
She leaves here on Monday. We are both staying with Diana. Then I go to David &
Tamara. [1]
   We saw a magnificent Czech Film called *Erotikon*.
   Also innumerable dress shows.

And I have eaten a lot of nice food.
I was sick in that aeroplane.

Everyone sends love,
Evelyn.

Nancy does not *expect* to go to Oxford or know that I am asking so it would not matter if you don't want her. But if you do write to her at High Wycombe and I know it would delight her.

[1] Tamara Abelson married David Talbot Rice (1903–74). He was Professor of the History of Art at the University of Edinburgh from 1934.

3 Divorce and Remarriage
1929-1939

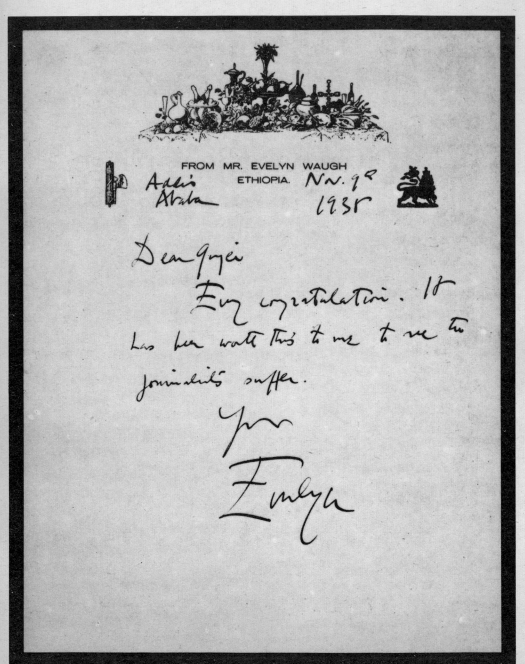

FROM MR. EVELYN WAUGH
ETHIOPIA.

Addis
Ababa

Nov. 9ᵉ
1935

Dear Joyce

Every congratulation. It
has been worth this to me to see two
journalists suffer.

Yours

Evelyn

To Hubert Knickerbocker, 9 November 1935

Introduction

The failure of his marriage and the success of his book changed Waugh's life completely. After he had lost his first wife and before he had found his second he had no home. For eight years he stayed at the Savile Club or with his parents in London, at pubs or with friends in the country. Alec Waugh had discovered the Easton Court Hotel near Chagford in Devon, and told Patrick Balfour, who introduced Waugh to it. A fourteenth-century thatched farmhouse with low dark rooms and small windows, it was run by a young Englishman called Norman Webb in partnership with Mrs Postlethwaite Cobb, an American divorcée with a bit of money, whom he had met in Morocco. Alec Waugh says that there was a steady stream of bohemian writers and that 'unofficial ladies' were made to feel at home. His brother used the hotel only as a cheap quiet place to get on with work, rarely mentioning other guests.

Waugh's previous travels had been conventional; he had scarcely strayed from Europe or the beaten track. Now he sought adventure and discomfort in Ethiopia (twice), British Guiana and Brazil and, virtually, the North Pole. These trips were made almost at random, not in response to a long-felt interest in the countries visited. He paid for them by working as a war-correspondent in Africa and by writing travel books or articles as well as novels. The breakthrough of *Decline and Fall* was reinforced with eight books in the next eight years. The four novels, *Vile Bodies,* 1930 (a great success), *Black Mischief,* 1932, *A Handful of Dust,* 1934, and *Scoop,* 1938, remain the most admired; but there were also four books based on his foreign experiences and a religious biography, *Edmund Campion,* 1935. *Labels, A Mediterranean Journal,* 1930, based on his delayed honeymoon, was written as if he had been alone and is actually called *A Bachelor Abroad* in the American edition.

His conversion to Roman Catholicism in 1930 was certainly seen by Waugh as the most important event in his life. Though it is widely ascribed to his unhappiness, Father D'Arcy, who instructed him, found him far from emotional: 'Evelyn never spoke of experience or feelings. He had come to learn and understand what we believe to be God's revelation and this made talking with him an interesting discussion based primarily on reason. I have never myself met a convert who so strongly based his assents on truth.'[1] Waugh thought that he would never be able to marry again or have children. It was by chance that he was told of a case similar to his own where an annulment had been granted. He made enquiries, but only two years later started proceedings which, after many delays, achieved in 1936 the declaration that allowed him to marry Laura Herbert in the following year. All this did not prevent his falling in love in the meantime.

Accusations of snobbery are frequently made and, as with every charge concerning motive, hard to disprove. His new fame ensured that he was asked 'everywhere'. His new freedom left him eager to accept. His new success meant that money was sometimes available. So he dined with Lady Cunard, though not often. There he met Lady Diana Cooper, and formed perhaps the closest and most lasting of all his friendships. He particularly liked worldly, witty women who had the confidence not to allow themselves to be bullied. Another such was Nancy Mitford, who, like the Lambs, after the divorce became a friend of his rather than of his wife. But most of all Waugh saw a new set encountered in the country at Malvern where he was learning to ride. The Lygon brothers, Lord Elmley and Hugh, he had known at Oxford; in 1931 he met their sisters Lady Lettice, Lady Sibell, Lady Mary and Lady Dorothy. Once more he fell in love with a family, but one without its head. The father, Earl Beauchamp, was homosexual. There had been a scandal and he had gone into almost permanent exile that year; their mother retired to live with her brother. So the children were left with money, youth, gaiety and freedom. Their large house, Madresfield Court, became the nearest thing to a centre in Waugh's volatile existence.

His letters to Laura are usually undated; their placing is often guesswork. After their marriage in April 1937 there are, understandably, few to anyone. In September they moved into Piers Court in Gloucestershire and Laura had a child (Teresa) the next year and another (Auberon) the year after. *Scoop* was written between April 1937 and February 1938 with more revision than usual, and came out at the end of May to the now accustomed acclaim. It was his fourth book to draw on his Ethiopian experiences, but no lack of freshness was noticed.

The earlier years are dominated by letters to the two Lygon sisters to whom he became and remained closest, Mary and Dorothy, known as Maimie and Coote to most, Blondy and Poll to Waugh. As the nicknames hint, they are written in a private language that is at times impenetrable. Letters to Teresa Jungman and Father D'Arcy exist but are not available. Letters to Lady Pansy Lamb and the great majority of those to Lady Diana Cooper are lost.

---

[1] Martin D'Arcy SJ, 'The Religion of Evelyn Waugh', *Evelyn Waugh and his World*.

TO A. D. PETERS   Paris.
[1929]

Yes, I will certainly do *John Bull's* article. I heard an interesting story the other evening from a Russian refugee but it occurs to me that a paper as British as *J.B.* might not want this. Could you ring them up and give them the choice of that or a humorous confession of my own life called 'a career founded by drink' or something like that describing how I was saved from being a successful school-master by a lapse into drunkenness & driven into authorship. I think I could make that funny.

I should also love to do some more for the *Mail*. Would they like (1) 'the Truth about Port Said' describing my visit there hoping to discover a sink of iniquity and finding a sort of Bournemouth (funny) or (2) an article of English Night Life contrasting it with Paris all to the advantage of London saying how much zest D.O.R.A. [1] adds to dissipation (funny) or (3) an article on Superstitions pointing out how people who think themselves enlightened & free thinkers are far more superstitious than religious people (more or less serious) or (4) 'Why people become authors' (satirical but rather serious) or (5) 'They do it better in France(?)' pointing out the number of superior refinements & comforts London has to offer over Paris or (6) 'Comfort in Travelling' about the sort of snobbery which makes the English, in their terror of being thought tourists, go through every sort of agony & dirt.

I return at the end of the week. Could you let me know any news of these suggestions to 145 North End Road

                              A hug & kisses to 'Roughhead'
                              Evelyn W.

[1] Defence of the Realm Act imposed regulations on drinking hours.

TO A. D. PETERS   Barford House,
[1929]   Warwick.

Here is the *John Bull* story. Will they mind it being in handwriting?
   Could you ask them to send proofs to this address.

                              Love to 'Roughhead'
                              E.W.

Another subject for possible article. The change that has come over snobbery about country & town hospitality. In Thackeray's time there are continual jokes about people who think friends good enough to know in the country but cut when they come to town. Lately I heard a hostess say about someone, that she didn't mind knowing him in London but didn't care to see him in the country. Would any paper like that bright thought?

To A.D.PETERS   Barford House,
[9 November 1929]   Warwick.
Postcard

I will deliver the *Daily Mail* & the *Harper's Bazaar* articles by the end of the week. I will do as many illustrations as *H.B.* like to pay for. Will you find out from the art editor size & price. By the way if you are having any casual chat with editors of daily papers will you tell them that I am *investigating 'emigration' conditions on my own Jan-March & will accept commissions to write about it.*

Love to Roughhead
E.W.

[November? 1929]   145 North End Road, N.W.11.
Postcard

I have left Barford so could you please let me know about the *Harper's* illustrations at this address.

By the way I am rather starving. Do you think that amiable Miss Reynolds[1] would give me £50 or so in advance?

Evelyn W.

[1] Miss Joyce Reynolds was an editor of *Harper's Bazaar* until the war.

To MAX BEERBOHM[1]   145 North End Road, N.W.11.
[1929]

Dear Mr Beerbohm,
    How very kind indeed of you to write to me.
    Of course I could not expect to be recognized from one crowded meeting & it was simply hero worship which impelled me to claim your acquaintance.
    I am more proud of your kind reference to my writing than of all the sales.
    My father sends you his warm regards.

Yours v. sincerely
Evelyn Waugh

[1] Max Beerbohm (1872–1956). Wit, dandy, writer and cartoonist. Knighted in 1939.

To Harold Acton
[23 January 1930]
Postcard

I have just read *Brothers & Sisters*[1] through twice & think it magnificently humorous and well managed. Do try it again & tell me what you think.

Evelyn

[1] I. Compton-Burnett, *Brothers and Sisters*, 1929.

In a Souvenir Programme for the New Theatre, Oxford
28 February 1930

RECOMMENDATION
to those who wish to preserve Oxford

Gentlemen,

You tell me you are going to act a play in order to preserve Oxford and I wish you every success for your performance. But will you, before it is too late, allow one who, like yourselves, has suffered the rigours and asperities of Oxford education, to suggest an alternative means of employing the ample funds which, I am confident, you will collect? If it is a question of 'Amenities', would it not be better to pursue a policy less of Preservation than of judicious destruction? A very small expenditure on dynamite should be enough to rid us for ever of the clock tower at Carfax, the Town Hall, the Indian Institute, the High Street front of Oriel, the Holywell front of New College and the whole of Hertford, thus changing Oxford from a comparatively ugly city to a comparatively beautiful one. All that is then necessary is to isolate it from through traffic by the destruction of Folly and Magdalen Bridges. Magdalen Bridge is a pretty structure and its total demolition is unnecessary; one arch would be enough. It could then stand like the bridge at Avignon pointing across an impassable gulf to the Morris Works and the Boer War Memorial and Oxford could lapse into repose, undisturbed except for the brawling of the dons.[1]

Your obedient servant,
EVELYN WAUGH

[1] Henry Yorke in a letter, 19 March 1929, to Waugh: '[Robert Byron] has published in the *Architectural Review* by far the most amusing article he's ever done, saying that the Oxford Preservation Fund ought not to preserve but demolish every building Ruskin put up in the town, and anything he smiled on as well.'

To A.D. Peters
[12 September 1930]
Postcard

Pakenham Hall,
Castlepollard,
Westmeath.

I want very much to go to Abyssinia[1] for the coronation of the Emperor. Could you get a paper to send me as special correspondent. If needs be I could pay $\frac{1}{2}$ my expenses. I think I am going anyway.

Evelyn Waugh

P.S. This is a serious suggestion.

[1] Waugh knew nothing of Ethiopia. He wanted to travel and one evening Alastair Graham suggested this expedition.

To Tom Driberg
[September 1930]

At
145 North End Road,
Hampstead.

My Dear Tom

Someone told me that your big brother[1] is in Abyssinia. Is this true because, if so, will you give me a letter to him? I go to Addis Ababa next month for the coronation and should like very much to find someone there who will help me if I get put into prison.

How are you? Why not ring up & suggest a meal sometime.

Do you see that Max Mallowan an old school chum of ours, has married Agatha Christie.

I missed you at Renishaw[2] by only a few days.

Yours
Evelyn

[1] Jack Driberg spoke eleven African languages and ate human flesh twice. Reluctant to burn villages in the Southern Sudan in 1921, he had merely reported that he had done so. The truth emerged, his career in the Colonial Service ended and he became an academic.
[2] Home of the Sitwells.

To W.N. Roughead
[September 1930]

Rolls Park[1],
Chigwell,
Essex.

Dear Roughy

Tell those Americans not to be bores! I shall send them my book when I feel inclined to – not before.

Also tell them not to cable so much. It all comes from hysteria & laziness. There is not such a frantic hurry that they cant write letters – as the cables are charged to me I object strongly.

Best wishes for the ju jitsu season
Evelyn

[1] Home of Sir Alexander Spearman.

To Henry Yorke   Hotel de France,
[November 1930]   Addis Ababa.

Dear Henry,
    I don't know when you will get this card. Posts are incalculable and
correspondence is always liable to destruction by government or diplomatic agents.
Life here is inconceivable – quite enough to cure anyone of that English feeling that
there is something attractive & amusing about disorder. But no part of the world can
be very foreign after Westmeath. This morning we all spent in Church from 6.30-12
with interminable coptic liturgy being sung. I wish you could have watched, as I
did, the Duke of Gloucester[1] sitting it out dressed up as colonel 10 Hussars. Public
castration which is the usual punishment for most infringements of law has been
stopped until the departure of the distinguished visitors. I have rarely seen anything
so hysterical as the British legation all this last week – or so incompetent to cope
with their duties. A half-baked consul called Barton[2] is minister. Irene Ravensdale[3]
& Charles Drage[?] are the only possible people in the town. I go to very stiff
diplomatic parties where I am approached by colonial governors who invariably
begin 'I say Waugh I hope you aren't going to say anything about that muddle this
morning. . . .' I don't know when I shall return. Not before Christmas I think. I go
on to Zanzibar as soon as the rains [?] are over. Please give my love to all our friends.
I long to hear all your scandal. I have not even Patrick's column[4] to keep me in
touch with acquaintances. I've seen no newspapers since I left. Love to Dig.

                                                              Evelyn

[1] Duke of Gloucester (1900–1974). Uncle of Elizabeth II.
[2] Sir Sidney Barton (1876–1946). Envoy Extraordinary and Minister Plenipotentiary to Abyssinia
1929–37.
[3] Lady Ravensdale (1896–1960). Daughter of first Marquess Curzon.
[4] Mr Gossip in the *Daily Sketch*.

To Catherine and Arthur Waugh   Grand Hotel Continental
16 November 1930   Dire-Daoua,
                                          Abyssinia.

Dear Mother & Father,
    I am stopping the night here – Dire-Daoua – on my way to Harar for a few days. I
am not sorry to have left Addis. Irene Ravensdale left me this morning for
Khartoum & I go on alone with two native servants. It is a 2 days ride to Harar. You
will see a railway marked there on the map but that is one of the many cartographical
jokes of the country. When I get there I sleep three nights in a tent in the consulate
garden. I leave here again 22nd sailing from Djibouti 25th for Zanzibar. I am going
up with a very decent German called Baron Von Plesen who was one of the special
mission for the coronation. How dutiful I am to tell you all this. I expect to be back
about Jan. 10th. I will keep you informed of my movements. I have the plot of a first
rate novel.

I went to Debra Libanos for a night with a bogus American professor[1]. It was not a monastery in the Western sense. All the monks had mistresses & children & most of them carried rifles & swords. None of them went to Church. All this trip is interesting me enormously. I think it is money well spent. As a matter of fact now I've left Addis it isn't costing very much. My two servants together only cost me about seven shillings a week. I have collected a great many Abyssinian paintings of little merit.

Best love
Evelyn

[1] Professor Thomas Whittemore. Leading authority on Byzantine art, friend of Henry James.

TO PATRICK BALFOUR   145, North End Road, N.W.11.
[12 July 1931]

Dear Patrick

It is OK about Ireland. You are to go there at the end of August. The address is Pakenham Hall, Castlepollard, Westmeath. The station is Mullingar.

I gave Betjeman[1] those photographs.

It is very nasty in London. I go back to France Canadel près Lavandou on Wednesday.

There is a new restaurant called Malmaison so much worse than all other restaurants & that is where we spend every evening.

Franks entanglement[2] is causing me a great deal of work but I hope to bring it to a happy conclusion.

Hazel[3] got so drunk at a cocktail party.

Gerald Berners[4] had an exhibition of pictures & sold them all on the first day which shows what a good thing it is to be a Baron. Why dont you take to painting. There was a picture of me in *Tatler* without my clothes. There was an article by you about Gentlemen in the *Daily Express*. Arthur Waugh thought it unoriginal.

I have not seen [shit Loundes?] but I went to some Rothschilds' and who do you think was there why Foster so he must be a Jew dont you think[5]. There was a special sort of strawberry kept for him.

I am quite losing the use of the pen.

I met a pretty heiress called Lorraine Berry[6]. Well I mean to say why dont you marry her because it would help journalism too, daughter dead Baron Buckland of Belch.

Gloomy Beatrice[7] gave a great banquet for Harman[8] & all the people were frightening ones just eight years older than Harman you know the sort I mean & she said 'I'm sure Miss Harman knows *nobody* here' and led her round like royalty & afterwards said 'Well, we haven't had time to make *real* friends yet have we'. And Baby[9] wasnt at that party so I thought it was all right but Harman met Baby at Lady Howard de Walden's [10] and there she made such bad blood about David Cecil[11] & Wanda[12] & Baby that now Baby thinks shes a sweet girl.

Mary Pakenham[13] is offering 5–1 on the wedding & not finding many takers. I pretend to have schemes up my sleeve but I havent any really I just trust in GOD.

When Hazel was so tight she asked everyone in the room to luncheon next day at three o'clock.

Freddy Birkenhead[14], Furneaux as was, is in love with Georgia[15] & she likes that.

And I took Father d'Arcy[16] to luncheon at the Ritz & there he saw Hamish[17] with Susan Carnegie so that shocked him so then Wanda came & kissed me a lot and that shocked him.

One good thing about London is after all one doesnt see Winter[18] or anyone like that.

I got a letter from Gerald Wellesley[19] saying he was at Calais & would I lunch with him – too late.

Doreen Jessel[20] & George Katani[21] alone together at Malmaison last night.

Caught Gloomy B recently with gigolo.

Caught David Cecil secretly with Mary Pakenham. I think that is a case.

. . . I was sick the other night.

Now I am going to stay with Cecil Beaton[22] in the country & Lady Colefax[23] will be there.

Shops dont seem to want Firbank.

. . . Veronica Blackwood[24] gave black eye to Hamish Erskine.

Nancy Mit. says she will marry Erskine yet. Erskine says no.

Sutro behaved monstrously in deep and complicated intrigues over Catholic club named Unicorn and has done himself much damage in highly valued Sykes-Elwes connexion.[25]

David Greene has come back no money bad clap like Hans very sorry for himself also he has diabetes.

Harman says Goldsmith[26] could come to Liberia will he? Scherhoff[27] still in London not Birmingham [?] job losing support Yorkes.

I am going to call the African book 'They Were Still Dancing' because those are the first words of it.[28]

Robert is hated by D. Guinness now.[29]

B. Guinness has written poem and Powell, author of *Afternoon Men* has got him to pay to publish them I mean think of it it is bad enough having to write for cash but to pay to write were MADNESS.[30]

Alexander is off to Borneo with an American girl.

Mary Erskine[31] is sunk very low now.

Yrs
Evelyn

[1] John Betjeman (1906–   ). Knighted in 1969. Poet Laureate since 1972. See Appendix of Names.

[2] Frank Pakenham (1905–   ). Politician and author. Married Elizabeth Harman in November 1931. Succeeded his brother as Earl of Longford in 1961.

[3] Hazel Martyn (1897–1935). An American, she had married Sir John Lavery in 1910. The colleen with harp and shawl on the Irish pound notes was drawn from her.

[4] Lord Berners (1883–1950). Composer, painter and writer.

[5] John Foster (1904–   ). Fellow of All Souls 1924. Conservative MP 1945–74. QC 1950. Knighted in 1964.

[6] Lorraine Berry, daughter of Henry Seymour Berry, who was created Lord Buckland of Bwlch.

[7] Beatrice Mackay, married to Nico Jungman 1900–1918, was the mother of Teresa and Zita. Soon after the war she married Richard Guinness. Died 1942.

[8] Elizabeth Harman (1906–   ). Historian.

[9] Teresa Jungman (1907–   ). A devout Roman Catholic and a Bright Young Thing. Waugh was in love with her, as were many others. As she was Dutch and resisted his advances, he came to use the word 'Dutch' to mean inconvenient or awkward.

[10] Margherita van Raalte (1890–1974) married Lord Howard de Walden in 1912.

[11] Lord David Cecil (1902–   ). Writer and Oxford don. Publications include *Lord M*, *The Stricken Deer* and *Hardy the Novelist*.

[12] Wanda Holden was married to Charles Baillie-Hamilton, Conservative MP 1929–39. Elizabeth Harman had never met her. Perhaps the original of Sonia Digby-Vane-Trumpington.

[13] Lady Mary Pakenham (1907–   ). Writer. Sister of Frank, Pansy and Violet. Married 1939–43 to Meysey Clive.

[14] Earl of Birkenhead (1907–75). Biographer of, among others, Kipling and F.E.Smith. Had succeeded to the title the year before.

[15] Georgia Doble (died 1980) A Canadian who had married Sacheverell Sitwell in 1925.

[16] Father Martin D'Arcy (1888–1977). The Master of Campion Hall, Oxford, 1932–45. Provincial of English Province of Society of Jesus 1945–50. Instructed Waugh.

[17] Hamish St Clair-Erskine.

[18] Keith Winter had published a novel, *Other Men's Saucers*. He had a red shirt with white spots and when visitors arrived Waugh shouted up to his window, 'Winter, come out on the balcony and show these visitors your shirt.' Alec Waugh, *A Year to Remember*, 1975. He was to have written the script for the projected Hollywood film of *Brideshead Revisited* in 1947.

[19] Gerald Wellesley (1885–1972). Succeeded as Duke of Wellington in 1943.

[20] Doreen Jessel (1909–   ). Sister of Teddy Jessel, married Sir Geoffrey Agnew in 1934. She has said there could have been no question of her dining alone at this time with George Cattavi.

[21] George Cattavi worked in the Egyptian embassy, knew Proust and wrote several books on him.

[22] Cecil Beaton (1904–1980). Photographer, theatrical designer and writer. Waugh stuck pins into him at their private school in 1914. 'The tears on his long eyelashes used to provoke the sadism of youth.' *A Little Learning*, p. 90. Knighted 1972.

[23] Sybil Halsey (died 1950). Married Sir Arthur Colefax in 1901. Hostess. 'Although an insatiable appetite for life and a corresponding reluctance to suffer the smallest twinge of boredom might momentarily occlude a great natural kindliness her gift for creating an atmosphere of intelligent pleasure was among the most eminent of her time.' *Times* obituary. Started successful decorating business in 1936.

[24] Veronica Blackwood (1910–   ). Sister of the Marquis of Dufferin and Ava. Married to Anthony (Roger) Hornby 1931–40.

[25] Freya Sykes, sister of Christopher, married Sir Richard Elwes in 1926. Both families were Roman Catholics.

[26] Sir Henry d'Avigdor-Goldsmid (1909–76). Conservative MP 1955–74.

[27] George Shuchoff, a German friend from Oxford, had stayed with Henry Yorke in January.

[28] *Remote People* appeared as *They Were Still Dancing* in the United States.

[29] Presumably Robert Byron and Diana Guinness.

[30] In fact Tom Balston of Duckworth accepted various commissioned volumes referred to by Constant Lambert as 'Poor Poems by Rich Poets'.

[31] Lady Mary Erskine (1912–   ). Sister of Hamish. Married 1933–44 to Philip Dunn, 1946–59 to Robin Campbell, 1962–9 to Charles McCabe and 1969 until his death to Philip Dunn again, who had meanwhile succeeded as second baronet. 'She was then eighteen years old and looked like a pretty and impertinent schoolgirl dressed up in her mother's clothes.' Daphne Fielding in *Mercury Presides*.

To Henry Yorke
[Summer 1931]

Chez M. le Curé,
Cabris,
Près de Grasse,
Alpes Maritimes.

Deary Henry,

Canadel on whenever you like. Do engage a room for me & let me know the address of the hotel so that I can make arrangements.

I shall probably be there awaiting you. I got claustrophobia in the Nina[1]–Maugham[2] milieu and so came here into the hills where I am living in great discomfort with a crazy priest. He talks very fluently about wars all the time – sometimes the last one and sometimes the next. I never quite know which he means. Lloyd George is responsible for both apparently.

Patrick[3] fell into bad company at the sea-side.

I am finishing that very dull travel book[4] & shall soon begin on a novel which is genuinely exciting for me.

I know what you must feel about your office. I have a corresponding longing for some kind of routine in my life.

How well do you speak French? I can't say anything at all.

Love to you both,
E

[1] Countess of Seafield (1906–69). Cyril Connolly wrote of her twenty years later, 'She has red hair, blue eyes, an attractive stubby figure, a lovely stammer and a gasping kind of speech.'

[2] Somerset Maugham (1874–1965). He had a house, the Villa Mauresque, at Cap Ferrat.

[3] Patrick Balfour. His father had paid his debts on condition that he resign as Mr Gossip of the *Daily Sketch*.

[4] *Remote People*, 1931. In the United States *They Were Still Dancing*, 1932.

To Henry Yorke
[Summer 1931]   [Villefranche]

Dear Henry,

I have dragged Patrick away from Mont Parnasse and we are at present staying at the Welcome at Villefranche.

I look forward so much to your coming to St Tropez. When you write for rooms do book one for me – a large one if possible. I hope those fine Misses Ruthven[1] (?) are coming too. The district is full of chums, Connolly[2], Aldous H[3], Willy Maugham, Nina, Eddie S-West[4], Alex Waugh, etc. I meant to do work but it is all very gay and we bathe a lot and get sleepy.

Do write and tell us some gossip.

We are going to live on an island at the end of the week but this address will be

Welcome Hotel
Villefranche sur Mer
Alpes maritimes.

An awful afternoon man called Keith Winter has arrived. Also Godfrey Wynne[5] also Tennyson Jesse[6] – too literary by half.
Will it make Dig shy if I appear in fisherman's clothes.
I have more scandal and baddish blood about Robert [Byron] in Paris.
I have found out more very shady things about Maurice's continental relaxation. Do write,

Love,
Evelyn

[1] 'Alison and Margaret Ruthven, generally known as "A" and "P". These identical twins, with their wonderful figures and fascinating sultry faces that just missed being beautiful, had an individual barbaric chic.' Daphne Fielding in *Mercury Presides.*
[2] Cyril Connolly (1903–74). Critic and author. He had not yet published a book.
[3] Aldous Huxley (1894–1963). *Point Counter Point* had been published in 1928, *Brave New World* was published in 1932.
[4] Edward Sackville-West (1901–65). Novelist, critic, musician. Succeeded as Lord Sackville in 1962.
[5] Godfrey Winn, (1908–71). Popular journalist and author.
[6] Fryn Tennyson Jesse (1888–1958). Writer, mostly about murder.

To LADY MARY AND LADY DOROTHY LYGON[1]   The County Hotel,
[1931]   Malvern[2].

Dearest Blondy & Pollen,
    It was delightful to get a letter from you. I miss you both very much at school and in play time. Malvern is not the same by a long chalk and all those girls get very uppish without you to keep them in their proper stations. As for Miss Nicholson, well, there was a very ugly scene on the first morning when she was upbraided for idleness and disobedience and the Captain[3] left the school in a rage. However they had a jolly up after that which ended in the Captain calling her Beryl. Then this afternoon she wanted to take his photograph and said oh but it must be with your whip in your hand and then she said please raise it as if you were going to hit me – so all my worst suspicions are confirmed. It is what is called Masochism and if you ask Elmley[4] & he thinks you are old enough he will explain what that means.
    I saw in my paper that Elmley's opponent had withdrawn & at first I thought Good & then I realised that it means now that there will be only one candidate for the bolsheviks to throw bombs at and those poor girls are bound to be blown sky-high so I am sorrier.

I wrote this before dinner. My dears, what do you think? May & I went in to find the Captain drinking champagne with a one armed chum.

I may say that the Captain is dead nuts on me. He talks to me all the time not only about riding but politics & art & everything. He smokes my cigars. Mrs Captain & Jacky[5] came & had cocktails with me this morning & Mrs Captain told me that Jacky's teeth were false – did you know? – having been rolled out by a horse when she was 14. She also gave me a bright red ointment which cures stiffness so I am well in with that family. Reggie[6] promised me some straps to wear on my trousers so I am very classy[?] now. Also I have been promoted from Master to a finer & gayer horse.

Give Elmley a rousing cheer from his old Varsity chum.

Best love & xxxxxxxxx
Boaz[7]

P.S. I bought a book today called *Twice round the World with the Holy Ghost*. This is perfectly true.

E

[1] Daughters of seventh Earl Beauchamp. Lady Mary (1910–) often known as Maimie or Blondy, Lady Dorothy (1912–) as Coote or Poll. Their home, Madresfield Court, was near Malvern. Waugh had known at Oxford their brothers, for the eldest of whom they were now canvassing. See Appendix of Names.

[2] Waugh was doing a course at the Riding Academy.

[3] Captain J.H.Hance, Waugh's riding instructor. 'G.B.H.', standing for 'God Bless Him', is often attached to his name.

[4] Their brother Viscount Elmley (1903–79). Succeeded as Earl Beauchamp in 1938. He was elected with a greatly increased majority and held the seat until then.

[5] Daughter of Captain Hance.

[6] Son of Captain Hance.

[7] Boaz or Boas was Waugh's nickname.

To Lady Mary and Lady Dorothy Lygon [1931?]

The County Hotel,
Malvern.

[Letter headed with Star of David]

Dearest Blondy & Pollen,

. . . Nicholson said to me today 'Whyever are you trying to learn to ride' so I said it had been prescribed as a cure and she said and for what and I said drink.

Diana Coventry[1] is going to dine with me tomorrow at least she says so. I have talked to Frisky[2] a bit on the telephone and I tried to make chums with Pearson.

The Captain has more photographers coming and he is wreathing all the jumps with barbed wire and poor Jacky is as frightened as hell.

As for poor Boaz his stock has fallen pretty seriously at the Academy. First, on Saturday, a little horse called Tom Tit threw me on my head over a fence. All the sluts laughed except Miss Jagger[3] who was sympathetic. Then this morning on

Gingerbread I muddled up all the school & was in deep disgrace. So I tried to have a come back by tippling with the Captain. That went fairly well for a bit but he said Do you know So-&-So and I said no so he said He must have been at Eton about your time and I said I wasn't at Eton and the Captain was shocked and finished his glass and strode straight out of the bar and now he doesn't even like me as a chap. I have also strained my back in a place between my shoulders where I can't reach it with Ma's red ointment and it hurts like nothing on earth and I do wish you were here to rub it for me. So what with one thing & another I feel pretty low. So I shall drink a bottle of champagne at dinner to your healths and Grainger's[4] & Elmley's & Friskys.

Love & xxxx
Boaz

Drank the champagne & do feel better. I forgot to say that I am going to Maud Yorke's[5] on 30th for ten days so perhaps I shall see you again after all.

[Signed with a swastika]

[1] Local friend of Waugh's.

[2] Arthur Windham Baldwin (1904–78). Writer and lasting friend. Son of the Prime Minister, succeeded as third Earl Baldwin in 1958. See Appendix of Names.

[3] Miss Jagger lived with the Lygons and her name was used for anyone happy to run errands or organize things, sometimes but not always in a sycophantic way.

[4] Lady Mary's one-eyed pekinese.

[5] Mrs Vincent Yorke (1874–1963). Mother of Henry.

To Arthur Baldwin

Forthampton Court[1],
Tewkesbury.

Dear Frisky,

I am sorry I made bad blood with Teresa [Jungman] but you must know, old boy, that alls fair in love. Anyway I can tell you this that whenever I plot & make bad blood – as I do pretty often I may say – it is always I who lose by it in the end.

I am coming to stay with you.

I will wire the train later.

Boas

[1] Home of Vincent and Maud Yorke.

To Lady Sibell, Lady Mary and Lady Dorothy Lygon
5 November [1931]

Savile Club
69 Brook Street, W.1.

Darling Lady Sibell[1], Blondy and Pollen,

Well this is the last time I shall write for days. I'll tell you why, you see I find suddenly there is no more money in my bank and about six tradesmen have written to say look here this bill is going too far what about it. So I went to my agent & said give me some money and he said well if it comes to that you owe *me* quite a bit one way and another. So I am broke. Well what I am going to do is to go to a boarding house called Easton Court Hotel, Chagford, Devon (where you must write to me) because Patrick Balfour lives there & I argue that if he can so can I because he is worse broke even than me. Well at Chagford I pretend to my London chums that I am going to hunt stags but to you who are intimates & confidantes I dont mind saying that I shall sit all day in my bedroom writing books, articles, short stories, reviews, plays, cinema scenarios, etc. etc. until I have got a lot more money. So I shan't have time even to write anything I am not paid for besides there is the expense of postage so you must [not] think it is lack of love if I don't write & you must please go on writing to me because I shall need some uplifting in spirits.

I hope Lord E [Elmley] will dress up as Father Xmas & go round putting oranges in stockings. May I bring fireworks.

I gave a little luncheon party and escaped from the restaurant without paying. Clever that.

I was usher at a wedding and I detected in church Billy Clonmore [2] (a) improperly dressed (b) drunk (c) uninvited. That wont amuse you much but tell Hugh [Lygon] because they were chums once.

xxx B

Clare Elwes says she knows Capt. Is this a lie?

[1] Lady Sibell Lygon (1907–   ). An elder sister, married 1939–52 to Flight Lieutenant Michael Rowley.

[2] Lord Clonmore (1902–78). Succeeded as Earl of Wicklow in 1946. An Oxford friend 'whose extravagances were refined by a slightly antiquated habit of speech and infused with a Christian piety that was unique among us and lay hidden behind his stylish eccentricities. Billy was a reckless roof-climber and quick in a quarrel.' *A Little Learning*, p. 200.

To Lady Mary Lygon
Chagford.
[12 November 1931]
Postcard
[Drawing]

Very depressed. Rain all day. No money. Can't write. Fire smokes. Filthy beams, pewter, lustreware and every antique horror. Patrick usually drunk. He left the tap of the beer barrel open last night and flooded the cellar. I ride a little horse called Evergreen. Looking forward to Yuletide.

B

To Lady Mary Lygon   English Club, Zanzibar.
[November, December? 1931]

... You must not suppose that I am in Zanzibar or in Nice. To tell you the truth I am back at Chagford. When I got back I found a letter from you. That cheered me up and I needed cheering I can tell you.

Mr Balfour's hearing is restored but he has lost his luggage.

We were interested in your comments on Mr B's obscene p.c. because I said you can't possibly send that obscene p.c. to those sweet orphan girls and he said yes and I said No. Well apparently he was right. Oh dear what the younger generation are coming to to be sure.

I think I will tell you about this hotel well it is very odd. Kept by a deserter from the Foreign Legion[1] and an American lady named Mrs Postlethwaite Cobb who mixes menthol with her cigarettes. And we drink rye whisky in her bed room and there are heaps of New York magazines & rather good, sophisticated food. I think it is a distributing centre for white slaves or cocaine or something like that. They never give one a bill. Mr B. hasn't had one since he came six weeks ago. And there are two odious dogs.

How is Grainger?

I'm sorry your SOCIETY wasn't more fun.

Today I shall ride a mare called Chiko and tomorrow I shall catch foxes and next week end I will write to you again.

Now I must write some more of a dull short story about a honeymoon which I have sold to Lady Sibells Bazaar[2].

Tell Lady Sibell to say that all the smart set are reading *Remote People* the brilliant book by that well known hunting gent E.W.

Dont let Jacky forget me.

[1] Norman Webb had been employed helping African animals in Morocco when he met Mrs Cobb, a divorcée with money.

[2] *Harper's Bazaar*, in which Lady Sibell wrote a column.

To Arthur Baldwin   L6, Albany,
14 January [1932]   Piccadilly, W.1.

My Dear Frisky,

I insist on answering, but as I am dictating, you will not be embarrassed by those deep man-to-man intimacies which we reserve for the Madresfield Crème de Menthe.

Good old Duff Cooper[1]. There's a man for you. Him, and his pretty wife[2] too. Man of Affairs; and Man of Taste; though why he qualifies his praise in that way I can't imagine.

Jolly sporting of you not to put Boaz in the moat[3], old boy. The more we stick together the happier the New Year will be!

What can I tell you? Well, I am living like a swell, in Albany, as it might be Lord Byron, Lord Macaulay, Lord Lytton, or any real slap up writer!

I have been trying to recreate Worcestershire in London – an evening with Barbara Lea[4], drinks with Duggan[5], *Cavalcade* with Sibell (both she and Lady Ursula Filmer-Sankey[6] in tears) and during the last three days, the malignant Cyclopean-eye of Grainger winking across the Ritz lounge – but it isn't the same, old boy, away from the Captain, (God bless him!).

As for Pekin – I don't believe I am going really now, because I have joined a rattling sporting chap, name of Dean[7], making Movie Pictures. I hope you will soon be seeing our work at the Astley Palace, or the Stourport Empire.[8]

Mrs Reginald Marix[9] is back in London, Teresa is hunting in Leicestershire.

Make the best you can from these Words to the Wise. – (Verb Sap)

Yours,
Boaz

[1] Alfred Duff Cooper (1890–1954). Politician and writer. Minister of Information 1941–2, Ambassador to France 1944–7, created Viscount Norwich 1952. Publications include *Talleyrand*, 1932, and *Old Men Forget*, 1953.

[2] Lady Diana Manners (1892–   ). Actress and beauty. Married Duff Cooper 1919. See Appendix of Names.

[3] Madresfield Court had a moat.

[4] Barbara Pell (1903–45). Married Thomas Lea in 1924.

[5] Hubert Duggan (1904–43). Oxford friend. Born in Buenos Aires of Argentinian, American and Irish descent, step-son of Lord Curzon. Household Cavalry 1924–8. Conservative MP 1941–3.

[6] Lady Ursula Filmer-Sankey (1902–78). Daughter of the Duke of Westminster and a cousin of the Lygons. Married to William Filmer-Sankey 1924–40, and later to Major Stephen Vernon.

[7] Basil Dean, founder and chairman of Ealing Studios 1929–36. Died 1978.

[8] Arthur Baldwin lived at Astley Hall near Stourport-on-Severn.

[9] Both Waugh and Arthur Baldwin had been attracted to 'Pixie' Marix.

To Lady Dorothy Lygon   Savile Club,
16 April 1932   69, Brook Street, W.1.

Darling Poll

Well I never stop thinking of your sufferings[1] and I am putting up a tasteful little monument to your bravery & popularity. It consists of a pedestal of oxidized zinc fifty feet high decorated with porcelain & mother o pearl. Then there are four columns of different coloured cement topped with a gothic tower of cast iron and putty and a little Indian dome of gilt cork. I hope you will like it. Meanwhile I hope that you realise the great opportunities afforded to you to ennoble the soul. Nothing like suffering for sweetening the character. If you would like some books of meditation just ring up Lord Clonmore and he will send you dozens.

My life is great burden to me on account of this play.[2] Lady Cunard (whom God preserve) has just been given seats in the 18th row and is gibbering down the telephone saying 'How can I take Prince George[3] to the 18th row?' so I have confiscated all poor Maud Yorkes tickets and given them to the old trout. Snobbish cad you will say no I answer it is respect for the CROWN. Then there was lady Castlerosse[4] who wont pay for her tickets oh dear these great ladies. Still it makes me feel a social figure which is good for my low spirits because no one knows how despised I am in the theatre. Then Mr Bradley who wrote the play says I must give him £95 and I cant even if I wanted to which I dont.

So I went to a disgusting thing called *Miracle*[5] and the young lady's father who took me I mean the father of the young lady who took me had paid three guineas each for our seats so I said how sickeningly bored I was and she thought damned ungrateful chap wont take him out again. And I sat next to the Duke of Norfolk. He didnt know me but I knew him & I thought here is the man I respect as the natural leader of English Catholics and why is he at this blasphemous play because it is full of blasphemy as an egg is full of meat.

Perhaps you would like to hear who will be in my party on Friday well first & foremost little Blondy then that dashing Major D[6], then the lovely Lady Lavery, then BARONESS Ravensdale, then Lady Eleanor Smith[7] the famous novelist, then Lord Clonmore the unfrocked curate[8], then Mr H. Yorke the lavatory king[9] and his pretty wife then poor Frank Pakenham who married beneath him and the Hon. Mrs P[akenham] who married above herself, then Mr Raymond de Trafford[10] the gambler and lover. So perhaps they will be photographed for the newspapers and you on your sick bed will think God how sad not to be there or alternatively my I would sooner have a broken bone than be there.

My point in writing this letter is less to produce high class literary composition than amuse tiny patient . . . . [incomplete]

[1] Lady Dorothy had broken her collar-bone.

[2] *Vile Bodies*, dramatized by Dennis Bradley. It had been on at the Arts Theatre for twelve nights the year before and now ran at the Vaudeville from 15 April to 30 May. In 1954 Waugh thought of making a dramatic version himself but nothing came of it.

[3] Prince George (1902–42). Created Duke of Kent 1934.

[4] Doris Delavigne (1900–1942). Married to Viscount Castlerosse 1928–38.

[5] *The Miracle* had opened on 9 April. A wordless 'mystery spectacle' with music by Humperdinck, produced by Max Reinhardt, it had failed in London in 1910, succeeded in New York in 1924 and now succeeded in London with Lady Diana Cooper as the Madonna.

[6] Hubert Duggan.

[7] Lady Eleanor Smith (1902–45). Novelist. Daughter of F.E.Smith.

[8] Lord Clonmore had been a deacon in the Church of England, and became a Roman Catholic.

[9] The Yorke's family firm, Pontifex, made lavatories.

[10] Raymond de Trafford (1900–1971). Married 1932–8 to Alice Silverthorne, an American formerly married to the Comte de Janzé. In 1927, while lunching in Paris, he suddenly told her he must leave. On the way to the station she stopped and bought a gun. At the Gare du Nord she shot first de Trafford and then herself. Both were dangerously hurt, but recovered. At her trial, he gave evidence on her behalf; she was fined the equivalent of 16s 6d and given a six-month sentence, but was immediately freed under the First Offenders Act.

To Arthur Baldwin   Savile Club
[16 April 1932]   69 Brook Street, W.1.

Dear Frisky

Well I call that downright pally and no mistake. Did little Miss [Teresa] Jungman send me a line of good wishes from Ireland? Not on your life. And did I look through a sheaf of telegrams with trembling hands looking for one loved name and was I surprised at its absence. I can't say I was.

The slow extermination of our Lygon chums saddens me. First little Blondy's arse. Now Pollen's breast bone. Blondy came to see my play but went away in great pain before supper.

So Boaz is momentarily a social lion and Lady Cunard (whom God preserve) calls him Evelyn and makes him sit on her right hand at luncheon & dinner every day of the week but is his head turned by these favours. No he remains the same simple lad who bounced round the Malvern Academy on the broad back of Mater (God bless her).

Well at 3.30 today I take a train for Devon and shall be there four weeks finishing a book.[1] Then heigh ho for Sunny Italy with a fine desperado called Raymond de Trafford.

I met a nice chum of yours named Lady Patricia Ward and she came to a dress rehearsal of my play.

Teresa & me went to a very terrible thing called *Miracle*. Then she popped off to Ireland.

All the best old son
Boaz

[1] *Black Mischief*, 1932.

To Lady Dorothy Lygon   Easton Court Hotel,
[April 1932]   Chagford,
                                                     Devon.

Sweet Poll,

Golly what a family. Hugh in a mad house and now Sibell at my ex-aunt Almina's abortionist parlour[1]. How my heart bleeds for you all.

... Now I will tell you about the sermon I heard on Sunday. First the priest said that it was soon the feast of the Blessed Margaret Clitheroe and the English Martyrs and he told us how they had their arses cut off with red-hot scissors & things like that. Then he said But they are not the only good Catholics who are persecuted. WHAT ABOUT ME he said very loud, why only yesterday I received a blackmailing letter from one of this very congregation accusing me of UNCHASTITY. Goodness we all felt embarrassed. I hadnt sent him the letter but everyone looked at me as though I had. YOU'D BETTER BE CAREFUL he said looking straight at me IT IS MORTAL SIN TO SPEAK ILL OF A PRIEST. Why he said I knew a man quite well who sat down to write an impertinent letter to a priest and as he stretched out his hand for the pen, it (hand not pen) fell lifeless to his side & he has never used it again. And I know another man, he said, who went to strike a priest and he (man not priest) FELL DOWN DEAD.

Pretty frightening, eh.

Well before Sunday (this letter is going rather backwards isn't it) I spent a week doing book writing about my Emperor and one day I rode 20 miles and my horse broke her bridle but I told all that to Thommie[2] and I daresay he has told you.

Before that I was in London and v. POPULAR and I gave a little ball but it was all spoilt because little Blondy's bottom was sore and she went home.

My word I am glad Hugh is coming to Italy because between you and me and the w.c. Raymond de T. is something of a handful v. nice but so BAD and he fights & fucks and gambles and get D.D.[3] all the time. But Hugh & I will be quiet & chaste and economical & sober.

Did Teresa send me a telegram to wish my Interesting Play well? Not her.

Perhaps you would like to hear about ——. Well he keeps a pub at a place called South Zeal and is a fairy and claims to be descended from ST THOMAS OF CANTERBURY or I could tell you about Mrs Postlewaite Cobb or Mr Norman Webb or Major VIPANS all friends of mine. But I wont.

GOD BE WITH YOU TILL WE MEET AGAIN. BOAZ.

[1] Lady Sibell was having her wisdom teeth removed at a nursing-home in Portland Place started by Lady Carnarvon, wife of the fifth Earl, who had married Evelyn Gardner's uncle.

[2] Sir Thomas Lea (1901–　).

[3] Disgustingly drunk.

TO LADY MARY LYGON
[August? 1932]

Savile Club,
69 Brook Street, W.1.

Very very sorry for lacocking[1] tea

_____

If you cant see this joke read it aloud
THE IDEAL HUSBAND
BY
HUGH GEOFFREY KNIGHT.

_____

Sexy Cooper[2] told me that one.

Mr Boaz

[1] 'Lacocking' or 'laycocking' means 'chucking'. Robert Laycock is often referred to as 'Chucker'.

[2] Duff Cooper.

To A.D.Peters
[October? 1932]

Easton Court Hotel,
Chagford,
Devon.

Here is Reynolds first story for Xmas. Hope she can sell it U.S.

Will you please take any orders for travel articles – far flung stuff impenetrable Guiana forests, toughs in Diamond mines, Devils Island, Venezuela. Particularly require payment on embarkation if possible.

To Lady Mary and Lady Dorothy Lygon
[1932?]

Ritz Hotel,
Piccadilly,
London W.1.

Dearest Blondy and Pollen

First I will tell you about Malvern. I didn't ride again after I wrote because I found I had broken my back so I went to the stables with Reggie and learned to be a groom and stood about with the Captain (G.B.H.) and heard all his confidences. Miss Bennet – that is the pretty steeplechaser with the fringe   got into better favour through good flexing. Then that evening Diana Coventry came to dinner with me and the telephone went and who do you think it was Hugh so we went to Madresfield to see him. Well I hate to say it but the truth is that Hugh had been at the bottle and he was walking about the house with a red candle saying he thought the lights might go out. Well we had some brandy with him and he got a little despondent about not having any money and having bought so many racehorses he can't pay for so we went upstairs and there was Lady Sibell in her bed also despondent because she was ill and couldn't think of what to say in her gossip column. So next day I went to dinner with Lady Sibell and she was still in bed but not so despondent and Frisky was there and he came back to the hotel and ate ham in my bedroom and said he knew there was no such person as God. Oh but much more important I went to tea with the Captain and Miss (G.B.T.). and ate lettuce and there was a girl called Olive who had broken her back too *and* cracked her skull into the bargain and Olive was very fresh and kicked the Captain and punched his arm and Robert Bartleet[1] was there and he talked knowingly about art so Jackie and I felt small and sat in the corner and I think Jackie is in love with me only I often think this about girls and it is hardly ever true so I daresay she isn't.

The next day I came to London and in the train was Miss Penrose so I had to go third class and couldn't sleep as I'd meant to because I'd got up at 7.30 and I packed in such a hurry that I had no evening collars and had to borrow one from a footman at my club and it didn't fit and that rather spoiled my dinner.

When I got to London I went to an accomplished lady called Miss Hector who gave me electric shocks in the back and made it much worse. Gloomy B recommended her. Then I found some people in a motorcar who said you must come to Acton to bully the poor so off I went and that was absolute hell because the people of Acton jolly well know how to look after themselves. So then I thought I'd like some SOCIETY so I found out that there was a lady giving a dinner party and I rang her up and said may I come and she said well I don't much want you to because the numbers would be wrong and anyway I don't much like you but I said 'Please let me come because my back is broken and I must have some SOCIETY' so she said well all right if you must so I came and I sat between the Ladies Birkenhead and Colefax and told them about the Captain (GBH) till they thought Golly what a dull young man so that was my SOCIETY.

Then today I had more excruciating shocks from Miss Hector and she says I am cured so that's all right. Then I went to lunch with Gloomy and I thought how nice now I shall talk to Teresa but not a bit of it. I was put all by myself at a little table with a Crockford's queen called Mary Montagu so I told her about the Captain til she thought Golly what a dull young man and Therese wouldn't look at me because she was fancying a South African gink called Sonny. So now I am waiting at the Ritz for a young lady who said she was coming to tea with me and she hasn't so isn't London awful and how I wish I was at Malvern and tonight I am going to Hampstead to have dinner with my papa who is feeling the cold terribly.

I have been asked to dinner tomorrow to meet Grandi[2]. I think I will go but I shan't dare tell them at the Academy.

> Lots of love and XXXXXXXXX
> Boas

Well you will say how Bo must have hated staying with me this week-end. However, no, not at all, quite the reverse. I love it and will look back on the noble line of the Malvern Hills that I love so dearly and

So I was interrupted by the lady I was to take tiffin with and now I am in the Savile Club. I was going on to enumerate all the glories of Malvern then I would say how wistfully and with heartache I would look back on them from the jungle.[3] We are both going to suffer rather a lot in the next few weeks but when we meet again it will be gay and terribly exciting and not at all like a biscuit box.

WY LIKE A BISKIT BOCKS PLESE?

Wait till you are a little older Tommy[4] and you will understand.

Well I am living with the bright young Yorkes.

Last night I saw a terribly drunk man with a prostitute.

WOTS A POSTATUTE PLESE?

Ask your little playfellow ——, she will show you, Tommy.

Then tonight I am going to dinner with the Pouncers[5]. I had luncheon with B. Guinness. Goodness he was gloomy.

Well soon I will whiten the sands of another continent and no broken hearted woman will tend the marble cross below the town[6] but I expect Katchin[7] will shed a tear or so just as it might be Mr Hanson[8]. All love to little Poll and Lady Sibell.

> BO

---

[1] Robert Bartleet was the vicar's son.
[2] Conte Dino Grandi, Italian Ambassador in London 1932–9.
[3] Waugh was going to British Guiana.
[4] Tommy MacDougal, a dashing MFH whom Waugh affected to believe illiterate.

[5] Simon Elwes (1902–75) married Gloria Rodd in 1926. He was a portrait painter who first exhibited in 1927, with a picture of Lady Lettice Lygon at the Royal Academy. He disliked the nickname 'Pouncer' which he thought unfair and unfortunate: 'People won't come to have their portraits painted.'

[6] One of several references to 'The Green Eye of the Little Yellow God' by Milton Hayes, which contains the lines:

'There's a one-eyed yellow idol to the North of Katmandu;

There's a little wooden cross beneath the town;

There's a broken-hearted woman tends the grave of mad Carew –

And the yellow God forever gazes down.'

[7] Rudolf Kommer (von Czernowitz), a Romanian Jew who was assistant to Max Reinhardt, and thus became a friend of Lady Diana Cooper. Called 'Kaetchen' because once in a restaurant he picked up a dog and said, 'Ah Kaetchen, Kaetchen, you mustn't crowl and park at the lady.'

[8] Mr Hanson owned a pub called the Hornyold and a hotel called the Essington Arms often visited by the Lygons.

To Lady Mary Lygon
[26 December 1932]

Hotel Tower,
Lots 74 & 75,
Main Street,
Georgetown,
Demerara.

Darling Blondy

Why you will say Bo is living in a town but no not at all quite the reverse – it is a one storied wood house but it is most up to date with a shower bath and a panatrope which plays Harry Lauder records all day. And there is a verandah where I am sitting now and next to me is an elderly gentleman talking in his sleep and he says 'Buy something, fuck you! Why don't you buy something?'

So yesterday it was Christmas and we had very far flung stuff – turkey and mince pies and paper hats at Government House and we drank to 'Absent Friends' and everyone cried like Mr Hanson and I thought of you and little Poll and Lady Sibell and Hughie and Lord Elmley and Mr and Mrs Arthur Waugh, and Mr and Mrs Alec Waugh and the Capt. G.B.H. and Min and Jackie and Reggie and Bartleet, and Diana[1] and the Dutch girl[2] and the tarts or pouncers and bubblesses[3] and mannerlesses[4] and Knatchie and Mr Conrad[5] and Frisky and Tommy[6] and poor TOMIE etc etc etc.

God how S[ad].

Now you would like to hear of my new friends. Well there is a lascivious beast[7] called Weld and an Irish-Portuguese called Hernandez and a Belgo-Indian called Williams and a Captain (not G.B.H.) shorter than me called Surridge[?] and goodness how Surridge sweats – worse than Lady Juliet at Venice.[8]

Well I went as I tell you to dinner at G. House and it was very hot on account of the sun never setting and so the Governor said it is so hot on account of the sun never setting that I must go away for a little in my yacht and will you come too so I said yes so I am going. [9]

Well I will write some more soon.

Love to that drunk man.

xxxxx Bo

Don't on any account let the Major go to Trinidad. There is a full cocktail bar with steel furniture like the New Age[10], Hereford where Dr Siegert gives everyone drinks to advertise his bitters. It would be the death of the·Major.

[1] Diana Coventry.

[2] Teresa Jungman.

[3] Jean Kinloch (1898–1945) married in 1919 Richard Norton (1892–1954) who succeeded as Lord Grantley in 1943.

[4] Maureen Guinness (1907–   ) married in 1930 the Marquess of Dufferin and Ava (1909–45).

[5] Conrad Russell (1878–1947). A contented Somerset dairy farmer and friend of Lady Diana Cooper. 'His forget-me-not eyes looked at one in a penetrating gaze over the top of his spectacles. His cheeks were fresh pink and his hair pure white.' Daphne Fielding in *Mercury Presides*.

[6] Sir Thomas Lea.

[7] 'lascivious beast' means a priest – from the limerick :

There was a young choirboy of Devon
Who was raped in the vestry by seven
Anglican priests –
Lascivious beasts –
Of such is the Kingdom of Heaven.

[8] Lady Juliet Duff (1881–1965). Daughter of the Earl of Lonsdale. Married to Sir Robin Duff 1903–14, and to Major Keith Trevor 1919–26. Lady Cunard had remarked of her in Venice: 'Juliet smells like a pub.'

[9] According to his diary he did go to Mazaruni with the Governor in a large steam launch.

[10] Pub.

To Lady Dorothy Lygon
1 January 1933

Georgetown Club,
British Guiana.

Dear Poll

It is only five weeks since I left Madresfield. Now I am four thousand miles away and oh what a changed world. Instead of the smiling meadows of Worcestershire and the noble line of the Malvern hills that I love so dearly, I look out upon a limitless swamp broken only by primaeval forest, desert and mountain. This club, if club it can be called so different is it from the gracious calm of Bucks & Punchs, is a log shack on the edge of the jungle. A single oil lamp sways from the rotting beam and so thick are the mosquitoes round it that it sheds only a pale glow. The table has long ago been devoured by ants and I write on my knees crouching on an empty cask. Around me corrupt officials gamble away the bribes they have taken during the day and a few traders and missionaries seek release from their sufferings in the anodyne of rum. Outside in the night air I can hear the tom-toms of hostile Indians encamped around us and the rhythmic rise & fall of the lash with which a drink crazed planter is flogging his half caste mistress.

There are few inhabitants. The Governor, if Governor he can be called, is a man prematurely aged whose unhinged mind belies his venerable white beard. He came out here as a mere lad in the service of a bookmakers company. All his companions have paid toll to the dread Yellow Jack or still dreader Black Jack. He alone remains. He is sitting in the corner now mechanically dealing out the greasy cards in a game of patience that will never come out because the three of clubs was stolen many years ago by a Portuguese adventurer who needed it for a hand of poker. But thank God the Union Jack still flies over what was once Government House.

The missionaries have long forsaken their vows & live openly with native women infecting them with hideous diseases.

The Medical Officer is a leper.

... As I write a crocodile snaps viciously at my feet and a cobra coils itself about the pen so I must stop and say goodbye and G.B.Y.

B.O.

To Catherine and Arthur Waugh
[2? January 1933]

Georgetown Club,
British Guiana.

Dear Mother & Father

I am afraid that I shant be able to write for a long time as I am going on a trip up country where there arent any post offices[1]. So dont imagine that anything untoward has happened if you dont hear for two months or even longer. It is all perfectly safe & healthy. The only trouble is no communications. I am travelling up with the Commissioner for the Rupununi district – a Mr Haynes[2] – we ride from the Berbice River to the Essequibo. It ought to be very interesting. After that my movements depend on who is going anywhere else. I hope to get to Takutu to a mission there. Anyway even if I dont get as far as that it should be an interesting trip & give me material for writing.

New Years eve was celebrated with numerous dances. Drunks sang until seven under my window with the result that I feel a little tired.

Best love. I'll come home by All Fools Day or thereabouts I hope.

Evelyn

[1] To Boa Vista, which he reached on 4 February. He arrived back at Georgetown at the beginning of April.
[2] Appears as Mr Bain in *Ninety-Two Days*.

To Lady Mary and Lady Dorothy Lygon
10 February [1933]

[Boa Vista,
Rio Bianco,
Brazil]

Darling Blondy & Poll

Well I have gone too far as usual & now I am in Brazil. Do come out & visit me. It is easy to find on account of it being the most vast of the republics of South America with an area of over eight million square kilometres and a federal constitution based on that of the United States of America. You go up the Amazon, easily recognisable on account of its being the largest river in the world, then right at Rio Negro (easily recognisable on account of being black) right again at Rio Bianco (e.r. on account of being white) and you cannot miss this village on account of its being the only one. The streets are entirely paved with gold which gives a very pretty effect especially towards sunset. But otherwise it is rather dull. The only other Englishman here is Lord Ebrington [1] & he spends his entire day on the telephone. None of the damned dagos can speak the Kings English and the lascivious beast who is Swiss is too ill with fever to talk any language at all. So I am rather lonely and have to wait here for some weeks until it rains & there is enough water in the river to go to Manaos. When I get there it is quite near Malvern & I will come over if you will have me & take a glass of beer with you & Bartleet at the Hornyold.

Tell Bartleet the local beer is called Superale Amazona and is rather nasty on account of it being so warm. No one drinks here so it would be a good place to send poor Major Duggan. They have the mescal[?] habit and drink an aphrodisiac called maté instead.

There are 30 soldiers here but the government forgot to send them any uniforms so they go about in pyjamas & straw boaters.

Everyone here is very poor like Balfour.

I shall have to learn to ride again because I have been so long riding dago horses & they behave in a quite contrary way to Captain Hances (G.B.H.) and are differently saddled & bridled in fact you would hardly know they were horses at all they behave so oddly. One lay down on top of me but luckily he was so small that it did not kill me outright.

How sad poor Dr Komma [2] must be without me.

Well I will ring you up when I get to Manaos and we will have some fun.

Perhaps you are dead & will never get this. How sad. How sad.

All love
BOAZ

What do you think. I found the name Father Hornyold among a list of lascivious beasts who had been in Guiana

[1] Hugh, Viscount Ebrington (1888–1950), had in fact become fifth Earl Fortescue in 1932.
[2] Rudolf Kommer.

To Lady Mary and Lady Dorothy Lygon
April 1933

Hotel Tower,
Georgetown,
British Guiana.

Darling Blondy & Poll

Well I am back in Georgetown & all the world is Highclere [1]. So there was a little hotel kept by a black man at a place named Kangaruma & there was no bed & 3 scorpions on the floor and only corn beef to eat & no bread and he brought out an old exercise book like the ones Tommy McDougal does his spelling lessons in & said would I write in it a testimonial so I wrote 'Exactly like Highclere' & he was very puzzled & scratched his wool.

The delight of these simple people at my return is very touching. A public holiday has been declared and all the men & women prostrate themselves in the dust & bring me their children to bless; great banners & bonfires decorate all the streets & several elderly niggers have already died of excitement. This afternoon the Governor is going to recite an ode which he has composed in my honour. Special services are being held in my honour at the Catholic & Protestant Cathedrals & the Mormon Mission and a banquet is being given by the police to the convicts at the Penal Settlements. Congratulatory wires have come from the King, the Pope, Miss Amy Johnson & Mussolini – but if I tell you more you may think I am boasting.

Tell Grainger I had luncheon in a Chinese restaurant yesterday & ate a birds nest.

I long to hear of the meeting of Sexy [Cecil] Beaton & Capt.G.B.H. If he laid so much as a finger on Jackie's ——— [sic] he will have to answer to me for the consequences. I have got so thin on account of starvation that I have to put a cushion in my trousers to keep them up.

The A.D.C. at G. House got sunstroke on account of never setting & sent a letter back to you please keep it for me to read.

Will you lunch with me at 1.30 on May 7th & bring Poll only give her a steak or two first and some plum pudding and a little ham and a pipe or 2 of port because it will be so expensive otherwise & I have spent all my money on stuffed alligators for my god-children. Would you like one?

I suppose that I shall not be able to understand any Madresfield jokes by the time I get home.

I wont say how delighted I am that you have expelled Miss Coventry because obviously by now you are bosom friends again.

I have some terrific tobacco for Capt. G.B.H.

All love & xs
Bo

[1] Highclere Castle is the home of Lord Carnarvon. Lady Sibell Lygon had stayed there and referred to its splendour afterwards. The name was taken up and used to mean any grand house or sometimes any house at all.

TO HENRY YORKE
[May 1933]

Grand Pump Room Hotel, Bath.

Dear Henry

Just back after a journey of the greatest misery. So I came to Bath which was absolutely right and live in a suite of rooms overlooking a colonnade with servants as it might be a club and a decanter of Crofts 1907 always on my sideboard and am getting rid of some of the horrors of life in the forest. Soon I hope to feel up to

London – on the 15th in fact when I shall arrive at the Savile & mean to stay intermittently until the end of July at least. I am longing to see you & Dig again. So much to discuss. Guinness – well it will keep. I've seen literally no one except my parents for a brief passage – five months mail to go through mostly Christmas cards and press cuttings all requiring legal action. Heavy Catholic trouble. Income Tax, dentist and so on. Now Bath is most satisfactory.

Woodruff married. [1]

Don't tell Hazel [Lavery] I am back.

Think of the horror of finding an article you wrote describing the Rupununi cattle district rechristened MY ESCAPE FROM MAYFAIR. I have written to Esmond Harmsworth [2] about it and hope to get an apology.

Do both write to me & tell me scandal

Yours
Evelyn

[1] Douglas Woodruff (1897–1978) married Marie (Mia) Acton (1905–   ). He was editor of *The Tablet* 1936–67.

[2] Esmond Harmsworth (1898–1978). Chairman of *Daily Mail* and General Trust Ltd 1932–71. Succeeded as Viscount Rothermere 1940.

An Open Letter to His Eminence The Cardinal Archbishop of Westminster [1]
May 1933

The Savile Club,
Brook Street, W.1.

My Lord Cardinal,

I lately returned from abroad to find awaiting me extracts from the Press, some months old in date but new and extremely surprising to myself. They deal with a novel, a copy of which is enclosed with this letter, written by me and published last October under the title of *Black Mischief*, and were occasioned by the following announcement in *The Tablet* of January 7th.

A year or two ago, paragraphs appeared in various newspapers announcing that Mr. Evelyn Waugh, a novelist, had been received into the Church. Whether Mr. Waugh still considers himself a Catholic, *The Tablet* does not know; but, in case he is so regarded by booksellers, librarians, and novel-readers in general, we hereby state that his latest novel would be a disgrace to anybody professing the Catholic name. We refuse to print its title or to mention its publishers. Indeed, this paragraph is not to be read as a review. We are mentioning Mr. Evelyn Waugh's work only because it would not be fair on *The Tablet*'s part to condemn coarseness and foulness in non-Catholic writers while glossing over equally outrageous lapses in those who are, or are supposed to be, our co-religionists.

This was followed by a joint letter of protest signed by twelve prominent English Catholics (and in case the word "friends" used later by the Editor [2] should be misinterpreted, may I mention that several of them are unknown to me personally?) The Editor then particularized his objections to my book and added to the terms of obloquy already employed. Here, except for irresponsible but extensive comment, the matter has rested pending my return.

... Before venturing upon any comments of my own let me quote in full *The Tablet*'s description of the book:

The novel in question is about an imaginary island in the Indian Ocean, ruled by a black Emperor. Prudence, daughter of the British Minister at the Emperor's court, goes up to the unsavoury room (the soapy water unemptied) of Basil, a man she hardly knows, and, after saying, "You might have shaved" and "Please help with my boots," stays till there is "a banging on the door." In the end, Basil, at a cannibal feast, unwittingly helps to eat the body of Prudence "stewed to pulp amid peppers and aromatic roots." In working out this foul invention, Mr. Waugh gives us disgusting passages. We are introduced to a young couple dining in bed, with "a bull terrier and a chow flirting on their feet." The young wife suddenly calls out "Oh God, he's made a mess again"; and Basil exclaims "How dirty the bed is." These nasty details are not necessary to the story. A dozen silly pages are devoted to a Birth Control Pageant, announced by posters which flaunt all over the island "a detailed drawing of some up-to-date contraceptive apparatus." The Emperor "re-names the site of the Anglican Cathedral 'Place Marie Stopes.'" Two humane ladies are ridiculed; in one place so indelicately that the passage cannot be described by us. There is a comic description of a Nestorian monastery with a venerated cross "which had fallen from heaven quite unexpectedly during Good Friday luncheon, some years back." If the twelve signatories of the above protest find nothing wrong with "during Good Friday luncheon" we cannot help them.

These are the grounds upon which my novel is condemned as obscene and blasphemous and the sincerity of my Faith is called in question.

I can imagine no task more repugnant to the sensibilities of the Editor of *The Tablet* than the painstaking page-by-page examination which he was obliged to conduct in search of the offensive, but I will do him the justice to suppose that he performed his disagreeable task with care. These extracts were printed after, and to justify, the original accusation, in reply to the letter of protest sent by twelve distinguished Catholics; when they were made the Editor was himself on the defensive, attempting to find grounds for the gross language he had employed towards me. It is true that in order to create an atmosphere prejudicial to me he hints darkly at the existence of evidence too hideous to be revealed – an ancient and unscrupulous forensic trick – but I think that I may take it that these quotations constitute the worst he can find against me, and are the result of careful selection in order to establish his case.

The accusation is one of blasphemy and obscenity, so let me first deal with the charge that falls under neither of these heads: that of ridiculing two humane ladies. Now had the ladies in question been real people, and had they been genuinely humane, I can conceive that it might be wrong to ridicule them, not certainly on grounds of blasphemy or obscenity, but of lack of charity. But these, my Lord Cardinal, are wholly fictitious characters, and the reason for which they are held up to ridicule is solely that they were *not* humane; that while they professed an exaggerated solicitude for the welfare of animals, they treated each other and all the human beings with whom they came into contact with a gross lack of consideration.

If anything were needed to expose the weakness of the argument surely it would be this: that after a detailed scrutiny of my work to substantiate his charges, the Editor of *The Tablet* is obliged to include this in his brief list of quotations, and to add to the calendar of sins that of an author exposing to ridicule the hypocrisy of his own characters. And this is one of the grounds upon which my novel is described as a "disgrace to anyone professing the Catholic name," "an outrageous lapse," and a work "outrageous not only to Catholic but to ordinary standards of modesty."

Perhaps, in passing, I may profitably specify the other charge associated with the humane ladies, that, besides ridiculing them, it is done "in one place so indelicately that the passage cannot be described." It is easy enough to make a charge of this kind and then leave the reader to fill in the gap according to his own imagination or experience. I have re-read the passages where the humane ladies appear and can find only this: a remark made during a riot by one of the characters, who is in search of them: "I daresay they've been raped," and the reply, "I hope so." I shall return to this later when I come to discuss the charge of immodesty. I merely mention it here to dispel the deliberately vague impression made by the insinuation in the text quoted.

I think it would be just to my opponent to include under the charge of blasphemy not only what is irreverent towards Catholic belief, but also flippant towards such Catholic practices as may not be essential, but are entitled, at the least, to reticent treatment. Had I erred in this latter case I think that though certainly not censurable in the vile terms employed towards me, I might be regarded as guilty of mild indiscretion and disloyalty. In point of fact my conscience is clear upon both grounds. I could point out that the only wholly admirable character is the only Catholic, a White Father missionary, and the only wholly contemptible one a French atheist; but that is beside the point. It is not required of me to prove that mine is an actively propagandist work, but merely that it is undeserving of the language used about it. Now the quotation upon which he bases his charge – and he obviously regards it as important since he reverts to it – is the one dealing with the venerated cross at the Nestorian Monastery. Let me quote my own words in full:

Here too were preserved, among relics of less certain authenticity, David's stone prised out of the forehead of Goliath (a boulder of astonishing dimensions), a leaf from the barren Fig Tree, the rib from which Eve had been created, and a wooden cross which had fallen from heaven quite unexpectedly during Good Friday luncheon some years back.

I think we must be in agreement that it does not constitute blasphemy to impute superstitious reverence for relics to a notoriously superstitious heretical Church but the Editor of *The Tablet*'s obviously confident denunciation of this passage has set me to reconsider it carefully and I can find only two reasons to account for his displeasure. Neither is particularly flattering to his intelligence, but I can conceive of no others.

It occurs to me that he may have misunderstood the slightly facetious form of the sentence and with a literal-mindedness that is scarcely sane, thought that they are genuine relics to which I am referring. It is painful to have to explain one's jokes. The phrase "among relics of less certain authenticity" is not intended to convey –

nor, I am convinced, would it convey to a reader who was not either semi-literate or else ill-intentioned – that those mentioned are authentic, but that those not mentioned are still more fantastic. Perhaps I should have qualified each item: "the stone (as they supposed) prised out of the forehead of Goliath," "a leaf (so they thought) from the barren Fig Tree," "the rib, erroneously described by them as that from which Eve had been created," "a cross which according to their wholly unreliable statement, had fallen. . . ." But really; one must in courtesy postulate some intelligence to one's reader. No doubt my publishers were at fault in sending a copy of the book to *The Tablet*, but how were they to know that a once leading Catholic paper was under such ingenuous management.

Or perhaps it is more charitable to attribute the misunderstanding not to puerility, but to ignorance. It may well be that the Editor of *The Tablet* has never heard of the Nestorians and taking the name to be a disguise for a Latin order of monks, read the passage as though I had accused a Carthusian or Benedictine house of such credulity. But again, is it seemly that such ignorance should be allowed to expose itself in the pages of *The Tablet*?

No other evidence is offered of blasphemy or irreverence.

The question of modesty is one of peculiar complexity. Here, as Your Eminence well knows, we are not dealing with any definite and absolute rules. An absence of clothing which is unexceptionable in Central Africa would be immodest in Europe; habits of speech and conduct that would be immodest in a child are normal in an adult. In parts of Italy ladies are refused admittance to Church in costume that would attract no comment at Westminster Cathedral; in many parts of Ireland it is held to be the height of impropriety for men and women to walk home together from Mass. There are different standards of modesty in every period, and every country, and to individuals of different races, ages, classes and sexes. It is one of the questions on which, owing to the great difference of their environment, it is often difficult for the clergy to understand the attitude of the laity. In writing a novel the problem is always present in a confusing degree. The author is reporting, say, the speech of a stoker who, he knows, would employ a great number of expressions unacceptable to gentle readers, and is accordingly constrained to various often ingenious devices by which he can retain the flavour of the original while purging it of offence. Thus in reporting the conversation of General Connolly I had often to alter and re-edit what would have been his actual words. By common consent certain oaths such as, for instance, "Oh, God" are regarded as tolerable, while others often far less offensive in their original meaning, are held to be unprintable. It is a matter of fashion and convention; the offence lies in transgressing the standards applicable to the author, irrespective of their absolute value. It is often as difficult for people of one generation to understand the standards of modesty of another, as for a traveller to accustom himself to the manners of a foreign country, and in order to avoid giving pain to any reader I refrained, in writing *Black Mischief*, from pushing to extremes the somewhat elastic conventions of my own era. No well-bred person to-day would feel the smallest embarrassment in mentioning the fact that a dog had "made a mess," few would take exception to a flippant reference to rape. Accordingly when the effect I aimed at required it (in the first case to convey the irregularity and discomfort of the menage of two of my characters, in the second to give expression, in mildly arresting form, to the callousness with which the officials regarded the fate of the two humane ladies) I did not scruple to employ the expressions.

There is in my book, as *The Tablet* points out, a Pageant of Birth Control. Perhaps the pages describing it *are* "silly", but it is not for silliness, surely, that I am being vilified? Like all Catholics I regard Birth Control as a practice which is a personal sin and an insidious social evil, but I know, and the Editor of *The Tablet* must also know if he ever spares himself time from insulting his fellow Catholics to converse with ordinary people of the world, that it is not so regarded by the vast majority of educated Englishmen and women to-day. In its principles and details it is accepted and discussed as one of the normal developments of modern society. In these circumstances I cannot regard it as an offence to introduce the subject, and that is the only offence with which I can be charged. There are two ways of meeting an evil of the kind – either by serious denunciation which is fitting for the clergy (and possibly for the journalists who regard Catholic employment as giving them authority to speak as though in the pulpit) or by ridicule. I chose the latter course as more becoming to a novelist and regarded and still regard my "silly" pages as an attempt, however ineffectual, to prosper the cause which we all have so closely at heart.

The Tablet quotes a scene occurring in an hotel bedroom and I readily admit that the impression I wished to convey was that the woman in question was the man's mistress. I do not write for children and I so phrased this statement, essential to the structure of my book, that it would only be intelligible to an adult reader. Now if it be "outrageous not only to Catholic but to ordinary standards of modesty" to write about a character who keeps a mistress, then not only am I guilty but practically every writer in every language and in every century.

It is often remarked with surprise by uninstructed observers, that whereas all other grave sins – murder, theft, suicide and so on – are universally regarded as suitable literary material, there will always be found in England and parts of America a vociferous protest if sins of impurity are so treated. The orthodox solution of the riddle is that many people are psychologically ill-balanced in sexual matters and that although the description of a masterly piece of house-breaking is unlikely to lead the reader to burglary, it is quite possible that a piece of erotic writing may excite him to sexual sin. Now there is nothing in my statement of Basil and Prudence's relationship which could be taken as inflammatory by the most prurient. The few details I give of the occurrence all tend in exactly the opposite direction, and the Editor of *The Tablet*, surely, weakens his case by quoting them? He does more than weaken his case; he gives us some indication of his own nature. The concomitants are disagreeable – Basil is unshaven, the room is "unsavoury", the soapy water has not been emptied. All these details are quoted with triumph. It is remarked (without foundation, as it happens, in the text of the novel) that they "hardly know" each other as though a sin were less culpable between old friends. What is the inference of these carefully extracted details? That in order to preserve modesty I should have staged the illicit meeting among silk sheets, soft music, expensive perfumery and all the shoddy stock-in-trade of pornography? What a picture this editor draws of himself, as one avid to nose out impurity yet doubly enraged to find it in unattractive guise!

There remains the climax of the story, when Prudence is eaten at a cannibal feast. Several critics whose opinion I respect more than the Editor of *The Tablet* have told me that they regard this as a disagreeable incident. It was meant to be. *The Tablet* quotes the fact that she was stewed with pepper, as being in some way a particularly lubricious process. But this is a peculiar prejudice of the Editor's, attributable perhaps, like much of his criticism, to defective digestion. It cannot matter whether she was roasted, grilled, braised or pickled, cut into sandwiches or devoured hot on toast as a savoury; the fact is that the wretched girl was cooked and eaten, and that is obviously and admittedly a disagreeable end. Though it forces me into the slightly ludicrous position of reviewing my own book, I hope Your Eminence will give me leave to explain my intention.

The story deals with the conflict of civilisation, with all its attendant and deplorable ills, and barbarism. The plan of my book throughout was to keep the darker aspects of barbarism continually and unobtrusively present, a black and mischievous background against which the civilized and semi-civilized characters performed their parts: I wished it to be like the continuous, remote throbbing of those hand drums, constantly audible, never visible, which every traveller in Africa will remember as one of his most haunting impressions. I introduced the cannibal theme in the first chapter and repeated it in another key in the incident of the soldiers eating their boots, thus hoping to prepare the reader for the sudden tragedy when barbarism at last emerges from the shadows and usurps the stage. It is not unlikely that I failed in this; that the transition was too rapid, the catastrophe too large. As I say, this opinion has been represented to me by many whom I respect, and if they are right, as they very well may be, I must plead guilty to an artistic mistake. But it is not the artistry or the silliness of my book that is under discussion. I am forced into this embarrassing explanation of my own artistic motives in order that I may defend myself against very different charges; charges against my personal honour, and my moral conduct in the exercise of my trade. They are not charges that can be founded on any artistic lapse, were it infinitely more serious than I am disposed to think the present one.

This, my Lord Cardinal, is my case against your employee, the present editor of *The Tablet*. I have attempted to state it with humility and restraint, but is it not an intolerable scandal that this letter should ever have been necessary; that by reason, and solely by reason, of his being a Catholic resident in the arch-diocese of Westminster, a writer should be obliged to interrupt a decent and inconspicuous life among people of his own kind to defend himself against public attack so ignorant and ill-judged; that he should find himself in the degrading position of reviewing his own books and explaining his own jokes, of haggling about the ridicule of humane ladies and the superstitions of the Nestorians with an opponent of this character? No one can practise the trade of writing, however obscurely, without, on occasion, being the object of stupid abuse. Had the Editor of *The Tablet* found, as I hope he may shortly find, employment more suited to his temper, and had his attack on me appeared in an organ where its tone would have been less inappropriate, I should have known how to treat it and should not now find myself dragged into this distasteful quarrel. Your Eminence's patronage alone renders this base man considerable, and it is with the earnest petition, as much for the good name of the Faith as for the comfort of all intelligent English Catholics, that a scandalous misuse of your patronage may be corrected, that I ascribe myself,

Your Eminence's very humble and obedient servant,

EVELYN WAUGH

[1] Cardinal Bourne (1861–1935).
[2] Ernest Oldmeadow remained Editor until 1936.

To Lady Mary Lygon
[July 1933]
Postcard

Breccles Hall[1],
Attleborough,
Norfolk.

So sorry I was mad carew[2] Fri. Longing to see the dignity prosperity and peace of Mad[resfield] again. Will come Tues and let you know with telegrams. So John Julius[3] had a book he kept showing to Capt McDougal and it was called *Reading Without Tears*. So I went too far teasing Capt Mac and was not like a gentleman.

Bo

[1] Home of Venetia Montagu (1887–1948). Married 1915–24 to Edwin Montagu. Friend and correspondent of Herbert Asquith.
[2] Mad Carew: from 'The Green Eye of the Little Yellow God'.
[3] John Julius Cooper (1929–). Only child of Duff and Lady Diana Cooper. Succeeded as Viscount Norwich 1954.

To Katharine Asquith[1]
[1933?]

Savile Club.

Dear Catherine,

I sent off two books to you today Remoters & Blackers[2]. Well I dont know what the effect will be. I dont think there's much to bring a blush in Remoters & yet I don't know – is it justified teleologically? As for Blackers there are bits in that to make your hair stand on end worse than Garnett[3], or Maugham. But what was I to do? There the books were and any minute you might come across them & the fat would be in the fire, cat out of bag etc. So it seemed best to take a risk & send them on and perhaps the result will be no more lovely week ends like the last.

Anyway I have had that, and it was the most enjoyable in years.

Diana [Cooper] just cant believe you like me.

Love from
Evelyn

[1] Katharine Asquith (1885-1977). Widow of Raymond Asquith, son of the Prime Minister. See Appendix of Names.

[2] *Remote People* and *Black Michief*.

[3] David Garnett (1892-   ). Writer.

To Lady Mary and Lady Dorothy Lygon

[September 1933]   S.S. *Kraljica Marija (Queen Mary)*

Darling Blondy & Poll,

So I am in the sea of Marmora and it is very calm & warm and there are lots of new & old chums on board and I have seen numbers of new & old places and am enjoying myself top-hole.

I had only $2\frac{1}{2}$ minutes in Venice so couldnt buy bad taste shoes but hope to do so on return journey.

Alfred[1] (brother of bald dago) has behaved very well so far except for once farting at Lady Lovat[2].

Lady Lavery missed the ship and so did Mr Yorke but instead there came those decent Bobbities[3]. The ship is full of people of high rank including two princesses of ROYAL BLOOD. There is not much rogering so far as I have seen and the food is appalling. Everyone except me ate a lobster and it poisoned them. God they were sick.

There are several beasts of various religions & they are jealous of each other and there is a Protestant Canon[4] with a beard who talked to one of the princesses with his fly buttons undone and she was disgusted.

I went to Athens which was full of wily Greeks & now go on to Istanbul which is full of terrible Turks. My jagger is called Collon god he is contemptible. Collon and I went to the mountains to see a very good taste church and were bitten by bugs such as you wouldnt believe possible. The lovely Magdalen Fraser[5] is ugly as hell and dull as mud. There is a decent cousin of Porchy called Gabriel Herbert[6]. She got drunk on gin for the first time & is a little sheepish about it.

Perhaps that handsome Dutch girl is staying with you. . . . Give her my love & a kiss on the arse and take one each for yourselves too.

Bo

And kiss Lady Sibells arse too if she is with you

And Mims

And Jackies

I don't think Mr Hood[7] would like it but give him one if he would.

[1] Alfred Duggan (1903-64). Novelist.

[2] Laura Lister (died 1965) married Lord Lovat in 1910.

[3] Viscount Cranborne (1893–1972) married in 1915 Elizabeth Cavendish (1897–   ). In 1947 he succeeded as Marquess of Salisbury. Conservative statesman.

[4] Canon William Ainger Wigram (1872–1953) of St Paul's, Malton, 1928–36.

[5] Magdalen Fraser (1913–69). Daughter of Lord Lovat. Married the Earl of Eldon in 1934.

[6] Gabriel Herbert (1911–   ). Married in 1943 Alexander (Alick) Dru. Her younger sister Laura was to marry Waugh. Their father was the younger brother of the fifth Earl of Carnarvon.

[7] A boxer from Birmingham who trained at Malvern with Wally Weston.

To Katharine Asquith[1] and the Earl of Oxford and Asquith[2]

[Portofino.]

[September 1933]

Dear Catherine & Trim,

A fine picture of Milan station. My journey went on as it began with dense crowds & discomfort.

However it is most enjoyable here tho you understated the dangers. Life a constant struggle with malignant natural forces – another Guiana for insects – landslides, heavy exertion. Delicious simple food and the wine not at all as you described it.

There are here: chap called Francis[3] of great beauty whose brother I used to know until he died in an edifying way; Jewish giantess called Eva[4] who plays oboe & concertina; bald, crazy mural decorator named Johnny[5]; white mouse named Laura[6]; fat girl full of sex appeal named Bridget[7]; gawky youth named David[8] courting her unsuccessfully; a dishevelled Scottish giantess called Magdalen [Fraser] who sometimes stops giggling to sing madrigals; very decent hostess[9] who barks like Mr Lunn; astute urchin with neurotic tendencies called Auberon[10]; decent chap called Peter[11] who has only woken up once & then to complain of seeing a ghost.

Returning Rome Express Thursday. At Juliets Fri-Monday & will ring you up.

Love from
Evelyn

[1] Katharine Asquith had been on the cruise with her son, and Waugh spent a week sightseeing with them in Ravenna and Bologna before going to stay with the Herberts at Portofino.

[2] Her son Julian (Trim), who had succeeded to his grandfather's title in 1928.

[3] Francis Howard (1905–   ). Succeeded as Lord Howard of Penrith 1939.

[4] Eve Myers, daughter of Leopold Myers, the writer.

[5] John Spencer Churchill (1909–   ). Composer, painter, sculptor.

[6] Laura Herbert (1916–73). Married Waugh in 1937.

[7] Bridget Herbert (1914–   ). Laura's sister. Married to Edward Grant 1935–47.

[8] David Peel (1910–44).

[9] Mary Vesey (1889–1970). Married 1910–23 to Aubrey Herbert. Laura's mother.

[10] Auberon Herbert (1922–74). Laura's brother.

[11] Peter Acton (1909–46). Brother of Lord Acton.

To Lady Mary Lygon
[October 1933?]

Darling

God how sad not to see you and say thank you thank you for all your kind hospitality. It has been lovely staying with you. Thank you. Thank you.

Just heard yesterday that my divorce comes on today so was elated and popped question to Dutch girl [Teresa Jungman] and got raspberry. So that is that, eh. Stiff upper lip and dropped cock. Now I must go. How sad, how sad. I wont sponge any more but I'll be in London next week at Savile and hope you will sponge on me for luncheon or dinner whenever Letty[1] frees you.

Now I will go to Mells[2].

BO

Good about Chetty[3].

[1] Lady Lettice Lygon (1906–1973). The eldest of the sisters. Married to Sir Richard Cotterell 1930–58.

[2] Home of the Asquith family.

[3] Roger Chetwode (1906–40). A close friend of Lady Mary's.

To Lady Mary Lygon
[October? 1933]
Postcard

That was a decent letter. Well at Victoria at nine they said you mcdougal your train is at nine thirty. Then I wrote[1] and wrote and wrote for 3 days and once I went to Chichester in a bus hoping to find a Cinema but there wasn't one then I thought well at least I can have muffins for tea but there weren't any, so I had my hair cut in a bad taste way and came back to solitude and sorrow and my tear drenched pillow. Yesterday I couldn't stand the disillusion, bitterness, death any more so I went to see a Mr Plunket Greene whom I know and he was decent and showed me a huge green house where he is going to grow tomatoes for the market and call it Plunket Greene Houses Ltd. Ha. Ha. I will see you on Wed when the sun has just passed his zenith. In the evening unless she is dutch I shall be with Miss J. can't help loving that girl. An aeroplane keeps roaring over my head oh dear oh dear I wish I was dead like Reggie Beaton[2] and the legless Jagger[3] at your gates. Tell Grainger I think of him always the lascivious beast.

Boaz

[1] *Ninety-Two Days.*

[2] Reggie Beaton, elder brother of Cecil, threw himself under a tube train on 16 October 1933.

[3] Wally Weston, a friend of Hugh Lygon, who ran a training gymnasium. He lost a leg in the First World War and kept a pub

To L.A.G.Strong [1]   Easton Court Hotel,
[26 November 1933?]   Chagford,
                                                       Devon.

Dear Strong
    Many thanks for your kind invitation to contribute to 'How I began'. I wish I
could accept but I am in the middle of a book & cant interrupt it.

                                                   Yours sincerely
                                                   Evelyn Waugh

By the way I have an idea that the title has been used for a book of sex instruction for
children.

    [1] Leonard Strong wrote or edited over a hundred books. *Beginnings*, essays by writers of fiction on
their literary beginnings, was published in 1935.

To Lady Mary and Lady Dorothy Lygon   [Fez, Morocco.]
[January 1934]

Darling Blondy & Poll,
    How very decent & surprising to get letters from you both so soon. It made me
feel less than a thousand miles away. Perhaps you will both come & visit me
tomorrow or the day after and you will find a warm welcome I promise you.
    Well it was a dull voyage out because all the pretty people were sick all the time
and only one man was drunk on new years eve and he was very small and low class
and had pinch-noses and he tried to conduct the band and no one thought that
funny except an old German lady who laughed fit to bust. It was very cold in the
ship.
    Then I came to Tangier and a black man confiscated all my cigars though I had
not tried to smuggle them. That was very sad indeed. I sat in Tangier for nine hours
and no one spoke to me except a boy who wanted to clean my shoes but I was too
mean to let him.
    Then I took a night train to Fez.
    It is a very decent town – with little streams running all through it & very old
houses with walled gardens & shops selling some of the worst taste objects I ever
saw. There are 100,000 Arabs and 30,000 Jews and about 3 white people. The white
people have a town of their own five miles away like the New Age at Hereford.
There are a great many soldiers, some black and some foreign legion. There is a
foreign legion of women too but they have no banners, no uniforms, no medals
when they are brave, no wounded stripes when they are hurt.
    I made friends with a froggy taxi driver called Joseph and he took me round the
—— quarter. It was very gay and there were little Arab girls of fifteen & sixteen for
ten francs each & a cup of mint tea. So I bought one but I didn't enjoy her very much
because she had a skin like sandpaper and a huge stomach which didn't show until
she took off her clothes & then it was too late.

It is not at all hot in fact it is cold & there are no fires or hot water pipes in the hotel. But the wine is free & rather nasty & there is lots of food. I have begun the novel[1] and it is excellent, first about sponger[2] and then about some imaginary people who are happy to be married but not for long.

The five to two's[3] have their own part of the town because the Arabs think they smell so it is like Madresfield at Xmas.

There was a shameless blonde (English I think) in evening dress with a thing in her hair going round the brothels just as did Mme de Janzé[4] and the tarts despised her terribly & made her pay double for her mint tea.

There is also a brothel full of white ladies very cleverly named Maison Blanche but they cost 30 francs each so I haven't bought any of them.

When I have finished this novel I think I will go to Jerusalem for a pilgrimage to become holy.

I will not put anything in this letter about your affaires because it might not be discreet but I hope all is going like a house afire or a hot cake or what you will.

It is a lie that Major Duggan had lunch with me. It was a night cinema but I expect he was too drunk to know the difference, poor sot.

Little Diana[5] was like Poll and saw me off.

No love to anyone except your dear selves.

BO

[1] *A Handful of Dust*, September 1934.
[2] Murrough O'Brien (1910–). Major in the Irish Guards.
[3] Jews.
[4] Phillis Boyd married the Comte de Janzé in 1922. 'One of the first women ever to wear a short skirt ... the face of a puma ... the fastidious walk of a crane.' Cecil Beaton, *The Glass of Fashion*.
[5] Lady Diana Cooper.

To KATHARINE ASQUITH   c/o British Consulate,
[January 1934]   Fez.

Dear Katherine

Well I have been here a week now and I very much wish you were all here to enjoy it too. It is a city of astonishing beauty with running streams & fountains everywhere and enormous covered gateways in very narrow streets – no wheeled traffic, miles of bazaar, elaborate medieval fortifications, hills all round dotted with forts, olive trees, sand cliffs & spring grass, waterfalls. Dense crowds of moors and a few French soldiers – mostly Senegalese or Foreign Legion – practically no touting for tourists.

I haven't done anything about taking a house yet as its too cold. I live in a French pension just outside the walls where the officers come in to play a kind of billiards. Good cooking & tolerable local wine. When it gets warmer I will look for an Arab house & then you can come & stay with me.

Some French Franciscans have made a chapel a kilometre away so I haven't got away from that. It is in an old moorish house with alabaster floors and tiled walls &

very pretty too & they say mass for two nuns and a dozen criminal looking orphan boys with shaved heads and skin diseases.

All my cigars, many pounds worth, got confiscated at Tangier which has put me out very much.

I peg away at the novel which seems to me faultless of its kind. Very difficult to write because for the first time I am trying to deal with normal people instead of eccentrics. Comic English character parts too easy when one gets to be thirty.

I don't see any papers here so please let me know the result of Trim's exam, in a post card if you have the time.

Reading the life of Charles de Foucauld – so thats edifying.

My love to Helen[1] & Trim & your mother and Conrad [Russell].

Evelyn

[1] Lady Helen Asquith (1908–   ). Katharine's daughter.

To Lady Mary Lygon   Fez.
[1934]

Darling Blondy

Decent to hear from you. I suppose that by now the pauper prince[1] will be on the high seas and you will be in the soup or perhaps Chetty again. I am sorry to read of Lulu's[2] death, the more so as I have just described him fully in my filthy novel and now that will be bad taste. I have written 18,500 words. It is excellent – very grim. About adultery so far. I am so afraid Periwinkle[3] will think it is about him – it isn't but bits of it are like.

Last night I was having a drink with the consul when I saw a newspaper which was the first I had seen since I left & there was a huge photograph of Lady Sibell on the front and DUKE SUES NIECE[4] and I said 'Oh' and looked at it & the consul's wife said, 'let me see, Lady Sibell Lygon is the Duke of Westminster's *fourth* wife, isn't she?'

The evenings are v. dull as there is nowhere to go or to talk to except froggy soldiers & they don't talk to me much so I go most evenings & take my coffee in a brothel where I have formed an attachment to a young lady called Fatima. She is not at all Dutch[5] in her ways. She is brown in colour and her face is tatooed all over with blue patterns v. pretty but does not play the piano beautifully, she has a gold tooth she is very proud of but as we can't talk each others language there is not much to do in between rogering. I gave Fatima that milk ring you gave me, so now if you are angry I shant be able to send it back & be forgiven. I don't think F. thinks much of it as her taste runs to gold & silver.

I may go to a place called Marrakesh soon but keep on writing to Fez and I shall get it all right. Keep writing all the news as I don't see papers.

Fatima is a teetotaler but she drinks a lot of peppermint tea. Tell Bartleet the beer is no good here. It is made in Rabat & called Cigogne.

Best love to Mr Grainger & your dear sisters.

Bo

[1] Prince George.

[2] A white pekinese belonging to Phillis de Janzé. In *A Handful of Dust* Djinn is 'quite colourless with pink nose and lips and pink circles of bald flesh round his eyes'.

[3] Or 'Perry' or 'Winkle', from Peregrine. Lord Brownlow (1899–1978) was personal Lord-in-Waiting to Edward VIII at the time of the abdication and drove Mrs Simpson across France, pursued by the press, the week before the final announcement.

[4] The Duke of Westminster, Lady Sibell's uncle, sued her for libel.

[5] Uncooperative.

To Katharine Asquith   [Morocco]
[1934]

Dear Katherine

Your letter arrived this morning with the news from Balliol[1]. How I wish I was in England to congratulate you all & see your delight.

It is the best thing thats happened for years – I couldn't be more excited if they had caught the Loch Ness monster or Lady Lovat had grown a beard.

By the way how does Trim like having his success, won by exalted abilities & unremitting toil, attributed solely to prayer? If I was he I should not have those nuns mentioned too much. Anyhow we all know nuns can get what they want, but we didn't suspect that monks could coach Balliol scholars. That seems to me one of the most stimulating disclosures – or is Helen taking all credit for the tutoring? Are you going to keep him at school those two terms? If I ever have a son who gets a scholarship (a possibility which seems fairly remote) my inclination will be to pack him off round the world or into some sort of job between school & university – or anyway put him out abroad to learn a language. But then I suppose there is the chance of his losing the taste for reading.

I think of going to Jerusalem for Easter. Why not come there instead of Rome?

> Best love to you all
> Evelyn

The novel drags on at 10,000 words a week. I have just killed a little boy at a lawn meet & made his mother commit adultery & his father get drunk so perhaps you won't like it after all.

[1] Her son had taken a scholarship from Ampleforth.

To Lady Mary Lygon   Fez.
[January? 1934]

Darling Blondy

I have been away for a weeks well earned holiday & I came back to find 2 letters from you. That was decent.

My good taste book is ⅔ done. I think that I shall finish it in 3 weeks and then I shall come to England for a day or two & hope to see you & Poll and that ill-behaved Lady Sibell.

God how sad about Jackie. It is a pity she cant learn to ride better poor child but of course she never had a chance, being brought up with that very incompetent fat man Captain Hance and that very cowardly woman Min. God what am I saying? I think I must have taken a touch of the sun.

So I went to Casa Blanca WOT? KARSA BLANKER? It is a large town on the Atlantic coast of Morocco, Tommy, WAS IT DESINT No Tommy it was bloody. Then I went to a place named Marrakesh where there was a pretty town and a lot of black buggers. Tell Phillis that & she will know I enjoyed myself with them[1]. There was an hotel like Highclere so I said give me your very finest rooms and when I got the bill I nearly died of it. Then I went to Rabat where I drank with some pauper royalty called Nemours[2]. The Duke suffers terribly from the Demon and his American Duchess beat him for drinking 2 glasses of port just like W. Weston.

If you are coming to 5 to 2 land[3] for Easter you must start packing your pessaries now.

I have been reading Dalroy[4] regularly with great interest.

The poor frogs here are so excited about the Stavisky scandal[5] WOTS THAT WAS IT HIS KOK No Tommy it is to do with finance & politics.

Please tell me if it is true that the bright young Yorkes have a son[6] & how Dig is for my newspapers don't say anything of it.

Lots of love to all & sundry and an x for Grainger

Boaz

[1] According to Waugh, Phillis de Janzé thought him homosexual.
[2] Charles Philippe Duc de Nemours (1905–70). Descended from Louis Philippe of France; he married Marguerite Watson.
[3] Palestine.
[4] A gossip columnist in the *Daily Sketch*.
[5] Alexandre Stavisky (1886–1934), whose dealings caused a scandal that led to his own death and contributed to the fall of the French Government.
[6] Sebastian Yorke was born 24 January 1934.

To Lady Mary Lygon
[March? 1934]

[Easton Court Hotel,
Chagford,
Devon.]

Darling Blondy

So I am back in G.B. but still must work as I havent finished my good taste book yet so I am at Chagford Easton Court Hotel Devon. I saw Charlie B.H.[1] at Gibraltar and I have learned to play dominoes. I was taught by a lady named Mrs Brown on a Japanese ship from that very small country. It is a good & easy game & I will teach you & Poll. I see they have let Lady Sibell[2] out of prison.

I have got a pipe for you to smoke hashish in and if you havent any hashish I will give you some but it doesn't make me feel d d or anything, v disappointing.

Tootle oo
Bo

[1] Charles Baillie-Hamilton (1900–39). MP for Bath 1929–31.
[2] Lady Sibell Lygon was never in prison. Presumably a reference to the Duke of Westminster libel case.

To A.D.PETERS
[March? 1934]

Easton Court Hotel,
Chagford,
Devon.

Dear Peter

I am back & this is my address until the novel is finished.

I here return the dramatic version of *S.Blandish*[1] which I have kept too long. I don't see any possibilities in it.

The name of the novel is A HANDFUL OF ASHES[2].

If you have your copy, could you send it to me here to put into order for book publication. I won't do anything about arranging it for serial until I hear from you. If those Americans wrongly called cosmopolitan take it there must be no monkeying with the text. The serial form, as I see it, would have an additional chapter of about 5,000 words making 50,000 in all, at the end of the scene where Tony refuses to be divorced. The chapter will describe reconciliation[3].

Yours
Evelyn

P.S. There was an article of mine about debunking the bush came out in December in a crook paper called *Oxford & Cambridge* and another in U.S.A. called, I think, *Virginia Quarterly*[4]. If they have paid up could you let me have the cash, dough, tin, spondulicks, ready, oof, doings or whatever it is. Read *Decameron* & see no possibility of modernisation. *V* sorry to have wasted so much of your time over that.

Want to write a 'Great Life' of Gregory the Great when novel is done. Perhaps you'd see what Balston will pay. Could you let me know how much advance I am likely to get on *Handful of Dust* & how soon? WHAT ABOUT THAT PORTRAIT OF EMPEROR OF ABYSSINIA MRS BRAND STOLE[5]

[1] *Serena Blandish or the Difficulty of Getting Married*, by A Lady of Quality (Enid Bagnold), 1924.
[2] Not just a slip. This title had been considered, as had 'Fourth Decade'.
[3] *Harper's Bazaar* printed five extracts from *A Handful of Dust* in America, with a specially written happy ending. The real ending had originally come from Waugh's short story 'The Man Who Liked Dickens', so it was possible to put asunder what had been joined together.
[4] 'Rough Life', *Virginia Quarterly Review*, 1934.
[5] Carl Brandt married another American agent, Carol Hill. Waugh found her 'a secretary raised to its highest power'. *Diaries*.

To Tom Driberg   Savile Club.
[September 1934]

Dear Tom

Here is my new novel[1]. I hope you will like it. I think it is better than the others.
At any rate the frontispiece might amuse you. I instructed the architect to design the
worst possible 1860 and I think he has done well.

It comes out on Monday.

Just back from Spitzbergen which was hell – a fiasco very narrowly retrieved
from disaster.[2]

                                                        Yours
                                                        Evelyn

[1] *A Handful of Dust* appeared that month.

[2] Waugh had run into Hugh Lygon on 5 July and heard that he was off with the Oxford University
Arctic Expedition. They left with Alexander Glen (1912–   ) two days later and reached West
Spitzbergen by various boats, some intended for seal-trapping, but an unexpected thaw drove them
back. They were away over seven weeks. According to Alec, Waugh was nearly killed and thought with
relief, 'So this is it.' He contributed 'The First Time I Went to the North. Fiasco in the Arctic' to *The First
Time I* ..., 1935, an anthology edited and illustrated by Theodora Benson.

To Henry Yorke   14A Hampstead Lane,
[September 1934]   Highgate, N.6.

Dear Henry,

Very many thanks for your letter of criticism[1].

You must remember that to me the savages come into the category of 'people one
has met and may at any moment meet again.' I think they appear fake to you largely
because you don't really believe they exist. The reason they didn't take the stores
was not honesty in any Sunday school sense. I think it is that they couldnt do two
things at once. Going home meant going complete with their own belongings – an
act of theft, though not at all repugnant, would have been a different kind of action –
and they were impelled by the mechanical [motive?] simply to go home.

I think I agree that the Todd episode is fantastic. It is a 'conceit' in the Webster
manner – wishing to bring Tony to a sad end I made it an elaborate & improbable
one. I think too the sentimental episode with Therese in the ship is probably a
mistake. But the Amazon stuff had to be there. The scheme was a Gothic man in the
hands of savages – first Mrs Beaver etc. then the real ones, finally the silver foxes at
Hetton. All that quest for a city seems to me justifiable symbolism.

                                                   Best love to you both
                                                   Evelyn

[1] Henry Yorke had written of *A Handful of Dust*: 'I feel the end is so fantastic that it throws the rest
out of proportion. Aren't you mixing two things together? The first part is convincing, a real picture of
people one has met and may at any moment meet again .... But then to let Tony be detained by some

madman introduces an entirely fresh note and we are in fantasy ... you spent far too much time on the trip. You have 348 pages, roughly 100 of these are concerned with Tony running away ... my whole mind is clouded by the Amazon. To tell you the truth I was furious that the natives did not steal all the stores. I can't and won't believe that natives are honest, it's too much. So you see in what a pathetic case I am.' The English scenes are praised as 'perfectly possible, very moving and beautifully written'.

TO LADY MARY LYGON   14A Hampstead Lane
[September? 1934]   Highgate, N.6.

Darling Blondy

So I too am staying with my Boom[1]. At present it is all dignity & peace but I expect we shall soon have a quarrel & black each others eyes & tear our hair & flog each other with hunting crops like the lovely Lygon sisters.

I am going to spend a very studious autumn writing the life of a dead beast[2]. I think I shall stay here so that I shall not be tempted to the demon at the Savile and to go out with whores & make myself ill as I do if I am away from good parents.

That good taste book I wrote about sponger is being a success and wherever I go the people shout Long Live Bo & throw garlands of flowers in my path and I have a brass band to play to me in my bath.

My Alfreds wife[3] has just inherited a fortune & is looking for a Highclere. Do you know of one for sale. I thought Lowesby might do but they want to be on the Great Weston Railway. Do you see that joke or did you think it just McDougal. You see Wally [Weston] worked on the railway. Oh I see ha ha ha.

I had dinner with Dig & Henry. Henry loved your Boom but God he was in a bad Temper.

Mr Reggie Hance is to marry a Welsh girl.

I have got fat again. I wish you had seen me at the N. Pole I had great sex appeal – thin as Bartleet.

I have just had a letter asking for the Dutch rights of *Black Mischief*. What a difficult book it will be – bound upside down with the pages in wrong order & bits left out I must send a copy to poor Tommy McD.

I hear you are never to be seen with English people now – Russians, Americans, natives etc. Well thats what comes of living abroad. The South has got you.

I am going to have a little holiday on Oct. 8th for the pony fair & last round up at Chagford. Will you come?

XXXXXXX
Bo

[1] Waugh's father. Lord Beauchamp, father of the Lygons, was nicknamed 'Boom', and so it became the word for any father.
[2] *Edmund Campion*, September 1935.
[3] Alfred came to mean 'brother', from Alfred and Hubert Duggan. Alec Waugh had married Joan Chirnside, an Australian, in 1932. In June 1934 they heard that she had inherited a quarter of a million pounds.

To Lady Mary Lygon   Newton Ferrers[1],
[1934]   Callington,
                                                       Cornwall.

... So it was decent to get a letter and to hear that your great cowardice re the horse
is overcome. There was a picture of Jackie walking along with Miss Churcher and the
Captain (G.B.H.)'s right eye

So yesterday talking of this & that what should I mention but fucking. Oh said Sir
Robert in great pain with crocodile tears coursing down cheeks, oh you have a *low*
view of love. *I* am so high minded I never think of a thing like fucking. To *me*, he
said, love is a spiritual and aesthetic matter, the worship of beauty and noble soul.
How much much better I am than you, he said.

Did I give him away & expose his great pouncing before Lady D.? No.
Gentlemanly Bo was silent and bore these undeserved reproaches without a
murmur.

So today I go to Easton Court Hotel Chagford. I shall be in London all next
week and hope eagerly for some jolly times with you.

So I have been to luncheon with a lot of cornish lords & ladies and they eat rather
dull food & Abdy's chef has laycocked them & they have a female saint instead but
goodness how badly she cooks.

I have given up tobacco for lent. Like frisky you will say. No not like frisky.

XXXXXX

Bo

[1] The house of Sir Robert Abdy (1896–1976) who in 1930 had married Lady Diana Bridgeman
(1907–67). Admirer of France, collector of French books, paintings and furniture.

To Lady Dorothy Lygon   Easton Court Hotel,
[October 1934]   Chagford,
                                                       Devon.

Darling Poll,

Did you know that in the glorious epoch 1900–1914 the word 'poll' was used by
our gallant boys, (so soon to pay the supreme sacrifice & lay down their lives for you
and me on foreign soil,) to mean a tart? Is not that sad & interesting? I was told it
yesterday. So now I shall give up calling you Poll on account of it being disrespectful.

Darling Dorothy, I have been living for quite a time at Chagford and it is decent.
Mrs Postlethwaite-Cobb is going to America this week. There is a yankee bugger
here named Mr Rupture[?]. He has been here since April on account of not being
able to pay his bill and he writes short stories about the foreign legion that are very
hard to read. That very poor Mr Balfour is coming next week with a viscountess not
Castlerosse. I went to Longleat yesterday and thought it a bad taste house and there
was a poor lonely old man called Lord Bath[1] and he had his little dinner laid out on
the table god it was sad why not marry him? There is a very nice midget who lives in

Cornwall called Diana[2] & I go to stay with her sometimes. She has a smutty frog book called *Le jardin parfumé*[3] it says that in rogering the cock should never be withdrawn so much as a millimetre and this gives the maximum pleasure to the lady on account of pressing her bladder. Do you remember a wicked man called Arthur Elliot who ran a cocktail club? Well he has a brother called Monty St Germains[4] who is a great gentleman in these parts and M.St G showed us a chapel where there was a stained glass window with a portrait of himself as a child, as it might be Elmley etc. at Mad[resfield], so I said 'I suppose that little angel is Arthur' and he said nothing so I said louder 'I expect that the little angel is your brother Arthur' and still he said nothing so I shouted 'IS THAT YOUR BROTHER ARTHUR?' and he stamped away & locked up the chapel so perhaps he is ashamed of his brother. God how sad. I have been hunting and it made me so stiff I could not tie up my shoe laces for three days. Our opening meet is Sat. week. Last Sat-Mon I went to Mells & that was very nice except for a lady called Violet Bonham-Carter[5] who thought me very common because I like Nathaniel Gubbins[6]. She thought that to read a Sunday newspaper of that kind was too bad-taste even to make jokes about. Next Sat-Mon I go to my midget for a birthday treat. Will you please send me a pretty card for my birthday because last year I got none and it made me very sad. It is on Sunday so you must post it Fri. I would like one best with some frost on it. Tell Hughie to hurry up & have catholic lessons. I wrote a funny short story about a looney bin[7] and a very dull one about a dog who bit a lady's nose.[8] That dog was rather like Grainger only not so intellectual perhaps more like Wincey[9] but god it was a bad story.

Please give my best love to your sweet sisters and your disgusting friends.

XXXXX
Bo

[1] Fifth Marquess of Bath (1862–1946).
[2] Lady Diana Abdy.
[3] *The Scented Garden,* an Arabic guide to love-making.
[4] Eighth Earl of St Germans (1870–1960).
[5] Lady Violet Asquith (1887–1969). Daughter of the Prime Minister's first marriage. She married Sir Maurice (Bongie) Bonham-Carter in 1915. Baroness Asquith 1964.
[6] Norman Gubbins wrote a column under that name 1930–53 in the *Sunday Express.*
[7] 'Mr Loveday's Little Outing'.
[8] 'On Guard'.
[9] Teresa Jungman's Blenheim spaniel, given to her by the ninth Duke of Marlborough.

TO LAURA HERBERT
[1934?]

St James' Club,
Piccadilly, W.1

Darling Laura

I am sad and bored and need your company. If you have a spare evening between now and when you leave London, please come out with me. Any time will suit me as I have no engagements that I cannot gladly break.

Ask your mother[1] first and tell her I wanted you to ask.

That is, supposing you want to come. Perhaps you don't.

I don't know where I shall be in the autumn so it may be a long time before we meet. Please come. I will behave respectfully, I promise.

Love
Evelyn

[1] An undated but later letter from Laura Herbert to Waugh says, 'I think I may be able to see you then because Mother agreed to it before she left for Ireland but when she got back today she was in a filthy temper and very tired and seemed to want to take it all back.'

TO W.N.ROUGHEAD
[4 November 1934]
Postcard

B.B.C. L.S.D. N.B.G. [1]

E.W.

[1] Waugh had asked Roughead to discover how much the BBC would pay for a proposed talk. Fifteen guineas was considered inadequate.

TO LADY MARY LYGON
[January? 1935]

The Manor House,
Mells,
Frome.

Darling Blondy

... I feel sad at Hazel[1] being dead on account of having been very Dutch to her and so I feel a shit. So to beat myself I am having a mass said at 7.30 which means being called at 6.30 and driving 6 miles in the cold & dark but the person who gets most beating by that is poor Lord Oxford because he has to get up to drive me and he was never dutch to Hazel so that is unfair.

I have taken a *great* fancy to a young lady named Laura. What is she like? Well fair, very pretty, plays peggoty beautifully. We met on a house party in Somerset. She has rather a long thin nose and skin as thin as bromo as she is very thin and might be dying of consumption to look at her and she has her hair in a little bun at the back of her neck but it is not very tidy and she is only 18 years old, virgin, Catholic, quiet & astute. So it is difficult. I have not made much progress yet except to pinch her twice in a charade and lean against her thigh in pretending to help her at peggoty.

My sister in law has taken it into her head to give a ball on Wednesday night. I cant make up my mind whether to go to it. Will you be in London. We might go & get d.d.

You must read good taste book named *Earth Stopped*[2].

xxxx

x for Poll   Bo   x for Sibell

[drawing] This is shaking hands but is not well drawn for Hughie

[1] Hazel Lavery. Her husband, Sir John, painted a last picture of her as she lay dying.

[2] T.H.White, *Earth Stopped: or Mr Morse's Sporting Tour*, 1934.

To Lady Mary Lygon   Savile Club.
[February 1935]

Darling LB

Decent you are coming to London I live there too and it is very cold & cheerless. So on 12th J's boy has an orgy for us to steal his wedding presents[1]. We will go together it is the pm and then later for your birthday we will have a stately orgy.

The young lady of whom I spoke to you named Laura came to London with me yesterday but it was not a success for I had a hangover & could only eat 3 oysters and some soda water and I was sick a good deal on the table so perhaps that romance is shattered.

Why had I hangover? Well I know a major and he and I went to have one drink so as to see the result of Randolph's[2] election and one drink led to another and it was the downward path for both of us.

Farter[3] gave a party in aid of Duff Assheton Smith[4] and the D of W[estminster] gave one in aid of the Duchess but I went to neither on account of F's great smell and the D not asking me to go.

I set my booms house on fire last Monday.

xxxxx
Bo

Bernini is O.K.

Bring me some DIAL

[1] Edward Jessel (1904–) married Lady Helen Vane-Tempest-Stewart on 14 February 1935. Succeeded as 2nd baron 1950.

[2] Randolph Churchill (1911–68). Journalist. Unsuccessful in 1935, he stood for Parliament seven times and was elected as a Conservative 1940–45. See Appendix of Names.

[3] Syrie Barnardo (1879 1955). Daughter of the founder of homes for orphans. Married to Somerset Maugham 1916–27. Fashionable decorator.

[4] Sir Michael Duff (1907–80) assumed the names Assheton-Smith in 1928, relinquished them in 1945.

To Lady Mary Lygon   Midland Grand Hotel,
London, N.W.1.

I missed that train so I have to wait wait wait wait god it is sad Hugh D Makingtosh[1]

H.D.M. Hugh D Hugh D I think I am about to die I missed the train What will Laura say? say? Hugh D Mackingtosh Grainger is impuissant as the frogs ... GRAINGER CANT FUCK.

[1] Hugh Mackintosh was an Australian businessman, a friend of Lord Beauchamp's whom his daughters found boring.

To Laura Herbert
[3 May 1935]

Belton House [1],
Grantham.

Darling Laura

Its discouraging that we never meet. I begin to despair of ever seeing you again.

Best wishes for Academy exam.[2] I am sure you will pass effortlessly. Don't believe that governess.

Party over here. In fact even my host and hostess have left. Their daughter[3], aged seven, says to me 'Why are you still here? When are you going to go?'

I'm pegging away at Campion. Hope to arrest him this afternoon and rack him before I leave. Then I will hang, draw & quarter him at Mells.

xxx
Evelyn

[1] Lord Brownlow's house.
[2] Laura Herbert was studying acting at RADA.
[3] Caroline Cust (1928–   ). Married John Partridge 1954.

To Katharine Asquith
Sunday [24 June 1935]

Lytham Hall,
Lytham,
Lancashire.

Dear Katharine,

A very beautiful house by Kent or someone like him with first class Italian plaster work. A lap of luxury flowing with champagne & elaborate cookery. Mrs Clifton, Easter (or so she seems to be called), Orsa, Michael a youth seven feet high with a moustache who plays with a clockwork motorcar and an accordion. The above all Cliftons all tearing mad[1]. The children bright & giggling, Mrs C. more sombre & full of soul. Tom Burns[2] who is a great favourite with these. Then there is a pie-faced debutante walking out with Michael. Large park entirely surrounded by trams & villas. Adam dining room. Five hideous Catholic churches on estate.

It was awful when you said you thought I was good. It shows what a hypocrite I must be at Mells.

No hypocrisy Friday night after seeing you off. Very low life.

All sitting at separate little tables at meals. Two or three good pictures including a Renoir. Went to Blackpool yesterday evening. That is a good place. Missed Rector of Stiffkey by two days. He had been starving in a glass case.[3]

Estranged is the word re M[iss] Herbert. High estimate of her character & charm undiminished but not able to see her without embarrassment.

Appalling heat. All sitting in sun with a dozen aeroplanes overhead & the gardens open to public.

Evelyn

[1] Violet Beauclerk married John Talbot Clifton and had five children including Mariel Easter Daffodil (1914–78), Yseult (1908–   ) and Michael (1917–   ). An elder brother, Harry, knew Waugh at Oxford.

[2] Tom Burns (1906–   ). Publisher. While at Longman's Green he commissioned *Waugh in Abyssinia*. Chairman of Burns & Oates 1948–67. Director of *The Tablet* publishing company from 1936, editor of *The Tablet* since 1967.

[3] Harold Davidson (1876–1937). Had been charged and defrocked for his relationships with many young girls. He was found not guilty of attempted suicide for fasting at Blackpool. Two years later he spoke from a lion's cage in Skegness and the lion killed him.

To Laura Herbert

Adelphi Hotel,
Liverpool.

Darling

A sunny comfortable train journey. We came to Crewe and I looked on the map and there was no way from Crewe to Liverpool so I began to be afraid that I had made a mistake as on Saturday. Then I came to a station called 'Alight here for the Zoo' that was alarming. Then to one called Lime Street so I leapt out and it *was* Liverpool. Then I went to see the new Scott Cathedral[1] again & thought it worse than ever – then I found some decent Bloomsbury houses. Then I had dinner. Cantaloupes, Morecambe Bay Shrimps, Steak, Cheese Soufflé – Mouton Rothschild 1916. Very decent. All round tough business men. It was fun seeing the waiters make them order what they wanted like conjurers forcing cards. Now I am off to my ship.

Darling darling Laura please dont find that you are just as happy without me. I am not nearly as happy without you. Bless you my darling love child

E

[1] The Anglican Cathedral in Liverpool (architect Sir Giles Gilbert Scott) was started in 1903 and completed in 1978.

To Laura Herbert

[On board to Djibouti]

[Typewritten]
[August 1935]

DARLING LAURA

The Daily Mail have given me a type writer and told me I mwust learn to use it so I thought it bestbt to practuce on you.[1] It is really quite easy if tou go slow and know how to spell. That is my difficulty as up till now I have used non commital letters when in doubt and there dont seem to be any on the type writer. I will give you one when I come back and you will b eable to type all my booksand send long letters to SIr franky about mo tor cars and the stock Exchange and the great comfort of the stately homes of ENGland. ihope you realise that Iam using all eight fingers and noxx and then the thumb and that it isthe first day so it it is not bab at all.

This is a very decent ship but the people very dull all French colonials except for another journalist going to Abyssinia[2], called Emeny you will think I have spelled that wrong but no it is his name. He is a married man and does not want much to be killed and has a gas mask and a helmet and a medicine chest twice the size of all my luggage and I have told him so often that he is going to certain death that I have begun to believe it myself.

No one at all pretty on board except a half-caste girl in the second-class and I have not been able to find her since we sailed.

We have to stop at Haifa to land some Jews so shant reach Djibouti until 20th and Addis not till about 24th probably. Soon it will be too hot to type.

Shall I put in some affectionate bits now xxxxxxxxxxxxx? no? All right that can wait till I get back.

Tell you what write me one letter it may get through before they bust up the railway. Send it poste restante Addis Ababa.

I dont at all like the idea of you in the hands of those barbarous wops if they are ready to kill poor Mr Emeny what will they do to you?[3]

xxxxxxx

All my love

Evelyn

[1] First paragraph is reproduced letter for letter. Later typewritten letters are minimally corrected.

[2] Waugh was on his way to Ethiopia to report the war against the Italians for the *Daily Mail*. He had no experience as a war correspondent and little as a reporter, and had been rejected by the *Daily Express;* but 'anyone who had actually spent a few weeks in Abyssinia itself, and had read the dozen or so books which contributed the entire English bibliography of the subject, might claim to be an expert . . . .' *Waugh in Abyssinia*, p. 49.

[3] Laura was in Portofino.

To Penelope Betjeman[1]   Red Sea
[August 1935]

Dear Penelope,

Can you find out for me anything about a man who should be a neighbour of yours, named Rickets[2]? He says he is master of the Craven & lives near Newbury. I want particularly to know how he earns his living, whether he is in the British secret service and whether he is connected with Vickers or Imperial Chemicals. Don't on any account mention my name in your enquiry. Be a good girl about this and I will reward you ... when I get back

Reply poste restante Addis Ababa

xxx
Evelyn

[1] Penelope Chetwode (1910–   ). Married John Betjeman in 1933. See Appendix of Names.

[2] Francis W. Rickett, a British entrepreneur secretly representing American oil interests, to whom Haile Selassie signed over exclusive concessions to a large part of Abyssinia. He had joined the ship at Port Said. When he received coded cables he said 'From my huntsman. He says the prospect of cubbin' are excellent.' Waugh thought him an arms dealer. The veteran Sir Percival Phillips broke the story on 30 August in the *Daily Telegraph* – the biggest 'scoop' of the war. Nothing resulted from the deal.

To Laura Herbert
Addis Ababa.

24 August [1935]

My Darling Laura,

I've given up the typewriter. I couldnt use it and the noise disgusted me.

I wonder how you are. In fact I wonder about you most of the day when I have any time to think of anything except fixing meetings with Ethiopian officials to which they dont turn up. The thing I think about most is your eyelashes making a noise like a bat on the pillow. How compromising that sounds – you know what I mean, but the Ethiopians wont who read all my correspondence & telegrams. I am universally regarded as an Italian spy. In fact my name is mud all round – with the Legation because of a novel[1] I wrote which they think was about them (it wasnt) with the Ethiopians because of the *Mail*'s policy[2], with the other journalists because I'm not really a journalist and it is black leg labour. Fortunately an old chum name of Balfour[3] is here and that makes all the difference in the world.

Nothing could be less romantic than my circumstances at present. There are something like 50 press people in the town, photographers etc. all told. There is no news and no possibility of getting any, and my idiot editor keeps cabling me to know exactly what arrangements I am making for cabling news in the event of the destruction of all means of communication. There is a pleasant enough mob of cosmopolitan, polyglot adventurers, spies, armament touts, soldiers of fortune etc. The only people who are not at all disturbed in the routine of their lives are the Abyssinians themselves who are absolutely self satisfied and confident of victory, not only of maintaining their independence but driving the Italians to the sea & conquering the Red Sea coast.

But if you are interested you will have read all this in the papers weeks before you get this and if you arent interested why should I tell it all to you now. Any news I can give you will be old news. Did you follow the Muzi Falconi shooting incident? The truth of that was that he attempted suicide. Vinci[4] the minister kept trying to get him back to his post in the interior to be assassinated so as to have an 'incident', but he couldn't get through on account of the floods. This preyed on his mind a bit. Also he was in wrong with his wife. Also she is daughter of Barton[5], British Minister here, so that was embarrassing with international things as they are. So he shot himself in the lung but didn't die. Sad story.

I have engaged a Greek spy named Mr Galatis who whispers wholly incredible stories into my ears in wholly unintelligible French. I am off to the Moslem country for a few days to investigate one of these stories, doubtless a lie, about dissemination of Arabic anti-Abyssinian propaganda.

Darling child I feel very far away from you. I cant think much about soft & delicate things in all this scramble.

I expect I shall be able to write again once or twice before the war starts. I will if I can. Bless you lovely girl. All my love.

Evelyn

My love to Gabriel, Bridget & of course your mother. I hope Bridget will be married before I get back. [6]

I hope there have been thousands of protective pimplies at Porto Fino. Every report of British anti-Italian policy has made me fear for you. It is idle to pretend I should like you so much if they ruin your face.

[1] *Black Mischief*. 'I witnessed the reunion of Waugh and "Prudence" in one of the capital's two dreadful cinema clubs, and it is the only time I have seen a woman dash a glass of champagne in a man's face.' William Deedes in *Spectator*, 5 May 1979.

[2] The *Daily Mail* was unusual in being pro-Italian.

[3] Patrick Balfour was special correspondent for the *Evening Standard*.

[4] Count Vinci, the Italian minister accredited to Haile Selassie.

[5] Sir Sidney Barton. His elder daughter Marion married Falconi.

[6] Laura's sister Bridget married Eddie Grant on 20 November 1935 after a long engagement.

TO KATHARINE ASQUITH   Deutsche Haus,
5 September [1935]   Addis Ababa.

Dear Katharine,

So by the time you get this you will know if there is to be a war or not which I don't know, but I think yes on account of that Mussolini's bughouse. Well I shouldn't say that when you are in Italy, but I daresay you are back at Mells. The journalists are lousy competitive hysterical lying. It makes me unhappy to be one of them but that will soon be O.K. as the *Daily Mail* don't like the messages I send them and I don't like what they send me but I don't want to chuck them on account of honour because they have given me this holiday at great expense and would be left in soup if I stopped sending even my unsatisfactory messages; they don't want to sack me for identical reason. So it is deadlock and we telegraph abuse at 4 and something a word.

But another chum has turned up named Charles Milnes-Gaskell[1] so now there are three of us who can enjoy it. Charles has no job here on account he is rich. We went to JIJIGGA and arrived by accident in the middle of a first class spy story[2] and we got all the details and it was sensational and we thought at last *D. Mail* will be pleased but not at all, there had been a bigger excitement with a crook named Rickett at Addis and they were furious I had missed that. Still it was delightful at Jijigga. There were Patrick and Charles and I and two askaris with antiquated rifles lent us by the Governor of Harar and our Abyssinian servant who was stiff with dope all the time and thought he was the Belgian Minister. Well he had been chewing khat all the way from Dirredowa and was full of it. It upset him very much when he heard of the Queen's death, and an Arab spy of Patrick's now in jug and an Afghan spy of mine named Wazir Ali Beg, very dignified but liable to err as when he told me the Italian consul had filled the foundations of the Harar Palace with dynamite and would blow it up on Sept 8. But this is no odder than what the journalists write every day. When I was in Jijigga I asked if there were any Europeans anywhere near. Yes the Arab spy said there were five Maltese Popes, so I went and found a little huddle of Franciscans living in frightful squalor and expecting to be arrested any minute for complicity in the Roquefeuil plot. They lived on boiled beads out of their rosaries.

No letters, but that's my fault as I told everyone it was no good writing. Make Desmond review *Campion*.[3] Best love to everyone.

Evelyn

[1] Charles Milnes-Gaskell 'had come out primarily in search of amusement'. *Waugh in Abyssinia*, p. 88.

[2] Count and Countess Maurice de Roquefeuil du Bousquet, a French couple, were arrested when she was found to have a roll of film in her armpit, destined, she confessed, for the Italian Consulate at Harar. Patrick Balfour's spy, nicknamed Mata Hari, informed them.

[3] *Edmund Campion* was not reviewed by Desmond MacCarthy.

To Laura Herbert   [Addis Ababa.]
[Typewritten]
October 1935

Darling this letter will be opened and read by a ludicrous little Belgian who has deserted his army and been made censor here. Fortunately he speaks little English so he will not understand much of it but like all ignorant and vulgar people he is liable to condemn all he doesnt understand. That is for his benefit.

It seems as though this job were nearly over. They began their war last week and for a day or two things here were quite gay with air raid scares and the Americans losing nerve and poor Mr Emeny. We had our first death too and a latter day adventist funeral with extempore prayers by an american minister 'O god please help us the late departed's sorrowing colleagues and do the best thou canst o god to cheer up his poor wife I know its hard for you o god but have a try. O god thou hast appointed three score years and ten as mans allotted span but O god statistics go to prove that comparatively few ever attain that age' and so on well that was fun but now things have settled down again just as before except that there is no news and if there wrew wr were funny how hard that word is to get right wr were gotvit were

were were were were if there were we should not be allowed to send it by the censor whom i have tild tou about. The telephone to the north is cut and the only news we get comes on the wireless from europe via Eritrea. No one is allowed to leave Addis so all those adventures I came for will not happen. Sad. Still all this will make a funny novel so it isn't wasted. The only trouble is there is no chance of making a serious war book as I hoped. It seems certain that the journalists will all be recalled preetty pretty soon. I cant decide if I shall go too or not. It is just possible that things might become exciting when all these americans leave. Vinci the wop minister leaves tomorrow and then I shall have no friends and no sources of information.

When i get home i shall buy a cottage. Please find me one. Dorset or Somerset near water sea or river long way main road but near main line station. I wouldnt mind the Berners Betjeman country. On no account the Juliet Beaton Pembroke country. [1] No pine trees. Sanitation light etc no consideration. Find me a house like that theres a poppet preferably thatch but not beams. Think of Mr Beverley Nichols famous cottage [2] and get the opposite. How about the Minehead district then you could come and visit me.

So I suppose you are acting now and falling down and elocuting and so on. well it is one better than being journalist and I know you do it better than I do my job. Goodness how stale and meagre my cables are. I got thirty *Daily Mails* last week and nearly died of them I hope you havent been trying to read them.

How very sad about Eddie [3]. I hope he is now settled all right. How are all your pimplies.

I had a baboon but he seemed incapable of affection and he kept me awake in the afternoons so I threw him away. I will try and bring you back some antelopes and ostriches.

You will have received a copy of *Campion* by now dont try and read it put it on the shelf and wait for the novel about journalists. all my love to you lovely poppet XXXXXXX evelyn

ps it is odd i dont say more about love to your mother and gabriel etc that is to be taken for granted. it is very sincere love so please tell them

[1] North Wiltshire or Berkshire rather than south Wiltshire.

[2] Beverley Nichols (1901–) had written *Down the Garden Path*, 1932, and *A Thatched Roof*, 1933, about his country cottage.

[3] Eddie Grant had left the publishers, Peter Davies, with whom he had been in partnership.

To LAURA HERBERT   [Ethiopia]
[Typewritten]
[October 1935]

... It is not proving so easy to leave the *Mail* as they have made themselves so unpopular by abusing the Abyssinians that they cant get a visa for another chap to come in. They sent a chap but he is stuck at Djibouti and that is no place to be stuck in it is about the worst place in the world next to london and this particular chap has gone bats on account of the heat and thinks he is a lepper. So I cant very well leave them flat without anyone here at all and it looks as if i shall die in harness as they say. I am sure you will sympathise because you are lazy too.

So there was a very sad banquet at the palace the night before last & the lights failed 5 times & we all talked on as if nothing had happened except P Balfour who laughed & all the americans thought it very bad taste but he was laughing because a Spaniard said to him I wish you were a girl then I could pinch you So I read in the paper that Bridget is to marry Capt grant. I have bought a picture of the battle of Adowa it is rather disgusting so i will give it to D[iana] Abdy not you. . . .

TO LADY MARY LYGON   Harar,
[Typewritten]   Ethiopia.
26 October 1935

Darling i can think of no reason why you should not write except that you hate me and no reason why you should hate me so I am puzzled as macdougal. I am sick to death of this country and these lousy blackamoors so I will soon come home. Perhaps in time for Xmas. Will you ask me to visit you at mad?

Pauper[1] has gone away and I am lonely.

                                                          BO XXXXX

My chief object in writing is to give you some of this good taste paper for your scrap book

                                                    love to mr grainger

[1] Patrick Balfour.

TO CATHERINE AND ARTHUR WAUGH   Dessye,
26 November [1935]   Wollo.

Dear Mother and Father,

There is a chance this may reach you for Christmas. I hope it does to give you all my love. I wish I was with you. I dont know when it will be possible to get back now. I am living in camp in the mountains with about thirty other whites of various nationalities. Mostly American and German. It is deadly cold and dull. We came here in the hope of going to the front but cant even move out of town.

We get absolutely no news from outside. The war may be over for all we know. So my opinion is worth less than anyones but I believe the Italians are beaten[1]. Not by sanctions but because they never contemplated the necessity of military conquest on a large scale and entirely miscalculated the spirit of the people. They had been giving away money to chiefs for years, knew the Emperor was unpopular and imagined that the moment they appeared in impressive strength the majority of the country would join them

Best love to Alec Joan children etc. It was good news about Cruttwell[2].

Evelyn

[1] Italian troops entered Addis Ababa on 5 May 1936.

[2] Joan Waugh had written that C.R.M.F.Cruttwell (1887–1941), Waugh's history tutor at Hertford and old enemy, had stood for Parliament as a Conservative at Oxford and been defeated by A.P.Herbert. 'A tongue like a whiplash': A.L.Rowse, *A Cornishman at Oxford*, 1965.

TO PENELOPE BETJEMAN
[Typewritten]
[November 1935]   in camp dessye wollo province ethiopia

darling penelope ungrateful bitch I gave you a rare copy of my excellent book named E Campion and not one word of thanks do I get. . . . I am celibate since Aug 1st on account of the altitude which reduces the carnal appetite, the great ugliness and disease of Abyssinian women, & my love for Miss L Herbert. . . . Send Xmas pudding to me at Deutsches Haus Addis Ababa. Patrick is in Araby. I am in a bitterly cold mountain with a boring hypochondriac socialist God I could kill him. The telegraph very sensibly refuses to accept press cables any more. I am a very bad journalist, well only a shit could be good on this particular job. We had a dinner for Thanksgiving Day given by a yank it was beastly & no wine for fear of the great sensibilities of 7th day adventist clergy. I have a lion skin coat it smells like a corpse. Give my love to Gerald[1]. Funny re Anthony Jenkinson[2]. I will take that cottage I saw when I come back. Evelyn[3]

[1] Lord Berners.

[2] Probably John Anthony Jenkinson (1909–35). Married Joan Dunn, sister of Philip. He killed himself.

[3] Waugh resigned in December when his replacement finally arrived. He went to Palestine and spent Christmas in Bethlehem.

TO KATHARINE ASQUITH   [Jerusalem]
23 December [1935]
Postcard

Gradually getting the smell of the *Daily Mail* out of my whiskers. Spending four days penance for the shame of the last four months in intense discomfort at Franciscan Monastery. Moving to hotel on Xmas day. Tomorrow night at Bethlehem. I half hate Jerusalem. For me Christianity begins with the Counter-reformation & the Orientalism makes me itch. New buildings here without exception excellent. Best I've seen anywhere. Hope to get down to Petra next week. Then I thought of going to Bagdad for a bit but have made no plans. The politics of Geneva, Rome, London, Paris horrify me. I have long ceased to be proud of being

English – now we must cease to be proud of being European. They have a wall here where the Jews blub. V. sensible idea. Dome of Rock good building.

E.

To KATHARINE ASQUITH
28 December 1935

King David Hotel,
Jerusalem.

Dear Katharine,

I wrote you a post card and said I half-hated Jerusalem. Well that is all over and I love it dearly.

It has even made me love the Abyssinians a little to find them living in frightful squalor in a collection of huts *on the roof* of the Holy Sepulchre. Bits of meat lying about and dirty clothes and their pathetic éloigné black faces.

It was decent to have Christmas without the Hitlerite adjuncts of yule logs and reindeer and Santa Claus and conifers. But I was appalled to discover that we have no altar at all in the basilica at Bethlehem – built by Constantine and Justinian where Baldwin I was crowned and Edward IV of England sent lead to repair the roof. The Midnight Mass they broadcast and Americans come to hear doesn't take place in the Church of the Nativity at all but in an execrably ugly, totally modern Church of St Katharine (well I suppose that bit is all right) next door. Did you realise that?

I feel obliged to write a history of England and the Holy Places. You see St Helena, Baldwin, Lord Stratford de Redcliffe, General Gordon etc. all English.

Off tomorrow to try and get to Petra – but that is difficult except at great expense. After that Damascus. Then I don't know. I don't really want to return to Europe until I know one way or the other about my annulment and can arrange things accordingly.

. . . Best love to you all,
Evelyn

To LAURA HERBERT
[Spring 1936]

Bridgewater Estate Office[1]
Ellesmere,
Salop.

Sweetie. Another letter last night. It is noble of you. I wish I could show how grateful I am by writing six pages of vivid description of my last twenty-four hours. Well I dont think I can because you see I havent left my rooms. Mrs Whitefield told me about a woman who got drowned in the lake but that was some time ago and not particularly exciting – she was 'skylarking' in a boat and they dragged the lake all day before they brought her in.

I am delighted that you were punished with a dislocated hip for entertaining pimplies. I hope it hurt acutely and is now quite well. Down with O'Neil and Cheatham.

I am pegging away with *Abyssinia*² and the X words – all right Saturday, two words missing yesterday. I dreamed that I was having dinner with the King at Fort Belvedere and jaggering him madly and he suddenly said, 'the whole object of the Abyssinian campaign is to separate the Herbert family'. I laughed immoderately at the time but when I woke up it did not seem particularly witty.

Tell you what you might do while you are alone at Pixton. You might think about me a bit & whether, if those wop priests ever come to a decent decision, you could bear the idea of marrying me. Of course you haven't got to decide, but think about it. I can't advise you in my favour because I think it would be beastly for you, but think how nice it would be for me. I am restless & moody & misanthropic & lazy & have no money except what I earn and if I got ill you would starve. In fact its a lousy proposition. On the other hand I think I could do a Grant and reform & become quite strict about not getting drunk and I am pretty sure I should be faithful. Also there is always a fair chance that there will be another bigger economic crash in which case if you had married a nobleman with a great house you might find yourself starving, while I am very clever and could probably earn a living of some sort somewhere. Also though you would be taking on an elderly buffer, I am one without fixed habits. You wouldn't find yourself confined to any particular place or group. Also I have practically no living relatives except one brother whom I scarcely know. You would not find yourself involved in a large family & all their rows & you would not be patronized & interfered with by odious sisters in law & aunts as often happens. All these are very small advantages compared with the awfulness of my character. I have always tried to be nice to you and you may have got it into your head that I am nice really, but that is all rot. It is only to you & for you. I am jealous & impatient – but there is no point in going into a whole list of my vices. You are a critical girl and I've no doubt that you know them all and a great many I don't know myself. But the point I wanted to make is that if you marry most people, you are marrying a great number of objects & other people as well, well if you marry me there is nothing else involved, and that is an advantage as well as a disadvantage. My only tie of any kind is my work. That means that for several months each year we shall have to separate or you would have to share some very lonely place with me. But apart from that we could do what we liked & go where we liked – and if you married a soldier or stockbroker or member of parliament or master of hounds you would be more tied. When I tell my friends that I am in love with a girl of 19 they looked shocked and say 'wretched child' but I dont look on you as very young even in your beauty and I dont think there is any sense in the line that you cannot possibly commit yourself to a decision that affects your whole life for years yet. But anyway there is no point in your deciding or even answering. I may never get free of your cousin Evelyn. Above all things, darling, dont fret at all. But just turn the matter over in your dear head.

All this reminds me of poor Miss Churcher. I sent her a long, very serious letter of advice telling her to jump at the doctors son & be a good wife to him & told her how to be a good wife & keep his affections – it was rather like Viola Tree's column, but it didn't go down well with Miss Churcher, whose pride was hurt. She wants me to know that the doctors son is an idealist & that she is his ideal. So I am afraid that their outlook is rather black. They will be married on May 9th at Brixton but we wont go.

Eight days from now I shall be with you again, darling heart. I don't think of much else.

All my love
Evelyn

[1] Belonging to Lord Brownlow.
[2] *Waugh in Abyssinia*, 1936.

TO LADY MARY LYGON
[April 1936]

Bridgewater Estate Office,
Ellesmere,
Salop.

Darling

So I hope your low Sunday party is a great success & that there are plenty of guests from the Low countries cracking low jokes and looking at Low's cartoons ha ha ha. So now I live here looking after the great Ellesmere estates god it is a responsibility I have afforested & deforested & distrained & debentured & still it wont come right. Write to me a lot please as I am all alone like M Lafone[1]. God what a lot of jokes I can remember. I am writing a v sad book re Abyssinia. The people of Ellesmere are very ugly.

I went to a common play named *Promise*[2] and Miss Best came to supper but the worst happened ha ha Lady Juliet [Duff] joined us & guzzled.

Is Poll dead yet.

Good bye
Bo

[1] Michael Lafone (1900–   ). Man about town, Captain in the King's African Rifles.
[2] By Henry Bernstein with Edna Best.

TO LADY MARY LYGON
[May? 1936]

Bridgewater Estate Office,
Ellesmere,
Salop.
Bureau de Propriété Bridgewater

Ma plus chère cherie,

Je le trouve bien convenable que vous m'avez écrit une si salle lettre française. Comme j'adore les grenouilles et leures elections generales bien commises. J'espère que tous les juifs et maçoniers sont gravement batus par les bons camelots du roi, catholiques et autres personnes de bon volonté. J'espère que votre aimable et beau père se trouve bien avec tous ses aimants. Ayez la bonté de lui donner mes sentiments les plus distingués. Sans doute le petit chien chinois, Grainger, est triste sans vous. Malheuresement je ne peux pas assister chez lui le mercredi à cause de mon absence de Londres.

J'ai passé la Dimanche chez le Milord Acton. Le Samedi nous avons buvé une grande quantité de Sherry, Hock, Bougogne, Champagne et Porto. Moi, j'ai souffert des peines épouvantables le lendemain. Comme j'étais malade à la messe!

Maintenant il me faut écrire le livre sanglant de quoi je m'occupe.

C'est des nouvelles tristes pour tous ses amis que M. de Trafford s'est rendu en Europe. Demandez lui s'il a reçu un cadeau le livre de bon gout, *Edmund Campion* de moi il y a six mois.

M. Jackson a coupé un 'arser' dans les cours de chevaux à Worcester.

La jeune fille paresseuse, Mlle Herbert, a écrit beaucoup de lettres plein d'amour mais elle les a addressé à Staffordshire en place de Shropshire.

On m'a donné un prix, qui s'appelle le 'Hawthornden'[1], à cause de la bon gout de mon livre *Edmund Campion* mais il ne faut pas lire ça avant que la présentation officielle en Juin, mais je suis bien content de cette affaire parce qu'il me fera beaucoup de bon avec Mde Herbert la mère de la jeune fille paresseuse au nez énorme.

L'amour, les embrasses sans nombre, à toi ma chérie

Bo

[1] A prize worth £100 awarded annually for a work of imaginative literature by a British author under forty-one.

To Katharine Asquith   St James' Club,
[June? 1936]   Piccadilly, W.1.

Dear Katharine

Very many thanks for your telegram. I will go down to the cottage tomorrow evening, probably rather late as Laura has a day off the Academy[1]. I'll get a taxi at Frome and slip into the cottage unobtrusively without disturbing the household.

Why not ask L Herbert for Sunday?

I loved the week end at Mells. I've seen far too little of you all since I came back from Africa. It was delightful being with you again.

Julian wore a white chef's cap in the motor car on the way to Oxford. They made me stop at Faringdon so that they could see the wicked Lord Berners. He was not at all pleased to see us & Mrs G Ansell[2] was there so we had some drinks and then were late at Oxford 6.50 dining at 7. Fr Knox[3] in great agitation. Shown into infamous bed room without looking glass, chest of drawers or wash hand stand, hideous oak beams, a crooked floor and a bed which I think he must have bought from C.Hollis[4]. No one to unpack, distant bath room. Changed in frightful discomfort and was downstairs by 7. R. Knox still in great agitation expecting other guests. Sat down two short in his dining room. Repulsive food, no servants a glass of tasteless sauterne. Sat with empty chair on one side and a nit-wit Canadian on the other. Feeling bad about not having prepared speech. Only thing that could have made it

all right would have been good dinner and lots to drink. No time to smoke. Hustled
into crowded lecture room[5]. Had expected only pimply undergraduates, to horror
saw (a) chums – Billy Clonmore, Woodruffs, entire Acton family, Strutts[6],
Lindsays[7] etc (b) distinguished guests – Ned Lutyens[8], Algernon Cecil[9],
O'Sullivan[10] etc. Well that was hell. So I began to speak but words would not come
and I got lost in my arguments & confused in grammar and it was as bad a lecture as
I ever heard. Then I looked at my watch, saw with delight that I had been speaking
for 43 minutes so sat down sharp. Felt a bit better and lit cigar. Then they began
asking questions. I was admirable. It was like a ventriloquist & his dummy. We kept
that up for an hour, wise crack back chat, & everyone laughed a lot & went away
thinking the evening had been all right. Then some tepid ale and insufferable
conversation with O'Sullivan etc upstairs and then to my sordid bed room & at six
some men began to lay slates on the roof. So then I came to London saw my agent
who dashed all hopes of solvency. Luncheon Laura. Now I must go & order a
pressed duck for her dinner.

Best love
Evelyn

Julian of course no trouble with dons on Saturday night

[1] Royal Academy of Dramatic Art.

[2] Gracie Ansell, an Australian who was divorced for adultery by a South African gold magnate before
the First World War – 'No woman would speak to me'. She left England but returned in the 1920s.

[3] Monsignor Ronald Knox (1888–1957). Catholic Chaplain at the University of Oxford 1926–39.
Writer and scholar, greatly admired by Waugh who wrote his biography in 1959.

[4] Christopher Hollis (1902–77). Writer, schoolmaster, Conservative MP.

[5] For a meeting of the Newman Society.

[6] Daphne Strutt (1911–) had married Lord Acton in 1931, so the families were connected.

[7] Probably Thomas Fanshawe Lindsay, assistant on *The Tablet* to Douglas Woodruff.

[8] Sir Edwin Lutyens (1869–1944). Architect.

[9] Algernon Cecil (1879–1953). Historian.

[10] Richard O'Sullivan, a lawyer who ran the Thomas More Society.

To Laura Herbert

St James' Club,
Piccadilly, W.1.

My darling Laura

I was sad leaving you at Gower Street[1] and I have got sadder since. But you see I
must not start interfering with your routine. My only excuse for seeing you at all, is
that I dont do that. Well I wont go on about that. All I want to say is how sad I am
not to be with you. Lovely child, you have been sweet to me all this last week and I
have loved it all and I look forward tenderly to Monday. Don't go getting put in
prison in night club raids. I shall think of you for about 17 hours in the 24 and dream
of you for the other five. Darling Laura. I love you. Thank you for loving me.

E

[1] Where Laura Herbert attended R.A.D.A.

To Lady Mary Lygon
[July? 1936]

Darling

V. sorry to hear of Letty & Grainger's illnesses.

So I am trying to write some more about Abyssinia & God am I sick of it.

You will be greatly surprised to hear I have got engaged to be married to Miss L. Herbert. I don't think I have ever told you about her. She is lazy with a long nose but otherwise jolly decent. When I say engaged Miss H. and the Pope[1] and I and Gabriel have made up our minds but it is not to be announced until after Xmas because Gabriel is so busy selling a house and settling the civil war in Spain and getting a plague of fleas fumigated in Captain E. Grants house and such things that she can't be bothered to pimp for Laura for a bit. Also she is rather ashamed of me on account I move in a very undesirable set and it will take her some time to break the news gently to her high-born relations. So I shant be married for a long time. That is sad. Also Gabriel thinks it is wrong to fuck in Lent. So you must not tell people I am engaged or Driberg will put it in the papers. And dont tell pauper[2] as he will spread foul lies about Miss H. in his unchivalrous way. And don't tell Capt. Hance or he will take Miss H. away from me on account of his superior sex appeal.

There is a strike of the coal miners here because Lady Horner very kindly brought them an expensive new machine which chokes them & gives them diseases of the lungs & they are ungrateful and wont use it, which shows what the lower classes have come to.

Well you have only to read the paper and see what is happening in Spain where the lower classes have the upper hand.

What is Frisky Baldwin's young lady[3] like. Is she as pretty as L. Herbert.

I long to see you and Major Duggan again and little Poll.

XXXXX
Bo

[1] Waugh had received a telegram on 7 July to say that his plea for an annulment had been allowed in Rome.
[2] Patrick Balfour.
[3] Arthur Baldwin married Elspeth Tomes of New York that year.

To Graham Greene[1]
Thursday night [30 July 1936]

Grand Hotel de Russie, Rome.[2]

Dear Greene

I am afraid I did not make much sense on the telephone yesterday. I had gone to bed very late & tipsy, got up early & still tipsy, was packing for an indefinite trip to Africa, and not in the best shape for talking business.

I think there are possibilities in your plan. I think that it should be a race not in time but economy. Each competitor to start with no luggage and a limited sum – say £100 – and the one who arrives with most cash in hand to get a prize. And more competitors. Five at least. How about Robert Byron if he's in England. In fact it might be open to anyone who cares to put up his own stake – three or four professional tourists like ourselves to get paid for. Why not in November? Don't answer until October as I have no address.

Yours
Evelyn Waugh

[1] Graham Greene (1904–   ). Novelist and lasting friend. See Appendix of Names.
[2] Waugh was on his way to revisit Ethiopia, now controlled by the Italians.

To KATHARINE ASQUITH   Grand Hotel Subasio,
4 August [1936]   Assisi.

... This is about the most agreeable hotel I ever stayed in. The head waiter told me riveting story about an English protestant dressed as a Franciscan. Contrary to expectation he (h.w.) vastly impressed. Said he was the cleverest man he ever met and he had more letters daily than anyone else in the hotel which proved he was highest political importance.

Off to Africa Friday full of the gloomiest forebodings I am sick of Abyssinia and my book about it. It was fun being pro-Italian when it was an unpopular and (I thought) losing cause. I have little sympathy with these exultant fascists now. I hope to be back in October when I would like to come and live at Mrs Whats-her-names' – the Belgian at Mells.

Missing L. Herbert a lot. . . .

To LAURA HERBERT   Grand Hotel Subasio,
Tuesday [4 August 1936]   Assisi.

My Darling Laura

How I wish you were here. It is a lovely little town – full of sun, you would like that, and bulls and Giottos (he is a famous dead painter). A charming little hotel, a room with a big stone balcony giving onto an empty colonnaded square with directly opposite the church of St Francis. (He is a famous dead saint who put this town on the map.) Good cooking & wine on a terrace from which we can see the whole of Umbria. A delightful maître d'hôtel whom I found telling my full life story. Mosquitos all night. Otherwise perfect. If I ever marry I shall bring my wife here for a bit.

Sweet poppet it seems such a waste to see lovely things & not be with you. It is like being one-eyed & goggling out of focus. I miss you & need you all the time. Most of all when I'm happy.

E

To Laura Herbert   Grand Hotel Subasio,
Wednesday night [5 August 1936]   Assisi.

My darling,

It is a night of inconceivable beauty – cool after a stifling day. They have put on the lights in the garden for the first time since I've been here and are proud of them. 'The garden' is a little terrace roofed in leaves with a monkey in a cage and two doves in another. There is an absurd little fountain – a single jet of water three foot high & they have lit that up too so that it looks like a damp firework. From the terrace one can see the lights of Perugia and all the Umbrian plain and, quite near, the cloister of the Franciscans jutting out over the cliff and they are having their hour of recreation & making a noise as if it is an orgy. Am I writing like a guide book? I hope not. It is just that I feel transported with the beauty of the night & wish you were here to share it. Assisi seems to be full of the Grace of God. Darling Laura I do so wish you were here.

I thought it was going to be easy to leave you for a time. Don't get that wrong. What I mean is that I thought it would be easier for me than you, that I should be seeing so many different things & people that I should not be all the time longing for you. Well I was wrong. I need you all the time – when I'm vexed and uncertain & tired – but more than ever on a night like this when everything is unearthly & lovely.

You see, darling child, so often when people fall in love & want to be married, it is because they foresee a particular kind of life to which the other is necessary. But I dont feel that. Sometimes I think it would be lovely to lead the sort of life with you that I have led alone for the last ten years – no possessions, no home, sometimes extravagant & luxurious, sometimes lying low & working hard. At other times I picture a settled patriarchal life with a large household, rather ceremonious & rather frugal, and sometimes a minute house, and few friends, and little work & leisure & love. But what I do know is that I cant picture any sort of life without you. I have left half of myself behind in England and I am only dragging about a bit of myself now.

And I don't at all regret the haphazard, unhappy life I've led up till now because I don't think that without it I could love you so much. Goodnight my blessed child. I love you more than I can find words to tell you.

                                                              E

To Lady Mary Lygon   As from Mells Manor,
[12? September 1936]   Frome,
                                                   Somerset.

Darling Blondy

I have just got back and have learned for the first time the tragic news of Hughie's death[1]. At least I have heard as much [as] my parents remember from the newspaper report. Do write & tell me what happened.

It is the saddest news I ever heard. I shall miss him bitterly. It is so particularly tragic that he should have died just when he was setting up house and seemed happier than he had been for many years. I know what a loss it will be to all of you and to Boom. Please accept my deepest sympathy. I am having Mass said for him at Farm Street.

I go down to Mells for a fortnight to finish the book about Abyssinia. Will you write to me there. I got no letters in Addis Ababa as I left before the mail. I long to see you again in October.

My dearest love to you
Bo

[1] Hugh Lygon, travelling in Germany, got out of a car, fell downhill and hit his head. He was thought to have had sunstroke.

To Alec Waugh
[1936]

Dear Alec

Many thanks for you letter of congratulation.

I look forward greatly to bringing Laura to see you when next all three of us are in London together. She is thin & silent, long nose, no literary ambitions, temperate but not very industrious. I think she will suit me o.k. and I am very keen on her. Wedding probably in February in the country. Joan is very kindly standing me the honeymoon. Busy looking at houses which I find very pleasant indeed. Have found a lovely one but dont know if I can get hold of it

Regards to your children
Evelyn

To Lady Mary Lygon   Savile Club.
[1936?]

My Darling Blondy

I am afraid I was like Bloggs & Teresa and worse about coming down this week end. I didnt know what would be most helpful for you so ended as usual by doing nothing. And I dont know what I can say that would not be impertinent.

But listen. I know from experience that being very unhappy is necessarily lonely & that friends can't help & that sympathy means very little – but please remember always that if there is ever anything I can do to help you have only to tell me, and I will chuck anything or do anything. The sort of dislocation you have had is a pain which cant be shared – but being unhappy is not *all* loss and I know you have the sort of nature that wont be spoilt.

I only dare to say this because I was unhappy some years ago in rather the same way as you are now.

> All my love – don't answer
> Bo

To Tom Driberg
7 January 1937

Pixton Park,
Dulverton.

My Dear Tom,

I have got engaged to be married & shall be announcing the fact early next week. I don't imagine the story will be of great news value but if you care to publish it you can have it a day ahead of *The Times*. In return could you oblige me in one particular? I think that by now most people have forgotten or have never known that I was married before. That marriage has been annulled by the papal courts and it would be very painful both to me & my young lady to have it referred to. (1) because in ecclesiastical circles they get embarrassed if annulments are given publicity (2) because my future wife is a near relative of my former wife's and there are numerous mutual aunts who would be upset. So may I rely on you not to bring the topic up?

Apart from that you can have all the details you need. She is named Laura Herbert, 20 years old, student at Academy of Dramatic Art, in my opinion a great beauty. Youngest daughter of (late) Aubrey Herbert who was a famous chap in his day. I can give you a photograph of her if you want one for Tuesdays paper – announcement Wednesday. . . .

> Kindest regards
> Yours
> Evelyn (Waugh)

To Laura Herbert
[January 1937?]

Easton Court Hotel,
Chagford,
Devon.

Darling

Two sweet letters from you this morning from Paris[1]. I wonder if you ever got any of mine?

I am coming to London definitely on Thursday. I cant promise how much I shall be free. It depends on Korda.[2]

. . . Mr Colonel[3] is fairly nice but absolutely useless. He had made absolutely no contribution yet to the film. Yesterday I sent him up to his room to think up some wisecracks and he turned up after $1\frac{1}{2}$ hours & said 'How would it be if one of the girls said to a policeman "I wish I had stilts, then I'd come up & see ya some time"'.

His only use is that he makes someone to talk to about the film. I think he may have murdered the real Mr Colonel and come instead of him. I can't believe he was ever really in Hollywood.

I bought you a very fine iron & brass 18th century grate today for £4 in the village shop. It will do for dining room or library or drawing room.

All my love
Evelyn

[1] Laura had gone to Paris to buy her trousseau.

[2] Through John Sutro, Alexander Korda had hired Waugh to work on *Lovelies from America*, later retitled *Lovelies over London*.

[3] An American called Kernel, sent by Alexander Korda. Their treatment was accepted but the film was never made.

To GRAHAM GREENE
St James' Club.
[March or April? 1937]

Dear Greene

Many thanks for your letter. I thought that at the moment you would be racing Theodora Benson[1] across the Gobi desert.

It is nice of you to think of me in connexion with your new paper[2] & I like the idea of dramatic criticism. The trouble is that I cant bind myself to be in London every week. Could you find a second chap to do it, irregularly, turn & turn about with me. . . . How does that suit you?

Yours
Evelyn Waugh

I remember being approached in 1929 by a London *New Yorker* that never materialized. Is yours soundly backed?

[1] Eleanor Theodora Benson wrote several books, some in collaboration with Betty Askwith. That year she published *How to be Famous; or The Great in a Nutshell*.

[2] *Night and Day*, an imitation of the *New Yorker*, which lasted from 1 July to 23 December 1937. Greene was the film critic. In the end Waugh reviewed books.

To LADY DOROTHY LYGON
Villa Altachiara[1]
[April 1937]
Porto Fino Mare,
Postcard
Wopland.

Darling Poll,

So it is very decent to be married, very decent indeed. We are staying at a great house called Altachiara – translate that into English and you will laugh. We were very sorry about your great illness at the time of our wedding and all the more profoundly moved and touched at your appearance there. A bas milady Sibell et ses jockeys. We went to Rome and saw a great deal of porphyry. God it was pretty. Then to Assisi & then to Firenze where we saw a great football match v. bad taste in fancy costume. We will come back in June & hope & pray that you will stay with us. Meanwhile please write one of your long famous & libellous letters. All love Bo

[1] The Herberts' house. The fourth Earl of Carnarvon, who built it, translated the name of his English home Highclere. Waugh had been married on 17 April.

To Alec Waugh
[1937]

Mells,
Frome,
Somerset.

My dear Alec

Many thanks for the cigars. I was sorry to miss you again in London. I tried to fix a meeting with Joan but times didn't fit. I hope you are happy at 21 Cambridge Square, where I have spent many happy hours.

Now that I am marrying procreating & purchasing property there is a thing which excites my curiosity – which you as the elder & wealthier of us might think it worth investigating – the validity of our coat of arms & crest. I may want to use it at my house, d'Arcy talks of putting it up in Campion Hall, you have it on a lot of silver. I have always had some doubts about whether we are entitled to it. We have certainly used it since the end of the 18th century. I have some bookplates of your great-great-grandfather with it engraved. But stationers at that time had a way of inventing arms without reference to the College of Heralds. Do you think it worth asking them, and, if it proves spurious, having a grant made? It would be made to our father so that we should both be entitled to it and I would share the expense – about £80 I believe. The usual thing in such cases is to grant the arms previously borne with some slight difference. I would suggest a border to the shield.

There is a further point. Since Robert Raban has become an American the Raban family will be extinct in the male line in England. In the circumstances I think that – mother being the only married daughter – we are entitled to quarter her arms, which are certainly genuine with ours. That is more ornamental and I think well worth doing. The College of Heralds would register this for us at the same time. It seems to me the kind of thing which isn't important now but which our children might well be grateful for if there were a change of fashion & heraldry came into general use again. [1]

The Waugh Coat may be registered in Edinburgh.

Best wishes to *Jill Somerset* [2] & Malcolm Somerset [3] from Somerset.

Evelyn

[1] Waugh had his coat of arms carved in stone and placed on the façade of the house he bought this year.
[2] Alec Waugh, *Jill Somerset*, 1936.
[3] Malcolm Somerset had been at Sherborne a few years ahead of Alec. He worked at Dunhill's and Selfridge's tobacco department. A fascist. He became poor and, not wishing to embarrass his friends, disappeared, answering no letters.

To Graham Greene   Pixton Park,
[August 1937]   Dulverton.
                                          as from Piers Court [1],
                                          Stinchcombe,
                                          nr Dursley,
                                          Glos.

Dear Greene

I'm afraid this is below length. I'll do a full article next week, when I want to do Calder-Marshall at some length. I could fit in a novel too.

There's nothing to take hold of in Brett Young – just flabby longwinded stuff. Not enough character to attack. A cushion not a bubble to prick. [2]

                                          Yours
                                          E.W.

[1] It was a wedding present from Lady de Vesci, Laura's grandmother. Waugh wrote nineteen years later, when selling it, 'Piers Court, occupying a lovely position overlooking the beautiful Berkeley vale, is a fine example of an 18th-century Manor House . . . an extremely fine façade . . . . The garden and grounds are easily maintained and include TT Attested Farm Buildings and extend in all to 41 acres.'

[2] Nothing on Francis Brett Young appeared. *The Changing Scene* by Arthur Calder-Marshall, which concerned the state of Britain and its possible improvement under communism, received an unfavourable review on 9 September. A collection of stories, *A Date with a Duchess,* also by Calder-Marshall, was highly praised the week after.

To the Editor of The Tablet
[4 December 1937]

Sir, – I have a keen appetite for marvels and do not doubt that we constantly fail in gratitude by attributing providential interpositions to chance or to natural causes, but I must confess to being somewhat nonplussed by the tale, in your issue of today, of Canon Campana and the viper. Where, precisely, did the late Miss Higginson [1] come to the Canon's assistance?

As I understand his story, he began his office in the confidence of supernatural protection from vipers; sometime later he found one coiled in his breast with its head already inside his suit. I do not know how common these reptiles may be in his district, nor how high the local rate of mortality from snake bite, but we have the Canon's assurance that this particular viper was of the most dangerous kind, and it seems clear that, so far from being protected, he had been subjected to more than ordinary annoyance. He rid himself of the snake by tossing it in the air with a cane and, in falling, it 'descended obliquely' and missed his head. He certainly had a narrow shave; of the two dangers – that of the snake nestling in his bosom and of its falling on his face – the former, which he averted by his own dexterity, seems far more grave. Is it not possible that, in his natural agitation, he 'trembled for fear where there was no fear'; that he had thrown the snake further and truer than he knew and that when it seemed to be poised immediately overhead, it was in reality proceeding in a narrow parabola to a safe distance? Should stories such as these be allowed to discourage critical and precise investigation in a question of first importance?

Yours faithfully

EVELYN WAUGH

[1] Teresa Higginson (1844–1905) had been suggested for preliminary canonical inquiry, and books were written in her support, leading to letters both for and against in *The Tablet*. Canon Campana, Professor of Dogma in the University of Lugano, related how he personally had been saved by her intervention, ending, 'So I am not surprised that Teresa Higginson should have delivered many poor Africans from the jaws of the infernal serpents.' It is this letter that Waugh is answering. Her name did not go forward.

To VIVIEN GREENE [1]
Piers Court.
8 March [1938]

Dear Mrs Greene,

... Yes, I normally wear a dinner jacket in the evenings, Laura a dressing gown. Do whatever is most convenient. I have asked a particular fan of Grahams & I am sure he will dress for the meeting.

Yours sincerely
Evelyn Waugh

[1] Vivien Dayrell-Browning married Graham Greene in 1927. 'Mrs Greene, handsome with black hair, was placid and sedate like a young Spanish matron'. J.Maclaren Ross, *Memoirs of the Forties*, 1965.

To A.D.PETERS
16 Cornwall Terrace, N.W.1.
10 March 1938

Dear Peter,

... This is the letter I wrote about 'Fascism' [1] & would like to expand into an article title 'Panic on the Left'.

Perhaps you would show it to P.Monkhouse & others. Laura's baby [2] was born yesterday morning. She was only ill for 9 hours and is now very well. The daughter huge & loud. No one has had the insolence to suggest it is like me.

I hope you agree I was wise to turn down *Sketch*.

Evelyn

[1] Published 5 March 1938 in the *New Statesman and Nation*. It complains of indiscriminate use of the word 'Fascist'.
[2] Maria Teresa.

To David Jones [2]   West House [1],
[June? 1938]   Aldwick,
                                                      Bognor Regis.

Dear David,

   Laura and I were absolutely delighted to see that you had got the Hawthornden
Prize. Yours is not only the *sort* of book that ought to get it – it is *the* book [2], and the
news is all the more delightful as we had heard from someone on the committee that
a different choice had been made. I hope the presentation was not too embarrassing
& that you enjoyed Miss Warrender [3] & Lady Hall.

   It certainly adds vastly to my pride in having got the prize to find myself in such
good company.

                                                      Yours,
                                                      Evelyn Waugh

   [1] The Sussex home of Duff and Lady Diana Cooper.
   [2] David Jones (1895–1974) wrote *In Parenthesis*, 1937. Waugh had praised it in *Night and Day*:
'Admirable . . . it is about battle rather than war . . . as though Mr T.S.Eliot had written *The Better 'Ole*.'
   [3] Founder of the Hawthornden Prize.

To Alexander Comfort [1]   Piers Court.
29 June [1938]

Dear Mr Comfort,

   I am returning to you under separate cover the manuscript of *Send Forth the
Sickle* which you submitted to Chapman & Halls & which was sent on to me for a
final opinion. I should like first to thank you for the great interest which its reading
afforded me.

   I gather from your letter, which was enclosed with it, that you have some doubts
about the book yourself & feel that it needs revision. The advice I am going to give
you must seem drastic: it is to put the book away for five years and not look at it until
you have written a second book. You may then find in it much valuable material
which, with your greater skill & experience, you may be able to put to a new use. At
present I believe the book to have defects which will prove fatal to its success. Too
hasty publication would be a discouragement to you now and an embarrassment in
the future.

   It has many good qualities of vigorous narrative and keen observation. It is clear
from it that you have a gift for writing that, properly developed, should be of great
use to you later. But the book must be judged on its merits as a single work. It seems
to me to fail because it has the air of being a *tour de force*. You are dealing with a
historical period of which you have no first hand acquaintance and the general issues
seem to me imperfectly understood. I have some acquaintance with the county
about which you are writing and, I must tell you, the atmosphere of your story
seems very false to my own experience. In particular the incident of d'Arcy going
poaching with a tramp appears wildly improbable. Very likely it is based on some

actual occurrence; half the problem of a novelist is to make real life credible, and you have certainly failed in this case. The conversations of another class are always peculiarly difficult to report. I think it was audacious of you to try rural dialect; even when well done, it is sometimes tedious, and, frankly, I do not think yours very well done. The book as a whole, moreover, seems to lack a unifying theme. You call it 'the General Dissection of a Character', but it seems to me to fall far short of this & become, in many places, a mere succession of rather melodramatic incidents. I am afraid I found Ridgway a great bore – the pseudo-Bohemian of the film – *Beloved Vagabond* type, and, I am sure, not drawn from the life.

My real criticism is that the book owes its origin to an impulse to write *a* book, not this particular book. Your imagination was not so obsessed by your subject that it had to find literary expression. And that is the only way – at least while you are learning the trade – that a good book can result.

I believe that any good writer has, in his early life, scrapped at least one book. It would not be a good sign if he started doing competent work at once, that way lies the mechanical prosperity of the higher journalists. Above all please do not think that a single minute of the long hours you have spent on this book has been wasted. The time has been as well spent as if the book were published. Let me also advise you, not as a publisher but as a fellow writer, not to send it to other publishers. It is possible you might get one to take it, but I am sure the results would be disappointing for you in the long run and perhaps harmful to your development as a writer.[2]

> With best wishes,
> Yours sincerely,
> Evelyn Waugh

[1] Alexander Comfort (1920–   ). Biologist and writer.

[2] The book was scrapped. Dr Comfort published a novel, *No Such Liberty*, in 1941 and, among many other books, the enormously successful *The Joy of Sex* in 1973.

To Henry Yorke
[August? 1938]

Hotel Ritz,
Mexico D.F.[1]

Dear Henry,

I can't tell you what a help your introductions have been to us on our journey. Your New York agent came to the ship to see us off & tell the captain to look after us. Another agent met us at Vera Cruz and led us off the ship first in front of three American vice-consuls and a dozen Mexican deputies, and put us in a drawing-room for the journey to Mexico. Holmes[2] has been charming to us. We spent last Sunday with him at Cuernavaca and took a particular liking to his wife. Laura joins in sending our keenest gratitude.

New York was 93° and felt like 193°. The *Silony* packed with jewesses. Your father was affectionately remembered by all the crew & stewards. In particular they remembered him as a popular one with the girls.

I join with you in dislike of Mrs Conway whom we lunched with & with whom we are committed to a picnic which I rather dread.

I can't say what I feel about Mexico yet either because I am punch-drunk to new travel impressions or because it is a prodigious mouthful to chew. Of course the spectacle is enchanting but I feel very remote from it at present. Everyone seems to want to talk finance-politics.

I wait anxiously to hear what Chapman & Hall decide about your novel [3]. It would be a great thing for us to publish it but they have the minds of grocers & I was rather afraid from what I heard, that they hadn't taken it in.

We could not escape from lyrical accounts of Dig's party. The *Aquitania* hummed with it – notably Victor Mallet [4].

Love to you both,
Evelyn

[1] Waugh had been commissioned to write a book on Mexico by Clive Pearson, son of the first Lord Cowdray. The left-wing government of General Cardenas was hostile to the extensive Cowdray interests in Mexico and Pearson wanted 'the truth' to be known. *Robbery Under Law: The Mexican Object-Lesson* was published in 1939; it was called *Mexico: An Object Lesson* in the United States.

[2] Holmes worked for the Mexican Railway, then British-owned, of which Henry Yorke's father was a director.

[3] *Party Going*, 1939, was published by the Hogarth Press.

[4] Sir Victor Mallet (1893–1969). Diplomat, Ambassador in Madrid 1945–6, Ambassador in Rome 1947–53. Sometimes referred to as 'Sexy', as are Cecil Beaton and Duff Cooper.

To A.D.Peters   Piers Court.
[25 October 1938]
Postcard

I find on unpacking that I have lost from my luggage one tie value 10/6, and an ivory backed clothes brush value £2.10. Can I claim this from insurance.

Also Laura is now laid up with appendicitis. Does her health insurance cover this? The doctor thinks operation desirable but not essential. It might be worth having it done now if the insurance are still liable.

E

To A.D.Peters   Piers Court.
[Received 25 January 1939]

Dear Peter,
(a)

Poor Laura had another attack of appendicitis on Sunday & was operated on that evening. Does Uncle Clive's insurance still stand?

She is very well & cheerful, eating something fairly like food & sharing an interest in the crossword. I am living in Bristol for the time being to be near her, so that is another weeks postponement of poor Uncle Clive's books.

(b)

The Jesuits have a centenary in 1940. Tom Burns wants a book about it. A stunt book addressed to general, non-Catholic readers. He thinks it will be a great success. It would be a years work for me & very little chance of serialising it so that I should need a years wages. I suggest quarterly instalments of £500 making £2000. I expect that will seem a lot to him. It does to me. I dont think it could be done under £1500. What do you think? What does he think?[1]

Yours
Evelyn

[1] Waugh also wrote to Peters that month, 'I still have the book of Heroes in mind. Did we ever discuss it with Burns? How would it be to offer him both that and the Jesuits?' Neither book was written.

TO THE EDITOR OF THE SPECTATOR   Piers Court.
[21 April 1939]

"JOURNEY TO A WAR"

Sir, – By mischance your issue of March 31st did not reach me until April 14th. Will you allow me, thus tardily, to reply to Mr. Stephen Spender's[1] letter about my review of Mr. Isherwood's and Mr. Auden's book?[2]

Mr. Spender misunderstands me when he speaks of my attacking those whom I believe to be down. It was precisely because I believed Mr. Auden to be so very much up that I allowed myself the pleasure of a few sharp expressions. Moreover, I find no satisfaction in the general apathy to poetry; what Mr. Spender takes for complacency was intended as irony. But I think that this apathy does in fact exist, and that as a result of it the English public is particularly gullible with regard to poetic reputations. In my opinion Mr. Auden is a case in point. I find him a very dull and awkward writer. Mr. Spender disagrees. This is not the place to dispute the matter in detail. Since, however, Mr. Spender imputes personal malice to me, I am entitled to ask: which of us is the more likely to be prejudiced – I, who have never met Mr. Auden nor, so far as I know, set eyes on him, or Mr. Spender, who is, I understand, his intimate friend?

I cannot affect any patience with Mr. Spender's final argument that it is evidence of poetic merit to be unfavourably reviewed; nor, I think, would he care to pursue it when his agitation has subsided.

I am replying to Mr. Spender mainly because his letter forms an example of the attitude towards Mr Auden of a certain group of writers. As I said before, it is their fault, not his, that he is a public bore. He writes mediocre verse, as do a multitude of quite decent young men. No particular shame attaches to that. But a group of his friends seem to have conspired to make a booby of him. At a guess, I should say that the literature they have produced about him is, in bulk, about ten times his own work. That is shockingly bad for a man still young, alive and, I fear, productive. But what is far worse is that they assume any dissension to spring from ignoble motives of personal malice. That is intolerable.

Your obedient servant,
EVELYN WAUGH

[1] Stephen Spender (1909–). Poet and critic.
[2] *Journey to a War*.

4 The War
3 September 1939-8 May 1945

Darling,

Matlock is a dull, decent little Town. I am glad to be outside the Glasgow area for a bit. We live in an absolutely enormous, gloomy Hydro. There are two or three other courses in the same building and a great collection of half baked officers and a great number of Americans & Canadians. The messing is my bad idea and I am suffering greatly from malnutrition. I share a small bed room & live on a my hard bed.

My telephone manner is my glorious.

There is one question and one answer. Obscure undistinguished regiments & undistinguished men.

Graham Eyres Monsell is here as an instructor. He was never particularly a friend of mine but we fell on each others necks in the way one does nowadays with people who in the old days would not have liked it was to be Party to speak to one another.

I go to Renishaw this week-end with keen anticipation.

Air Photograph Interpretation is quite difficult and quite interesting. My eyes & head are very wrong by the end of the day.

I wrote to H. Duggan asking him to be Margarets god father.

I will write you a real letter next week-end.

All love   Evelyn

Introduction

In his diary for 29 June 1939 Waugh wrote: 'At dinner Diana tried to talk about crisis but was deflected rather abruptly.' In a letter Lady Diana Cooper reported the deflection and asked for an explanation of this 'nasty snub':

D: 'How strange that we should be ending dinner without speaking of the world situation.'
E: Grunt.
D: 'With us it is always referred to as being so much on one's mind.'
E: 'So I've noticed. Did you get the long word down in the crossword puzzle?' I saw both butlers blench at your tone. Why is it Bo?

No answer survives. Lady Diana had to catch news bulletins seated in her car, for Waugh still took pride in not listening to the radio. He would not discuss European politics and they are rarely mentioned in his diary. Nevertheless, before war was declared, he had applied to, and been refused by, the Ministry of Information. He had also noted that both as a writer and as a patriot his best course was to join up as a private. The war was foreseen even if it was not to be discussed. Though almost thirty-six he wanted to fight. However his brushes with the enemy were not to be as he hoped: evasion, retreat and waiting around were his lot rather than confrontation. The division between the good and the bad blurred when the Russians became our allies. There were sufficient interludes for Waugh to work on one novel, complete two more and begin a fourth.

His energetic efforts to find himself employment of any sort were not immediately successful. Public Relations at the War Office, naval intelligence and the Welsh Guards found in turn that they could not use him. Depressed, Waugh returned to his novel, which was published unfinished as *Work Suspended* in 1942. Then in December 1939, with Brendan Bracken and Winston Churchill supporting him, he joined the Royal Marines as a Second Lieutenant. This meant training at Chatham, then at Deal in Kent, then at Bisley, near Aldershot. In July 1941 he went to Wales and embarked to prevent German troops landing in Ireland. Then he was moved on to defend Cornwall. Next there was more training, this time at Scapa Flow. In August, now a captain and intelligence officer, Waugh set off on an expedition to seize Dakar in West Africa. It was not a success. His battalion retreated without ever landing.

Before sailing, Waugh had already approached Colonel Robert Laycock, and he was seconded in November 1940 to No. 8 Commando and a little later from the

Royal Marines to the Royal Horse Guards. With several old friends, he was stationed at Largs in Ayrshire and in February 1941 they sailed to the Middle East. In April he was on a night raid against Bardia on the Libyan coast. His most violent confrontation with the enemy was the Battle of Crete at the end of May, a rearguard action after defeat. No. 8 Commando was disbanded and Waugh returned from Egypt via the Cape, once more a Marine. On the way he wrote *Put Out More Flags*.

After a course in Edinburgh Waugh again welcomed his transfer to the Commandos, which meant Hawick, Ardrossan and, finally out of Scotland, Sherborne in Dorset. But when in June 1943 Laycock sailed for Italy, Waugh was left behind. He minded bitterly; there was no longer any future there and in July he resigned.

He seemed to have become unemployable, but Colonel William Stirling was raising a new unit and in October he joined the 2nd Special Air Service Regiment. When Allied successes meant that they did not go to North Africa, there was a dispiriting stint at Windsor. In December he went on a parachute course and hurt his leg. He no longer wanted to fight. When a request to Brendan Bracken, now Minister of Information, was successful and he was given leave, he used it to write *Brideshead Revisited*, which contains an ungrateful caricature of his liberator as Rex Mottram. His freedom was extended; his knee injury was exploited, and the generals who wanted him as an ADC were repulsed.

In June 1944 Waugh was recalled to Scotland to the 2nd SAS, now commanded by Colonel Brian Franks. They did not want him and he did not want to go so all were pleased when Randolph Churchill invited him to join the 37th Military Mission to Yugoslavia. The aim was to support the Resistance led by Marshal Tito, a Communist; Waugh was chosen because many of the Croatian Resistance leaders were Catholic. That is the simplest of the local contradictions. He stayed with the mission until early December, when he went to Dubrovnik as liaison officer between the British and the Yugoslavs. In February 1945 he returned to Italy, in March to London. He started to write *Helena*. In September he was demobilized.

The events of his own life are closely followed in *The Sword of Honour* trilogy. Christopher Sykes has warned against assuming that Waugh shared Guy Crouchback's initial enthusiasm for the army, but it does seem a story of mounting disillusion. The letters are almost exclusively to Laura. As he was never away so much again, they form the bulk of those written to her and show a side of him not previously seen. At the same time travel arrangements, censorship and discretion, and a drab, monotonous life do not make for sparkling correspondence, so many letters have been omitted.

To John Betjeman   Piers Court.
[September? 1939]

Dear John

Many thanks for the delightful poem. I hope it does not mean that you subscribe to the nonsensical ideas of Connolly that the rich are more selfish & nervous than the poor.

The war seems to be developing into ourselves against the world so we shall all have some fighting to do between our 40th and our 80th birthdays. Meanwhile no one wants us for any purpose except paying taxes. Mr Popkin[1] sent me a delightful letter saying that in these difficult times the revenue officers looked to him to carry on his national work.

Have you considered Evacuation as a theme for a major work ideally suited to yourself.

I enclose the first chapter of a novel[2] I was writing & have discontinued. It would have been O.K.

Do you know anyone who would like to take this house furnished for the duration?

                                                   Yours
                                                     E.

Please return chapter of novel

[1] Waugh's accountant.
[2] *Work Suspended.* The fragment of about 35,000 words was published in 1942.

To W.N. Roughead   Piers Court.
[October? 1939]

Dear Roughie

. . . Re novel. About 15,000 words were done & jolly well done before the war. Its fate depends on mine. If no one wants my patriotic services at once I think I may retire to the Faro islands & finish it.

Laura is having another baby[1] shortly, the house is to let and I am feverishly planting box hedges in the hope that in ten years or so, when I return, they may afford some shelter to my feeble frame.

Yours
Evelyn

[1] Auberon Alexander, named after both his parents' brothers, was born on 17 November 1939. Waugh wrote in an undated letter, possibly this year, 'I am fretting about your anti-daughter feeling. You must not mind when this new baby is a daughter. Daughters are a great comfort to their parents, compared that is with sons.'

TO LAURA WAUGH   [Highgate?]
Sunday [10 December 1939][1]

My darling Laura

I am in London for 24 hours and at last have the opportunity of writing. Till now, though we have not begun our real work yet, we have been busy all day long and in the evenings, until the post has gone, the three writing tables in the mess are always occupied. Tomorrow I shall try & get to a shop & buy pens, ink & paper. We are some way out of the shopping area of the town & never get off work until after the black out.

First, an important practical point. Has my despatch case been found? It contains, among other things, the certificate of our marriage & Maria Teresa's birth certificate. I must have these, and also Auberon Alexander's in order to claim my marriage allowances. If the despatch case has not been found it will mean getting copies at Somerset House. Please get A.A. registered & send me all these certificates as soon as you can. It is odd that the Admiralty will not take our word for it & suspect that, having given up lucrative jobs to serve we would then perjure ourselves for a shilling or two a day, but that apparently is the assumption.

. . . So far I have enjoyed myself very much. In the train at Victoria I recognized one of the men who had been to the medical exam. at the same time as I. We travelled down together. He was younger than me but looked as old on account of having lost his wool. He was the type I expected to find – a Plymouth solicitor named Bennett[2] who spent all his spare time sailing round Iceland. The rest of our draft, however, are a great surprise. There are 12 of us chosen out of our 2,000 applicants, no one least of all ourselves can conceive how. It is the main topic of speculation. I will not tell you all names and histories now. I do not know them yet. There is an apoplectic gentleman named Hedley[3], who looks just like Alfred [Duggan] and is, in fact, a North Country wine merchant. There is a gentle soul called St John[4] who is reading *The Way of All Flesh* for the first time and suffers from weakness of the bladder. There is an ashen faced bank clerk and a sporting journalist who has never had a military training of any kind and simply does not know what any of the elementary terms mean. There is a Welsh father of twins[5] with enormous cavalry moustaches but, so far, no uniform. And so on. In fact the kind of nondescript body one might have conscripted out of the first omnibus one saw in the Strand. However they are all in their several ways very agreeable people. The solicitor, the wine merchant & the chap with the defective bladder are so far my chief companions.

The regular Marines are very pleasant, hospitable people obsessed by their own obscurity. So far from the critical reception I expected from Eddie's favourite book[6], the atmosphere has been one of ceaseless apology & self-deprecation in the Chinese style of courtesy 'Will noble and honourable second lieutenants deign to enter our unworthy mess and meet our ill-favoured Brigade Major?' As soon as we arrived we were surrounded by jaggering colonels & majors who stood us drinks continually from 12 noon until 11 pm.

The commandant made us a speech which was one long apology for everything – our beds, our servants, the fact that the mess paintings & silver were stored away underground. He said, 'Once you use the mess all differences of rank cease to exist. All we expect is the deference which youth naturally pays to age.' Since I am considerably older than most of the captains that suits me well enough. As it happens there is absolutely nothing to apologise for. I have a large bed-room to myself with a fire continually blazing in it; the architecture of the barracks is admirable – Georgian brick; there is a fine portrait of William IV with contemporary frame carved with naval trophies; we drink out of splendid silver goblets; the food is absolutely excellent. On the first evening there was a cold supper on account of a play which was being given us in our own theatre. I was led to the supper table with profuse apologies and found lobster, fresh salmon, cold birds, hams, brawn exactly like the cold table at the St James'. Afterwards several rounds of excellent vintage port. Everything a great deal better than an Oxford Senior Common Room but rather like it.

We haven't started work yet but I think that will be rather gruelling. We are doing a six weeks infantry course which normally takes six months. It includes map-making, sanitation, small-arms, military law and of course endless arms drill & P.T. The Brigade will be formed in February & will have three battalions, one for each Marine division – Chatham, Portsmouth, Plymouth. I am in Chatham (I mean that I shall be in the Chatham battalion when it forms. The fact that I am training there does not necessitate this). The company commander & staff are in training somewhere else, the men somewhere else. The idea is that we shall all know a certain amount about our work before we meet one another. It has not yet been decided where the Brigade will form. They are looking for a suitable sea-side town. It is rumoured we may go to a Borstal Institute quite near Chatham. I hope not.

So far our routine has consisted in drawing large quantities of equipment, going through gas-chambers, being marched over the barracks & shown the topography etc. We got leave from after luncheon yesterday until tonight so I came up, slept the night at Highgate and am lunching with Hubert [Duggan] & Phillis [de Janzé]. My hair is cut like a convicts. I do not look very impressive in uniform except in my great coat which is [a] fine garment.

I think I was suffering from 'pink-eye' when I left Pixton. I have been treating it with some stuff I bought at Perkins's & it is getting better. Apart from that I am very well.

You must not expect a letter on Tuesday but I will write, if I can, tomorrow night so that you will get it on Wednesday morning. Till then, all my love.

E

[1] Waugh had just become a Second Lieutenant in the Royal Marines.
[2] Michael Messer-Bennetts.
[3] Described in the diaries as 'choleric-looking' and 'of great girth'.
[4] John St John, trained as a chartered accountant before the war, a journalist and publisher afterwards. Denies that he ever had a weak bladder. Published *To the War with Waugh*, 1973.
[5] Griffiths, a schoolmaster.
[6] A. W. Smith, *Captains Departed*, 1934.

TO LAURA WAUGH   R.M. Barracks,
[14? December 1939]   Chatham.

My darling Laura

. . . Last night I went to the music hall with Mr St John, Mr Bennett & Mr Sanders. We saw a lot of young ladies in pink tights pretending to be nude statues. Also a jew named Lotinga[1] who kept getting struck in the face by his wife.

Will you thank Bridget very much for her letter.

There seems a probability of our going to Deal on Jan 15th.

Mr Cowan fell asleep tonight while Sergeant Fuller was lecturing upon company drill. Mr Cowan hates S. Fuller on account S. Fuller always calls him Mr Cohen. I do not hate anyone much except a Mr Grindle who tells me too much about a cross country running club he belongs to at Bromley. He is a weedy youth with a cockney accent and he croons to himself & snaps his fingers. There is to be a great dinner here for wives on Dec 31st but I shant be here till too late.

You might suppose that the naval battle in S. Atlantic[2] caused interest here, but you would be wrong. The war seems just as remote as home.

Mr Betjeman thinks he can get a good architect to do Previtt's flat[3] cheaply.

I am giving *no* Xmas presents this year to anyone, but I have bought 6 regimental Xmas cards for the servants & nuns.

Mr Bailley has been so badly affected by vaccination that he has to change his pyjamas 6 times a night on account of sweating so much.

All my love
E.

[1] Ernie Lotinga, British comedian, star of *Josser joins the Navy* and other films.
[2] The pursuit and sinking of the *Graf Spee*.
[3] At Piers Court, now rented to nuns as a school.

To Lady Diana Cooper   Pixton Park,
Christmas Eve [1939]   Dulverton.

Dearest Diana

What can a Netherland Plaza[1] be? I suppose a relic of the great Duke of Alba.

It was nice to be thought of. My heart bleeds for you & Duff.[2] I can think of no more painful time to be among Americans & to be obliged by your duties to pay attention to their ghastly opinions. My poor friend Father d'Arcy is in precisely similar circumstances at Fordham University N.Y. Do get into touch with him when you want to hear a civilized voice; it would be a great kindness to him.

You ask for news of *myself* underlined. Well I am having a spot of leave at Pixton; it is a rough transition from the comfort & order of barracks but there was no alternative, as Laura is still bed-ridden. She had the baby quite happily (a son) and was making a good recovery when she contracted pleurisy and is only now beginning to sit up for an hour a day. Pixton is full of slum children; eight professional spinsters, ironically termed 'helpers' sit down to dinner with Mary. I eat on a tray in Laura's room. It is all highly disagreeable.

Stinkers[3] is a girls school but the convent have taken it for only six months and unless we get some decent raids early in the new year I am very much afraid that they will not take up their option of renewal.

I had an unsatisfactory first six weeks of war flirting with embusqués but am now in a very fine force which Winston is raising in order to provide himself with material for his broadcasts. It is called the Marine Infantry Brigade. We are in training, at present, at Chatham in charming befogged Georgian barracks, excellent cellar, tolerable & tolerant company, wholly delightful routine except for P.T. which is a degrading & deleterious business. We are to be used for what are called 'combined operations' & given posthumous medals but at present there is no suitable coast for us so it is very cosy.

Everyone I see, but that is very few outside the Marines, is enjoying the war top hole. The highbrows have split – half have become U.S. citizens, the other half have grown beards & talk of surviving to salvage European culture. It is true about the beards & very curious – even Algernon Cecil has got one. Robert Byron & Michael Rosse have started a thing called Federal Union which consists of all the old figures of my adolescence in the '20s – Elizabeth Ponsonby, Harold Acton, Brenda Dean Paul[4] etc. – they have meetings together and publish a very serious paper under the editorship of John Sutro. Lady Kinross (Mrs Patrick Balfour[5]) has a salon for spies. Alfred Duggan is a private in London Irish (a force recruited entirely from the race gangs of Battersea). He was ask[ed] by the chaplain to become his batman under the supposition that it would be a slightly more civilized job. He said he was very sorry but he couldn't afford it; he paid out his entire wages as it was to his corporal to clean his uniform & couldn't undertake anything more. He had a spot of Christmas leave too & telephoned his mother to meet him for dinner at the Dorchester. She came up to London, got some jewels out of pawn, bought seats at a theatre determined to do Alfred proud & sat from 8 until midnight waiting for him. At 4.30 she was awoken 'Will Lady Curzon come at once to the Slip-in bringing £4.12 &

remove Mr Duggan'. Hubert is as fit as a flea, hair short, smart uniform, sitting on court martials and examining meat rations.

Eddie Grant is A.D.C. to Andre Maurois. [6]

I have had to leave $\frac{1}{4}$ of a novel I was working on. It was very good indeed.

By the time you are home I shall be at Deal I think.

Would you like to have Stinkers for the duration at cost price – ie rates taxes gardeners wages about £5 a week in all?

Best Love
Evelyn

[1] A hotel in New York.

[2] Duff Cooper was on a six-month lecture tour planned before war was declared. Supposed to stick to Keats and Shelley, he spoke mainly of politics.

[3] Piers Court, Stinchcombe.

[4] Brenda Dean Paul (1907–49). Found guilty on a drugs charge that year and again later.

[5] Angela Culme-Seymour (1912–   ). Married 1938–42 to Patrick Balfour who succeeded as Lord Kinross in 1939. Half-sister of Janetta Woolley, who married Derek Jackson.

[6] Grant was at this stage in charge of journalists of whom André Maurois, an old friend, was one. Later he was a liaison officer between the retreating French and English armies and was at Dunkirk.

TO LAURA WAUGH   [Chatham]
[5–7 January 1940]

Darling Laura

The pantomime was very good indeed particularly Widow Twanky. And after it poor Mr St John was ill with a pain in his stomach so I nobly lent him my hot water bottle. Then at 12.30 he came into my room and said his pain was agonising so I dressed and went out to find him a doctor & walked all over the barracks & Melville Barracks too & at last found that there was one immediately over our rooms. He took St John away to a Naval Hospital and I went back to bed.

Today we had lessons about the Bren gun which is rather like the noisy automatic rifle we saw in G. Men institute at Washington. When C. Sergeant Greensmith had taken it all to bits & put it together again & explained its ingenuity for 6 hours he said with great feeling 'Think of anyone inventing all this. I bet he's mad.' 'Mad, colour sergeant?' 'Well unnatural.'

This evening we went to the gymnasium for our P.T. and found it dark & empty and all the officers said what are we to do so I exerted my powers of leadership and said Do? Bugger off quick. So we buggered off.

Tonight there is a music hall show in our theatre.

All love
Evelyn

To Laura Waugh   [Chatham]
Sunday night [7 January 1940]

My Darling

It has been an intolerably long week. I find it impossible to realise that it was only last Sunday that I said goodbye to you. The next fortnight is going to be interminable.

I went to London yesterday & spent the night at Mr Burns' house. We had a nice unmarine dinner of snails and were joined by an argumentative typographer called Stanley Morison[1] who was very nice. Burns plans to end the war in two months by raising the catholics of Germany in rebellion against Hitler. Mr Morison & I thought he would not succeed. I went to see Anne Bowes-Lyon[2] in bed with ague and to cocktails at Great Cumberland Place. Gloomy[3] burned her belly with a bursting hot water bottle and tried to buy stuff called tulle de gras for it which no chemist had heard of. The Dutch girl, like so many other people, has got a new youth out of the war (and the death of her Blenheim spaniel). She dances with Canadian soldiers at night clubs three nights a week and sits up in an A.R.P. post the other four.[4] Zita [Jungman] is going to France with Gabriel[5] to upset the poor Poles – so Tancred[6] says. Jimmy Smith[7] was there in battle dress and, oddly enough, rows of medal ribbons.

Today I lunched with Maimie. T. Jessel was there. He cant be made a soldier and was very jealous of me. I drank a lot of good wines & talked smut with Prince Vsevolode[8] until tea time. Then back here.

Mr St John's great pain is a gall stone.

All my love
E

[1] Stanley Morison (1889–1967). Scholar and typographer. Designed typeface of *The Times* 1932.

[2] Anne Bowes-Lyon (1917–   ), cousin of the Queen. Married 1938–48 to Viscount Anson, and in 1950 to Prince George of Denmark.

[3] Teresa Jungman's mother.

[4] Teresa Jungman was married 1940–45 to Graham Cuthbertson, a Scot in a Canadian regiment.

[5] Gabriel Herbert, Waugh's sister-in-law.

[6] Tancred Borenius (1885–1948). Editor of the *Burlington Magazine* 1940–45. A Finn. 'The most gallant social butterfly possible': Adrian Daintrey, *I Must Say*, 1963.

[7] James Smith (1906–   ). Director of W.H. Smith, the newsagents. Possibly wearing one order.

[8] Lady Mary Lygon had married H.H. Prince Vsevolode Joannovitch of Russia in 1939.

To Laura Waugh   St James' Club.
[14 January 1940]

Darling,

It was a beautiful leave. Thank you for being continually so sweet.

If I write about Wickham it means 'abroad immediately' if about Winstanley it means 'training for a week or two, then probably abroad' if about Abercrombie 'all plans still perfectly vague'.

All love
E

To Laura Waugh   Deal & Walmer Union Club,
[15 January 1940]   Walmer.

Darling Laura

Thank you for a lovely leave, I think the happiest two days of my life.

Kingsdown is lousy. It is a hideous, derelict Victorian villa without carpets, curtains or furniture, one bath, one w.c. without a seat and another without a plug. Surrounding it is a collection of huts built of one thickness of asbestos for use in the summer as a holiday camp. The cold is intense. There are about 60 officers assembled for our tactical course. In the absence of carpets the noise is overwhelming – we have two rooms in the mess, one with a ping-pong table, the other a wireless. We eat in an asbestos extension built out. There are three or four easy chairs, and a number of little hard ones, but everyone stamps up and down the bare boards to keep warm. I am in a bed room in the house with 4 others & nowhere to hang an overcoat.

So Hedley & I set out this afternoon and found this club for retired buffers and became members for a guinea. There is a bath room which will be useful & Mr Hedley is very happy to find some old bores to talk to. I do not know if it will be worth a guinea. I think it will be because it will be somewhere to come & sit when otherwise I should have to go to a Cinema or an hotel.

Our brigadier St Clair Morford [1] looks like something escaped from Sing-Sing & talks like a schoolboy in the lower-fourth.

Mr Belloc's son [2] is like a Chinese to look at & rather affectedly gay to talk to. At least he was last night. This morning he was taken ill & removed in an ambulance in great pain with a high temperature. Some diagnosed pleurisy, like you had (as H. Yorke would write). I do not want to go back to Kingsdown at all. This will be a sad month.

All love
E

[1] Major General Albert St Clair-Morford (1893–1945). Wounded four times and received MC in the First World War. Commanded Royal Marines Brigade 1940–41. Sent to India 1942–3. Described his recreation as 'most games'. The model for Ritchie-Hook in *Men at Arms*.

[2] Peter Belloc (1905–41). Journalist. Used to go sailing with A. D. Peters, William Roughead and Lord Stanley. Died suddenly of pneumonia.

To Laura Waugh   Deal & Walmer Union Club.
22 January 1940

Darling Laura

You have been good about writing. I love your letters. Thank you very much for them.

Kingsdown is now cut off from wheeled traffic and we have to trudge to & fro. This is not as bad as it sounds since I have taken up with a highbrow gentleman who has rubber soles on his boots. Every ten yards or so he falls flat on his back and it is very enjoyable as he never interrupts his conversation and goes on talking about education and culture and psychology from the road. He is called Mr Spencer and is bald. He has been on the BBC in fact he is very like Mr Stucley and he is a professor in U.S.A. too like Mr Hollis (who by the way had no business to ask us to have passages in *The Tablet* transcribed for him). He loves young men and is keenly looking forward to meeting his platoon of militia. He introduced me to an Italian restaurant in Deal which is very cheap & nice.

. . . So on Thursday night I went to dinner with Mr Wooley and his wife. Mr Wooley is one of the Deal detachment and looks exactly like Anthony Eden and is a very dull gentleman indeed. His wife is like a bird and he has a daughter & they are all in an hotel at Walmer & they said I must bring you too & then they could share a sitting room with us. Well I do not think you would like that very much but I do not think I can put you in another hotel without causing offence.

Princess Opitubitch-Buggerof [1] sent me some letters of introduction to local residents and I tramped through the snow to deliver them but most of the houses were shuttered up for the winter so I dont think much will come of them. I am trying to get Lady Chetwode [2] to write to the Birdwoods on her behalf.

Mr St John has come back with his pain cured. Also P. Belloc. I met P. Belloc in church & he took me to some public houses where he was jaunty as be damned calling the barmaid 'beautiful' and referring to 'my lady-wife'. He hates his brothers & sisters.

I had lunch with Messer-Bennetts who has his wife here for the week end. She was very pretty & very nice so I asked them to share a house with us at Bisley putting them into precisely the same condition of embarrassment as Wooley put me. . . .

Marine Rose [3] is rapidly failing in health. I have lent him my oil stove but it does little to cheer him up. I think he will die very soon and his blood will not be on my head.

I wrote a long & offensive memorandum on the disorganization of the camp for the camp commandant which will either result in my expulsion from the brigade or my being marked for staff promotion.

Mrs Messer-Bennetts kissed Mr Messer-Bennetts' hard after luncheon. She was in a highly sexy state. I thought perhaps they spend their Sunday afternoons in a way I understand, so I came here through the snow and left them to it.

Will you please deal with the cutlery problem?

All love
Evelyn

Mr Owen Griffiths has a poisoned leg. Mr Newman had a hangover which kept him in bed for two days.

There are 2 jews in this club. They talk of food & women in a shocking way.

[1] Lady Mary Lygon.
[2] Alice Cotton married Lord Chetwode in 1899, died 1946. Mother of Penelope Betjeman.
[3] Waugh's servant.

TO LAURA WAUGH   Kingsdown House,
[23? January 1940]   Walmer,
                                                     Kent.
Darling,

It is snowing & freezing & the Dover road is blocked but our training goes on unchanged. Much of it consists in standing on a hill top with maps & identifying topographical features. We did that yesterday in a blizzard with visibility about two yards.

I am o.k. at tactics. Yesterday in the first problem they announced 'Waugh has pin pointed the staff plan' which meant I had placed my Bren gun in the precise spot that the general staff had chosen as the right answer. This morning I pin-pointed the plan with three platoons and the enthusiasm was tempered with suspicion that I had got at the answers.

I have moved out of the dormitory into an asbestos hut so as to be alone. It is better in some ways but worse in others – notably acute cold & the fear of the building blowing away.

I am on the mess committee & am trying to suppress the wireless, ping-pong table & other, rare recreations of my juniors. So far my only victory is to insist on correct dress at dinner & grace said by the mess president.

Please make your mother – even before she writes to thank me for giving her sherry – write to anyone she knows in this locality – but unless in a town on the railway four or five miles is the limit – giving them my address & asking them to ask me out. I am free for dinner every evening.

I am in correspondence with Trim. We think you & Katharine might come to Dover the week-end after·next.

Did you see that sexy Mallet has been made minister to Sweden.[1] A ticklish job at the moment.

I still brood constantly about our visit to London

                                                     All my love
                                                     Evelyn

[1] Sir Victor Mallet was Minister to Stockholm 1940–45.

To A.D. PETERS   Kingsdown House Camp.
[Received 23 February 1940]

Dear Peter

It is clear to me that I shall not resume my novel for the duration. Is there a chance of selling the two chapters under the title 'Work not in Progress' or 'Work Suspended' to a high-brow paper. [Cyril] Connolly has started one backed by a pansy of means named Watson[1]. Could they be induced to pay, say £50 for the serial rights of the fragment? I should think they might.

I still enjoy every feature of military life except the wages. They have just knocked 3/- a day off our marriage allowances.

There is no possibility of my doing any writing at all in present circumstances.

I come to London quite often at week-ends. It would be very nice to see you & Henrie[2]. Have you a spare bed where I might sometimes spend Saturday nights?

                                                           Evelyn

[1] Victor William Watson (1906–56). Called Peter. He inherited a fortune made from margarine in the First World War. He spent some of it on a collection of modern pictures and the magazine *Horizon*, of which Connolly was editor and he was arts editor. Stephen Spender was a co-editor for the first two years.

[2] Mrs Peters disliked her given names of Lucy Margaret and chose to be 'Henrie'.

To LAURA WAUGH   [Bisley.]
[25 February 1940]

Darling Laura

. . . My stock is high. I gave a twenty-minute lecture on reconnaissance patrols which was greeted with universal acclaim. On the other hand I was overheard by Major Cornwall speaking with contempt of the head of the Hythe School of Small Arms and was rebuked, so that may have put me down a bit.

Yesterday was an alarming day. The Brigadier suddenly accosted Messer-Bennetts & me & said, 'I hear you are staying in camp for the week-end. You will spend the day with me.' So at 12.30 he picked us up in his motor-car and drove all over the road to his house which was the lowest type of stockbroker's Tudor and I said in a jaggering way 'Did you build this house, sir?' and he said 'Build it! It's 400 years old!' The Brigadier's madam is kept very much in her place and ordered about with great shouts 'Woman, go up to my cabin and get my boots'. More peculiar, she is subject to booby-traps. He told us with great relish how the night before she had had to get up several times in the night to look after a daughter who was ill and how, each time she returned, he had fixed up some new horror to injure her – a string across the door, a jug of water on top of it etc. However she seemed to thrive on this treatment & was very healthy & bright with countless children.

So after luncheon we were taken for a walk with the Brigadier who kept saying 'Don't call me "sir".' He told us how when he had a disciplinary case he always said, 'Will you be court martialled or take it from me'. The men said, 'Take it from you, sir,' so 'I bend 'em over and give 'em ten of the best with a cane.'

When we came back from our walk he showed me a most embarrassing book of rhymes & drawings composed by himself and his madam in imitation of *Just So Stories*, for one of his daughters. I had to read them all with him breathing stertorously down my neck. Then we did the cross-word puzzle until a daughter arrived from London where she is secretary to a dentist. She told me she had been a lift girl at the Times Book Club and had lost her job because at Christmas time, she hung mistletoe in the lift. The Brigadier thought this a most unsuitable story to tell me. When he is in a rage he turns slate grey instead of red. He was in an almost continuous rage with this daughter who is by a previous, dead madam. After that she & I talked about low night clubs until I thought the Brigadiers colour so unhealthy that I ought to stop. Most of the madam's reminiscences dealt with appalling injuries to one or other member of the family through their holiday exercises. The Brigadier says that the only fault he has to find with the war is that he misses his hockey. A very complex character. A lot of majors & their madams came to dinner; oddly enough all foreign – a Russian, a German and a Swede – a fact on which the Brigadier never ceased to comment adding 'I suppose I can't really tell 'em what I think of their benighted countries.' Then he asked very loudly whether it was true that he ought not to smoke his pipe with vintage port and if so why, so I told him and he got a bit grey again.

He said, 'There's only one man in Egypt you can trust. Hassanin Bey[1]. Luckily he's chief adviser to the King. He is a white man. I'll tell you something that'll show you the kind of chap he is. He and I were alone in a carriage going from Luxor to Suez – narrow gauge, single track line, desert on both sides, blazing heat. Ten hours with nothing to do. I thought I should go mad. Luckily I had a golf ball with me. So I made Hassanin stand one end of the corridor and we threw that ball backwards & forwards as hard as we could the whole day – threw it so that it really hurt. Not many Gyppies would stand up to that. Ever since then I've known there was at least one Gyppy we could trust.'

Your friend Bailey came very near being expelled from the Brigade owing [to] the worst possible reports from all his instructors but has been given a second chance. The Brigadier said, 'I hope I'm not giving away his identity when I tell you I meant to turn one of you out. Then he said he'd been a reporter on the *Star* in civil life and I thought that a good enough excuse'. I said, 'You have given away his identity but I can assure you he is all right.' 'Yes, he spoke up for himself very well'. I did not like to ask whether he had caned him.

Capt. Macdonell has just been in here with his madam. He says he thinks that it will be o.k. for us to live out in a week or two. Yesterday he told me the Colonel had said no one was to live out. That shows how things change from day to day.

He also said, 'I hope you aren't taking a lot of notes about us all to make fun of us in a book. There was a nasty bloke called Graves wrote a book called *Goodbye To All That*. Made fun of his brigadier. Bad show!' I thought it lucky he did not know what was in this letter.

All love
Evelyn

Don't forget to ask Eddie [Grant] to give me a sumptuous dinner on Thursday if he is in London.

¹ Ahmad Hasanayn was appointed chief of the Royal Cabinet in August. He was killed in a car accident in 1946.

TO LAURA WAUGH
[April 1940]

Darling,

It is sad news for you that you are having another baby and I am sad at your sorrow. For myself, surrounded with the spectacle of a world organized to kill, I cannot help feeling some consolation in the knowledge that new life is being given. Your suffering will be to give life, ours, if we have to suffer, to take it. A child that is a danger & distress now may be your greatest happiness in the future. If I do not live through this war, you will have your childrens love & their need of you. I am writing this in my orderly room with marines coming in and out. It could be better expressed but try & see what I mean. I know your patience & resignation will be needed to the full in the coming year, and I thank God that you have them.

. . . Orange peel in the lines this morning, unauthorized clothes lines, dirty plates in the mess tent and 50 other tiresome little questions.

All love
E

TO LAURA WAUGH
13 September [1940]   [Posted Freetown¹]

Darling Laura,

Tomorrow we arrive at a port of call where there is the chance of posting a letter. It is very tiresome not being allowed to tell you about our expedition which is full of oddities & follies. My own position is rather peculiar. There was an untoward incident at Liverpool when the marine in charge of the officers incoming mail emptied it all down the rubbish chute. Presumably my transfer to the 'commando' was in that bag. Anyway we heard nothing up to the time of sailing & meanwhile a Major had been sent from another division to take over my company. I had had a lovers' quarrel & reconciliation with Col. Lushington² and was feeling very deeply devoted to him. So I had the choice of taking on Brigade Intelligence or going back to Plymouth to wait news of the transfer. Well the former would mean leaving the battalion & working with the Brigadier instead of my loved Colonel, and the latter carried the stigma of leaving the expedition just when it might be going into action (Newman & Ely had been packed off and I did not want to be in the same boat as they). So I refused both and as the Colonel was very loving to me just then he took me on as Br. Intelligence which really means 1st class passenger observer. I am keeping my rank at captain but the Admiralty may complain about my getting paid for doing a lieutenants job. The Col. (God bless him) cannot believe that any movement we make will not result in enormous casualties so he cheerfully speaks of my probably being the only serving officer & bringing home the battalion. Anyway I have had a very pleasant three weeks. I am glad to have a rest from troops for a short time.

I do not know what else was lost with the mail. It is no use your writing or forwarding letters. Will you open everything that comes for me, and if needs be deal with it. I may be home in a month but there is absolutely no certainty about anything. I may be away a year, but that is unlikely.

I have not made a will because the covenanted payment to your marriage settlement engulfs everything I shall leave. In the event of my not coming back I should like you to hold onto Stinkers for Bron just so long as it is habitable. That is to say supposing Dursley grows and other factories spring up along the Severn and the place becomes an industrial district sell out by all means. If it remains rural let the house for what you can get to anyone who will keep it in order until Bron is earning enough to take over.

In the event of the Germans overrunning England before I get back, try & get to Canada, leaving the nuns in possession rent free. I presume that if England were successfully invaded all troops outside England at the time would concentrate somewhere in the Empire, probably Canada.

Major Teck has grown a little black moustache & looks terrible. His sole duty on board is running the daily sweepstake.

We play a lot of that game you enjoyed in the *Aquitania* and it brings tears to my eyes to think of you at the table. . . .

We are all on good terms with one another & the enmities which broke out at Liskeard are healed. There is heavy drinking as gin is $2\frac{1}{2}$d a glass.

I have a lot of time on my hands now & I spend most of it thinking of you. My worst fear is that England gets into German hands & I shall not be able to get to you. There is a nice French officer serving with us in just that position. He has heard nothing of his wife & family since June. If the invasion comes, stay put at Pixton at first, then at your leisure make for Quebec.

The Brigadier is in the same ship with us. He and Col. Lushington fall into terrible rages with each other.

All my love.
E

[1] Waugh was on his way to attack Dakar.

[2] Major General Godfrey Wildman-Lushington (1897–1970). Chief of Staff to Chief of Combined Operations 1942–3. G.O.C. Commando Group 1945.

To Laura Waugh   P & O SS.
26 September [1940]

My Darling,

Whiskereal[1] prayers are still exercising a decisive influence on the fortunes of the Royal Marine Brigade and, for that matter on the larger strategy of the war. Bloodshed has been avoided at the cost of honour. My lips are sealed except to say that our future is uncertain but probably safe & boring. My own position is very peculiar but quite agreeable. In the hours when it seemed likely we were going into a very hazardous operation, my thoughts were with you, & with you only, all the time. Absence, as you have observed, makes the heart grow fonder.

Major Teck's moustache is terrible. Mr Grindle has had terrible outbreakings of boils. There is nothing I can write because all subjects are forbidden. I love you devoutly, more & more.

                                                                    E

[1] Waugh sometimes called Laura 'Whiskers'.

To Laura Waugh   P & O Cathay
28 September [1940]

Darling Laura,

My duties as I.O. were never very heavy. At the moment they have practically ceased. We are in harbour awaiting orders. I have written again to London asking for a transfer from the Brigade because it seems clear to me that we are never going to be employed in a way I can be proud of. Also I want to see you.

Mr St John writes pages to his artistic girl & when asked what about said 'love'. I am afraid I do not know how to write that kind of letter but I can tell you this – during the time when we expected to be sent into an operation which could only be disastrous, I realised how much you have changed me, because I could no longer look at death with indifference. I wanted to live & I was pleased when we ran away.[1] That is a bad state of affairs for a marine, but I believe most of the marines felt the same. Perhaps that is a bad thing for the country. I dont know. I know that one goes into a war for reasons of honour & soon finds oneself called on to do very dishonourable things. I do not like the R.M. Brigades part in this war and I do not like the war, but I want to be back in Europe fighting Germans.

It is no good your writing to me or forwarding anything.

It is time Poltening [?] paid his rent. He never does so when reminded. Write to him cordially & say that as I am away you are taking charge & will he pay his half-yearly rent to you.

                                                            All love
                                                                    E

[1] An Anglo-French attempt to install General de Gaulle at Dakar in French West Africa never began to succeed. Waugh's battalion did not land; but 'ran away' is not true.

To Laura Waugh   P & O SS.
13 October [1940]

My Darling Laura

. . . We have been in this ship so long that we have drunk all the wine & smoked all the cigars & eaten most of the food. We are rationed for water & rather tired of one anothers company. I have never before been for so long in the same, unvaried society, & though I love the marines still I sometimes wish one or two of them understood my kind of joke. We act charades in the evenings beside which Mrs Bullivant's appear infinitely subtle & polished. EVE-ILL-INN-WAR all in dumb show.

I have read all the detective stories in the library. The C.O. with innocent, troubled eyes complains of signs of stagnation in his battalion.

We have had a number of cases of unnatural vice. In one there was a court martial and the elder sinner chose me as defending officer. That gave us a lively two days. He got 8 months. His companion in sin got 11 so I feel I did fairly well for him. The details of the crime were disgusting.

Don't forward anything of importance as submarines sink so many ships but write to me about yourself to Army Post Office 600. I may or may not get it.

A black man's pigeon English description of air raid 'Steam chicken topside make plenty plenty no good.'[1]

Capt. Bell & I are friends again. In fact I am friends with all on board but I do wish sometimes I could meet an adult. They are all little boys. Some of them naughty little boys like the Brigadier, most of them delicious & just what I want Bron to be at the age of ten, but not one of them a mature man.

You are never out of my thoughts my darling.

Are the nuns paying their rent? They sometimes pay by cheque & sometimes pay straight to my bank. If you have not had any cheques from them will you enquire from my bank. Life is fairly cheap on board & I hope to have reduced my overdraft a little by the time I reach England.

What arrangements have you made about the birth of your baby? London is off presumably. Please don't have Collins[2] again. Make Bridget take care of you.

Has Highgate been bombed? Are you short of money?

What is the good of my asking these questions? I shall never get an answer until I get home. We always move before the mail.

All my love

E

[1] Censored for Laura. In his diary the sentence ends 'plenty no good shit'.
[2] The local doctor. Their child, christened Mary, was born 1 December and died the next day.

To Laura Waugh   [Highgate?]
Monday [11 November 1940]

Darling Laura,

It is now fixed up for me to go to Laycock[1]. My address will be Marine Hotel

Largs, Ayrshire & I go there as soon as I can get the Marine Office to sign my discharge.

. . . London looks much the same as it always did, the bomb craters at first sight might be the usual repairs & demolitions that are always going on. Peoples lives, on the other hand, are quite different. My first evening I dined at the Dorchester. Everyone was there from the Halifaxes[2] to Bob Boothby[3] and I had an agreeable evening meeting only friends. Phillis[4] spends the day at Chapel Street, moves into the Dorchester in a room on the VIII floor at 6.30, moves down to the vestibule of Odham's suit & sleeps there from 11 until 7. Moves up to the VIII floor from 7 until 10. Others vary this routine by sleeping in the Turkish Bath instead of Odhams. There is absolutely no reason why the Dorchester should be any more secure than anywhere else but they feel happier near each other. A Fifth Column whispers that the hotel is not 'steel framed' and that the Turkish Bath has only two feet of rubble between it & the surface of Park Lane. Miss Wade, Diana's beastly maid, is more or less manageress of the hotel. When one asks for a room there is no question of paying. Phillis & Dr Borenius offer one a choice 'There's Teeny Cazalet's[5] bunk in the Turkish bath or Duffs ante-room or Barbara Rothschild's[6] bed.' I took B. Rothschilds bed – very comfortable.[7]

Next day I went to see Maimie who has moved from her big house to a cottage behind Brompton Oratory. She is living a life of serene detachment among acres of ruin. Her minute house full of opulent furniture, a disorder of luxury – lap dogs, orchids, dishes of grapes, boxes of chocolates, about 50 mechanical toys with which she and Vsevolode play in the evenings. She, very stout, and oddly dressed, exactly like eccentric royalty. She was giving a cocktail party at 12 in the morning 'because people are so dutch about jaggering me at night', full of cosmopolitans who kissed her hand. Pam Chichester[8] was staying there with a broken rib having been blown out of two houses. When the party left we had a great luncheon of oysters & gruyère cheese, with two bottles of very old champagne. Then Vsevolode and I smoking cigars a yard long & Maimie smoking one of a good six inches, we went to a matinée. It is not at all London life as Hitler imagines it.

Then I came to Highgate for two dutiful nights. My mothers nerves are rather shaken but my father placid, reading de Maupassant & hearing nothing of the raids.

Today I must renew my persecution of the R.M. Office.

Various bits of gossip. . . . Alec Waugh has three girls living with him in Buckingham Street – all admirals' daughters. He takes them out to dinner at Boulestin's in rotation. By day he experiments with a flame thrower. Elmley sits at Madresfield in the crypt of the chapel, in a bomb proof waistcoat. Hamish Erskine has got a commission after serving six months in the ranks in the Coldstream. Miss Joan Duff (the Chagford giantess) has been expelled from the secret service for spreading consternation & alarm at a cocktail party of Alec's. Lady Curzon[9] is working as a blood donor. Calder-Marshall is driving a motor truck.

I hope to go North tomorrow, with little relish for the endless train journey. There is no shortage of anything in London except lemons. Oysters are plentiful and are not 'fish'; neither are whitebait.[10]

St James' Piccadilly is bust up, also In and Out Club and a corner of Horse Guards. Otherwise no serious architectural losses that I saw.

> All my love,
> E

[1] Robert Laycock (1907–68). Waugh's understanding patron and sometimes his commanding officer. Chief of Combined Operations 1943–7, he was made a Major General.

[2] Earl and Countess of Halifax. He was Secretary of State for Foreign Affairs and about to be Ambassador at Washington.

[3] Lord Boothby (1900–   ). Unionist MP 1924–58.

[4] Phillis de Janzé.

[5] Victor Cazalet (1896–1943). Political Liaison Officer to General Sikorski with whom he was killed. Unionist MP since 1924. Squash amateur champion, tennis and racquets blue.

[6] Barbara St John Hutchinson, married to Victor Rothschild 1933–46. He succeeded as Lord Rothschild in 1937.

[7] Among those who had permanent suites at the Dorchester were Duff and Lady Diana Cooper, Lady Cunard, Mr and Mrs Charles Sweeny and Mrs Ronnie Greville.

[8] Pamela Peel (1900–   ) married to Charles Chichester 1924–8.

[9] Grace Hinds (1877–1958). Married Alfred Duggan, an Argentinian ranch-owner, and had Alfred and Hubert. After his death she married Lord Curzon, Foreign Secretary and Viceroy of India, who died in 1925. Published *Reminiscences* 1955.

[10] The number of courses a restaurant was allowed to serve during the war was restricted.

TO HENRY YORKE
[13 November 1940]

[Written on Central Hotel, Glasgow, paper with the address crossed out.]

Dear Henry,

I am writing to Forthampton[1] – tho I suppose it is now an asylum of some kind – because I tried to telephone you in London & to trace you in other ways, but without result.

The Hogarth Press sent me a copy of your book[2] 'for review' but as I don't review now I take it to be a present from you & thank you very much indeed.

I read it in increasing delight. It got better and better, I thought, towards the end. I never tire of hearing you talk about women & I wish there had been very much more indeed about them & the extraordinary things they say. Thank you by the way for 'charlies' an entirely new word to me.

I wish there had been twice as much about Oxford, four times as much about hunt balls, twice as much about the factory.

Only one thing disconcerted me – more in this book than any of the novels. The proletarian grammar – the 'likes' for 'ases', the 'bikes' for bicycles, 'hims' for 'hes' etc. and then the sudden resumption of gentleman's language whenever you write of sport. And I thought the school 'down the river'[3] a pity – as tho' you hadn't got over snobbery. Both these things upset me – school 'by the river' and the correct hunting terms. But it was a book no one else could have written and it makes me feel I know [you?] far less well than I did before which, in a way, I take to be its purpose.

I hope the shadow of death that hangs over it has lightened. You must be finding plenty to do with your hands. After returning with head unbloody but bowed from Dakar, marine life became too humiliating and I have transferred to something more unusual under Bob Laycock whom you may remember in the first post-Duggan Maimie period. It is corps of Buck's toughs doomed no doubt to ignominy like the marines, but at the moment promising. Anyway a change.

Laura is having another baby at Xmas poor girl – regretted by all. I saw her for a week at Pixton.

My fondest love to Dig.

(There is a chap called Biddulph in my commando. Any relation?)

Evelyn

[1] The Yorkes' family home.
[2] Henry Green, *Pack My Bag*, autobiography, 1940.
[3] Henry Yorke wrote about Eton without naming it.

To Laura Waugh
[November 1940]

Marine Hotel,[1]
Largs,
Ayr.

Darling Laura,

You need have no misgivings about my prestige.[2] Everyone in the army is competing feverishly to get into a commando and it is more glorious to be a subaltern here than a captain in the R.M. Brigade. It is also a great deal more enjoyable. The officers are divided more or less equally into dandies and highly efficient professional soldiers. It is a good mixture, and both parties are said to have got on very cordially together until Mary Gore[3], that lovely girl arrived. There is one rather unhappy man called Godfrey Nicholson[4] who does not fit into either category. I have known him for 18 years and he is a good, dull fellow, a member of parliament, captain in the territorial army, rejected suitor of Pansy's[5] and now, like most Englishmen, married to a cousin of yours[6], rich, bald, very highminded. So on her first evening here he poured out his heart to Mary & said how shocked he was by the dissolute habits of the dandies; he called them 'scum'. Then Mary met the dandies and she had not met people like them before and it over-excited her a little so she told them all Godfrey had said. So everyone hates poor Godfrey who combines his high mindedness with very low efficiency and he has the only shit in the commando as one of his subalterns. Randolph was his other subaltern, but after the great 'scum' revelation, he went to Bob and said that now he was an M.P. he could not serve under another M.P. with whom he was in political disagreement and asked to join Peter Milton[7] who is a king dandy & scum. Bob said audibly, 'So you prefer the upper house' but let him go. Then Godfrey asked me to join him but I said no, I was waiting for a vacancy in the troop which takes charge of the boats and Godfrey said, 'I quite understand.'

At present I am a liaison officer with Harry Stavordale[8] & Robin[9], who is improved out of all knowledge by military training and a very companionable man. Liaison officer really means being on the waiting list for a job. I have done nothing so far except take a cuckoo clock to pieces & play a lot of ludo. All the officers have very long hair & lap dogs & cigars & they wear whatever uniform they like. One very nice grenadier called Frank can hardly ever be persuaded to wear uniform at all.

We rise above all the troubles of normal administration. The troops are simply given large sums of money & told to arrange their own food & lodging. There are no punishments because if anyone is a nuisance he is simply sent back to his regiment. In these ways Bob[10] has got what looks like being a really formidable fighting force. It will be lovely for us because as soon as you are well (Pam Churchill[11] was here three weeks after the birth of little Winston[12]) you can join me & we can live together in rooms exactly as you have always wanted to. There is long leave every week end. We expect to move South, somewhere in the Isle of Wight area, before Christmas.

Money is not going to be quite as difficult as I feared. As a result of so many chaps being so very rich I have been able to set myself up as a poor man. We get 13/4 a day allowance for food & lodging & make slightly on it instead of paying mess bills. What I do not yet know, is whether I shall get marine 9/- or army 14/- pay. I will manage your £15 a month without privation.

I do congratulate you with all my heart on your resolution in not having Teresa maltreated by Collins. I am only sorry he was ever consulted. I understood that you had given him up altogether. Will you please write to the nuns & tell them to air my books. That is to say take them all out shelf by shelf, dust them, open the leaves & bang them together. Otherwise they will get worm & damp in them.

I thought I detected a note of asperity in your letter & put it down to your thinking I should have returned to Pixton instead of staying in London. That is all balls. I had to be in touch with the Marine Office & the Special Service Brigade daily. It was not until midday on Monday that my business was completed and I left at dawn on Tuesday, after dining with Diana [Cooper] & Hutchy[13], Walter Monkton[14], Jean Norton – and sleeping in Phillis' bed. She was planning to go to Faringdon when Hubert – a lieutenant again – went to Windsor. Bertie has been a captain three times during this war. You must realise that the changes are normal.

This is the hotel which the 'scum' like but the food is beastly. They do not notice because they dine in Glasgow most nights, but I think I shall move. Largs is a sea side resort with many hotels, cinemas & churches, with fine hills all round and an island in front.

Col. Lushington came to London with Bob & was quite loving to me. 1 R.M. is still getting the worst of everything and is quartered in a slum in Renfrew. Cowan has fallen on his feet and is in charge of the *Ettrick*[15] alone, with his lady wife ashore next to him. Grindle keeps ringing up to ask if I have stolen some pins from the intelligence service stores. It is a sad & remarkable thing that I leave the Br. without a tinge of regret. It is only now I realise how heavily they had come to oppress me and how grim & fidgety the whole routine was.

I think I shall start writing a book, for my own pleasure, probably not for publication – a kind of modern Arcadia. I will soon send you Henry Yorke's autobiography, which is very disappointing. The Eton part a very poor second to Connolly and the later part, which might have been delicious, badly scamped.

I am in keen demand as a lecturer on the Dakar fiasco.

Randolph [Churchill] has a bet £50–£500 that he will swim to the island so that unless the Colonel stops it, which seems to me likely, that will be the last of him.

All love,
Evelyn
S.W.A.L.K.

[1] With No. 8 Commando.

[2] Waugh had been an acting temporary captain, was now once more a lieutenant.

[3] Mary Ormsby-Gore (1914–   ). Married 1936–46 to Robin Campbell, and in 1947 to (Alexander) Lee Mayall.

[4] Godfrey Nicholson (1901–   ). Conservative MP for thirty-three years. Created baronet 1958.

[5] Lady Pansy Lamb.

[6] Lady Katharine Lindsay, who had married in 1936.

[7] Earl Fitzwilliam (1910–48). He succeeded in 1943.

[8] Lord Stavordale (1901–64). Succeeded as Earl of Ilchester in 1959.

[9] Robin Campbell (1912–   ). Married 1936–46 to Mary Ormsby-Gore, 1946–59 to Lady Mary Erskine. Director of Art, Arts Council, since 1969.

[10] Robert Laycock.

[11] Pamela Digby (1920–   ). Married 1939–46 to Randolph Churchill, 1960–71 to Leland Hayward, and in 1971 to Averell Harriman.

[12] Winston Churchill (1940–   ). Conservative MP since 1970.

[13] John St John Hutchinson (1884–1942). Barrister.

[14] Walter Monckton (1891–1965). Barrister and Conservative MP. Created Viscount Monckton 1957.

[15] The *Ettrick* was the troop ship in which Waugh had sailed to West Africa.

To Laura Waugh
[1940]

Liaison Officer
No. 8 Commando,
[Largs.]

Darling Laura

It is very tantalizing to have long week-end leave & no chance of getting to you, so I am staying in Largs again over Sunday where it is not very gay because most of the commando are away and horrible parties drive out from Glasgow to spend the day at the Marine Hotel. The only lady now left is Lady Katharine Nicholson and she is no beauty. Mrs Randolph has freckles and a very friendly disposition. Mrs Campbell went from bad to worse, accusing a very senior grenadier captain of buggery. On Friday Robin had to go to London and Mary got tipsy and sat up until four with Lord Milton & Captain Milbank[1] and made such a noise that the hotel put up its prices for all commando members. The prices are really very severe. Randolph's bill for three weeks was £54. He had a great row with them. They charged him £1 a week for his pekinese dog. 'Do you realise my good woman that that is the interest on £2000?' To which she imprudently replied, 'What's a pound a week to you?' 'Ha, so your prices are based on what you think you can get, not on the service you give' and so on for some hours, in the course of which the manageress said, 'We should be very glad if you were all to go. There are plenty of nice people who want your rooms.' '*Nice* people. I suppose you mean evacuees from Glasgow'. 'No. People with estates'. A good time was had by all. Randolph nearly burst and paid £53.10 saying to the waiter 'I hope you make sure of getting the 10% charged in the bill. These seem to me the kind of people who would try and cheat you.'

But I shall only be there another six days as on Saturday Randolph & I are going North to a three weeks course of field training. Randolph has been on the course before but was expelled for heckling the instructors. Since then the instructors have been detected in peculation. It is said to be very uncomfortable but I have been trained in a hard school with 1 R.M. and I expect I shall find it luxurious in comparison with Dotheboys[2].

I do not think you take a great deal of interest in my commando yet, but I hope that this will come with time. I have not much else to write about at present. My lecture on Dakar has now been given for the 4th time. It wins me many good opinions.

I am trying to get Ellwood[3] here as my servant. I have written to him but do not know yet if he will come.

Have you read the books of Peter Cheyney? You would like them.

I expect that when I have finished at the training school in the North the commando will have moved to Isle of Wight area. I will join them there & wait until your baby is born before asking for leave. Then take a week, go to the commando & look for your rooms & we will live there all the winter in domestic bliss and dignified poverty.

> All my love
> E

[1] Mark Milbank (1907–). Succeeded as baronet in 1964.
[2] Kingsdown.
[3] Waugh's butler.

To Laura Waugh
Xmas Day [1940]

British India Steam Navigation Company Limited.[1]

Darling Laura

I am very sorry not to have written more often. We were living in very overcrowded circumstances when it was almost impossible to find space to write, but the main reason is that, under censorship, there is very little I can write without embarrassment. Now they have moved us for Christmas into a large and, for officers & sergeants, comfortable ship. Our lives are still frustrated at every turn but I have come to believe that all service life is like this, the only difference being whether one is in amusing company or not. Robin now lives a life among staff officers & we see very little of him. Harry[2] maintains unfailing humour – a most delicious character. We never see Bob. David Stirling[3] has joined us – a gentleman obsessed by the pleasures of chance. He effectively wrecked Ludo as a game of skill & honour. Now we race clockwork motor cars. At present I am well up on the betting.

I was very pleased indeed that Penguin are going to publish *Work Suspended*. There is too much good material there to let it disappear.

I wish I could get leave but it does not seem likely at the moment.

Is the Admiralty still paying you your £15 a month? I have not seen my pass book for months & do not know whether I am getting any pay at all. I have sent for Ellwood & hope to have him with me in a week. It will be a pleasant link with Stinchcombe.

All my love
Evelyn

[1] No. 8 Commando was on its way to Egypt via South Africa on *Glenroy*.
[2] Lord Stavordale.
[3] David Stirling (1915–   ). Colonel in Scots Guards. DSO 1942. Created the SAS. Chairman of Television International Enterprises.

To Laura Waugh
18 February [1941]

(On board *Glenroy*, en route to Egypt]

Dearest Laura,

. . . My beard looks very horrible at present. I have had a photograph taken of it to send you. It is not yet developed – neither the photograph nor the beard. There are very few topics except this beard to write about. Indeed it forms the basis of most of the letters sent home from the commando. We are afraid that the censors may think it is a code word. Anyway it gives me a hobby sadly needed during the voyage, like a pet or a pot plant whose progress I can watch day by day.

As the voyage goes on gambling gets formidably high. Chemin de fer most nights with banks never lower than £50. Randolph lost over £400 last night. I do not play at this table but have a little poker game with the poor from whom I consistently win small sums.

I lecture on Abyssinia until I am in a frenzy of boredom with the subject. Most of the day goes in sleep.

David Stirling rarely appears before dinner.

We have run out of most drinks so I am very sober these evenings. We hope to replenish stocks at the next port of call.

If you are ever in any anxiety about our welfare do not hesitate to apply to Pamela [Churchill] for information, of which, in the nature of things, she has great superiority.

I read a book called *Fanny by Gaslight*[1] which I liked. Also one about Angela Balfour named *Manon Lescaut*[2].

> All my love
> Evelyn

[1] By Michael Sadleir, 1940.
[2] By l'Abbé Prévost, 1731; about a young man who ruins his life for a courtesan.

To LAURA WAUGH   [On board
23 February [1941]   *Glenroy*]

Darling Laura,

Here is another small cheque to pay into your account.

As the voyage goes on the commando gets more & more like the Russian cavalry of Tolstoy's *War & Peace*. At the last settling day for gambling poor Randolph was £800 down. Poor Pamela will have to go to work. I do not play these high stakes and continue to win steadily. The promotion has not yet come about, will at our destination I hope.[1]

We had a very enjoyable two days at our last port of call[2]. The Glenconners[3] were there. I asked Elizabeth to write to you and say I was well, as they were likely to be home before my cable. The inhabitants of this town excelled all I have ever heard of colonial hospitality, taking the troops for drives in their motor cars, & feeding them on peaches & grapes. Randolph & I found a sugar-daddy who crammed us with rich foods & let Randolph tell him all about the political situation. One sad feature of this situation was that to grow a beard in that country is the sign of a Nazi so I got some ugly looks. My beard is terrible.

Ed Stanley & Robin Mount[5] are in a neighbouring ship so we see them at ports. Bones Sudeley[6] is behaving in a very reprehensible way, living in an uxorious stupour. Harry was very cruel at the zoo, chasing the peacocks & trying by insults to make the ostriches bury their heads in the sand. Robin is very gay & amusing. He has found his own level & now plays cards with me. David Stirling bought us a great quantity of quite undrinkable wine and is in very bad odour.

My tropical clothes do not fit. I look terrible. The young ladies at our last port were not tempting.

I hope that you have not abandoned your plan of going to Stinkers to work on the trees & hedges.

> All my love,
> Evelyn

[1] Waugh hoped to become Robert Laycock's adjutant.
[2] Cape Town.
[3] Elizabeth Harcourt Powell married in 1935 Lord Glenconner (1899–   ).
[4] Lord Stanley of Alderley (1907–71).
[5] Robin Mount (1907–69). Amateur jockey and writer.
[6] Lord Sudeley (1911–41) had married Elizabeth Bromley in 1940.

To Laura Waugh   Layforce H.Q.[1]
25 April 1941   MEF

Darling Laura,

... I am being comparatively parsimonious here – comparatively with the lavish
standard of life of Pete Milton, Harry, Phil[2] etc all of whom have bought racehorses
– feel ashamed to be eating so much delicious food while you are rationed and of
bathing in brilliant sun while you are cold. None of these things give me any real
pleasure without you to share them. I have been in one very minor action[3] & emerged
safely with considerable good fortune to be grateful for. The Brigade Major who is
an unnaturally hairy man, a kind of Rumanian, has his wife arriving today and I am
consumed with envy. I read E.M.Forster's *Guide to Alexandria* which is the best of
all guide books. I went to my Easter confession & had to have the priest arrested for
asking questions of military significance. My love to my children & to all your
family.

                                                        Evelyn

[1] No. 8 Commando had become B Battalion, Robert Laycock a colonel, and Waugh, not Laycock's
adjutant as he had hoped, but intelligence officer and a captain. They had reached Sidi Bish near
Alexandria by way of the Suez Canal.

[2] Philip Dunne (1904–65). Unionist MP 1935–7.

[3] Presumably the Bardia raid, which began on 19 April, a shambles in which a sea-attack on a town that
turned out to be deserted was hopelessly uncoordinated.

To Laura Waugh   [Egypt.]
7 May [1941]

My Darling Laura,

I got a letter from you this afternoon – very sad & affectionate and, it seemed,
written very soon after I left England. You told me Euan Wallace[1] was dead but I
cannot remember when that was. Anyway it was lovely to get a letter. I daresay
others will find me eventually if we stay in one place & retain one name for a little
longer. A soldier in one of the Battalions was found to have written on the troopdeck
wall 'Never before in the history of human endeavour have so few been so buggered
about by so many'. It is funnier if you are as familiar as Randolph makes us with
Winston's speeches. Poor Randolph has had a letter from Pam about his losses at
cards & she is very vexed with him. She has let her house so you cannot go & stay
with her.

Yesterday I spent in the Union Club here looking at the *Country Life* books of
country houses in an orgy of homesickness. Phil Dunne & I found a large scale map
of England & it marked Stinkers & his village & we nearly died of maudlinness.
Everyone is very sad; even Randolph less exuberant than usual. Harry's brother[2] is
a prisoner & David Stirling's[3] thought dead. I have been able to get no news of
Trim. I presume that he is somewhere in this country but sappers are very elusive
as they have no regiments of their own but get attached to others like hermit crabs.

I live with headquarters and only see my beloved 8 Commando when I go into Alexandria to dine which I do rarely on account of economy. Headquarters are very dull. I thought I liked the pansy C of E. chaplain at first but now he has become very tedious to me. Bob is very lonely in his scarlet & rather wistful. There has been a strong movement against him in No. 8. led by Phil & he has begun to notice it. He is rather touching, reading jokes from Angie's[4] letters & engaging in intellectual conversation. Robin Campbell is the saddest of us all. Pete Beatty[5] the least changed. He woke me up the other evening to tell me we had had a great victory *over* the Greeks.

The food in Alexandria is delicious – we live on quails & prawns & wood strawberries. But wine is very expensive. I have given up drinking except for a little Chianti. There is a cinema in the camp with a change of film every night. There is superb bathing. All this while you are living in a state of siege.

I see no women. Celibacy is not so irksome as the lack of female company. The pansy clergyman does not really fill their place.

I hope you are seeing some friends. Do keep in touch with them. It might be worth your while consulting Angie & Pam about means of writing letters. They seem to find ways of getting letters sent out by diplomats etc.

The Brigade Major had his wife here for a fortnight goodness how ugly & how we envied him. Now she has been expelled & he is so sad he is playing the bagpipes. I may not be as demonstrative but I feel very strongly too. I am becoming indolent & full of habits. If you see me again you will find a man of middle-aged, uncertain temper & failing powers – but a very loving one.

Please give my love to our children & to all your family. Will you sometimes write to my parents & tell them I am well. Should they not be evacuated? I am afraid my mother must find the raids upsetting.

All my love
Evelyn

[1] Euan Wallace (1872–1941). Minister of Transport 1934–41.
[2] John Fox-Strangways (1908–61). Badly wounded and taken prisoner. After the war he kicked Aneurin Bevan on the steps of White's.
[3] Hugh Stirling (1917–41). Killed in action in Egypt.
[4] Angela Dudley Ward (1916–   ). Married Robert Laycock in 1935.
[5] Peter Beatty (1910–49). Son of Admiral Sir David Beatty.

To Laura Waugh   [Egypt.]
2 June 1941

Darling Laura,

I sent you a birthday present of cigarettes by Peter Fleming, who was going home for the week-end. I hope it arrived. I should have liked to send eggs and chocolate and quails and silk stockings & all the things which you must need but he could carry so little I thought Lucky Strike the most acceptable thing. By the way, if you hear any damaging stories about Peter's behaviour in Greece you are to give them the lie direct as Mr Belloc would say; they are spread by a bad Lord Forbes[1] and are untrue. Since I wrote last to you I have been in a serious battle[2] and have decided I abominate military life. It was tedious & futile & fatiguing. I found I was not at all frightened; only very bored & very weary. For the time being I am delivered from countless perils to life & liberty. I shall have a great deal to tell you when we meet which I cannot write now. Meanwhile be profoundly grateful to God & his saints for my preservation during the days May 28–June 1st (operating largely through the forceful personality of Bob Laycock). My Mr Tanner turned out heroic, in a minor way, & is having his name sent to the C in C. The thing about battle is that it is no different at all from manoeuvres with Col. Lushington on Bagshot heath – just as confused & purposeless. In case I don't see Auberon again tell him when he goes to war that the *most* important thing an officer can carry with him is a pillow. I stuck to mine to the end after I had jettisoned gas-mask & steel helmet & blanket etc & blessed it every hour. I have come back a great deal thinner but am rapidly repairing my losses.

I went to Cairo on duty last week & to my delight ran into Trim (also very lean & rather clean). We dined together with Anne Palairet[3]. My word she is sex repressed. She fell down stairs after dinner, not on account of drink but of love for Trim.

Randolph dined with the Lampsons[4] the other evening & Lampson sent a pompous & jaggering cable to Winston 'Your son is at my house. He has the light of battle in his eye'. Unhappily the cypher group got it wrong & it arrived 'light of BOTTLE'. All too true.

I dined with Henry Howard[5] the other day & the son of that blackguard Persina[?].

I got two lovely letters from you about your life in Northants with R.A.F. and boiled eggs on the bacon. They cheered me enormously.

What a lot we shall have to say to each other when we meet. I feel that all our future life will be spent in telling how we have spent this year apart. In danger I have only one fear, that it means further separation from you.

I have written this very small, perhaps illegibly, so as to be able to say a lot, and now I can think of no more to say. All my love to you, my darling. I read a book *Old Curiosity Shop* in which there was a pony called Whisker & it brought me near to tears.

Evelyn

[1] Earl of Granard (1915–). An Air Commodore.

[2] The battle of Crete. The British held Crete, which was supposed to be tactically essential. On 20 May the Germans attacked by parachute for the first and last time. The British were unprepared for this and a week later their forces were withdrawn, 12,000 being left behind to become prisoners. Laycock was sent to reinforce the garrison and organized the retreat. Waugh, his intelligence officer, considered that he had taken part in a military disgrace, and that the British could have remained.

[3] Anne Palairet married the Earl of Oxford and Asquith ('Trim') in 1947.

[4] Miles Lampson (1880–1964). Had married Jacqueline Castellani, an Italian, in 1934. He was Ambassador to Egypt 1936–46, created Lord Killearn 1943.

[5] Henry Howard (1913–). Brother of Lord Howard of Penrith. Administrator of St Kitts, Nevis and Anguilla 1958–65.

To Randolph Churchill   St James' Club.
26 September [1941][1]

Dear Randolph,

I hear you have been made a major & congratulate you with all my stuffy heart. Your father too has had a leg up and is Warden of the Cinque Ports. On looking the list up I find it very much more considerable than that of Prime Ministers. Always glad to see Churchills doing well.

I have seen Pamela – her kitten eyes full of innocent fun. She is showing exemplary patience with the Americans who now have the place in England which the Germans had in Italy in 1939. They are ubiquitous & boisterous and everyone hides his impatience splendidly.

I went to Bones's[2] memorial service where many patriotic tunes were sung and P. Dunne was moved to tears.

I finished the book[3], dedicated to you, & it is quite funny but paper is so short that it will not appear until it has lost all point.

England is very uncomfortable & everything is being done by the bureaucrats to aggravate the discomfort. There is a splendid new idea called 'equality of sacrifice' which means that life is reduced to the level of a pre-war unemployed miner – in every sense for extreme idleness is combined with privation.

The only place where one feels at peace is Marine Barracks – I spent a delightful two days at Plymouth – band playing, drill sergeants strutting about the parade ground, old old colonels saying, rightly, that the Fonseca '22 does not compare with the Campbell '12 which the temporary officers intemperately consumed.

Your chum Maisky[4] goes to Church to celebrate the coming of age of the King of Serbia and munition factories fly the red flag & sing 'internationale' when he visits them. Maimie expects to be called to the throne of All the Russias[5] any day & has become gloriously sedate.

I have seen most commando wives, Angie, Nell[6], P.Dunne. I left Beatty's name at the door of Bones's funeral and it was printed in *The Times* as the Hon. Mrs Beatty, so I suppose he counts as a wife too.

I have a company of juvenile marines in barbarous surroundings at Hayling Island. Laura drives a tractor and garners thistles in large quantities.

We seem both to have become members of White's in our absence & I eat heavily there under the portrait of Frederick Duke of York feeling a little less warlike.

Berners has written the dullest book[7] yet seen.

Phillis sends you her deep love, whatever that may be.

Maureen[8] raided V. Cowles's[9] flat and stole all the sheets. Laura Long[10] went to Grosvenor Place to claim them and lost a long battle with E. Guinness's[11] secretary.

B. Jungman has a baby.[12]

Honor[13] has left Chips [Channon] for the bailiff – like Lady Chatterley in every respect.

                                                              Yours
                                                              Evelyn

[1] No. 8 Commando was temporarily disbanded and Waugh, once more a Royal Marine, reached Liverpool via South Africa and Iceland on 3 September 1941.

[2] Lord Sudeley had died in the Red Sea.

[3] *Put Out More Flags*, written on the voyage home.

[4] Ivan Maisky (1884–1975). Russian Ambassador in London 1932–43. Member of the Athenaeum.

[5] Lady Mary Lygon's husband, Prince Vsevolode, had a serious claim to the throne of Russia. He died in 1973.

[6] Helen Ward (1907–70). Married Lord Stavordale in 1931.

[7] Lord Berners published four books that year.

[8] Maureen Guinness (1907–   ). Married to the Marquess of Dufferin and Ava 1930–45.

[9] Virginia Cowles (1912–   ). American journalist, married Aidan Crawley in 1945.

[10] Laura Charteris (1915–   ). Married 1933–43 to Viscount Long, 1943–54 to the Earl of Dudley, 1960–69 to Michael Canfield, 1972 to the Duke of Marlborough.

[11] Ernest Guinness (1876–1949). Maureen's father.

[12] Richard Cuthbertson, killed in a car accident in 1964.

[13] Honor Guinness (1909–76). Married to Henry Channon 1933–45 and in 1946 to Flight Lieutenant Frantisek Svejdar.

To Laura Waugh   St James' Club.
Saturday [October? 1941]

Darling Laura,

. . . I have been considerably buggered about since last Tuesday. Wednesday was not bad as one feels further from the war in Marine barracks than anywhere else on earth. I spent the morning looking at the Royal Victualling Yard which cultivated people say is an architectural masterpiece. Well it is all right, notably two grand & graceful chimneys which anticipate Battersea Power Station by a century. Major Sinclair was charming. I had overstayed leave by 24 hrs but he said just keep quiet about it. In the evening instead of dining in mess as I should have liked I had a painful evening with a staff major, rather like myself in figure but uglier who asked me to dinner in his quarters saying we should have a bottle or two of wine & some older officers who would like to hear about the Middle East. When I got there there was only himself, a bottle of beer, cold beef & uncooked blackberries, and he talked all the time about spiritualism. . . . So yesterday I drove to Hayling to find about 40 men. The rest were on leave or at a previous camp some miles away. Their C.O. was on leave. Hayling Island is without exception the most obnoxious place I ever saw, a flat, bedraggled suburb rather like the country near Diana [Cooper] at Bognor. In this awful place I met Spencer, the highbrow you may remember from Deal days. He too was being buggered about, had lately been a major in a mechanized unit & was now fast descending. I hope his descent ends him in the infantry. Well then I drove to find the second in command who was in the half struck camp some miles away. He had no instructions for me except that I was coming. He is already overstrength. His officers are like young corporals, all very young and very plebeian. There was nothing for me to do until the C.O. returned from leave and the prospect of two days idleness, miles from anywhere, with these horrible young barbarians was terrible. So I asked for, and obtained leave, during which I hope to write the article for *Time*, for which Peters has obtained brilliant terms (£50 down whatever it is like, another £50 if it passes the censor, and then £100 if the Americans print it. The £50 down is the best part).[1] I have not yet heard anything from Chapman & Hall. I suppose they discussed me yesterday. I arrived late last night in a train which had no lights at all.

I have written to Morford & Lushington begging to be taken back to the old party. The new party is still in training & unlikely to be used until the new year if then.

I miss you unspeakably.

I have lost my beautifully carved stick.

I am very sad indeed.

E

[1] Waugh wrote an article for *Life* on the Commandos, which included an account of the Bardia raid, and was paid £200. He had received clearance from Brendan Bracken, Minister of Information. Peters sold it to the *Evening Standard*, other papers complained, and the War Office issued it as a bulletin. Waugh was reprimanded.

To Laura Waugh
[October 1941]

12th R.M. Bn. Officers' Mess,
Sherborne House,
South Hayling,
Hants.

Darling,

So when I got back I thought how nice it would be to see Capt Spencer & went to call on him. He had shot himself dead the evening before.

I have not begun work here yet as the C.O. is still on leave. . . .

Very sad
E

To Laura Waugh
Sunday evening [October 1941]

St James' Club.

My dearest Laura,

I am still missing you unbearably. It is lucky I came to London as I think I should have died of grief at 12 R.M. As it is I am only half alive.

Alec Waugh went off last night to embark for Syria. It is sad for my parents & for me as it means I now have them on my conscience. He gave a champagne orgy to his pipe lines[1] in White House. I saw Calder-Marshall who is behaving in a very unpatriotic fashion; also Christina Hastings[2], Claud Cockburn[3] & others. I dined with Henry [Yorke] who told me things about the fire brigade which make it clear that they are much braver fellows & have seen more real action than the army. At church this morning the priest lost his memory for about three minutes & stood gaping at us like a fish quite silent. It was embarrassing. I go back early tomorrow morning to Hayling Island with the most profound misgivings.

I have not finished the article yet so I must sit up & do it late & my mind is empty of ideas & everything I try to write comes out in clichés.

I suppose Mussolini is sadder & possibly Budieny[4] but I am third saddest man in the world. I wish I could recapture some of that adventurous spirit with which I joined at Chatham.

All love
E

[1] 'Pipe line to youth' meaning young girls.

[2] Christina Casati, married 1925–43 to Francis Hastings who had succeeded as Earl of Huntingdon in 1939.

[3] Claud Cockburn (1904–   ). Journalist. Editor of *The Week* 1933–46. Cousin of Waugh's.

[4] General Simeon Budenny was in command of the Russian reserve force on the south-west front which had just been destroyed by the Germans.

To Laura Waugh   [Hawick][1]
16 November 1941

My darling wife,

It is still very disagreeable here. One day in four it is intensely cold with a high wind, for the rest of the week it rains heavily & continuously. I am always wet, cold and bored. In the mess the wireless plays ceaselessly. My hut is too dark & cold to sit in. Hawick is five miles away & full of soldiers. There is no one here with any sense of humour but they never stop laughing. It is what your books call a mirthless laugh. Reading[2] is intolerably smug, cocksure, charmless. The only man I have to talk to is the doctor who is a Glasgow communist and he is trying to get sent to sea. The Catholic priest in Hawick is trying to start a sword of the spirit here. It sounds like a lot of hot air to me.

. . . Tomorrow a company competition has been ordered on a run-&-walk (200 yards marching, 200 yds doubling) over a five mile cross country course in full equipment. I think this will be the death of me.

I got a loving letter from you dated 19 May. Thank you for it, and also for your other sweet letters & for all the things you have sent. The warm clothing & fur rug have made an enormous difference.

The *Spectator* & *Tablet* have sent me some books for review so I have something to read. Cigars & red wine are lasting out. A man who was in my company in the first battalion has asked to come to me as a servant. I am quite a success in the company here and Major Tailyour[3] is very decent. These are the best things. There is also a hope of the Bde Major fixing a move for me.

All love
Evelyn

[1] In remote Roxburgh for further training with the Royal Marines.

[2] Colonel Reading was also 'an able, ambitious, smug, conceited, active, quick-witted little man with no single interest outside his profession'. *Diaries*, p. 517.

[3] Norman Tailyour (1914–79). Knighted 1966. Commandant-General of the Royal Marines 1965–8.

To A.D. Peters
[Received 17 November 1941]

5 R.M.
Hawick,
Roxburghshire.

Captain no longer. Plain Mr.

Yes the Marine Office made a fuss this end about that article. I simply replied 'special permission Rt. Hon. B. Bracken' that has held them off for the present.

I'd like to sue the War Office for plagiarism. Shall I try?[1]

Evelyn Waugh

[1] See Note 1, p. 156.

To Arthur Waugh
[5 December 1941]

[Hawick.]

Dear Father,

I am very sorry to hear of the death of your poodle. You speak of it as having happened some time ago. This is the first news I have had. Please accept my warmest sympathy. I hope you will soon find another who will take his place in your hearts.

Glad you liked most of *Put Out More Flags*. It is a minor work dashed off to occupy a tedious voyage, but it has good bits such as the half incestuous relationship of Basil and Barbara. My major work, unfinished in 1939, appears shortly as a fragment in Penguin. A fragment of this fragment is in this issue of *Horizon*. It is about a father with whom you will be unable to trace any similarities.

I am commanding a company again, living in squalor. We returned yesterday from a happy week at sea and re-embark next week.

A letter of yours was enclosed in your letter to me probably in error. It dealt with Beverley Nichols. Do you want this back? His inaccurate gossip about me caused pleasure on the lower deck but nowhere else.

You cannot expect to hear from Alec for sometime after he arrives. I expect he is warm and content and in good company. We seem to have forestalled the German offensive in Cyrenia. I can't think what possessed the papers to forecast a triumphal advance to Tunis. We are lucky to hold the enemy at all. Syria should now be safe until early Spring so don't fret about Alec.

Love
Evelyn

TO A.D. PETERS   The Manor House,
[4? April 1942]   Mells,
                                                        Frome.

Dear Peter,
    A very funny incident occurred over this B.B.C. payment. The *Brains Trust* were smugly saying that anyone ought to be paid equal wages with soldiers and it seemed to me that too many people at the moment are anxious to take money away from others, so I suggested that we made a start by each accepting $\frac{1}{3}$ for his afternoons work. They were aghast but ashamed to dissent so I left them with that decision but the certainty in my mind that they would rat as soon as my back was turned.
    Will you please find out if they did rat? If so receive my £21 + 1st return fare Hawick-London. If they ratted I shall give the press the full story with details and I hope do something to discredit Joad [1] (which is greatly in the national interest). I go to Pixton Monday-Wednesday. Could you send me a telegram there saying 'ratted' or no. [2]

Yours
Evelyn

[1] Professor C.E.M. Joad (1891–1953). A regular member of the Brains Trust, on which he gained a national reputation as a sage answering listeners' questions.
[2] They ratted.

TO LAURA WAUGH   St James' Club.
[May 1942]

Darling Laura,
    Mr Sanders is Mr Beeding – or at any rate a half of him. I do not know quite how much of your esteem & gratitude is his & how much his colleagues. Their method of work is that Mr Sanders supplies plot, political & topographical material & his friend character & jokes. They discuss the proposed book in detail & produce together a pile of notes. Mr Sanders then retires with them & without drawing breath dictates a novel in which the wines are correctly named & the train for Basle leaves the right station in Paris. This is passed to his chum who re-dictates the book putting in jokes & personal items. Mr Sanders never sees his story after it leaves his hands until the bound copy of Mr Beedings work arrives on his breakfast table.

Neither Bob, Phillip, Henriques, Cliffe nor anyone else I could find in C.C.O. H.Q. had ever read a book by Mr Beeding.[1]

I have moved into a very small room. I found it full of whiskerial litter – razor, a bottle of blue-green matter, some pretty buttons which, since you dont want them, I gave to a passing whore, some very low-class literature. I am making a little bonfire of them.

Yesterday evening I went to call on Randolph & Panto. It was very interesting. At first Lord Digby[2] was there & he & Panto went into the bed room for a long conference. Was he attempting to adjust a difference between the young couple, I ask myself. Randolph was exuberant & vociferous. Panto hates him so much that she cant sit in a room with him but paced up & down the minute hall outside the door after her father had gone. When we (Sexy Beaton, Phil & I) obliged her to come in she could not look at him & simply said over her shoulder in acid tones 'Ought you not to be resting?' whenever he became particularly jolly. She was looking very pretty & full of mischief.

I breakfasted here today, sumptuously, for 2/2, dined last night, well, for 10/- including 1924 claret. Today I hope to visit that Red X exhibition. If I see any better buttons than those I gave the whore I will put in a bid for them.

Randolph tells me that *Put Out More Flags* is 'sweeping America' but I take this only to mean that Mona Williams[3] has read it.

I had a very funny interview with Casa Maury[4] yesterday. He gave me an intelligence report saying 'You will find it quite captivating. It tells you just who is sleeping with whom in the village.'

He also wagged a finger saying 'You write me the most terrible letters' and in front of a lot of very serious staff officers fell into light gossip about the Abdies.

Write to me at SEAFIELD TOWERS   ARDROSSAN

All love
E

[1] The resulting detective stories were published under the name Francis Beeding.

[2] Lord Digby (1894–1964). Father of Pamela Churchill.

[3] Mrs Harrison Williams, later Countess Bismarck. 'What do I care if Mrs Harrison Williams is the best dressed woman in town? What do I care if Countess Barbara Hutton has a Rolls Royce built for each gown?' 'Ridin' High', from *Red Hot and Blue* by Cole Porter, 1936. Mr Williams was a banker with houses in Palm Beach, Paris and Capri.

[4] Marquis de Casa Maury, a Spaniard, had married Freda Dudley Ward in 1937 and so was Angela Laycock's stepfather. He died in 1968.

To Laura Waugh   [Glasgow][1]
31 May 1942

Darling

It was a great joy to get a letter from you. I thought you had been swallowed up in some Pixton plague.

Do you know Ellwoods[2] address? I wrote to him care Harper – no answer.

Miss Cowles leaves tonight. Everyone except me will be sorry. I have had to arrange all her movements and it has been a great deal of trouble. She is a cheerful, unprincipled young woman. She wants to be made Colonel in chief of the commando so I have suggested Princess Margaret Rose instead. Bob eats out of my hand at the moment.

So No. 3 Cmdo were very anxious to be chums with Lord Glasgow [3] so they offered to blow up an old tree stump for him and he was very grateful and he said dont spoil the plantation of young trees near it because that is the apple of my eye and they said no of course not we can blow a tree down so that it falls on a sixpence and Lord Glasgow said goodness you are clever and he asked them all to luncheon for the great explosion. So Col. Durnford-Slater [4] D.S.O. said to his subaltern, have you put enough explosive in the tree. Yes, sir, 75 lbs. Is that enough? Yes sir I worked it out by mathematics it is exactly right. Well better put a bit more. Very good sir.

And when Col. D. Slater D.S.O. had had his port he sent for the subaltern and said subaltern better put a bit more explosive in that tree. I don't want to disappoint Lord Glasgow. Very good sir.

Then they all went out to see the explosion and Col. D.S. D.S.O. said you will see that tree fall flat at just that angle where it will hurt no young trees and Lord Glasgow said goodness you are clever.

So soon the[y] lit the fuse and waited for the explosion and presently the tree, instead of falling quietly sideways, rose 50 feet into the air taking with it $\frac{1}{2}$ acre of soil and the whole of the young plantation.

And the subaltern said Sir I made a mistake, it should have been $7\frac{1}{2}$ lbs not 75.

Lord Glasgow was so upset he walked in dead silence back to his castle and when they came to the turn of the drive in sight of his castle what should they find but that every pane of glass in the building was broken.

So Lord Glasgow gave a little cry & ran to hide his emotion in the lavatory and there when he pulled the plug the entire ceiling, loosened by the explosion, fell on his head.

This is quite true.

E

[1] Waugh had been transferred to Laycock once more to his great relief and was a temporary acting captain in the Royal Horse Guards.

[2] The butler at Piers Court and then Waugh's soldier-servant.

[3] Earl of Glasgow (1874–1963).

[4] John Durnford-Slater, author of *Commando*, 1953.

To Nancy Mitford [1]   [Ardrossan,
[31 May 1942]   Ayrshire.]

Darling Nancy,

What a very nice parcel. There is only one book I am too proud to read, which I enclose. May I please have something educative instead?

I am back with Bob Laycock after a winter of great austerity with the marines in Scotland &, before that, some months of the ineffable longueurs that are ironically termed 'action'.

I have grapefruit & omelette for breakfast every day on account they do not believe in rationing in these parts. I never thought of eating grapefruit before the war nor I suppose did you. What with these grapefruit & other things I am not really enjoying the war as much as I used to. I daresay it will get better in a year or two when they have killed off some of our soldiers and you and me and Connolly are left to defend culture without interference.

When I come to London I will pop into H. Hill Ltd. Will you be there?

I think these books will make an interesting shelf for my grand children (supposing they can read which is not likely). I will say these were the books chosen at the height of the Great-great War by a great novelist and an eminent critic. Well it would be jolly interesting to see the parcel of books chosen by Southey to send a captain of marines during Napoleonic wars, wouldn't it?

We have just had Miss V. Cowles here for a long visit – an amiable but unprincipled young woman.

Are you writing the life of Robert Byron? I think it your plain duty.

I think letters of T.E. Lawrence sounds the best of the books you mention. I read E. Gill's autobiography[2] with great pleasure & admiration & I think life at Piers Court will be quite different as a result.

> Best love
> Evelyn

[1] Nancy Mitford was to become Waugh's chief correspondent. In 1942 she had little money and had just started working in Heywood Hill's bookshop in Curzon Street. She had published four novels but had not yet had a best-seller. The war parted her from her husband Peter Rodd and they never really lived together again.

[2] Eric Gill, *Autobiography*, 1940.

TO LAURA WAUGH
20 June 1942

Renishaw Hall,[1]
Renishaw,
nr Sheffield.

My darling Laura,

I have not done well in writing to you and I am very sorry for it.[2] My excuse – and a poor one – is that there is nowhere at Matlock[3] to sit & write and that by the end of the day my eyes are so dazzled by scrutinizing photographs that all I have in mind to do is sit in the twilight drinking beer. The course is interesting & I am doing quite well at it. It will be useful to have some technical military accomplishment to fall back on when I get too stiff in the joints & short in the wind to be an active soldier.

Thank you very much indeed for the beautifully mended shirt and for the fine hat. It is like a royal marines, red band on blue with a peak almost entirely covered with gold lace. I wore it for the first time coming here in the back of a hired Daimler & scowled at the poor on the way.

Renishaw is just as you saw it. Shabbier outside with the lawns grown long & the hedges ragged so that you might think the house deserted till you come inside. There everything is open; no evacuees or billetted soldiers; no dust sheets except in the ball room. Banks of potted plants & bowls of roses; piles of new & old books & delicious cooking. Osbert [4] & Edith [5] & Robbins [6] are full of loving messages to you. There is an extremely charming artist called Piper [7] staying here making a series of drawings of the house. Osbert bland & genial; Edith alternating between extremes of [venom?] and compassion. They have done what I most hoped they would do – left me alone for the afternoon.

. . . At the opening lecture a beastly don named Casson [8] gave an address in which he quoted among examples of bad intelligence the Rommel raid saying that those in charge of it did not trouble to consult the intelligence corps who could have told them R. was away. I wrote & reported this insolence to Bob & hope the don will be punished.

I share a room with a very gloomy but deferential man called White who comes back every evening a little tipsy and says he always feels on top of his form at midnight & how he hates the provinces & wants to dance with beautiful blondes at select night clubs. The intelligence officers are mostly very unmilitary & no one ever gives an order – They say 'I say would you mind kind of gathering round'.

All my love
Evelyn

[1] Home of the Sitwell family.

[2] Margaret Waugh had been born ten days before.

[3] In Derbyshire. Waugh was on an Intelligence course.

[4] Osbert Sitwell (1892–1969). Author and champion of the arts. Succeeded as baronet 1943. His publications include an autobiography in five volumes, 1945–50.

[5] Edith Sitwell (1887–1964). Poet. Dame of the British Empire 1954.

[6] F. Robbins, Osbert's soldier-servant in the First World War who became the butler.

[7] John Piper (1903–   ). Painter and writer.

[8] Stanley Casson (1889–1944). Reader in Classical Archaeology at Oxford. His memorial at New College has the inscription 'Killed flying to the aid of Greece . . . .'

To Laura Waugh   White's.
27 October [1942]
One day before my birthday

Darling

So I had a very happy week-end. On Friday the boys of Sherborne [1] school were having an exercise so we all went to umpire it & goodness it was a dull exercise and the boys showed very little fighting spirit so when it got dark we all slipped away & left them & having no umpires the scheme was a balls up but we had our dinner in peace & Basil [2] & I drank a bottle of vintage port before dinner & another afterwards.

Then we remembered that the chief schoolmaster Col. Randolph (who will not whip the boys in his house) had asked us to beer & sandwiches so we went to find him & got lost among the architectural beauties of Sherborne & did not arrive until about ten & we had great cigars in our mouths & an unhealthy flush & Col. Randolph had put about eight hundred sandwiches for us to eat but we had dined so ate none & the Randolph family will live off sandwiches for a week. I thought our social call a great success but Brian [3] & Basil say no. Col. Atkinson funked it altogether. He is losing his grip more & more. The other evening the organist was going to play the march which N. Coward has written for us, in the Abbey. So that afternoon Col. Atkinson said 'I say I have to go to the Abbey this evening. Will you take me there now so that I shall know my way in.'

Then on Sunday we went with the merry wives of Wessex and had luncheon & dinner at Harry's & got very drunk. I fell down & hurt my knee. Harry fell asleep & waking up thought he was at the Bag of Nails, fixed Nell & Daphne [4] with a gloomy eye and said, '*Those* women can go home. Tell Milly to send up some new ones.' Then a message came that I must go to London urgently so after getting to bed at 2.a.m. I got up at 6 still very drunk & began to drive to London and at Camberley we had a collision & totally destroyed our motor car but no bloodshed & I got a lift to Mr Perkins. Then I had a great hangover all day but I had some oysters with Maimie & I dined with Bill Stirling at this glorious place, slept at Maimie's and now I feel very well again. But you see I do get into mischief when I am whiskerless do I not.

Vsevolode is being made a major in the Serbian army and is so excited about it he was sick at Lady Crewe's.

It is a beautiful day. Tonight I return to Sherborne.

All my love
E

[1] Laycock decided to move Brigade Headquarters to Dorset and Waugh was among those who went ahead to make arrangements.

[2] Basil Bennet (1894–1966). He was Camp Commandant and sharing a house with Waugh. Later Chairman of Hyde Park Hotel.

[3] Colonel Franks (1910–   ). Hotelier 1929–72. Managing director of the Hyde Park Hotel from 1939.

[4] Daphne Vivian (1904–   ). Writer. Married 1926–53 to Viscount Weymouth, who succeeded as Marquess of Bath in 1946. See Appendix of Names.

TO LAURA WAUGH   [Sherborne?]
[28 December 1942]

Dearest Laura

Christmas was rather better than was feared but very exhausting and I find it difficult to hold the pen which behaves rather like an ouija board. There has been much heavy drinking.

Zoe Franks [1] who is an absolutely crashing bore and Angie whom I am keen on came to stay at the Plume of Feathers. I went to Daphne Weymouth's for one night.

Duff, Diana, Conrad [Russell], the Cavendish boys[2] – an excellent pair – Debo[3], Rex Whistler[4] and many nameless foot guards. Great drunkenness. I went to call next morning on your cousin Olivia Greene & found her with no trousers on completely drunk and Gwen blacking the grate. Then I came back to Sherborne and off we went again, to a great dinner party given by Bill Stirling & Peter Milton. Last night I suffered from the delusion that black rooks were flying round and round my bed room.

Phil has behaved abominably & stolen a most delicious excursion from me. I will tell you about it when we meet.

... Mrs M's[5] latest eccentricity is to put bricks in the lavatory cisterns to save water.

All love
E

[1] Married to Brian Franks 1939–53.
[2] Marquess of Hartington (1917–44) and Lord Andrew Cavendish (1920–   ) who succeeded as Duke of Devonshire in 1950.
[3] Deborah Mitford (1920–   ). Nancy's sister, had married Andrew Cavendish in 1941.
[4] Rex Whistler (1905–44). Painter and engraver.
[5] Mrs Maxwell, Waugh's landlady.

TO LAURA WAUGH   [Westbridge House,
[March? 1943]   Sherborne.]

Darling Laura

So when I came home on Thursday after a long day of explosions in the cold there was nothing for dinner except a cold Spam pie. So next day we said to Louie that if she must go out she must choose days when we were away as that was not the kind of dinner we could eat in war time. So Louie said 'I told Mrs Maxwell so and she said "If they are hungry they will eat it."'

That evening Foster came in and said 'What have you been saying to Louie? She's fair on the war path. She isn't half going to give it to Mrs Maxwell. She said your cold pie wasn't fit for pigs and Mrs Maxwell would lose you if she wasn't careful.'

Since then we have had three or four very elaborate courses for each meal but there is a further complication because Basil had not paid his bill since Jan 25 and couldn't be got to do it and I couldn't let Mrs M. have any excuse for her negligence so I paid it myself. This caused Basil deep guilt in his cups so he reeled into Mrs M. and said he had had a grave financial reverse and was now living on my bounty and she believed him and now he is embarrassed. So on Saturday he took me to lunch at Weymouth and we got tipsy. It is a very beautiful town. Would you like to come there for a week end with me? Far better than London in every way in fact another Hawick.

Bob, Phil & Brian & Snake[1] came back today.

On Sunday Vile T. Churchill[2] took a car to Swindon to see his wife. He has sulked ever since I beat him.

The explosions were very dangerous and bits of steel flew about our ears.

Basil has gone to live at Weymouth with his wife & daughter until Saturday.

I have written to Alick[3] about his mesalliance and will telegraph Gabriel on the same subject.

You are welcome to the Green Chartreuse and so is dear Fuckable.

I walked far & fast today and am weary.

All love
E

[1] One of the Laycocks, usually Angela.

[2] Major General Thomas Churchill (1907–   ). GSOI Commandos, Sicily and Salerno landings. Married Gwendolen Williams in 1934.

[3] Alexander (Alick) Dru married Laura's sister Gabriel on 6 March. Friend of Anthony Powell. Edited and translated *The Journals of Søren Kierkegaard*, 1938.

TO LAURA WAUGH   St James' Club.
[May 1943]

Darling

Still here.[1] I had an ugly shock yesterday to find Auberon[2] lurking in a corner. I gave the boy a glass of vintage port & left him without hard words.

Has Maria Teresa[3] read a book called *The Marmalade Cat*. If not, will you write to Nancy [Mitford] Rodd at Heywood Hill Ltd, Booksellers, Curzon Street, W.1. ordering a copy for her, to be charged to me. It has very pretty pictures & deals almost entirely with food.

I dined last night with Alick and a Pole at his flat. Baby Jungman has come to London with a vast baby solely in her charge. She sends you much love. She has changed a great deal with contact with rough Canadians and loss of virginity and is now frank in thought, coarse in speech & likes a stiff whisky. Very surprising.

I have just seen Auberon again. By the colour of his face I think he has been drinking last night. Well who am I to criticise him for that.

Bob is in love with a chorus girl named Iris. That is the reason for our hanging about London.

Capt. Hedley is in London, lame. I am to see him soon.

It is maddening that you should be away but I can't suggest your returning as at any moment my love-sick brigadier may recover his self control & whisk me off.[4]

All love
E

[1] Waugh was at the Combined Operations HQ. It was in March that Laycock had told him that he was 'so unpopular as to be unemployable'.

[2] Auberon Herbert, Laura's brother. Failing his medical for the British army, he joined the Poles.

Waugh became so hostile that later, when they were neighbours, the brother and sister used to arrange secret meetings.

[3] The eldest of the children, now five.

[4] On 24 June Arthur Waugh died. The same day Robert Laycock set out for Italy on 'Operation Husky', leaving Waugh behind. He had overruled protests that Waugh would prove a disruptive element and left written instructions that he should be sent in the first reinforcements. Lord Lovat blocked the order. Angry letters and interviews followed. Pressure was brought to bear and, firing off what he later called 'a fine pompous letter to Lord Louis Mountbatten', Waugh resigned on 17 July. He saw no more action.

To Laura Waugh   White's.
[August 1943]

My very dear Laura

I was lonely on Thursday when you left. I got tipsy at luncheon, slept & then dined with Maimie where, by good chance, Vsevolode became ill & left the dinner table and us to two hours gossip. Then back to an empty bed room.

On Friday I went down to Bognor. No guests except Loelia Westminster[1]. Diana [Cooper] so busy feeding starving animals & birds that I scarcely saw her. *Vice Versa* aloud, gin rummy and only one row with Duff and that a mild one. On Saturday we went to tea with the Bishop of Chichester which was *most* enjoyable. Good, old fashioned, conservative cathedral clergy in breeches & gaiters & a fine palace. Good wine at Coopers.

Then I came back and am lonely again. No news of my posting to Windsor.

It was very sweet of you to give up so much of your summer to looking after a lazy husband in London. I miss you sorely.

I went to see my mother on Friday afternoon when I was drunk but I don't think she knew.

All my love
E

[1] Loelia Ponsonby (1902–   ). Married 1930–47 to the second Duke of Westminster.

To Laura Waugh   White's.
[15 August 1943]

Darling Laura

I miss you very much. I have no heart for the cross word puzzle and the stretch of carpet by my bed is desolate. Even Whites loses its glamour when there is no whisker waiting impatiently for my return.

Mia [Woodruff] lunched with me today bringing a brace of grouse, but they had been cooked too soon & kept too long on the ice and were hard & tasteless. Then we went to a Cinema but she had to leave before the end so I do not know what became of the wicked earl with which it dealt.

Tonight I dine with Basil but we shall both miss your silent gluttony.

Tomorrow I go to Bognor for another night & Hall is received into the Church.

All I have to look forward to is Bob's[1] proof of my fathers book-plate.

It has grown hot suddenly & I weary.

All my love
Evelyn

[1] Robert Ormond (1874–1959). 'An aged but brilliant engraver called Ormond.' *Diaries*, p. 539.

To Laura Waugh   [Windsor.][1]
24 August [1943]

Darling Laura

It would be idle to pretend that I have been a good correspondent lately. The troubles have been wireless in the ante room and Corah in the bedroom. Corah is not as you would think a young woman but a young man of repulsive appearance who has taken the Pelman course in personality and how to make friends and he practises on me. Now the adjutant has sent him on a course for a happy week.

The Colonel has been shooting grouse in Scotland so I have not seen him yet. When I do I expect to know more of my future. The elderly officers are very sad and companionable; not so the young. Your cousin Porchester[2] is one of them. . . . He seems a vacant youth. I have spoken to him once or twice & found him civil. Mick Dillon[3] remains the most likeable.

I dined with Angie one evening. Melon, grouse, an ice, good claret, Bobby Casa Maury. Her new daughter is a negress.[4] I also dined with two Grenadiers and got very drunk. Otherwise I have spent every evening here.

Fusilier Hall is now Trooper Hall with a peaked cap. He has got on my nerves a little as the result of undue devotion.

I have found a good bookshop in Eton and bought what I take to be a first edition of Palladio, 1570, in perfect condition. Will you please go to your mother's edition and write down for me the date, printer and number of pages in each book please.

I have also bought a number of other less sensational but bulky books.

Basil is said to have defeated Shimi[5] and secured his passage to Sicily.

Windsor Castle is very ugly outside. They won't let you inside. There are objects of interest in St George's Chapel.

I am getting a suit of blues to wear of an evening.

White's is shut so I have no wish to go to London.

I enclose some money for your ma and a note for her. Please give it to her.

All love
Evelyn

On second thoughts I send your ma's cheque separately. I hope my ma is enjoying herself & not being a bore.

¹ Waugh was now with the Royal Horse Guards at Windsor with little to do.
² Lord Porchester (1924–   ). Son of sixth Earl of Carnarvon.
³ Viscount Dillon (1911–   ).
⁴ Emma Laycock (1943–   ). Married Richard Temple, owner of the Temple Gallery in Chelsea. Not a negress.
⁵ Lord Lovat (1911–   ). The man who stopped Waugh going abroad to Robert Laycock, and so his enemy.

To Laura Waugh   White's. ¹
19 September [1943]

My darling Laura

I do hope that your nursery life is not proving unendurable. I think I have not said enough about how deeply I admire your patience & resignation in this and in the threat to your future happiness in the birth of another child. If I have seemed to make light of it, that is my rough manner; my heart is all yours & sorrowing for you. This life of separation & endurance is not what I planned for you when I married. There was a brief time when I seemed to be having the worse of the war; now I live luxuriously & without responsibility & you bear the full weight of the times. I love you the more for it but wish we could change the roles – for a little at any rate.

I have had an uneventful week, living at St James's club. On Monday I went to dinner at Highgate & found my mother painfully futile and slipping effortlessly into a life of pottering & havering.

On Tuesday I dined at what should have been a very gay bachelor dinner in honour of Maurice Bowra, given by Osbert Lancaster², Freddie³ & John Betjeman the other guests. But there was not enough to drink. We went on to Pratts and had one bottle of port between us & waited for jokes. I was reminded of the literary breakfast parties in *Don't Mr Disraeli*⁴.

On Wednesday this glorious place reopened. I had Maurice [Bowra] to luncheon (he sent you particularly cordial messages) and we got very drunk. Then I went to dine & sleep at Maimie & Vsevolode's. Mrs Lea has written some nauseating love poetry.

Bill Stirling⁵ arrived at Whites unexpectedly and said he has an appointment for me. Since then I have seen him repeatedly but always in mixed circles and never in circumstances which make it possible to clinch matters. I should greatly prefer to go to him but I am keeping negotiations open with PWE⁶ in case he goes back to Africa suddenly without me. I have had several cordial interviews with PWE and am bidden to another on Thursday afternoon.

On Friday I lunched with Christopher & Camilla⁷ and dined with Cyril Connolly. His mistress⁸ loves me still. Nancy there too. Truffles and lobsters. Then to a party of Bills.

On Thursday I went down to Bray with Angie for the Christening of Emma.

Lord & Lady & Miss Mountbatten[9], Lorraine Morgan Jones, John Selwyn's father & mother & sister[10] – odd party. Luncheon afterwards at Hind's Head. Lord Louis very jaggering. I have also dined & lunched with Ran & Angela[11], today I go to luncheon with Woodruffs & dine with Nancy.

I have a new bibliophilic fantasy – the illuminated books of Owen Jones, circa 1845, in imitation carved wood covers – *very* pretty and, at the moment, cheap.

After tonight I have nowhere to sleep. I am shy of returning to Maimie as I accused Vsevolode of being a spy when I was drunk.

The Duchess of Roxburgh[12] sends you her love.

Peter Laycock[13] is trying to join Bill too & like me cant get him alone.

Susan Stirling[14] is really rather a dreary girl.

Angie sends you loving messages and will try to get you a nanny. She says friends of hers, advertising, have received countless replies. I should put an advertisement saying 'Catholic preferred, care *Hon*. Mrs Aubrey Herbert, Pixton Park, Dulverton' dont be servile when dealing with applicants. They dont respect it & good servants dont want a servile mistress.

If by any chance my children should die, do come to London. I miss you every hour.

I went to see my ma again yesterday. Golly she was flabby.

Miss Silk[15] has been commissioned to wash a picture for Fr Alfred Gilbey.

Bugger Powys[16] is to marry Miss 'Waughtefall' Myers.

I think Connolly should seriously consider marrying Alice V Hoffmanstahl[17] & giving his mistress to Bowra. He, Connolly, has been expelled from the *Observer* in circumstances very like my expulsion from C.O.H.Q. He expects to be directed down the mines soon.

> All love my exquisite wife.
>
> E

[1] Waugh had been granted indefinite leave.

[2] Osbert Lancaster (1908–   ). Cartoonist for the *Daily Express* since 1939. Stage designer, author. Knighted in 1975.

[3] Earl of Birkenhead.

[4] By Caryl Brahms and S.J.Simon, 1940.

[5] William Stirling (1911–   ). Brother of David. Scottish landowner, farmer and businessman. He was raising a new force, the 2nd Special Air Service Regiment.

[6] Political Warfare Executive.

[7] Camilla Russell (1912–   ) married Christopher Sykes (1907–   ) in 1936. He is Waugh's biographer.

[8] Lys de la Tour Dunlop, married 1938–54 to Ian Lubbock. She worked on *Horizon* and took Connolly's name by deed-poll.

[9] Edwina Ashley married in 1922 Lord Louis Mountbatten. He became Supreme Allied Commander South-East Asia in 1943, Viceroy of India, and was created Earl Mountbatten of Burma 1947. They had two daughters: Patricia (1924–   ) married Lord Brabourne, and Pamela (1929–   ) married David Hicks, the interior decorator. Earl Mountbatten was killed in 1979.

[10] John Selwyn was the clergyman.

[11] Angela Sykes (1911–   ), sister of Christopher, married in 1934 the Earl of Antrim (1911–77).

[12] Lady Mary Crewe-Milnes, married to the Duke of Roxburghe 1935–53.

[13] Peter Laycock, younger brother of Robert, died 1978.

[14] Susan Bligh (1916–   ) married William Stirling in 1940.

[15] Muriel Silk, Arthur Waugh's secretary. Later a picture restorer and 'almost a daughter' to Catherine Waugh.

[16] Littleton Cowper Powys married the Catholic writer Elizabeth Myers. Her book *A Full Well of Leaves*, 1943, is dedicated to Arthur Waugh.

[17] Alice Astor was married to Prince Serge Obolensky in 1924, to Raimund von Hofmannstahl 1933–9, to Philip Harding 1940–45 and to David Pleydell Bouverie 1947–53.

To Laura Waugh   St James' Club.
[September 1943]

Darling

Two letters from you today have relieved me of impatience that was rapidly becoming frantic.

I have taken a room of very great squalor in Ebury Street. The sort of room a genius should inhabit before he is recognized, not after.

The news of Hubert is very bad indeed. He is allowed to see no one. I had a long talk with Ellen[1] about it. He never sleeps and drugs put him into a delirium but not to sleep. He is in the blackest melancholy and haunted by delusions. There is nothing which can be done for him medically. Supernatural aid needed.

Stirling is due back today or tomorrow from Scotland when I may know more of my movements. Meanwhile I sit in that glorious place. Ran [Antrim] is losing his reason. He now sits staring fixedly at the members coming and going making very loud comments about them to himself. 'Thats not a member. Whats more he's not a gentleman' 'That man has no neck' 'Those two look like card sharpers to me' 'What a gang of shits' etc.

I have bought a lot of very heavy books & put them in Hyde Park Hotel.

Lord Ormonde[2] on hearing of Valentine's[3] death hastily put down his glass and has been on the waggon ever since.

All love
Evelyn

[1] The Duggans' maid.
[2] Marquess of Ormonde (1893–1971).
[3] Earl of Kenmare (1891–1943). Journalist and friend of Beaverbrook; former Viscount Castlerosse.

To Laura Waugh   White's.
Tuesday night [28 September 1943]

Darling Laura

It has been a great sorrow to me to hear nothing of you. No anxiety: I am sure that if any disaster had happened I should have twenty zealous Herberts on my doorstep with the news. No particular interest in your doings: to hear that Teresa has sneezed or Bron fallen down or Gabriel bought a farm does not excite me. Still I should like to feel that once or twice a week you felt enough interest in me to write & say so. I am fighting the Giant Boredom as best I can. I have moved back to St James's which is a move for the better.

Most of my day is spent waiting for and on Bill Stirling. He is a great change as a master from Bob – vague, mystical, imaginative, unsmart, aristocratic – in every quality diametrically opposed to Bob and in many ways preferable. Susan alone is a very poor exchange for Angie – a sour, egotistical, awkward girl.

Shimi has won every point & escaped going to Far East & is just where he wants to be as Palais de Dance hero.

I have bought a very decent book called *Rustic Ornaments for Homes of Taste*.

I spent yesterday evening with my mother. She is more composed in her mind but very dull. Her conscience is beginning to prick her that she is living a life of pure self indulgence. Her social round in Highgate would make Colebox[1] dizzy.

> Come soon. Sad.
> Evelyn

[1] Lady Colefax.

To Laura Waugh
[14 October 1943]

White's.

Dearest Laura

I hope very much that you are better.

My spirits are a little higher. On my return[1] I found Bill had fled to Scotland without a word to me or to the Blues with whom he had promised to negotiate my attachment. So I sent him a peremptory telegram which I think has had an effect. I know nothing of my movements but believe it is possible that I may be going abroad for a longer visit than I suspected possibly six months. In that case I would give you authority to draw on my account. Will you send me some signatures for specimens. If I am going for long I will see you first.

Yesterday Hubert was thought to be on the point of death so I got a priest to him and he gave adequate signs of assent & comprehension. There was a good deal of family embarrassment with Marcella[2] & Ellen on one side with a disgusting Canadian doctor & Lady Curzon and I and the angels on the other side. He is still alive today but is not expected to recover consciousness.

Randolph is home and in great spirits. We lunched together yesterday & drank a lot. I dined with the FitzWilliams & Peter gave me a small box of huge cigars. Today I lunch with Scott[3] and dine with the Connollies.

Audrey[4] was tipsy last night. I have been soberer.

> Get well quick. All love.
> E

[1] From Pixton.
[2] Marcella Rice, Hubert's sister.
[3] Charles Scott.
[4] Audrey Rubin.

To Laura Waugh   White's.
Friday [5 November 1943]

My darling

Thank you for your sweet & grown up letter. I too loved my leave and am ashamed that I was often petulant and ungrateful. Thank you for being so funny & patient. I think there is no chance of my leaving before the 12th. If you would like to come to London do come. I don't think it would be as lovely as our time in the country. It is just a question of whether you prefer half a loaf to no bread as they say.

I have searched for a comb but found nothing better than this.

The Connolly party was off but the Robin[1] party was on and very enjoyable, organized by Randolph on a lavish scale. Oyster and turkey in a private room at the Savoy – fine champagne & brandy & Churchillian cigars. It turned into general abuse of Bob[2] who accepted it all with great magnanimity. He & I left the party early (1.30) and went to a night club. I rang up Randolph at 10 this morning to congratulate him on his good organisation but he had not yet returned so I think it must be either the cells or a house of ill fame. Robin was delightful. He has been well lionised – a week end at Chequers – and it has been a splendid home-coming for him.

I did not behave well at my mothers. We could of course sleep there if you liked but it would be fraught with dangers to temper.

Fr d'Arcy was very hospitable but the Jesuits sat round telling funny stories which made me long for the Herberts' great narrative gifts. There was an untoward incident at Hubert's requiem[3]. At the end the trumpets of the Life Guards sounded off Last post & Reveille and sounded them very well so that everyone who had not understood what the mass was about, was moved to tears of emotion. Suddenly the hush was broken by a stentor's voice saying 'In the 40 years I have held his majesty's commission I have never seen an officer fail to stand to attention when that was sounded'. I looked back and saw poor Basil getting a great rocket from an unknown old warrior in plain clothes. Instead of saying, as I should have, 'Sir, I have come to pray for my friend's soul. Kindly keep your parade ground truculence out of this sacred place' he said very lamely, 'I'm sorry I didn't recognize the tune'.

Baby has had a baby[4] and I am its god father. She sent many sincere messages of love to you.

Capt Wordsworth has been *most* helpful in fixing my passage.

                          All love and I mean all love
                          Evelyn

[1] Robin Campbell. He had been a prisoner of war and lost a leg.
[2] Robert Laycock, promoted to Major General and Chief of Combined Operations.
[3] On 25 October.
[4] Penelope Cuthbertson.

To Laura Waugh   [Manchester.][1]
[December 1943]

Darling

I have not been able to write on this course on account of its great secrecy. Nor have I had any letters so anything may have happened to you.

A lot has happened to me. First 'flu' with temp 104. Then I fell a great height twice and sprained my knee which is now in a splint. I think I shall leave without splint on Tuesday and if sick leave is suggested perhaps come to the Lion and the Lamb[2] for a few days. On the whole this course has been exhilarating.

Sykes has been very drunk all the time.

All love
Evelyn

[1] Waugh had achieved his aim and joined William Stirling's Special Air Service, a fighting unit. However, Allied successes meant that no reinforcements were needed in southern Europe and he was again unwanted. Christopher Sykes, with Laycock's backing, managed to get both of them on a parachute training course with the Special Operations Executive, which saved Waugh from an unwelcome return to Windsor.

[2] In Dulverton, near Pixton.

To Laura Waugh   YMCA
Monday [December 1943]   With His Majesty's Forces.
                                                       [Manchester]

Darling

So this morning I was X-rayed and I have cracked a minor bone in my shin. It is thought this will take 3 weeks or so to mend. I have moved to a RAF sick bay which is not at all what I am used to and I have asked to move back to the secret house I came from. The only disadvantage of that house is that you cant write to me there and a very great disadvantage that is. As soon as I get hurt I need you enormously and all the last four days I have thought of little else.

. . . Parachuting is without exception the most exhilarating thing I have ever done. All the tedium of the last months has been worthwhile for the few seconds of first leaving the aeroplane. I felt absolutely no reluctance to jump – less than in taking a cold bath. But hitting the earth was very shocking.

I telegraphed for my mail from Whites. Perhaps there will be a letter from you there. I hope so. Such a lot has happened in the past ten days that I feel as if I had been separated from you for a year.

Trooper Hall has jumped very well and is proud as a peacock.

All love
Evelyn

To Laura Waugh   [Manchester.]
Tuesday [7 December 1943]

Dearest Laura

Your telegram of this evening was a bitter and unexpected blow. I am unable to
telephone from here so it will be some time before I shall know why Bottle[1], Haig[2]
and a convent full of nuns are together unable to take charge of three children.

Meanwhile I do not know where to go. I am in pain & helpless and can't manage
the journey to Pixton; even if I could I should need more attention than I can ask in
the circumstances. Nor can I stay alone at a London hotel.

They put my leg in plaster tomorrow which may have the effect of rendering me
more mobile. Anyway I will let you know as soon as anything is decided. My love to
my children. I think mumps is not a grave trouble at their age.

                                                              Evelyn

[1] The nanny.
[2] Miss Joan Haig was in charge of evacuees at Pixton.

To Laura Waugh   36 Montpelier Walk, SW7.
[January 1944?]

Darling Laura

I am most distressed to hear of your illness. Had you telegraphed that news to me
instead of saying that your children had mumps, I should fully have understood
your refusal to come to London.

As you will see from this address Maimie has taken me in. As long as I remain in
bed I am in no pain. I will let you know my plans when I know them. I will certainly
not come to Pixton in the conditions you describe.

                                                              All love
                                                                E

To John Betjeman   White's.
10 January 1944

Dear John

I have imprudently promised Debo Cavendish – a girl of flawless beauty – a copy
of *Continual Dew*.[1]

As it might be a blue rose
Can you help?

                                                              Evelyn

Damn it I gave you a copy of Suspenders [*Work Suspended*] – a work of less merit but
almost equal scarcity.

[1] A book of poems by John Betjeman, 1933, reprinted 1977. Waugh fulfilled his promise.

To Laura Waugh   White's.
25 January 1944

Darling Laura

Many thanks for your two letters, the second giving a far happier account of your condition than the first. I am delighted that you are being properly looked after.

I still have an obstinate cough and am low in spirits. My knee is practically well & was passed as completely well by the doctor at Milbank this morning. I have written to Col. Ferguson asking for three months leave to write a book[1] & am going to the Ministry of Information this afternoon to try & enlist their support. It will be an enormous boon if it is granted. I do not dare hope for it too much.

. . . I did not explain why your plan to live with me in a cottage at Pixton would not do and may have seemed abrupt in turning it down. The reason is that I long for your company at all times except one. When I am working I must be alone. I should never be able to maintain the fervent preoccupation which is absolutely necessary to composition, if you were at close quarters with me. What I shall like to do would be to settle in some farm or inn & visit you for a night or so every fortnight. If I get my leave I shall see if they can take me at Chagford.

My mother has been ill too. I have not been to see her yet.

I got tipsy last night for the first time for some weeks. It made my cold worse.

I hope you succeed in getting a governess for your children. I am sure that one is needed.

All my love
Evelyn

[1] Waugh wrote that he was unsuited for duties with his regiment and that he had 'formed the plan of a new novel' of no propaganda value which would take three months to write. He sent a copy to Brendan Bracken, Minister of Information, and seems to have been given his freedom.

To Laura Waugh   [Chagford.]
[1 February 1944]

My Darling

So the nut started rather stiff & I had to write the first thousand words of magnum opus[1] three times before they came right but now things are going better and I have done 2,387 words in 1½ days. It shall be 3,000 this evening & soon I hope to get 2000 a day. It is v. high quality about Col. Cutler and how much I hate the army.

I have bought a very expensive concoction of calcium & halibut liver oil which the chemist thought would restore me to strength but on reading the label more closely I find it to be a cure for chilblains.

Carolyn & Norman were very welcoming. They have given me the room they call the 'middle lounge' as private sitting room but the fire smokes so badly that I have to choose between being blinded and being frozen.

The other guests in the hotel are all like old house-keepers. There are plenty of eggs. I have found an old man who will go to Stinkers to get me claret.

> More & more
> E

[1] *Brideshead Revisited.*

To A.D. Peters
8 February 1944

Easton Court Hotel,
Chagford,
Devon.

Dear Peter

Could you please tell me the new address of Mr McLachlan the typist?

I am busy on the novel, have done over 10,000 words and, if the military do not disturb me, should finish it by the middle of May. It would have a small public at any time. I should not think six Americans will understand it.

Would it be prudent to warn Gatfield[1] to expect a manuscript for his Christmas publication? He would then be able to reserve some paper.

I am concerned with the quality rather than the quantity of Gatfields work. I take it that the regulations only prescribe how big the margins shall be & how small the print? They do not categorically enforce bad typography? And is there any paper of better quality than others?

Would Littlebrown care to produce an edition de luxe or at least de propriété? I should like this book to be in decent form because it is *very* good. Failing all else can Gatfield get hand-made paper for twenty copies or so at my expense?

My salutes to Henrie. I am in better shape than when I last saw her and you.

> Yours ever
> Evelyn

Would it interest you to see the first 2 chapters in their first typed version or will you wait until it is finished? You might be able to guess how many yanks and Bevin-boys[2] will be able to understand it.

[1] Joint managing director of Chapman & Hall, who died in 1944.
[2] Those conscripted into the coalmines while Ernest Bevin was Minister of Labour 1940–45.

To Laura Waugh [Chagford.]
Ash Wednesday [23 February] 1944

Dearest Laura

Your visit was a great joy to me. Please come again soon.

When you left I wrote till 3.30 then walked until 6.30. Now I am weary and ill satisfied with my canonical collation. I hope you are feasting on sardine trifle or whatever delicacy Mrs Grant has now devised to welcome you home.

Carolyn has been in Torquay all day. I sit now in your chair with my back to the three old women but I hear all their vile conversation.

Do not forget the watch to G & S[1] or the books from HH[2].

You left a list of medical stores. Do you want it?

All love
E

[1] Perhaps the Goldsmiths' and Silversmiths' Co.
[2] Heywood Hill.

To Laura Waugh White's.
29 February 1944

Darling Laura

Thank you very much for your charming letter which reached me at the Hyde Park Hotel this morning.

This afternoon I go to Tenterden in Kent to be ADC to a general named Tomkins or Thompson.[1] It is an injudicious appointment as I warned Thomas or Tomlin and a rude interruption to my work, but I hope to assert my independence early and so get time for a little more writing. I lunched with Tom-Dick-or-Harry at Col. Ferguson's orders. He called me 'Emlyn' and the more I tried to render myself obnoxious to him, the more he liked me. I thought him a brave simpleton; I have since been told he is a man of ruthless ambition who has reached his present eminence by betraying his friends, insulting his subordinates and toadying his superiors. His present ambition is to become a member here. I have not yet put my name down for him. He little knows how unimportant my support will be. When I know my new address I will write & tell you. Margaret Vesey's[2] engagement is cancelled. T. Vesey[3] had a bomb on his greenhouse. The damage to London is negligible but the inhabitants are very frightened. Wiltons has disappeared and the biographies in the London Library are buried in plaster. Robin Campbell was blown unconscious in Perry Brownlow's flat but is conscious again now. I drank with Laycock and Harry Stavordale and Philip Dunne and Philip Dunn[4] last night.

B Bennett has had all his teeth knocked out by his daughter Vivian. Vsevolode has lost his nerve. The present Maimie sent to Whites is a very beautifully bound copy of Grays Poems with photographic illustrations. *Most* acceptable.

All my love

Evelyn

[1] The War Office had changed its mind about Waugh's leave. He was sent as ADC to Major General Ivor Thomas for a trial period.

[2] Margaret Vesey (1912–   ) married Major Herbert Quinton in 1946.

[3] Colonel Thomas Vesey (died 1946), brother of fifth Viscount de Vesci.

[4] Philip Dunn (1905–76). Inherited a Canadian fortune. Married Lady Mary Erskine twice.

To Laura Waugh

White's.

2 March [1944]

Dear Laura

A note to tell you that I have escaped from my general. He was a dull fellow & he did not enjoy my efforts to enliven his mess. The worst I did was to pour claret in his lap. [1]

So I am now back in London with future uncertain. All I want is to get back to Chagford and Mag Op. I shall bully M of I again but I think the most likely destination is Windsor.

All love

E

[1] 'The primary lack of sympathy seemed to come from my being slightly drunk in his mess on the first evening. I told him I could not change the habits of a lifetime for a whim of his.' *Diaries*, p. 559.

To Laura Waugh

White's.

[9 March 1944]

Darling

So the new general[1] is very much less assuming than Tomas & fully appreciates, or appears to appreciate, the importance of a gentleman leading his own life. In fact it seems possible that he may engage me & send me at once on five weeks leave to write my mag.op. which would be all one could hope for.

I enclose a letter for Teresa's birthday for you to read to her.

I enjoyed my visit to Pixton very much except for Mrs Grants 'orrible overcoat.

All love
E

[1] Major General Miles Graham (1895–1976). Knighted in 1945.

TO TERESA WAUGH   White's.
9 March 1944

Dearest Tess

Here is a little note to wish you every happiness on your birthday. Your mother will give you the present I have for you. It is some painting material and I want you to take great care of it & paint very carefully, because these colours and brushes are not made as toys but are the kind which real artists use, and when a thing is the best of its kind, even if it is only a little thing like a paint brush, it should be treated like a Sacred Animal. Always remember it is not the size or price of things that is valuable but the quality.

You have been a great happiness to your mother and me for five years. It is very sad that I see so little of you. I pray that before you are six[1] we shall be together at home once more

Ever your loving
Papa

[1] It was her sixth birthday.

TO LADY DOROTHY LYGON   As from White's.
23 March 1944

Darling Poll,

It was a delight to hear from you. I hope you will get this letter. I will try and make it suitable for the censor but my views nowadays are so different from what Brendan [Bracken] tries to make them that I may find myself in prison any moment. It would be a pity if I got you into prison too.

At the moment I am in Chagford having a little rest between military duties and in consequence working harder than I have done for nearly five years. I am writing a very beautiful book, to bring tears, about very rich, beautiful, high born people who live in palaces and have no troubles except what they make themselves and those are mainly the demons sex and drink which after all are easy to bear as troubles go nowadays.

I have suffered terribly from the latter demon lately. In fact in London it is not unfair to say I never draw a sober breath. I was beginning to lose my memory which for a man who lives entirely in the past, is to lose life itself. In fact I got a little anxious about it but I found all I needed was congenial work. I have been here six weeks, the nut has cleared and I am writing better than ever I did. Little Laura comes to see me sometimes. She is leading a life of startling heroism and is having another baby in a few weeks.

Since I saw you my military life has gone rather into the shadows. I drove a General mad, literally, and both he and I were expelled from that headquarters together. Then I became a parachutist. For one who values privacy there is no keener pleasure than the feeling of isolation as you float down, but it is all too short-lived, the ground is very hard and the doctors decided – as I could have told them – that I was too old to hope for many such pleasures. Christopher & Phil were both with me on this jumping course. Christopher is a worse dipsomaniac than yours truly. His liquor always takes him now so that he talks American, not very well but well enough to upset our teeming allies. Bob Riesman, by the way, has not made himself known to me, but I have been out of London for some time.

After my leg healed I was sent to be ADC to another General. That lasted 24 hours. I had the misfortune to upset a glass of claret in his lap at dinner. It is extraordinary how much wine there is in a glass & how far it spreads if it is thrown with gusto. He was a very dull man and I was well rid of him and he of me. Then I was engaged by another General of a slightly superior type – Miles not poor Malise Graham whom I knew vaguely of old. But either he was warned or himself sacked – anyhow I got a note hastily cancelling the appointment before I had taken it up. My patient colonel has now put the matter in the hands of the war office and it is just that having so often in the past suffered from their dilatoriness, I should now profit by it. There is great talk of manpower shortage but I meet nothing but unemployed. I suppose we know unemployables mostly. There is always a great line of them on the fender at White's, headed by Phil, most of them ex-employees of Chuckers, so much so that he dare not come there now because we bully him so much. He is very prosperous. Poor Angie is like the picture of Dorian Grey and seems to bear the stamp of all his iniquities.

What are the documents concealed at Mad? That [blot] is a thing expunged by bootleg gin.

I had a lovely time in bed with my broken leg. People came to see me in great numbers and cost me about £10 a day in drink.

Vsevolode is being a great grief to all who love Blondie. It is impossible ever to see her alone and he has not now any wine to sell one so there is no point to him at all.

If you ever go to Naples do visit Laura's cousin Margaret Vesey who is in a Catholic canteen – a very decent girl.

The only hostess in London now is Laura Long who lives . . . in the Dorchester Hotel; the only man of fashion is Peter Quennell. Sgt. Preston[1] is not as prominent as he was. The Duchess of Devonshire gave a ball two months ago. There have been some gambling parties which I don't frequent. Some enemy diplomats called Cacenau[2] or some such name also give parties but don't ask me. There is a great demand for what are laughingly called 'Brains Trusts' to amuse our allies. I did one. When I tell you that the dominant wit was Bill Astor[3] and the representative of cultural aristocracy Hugh Sherwood[4], you will see what I mean. To do them justice, our allies were madly bored. I went to dinner with a lot of Elweses to meet a socialist priest and I am to dine shortly to meet the new ArchBishop[5]. Cyril Connolly and his delightful mistress give dinner parties which I enjoy very much but it always means walking home from Bloomsbury. Phil & Peggy are thought to be finally split at last. Ran has gone abroad – a friend I can ill spare. Ed Stanley has married your late cousin, the widow Fairbanks[6]. Anthony Head[7] pretends to be very important but isn't. Freddy pretends to be very dim and is. Mannerless[8] lives in Perkins the chemist shop killing himself with patent medicines now. Nancy [Mitford] Rodd keeps a little lamp burning in Peter's cabin but he never comes home. Her bookshop is the one centre of old world gossip left. That is all the social news that I know.

Dado is wrong. You mean frieze.

Miss Jungman has another baby. She has become very proletarian.

Balfour was in London for a bit and is absolutely beastly. Very smug and ambitious and through being in the RAF thinks it entirely unique to be a lord.

Don't go East. Come back to us.

All love

Bo

[1] Stuart Preston was an art historian serving in the American army as a sergeant. Appears as 'the Loot' in *Sword of Honour*. Enjoyed an astonishing social success in wartime London.

[2] Miguel Carcano, the Argentinian Ambassador.

[3] William Waldorf Astor (1907–66). Succeeded as Viscount Astor in 1952.

[4] Lord Sherwood (1898–1970). Liberal MP 1923–4 and 1935–41.

[5] Cardinal Griffin, Archbishop of Westminster.

[6] Sylvia Hawkes, who had been married to Douglas Fairbanks, married Lord Stanley in 1944.

[7] Lord Head was Representative with Directors of Plans for Amphibious Operations 1943–5.

[8] The Marquess of Dufferin and Ava was killed in action in 1945.

To A.D. Peters
[Received 3 April 1944]

Easton Court Hotel,
Chagford,
Devon.

Dear Pete,

My Magnum Opus is turning into a jeroboam.

I have written 62,00 words of which I enclose half. The rest is typing. A problem vexes me on which I should value your advice: The original scheme of the book was three sections of which two are complete. The total length will be about 90,000 words. I now find that what I have written could be profitably enlarged and what I have to write could be an entire book. The leisure at my disposal is limited.

Should I be well advised to expand what I have written to 70,000 words & publish it as Vol I, leaving the second for next year? Supposing that by next year paper is again abundant we could publish a single volume of 120,000 words incorporating the first volume which would have had the limited circulation of the time. Expansion would be an artistic benefit.

Evelyn

Please retain MS for time being. It is a first draft requiring much alteration even if there is no expansion.

TO LAURA WAUGH   Chagford
12 May [1944]

Darling Laura

My heart is with you in this time of waiting. I pray God that by the time you get this you will be happily delivered.[1] I will come as soon after the birth as you think fit. I mustn't stay long as I am hard at magnum opus, interrupted by two nights in London.

Do you still want the Countess as a godmother?[2] With your permission I'd like to have Bill Stirling as Catholic god-father as I am now deeply indebted to him as I will explain later.

My interview was very funny. I found room 107 full of the gloomiest looking officers you ever saw – some of them old boys like Joey Atkinson, some horrible looking young hooligans who were clearly in disgrace with their regiments.

We were called in one by one and interviewed by a civil colonel. He said 'Well I have two jobs I'm trying to fill. Both very interesting ones. I don't know which you'll like the better. The first is adjutant to a transit camp in India. The other is assistant registrar in a military hospital.' I said well if I must choose one or the other I would be assistant registrar in a hospital. Then he said 'I say, are you educated?' 'Yes.' 'Well thats splendid. They're looking for an educated officer to be in charge of some chemicals at the War Office.' So I said well my education is all classics & history, not chemistry. 'Oh that doesn't matter. It's education they want.' So I was put down for that.

Then I beetled round to Richmond Terrace and saw Bob and said get me out of this quick. So he telephoned to the colonel and said that Bill Stirling had secret work of great importance for me. He was very loving and well conducted in the matter.

So Bill is going to let me have six weeks to finish mag. op. Hurrah. But will it work out like that I ask myself. If it fails I think Philip Hardwicke[3] will take me into a training unit he is forming for Bill. All the old gang is assembling round Bill. My chief fear is that he himself will fall and all of us be exposed.

Angie sent you many messages of sympathy & affection.

Harold [Acton] has given you a star sapphire. I do not know what you can do with it. It looks like a half sucked acid-drop.

The night of my great success Robin [Campbell] dined with me. He was drunk, not me – much. He wants to become a legless pilot & be killed. Perhaps this is a symptom of not liking Mrs C.

Kik Kennedy's apostasy[4] is a sad thing. Her heathen friends have persuaded her that it is a purely English law that her children must be brought up Catholic, and that she can get married in U.S.A. after the war. It is second front nerves has driven her to this grave sin and I am sorry for the girl.

I hope you are enjoying *The Semi-Detached House*[5]. It is a book you & Bridget would like to read to one another.

Sex repression is making mag.op. rather smutty.

Norman Webb goes to Second Front again on Sunday. Mrs P. Cobb has a great boil and is in state of nerves about Normans departure. She has received the reversion of half the Webb fortune.

Do not let the Herberts harrow me with information about your baby until it is born and you are well & happy. . . .

All love
E

[1] Harriet Waugh was born 13 May 1944.

[2] Countess Coudenhove, whose husband was an Austrian diplomat, was at Pixton when the war broke out and stayed for several years.

[3] The Earl of Hardwicke (1906–74).

[4] Kathleen Kennedy, the eldest sister of President Kennedy, agreed that any children from her marriage with the Marquess of Hartington, heir of the Duke of Devonshire, should be brought up as Protestants. In the event he was killed four months after their wedding in 1944 and no child was born. She was killed in an aeroplane accident in 1948.

[5] By Emily Eden, 1859, republished 1969.

To Laura Waugh   [Chagford.]
17 May [1944]

Darling

No letter from you today. I hoped you would have been well enough to scribble in pencil & tell me you were content or not as the case may be.

I long for Monday and my visit to you.

Mr B[everley] Nichols is behaving very well. Leaving me to work when I want to and telling me about 'Ivor' Novello & 'Willy' Maugham and 'Noel' Coward when I want relaxation. He believes he is a great musician rather than a great writer.

Mag. Op. steams along slowly at about 1500 words a day.

I announced the birth of your daughter in *The Times*. Did you know that 13 May is proverbially a very unlucky day?

The lilac has no smell here.

All my love. Till Monday
E

To A.D. Peters   [Chagford.]
[Received 20 May 1944]

Dear Pete

Many thanks for congratulations. Both well; no nanny.

How about 'Sacred and Profane' on the cover; *The Sacred & Profane Memories of Capt. Charles Ryder* on the title page?

Yes, Lady Marchmain is an enigma. I hoped the last conversation with Cordelia gave the theological clue. The whole thing is steeped in theology but I begin to agree that theologians wont recognise it.

Duck into hare shall stop. [1]

I wish I could dine but I am glad of the reason for not being able to. I am steaming ahead with the novel. It is becoming painfully erotic. [2]

Yours
Evelyn

[1] Perhaps the *caneton à la presse* that Charles Ryder had at the expense of Rex Mottram in Paris: *Brideshead Revisited* had turned it into hare on its second mention.

[2] *Brideshead Revisited* was finished on 16 June. Brian Franks replaced Bill Stirling as Waugh's commanding officer and reluctantly summoned him to Perthshire. The Second Front had opened on 6 June, and reinforcements would be needed.

However, Randolph Churchill was leading a military mission to Yugoslavia and wanted Waugh. Everyone was delighted by this idea and they left together on 4 July. The complexities of the country they approached defy simplification. Outside intervention obscured a civil war. The Germans and Italians had overrun Yugoslavia in 1941. The British had therefore helped the resistance and in particular Mihailovich, a Serbian and a Royalist. In 1943 support was switched to Tito, a more active partisan and a communist. The Americans unenthusiastically followed the British lead. Another of many splits among those who opposed the Germans was religious. Waugh was supposed, correctly as it turned out, to work more effectively with other Roman Catholics. An air base had been set up at Bari in Italy and missions to local partisan leaders established. Waugh's, the 37th, was to Topusko, their headquarters.

To Laura Waugh   British Embassy,
6 July [1944]   Algiers. [1]

Darling Laura,

A very luxurious trip here in an airplane in which they fed us on currants & sultanas & barley-sugar like animals in a zoo, every hour or so. Breakfast in Gibraltar, here in the early afternoon. A charming house in Arab style some of it old, with tiled courtyards not unlike Mexico and peacocks and palm & rubber trees, high above the town. An amusing house-party – Bloggs Baldwin, Victor Rothschild [2], Virginia Cowles, Mrs Hemingway [3] (awful), Randolph & me. Duff & Diana wonderfully unambassadorial, French & Americans & jews in & out all the time clearly enjoying it very much, D & D very popular & happy, good food, one lavatory, one bath, everyone in pyjamas all the morning, like Venice before the war. Yesterday I lunched in the town with Bloggs, today with Lady Ranfurly [4].

. . . Duff fell into one of his great rages with Bloggs last night & behaved as no host or ambassador should. The remarkable thing is he is so soon appeased. I should be agitated for a fortnight if I got so angry. Diana looks very elegant in lots of new clothes. . . .

> Sober, faithful & loving
> Evelyn

[1] Duff Cooper was British Representative to the Free French.

[2] Victor Rothschild (1910–   ). Succeeded as Baron 1937. Biologist and businessman.

[3] Martha Gellhorn, war correspondent and writer, was married to Ernest Hemingway.

[4] Hermione Llewellyn married the Earl of Ranfurly in 1939. He was personal secretary to General Wilson.

TO LAURA WAUGH
17 August [1944]

[5 Via Gregoriana, Rome.]

Darling Laura,

I have tried to keep you informed of my welfare by means of the Prime Minister, the Editor of the *News Chronicle*, Coote Lygon[1], Randolph, Mondi Howard[2] and others. I hope some of their messages reached you. I have had two narrow escapes from attempts on my life, the first by the RAF to incinerate me,[3] the second by RAMC[4] to poison me, but have survived and am now on the way to recovery, out of hospital, living in a charming flat with a view of Borromini's tower of S. Andrea del Frate, as the guest of John Rayner whom I neither knew well or particularly liked (he is Joan Eyres Monsell's husband)[5] but who has behaved very hospitably to me. The aeroplane accident is a complete blank to me as I was knocked unconscious at the time tho I understand that those of us who survived got out of the machine by our own efforts. My first memory is of walking in a cornfield by the light of the burning aeroplane & discussing the progress of the war in a detached manner with a totally strange officer who kept saying 'I say skipper hadn't you better lie down?' It was some hours before I remembered why I was in that particular country and, as I say, I do not yet remember anything of the fall. I was burned in several places, on both hands, legs & head, but as I was anaesthetized by shock my sufferings were negligible. They fetched us out after 36 hours and I was about a fortnight in hospital in Italy. Randolph made the ward exactly like *The Man Who Came to Dinner*[6] but it was an agreeable time. The chief annoyance of the incident was the total destruction of all my luggage most of it irreplacable. I still have no shoes except gymn shoes, of different sizes but made for the same foot. Then I came on sick leave to Rome and was at once struck down by a far worse trouble – a carbuncle on back of the neck – an affliction which I have hitherto regarded as slightly comic but which reduced me to an extremity of pain & depression. I was in hospital another fortnight in great discontent until I was liberated the day before yesterday. Now I am not as strong as a horse nor quite as happy as a lark, but taking things easy, seeing a number of friends, refreshing myself with good architecture. Randolph had housemaid's knee in both knees and slight derangement of the mind & went off to stay with Duff & Diana. I expect him back soon when I hope to resume our plans where they were interrupted.

. . . I feel I have been away many months tho it is less than two, and long to be with you again.

All my love to you & to my children.
Evelyn

[1] Lady Dorothy Lygon.

[2] Edmund Howard (1909–   ). Second Secretary in Rome 1947–51, Counsellor in Rome 1951–65.

[3] The aeroplane taking Churchill and Waugh from Bari to Croatia crashed at the airfield when they were landing.

[4] Royal Army Medical Corps.

[5] Joan Eyres Monsell (1912–   ) was married to John Rayner 1939–47. He was in Psychological Warfare. She married the writer Patrick Leigh Fermor in 1968.

[6] The play written by George Kauffman and Moss Hart concerns a loquacious and overbearing visitor, based on Alexander Woollcott.

To Laura Waugh   [Topusko,
16 September [1944]   Croatia.]

Darling Laura

Since I last wrote we have left our forest and set up house in a farm.[1] I miss the isolation & silence of the surroundings but the house itself, though reeking of the pig sty, has a substantial advantage – I get a room to myself away from Randolph, whose rhetoric in his cups I find a little wearisome. The entire work of the farm appears to be done by a little girl of Teresa's size.

We are on the outskirts of a small town which was once a spa. Indeed the baths still stand and we go there daily & sit in radio-active hot water which I find very enervating. The town has been laid out entirely for leisure, with neglected gardens and woodland promenades reminiscent of Matlock. It suits our leisured life well. We do very little & see little company except a partisan liaison officer, the secretary general of the communist party, the leader of the Peasant party & such people. We also arrange for the evacuation of distressed jews. There is a monsignore and an old parish priest in the town and no religious enthusiasm or persecution. We have great quantities of eggs to eat and some very tough meat to eat.

I am very hopeful of our work here being done before Christmas. I have sent Bron a 'pin-up' of myself. It will be slow in arriving because it has to go by ordinary mail.

All my love
Evelyn

[1] They had spent the first three days in Yugoslavia in a wood cabin.

To Laura Waugh   [Topusko.]
27 September [1944]

Darling Laura,

Time seems to stand still here. I believe that the war would have been over sooner if I had become assistant registrar of a hospital. I find nothing to do between meals & there is nothing to tell you. Our wireless operator has taken to drink with a frenzied zeal which is disconcerting in so small a community. I find the smell of rakia sickening, that & the local cigarette smoke are the characteristics of the place. My window is almost covered with vine leaves & I could not understand why, on waking and seeing the light come through the leaves, I spent the first quarter of an hour of every day thinking of Midsomer Norton. I thought it was because the pattern was like my aunt Constance's church needlework, or like the borders of nineteenth-century printed texts. Then I realised that it was quite simple & direct & that this was how the light came into the smoking-room through the vines on the verandah.

There was a great dinner party two nights ago in honour of an exchange of decorations with the Russians. It was midnight before the presentations began. Then at two, when I was a little weary of speeches in a strange tongue, a theatrical entertainment began of patriotic recitations, plays, and songs until four o'clock. As we are in the habit of going to bed sharp at ten o'clock, it was an unusual strain.

Yesterday we drove a great distance to see a battle. It was a splendid autumn day. The countryside is extraordinarily English, with little irregular woods & fields and hedges full of Travellers Joy and elderberries & blackberries & thorn. We picnicked on the side of a hill with a desultory, inconclusive little battle going on a mile below us & drove home by dusk & moonlight to find the telegraphist wandering about the farm without his trousers groaning as though in great pain.

Today has lasted about a week already and it is only 4.15 pm. We are like Chekhov characters.

At this moment a deputation of distressed jews has arrived. They come nearly every day. Randolph takes the sort of interest in them that Herberts take in Albanians. I think I prefer the Herbert interest.

There is also a wandering musician with an inflated pig's carcass playing jigs like a Highlander.

Now I must go and call on the General. It will only be half past five when I come back. Oh dear I wish I could go to sleep & wake up when the war was over.

All my love
Evelyn

To A.D. Peters   'M' Military Mission
30 September [1944]   C.M.F.
[Topusko.]

Dear Peter,
... Littlebrown must on no account change the title of *BR* without submitting

the alternative for my approval. I think it most unlikely I shall agree. He can call it 'A Household of the Faith' if he likes.

I am writing to Gatfield by this post asking for a set of galley proofs by air mail so that I can revise the first half. The changes may be extensive.

. . . Randolph does not want to write his war memoirs but will come & see you when he gets home to discuss doing business with you. You may find him offensive. Most people do. I seldom.

Time passes very slowly in this backwater.

Yours
Evelyn

TO LAURA WAUGH   [Topusko.]
14 October [1944]

Darling Laura,

Yesterday evening, Friday 13th, when I was sitting with Randolph & wondering how much longer I could bear his uninterrupted company, Freddy Birkenhead[1] suddenly arrived. He could not have been more unexpected if his coming had never been proposed; we had quite despaired of him. Randolph literally leaped for joy and I felt a great sense of pleasure & relief. He brought, for a short visit, another major a harmless fellow[2], also 100 cigars, 2 pairs of shoes, a pot of shaving cream, a pair of hair-brushes, razor blades and a letter from you. You are an exemplary wife, thank you very very much. It is a joy to smoke again, to feel shoes on my feet that fit & to look down & see a pair of human feet instead of the ludicrous appendages I have worn for two months, the shaving cream is unprocurable here or in Italy and greatly needed, the hair brushes are admirable quality – in fact you have done splendidly. The letter was written long ago but was none the less welcome. It was very loving and warmed my chilly old heart.

. . . It is a pleasure to have Freddy here to take Randolph off my hands for a bit but the result of his arrival has been to undo much of the good work I had done in subduing him. He bursts out in such exuberant, spontaneous, full-hearted joy that it should be a pleasure to see him – but it is no great pleasure to me. If Freddy likes it here I think I may propose moving in a fortnight or so to a wine-growing district. They all languish from over-work and office life in Bari – otherwise I might try & transfer there. I should like to settle down in some peaceful vinous place and do another months work on Magnum opus. I have asked Gatfield to send proofs via 10 Downing Street and I should like to rewrite the early-middle chapters before it is published.

I have lately read two books which I am sure you know about about an American lawyer called Perry Mason. Is he one of your favourite characters? I thought him rather like Mr A.D. Peters.

The rain which I thought would continue all the winter has stopped. The leaves are falling. Do you remember our catching leaves in the beech avenue at Mells?

The table cloth smells of rakia spilled by Randolph in his joy yesterday.

A little parcel of books came from Nancy.

We must be very rich as I am spending no money here. Please enjoy yourself and indulge yourself to the top of your bent. Buy an astrakhan coat, take a suite at the Ritz & entertain, have fun.

All my love & thank you again for sending me such nice things.

Evelyn

We have a splendid American gas bomb for killing flies.

[1] A friend of Churchill's from childhood, of Waugh's from Oxford, Lord Birkenhead was second in command.

[2] Major Stephen Clissold, an expert on the Partisans and fluent in Serbo-Croat. His 'charm and sanity were to ease many a grim situation': the Earl of Birkenhead in *Evelyn Waugh and his World*, p. 142.

TO LAURA WAUGH   [Topusko.]
17 October [1944]

Darling Laura,

I must write to you about an exciting new idea that has come to me and ask you what your opinion of it is. For some time I have been worried about how, after the war, we are going to reconcile your wish to farm and my wish to have the children brought up on a farm and in the country with my own ineradicable love of collecting bric-à-brac and my need for a harmonious place to write in. This is my idea. Why should we not dispose of Stinkers and buy you a simple farm house and property near Bridget for yourself & the children where I will live when not working, and for my work and collecting mania and your frequent visits retain my aunts house at Midsomer Norton. This will presumably be left equally between Alec, myself and my Tasmanian cousin. They would obviously wish to sell their shares which, freehold & contents could not amount to more than about a thousand pounds in all. I could then make the house into a museum of Victorian art, put Ellwood there as permanent housekeeper to look after me while I was there and of everything in my absence. I could keep my library there & write my novels there. It would be a secret house to which no guests would come. I have the photographs of the rooms as they were in 1870 & I could gradually restore them to that splendid state. It, and the tranquillity of a provincial town, would be precisely suited to the mood in which I work. After my death if none of sons in law or spinster daughters want to live there, I could make it into a public museum & memorial to myself. It will by that time, supposing that I live until 1970, be a unique spectacle. The more I think of this idea the more splendid it seems. What do you think?

Evelyn

You would of course be always eagerly welcomed there. It is not an attempt to set up a separate household, but I could not be happy with *only* a farm as my home. I could not work near my children, I could not live permanently near the Grants. I am quite sure you would never farm happily except near the Grants.

The £1000 would be my aunts legacy so we lose nothing by the idea – or rather we do not have the effort of finding any money.

TO LAURA WAUGH   [Topusko.]
24 October 1944[1]

Darling Laura

Major Clissold, the gentle ex-schoolmaster[2] who came to us on a three days visit, is still here after ten days. Some evenings he goes out to the airfield and waits for an hour or two, other evenings he just looks at the rain & stays at home. Meanwhile my letters to you pile up in his bag & will presumably reach you in a single post. I wonder if you do as I do with yours – open them all first, look at the dates & then read them in proper order. Freddy is still with us, alternately morose and drunkenly jolly. He is a great support in his jollity taking Randolph off my shoulders. The pair laugh a great deal but never at new jokes or even at their own; they retell endlessly the memorable retorts their respective fathers made at one time or another to various public personages. Even with that vast repertoire they repeat themselves every day or two, sometimes every hour or two. Then they recite memorable patches from Macaulay's essays, John Betjeman's poems and other classics. Of conversation as I love it, with anecdote occurring spontaneously & aptly, jokes growing & taking shape, fantasy – they know nothing. The good time of day for me is the first two hours of daylight before Randolph is awake. But all day is better than life with Col Cutler, or than any military life which seemed open to me six months ago so I must not repine. My health is admirable and my nut very clear – so clear that I hunger to rewrite Mag. Op and *Scoop*, and to write a child's history of Christendom and a short story, drawn from my present experience, of a man who gave up drink and became so clear sighted that he could not abide any of his friends & had to take to drink again.

We had a little air raid the other morning and the hot baths have been put out of order which is a grave loss to our comfort. American air crews keep drifting in, some of them lame from parachuting, and it is difficult to find room for them. There were great celebrations here for the fall of Belgrade, including a te deum in the church attended by all the communist bosses and later a drunken speech by Randolph. The partisans fired off all their available ammunition into the air & scared our cook. You must read a very funny penguin named *Bullet in the Ballet*[3]. I think my son's birthday is approaching. I can send him nothing but sage advice & that will keep another year. I think that soon I will go to Bari for a weeks leave & try and get down to Lecce which is said to be a town of great beauty & one which it is unlikely we will ever have the chance to visit as conveniently again.

My cigars are lasting out and are a pleasure three times a day. I don't think it is any good trying to send me any more unless we hear of someone coming out.

Our poor jews stay in increasing distress. The more airmen arrive the smaller their chances of getting out.

Please enjoy yourself as much as you can. Get rum from Vsevolode and Basil,[4] take Bridget to London, buy a house at Bude. Don't let winter & Pixton and my teeming family get you down.

All my love
Evelyn

[1] There had been an aerial attack two days before which precipitated a row with Churchill.
[2] In fact a lecturer at Zagreb University.
[3] By Caryl Brahms and S.J.Simon 1937.
[4] Prince Vsevolode worked for the wine-merchants Saccone & Speed, and Basil Bennett ran the Hyde Park Hotel.

To Laura Waugh   [Topusko.]
2 November [1944]

Darling Laura,

... My birthday was the glummest I have spent for eleven years. It rained continually. I did not leave the house except to visit the baths which we had been told would be working again. They were not. I thought perhaps you were thinking of me and that warmed me a little.

Yesterday, All Saints, the peasant women all came in to mass in gala dress & brought flowers to the graveyard.

I have got to the stage of disliking Randolph which is really more convenient than thinking I liked him & constantly trying to reconcile myself to his enormities. Now I can regard him as one of the evils of war like Col. Cutler or Tom Churchill or Roger Wakefield and so live with him more harmoniously. Freddy takes him away for some time most days but when travel is possible Freddy & Clissold both leave us.

... I am afraid it will be a gloomy winter for you, but I pray God the last we ever spend apart. On my birthday I thought it had been a good year – mostly due to you.

All my love
Evelyn

To Laura Waugh   [Topusko.]
5 November [1944]

Darling Laura

... We grow backwards in war time. First it was public school life in the Marines, then prep. school at COHQ, now nursery – with picnics postponed for rain, everyone with his nose pressed to the window, time dragging, occasional treats of sweets – literally of sweets – when we get a sortie.

Drunkenness is a very sad thing for the sober. Freddy is fuddled most evenings and, I suppose, just as he was in Whites when I thought him the wittiest of worm[1] friends – now I find him repetitive & trite. Randolph shouts himself into a stupor and often goes to bed before dinner. Oh dear.

Bloggs [Baldwin] has been moved from Bari which takes a large part of the glamour from it & I don't so much want to settle there now. People talk of things ending here in a few weeks but the war seems to me to have rolled itself in blubber like an eskimo & settled down for the winter. I don't see much hope of getting back before the spring.

The only good time of my day is 7.30 to 9.30 am before Randolph gets up, when I eat a delicious omelette and feel well & cheerful & can read or write. From 9.30-10 there is incessant noise; dusk at 5 and the light usually too weak to read. I go to bed at 10, think of you & usually sleep 10.30-6.30 which is fine.

All my love
Evelyn

[1] A phrase borrowed from Nathaniel Gubbins.

To Lady Dorothy Lygon   [Dubrovnik.][1]
25 December [1944]

Dearest Poll,

. . . The Pearl of the Adriatic is not improved by having all its renaissance façades daubed with communist slogans in red paint but it is still a handsome little town. I have a small, unheated house in the slums and a fine cook, several servants of different nationalities, unlimited quantities of tolerable wine, no superior officer nearer than Belgrade, so it is what you might call 'clover' or even 'easy street', but I do not think it will last long, when I shall be consoled by the hope of seeing you again. I am afraid I felt far from well when we last met. You will think I am an invalid, but it is not always so.

Christmas makes me think a lot about Malvern – Mr H[2] and the Capt [Hance] and the handsome presents Blondie made us give them, and Jessel's boy's foie gras and the time we went up to the top of the noble line after dinner and someone gave the late Maj. Duggan a push and he could not stop running until he reached the gates of St James girls school and you and me & Hamish [Erskine] popping into Lord Beauchamps Home for Impotent[3] Clergymen. Well well never again.

It seems hopeless our attempting to write to one another, but if this letter gets through, do try & send one back. It would be a treat to me.

Love from
Evelyn

[1] At the end of November Waugh was ordered to Dubrovnik, where his main interest was in discovering the extent of religious persecution.

[2] Harrison.

[3] Impoverished.

To Nancy Mitford   37 Military Mission
25 December 1944   CMF
                                             [Dubrovnik]

Darling Nancy

Your letter (written on the 12th) was my only Christmas mail – my only mail for some time – and very nice too.

The Curse of the Cecils – goodness. Is it something like haemophilia they can only give each other or is it like the common cold something they can give us? Come to think of it I think that M. Bowra must have had that curse for many years; the war cured it, hence his sudden frightful fertility. [1]

I have escaped from your cousin Randolph and am now on my own in the Pearl of the Adriatic which looks a little less pearlish with all the renaissance façades daubed with communist slogans in red paint. I have spent a solitary Christmas which next to having Laura's company or the few friends I can count on the toes of one foot, is just as I like it. I dined alone sitting opposite a looking glass & reflecting sadly that the years instead of transforming me into a personable man of middle age, have made me into a very ugly youth.

Well last Christmas I dined with Maimie & Vsevolode and M and I O'Brian [2] and some howling cads. It is better than that. But two years ago I was with D. Weymouth & first met Debo. It is a great thing not to be with my children at Pixton at this season. So I met Taffy Rodd [3] at that social centre Bari just out of Athens with alarming tales I have since learned to be untrue. And a Capt Elwes [4] called on me today. It is interesting that H. Hill has engaged a jew named Sutro to watch the till. I knew him well at the University. You will find he fits in beautifully to the Sergeant Preston life in Curzon Street. It is very good news that you may take up the pen again. Please give the results to Chapman & Hall. They love losing money & I will get you a substantial over advance. One thing about your letter saddens me. It does not say 'Thank you for your beautiful Xmas present of *Brideshead Revisited*. It is a beautiful work'. Is it too bad to mention or has V2 blown it up? You should have got it by now, and though I know it will shock you in parts on account of its piety, there are a few architectural bits you might like.

I wonder what *Grave* [5] is. Perhaps a book on its way to me? The last I had was an attempt to whitewash Bryan Guinness called *Belchamber* [6] which I enjoyed enormously. I lent it to Randolph who was so much moved that he said he could never commit adultery again – at any rate not with the same innocent delight.

... I went to a cocktail party of officers and there was not one who was not purely proletarian. It does not make them any more sympathetic to the partisans though.

The partisans are celebrating Xmas by firing off all their ammunition under my window. My nerves are not as steady as they were before my harrowing life with R.S. Churchill.

A very nice skier named Peter Lunn [7] claims close friendship with Dekka [8]. True? Do you remember the M.P. who tried to seduce Romilly in Madrid? He is here too.

                                             Love and kisses
                                             Evelyn

[1] Maurice Bowra published three books in two years: *The Heritage of Symbolism* and *A Book of Russian Verse* in 1943, *Sophoclean Tragedy* in 1944.

[2] Murrough and Irene O'Brien.

[3] Gustaf Rodd (1905–74). Brother of Peter. Served in the Royal Navy 1918–28 and 1934–45. Settled in Italy in 1945.

[4] Jeremy Elwes, nephew of Simon. Farmer, director and patron of the arts.

[5] Cyril Connolly, *The Unquiet Grave*, 1944–5.

[6] By Howard Sturgis, 1904.

[7] Peter Lunn (1914–   ). Son of Sir Arnold Lunn. Diplomat, and captain of the British Olympic ski team 1936.

[8] Jessica Mitford (1917–   ). Writer. Sister of Nancy, married to Esmond Romilly 1937–42, and to Robert Treuhaft in 1943.

TO LAURA WAUGH   37 Military Mission:
7 January 1945   [Dubrovnik]

Darling Laura, sweet whiskers, do try to write me better letters. Your last, dated 19 December received today, so eagerly expected, was a bitter disappointment. Do realize that a letter need not be a bald chronicle of events; I know you lead a dull life now, my heart bleeds for it, though I believe you could make it more interesting if you had the will. But that is no reason to make your letters as dull as your life. I simply am not interested in Bridget's children. Do grasp that. A letter should be a form of conversation; write as though you were talking to me.

For instance you say my Christmas presents have arrived and Eddie [Grant] is pleased. What do you think of the book? Your copy is still binding but you must have seen his. You know I have not seen one. Tell me what it is like. It is dedicated to you. Are you pleased to see it in this form? Are you curious to know what changes I have made in the final proofs. There are many changes in this copy from what you read before. Can you not see how it disappoints me that this book which I regard as my first important one, and have dedicated to you, should have no comment except that Eddie is pleased with it.

Has no wine come for you? I ordered some. Perhaps there is none left in London.

No Christmas present came from you to me.

Today is the Orthodox Christmas. I have just been to a 'tea party' to which I was invited at 3 pm. With savage peoples one knows so little what to expect, so after a heavy luncheon I set out and was given a place at a table already full. First I was given green chartreuse and ham, then tea and cakes then cherry brandy and cigarettes. It seemed the end but suddenly a whole cold roast sheep was brought in; there were red wine & speeches until 6.30 pm.

Do write & tell me what you are thinking & how you are looking. Be natural when you write. Don't send any more of these catalogues of family facts. Tell me what letters of mine you have had.

                                                            Evelyn

To NANCY MITFORD   37 Military Mission.
7 January 1945   [Dubrovnik]

Dearest Nancy,

Yes I know what you mean;[1] he *is* dim, but then he is telling the story and it is not his story. It is all right for Benvenuto Cellini to be undim but he is telling his own story and no one elses. I think the crucial question is: does Julia's love for him seem real or is he so dim that it falls flat; if the latter the book fails plainly. He was a bad painter. Well he was as bad at painting as Osbert [Sitwell] is at writing; for Christ's sake don't repeat the comparison to *anyone*.

Lady Marchmain, no I am not on her side; but God is, who suffers fools gladly; and the book is about God. Does that answer it?

Bad about the clip. Too late for the first edition & there are no second editions these days. I knew I should have submitted it to you for criticism. The definitive (ha ha) edition is substantially different from the first so if you really feel disposed to re-read it, as you say, wait a month or two for that.

A lovely parcel of books from you. Connolly's *Grave*. What he writes about Christianity is such twaddle – real twaddle – no sense or interest, that it shakes me. And he seems ashamed of the pleasant part of himself – as a soft, sceptical old good liver. I am shocked by the *Grave*. But I have read only five or six pages. My father was a better classical scholar than Connolly but he did not trot out his recondite quotations in at all that way. I think Connolly has lived too much with communist young ladies. He *must* spend more time in Whites.

... 50 copies of *Brideshead Revisited* went out, 40 of them to close friends of yours. Do please keep your ear to the ground & report what they say. For the first time since 1928, I am eager about a book.

                                                   Love
                                                   Evelyn

[1] Nancy Mitford had written of *Brideshead Revisited*, '... a great English classic in my humble opinion.... Are you or are you not on Lady Marchmain's side? I couldn't make out.... One dreadful error. Diamond clips were only invented about 1930, you wore a diamond *arrow* in your cloche. ... I think Charles [Ryder] might have had a little more glamour – I can't explain why but he seemed to me a tiny bit dim. ...' She continued in her next letter, 'I quite see how the person who tells is dim but then would Julia *and* her brother *and* her sister all be in love with him if he was? Well love is like that, and one never can tell.'

To LAURA WAUGH   37 Military Mission.
9 January 1945   [Dubrovnik]

Darling Laura

Another ship in with another letter from you written on 26th – a much better one. Its predecessor was so disappointing that I had to write & tell you so. I am delighted that you have read your Magnum Opus. All the passages, including the coarse phrases with the tarts, which upset d'Arcy have been cut out for the public version.

You do not say what Mrs Grant says about it. Please report fully, and what your mother says & Katharine. I have a deep interest in the welfare of this book. Three copies are being bound for you – page proofs, private edition, public edition – and will reach you in due course. Come to think of it only the two latter are for you. Page proofs belong to the house library but you may, must study them to see the changes.

. . . A lot of letters should be arriving at Pixton thanking for M.O. If you have not yet forwarded them, do not do so; keep them in a safe place – not loose in your drawer but in a tin box – and copy out on an Air Letter the most interesting sentences from each.

How did your ma come to be lunching at Downing Street?

When you write a letter take my last letters and read them through, see what questions I have asked and answer them. Try & look on correspondence as a conversation not a diary.

Have you ever considered how the Epiphany is the feast of artists. I thought so very strongly this year. After St Joseph and the angels and the shepherds and even the ox and the ass have had their share of the crib, twelve days later appears an exotic caravan with negro pages and ostrich plumes. They have come an enormous journey across a desert and the splendid gifts look much less splendid than they did when they were being packed in Babylon. The wise men committed every sort of bêtise – even asking the way of Herod & provoking the massacre of the innocents – but they got there in the end and their gifts *were* accepted.

I have always detested Christmas. Now I shall always celebrate the Epiphany instead.

How are you looking. Have you any fine new clothes. We are stinking rich. Do get magnificent furs if it is not a foolish time.

Did I send Gabriel M.O. in the end? I thought I did but you don't mention it.

I have written to Basil saying it is never too late to send booze to Pixton.

All my love
E

To Laura Waugh   [Dubrovnik]
23 January 1945

Darling Laura

. . . I am very well & happy. I do not well see how I could be happier granted that I have to lead a military life away from you. I have no commanding officer to bother me and my subordinates are soon to be reduced to one. My work consists solely in doing good. I distribute food to the needy and get a sense of vicarious generosity in the process. A great number of prayers are being put up on my behalf in consequence. I do not think there is any military appointment so congenial – good architecture, good food, wine, blameless life, and for once in my life a sense of being very popular.

My bust goes slowly because the poor old man making it believes his food ration will cease when the work is done, so he fiddles away making the nose longer and shorter by turns. I look very fat and placid, like a nineteenth-century Headmaster Bishop. It will be a preposterous possession. It is by having preposterous possessions that one can keep them at arms length. Well I have a preposterous wife have I not? I have not had a letter from you for some time as the weather has kept shipping away so I have not much to write about. Today it would seem from the news that the war is coming to an end. By all means buy that house near Taunton if you like. [1]

Peggy Dunne has given Mary Dunn £200 to buy new clothes for her honeymoon. Tomorrow I shall tell my Mr Paravicini that I will continue his food allowance after his work is done for I am tired of sitting to him.

. . . I do a great deal of illicit benefaction to the religious.

Who should turn up as head of the RASC[2] here but Zena Naylors half-brother[3] – not a very attractive youth, but the association has been worth some tons (literally) of food for the Dominican convent. It is an odd chain of circumstances from Alec's nymphomaniac mistress in London to a lorry load of army rations at a medieval convent in the Adriatic, is it not?

I have got very fat & noble looking – like a patrician Roman of Petronius's day. You do not tell me how you look. I hope that by now B Bennett has sent you some wine.

I have just read *Dombey and Son*. The worst book in the world.

All my love
Evelyn

[1] It was not bought.
[2] Royal Army Service Corps.
[3] Roddy Douglas.

TO LAURA WAUGH   [Dubrovnik]
29 January 1945

Darling Laura,

A charming letter from you with diagrams of M.O. [Magnum Opus] or (as Nancy prefers) G.E.C. (Great English Classic). How quick communications are now. It is like the telephone.

Did you ever get a letter from me asking you to put Bron down for Ampleforth? Please do so. Did you ever get an enquiry about an illuminated book from Maltby? Please answer.

I presume from your silence that B. Bennett has sent no wine. Very worrying.

When buying a new house, which I give you full authority to do as soon as you find one that suits you, please bear in mind that it must be very near a Catholic Church. I find it a great joy to be within two minutes walk of daily mass. I don't want our churchgoing to be a long weekly drive in the half dark. Did you ever get a letter from me expressing the wish to retain the little house at Midsomer Norton? You have never commented on that idea.

I had a long, charming letter from your ma. It is curious how that unliterary lady is most herself pen in hand – unlike her daughter whiskers.

My life here is really very full of incident. Yesterday a Chec Czek Czech how? woman came to accuse my predecessor of stealing 39 dollars from her and when I laughed stormed out saying 'Alors monsieur capitaine, vous êtes si gentil que je vais tuer ma mère'. Today a distracted Chilean engineer (as it might have been Burns[1]) came to tell me that his 17 year old daughter had stowed away on a British ship & would I please have her imprisoned? Then a few minutes later a Canadian subject was beaten up by the secret police. Never a dull moment. Goodness I wish you were here. I am on great good terms with the Bishop who believes I am a secret envoy from the Pope and laughs away all my disclaimers as modesty & guile. I have asked to be given full consular powers in which case I might have you shipped out here. Would you like it. Copious food & drink, constant excitement without danger. The architecture is not really good. It is an inferior people aping the Italian.

My bust has its good days and its bad days. Today was a good one. I have got 10 years younger and two stone lighter. When he starts on the stone I shall be more excited. The long sessions while he makes mud pies of my face are rather boring particularly as he will talk politics all the time. My French conversation is rather like your social conversation in English & like you I have learned to shut off $\frac{2}{3}$ of my mind from what is being said.

I am shocked that Pansy did not appreciate M.O., G.E.C. I think you take relish in repeating the unfavourable things – Beast.[2]

Sat Feb 3 is the great feast day here. As everyone is starving feast day is a sad expression.

My ma is O.K. She wrote a perfectly sane letter. Just lazy.

Andrew Waugh[3] is to be a sailor. A very good idea.

All my love
Evelyn

[1] Tom Burns was born in Valparaiso but left before his first birthday. He was never an engineer.

[2] Lady Pansy Lamb had written, '. . . But all the richness of your invention, the magical embroideries you fling around your characters cannot make me nostalgic about the world I knew in the 1920s. And yet it was the same world as you describe. . . . Nobody was brilliant, beautiful and rich and the owner of a wonderful house, though some were one or the other. . . . Oxford too, were Harold Acton and Co really as brilliant as that, or were there wonderful characters I never met? . . . You see English Society of the 20s as something baroque and magnificent on its last legs. . . . I fled from it because it seemed prosperous, bourgeois and practical and I believe it still is. . . .' Which lines Laura quoted is unknown.

[3] Andrew Waugh (1933–). Son of Alec.

To CATHERINE WAUGH [Dubrovnik]
5 February 1945

My Dear Mother,

I have had two letters from you now since I last wrote and am in your debt. Posts may be less frequent in future as there will be fewer ships in the coming weeks but please keep writing as your letters are a great pleasure, none the less so when they come in batches.

. . . I struggle so far as one bad tempered man and a wireless station can struggle to get the authorities in Italy to do something to relieve the distress here, but so far nothing has been done.

I am beginning to get letters thanking for *Brideshead Revisited*. It seems to be a success and I think it should be. Unfortunately it is not to be published until April because of shortage of paper and the delays in proof correcting due to my sojourn abroad. This is a pity because it is a book for winter reading. Also, I hope, in April everyone's mind will be on great events in Europe rather than novels of the past. But I believe it will go on being read for many years. The general criticism is that it is religious propaganda. That shows how opinion has changed in 80 years. No one now thinks a book which totally excludes religion is atheist propaganda. 80 years ago every novel included religion as part of the normal life of the people.

When do you return to Highgate? Are your tenants satisfactory? Are your financial affairs perfectly easy? Has Joan made any contribution yet?

I hope you have not forgotten your intention of making a Waugh genealogy. I think Aunt Connie could do a great deal of it from memory.

I remain well and as happy as it is possible to be surrounded by so much distress.

Best love to you all at Norton
Evelyn

To Laura Waugh   [Dubrovnik]
10 February 1945

Darling Laura,

. . . It is also sad about Auberon's arrest & ill treatment. I presume the police were Poles not British?[1]

My life has been clouded. I boasted too soon of my happy situation. The partisans are now seeking to expel me and I think they will succeed. Whether or no this leads me back to England is impossible to say. As always I assume the worst – a number of increasingly painful & undignified scenes here culminating in ignominious withdrawal. Then put into a pool of unemployed officers in Italy and being found some unsuitable and unacceptable post there. But there are other more pleasant possibilities including that of my return to England to you.

D'Arcy's letter about M.O. was most unsatisfactory. He says he has not formed an opinion. I thought he was struck of a heap by it. It seems to me that my book is designed for faded ladies of fashion – all of them rejoice in it but not many others. It will be interesting to see the reviews.

Will you please thank Teresa very much for her Christmas letter. I wonder why she chose a card of a dead soldier for me.

The bust has its days off and its days on. Lately it has been going well & has reached the stage that if I have to leave suddenly, it can be carved in stone without me. It has grown thinner & more bad tempered. [2]

Spring is here; splendid sunshine all day & cool nights. We even had an earthquake the other morning, not very severe. I slept through it but it destroyed the rock garden of two very sad Poles I befriend. But I cannot rejoice in the weather or even in the wine because the bloodiness of the partisans and my uncertain position depress me continually; more than that there are so many unhappy people who look to me for help which I can ill supply. It seems to comfort them to come & tell me how miserable they are; it saddens me. But is it not odd? Would you have thought of me as having a kind nature? I am renowned for my great kindness here. At our headquarters in Bari however I am looked on as very troublesome and offensive. [3]

I am sorry that my little Christmas present of drink coincides with Auberon's leave. I looked forward to thinking of you having several tipsy Sundays – not a single orgy.

. . . I have just had my weekly bath which I take in a neighbours house. It was very hot for once.

Has it occurred to you that the Poles are likely to become the criminal class of the world in the next decade, being uprooted hopeless and embittered so that Auberon is likely to be in & out of prison a lot. If he is still with you please give him my warmest congratulations on his commission.

All my love sweet whiskers

E

[1] Auberon Herbert, wearing the uniform of the Polish army, had been arrested as a spy by the Americans in Belgium. Two of his teeth were knocked out.

[2] The bust reached England eventually. Laura had copies made in plaster and terra cotta after Waugh's death.

[3] Waugh was forced out of Dubrovnik by the hostility of the Partisans, who understandably disliked his association with the clergy. He felt that he should come back as consul and continue the struggle but was relieved when his application was refused. On 20 February he sailed from Dubrovnik and never returned.

To Laura Waugh   [Bari]
8 March [1945]

Darling,

If things go as I expect I shall be with you at the end of the month. [1] I do not know for how long; possibly for ever; at any rate for a month. I must be in London for the first week & shall be busy seeing archbishops, Foreign Secretaries, and such people. I think it will be best for you to join me at the Hyde Park Hotel. We will have a Mayfair room[?] suite and try & induce Basil to give us champagne. Bring some books so that it will not be necessary for us to go out of doors often into those squalid & disorderly public streets.

I had a successful & happy week in Rome. Mia Woodruff turned up, very pretty &

. smart. I moved in high Vatican circles, having long discussions with the secretary of state & finally a private audience with the Pope in a week when he was seeing no one. [2] Please tell your children that he asked after them & gave them his personal blessing & sent them a rosary each. I told him there were four. I hope that was right.

The sad thing about Pope is that he loves talking English and has learned several elegant little speeches by heart parrotwise & delivers them with practically no accent, but he does not understand a word of the language so that people like Myron Taylor [3] leave thinking they have conveyed some essential information when in fact HH has not attempted to take in a word. It was a great sign of the importance he attached to what I had to say that he invited me to talk French, which I do with great grace & fluency. Then when the business was over he made a little English speech, inopportunely the one he keeps for sailors telling them how much he enjoyed a naval review at Portsmouth in 1920 something.

I have caught cold & feel a little low. Most of my friends are leaving this district. I have made up my differences with Randolph who is back in hospital in Rome having lost the use of his legs at a ball in Belgrade. . . .

All my love
E

[1] Things went as expected and Waugh flew home on 15 March and stayed. On 25 March one of the last rocket-bombs shattered the window of his room in the Hyde Park Hotel. He wrote a lengthy report entitled *Church and State in Liberated Croatia* which argued that 5,000,000 Roman Catholics were being persecuted in an area where the British had both responsibility and influence. It was handed to Fitzroy Maclean at the Foreign Office, where it caused some stir but did not alter policy. Christopher Sykes examines the matter in detail in *Evelyn Waugh*, pp. 273–6.

[2] The purpose of Waugh's audience with Pope Pius XII was to tell him about the unhappy situation of Roman Catholics in Yugoslavia. Waugh left him 'convinced that he had understood what I came for. That was all I asked.' Cardinal Tardini later conveyed to him that he had made a good impression.

[3] Myron Taylor (1874–1959). Personal representative of Roosevelt and Truman to Pius XII 1939–50.

5 A Family in the Country
1945-1956

May 12ᵗʰ 1956

Darling Hatty

Oh dear, I am ashamed of myself.
Tomorrow is your birthday & tomorrow is Sunday
so this letter will not get to you in time to
send you my love and good wishes. I shall think
of you at Mass & drink your health at
dinner, but that is not at all the same thing
as writing on the right day. No excuse. Please
forgive me.

I hope anyway that the cake I ordered for you
arrived in time & that you had a very happy day.

Introduction

In 1939 when Waugh joined the army he had one baby daughter; by the time he left it, he had a family of three girls and a boy. Before the war he had been a well-known novelist; with *Brideshead Revisited* he became internationally acclaimed. Though he did not attempt to follow up this success, most Americans had his earlier books to discover.

It took a little time to repossess Piers Court, so Waugh moved from Chagford to a house at Ickleford in Hertfordshire, which he shared, all squabbles forgotten, with Randolph Churchill. Laura stayed mostly at Pixton. He seriously considered moving to Ireland, but gradually settled down to a life in the country with his family and work, punctuated by raids on London and trips abroad. If this regime sounds placid, it must be remembered that it led to the crisis on which *The Ordeal of Gilbert Pinfold* is based.

Many more letters survive from this period and it is likely that more were written. The correspondence with Laura naturally stops, that with Nancy Mitford has just begun. I am aware of no major gaps that have not been mentioned.

To Ronald Knox   Pixton Park,
14 May 1945   Dulverton.

Dear Ronnie,

I dont know which I am the more grateful for – your letter or the list of misprints (some of which were no fault of the printer but plain bad spelling of my own). Thank you with all my heart for both.

I am delighted that you became reconciled to *B.R.* in the end. It was, of course, all about the death bed. I was present at almost exactly that scene[1], with less extravagant decor, when a friend of mine whom we thought in his final coma and stubbornly impenitent, whose womenfolk would only let the priest in because they thought him unconscious, did exactly that, making the sign of the cross. It was profoundly affecting and I wrote the book about that scene. (I have just had to look up the spelling of scene in a dictionary.)

Katharine who detested the book to the end & beyond, and expressed her disgust with feminine ruthlessness[2], had the same thing to say – that the characters did not exist either in real life or faery. The sad thing is that 'Metroland' is my world that I have grown up in & I don't know any other except at second hand or at a great distance. It would be as false for me to write about Maurice's[3] world as when Thomas Hardy tried London drawing rooms & Virginia Woolf successful business men. I thought & think all the characters highly companionable, except possibly Mulcaster & his awful sister.[4]

I have cut out of the published edition any turns of phrase which were hard to read aloud – at least I hope I have. I never quite know what terms are current outside Metroland.

Now I am writing an unhistorical life of St Helena[5] which absolutely no one will be able to bear. It keeps my mind off the Responsibilities of Peace.

                                          Yours very sincerely
                                          Evelyn Waugh

[1] The death of Hubert Duggan.

[2] Katharine Asquith had written: 'It's beautifully written and some of the bits about the house made me cry . . . . O Evelyn do do do write a book not a novel – yet not like Algernon's [Cecil, the historian]. I can hardly bear your writing about modern people. . . .'

[3] Maurice Baring.

[4] Knox had written that if he had stopped reading he would have felt, 'Yes its all very well, terribly amusing and well-written and the descriptions are poignant and all that; but I wish Evelyn would write

about characters whom one would like to meet in real life . . . . But once you reach the end, needless to say the whole cast – even Beryl – falls into place and the twitch of the thread happening in the very bowels of Metroland is inconceivably effective.' 'The twitch of the thread' is a fishing metaphor drawn from G.K.Chesterton's Father Brown stories, meaning that once someone has seen the Grace of God, however much time and space remove him, he can be retrieved.

[5] Waugh abandoned the biography of St Helena, discoverer of the Cross, but wrote her life as a novel in *Helena*, 1950.

To Laura Waugh   White's.
19 May 1945

Darling

I think I have just bought a castle. I hope you will approve. It is 20 miles from Arklow, about 15 bedrooms 5 reception, 80 acres of park, with as much farm land as you want. It belongs to Peter FitzWilliam who wants a friendly neighbour . . . .

All my love
Evelyn

To John Betjeman   Pixton Park,
Vigil of Corpus Christi   Dulverton.
[27 May] 1945

Dear John,

I am very glad you like *B.R.* I think it splendid. *Daily Herald* readers wont, unless you say it is a classic. Which it is. Funny their thinking you a Catholic.

I say is it wise to settle Penelope near a Mosque[1]. She is bound to fall in love with the Imam & she's a teetotaller already.

As I told you I am writing her life under the disguise of St Helena's. I haven't yet reached the middle Mystery Cult period. She is 16, sexy, full of horse fantasies. I want to get this right. Will you tell her to write to me fully about adolescent sex reveries connected with riding. I have no experience of such things, nor has Laura. I make her always the horse & the consummation when the rider subdues her. Is this correct? Please make her explain. And is riding enough or must she be driven? Are spurs important or only leather-work.

I don't much admire Piper's work[2] but know no one else. If he's too dear do you know anyone else to try? I went to the Academy in the hope of spotting an architectural draughtsman but they were all awful.

Please send address of Edinburgh book shop with illuminations.

I have duplicates of Day's *Parables of Jesus* 46.[3] Want to swap?

Vote for Pakenham[4] the old booby.

Evelyn

[1] The Betjemans were moving to Farnborough Rectory, near Wantage.

[2] John Piper drew the illustrations for *Brideshead Revisited*, but was dissatisfied and never submitted them to Waugh.

[3] Published by William Day, the Victorian lithographic firm.

[4] Frank Pakenham was not returned at the General Election as a Labour MP, but was created Baron Pakenham and became Parliamentary Under-Secretary of State in the War Office.

To A.D.Peters   Hyde Park Hotel.
28 June 1945

Dear Pete,

Thank you for your letter & enclosure.

This sum of money is very large. I do not see the advantage of making more than £5000 a year under present regime; that is to say 2000 from Korda and 3000 from USA. Supposing USA totals £15,000 in all, which seems likely,[1] that is five years salary. Can it be fixed thus? Meanwhile could you please see whether I shall have earned 5000 this year by next April & if not pay into my account whatever is needed to make it up to that figure. . . .

Yours
Evelyn

[1] *Brideshead Revisited* was a Book Society Choice and best-seller in the United States.

To Laura Waugh   [London?]
[14 July 1945]

Darling Laura,

It was sweet of you to come & stay with me. I miss you very much. I am afraid that in the agitation of getting you transport & luncheon I failed to thank you for all your patience and forbearance & to tell you how enormously I enjoyed your visit.

Rest at peace about Ireland. I will not, unless you change your mind, make you live at a distance with a sea-crossing from your children's school. I too hope we may find our home in the West of England.

I think it will be fun for him and a relief for you if I have Auberon to stay with me during his holidays[1]. We can fix times & details later. Randolph & Pam's nurse is able & willing to look after him for a week or so. Winston is a year younger but I will give a lot of my time to educating him.

I love you very much. I am just off to dine with Brian Franks and, alas, Zoe & then to Berry Ball perhaps. I will write & tell you about it. I do not deserve reproaches for being a bad correspondent.

All love
Evelyn

[1] At the house he was to share with Randolph Churchill at Ickleford, near Hitchin in Hertfordshire.

To Laura Waugh   [Hyde Park Hotel?]
24 July [1945]

Darling Laura

Many thanks for sending me my laundry. Also for your & Teresa's letters.

I am sorry you wont come up for the election. I should have thought Ann's[1] came very near the requirements of a whiskerial party. But there is no point in taking a long journey if you would not enjoy yourself at the end.

On Saturday I lunched with Diane[2] & the Cholmondeleys – a herring & water – and fainting with hunger went to the Wallace Collection with her. I returned later to White's to find Randolph playing drunken billiards with Ed. at £50 a game & complaining that his ball gave out a droning sound when struck. On Sunday I drove down to Hitchin to see Randolph's house which has only the furniture which Pam chose not to take.[3] My heart sank. We have a lame cook but no other servants so far. It is presumed that the Melchetts[4] will feed us whenever we are hungry. I do not know the Melchetts so I do not know how well justified this presumption may be.

I dined with Malcolm Bullock[5] at the Turf & went to bed early.

Yesterday I resumed my old round which will come to its end this week. Nancy's shop, Whites, Beefsteak, sleep, Whites, then a call with Basil on Angie. Bed 3 am.

This morning a bottle of Basil's champagne, luncheon with Bill Stirling, sleep. It is a very warm evening. Now I shall have a bath and go Whites, Beefsteak.

I cannot give clear instructions about Bron's visit until I have seen more of the menage at Hitchin. I think Winston comes in the latter half of the month for 10 days only.

Now that election results are imminent I have got quite excited about them.

All my love
Evelyn

[1] Ann Charteris (1913–   ). Married to Lord Rothermere 1945–52. See Appendix of Names.
[2] Lady Diana Abdy.
[3] The marriage of Pamela and Randolph Churchill was dissolved in 1946.
[4] Lord Melchett (1898–1949) married in 1920 Amy Wilson.
[5] Malcolm Bullock (1890–1966). Conservative MP 1923–53. Created baronet 1954.

To Laura Waugh   Old Rectory,
1 August [1945]   Ickleford,
                                                     Hitchin,
                                                     Herts.

Darling Laura,

You will be surprised to hear how I employed this time yesterday – inspecting a herd of Red Polls and their luxurious quarters. We went to luncheon with a neighbour variously named Audrey James-Coates-Marshall-Field-Pleydell-Bouverie[1] in a pretty Queen Anne house with a tutor lover & two pretty sons but whether Coates, Marshall-Fields, or Pleydell-Bouveries, search me. A delicious luncheon & good wine. Then the Red Polls, then back here.

I had been up to London for an almost sleepless night in Park West[2] where Douglas, Mia, Chris and I celebrated Chris's election[3]. Douglas & I had it in mind to give him advice about his proper conduct & appearance in Westminster but he was not receptive and I fear he is content to become a local rather than a national figure.

Our cook has come, a frail gnome of eighty or ninety brought here under false pretences in the belief that there were other servants. I dont think she will live long in the circumstances. So far we have had enough to eat & I sleep well but the house is comfortless & the telephone rings too often. Few of the doors have fastenings and the wind whistles through the house in Pixtonesque style. I am very cold. Please send my grey tweed herring-bone suit.

I am glad the sherry arrived. Your ma wrote to thank for it.

Randolph has recovered his good spirits and is intent on fighting bye-elections.[4]

I have had a letter from the nuns at Stinkers asking to be let off the rent for the last fortnight of their stay. They leave on 12 September.

Basil has given me a ream of this high class pre-war paper.[5]

Do not forget or neglect to send my tweed suit.

All my love
Evelyn

[1] Audrey James was married to Captain Muir Coats 1921–7, to Marshall Field 1930–34, and to Peter Pleydell-Bouverie 1938–46. She died in 1968. Her sons were adopted.

[2] Flats in Edgware Road.

[3] Christopher Hollis had been elected as a Conservative MP.

[4] Randolph Churchill failed to get elected at Preston.

[5] Cheap lined foolscap.

TO TOM DRIBERG
St James' Club.
11 August 1945

Dear Tom

Many thanks for your card. 'Revised' from an early edition for private circulation which had an immodest scene between C. Ryder & Celia in New York; also more of the father who took more than his due space; also more than 24 spelling mistakes in all languages.

My congratulations on retaining your seat. I rejoice that such swift justice befell Churchill for his betrayal of Poland & face the Hooper-Attlee terror with fortitude.[1]

Nancy Mitford sent me to see a *very ugly* picture you had bought. I suggest it goes to the Maclean Youth Centre at Stalingrad. I don't see *Reynold's News* normally but Nancy showed me your article & the picture & I laughed more than I had done since I read J.B.Priestley's contribution to *Horizon* French questionnaire.

Floreat Lancingia.
Evelyn

[1] Clement Attlee had formed a Labour Government on 26 July 1945.

To Laura Waugh   White's.
25 August 1945

Darling Laura

I have regretfully come to the conclusion that the boy Auberon is not yet a suitable companion for me.

Yesterday was a day of supreme self-sacrifice. I fetched him from Highgate, took him up the dome of St Pauls, gave him a packet of triangular stamps, took him to luncheon at the Hyde Park Hotel, took him on the roof of the hotel, took him to Harrods & let him buy vast quantities of toys (down to your account) took him to tea with Maimie who gave him a pound and a box of matches, took him back to Highgate, in a state (myself not the boy) of extreme exhaustion. My mother said 'Have you had a lovely day?' He replied 'A bit dull'. So that is the last time for some years I inconvenience myself for my children. You might rub that in to him.

I had a very enjoyable evening getting drunk at the House of Commons with Hollis & Fraser[1] and the widow Hartington[2] (who is in love with me I think) & Driberg & Nigel Birch[3] & Lord Morris[4] and Anthony Head & my communist cousin Claud Cockburn.

Last night I dined with Maimie. Vsevolode kept going to bed and coming down again.

London is fuller & noisier than ever.

                                                    All my love
                                                    Evelyn

[1] Hugh Fraser (1918–   ), brother of Lord Lovat, had been elected as a Conservative MP. Secretary of State for Air 1962–4.
[2] Kathleen Kennedy's husband the Marquess of Hartington had been killed in the war.
[3] Nigel Birch (1906–   ) had been elected as a Conservative MP. In 1970 he was created Lord Rhyl.
[4] Lord Morris (1903–75). Barrister.

To George Orwell[1]   White's.
30 August [1945]

Dear Mr Orwell,

I am most grateful to you for sending me a copy of your ingenious & delightful allegory.

It was, of course, one of the books I was seeking to buy, and, of course, finding sold-out everywhere.

                                                    Yours sincerely
                                                    Evelyn Waugh

[1] Eric Blair (1905–50). Novelist and essayist under the name George Orwell. *Animal Farm* appeared in 1945, *Nineteen Eighty-Four* in 1949. He intended at the time of his death to write a study of Waugh, using him as an example of the fallacy of the Marxist view that art can only be good if it is progressive.

To A.D.PETERS   Piers Court [1].
20 September 1945

Dear Pete

The answer to the antipodean offer of £75 for serial rights depends on the character of the journal. If it is (a) a struggling literary review (b) a Catholic newspaper – corresponding to *Horizon* or *Catholic Herald* in this country – I accept.

If it is a magazine specializing in fiction, a shiny pseudo-American beastliness; above all if it is illustrated, I refuse.

If it is just a small town evening paper or daily newspaper, it is plainly derisory for them to offer less than they give their local hacks. Do Australian journalists get paid less than £1 a thousand words? If so, and if the paper is respectable, let us accept. But illustrations are barred.

It is a great happiness to be under my own roof but the difficulties of home life are immense; it never stops raining and I have a heavy cold.

                                                          Yours
                                                          Evelyn

[1] The Waughs moved in on 10 September, the nuns moved out on 12 September.

To NANCY MITFORD   Piers Court.
25 September 1945

Darling Nancy

So I am back in my own home & dont give a fig for your Paris. Not that I do not suffer. The planners have diverted the village water supply so I spend most of the day carrying buckets of water from the well to the boilers[?]. The house is shabby & lacking many essential bits such as door keys. The garden is a bombed-site jungle. But there is a fair amount of wine in the cellar & heaps of books I forget having bought.

I went to London for one night for Philip Dunne's wedding [1] – the old number eight commando gang in force and champagne in cascades.

What I am really writing for is to keep a promise to your cousin Randolph. He is as you know now correspondent for an American series of newspapers. He wants what he (& other people) calls 'contacts'. He has seen some of your well-known letters & wants some for himself. He will pay two guineas a week for a weekly letter. I don't know if you would do this. I pass on the offer as he made it. Your name would not appear, your own words would not be quoted. He just wants gossip about Paris. What he writes only appears in U.S.A. No shame, no effort. If you like, write now your first letter to Whites.

I am sorry you have not been able to rewrite the unsatisfactory section of your book [2] in time for the first edition. Start rewriting it *now* for the Penguins. It is the difference (one of 1000 differences) between a real writer & a journalist that she cares to go on improving after the reviews are out & her friends have read it & there is nothing whatever to be gained by the extra work. There is a very good theme in the Spanish refugees camp and it was vicious to falsify the facts to make them fit. The contrast of Linda with her manorial soup and port benefactions and her communist husband with his zeal to re-equip the militant workers for the class struggle in Mexico could be excellent. It would give point to her bewilderment that the Spanish gentry did nothing to help. You could make a dramatic climax in the sailing of the evacuation ship with the communists taking off the distressed families in order to pack it with international thugs.

To revert to Randolph. He does not want you to reveal the state secrets of Fabrice[3] nor yet to say what Millicent Duchess of Sutherland is doing to her villa. Well you know what the boy will want.

The planners are making further cuts in paper imports.

Love from
Evelyn

[1] Philip Dunne married Audrey Rubin 18 September.

[2] *The Pursuit of Love*, 1945. Waugh had looked at the manuscript and made suggestions, including the title.

[3] Gaston Palewski (1901–   ). Directeur du Cabinet for de Gaulle 1942–6; remained loyal to de Gaulle and was President of the Constitutional Council 1965–74. Nancy Mitford's lover and the original of Fabrice in *The Pursuit of Love*.

To Randolph Churchill   Piers Court.
8 October 1945

This morning a rare and beautiful gift arrived for me. I thank you with all my heart. The cigars would have been a keen pleasure at any time; doubly so now for I am living in conditions of Balkan austerity. We have no servants; Laura broods despondently over the kitchen range and periodically raises columns of black smoke, announces that our meat ration has been incinerated, and drives me to dinner at a neighbouring inn. Most of her day is spent in cooking potatoes for the poultry – 27 hens who lay three eggs a day between them. The domestic hot water machine has burst and flooded the kitchen quarters. We have had no hot water for a week. But hungry and dirty as I am I shall now be content for an hour a day for 25 days thanks to your munificence. In 25 days my butler will be out of the army, the plumber will have put in a boiler, a cook may have been found and I may be equipped to invite you to visit me.

I come to London for the day on 26th of this month and will search White's for you.

To the Editor of The Times[1]   Piers Court.
18 December 1945

Sir, – Strong tea with what Mr. Dunlop describes as "a shot" of vodka is indeed a nauseating draught to those who are used to the fine wines of Titian and Velasquez. M. Saurat has the root of the matter but I think he does not draw the right conclusion: "mankind is disillusioned with itself," realizes it is incapable of the great feats of its ancestors, but instead of patiently relearning the forgotten lessons turns meanly towards "something new."

Señor Picasso's painting cannot be intelligently discussed in the terms used of the civilized masters. Our confusion is due to his admirers' constant use of an irrelevant aesthetic vocabulary. He can only be treated as crooners are treated by their devotees. In the United States the adolescents, speaking of music, do not ask: "What do you think of So-and-so?" They say: "Does So-and-so *send* you?" Modern art, whether it is Nazi oratory, band leadership, or painting, aims at a mesmeric trick and achieves either total success or total failure. The large number of otherwise cultured and intelligent people who fall victims to Señor Picasso are not posers. They are genuinely 'sent.' It may seem preposterous to those of us who are immune, but the process is apparently harmless. They emerge from their ecstasy as cultured and intelligent as ever. We may even envy them their experience. But do not let us confuse it with the sober and elevating happiness which we derive from the great masters.

I am, Sir, your obedient servant,
EVELYN WAUGH.

[1] An exhibition of Picasso and Matisse opened at the Victoria and Albert Museum on 5 December and caused a controversy.

To Robin Campbell   Piers Court.
27 December 1945

My dear Robin,
Many thanks for your letter which can only be answered by a complete apologia. In brief:

My letter to *The Times* newspaper[1] was far from being a hoax. It was an attempt to defend friends such as yourself from the charge of depravity and affectation. I believe that we all have a secondary and impure aesthetic sense. Tennyson delighted in smutty doggerel, Ruskin in Kate Greenaway, Betjeman in chapels and so on. I am keenly excited by 19th century book-illumination. I suggested that Picasso-addicts were similarly moved – that the excitement was harmless. Today I am not so sure. You have no doubt read Mr Hobson's[2] letter printed this morning. He claims to have suffered the Aristotelian purge and further says that he emerged from Picasso's exhibition 'dazed' and in a mood in which he could 'hardly bear to look' at the masterpieces of the middle ages and the renaissance. An appalling and significant admission. Mr Hobson's state is, of course, the very antithesis of purgation which must make all the perceptions sharper, the sense that the grass is greener and the birds singing more sweetly. An experience which dazes and leaves one blind to other beauties must be brutish.

To return to your letter. One must distinguish between uses of 'new'. There is the Easter sense in which all things are made new in the risen Christ. A tiny gleam of this is reflected in all true art. Every work of art is thus something new. Just as within the moral framework there is space for infinite variations of behaviour, so within the aesthetic framework. Most so-called innovators have in fact thought themselves revivalists, appealing to an earlier and purer virtue against what they consider the corruption of their immediate predecessors.

Picasso and his kind are attempting something new in the sense of something different in kind. Titian might have thought Frith intolerably common but he would have recognized that he was practising the same art as himself. He could not think this of Picasso. Chaucer, Henry James and, very humbly, myself are practising the same art. Miss Stein is not. She is outside the world-order in which words have a precise and ascertainable meaning and sentences a logical structure. She is aesthetically in the same position as, theologically, a mortal-sinner who has put himself outside the world order of God's mercy.

Picasso fails to be an artist in two essentials. First, in communication. He is hit-or-miss. Nothing is more ludicrous than the posturing of a Svengali who fails to put his Trilby under. The only criticisms valid for him are: 'Ooh, doesn't it make you feel funny inside' or 'the fellow's a charlatan'. You do not hear people say: 'I think the hand is coarsely painted, but what an exquisite angel's head in the left hand corner. And what a lovely landscape through the window.'

He fails, it seems, in the content. Here I must judge at second hand because he fails entirely to put me under, but his addicts tell me his message is one of Chaos and Despair. That is not the message of art. If it were any issue of the *Daily Mirror* would be a supreme aesthetic achievement. You cannot excuse him by saying it is the message of the age and at the same time deny that the age is decadent. Goya, incidentally, was an exact contemporary of Goethe.

It is entirely historical to believe that cultures decline and expire. I believe Western culture to be in rapid decay and that Picasso and Stein are glaring symptoms. You have no authority for saying so jauntily that 'there are a few million years yet'. It is one of the determining conditions of our existence that it may end at any moment, individually or generally but were it true, your assumption would have no bearing on the probability of a new ice-age. Incidentally again, I believe the sin the West is dying of to be Sloth not Wrath as is popularly assumed. It requires constant effort to keep within the world order and our contemporaries are too lazy to make the effort.

Poor Beachcomber[3], a man of high principle, a poet manqué, whom an imprudent marriage has drawn into drudgery. I shall not have his good reason if I develop his few defects. I would greatly prefer to have his virtues than Peter Watson's.

I hope your Christmas was not unduly overcast by the death of Lord Keyes[4].

> Yours ever
> Evelyn

I could write a great deal about primitives and Byzantine mosaics. There is, I believe, a grain of truth in the functionalist chaff; aesthetic value is often the by-product of the artist striving to do something else.

Did you see the exquisite replica of the *Railway Station* on sale in Mount Street? Will you join the Beefsteak?[5]

[1] Campbell had been prompted by Waugh's letter to *The Times* to write defending the new: 'Was it mean of Chaucer not to write like his predecessors? . . . Is it mean of you not to write like Henry James?' He mentions his admiration for Frith, but describes him as an illustrator. 'Is Turner a worse painter than Frith because there is less literary content in his subject matter? . . . Please Evelyn, do not become like Beachcomber . . . . It is most unhistorical to feel all art came to an end some time ago and will never revive. Take heart there are a few million years yet. This is a period which does not inspire "sober and elevating happiness" – nor was that in which Goya worked.

> Love
> Robin

P.S. Was your letter a hoax. . . .'

[2] G.D.Hobson, bibliographer and director of Sotheby's.

[3] J.B.Morton (1893–1979). Columnist in the *Daily Express* from 1924. Married Dr Mary O'Leary in 1927.

[4] Roger Keyes (1872–1945). Admiral of the Fleet 1930. Created Baron Keyes of Zeebrugge, 1943.

[5] Waugh had been elected to this London club on 19 May 1944.

To Nancy Mitford   Piers Court.
5 January 1946

Darling Nancy

Death is not certain; blindness & baldness are. Still it will save you from seeing Picasso & wigs are easier on girls than chaps.

Please, before your sight fails, order Mrs F Greene[1] to send you *The Tablet* and read my opening chapter of the life of the Empress Helena. I want your opinion on it.

This Prod-worship[2] is not healthy. Clever perhaps– good no. You must get a nun to nurse you through your fever. She will explain what goodness is.

I am very jealous of R. Mortimer[3] and Debo[4]. It was unfeeling of you to tell her he was like a wild beast. She was clearly very much over excited before his visit. I hope it was a bitter disappointment.

Picasso is the head of the counter-hons. I went to his disgusting exhibition to make sure. Klee rather old-maidish & sweet in a finicky way. It is a pity you do not read *The Times* Newspaper it has been full of tremendous art balls lately. I have had a great fan mail about Picasso – all from Surrey.

Miss Hunter Dunn is a real person.[5] Her sister is engaged to be married to a Major this morning.

With your resistance weakened by so many dinners at the Dorchester the fever may prove fatal.

My two eldest children are here and a great bore. The elder alternates between strict theology & utter silences; the boy lives for pleasure and is thought a great wit by his contemporaries. I have tried him drunk & I have tried him sober. ...

How nice to be able to read Proust in his own lingo. I tried in Scottish and couldn't get on at all. Take *Henrietta Temple* (Disraeli) to the lazar house.

I have just got to work again on Helena – now the Cinema company from whom I have been happily drawing money all these years suddenly demand my services. It is a great nuisance.

Yesterday I went to an excruciating Pantomime at Bristol. I asked Maria Teresa how she had enjoyed it. 'All except the jokes, papa.'

In a moment of Christmas sentiment I wrote to the nuns who had this house during the war to say I would let them off paying the damages & losses (assessed at £214 by the agents). The Mother Superior wrote to say that she was 'glad our little difficulty was forgotten'.

Our nursery maid at Pixton has fallen ill so Laura goes off there next week leaving me alone here.

A chap I know was lately possessed by the devil and has written a very interesting account of the experience.

I saw Bowra drunk in White's with Smarty[6]. Smarty never comes in now except on Saturdays when one is allowed a guest to luncheon.

The first thing Maria Teresa asked for on her arrival from her middle class convent was a 'serviette-ring'.

Counter Hon Quennell behaved well about *Love* in his *Daily Mail*, I was glad to see. I look for other reviews but don't see them. Your cousin Ed[7] thought the communist part particularly good.

Try not to die. It is the strong ones who go under easiest.

Love
Evelyn

Death to Picasso the head of the Counter Hons.

[1] Molly Friese-Greene had worked at Heywood Hill's bookshop since 1942. Handasyde Buchanan came in 1945. In 1948 they married and in 1959 he became a partner.

[2] Prod is Peter Rodd, Nancy Mitford's husband.

[3] Raymond Mortimer, the literary critic.

[4] Deborah Mitford, now Marchioness of Hartington.

[5] As well as the heroine of a poem by John Betjeman.

[6] Short for Smartyboots, a nickname bestowed on Cyril Connolly by Virginia Woolf.

[7] Lord Stanley.

To PENELOPE BETJEMAN   Piers Court.
15 January [1946]

Darling Penelope

Many months ago I wrote to ask your help with the hipporastic passages of my life of Helena. *The Tablet* had the fruits of my unaided invention. I should welcome detailed criticism. The Empress loses her interest in such things when she is married. I describe her as hunting in the morning after her wedding night feeling the saddle as comforting her wounded maidenhead. Is that O.K.? After that she has no interest in sex.

I have one fan letter from a gentleman in Cheltenham named Meek. Is he a chum of old London life days?

I think it impolite of you to say the story 'came your way'. I sent it.

I also sent John a long letter & had no answer.

I lead a life of extreme ease, Laura one of martyrdom, milking, making beds, mucking out her horses. The only servant in the house is my pre war valet[1]. Laura makes his bed & cooks his meals. My two eldest children are going to suitable schools, (one kept by a conjuror named Dix[2]) the younger two are at their grandmothers. I had the two elder here for Christmas & took them to Bristol pantomime. My daughter complained there were too many jokes. So there were.

DEATH TO PICASSO THE KING OF THE COUNTERHONS

I was puzzled to notice in *The Times* newspaper that there is in fact a family named Hunter Dunn.

Love from
Evelyn

Maurice comes to London as the Guinness girls used to come to Oxford to get drunk.

[1] Ellwood.

[2] F.H.R.Dix, headmaster of All Hallows, was a member of the Magic Circle and sometimes did tricks for the boys.

To A.D.PETERS   Piers Court.
16 January 1946

Dear Pete

1.   Welcome Home
2.   Ghastly about our cigars
3.   Death to Picasso
4.   I have to pay £500 to the socialists. Have I got it?
5.   Here are the contracts. I know they cant force me to write but the dates may provoke them to send impudent letters. By 1952 I may be writing nothing but blank verse dramas or theological tracts.
6.   Thank you for the press-cuttings. Im glad we have shaken off Edmund Wilson at last.[1]
7.   Why should Littlebrown not publish *Campion* in the Spring? It is a book to keep in print & sell steadily for convent prize-givings. It needs no ballyhoo. *When the Going was Good*[2] does not deserve much notice. It is simply a mopping-up

operation. I have cut down the length still further (with benefit) and it is now at the press. I suggest we send Littlebrown a set of proofs as soon as they are available & he publish in the autumn in a modest way. Is he going to give the Jesuits any advance on *Campion*? They are putting up some execrable frescoes with the money & could use it on this deplorable work at once. I hear that Hollis & Carter are not as flush with their paper as is believed. Can we persuade any of the liberated nations to translate *Campion*?

8.   I must come to London to get my hair cut & change books at the London Library. Probably next week. I will tell you when.

9.   'The Quest of the Empress Dowager' is one third written & very good. No money in it for either of us. My wish is to publish it in an edition de grande luxe & perhaps reprint for the general public in five or six years time. Could you in odd moments sniff round & see if any of the private presses – Golden Cockerel, Nonesuch etc. are interested. The yanks will think it awful. If Littlejohn gets cocky we will send it to him as a novel.

10.   I had a very civil letter from Sir Alex Korda's successor. I would like to do my service with him as soon as 'The Quest' is finished. Say in May.

11.   Love to Henrie.

12.   What made Alex Waugh say that Robert Henriques[3] was a good writer?

13.   Emily Eden wrote only two novels, both admirable, at thirty years interval.[4]

Yours ever
Evelyn

[1] Edmund Wilson (1895–1972). The American critic. He discovered Waugh in 1943 and found him 'likely to figure as the only first-class comic genius that has appeared in England since Bernard Shaw': *New Yorker*, 4 March 1944. But *Brideshead Revisited*, which Waugh sent with a friendly note before publication, came 'as a bitter blow to this critic ... [it] turns out to be more or less disastrous': *New Yorker*, 5 January 1946.

[2] Extracts from the travel books, with the exception of *Robbery Under the Law*, published in one volume in England and America, 1946.

[3] Robert Henriques (1905–67). Writer and farmer.

[4] *The Semi-Detached House*, 1859 and *The Semi-Attached Couple*, published in 1860 but written in 1830.

To ROBERT HENRIQUES   Piers Court.
24 January 1946

Dear Robert,

I am at work on a description of the Empress Helena's visit to Jerusalem in about 330 AD. My authorities are all either Christian or atheist. Can you, I wonder, put me onto any Jewish books in English that would help? What I need is a description of the Jews in Palestine after the destruction of the temple and anything on the antiquities and authenticity of the sites. Do you know anything?

Also, can you tell me anything about the Wandering Jew? Is he purely a mediaeval Christian legend or does he correspond to any tradition of your Faith?

Please forgive me for pestering you in this way. You are the only religious Jew of my acquaintance.

Yours ever
Evelyn Waugh

To Nancy Mitford   Piers Court.
28 January [1946]

Dear Nancy,

My little trip to London passed in a sort of mist. Did I ever come to visit you again after my first sober afternoon. If so, I presume I owe you flowers. I left a trail of stunted & frightfully expensive hyacinths behind me. On the last evening I dimly remember a dinner party of cosmopolitan ladies where I think I must have been conspicuous. Were you there? I awoke with blood on my hands but found to my intense relief that it was my own. I sometimes think I am getting too old for this kind of thing.

I have just read an essay by a jew which explains the Mitford sobriety and other very peculiar manifestations of the family. You all live on a single plane. There is a lucid diagram of a flight of stairs to explain this. It is called *Yogi & Commisar II*[1] I believe this jew is a chum of S. Boots Esq & all the little bootses.

Business. I have got a working edition of Gibbon so only want 4to now. Are you a newsagent? If so please send me *Horizon, Polemic, Contact*, and all the Boots & counter Boots journals regularly. Please send E.M.Forster's lecture reviewed by Desmond yesterday.[2]

Please send the two Penguin pamphlets about counterhon painters[3] reviewed yesterday too. (*Sunday Times*).

Please get me sets of Cambridge Ancient Modern & Mediaeval History.

Also Oxford Books English & Victorian Verse.

Also Eliz. Bowen's book when published. End of Business.

I was asked to tea by Andrew to meet Debo but had the decency to refuse. She would have thought me a wilder beast than Mortimer.

I was sent a tiny box of completely unsmokable cigars on which I had to pay a prodigious fine by whom do you think? Sergeant P.

My great new friend B.H.Bennett has turned absolutely beastly to me.

Sykes seems the main source of the tale that the Bootses hate your charming book. I heard it several times but in each case traced it back to Sykes. It is generally said in Whites that your dedication to the Polish fascist[4] is a blind & that the real Fabrice is someone named Roy. I gave no opinion on this but nodded sagely.

I go today for two nights to my beloved Asquiths at Mells where Picasso is not mentioned. I am taking my unhappy little boy to his first boarding school. He is going in a high state of pleasurable excitement poor beast. I think he lives on one plane like the Mitfords.

Can you politely ask any of your jewish friends whether they know the sources of the Wandering Jew legend? Encyclopaedia Brit. is very weak on the subject. I am introducing him (B.Howard again) into the Helena book & would like to get the full facts.

I say is this all right; I am bringing out a book of extracts from my travel books & dedicating it to all the people the original books were dedicated to. One was Diana Mosley. Will she mind or be quite pleased? Should I ask her? I can't just say Diana because there is a second Diana (Cooper) so I have to put Mosley & that means I have to put Bryan Moyne. It is a point of delicacy but perhaps I am scrupulous[5].

I am having a very interesting correspondence with Mrs Betjeman about horses & sex. Half of it gets confiscated in the post by the socialists.

Death to Picasso. I had $\frac{1}{4}$ of wild beast Mortimer's article sent me by a press agency. What these wild beasts can't realise is that Picasso is old and has been at his dirty work for decades, so it is no use their saying 'You cannot appreciate this glorious genius because he is New and you are too crusted to receive new impressions.' The pure clear witness against him grows with the years. You are all either dupes or traitors. You are a traitor.

Love from
Evelyn

[1] Arthur Koestler, *The Yogi and the Commissar*, 1945.
[2] *The Developments of English Prose between 1918 and 1939.*
[3] *Edward Burra* by John Rothenstein and *Victor Pasmore* by Clive Bell.
[4] Gaston Palewski.
[5] *When the Going was Good* is dedicated to Bryan Moyne, Diana Mosley, Diana Cooper, Perry and Kitty Brownlow and the memory of Hazel Lavery.

To Mrs Reeve of Life Magazine [1]   Piers Court.
31 January 1946

Dear Madam:
I have read your letter of yesterday with curiosity and re-read it with compassion. I am afraid you are unfamiliar with the laws of my country. The situation is not that my co-operation is desirable, but that my permission is necessary, before you publish a series of photographs illustrating my books. I cannot find any phrase in your letter that can be construed as seeking permission.

You say: "Without consulting you the project will be like blind flying". I assure you it will be far more hazardous. I shall send a big blue incorruptible policeman to lock you up and the only "monumental" work Mr Scherman is likely to perform is breaking stones at Dartmoor (our Zing Zing).

Yours faithfully,
Evelyn Waugh

[1] A letter had arrived informing Waugh that *Life* magazine planned 'a photographic feature dramatizing character and scenes from your novels ... we face a monumental job ....'

To ROBERT HENRIQUES   Piers Court.
2 February 1946

Dear Robert,

It is very good of you to take so much trouble. As a novelist you will know the kind of material I want.

How far, for instance, was Hadrian's law putting Jerusalem out of bounds to Jews ever put into force? Did they begin to return by the third century? There seem to have been plenty about in the fourth century when the Emperor Julian began rebuilding the temple. Were they living outside the prohibited area in affluence and security? And so on. There are endless questions which the right books, if you can put me on to them, might solve. The period is fascinating.

The Wandering Jew is plainly a fairy tale and in its modern Matheson Lang[1] form is of reformation origin but there are glimpses of it in other shapes in the Christian middle ages. I wondered if there was any parallel in your folk lore – a Jewish Rip-Van-Winkle? One often finds identical stories in widely separated mythologies.

. . . I am delighted that you liked *Brideshead*. I was pleased with it at the time but I have been greatly shaken by its popularity in U.S.A.

My regards to your wife,

Yours ever,
Evelyn

[1] Matheson Lang (1879–1948). Actor who played Matthias in *The Wandering Jew* by Temple Thurston in 1920. The Jew was burnt at the stake.

To NANCY MITFORD   Piers Court.
4 February 1946

Dearest Nancy,

Since sending you a post-card today I purchased the *New Statesman*. I thought 'Reeds'[1] review of your book egregiously silly both in praise & blame. I love all the Mitford childhood, as you know, but to single out the buffoon father while totally ignoring the unique children's underground movement is brutish. He calls your one false character 'a brilliant sketch'[2]. You know better than I how wrong he is about Fabrice. The review irritated me greatly. I wonder who it is who writes it. Plainly a homosexual; perhaps a Lesbian?

I looked at other pages of the paper & was astounded that you take it in. I read Eddie [Sackville-West] describing the use of the word 'brothel' on the wireless as 'a refreshing experience which spoke eloquently of the intelligence, sanity and good feeling of ordinary people'. I read 'Nothing can stop big Powers bullying their small neighbours if they wish to do so'. Last time I had the paper in the house it was boiling to attack Germany & Italy for no other reason. I read the wild beast saying that Mr Sutherland's painting 'rivals butterflies wings in delicacy.'[3]

The only thing that made any sense in the paper was a grovelling apology to a soldier they had insulted, but that had been dictated, presumably, by some intelligent solicitor.

How can you read it? It explains all that modern trash that encumbers your shop.

Evelyn

[1] Henry Reed (1914–   ). Poet who worked for the BBC.
[2] Talbot, the middle-class communist in *The Pursuit of Love*.
[3] Raymond Mortimer was reviewing *The Approach to Painting* by Thomas Bodkin.

To Lady Mary Lygon   Piers Court.
4 February 1946

Darling Blondy

Thank you very much for your beautiful letter. I long to see you. I came to London for a day but behaved very badly owing to not being used to wine and I went to a dinner party of fashionable cosmopolitans & broke a brandy glass & cut my hand & a footman had to bandage it and I sat next to Serpent Laycock and I told her about a young gentleman who committed suicide by tying up his cock with catgut so that he could not pee and so burst & this sad true story instead of exciting compassion in the snake excited loathing of me though it was not I who tied up this young gentleman's cock. Then I kissed farter Mrs Maugham[1] and had to go away so I thought at least there is one person in the world who will not despise me for my pitiable condition & that is Captain Bennett so I went to his mean little room in his hotel but he despised me more than Snake and I thought God I have sunk low if I am despised for drunkenness by B.H.Bennett.

My book has been a great success in the United States which is upsetting because I thought it in good taste before and now I know it can't be and I shall not even have much money on account of the New Deal & the late Mr Roosevelt and the socialists here taking it all away.

So Tom Vesey[2] is dead R.I.P. In August 1939 he laughed fit to bust his pants when I asked him to make me a soldier. You're far too old and soft he said. Now he is dead & I am alive and kicking.

Your god-son behaved very well throughout his Christmas holidays so I have sent him to a boarding school for a reward. The headmaster is named Mr Dix and he does conjuring tricks. It is quite near where the railway bridge fell down yesterday so the papers tell me.

I think B.H.Bennett is intriguing to be made an alderman of the City of London that is why he is so pompous & smug & wholly detestable. My word if he becomes Lord Mayor we will mock his Show.

I am writing a very beautiful book about Penelope Betjeman's early sex life called 'The Life of the Empress Helena'. I think Constantine is a Saint in your Church[3]. He is a shit in my book so I expect you will be forbidden to read it.

I have a partridge and a woodcock for dinner tonight. Laura is to have half the partridge. Which is very generous of me but she does not often have anything to eat and she works very hard and is soon to have another baby and if you cut it cleverly you can leave half the breast on one's own half of the partridge. I shall also let her have $\frac{1}{4}$ bottle of claret so it will be a lovely evening for her and I will have $\frac{3}{4}$ so it will be lovely for me but there are not many such evenings in my home.

There is a hill near here called Hetty Pegler's Tump.

I will be in London on 22nd of this month & will try & see you and draw patterns with you for p.work quilts.

I do not think a table made of butterfly's wings will stand very hard wear unless it was a very big butterfly.

I hope you did not go & see the disgusting paintings by Picasso.

One good result of my humiliating success in U.S.A. is that the publishers send me havana cigars. I will bring you one. They are not very good but better than we are used to now.

This interesting coupon will enable you to write to America free or anywhere else. A yank sent it to me hoping for an answer but did he get one, no.

I fell in love with a film actress named Miss Todd dressed as a schoolgirl. [4]

Love and xxxs
Bo

[1] Syrie Maugham.
[2] Thomas Vesey (1885–1946). Brother of the fifth Viscount.
[3] The son of Helena is a saint in the Russian Orthodox Church.
[4] Ann Todd in *The Seventh Veil*.

To Nancy Mitford   Piers Court.
5 February [1946]

Darling Nancy

I seem to write to you twice a day.

£2000 is the least you should take, £5000 the most you can hope for for film rights. It will be a lump sum, not royalties. If you were not a socialist I should advise you to have it paid in two instalments on Apr. 6th 1947 and 1948 so that it does not all go to the State, but of course, that is what you like.

Whose ball? Why was I not asked? Why was Quennell asked? He should not be allowed to see, let alone meet, still less criticise a debutante.

Ever since I bought that terrible socialist paper I have been haunted by the image of Eddie sitting night after night beside his loud-speaker with strained face, waiting for the word 'brothel'. At last his vigil is rewarded and his faith in the decency of common humanity is restored. I know him so little. It does not at all square with Uncle Davey [1]. I re-read his essay on Mr Sutherland last night & studied the 'butterfly plumage' of the Penguin reproductions. [2]

You are all stark mad in London.

E

Commerce: No books have come tho several I ordered were modern trash.

[1] In *The Pursuit of Love*.

[2] Edward Sackville-West wrote a book on Graham Sutherland in the Penguin Modern Painters series.

To Life Magazine   Piers Court.
7 February 1946

Dear Mr Osborne:

I dont know how I have given you and Mrs Reeve and Mr Scherman the impression that I seek popularity for my books among those who cannot read. I have tried to give the literate all the information they need about my characters. If I have failed, I don't believe you can help me.

I am sure it is not your fault and that you are being bothered by some boss in the United States. Take heart; he has forgotten all about it already. I was once a journalist for seven weeks and I know about bosses. They are volatile creatures.

But if this preposterous project has become a fixed idea with the man and you would like to see me, by all means come. I cannot ask you to stay as I have no cook or housemaids; there is a neighbouring inn. Have you a bicycle? I live seven miles from Stroud station. I am always here and can give you a glass of port on your arrival and plenty of dry bread.

Please do not telephone.

Yours sincerely,
Evelyn Waugh

To A.D.Peters   Piers Court.
25 February [1946]

Dear Pete,

I have been bothered for some weeks by some yanks named Life & Time. Their first modest suggestion was that I should supply the names of all the people from whom the characters in my novels were drawn & arrange for them to sit for their photographs. No amount of rudeness has shaken off these pests & yesterday a feeble minded young man named Osborne arrived on my door-step. Their present proposition is more reasonable. That I should write them an article about my characters and supply help to an artist who will do sketches of them. This I think I can honourably do. I told the balmy fellow to apply to you for terms. Make them stiff. I am not particularly anxious to do it at all & would only do it for a sum that would leave an appreciable amount after tax was paid. Can they arrange to pay it in this country so as to avoid U.S. taxation? Can they pay it in kind?

Mr Osborne has an impediment in his speech perhaps due to drink.

Yours
Evelyn

To Randolph Churchill   Piers Court.
[April 1946]

Notes on Nuremberg

Surrealist spectacle. Two buildings standing – a luxury hotel & a luxury law-courts – amid acres of corpse scented rubble. Kaiser William baroque hall, functional light, functional furniture, a continuous parrot-house chatter of interpreters. Interpretation almost simultaneous. Curious sensation of seeing two big men bullyragging & their voices coming through the head phones in piping female tones with American accent. Obvious irony of Russian bullet-headed automata sitting on judges bench. Russian delegation all in top boots epaulets, everyone else in plain clothes. Russians sit immobile listening hard, quite bemused, as strange as renaissance Venetian ambassadors at the court of Persia. Whenever 'Russia' is spoken they all start guiltily & their spokesman leaps up to say 'I protest that that question is anti-democratic, irrelevant, fascist, cannibalistic & contrary to the Atlantic charter.' Then Lord Justice Lawrence[1] (an entirely admirable man) says: 'It is an entirely proper question' and the trial proceeds. The English are top dogs. Our lawyers six times abler than anyone else. French & Yanks openly admiring. Only obvious criminal in the dock is Kaltenbrunner[2] who is a cross between Noel Coward & Fitzroy Maclean (in appearance). Goering has much of Tito's matronly appeal. Ribbentrop was like a seedy schoolmaster being ragged. He knows he doesn't know the lesson & he knows the boys know. He has just worked out the sum wrong on the blackboard & is being heckled. He has lost his job but has pathetic hope that if he can hold out to the end of term he may get a 'character' to another worse school. He lies quite instinctively & without motive on quite unimportant points.

With six or seven exceptions the entire occupying force are [preposterously?] Jewish because the only Yanks who speak German are first generation immigrants. They spend the day photographing one another doing Nazi salutes on the rostrum at the Sports Palace.

Hundreds of languid, blasé, highly painted, rather hideous young women-secretaries make continuous round of cocktail parties & dinner parties. All in different corners of the same hotel. 'Oh dear I promised to go to the French and the Romanians & I must dress early for the Procurator General's. I must fly.' The flight is to cross the lounge to another group.

Unemployed barristers enjoying a free holiday V.I.P.

Surprising esprit de corps among English lawyers. They are not at all blasé. Working very hard & believing their work historically important.

Please do not quote me in any sense which would seem to show me ungrateful to my hosts or sceptical of their good work. In fact please do not quote me at all.

[1] Geoffrey Lawrence (1880–1971). President of the International Military Tribunal, Nuremberg, 1945–6. Created Baron Oaksey in 1947.

[2] Ernst Kaltenbrunner, Chief of Secret Police and so director of Himmler's organization.

To NANCY MITFORD   Piers Court.
Maundy Thursday [18 April] 1946

Darling Nancy

Paris was heaven but goodness it was exhausting. It so much overexcites me nowadays to meet new people that I cannot sleep after it. I should be neither genial nor génial after a second Thursday at Mme Bouquets. I still lie awake thinking of the adventuress who pouched the forks. As for the Colonel, he is never out of [my] thoughts – the Beauty.

I should like very much to know more of Quennell. At five a.m. on my last morning he had a seizure brought on by sexual excess.[1] Did he die of it?

I delivered the ribbon at Corporal Hill's[2] & had a civil letter of thanks from Mrs Friese-Green. With Debo I was less successful. I went to her slum & found her door surrounded by unemptied dustbins, dead flowers & empty bottles; all windows shut; a telephone ringing unanswered upstairs – plainly the scene of a sex-murder so I went away, wrote to her (to the scene of the outrage) saying the hat[3] was at White's to be called for, but have heard nothing since.

The customs-men were most obliging. I had a big cargo by the time I left – millinary, champagne, cheese, scent, toys, etc. They said: 'Lets call it a fiver'.

I have put myself on a Belsen diet for Holy Week & feel alternately faint & furious.

All my children are here for the holidays – merry, affectionate, madly boring – except Harriet who has such an aversion to me that she screams when she catches sight of me a hundred yards away.

My garden is not at all like Sir Leicester Kroesig's[4] at the moment. Laura has bought a minute tractor, like a doll's pram, and has ploughed every available rood up to the windows in order to grow kale & mangolds. I run behind collecting bulbs in full flower as she turns them up. I have been elected chairman of the Parish Council. I have also been to a cocktail party where the smart hunting set were segregated from the dowdy village worthies in two rooms. Laura & I were put in the dowdy room in spite of the fantasies in her hair.

Love from
Evelyn

[1] In fact a hangover.
[2] Heywood Hill.
[3] A white felt hat with stuffed doves and feathers which Waugh selected, tried on and gave to Lady Hartington, who wrote: 'It will be a giver of confidence when opening fêtes.'
[4] 'A lady water-colourist's heaven, herbaceous borders, rockeries and water-gardens were carried to a perfection of vulgarity and flaunted a riot of huge and hideous flowers. . . .' *The Pursuit of Love.*

To RANDOLPH CHURCHILL   Piers Court.
12 May 1946

Dear Randolph

You display the most exquisite delicacy in your attentions. The cheese reposes in a temperature of 65°, ripening gently. When it comes to the table there will be tears of gratitude in my eyes & in Laura's if I allow her a little piece. Thank you very much.

Lord FitzWilliam & Col Stirling are the chief movers in the cocacola plot.[1] I am told the concoction causes insomnia, garrulity and early impotence. Please denounce this obscene traffic.

Douglas Woodruff has been staying with me. I mentioned to him that you maintain a network of overpaid informers. I thought his ears pricked as though he might wish to enter your service.

> Yours affectionately
> Evelyn

[1] Negotiations for the Coca Cola franchise for the north of England were not completed.

To Maurice Bowra   Piers Court.
[May 1946]

Dear Maurice

An entirely delightful visit. Thank you with all my heart.

... I looked up effete. It means primarily 'having given birth'. The dictionary is an endless source of surprise and pleasure. Lady Pakenham is the archetype of effeteness rather than E Sackville-West, it seems.

> Yours ever
> Evelyn

To Nancy Mitford   Piers Court.
8 June [1946]

Darling Nancy

I am off to Spain next week so will you please ask Prod & Picasso & Huxley and all your bolshie chums to postpone their invasion until the second week in July when it will be all clear.

I suppose you will not come back to this country[1]. You are very wise. The food gets drearier & drearier. Today the Government are staging the most extraordinary masquerade[2]. Mr Attlee[3] & Mr Chuter Ede[4] (they and no others of the Cabinet) are driving round London in a carriage borrowed from the King, representing themselves to the lower classes as the men who won the war. It seems an odd choice even for Mr Attlee as he could have found two or three colleagues who were at least doing some kind of work however mischievous. But no Attlee & Ede it is. Behind them follow a ramshackle troop of Brazilians, Mexicans, Egyptians (Egyptians!)

Naafi waitresses etc. All the builders erect grandstands & triumphal arches for this exhibition of vanity.

The Stinchcombe Parish Council under my chairmanship voted that no celebrations were to be held here.

I have been reading your Stanley letters[5] again with intense delight. I think they should come out again soon. If you would like it I will mention it at Chapman & Halls. I rather favour an omnibus. Would you be ready to write a new introduction. The last was topical and subversive.

I long to hear about your American public. Are you greatly troubled by admirers.

Do you want any money? I owe you I dont know how much for Debo's hat. Shall I tell that tricky looking frog who publishes for me, to make some cash over to you? Would you like all my francs? I don't think there are many of them but you are welcome to what there are. It must be a great expense keeping the colonel[6].

I went to Oxford for their Eights Week Debate & stayed with Maurice [Bowra] in complete comfort. I should have thought my Union speech a great success if I had not heard the previous speakers & seen the audience falling off their benches with laughter at the most banal jokes. Then they rolled about for me too but it was not so gratifying as if I had been the only speaker and not known how easy technicians are to amuse. They all treated me with great respect & tenderness as a ghost from *Sinister Street*. I liked *that* very much.

If Spender or Quennell do not blow me up I return from Spain in July & set up at Hyde Park Hotel.

I went to London once to get my hair cut & hurried home aghast at all I saw. I looked into your shop. There was a woman like an elementary school teacher in your chair. Handycrafts[7] tried to make me pay 12 guineas for a book I had lately bought for 7/6. He has quite lost his reason about prices. Nothing under a tenner & most of his battered works £25 or £50.

Graham Greene has gone to live in Kenya.

I have written a treatise on wine – very bad – for Vsevolode. Maimie's nasty little dog was kidnapped & held to ransom. She paid up.

Laura has bought another cow & two pigs.

It never stops raining.

Do you know a very nice war hero called Bill Deakin[8]?

Can you get rubber corsets in Paris, Laura asks. It is very important to have them after having a baby.[9] If they are procurable do send her a pair by the next chap coming over. I will try in Salamanca but I do not speak *any* Spanish so shopping will be difficult. Also my memory is that Spanish shops are never open.

Your god-daughter[10] is wilfully backward & will not speak though her face is alive with malevolent intelligence.

I think of you with compassion every Thursday at 6 p.m. & with envy all the rest of the week.

Best love
Evelyn

---

[1] Nancy Mitford lived in France for the rest of her life.

[2] Victory Day Parade.

[3] Clement Attlee, Prime Minister 1945–51.

[4] J. Chuter Ede, Home Secretary. He had been Parliamentary Secretary to the Ministry of Education 1940–45.

[5] *The Stanleys of Alderley*, edited by Nancy Mitford, 1934. There was a new edition in 1968.

[6] Gaston Palewski.

[7] Handasyde Buchanan.

[8] F. W. Deakin (1913–   ). Led first British Military Mission to Tito, May 1943. Warden of St Antony's College, Oxford, 1950–68. Knighted 1975.

[9] James was not born until 30 June.

[10] Harriet, just two.

TO JOHN BETJEMAN   Piers Court.
11 June [1946]

My Dear John

There is nothing painful about writing letters provided one writes nothing else. I have given up work of all kind.

That is one objection to the proposal you kindly make. The whole suggestion is repugnant. (a) to lunching with Mr Burns. Where would he take me? Some ghastly London restaurant & starve & poison me I have no doubt & expose me to insult from socialist servants & make me see women in trousers with hair like rubber sponges, and give me no wine. No that would not do. (b) Broadcasting, supposing it could be arranged without a visit to the Dorchester Hotel, would still be obnoxious. You see the lower classes dont read books but they do listen to the wireless and when they have heard anyone speak they think this constitutes an introduction & warrants their leering knowingly ''Eard you on the air last night Mr Betjeman. Our Gladys said Why if that isn't Mr Betjemans voice and we looked it up in the paper and it was'.

Of course in order to earn a living (ha ha) it is unavoidable that one exposes oneself to ridicule & obloquy now & then but the BBC pay so little & expect so much time & trouble that it is not worth while. It is better to write occasionally for the magazines.

I have not forgiven you for deserting me at Oxford. In your place they put a facetious negro[1]. But I stayed two nights with Maurice in complete comfort, & bought a nice copy of Edmund Evans *Chronicle of England*[2] for 3/6 at the Turl Bookshop, so the expedition was a success.

. . . On Saturday d.v. I go to Salamanca to celebrate the fourth century of the death of a Thomist philosopher[3] whose name escapes me.

D'Arcy on Love[4] much harder to understand than Nancy Mitford on same subject.

Americans write to me by every post, O God.

My love to Penelope.

I shall be alone in London at Hyde Park Hotel all July. Ask me out, take me about, draw me out of myself, show me how the other half of the world lives.

Your rival reviewer Quennell had a seizure brought on by sexual excess[5] in the British Embassy Paris – the seizure was there not the excess.

Yours ever
Evelyn

[1] Professor Fernando Henriques (1916–77). Director of Centre for Multi-racial Studies at Sussex University since 1964. Committed suicide in 1977.
[2] James Doyle, *A Chronicle of England*, 1864, printed by Evans.
[3] Francisco de Vittoria (1485–1546).
[4] Martin D'Arcy sj, *The Mind and Heart of Love*, 1946.
[5] Hangover.

To Laura Waugh   Hotel Parador,
18 June [1946]   Condestable,
                                        Burgos.

Darling Laura,

I am very much ashamed to have let three days pass without writing. But they have been very curious days. Instead of the pious & peaceful retreat at Salamanca which I expected I find myself whirled round Castile to a series of mayoral receptions conducted tours & endless drives in a decrepit charabanc. The Pax Romana Congress is postponed a week so Douglas[1] & I have gate-crashed a quite different party of international jurists. We are addressed always as Professors. We have sharp alternations of starvation & gluttony which have knocked out two professors already but I am in good health & enjoying myself in a dazed kind of way. Mary Campbell[2] was on our aeroplane. I taxed her with not having answered your letter. She lied & said she had never had it, gave herself away, recovered with clumsy further lies & suffered, I think, in the process. She was travelling with a very pretty man rather like Robin. I shall not bring back much from Spain as the famine here is worse than England & prices are enormous. Even sherry is as expensive in Madrid as in London. The weather is delicious – not at all too hot. The correct dress for a country outing is a suit of black broadcloth, stiff white collar, no hat. Very odd. No signs of Liz[3]. A Miss Cope was put in my charge by her mother (of Bramshill) but I have lost her since the first day.[4]

All my love
Evelyn

[1] Douglas Woodruff organized the expedition.
[2] Robin Campbell's first wife, Mary Ormsby-Gore.
[3] Probably Lady Elizabeth Paget (1916–80). A niece of Lady Diana Cooper, she had married Raimund von Hofmannsthal in 1939.
[4] 'Miss Cope was met by friends.' *Diaries*.

To Nancy Mitford   Hyde Park Hotel.
7 August [1946]

Darling Nancy

My last day in London & goodness I am pleased. Without you at Heywood Hills my days have been empty. It is six weeks now I have been sitting about in hotels & clubs bored bored bored.

Last week was made hideous by the arrival of a Hungarian countess who pretended to be a French poet[1]. An egocentric maniac with the eyes of a witch. All the ladies fell at her feet to be hobbled over. I understood it in tender creatures like Diana & Miss Capel[2] but when I found stout old hearts like Venetia's[3] & Daphne's[4] bleeding, dripping oozing, I felt sick to the stomach. She is the Spirit of France. How I hate the French. They are sending us Camembert cheese made of UNRA dried milk. It turns to chalk & moss instead of melting. Also they are deliberately destroying all the Rhine vineyards. They have even stopped doing the one thing they are good at – making wine – and mix it all up in milk churns & send it to us labelled 'Burgundy' & 'Claret', quite simply. Down with the beastly French. At least you have had the better taste to choose a Pole.

... I have given a series of champagne parties hoping to make some nice new friends – old cronies turned up with gratifying regularity but no one new. Debo has disappeared from my life & heart.

I sent you my second barrel at Smarty boots[5]. I think I shook out a few feathers. His stock is *very* low even in the Dorchester Hotel.

Randy has been roaring round insulting Lords Kemsley, Camrose & Rothermere.[6]

I am rather keen on Miss Capel.

I went to a circus entirely run by half-witted boys. Such a good idea. They get on far better with the animals than sane people & tumble about as clowns with great seriousness.

Is the Heath case[7] reported in France. It has been a very clever move by the socialist government to take the housewife's mind off her troubles. Just as the French (Bah!) did with Landru at the time of the massacre at Smyrna. Strachey & Co got two loyal socialist girls & carved them up in the most imaginative way & are trying an airman who is the dead spit of Beverley Nichols for murder. No one now mentions bread rationing or Palestine.

Very sad & shocking about Diane.[8]

Maimie was burgled last night & lost 48 bottles of Pol Roget, 6 whiskey and a gold cigarette case.

I went with Harry to the Marx brothers. He fell fast asleep as he sat down & snored until we had to go. He said he found the film disappointing.

Not legible?

                                                        Best love
                                                        Evelyn

[1] Louise de Vilmorin (1902–69). French poet, playwright and novelist. Married Count Paul Palffy in 1937.

[2] June Capel (1920–   ). Married to Franz Osborn 1948–54, and to Lord Hutchinson since 1966.

[3] Venetia Montagu.

[4] Viscountess Weymouth.

[5] 'Palinurus in Never-Never Land', Waugh's review of Cyril Connolly's *The Unquiet Grave*, had been published in *The Tablet* on 27 July. 'A Pilot All at Sea' had appeared also in *The Tablet* on 10 November, 1945.

[6] Proprietors of the *Sunday Times*, the *Daily Telegraph* and the *Daily Mail*.

[7] Neville Heath was hanged in October for the murder of Margery Gardner.

[8] Lady Diana Abdy had had a serious car accident.

To Nancy Mitford   Piers Court.
26 August [1946]

Darling Nancy

Of course I revere saints. I mentioned them not as a further cause of complaint but as the one good thing about the frogs. But the saints, you see, are the opposite of modern French culture & they find it almost impossible to lead normal lives with their fellow countrymen, they have to go into convents or be missionaries. The French are absolutely splendid missionaries.

They are not 'low' in the way Hindus & Egyptians & most Americans are. They are an ingenious & discriminating people who have deliberately chosen the evil way. It comes out in anything they have done for centuries. One typical manifestation is their giving up everything that is meant by Chivalry – which was originally their invention. But of course when they are touched by Grace they are all the nobler for the qualities that make them so very vile in their corruption.

Saints are people who have a peculiar intimacy with God and as a result give evidence of sublime virtues and usually of miraculous powers. You can never understand them unless you start with God, then go to man as his creation – a special order of being with unique limitations, opportunities & obligations. Saints are simply men & women who have fulfilled their natural obligation which is to approach God. It is in that that all mankind has a different nature from the rest of the animal kingdom.

There is no such thing as a 'religious temperament' or a 'religious type'. Saints are as different from one another as it is possible for humans to be. St Thomas More, Bernadette, John of the Cross, etc. all wildly different. But some nations, probably in providence because of their greater spiritual dangers, tend to produce more saints than others. U.S.A. have not produced one except an Italian-born immigrant[1]. France hundreds, of all types. It is to make up for the Zolas & Gambettas[2] & Martys & Picassos. By the way a league has been formed 'to counteract the evil influence of French painting'. Headquarters suitably at Kelmscott Manor. I have joined you bet. It is called 'Rhodian'. Why?

———————

I have just come back from a week-end at Pamela Berry's.[3] Very luxurious. Betjeman came over & read poetry. Most enjoyable. I went to call on Peter Fleming who lives next door. Too extraordinary. He is very rich and has built himself the most hideous little Golders Green villa. He farms 2000 acres & never has an egg or a pat of butter & lives on rations from the local Cooperative Stores. He dresses in khaki shorts & military shirt. His wife[4] has had to leave the stage because they have no cook.

The Betjemans both put on Jaeger combinations on the 1st of September & keep them on for all purposes until the 2nd week of May. A horse sleeps in the kitchen.

What is a Mé. Cant find it in Cassells dictionary.

Daisy F[5] is said to have taught Gerald B[erners] to take cocaine.

Deauville is full of stranded chums who cant cash a cheque to get home.

The price of the vile French wine they send us is 3 times what good wine was in 1939. We all *hate* it. The Camembert cheese are all made of chalk & never ripen do what one will to them. No one here thinks them delicious but they are one better than Woolton-Strachey's 'Processed'.

There is a better Brogan than yours. Colm[6]. A brother?

Love from
Evelyn

[1] Mother Cabrini, born in Lombardy 1850, died in Chicago 1917.

[2] Léon Gambetta (1838–82). French republican politician.

[3] Lady Pamela Berry (1914–   ). Daughter of first Lord Birkenhead, married in 1936 Michael Berry who was created Baron Hartwell in 1968. She lived at Oving House near Aylesbury.

[4] Celia Johnson (1908–   ). She returned to the stage in the title role of *St Joan* the next year, after a five-year absence during which she made several films including *Brief Encounter* (1946).

[5] Marguerite, the daughter of the Duc de Decazes and the widow of Prince Jean de Broglie, married in 1919 Reginald Fellowes (1884–1953). Her fortune derived from Singer sewing-machines. Publicized as the best-dressed woman in the world. Died 1962.

[6] Colm Brogan (1902–   ). Journalist in Glasgow until 1946, then in London. Brother of Sir Denis Brogan the historian.

To A.D.Peters
Piers Court.

[Received 23 September 1946]

Dear Pete

Thank you for your letter & *The Bookseller*. The notice ought to annoy Sir Stanley Onion[1].

I should like to leave C & H lock stock & barrel but only for a firm like Macmillan. I suppose that legally I am free to go as they have broken their contract by allowing the books to go out of print, but I should not wish to take advantage of this, nor would a respectable firm I imagine.

If a deal could be arranged later by which I went to Macmillan or a firm of equal respectability, I should welcome it but it doesn't seem likely. Anyway I think we should wait a bit. I shant have another novel for them for a few years anyway[2]. . . .

Yours
Evelyn

[1] Sir Stanley Unwin (1884–1960). Chairman of Allen & Unwin. In *The Bookseller*, 12 September, it was announced that Evelyn Waugh was retiring as a director of Chapman & Hall.

[2] Waugh had protested about John McDougall, new to the firm, being promoted over F.B.Walker, who had been with them through the war. McDougall became a lifelong friend. See Appendix of Names.

To A.D.Peters   Piers Court.
3 October [1946]

Dear Pete

I have no insuperable artistic scruples about their filming any book except *Brideshead*. I should greatly prefer, however, to be allowed to write all additional dialogue.

I should like to take Laura for a jaunt to Hollywood in February. The sort of offer I should find most attractive would be a tax-free trip, lecture-free, with a minimum of work of any kind at the other end. Luxury not lionization is the thing. And all trouble spared me of getting permits & booking cabins etc.

The sum paid beyond that is not of great interest. I should like to have it by instalments if it is large. With enough pocket money for us to do some shopping in New York.

Yours
Evelyn

To Nancy Mitford   Piers Court.
16 October [1946]

Darling Nancy

It was indeed a bitter disappointment to us both to learn that we shall not see you. My only consolation is that my water supply failed last night so that your visit would not have been comfortable.

I must beg you with all earnestness if we are to continue friends, never use the word 'progressive' in writing to me. It upsets me more than 'note paper' upset your fastidious father. It makes me sick and agitated for hours to read it. Please please never again.

There was so much I wanted to talk about & was keeping for your visit. Now 'progressive' has dried up all my sympathy. I could have spoken with feeling about Debo's future love life.

I do not know your friend R.Mortimer. I understand. ... [a line destroyed] to having our novels labelled historical. After all they are very literally dated.

I foresee great professional difficulties for you. You have used your two great plots – Farve & Fabrice.[1] You have set yourself up in a style of life which only continuous success can support. You have isolated yourself among cosmopolitan riff-raff from the sufferings of your fellow countrymen. What will you write about unless you make yourself a historical writer of the 20s? You might perhaps start a genre of *San-Michele-Elizabeth-and-her G Garden* about exile in Paris.[2] But must drop that dirty word 'progressive' if you are to do that. How I wish you were back in Curzon Street. No one departure has left such a yawning (literally) hole in London as yours.

I am anxious to emigrate, Laura to remain & face the century of the common man. She is younger, braver & less imaginative than I. If only they would start blowing the place up with their atoms.

My lecture at Bristol was hell – to graduates of the University on book collecting. A Catholic assembly. I accepted as an act of piety. The secretary said he would call for me at 6.45 and drive me there. Would you not have supposed that such an invitation included some sort of meal? I met him with a keen appetite from having dug all day. 'What time is our meeting?' '7.30. Plenty of time.' So I lectured & a lot of Catholic ladies came & shook my hand trembling with hunger. Then he drove me back, arriving here at 10.30 with not so much as a bun or a cup of coffee. He was a perfectly civil, cultured young man. It is just that those who have grown up since 1939 have lost all idea of hospitality.

When you get back to Paris do write me a full account of all you have seen in England. Boots [Cyril Connolly]?

I go to Eton at John Julius's [Cooper] insistence to lecture to the Literary Society. Perhaps I shall see Jonathan[3]. What is the news from him.

Did you hear any complaints of my behaviour at Debo's ball?

How delighted the people in the Dorchester must have been to have that revolting cook & those insolent waiters on strike. Hyde Park remained loyal.

I am writing a dreary short story about Spain.[4]

Harriet had been shown her tea-pot for the first time in preparation for your coming & was overjoyed with it. Played with it continually. Now it has been taken away again & put in a drawer in tissue paper until your next visit. It is a comfort to think she will never be too old to enjoy it.

Is it not odd how Poppy [Thursby] goes to *all* funerals?

I am tempted to come to Paris after Christmas. Is it easy? Can one just go to Victoria & get in a train? I think I shall go to California in February. I am bored here by lack of company. If only country neighbours would talk like Jane Austen's characters about gossip & hobbies. Instead they all want to know about Molotov & de Gaulle.

What has become of Prodd?

Do write me a long informative letter. I know you cant do it in London but from Paris yes?

Love

Evelyn

[1] *The Pursuit of Love* contained portraits of her father (Farve) and Gaston Palewski (Fabrice).

[2] Dr Axel Munthe, a Swede who lived in Capri, wrote *The Story of San Michele*, 1930. Elizabeth von Arnim (née Beauchamp, later Lady Russell) a New Zealander who lived in Germany, wrote *Elizabeth and her German Garden*, 1898.

[3] Jonathan Guinness (1930–   ). Son of Lord Moyne and Nancy's sister Diana, later Lady Mosley. Waugh's godson. Chairman of Monday Club 1972–4.

[4] *Scott-King's Modern Europe*, 1947.

TO NANCY MITFORD   Piers Court.
24 October [1946]

Darling Nancy

It was charming of you to send Harriet the Walter Crane. She was allowed a few minutes fascinated glimpse of it before it disappeared into my library. She may be allowed to look at it again on Christmas day – also the tea pot. At present she has two oyster shells which she bangs together in the stable yard for hours at a time in apparent contentment.

You used the accursed word 'prog' in connexion with Farve[?]. The fact that you forget it convicts you of using it naturally. It is like the beasts who still write to *The Times* newspaper 'In these enlightened days. . . .' Can I say nothing to convey to you the contempt & loathing with which we English regard absentees like you and Prod who stir up class war and then bolt from the consequences of your frivolity and vice? I think of abjuring the realm and becoming Irish. Do you know anything of Gormanston Castle Co Meath now for sale? Seat of Lord G., 20 miles from Dublin, near the sea. It is advertised as having 'Ballroom unfinished' which might be exquisitely romantic. I am going over to see it soon & perhaps buy it.

It is really too disgusting about Ran[1] – a man I love & respect. Daphne[2] rocks about crooning 'Her mother was called Melanie'. Does Bridget[3] know her? I should think *that* acid might expose the base metal.

Your literary future is insoluble I think. You see even the most bookish & meditative minds, like A. Huxley's, decay in exile. He never wrote a good novel after *Antic Hay*. You are so topical and on the spot & so radically English that you must feed on a fresh English diet. As an English observer thinking foreigners absurd you might be able to write about them. As a cosmopolitan you are lost. But I am relieved & delighted to hear that you can support yourself & Fabrice for another 2 years. I imagined he had swiped the whole kitty already. As you say in 2 years anything may happen. You may well return to us like the Bolter[4] babbling the jargon of the 30s. 'Progressive. Antisocial. Fascist. Workers. Dear Mr Gollancz. Munich. Picasso.' You will be very welcome.

I think an insuperable difficulty of your writing a book about the French is the conversational language. Do you write idiomatic English and so make the characters English despite yourself or translate Gallicisms literally with scattered italic phrases? Henry James did the latter. So did the Parisian diarist in the *Bystander* in the 20s. I simply dont believe it is possible.

Next week I am 43. I have minded no birthday since my thirtieth. Now I strain forward to senility.

I think you have a possible theme for another historical novel in the Strand-on-the-Green[5] world of Basil[6] & Ancaret[7] & Silps[?] etc. but I do not think it would be popular at the moment. Avoid at all costs 'Britain can take it' and memories of how matey you were with the lower classes at the warden's post.

I have two shots in my locker left. My war novel and my autobiography. I suppose they will see me out.

I go to the Cinema 4 times a week. I suppose I have seen more bad films than any living man in the last six months. I forget them like dreams the moment I leave the building.

Patrick Balfour is coming to stay to Laura's horror.

My love to Bridget & my regards to Mrs Lubbock[8].

> Love from
> Evelyn

[1] Earl of Antrim, an admirer of Louise de Vilmorin, whose mother was called Melanie.
[2] Viscountess Weymouth.
[3] Lady Bridget Parsons (1907–72). Sister of the Earl of Rosse.
[4] In *The Pursuit of Love*.
[5] Nancy Mitford lived in Strand-on-the-Green after she married Peter Rodd in 1933.
[6] Basil Murray.
[7] Ankaret Howard (1900–1945). First cousin of Basil Murray, she married William Jackson in 1927 and was killed in a riding accident.
[8] Aselaide Stanley (1906–   ). A cousin of Nancy Mitford. Married Maurice Lubbock in 1926. Her son Eric was a Liberal MP 1962–70.

TO HENRY YORKE   Piers Court.
[November 1946]

My dear Henry,

I have finished reading *Back*[1] with intense interest. No one but you could have written it or any part of it (except the French pastiche of which hereafter). The ingenious symbolism – roses roses all the way – excited envy & I delighted in the gradual breaking of dawn from madness to normality which could not have been better done & which, I hope, symbolizes for you a cosmic process which is entirely invisible to me. And the 'married & lived happy ever after' was conclusive for your couple this time as it was not for that beastly butler.

I should have liked it clearer whether in fact there was a marked physical likeness between Rose & Nance. She hints once that she is constantly plagued by being mistaken for the half sister but no one except Charlie seems to see it & then only when he is deranged.

The office scenes and the episode of the secretary seemed perfect. In fact the story is a triumphant success.

From all this I must except the Grand Siècle interpolation. A story within a story is a tricky device & I don't think this comes off. It is as if you wanted to show you can jolly well write with old world elegance if you care to – and you cant. Sentences like '. . . as well born as he, ill as he is as well' are excruciating to me. Apart from the jingle of it the syntax 'well – ill – well' each time in different sense, 'as – as – as – as' all different again. People did not write like that in civilized ages. It is like the time you told me poor Andrew Scott was a 'cunt'.

I get encouraging reports of the house I am thinking of buying in Ireland so I think soon I shall shake off the dust of your industrial state for ever.

You will think me a prig of course for what I have said above. Well I suppose I am.

Love to Dig
Evelyn

[1] Henry Green, *Back*, 1946. He had written on 20 March praising *Brideshead Revisited*, though saying that the theme was 'not easy for me . . . . How curious it is that we should both now be writing on lines essentially odious to each other. Me with servants and children [*Loving*, 1945] you with the dilemmas of the church.' He wrote on 11 November that he was 'entirely delighted that you thought the book a success. I value your opinion and depend more than you know on your praise. As to the French "pastiche" this is of course a translation from the original. But I did have the greatest difficulty with the wording. You are right when you say I haven't brought it off.'

To Henry Yorke   Piers Court.
12 November [1946]

Dear Henry,

I confess I hadn't realized the 'pastiche' was authentic. I have re-read it & find my credulity strained. As a matter of literary morals should you not have put a note to this effect? To introduce someone elses work into your own fiction seems to me reprehensible.

The story is deep as a well and wide as a church door without it. If, as you kindly say, you value my opinion, do consider cutting it right out. Apart from its teeming inadequacies, it is, surely, false to the main story to make James read anything of that kind.

Laura and I greatly look foward to your visit. The only thing that might interfere with it, is our going to inspect the house in Ireland which I am thinking of buying. But if we go it will be for only a day or two. After 18th Dec all will be a slum here, with the return of my children from school, so come before then please.

Evelyn

To LADY MARY LYGON   Piers Court.
27 November [1946]

Darling Blondy

Please accept my congratulations on your election to the London Library – a
position you have won for yourself by your valuable contribution to English Letters
as the editress of *Diversion*.[1]

I hope you will always remember to behave with suitable decorum in those grave
precincts. Always go to the closet appointed for the purpose if you wish to make
water. Far too many female members have lately taken to squatting behind the
Genealogy section. Never write 'balls' with an indelible pencil on the margins of the
books provided. Do not solicit the female librarians to acts of unnatural vice. When
very drunk it is permissible to fall into a light doze but not to sing. Fireworks are
always welcome in the reading-room but they should be of a kind likely to divert the
older members rather than to cause permanent damage to the structure.

By observing a few simple rules such as the foregoing you will find yourself
perfectly acceptable to the more amorous scholars who abound in the darkened
bays.

I go shortly to Ireland to inspect a castle where I propose to immure my family. I
pass through London on my return journey on 6th of next month & hope to see you.

Christopher Sykes junior has written an exquisite life of Christopher Sykes
senior[2].

Your godson[3] told his headmaster that I had separated from Laura & 'lived
purely in Africa'.

I have to go under the surgeon's knife in January for a painful, costly & indelicate
operation.

There is a very beautiful character called Mr Cox[4] at the London Library. You
must not make jokes about his name.

All my love
BO

[1] *Diversion* was a book edited by Lady Mary Lygon and Hester Chapman to raise money for the
Yugoslav Relief Society.

[2] *Four Studies in Loyalty*, 1946, concerned Robert Byron, the author's great-uncle Christopher Sykes,
Bahram Kimani and various members of the French Resistance.

[3] Auberon Waugh.

[4] Frederick Cox (1865–1955). Worked for seventy years at the London Library.

To NANCY MITFORD   Piers Court.
27 November [1946]

Darling Nancy

I expect you have been very busy electioneering for the communists &
transhipping Jewish terrorists to Palestine. I hope you are gratified by your
successes.

I go to Ireland next week to inspect a castle where I hope to immure myself and family. Before that I have to go under the surgeons knife for a painful, costly & indelicate operation. I cannot say the word, can I write it, well – piles. That is to be my January. For February & March I go to Hollywood if the American civil war [1] has not cut all communications. Then I hope to my castle. Have I told you about it? Well I will when I have seen it. Rats leaving sinkers or birds of delicate plumage migrating to a more genial climate – however you care to look at it.

Since I last wrote I have been on for me an adventurous round. First to Oxford to wait on H.E. Cardinal Griffin [2] who is a Truman-Attlee-common-man. I dined sumptuously with Bowra the famous Stakhanovite [3] (?) scholar. Then to the Betjemans in a house which smelled like a village shop – oil, cheese, bacon, washing but the fare was not as frugal as Dorchester Hotel. Harness literally everywhere. Books to make Handy blink and seize a pencil & start writing £100 in each. Nasty talk about protestant clergymen. Then to Eton where at John Julius insistence I lectured to some bright civil boys. I met a dull master who worked in College. He said 'Guinness has turned the corner'. Jonathan came to my lecture but I failed to recognize him so sent him a sovereign. The house masters wife with whom I stayed with very pretty with purple finger nails. Then to London where it was just Whites & Hyde Park Hotel. Pansy Lamb came to dinner – thin old half-starved clever shy. A beast called Rayner Heppenstall [4] tried to make me go a round of Europe to broadcast a message of Xmas goodwill. Me of all people. I said £300, he said £50 so there the matter ended. I wonder whom they will send.

Here I have entertained Patrick Balfour, very bland & plump & bureaucratic, zealously coming to terms with the socialist state. Also Frank & Elizabeth Pakenham. I think he is seeing a glimmering of the disaster ahead which he has worked so hard to bring about. S Boots Connolly has fled the country. Some say from his debts. I see he has hired a woman to attack me in his absence.

I let your god daughter see your tea pot once more. It is in fragments. She is becoming a droll little girl. My son told his headmaster's wife that it was no good writing to me as I had left his mother & 'lived purely in Africa now'.

Christopher Sykes has written an exquisite life of his great uncle and a lot of balls about the late Robert Byron.

I was offered £50 for 50 words by a yank magazine on my favourite quotation. If I go to Ireland money will once more recover some value. I have written a very very long short story about my trip to Spain.

Who is the Mr Rodd who has bought Buckland Abbey?

How I dread Christmas. The operating theatre & nursing home will come as a welcome treat after it.

Do you see Picasso every day?

Yorke has written a book called *Back*. In the middle he inserts a long & irrelevant & inelegant translation from the French. Very mad. He & Dig frequent the night club where Heath met poor old Marge. [5]

Best love from
Evelyn

[1] A.D.Peters had written that America was embarking 'on the bloodiest strike in its history. Anything may happen.'

[2] Cardinal Griffin (1899–1956). Archbishop of Westminster.

[3] Exemplarily industrious. Bowra had published four books in three years.

[4] Rayner Heppenstall (1911–   ). Writer. BBC producer 1945–65.

[5] Neville Heath met his victim Margery Gardner at the Panama Club.

To JOHN BETJEMAN   Piers Court.
22 December 1946

My Dear John

Thank you very much for your Xmas card & the promise of *The Pavilion*. What you do not send & what I want very much is my article in *Life*. [1] Please please send it back.

I have been painfully shocked by a brochure named 'Five Sermons by Laymen'. Last time I met you you told me you did not believe in the Resurrection. Now I find you expounding Protestant devotional practices from the pulpit. This WILL NOT DO. You should be thinking of St Thomas More not of Henry Moore.

I understand that Penelope means to purchase you a years respite from uncongenial work. You must spend some of that time thinking. It is no good saying: 'I don't happen to be logical'. Logic is simply the architecture of human reason. If you try to base your life & hopes on logical absurdities YOU WILL GO MAD. No one goes mad because he works in a factory & eats tinned food, as you suggest, though these acts are symptoms of unreason. But people are going mad & talking balls to psychiatrists not because of accidents to the chamber-pot in the nursery, but because there is no logical structure to their beliefs. Vide Smarty-Boots-Connolly passim.

Your ecclesiastical position is entirely without reason. You cannot possibly be right. Marxist-Atheists might be. Zealous protestants may be (i.e. it is possible to say that from the word go the Church was all wrong & had misunderstood everything Our Lord told them, & that it required a new Divine Dispensation in the sixteenth century to put people on the right track again. That is just possible). What is inconceivable is that Christ was made flesh in order to found a Church, that He canalized his Grace in the sacraments, that He gave His promise to abide in the Church to the end of time, that He saw the Church as a human corporation, part of his Mystical Body, one with the Saints triumphant – and then to point to a handful of homosexual curates and say: 'That is the true Church.'

You & I cannot both be right. But every argument you can put forward for your little group in the Church of England is *a fortiori* an argument for me. This is so self-evident to me that I cannot expound it further.

You say you regard the question of Orders as the crucial question. Why? There is no conceivable doubt that the Catholic Church has valid orders; it is probable that the Orthodox have; also the various Eastern heretical bodies & the Ethiopians; it is highly improbable that the Church of England has. But even if they had they would not be free of the frightful sins of heresy & schism. Cranmer & Luther had valid orders. Did Calvin? I don't know. But valid orders do not confer impeccability or infallibility. Your communion would be sacrilegious if it were valid. A Church is a corporate human association. You cannot escape pollution from the blasphemous aberrations of most of your clergy by forming a little clique (even among whom I believe the most preposterous heresies are current).

You must not suppose that there is anything more than the most superficial resemblance between Catholics & Anglo-Catholics. They may look alike to you. An Australian, however well-informed, simply cannot distinguish between a piece of Trust House timbering and a genuine Tudor Building; an Englishman however uncultured knows at once.

The true Church is unique & indivisible & nothing is remotely like it. This may not be apparent from outside. But I think more violence is done to the Mystical Body by those who imitate it than by those who frankly hate it.

You will find an enormous number of features of the Catholic Church that are repugnant to you, for the very reason that it is sui generis. But I do implore you to spend your year in investigating. Then it will be a Year of Grace. You may not get another chance. It would be a pity to go to HELL because you prefer Henry Moore to Michelangelo.

THIS GOES FOR PENELOPE TOO.

Evelyn

[1] 'Fanfare', published in *Life* in April, was an answer to his fan-mail, a defence of *Brideshead Revisited* and an attack on his critics, in particular Edmund Wilson.

To Randolph Churchill
22 December [1946]   Piers Court.

Dear Randolph,

I am happy to say that you were elected to the Beefsteak without a dissentient vote. Hugh Sherwood addressed the committee in moving terms about your war heroism; the Duke of Devonshire sent a message that your chief characteristic was pious deference to older men; I said you would not use the club very often. On the opening of the box no blackball was discovered.

... I have put this house on the market and am negotiating to buy a castle in Ireland where I hope to find brief shelter from the Attlee terror; but Hic non habemus manentem civitatem.[1]

Yours ever
Evelyn

[1] Here we have no abiding city.

To John Betjeman   Hospital SS John & Elizabeth,
9 January 1947   NW8.

Dear John

God forbid that I should pronounce damnation on the people of Wantage. No one is damned except by his own deliberate act. Heresy is certainly one of the sins which can damn a man, but it is doubtful how many formal heretics really commit the sin of heresy – of seeing the truth and denying it. Many hereditary heretics are in a state of invincible ignorance. They may well receive some of the Grace & Mercy of God. I think it is even possible that devout Moslems & Jews are allowed to approach God in prayer.

The reason I wrote to you as I did was because *you* seem to me to be in a different position altogether – that you are being allowed to see a glimpse of the truth broad enough to damn you if you reject it now. Intellectual doubt is the least of all the causes of infidelity. Pride, sloth & cowardice all contribute more. I have not myself met the Catholics you speak of who are subject to assaults of doubt. I am sure they exist because there are Catholics of every kind. There is certainly a stage in the mystical life (of which I know nothing) when many saints have had to wrestle with doubt for years. But your doubts seem to me much more terre à terre. They are the natural eruptions of a thoroughly bad intellectual constitution. If you accept an absurdity, as you do in pretending the Church of Wantage is the Catholic Church, and luxuriate in sentimental raptures, you will naturally break out in boils & carbuncles & question the authenticity of the Incarnation. Catholics are irked by church discipline & puzzled by many logical problems but they do not, in my observation, have the sort of fundamental doubt you suffer from.

I have no patience whatever with the plea of duty to a sinking ship. If your group at Wantage are the Catholic Church they are not sinking. They are one with the angels & saints triumphant. If they are sinking it is because they should never have put to sea. There have been hundreds of mutinous ship loads in the last 2 thousand years who have set sail with a great hullaballoo & salutes of guns. 4 centuries is about their life afloat. Honour among thieves is complicity in crime. If you realise that you are in a pirate crew your only duty is to desert at once however endearing you find your ship mates.

You cannot rely on a death bed conversion. Every hour you spend outside the Church is an hour lost. I well know the vast handicap of having started my Catholic life 27 years too late. Think what it must be like for poor Charles II who only had a few minutes Catholic life!

I don't believe your wretched clergy have any faith themselves. I met a number of protestant chaplains in the war. None showed any special knowledge except some acquaintance with German textual critics – Tubingen 1870[1]. They had no grasp of moral theology & were swayed by any sort of 'feeling' in their opinions. Chris Hollis is peculiarly tender toward these people – pietas to Wells Cathedral Green combined with votes of Wiltshire rectors.

This is a rambling letter for I am on a sick bed. What I want really to say is that you must give yourself time to take lessons in the rudiments of theology. Don't follow emotions follow reason. The final step must be a step in the dark because you can have no conception of what the Church is like until you see it from inside. Father Devas at Farm Street[2] would be a good instructor in the catechism. Remember that anything the mystics wrote was written from *inside* the Church. All the structure & discipline of the Church is accepted as given, before they go on to higher speculations. If you read the utterances of the mystics from *outside* you will miss the point & incur dangers. So leave all that aside & get the elementary theology & history clear first. After that every luxury of devotion is available.

Perhaps this is not even legible. I will write again when my hand is steadier.

I am here another week. Pop in if you are passing.[3]

Evelyn

[1] The Eberhard-Karls University Catholic Theological Faculty.

[2] Father Devas, 'very quiet and simple and humble', had given Hubert Duggan absolution at Waugh's instigation. The headquarters of the Jesuits in London is at Farm Street.

[3] Betjeman's replies included the statement that 'What I cannot believe – this is a far more permanent carbuncle (you would call it) than my occasional doubts about the Resurrection – is that the C of E is *not* part of the Catholic Church. . . .'

To JOHN BETJEMAN   Hospital SS John & Elizabeth,
14 January 1947   NW8.

My Dear John,

Thank you for the handsome art publication. What a lot of ladies you know named Myfanwy![1] I suppose your poems bring you into correspondence with them. I admire your article very much also Wests. Not so keen on snails.

I am no expert on Anglican orders. It has never seemed to me an important question. It is certainly one on which we cannot get an infallible answer this side of the grave. The papal condemnation is simply their expert opinion. I do not even know what you believe their authenticity derives from – some renegade Dalmatian Bishop in the middle of the seventeenth century is it not? I don't know either how they jumped the two hundred years to Pusey[2] etc. Plainly 'intention' is an essential part of ordination. Otherwise it becomes simply magic like the people in fairy stories who rub a lamp by chance & find a genie at the elbow. Do you seriously believe that those periwigged 18th-century bishops intended to produce sacrificing priests? Do you believe that a genuine Bishop repeating the words of ordination in a hypnotic trance would produce a priest? Whether any trickle of divine power survived the reformation & when precisely it petered out are questions of fact to which there is no answer because the evidence is lacking. Anyway I don't see the importance. Almost all the great heresiarchs have had valid orders – Arius[3] etc.

Because the validity of a sacrament is objective not subjective, the personal virtue of the priest does not affect it. It would clearly be insane to think that Fr A's wafer was *more* the Body of Our Lord than Fr B's because Fr A is the worthier man. Thus a priest in mortal sin can say mass & give valid communion to a man also in mortal sin to the damnation of them both, whether the mortal sin is adultery or heresy.

I can't write the history of the Church of England for you but I presume we agree that it came into existence through a mixture of political, economic & domestic causes. The apostate priests who founded it and its earliest ministers were driven by a typical English confusion of wrong opinions culled from Luther, Calvin, Zwingli, etc. In order to achieve some sort of shape they accepted the principle that the King was the supreme temporal & spiritual authority & that his decisions on doctrine were the tests of orthodoxy. And to this day the head of your church becomes a Presbyterian the moment he crosses the Tweed. You would also agree, I take it, that many of your clergy, higher & lower, entertain extravagantly eccentric notions. You say that 2 to 1 are what you call Catholic. I am astounded, but I do not know many parsons & you know thousands so I must believe you. I was educated at Lancing which was said to be the most 'Catholic' protestant school. Many of the clergymen-masters were devout & virtuous but none at all like priests. The various chaplains I met in the war seemed to have no sense of the supernatural at all. I think the difference is that you genuinely don't know what Catholicism means. It is as I described it before in comparing you to an Australian unable to recognize the marks of genuine architecture.

Perhaps I was wrong to speak of a small group of homosexual curates. No doubt there are thousands of them at the moment but they are still a pretty small group when assembled with all their colleagues since the Act of Supremacy. And where are their Saints & Miracles. To call these people priests is like saying: 'Be a saint (or angel) and fill my glass as you're up!'

What you are saying is: 'When I am convinced of error I will receive instruction'. Are you expecting a divine revelation like Paul's. It is very presumptuous. How can you be convinced of error *without* instruction? And how can you expect a Cowley Father[4] to instruct you in the truth which he lacks himself. You say, 'What more can I learn at Farm Street than I learn at Wantage already?' I say 'everything'. But if you feel it disloyal to take instruction while you still have a 'confessor' I suggest this: Go to a Roman Catholic priest (I recommend Devas) and say to him: 'Don't teach me anything specifically anti-Anglican at the moment. Just go through the creeds with me & the catechism. Teach me the morals & the faith which I believe we have in common'. Then when you have had a few months of that ask yourself seriously 'Is this the Faith of Wantage or is there something here radically different?' I am sure you will peep into a different world.

But even if you see some similarities you still have to answer the question 'What are the Wantage group doing in the same galley as the Coventry Group?' If yours is a Church at all, which I don't think it is, it is a living corporation. We are members one of another and by adherence to Bishop Barnes etc. I am doing public violence to my convictions.

All this 'waiting for God's good time' is intolerably wet. Time is a human conception & limitation. We make God's time for him.

Almost everyone who becomes a Catholic makes sacrifices. Some very large ones. Yours I think would be greater than most for you have built your life & learning & art round the Church of England. I can well understand your reluctance to start a new life in middle-age with every literary & aesthetic predilection the other way. It is easy to say 'Well I'll just wait until an Archangel is sent to make the announcement to me personally in God's good time. Meanwhile I'll believe in the Incarnation on two days a week and continue my catalogue of Anglican Churches.'

Finally, do consider my first letter. (1) We may both be wrong (2) We can't both be right (3) You cannot be right and I wrong (4) If I am right you are wrong. Which of these statements do you deny? A real protestant could deny 3. But your Wantage waifs don't and can't.

But there is ten years painful transition ahead for you if you decide to follow your mind instead of your emotions. You may shirk them.[5]

Evelyn

[1] The only Myfanwy Sir John Betjeman remembers is Myfanwy Evans who married the painter John Piper in 1935.

[2] i.e. Anglo-Catholicism.

[3] A priest in the diocese of Alexandria at the beginning of the fourth century who did not believe in the divinity of Christ.

[4] Anglican order founded in 1865.

[5] Betjeman replied with a short letter on 23 January saying, 'All I can do now is to read pray and study the life of our Lord. That I am doing. I feel that it is not so much a matter of which church, as of loving God and I still think of us as *both* right.'

TO A.D.PETERS   Beverley Hills Hotel & Bungalows,
6 March [1947]   Beverly Hills,
                                 California.[1]

Dear Pete

Thanks to Charles Mendl[2], no thanks to MGM, I have at last got a fairly decent set of rooms.

I have had a telephone call from Knox's agent & frozen him out.

I am entirely obsessed by Forest Lawns & plan a long short story about it. I go there two or three times a week, am on easy terms with the chief embalmer & next week am to lunch with Dr HUBERT EATON himself. It is an entirely unique place — the *only* thing in California that is not a copy of something else. It is wonderful literary raw material. Aldous [Huxley] flirted with it in *After Many A Summer*[3] but only with the superficialities. I am at the heart of it. It will be a *very* good story.

... MGM bore me when I see them but I dont see them much.[4] They have been a help in getting me introductions to morticians who are the *only* people worth knowing.

Social life gay & refined. Not as generally described. Laura returns on *Q.E.* sailing 22nd. Probably I go with her.

Mr Mayer[5] cried when his horses were sold.

Did you know that the cadaver was referred to as 'the loved one' at F.L. I have seen dozens of loved ones half painted before the bereaved family saw them. In the Church of the Recessional at F.L. they have Enid Jones *National Velvet* in a glass case with a notice saying that it is comparable to *Alice in Wonderland* & was inspired by Rottingdean Church from which the Church of the Recessional derives. [6]

I will try & get one of Eatons books signed for you.

> Yours ever
> Evelyn

Randolph came for two days & behaved abominably. I thought he could never shock me any more but he did. Brutishly drunk all the time, soliciting respectable women at luncheon parties etc. His lecture, to which we went at Pasadena, was surprisingly good considering the grave condition he was in. He mocked the Jews to the sound of applause. I was not the least anti-Semitic before I came here. I am now. It is intolerable to see them enjoying themselves.

The news that weekly papers have closed down in England brought the crisis [7] home to us as nothing else had.

[1] On 27 January Waugh sailed for New York and on 6 February he reached Los Angeles. MGM were paying his expenses in order to discuss making a film of *Brideshead Revisited*.

[2] Sir Charles Mendl (1871–1958). Press attaché at the British Embassy in Paris 1926–40. Married to Elsie de Wolfe 1926–50.

[3] Published in 1939.

[4] Waugh eventually turned down an offer of $125,000 for the film rights of *Brideshead Revisited*.

[5] Louis B. Mayer (1885–1957). Vice-president and general manager of MGM.

[6] Enid Bagnold (1889–   ). Writer. She married Sir Roderick Jones in 1920, lived near Rottingdean in Sussex and wrote *National Velvet* in 1935.

[7] The intense and prolonged cold of the winter of 1947 caused power cuts.

To John Betjeman
[2 ? April 1947]

Dear John

Just back from Hollywood. Did you ever get the Forest Lawn album?

Thank you for the civil things you say of me in *Strand* magazine but why do you persist in cutting down my Catholic life. I was received in 1930.

O. Lancaster's sketch good in conception but poor in execution.

I am obsessed by american morticians (undertakers) and am starting a book about them.

Do you feel disposed to come on a house-hunting jaunt in Ireland with me at my expense soon after Easter?

I can't sleep. Can you?

Awful about your obduracy in schism and heresy. Hell hell hell. Eternal damnation.

Love to Penelope

> Evelyn

To the Editor of The Times   [Piers Court?][1]
[17 April 1947]

FOREIGN TRAVEL FOR YOUNG WRITERS

Sir, – I trust that Mr. Maugham has squared the police before disclosing his purpose of giving £500 yearly to a young writer to be spent in foreign travel; otherwise he will find his protégés, and perhaps himself, in chokey.

Supposing that the plan has state sanction, does Mr. Maugham realize what a huge temptation he is putting before elderly writers? To have £500 of our own – let alone of Mr. Maugham's – to spend abroad is beyond our dreams. We may not even spend the royalties on our translations in the countries where they are earned. What will we not do to qualify for Mr. Maugham's munificence? What forging of birth certificates, dyeing of whiskers, and lifting of faces! To what parodies of experimental styles will we not push our experienced pens!

Your obedient servant,
EVELYN WAUGH

[1] Waugh had returned from the United States on 7 April.

To Douglas Woodruff   White's.
[8 May 1947]

Dear Douglas

I was most surprised to learn from Speaight[1] that you are only now 50. I always supposed that when you came to Oxford, after your retirement from the Dutch consular service, you were at least that age. It is a great thing to be old and I am sorry you are not older. Still you have definitely passed the watershed & that is everything. Downhill now all the way into deep pasture & long evening shadows. I am still struggling up the last false crest & salute your vanishing silhouette.

Speaight's austerity dinner will be a sad occasion for all but I will loyally attend. Meanwhile here is a birthday present Maurice gave to Venetia [Montagu], from her as wedding present to Randolph, bought from him by me at the break up of his domestic life, now to you – a varied history.

Yours
Evelyn

[1] Robert Speaight (1904–76). Actor and author.

To John Betjeman
[May 1947][1]

Dear John

I wish you had come with me to Ireland. I saw three houses a day for a week and have boiled down the choice to three – Kiltinan, Tipperary, a romantic slum,

Lisnavagh, Carlow, a practical Early Victorian Collegiate building, and a fine ugly 1870 Italianate villa on Lough Derg called Slevyre, the home, believe it or not, of General Sir William Hickey. Lord Wicklow tried to avoid me but failed. When trapped he showed me a letter of yours from which it is plain that you have refused the aid I suggested in overcoming the pit dug for you by Dix.[2] I am appalled by the danger of your position. You have seen the light & rejected it.

Can you not see how preposterous it is to go for advice to the very people whose position is in question? I say 'They are impostors & I can prove it'. You say: 'Well I must ask them first whether it is all right to examine the proofs'.

One deep root of error is that you regard religion as the source of pleasurable emotions & sensations and ask the question 'Am I not getting just as much out of the Church of England as I should from Catholicism?' The question should be 'What am I giving to God?' Nothing less than complete abandonment is any good. His will is plain as a pikestaff that there shall be one fold & one shepherd and you spend all your time perpetuating a sixteenth century rift & influencing others to perpetuate it. I wouldnt give a thrushs egg for your chances of salvation at the moment.[3]

Yours
Evelyn

[1] Penelope Betjeman had written to Waugh in April:
'Dearest Evelyn

    I am very grateful to you for writing those letters to John tho' it is very disloyal of me to write to you and say that still I hope you will pray very hard indeed during the next few weeks for him because he is in a dreadful state he thinks you are the devil and wakes up in the middle of the night and raves and says he will leave me at once if I go over.... However put yourself in his position: suppose Laura were to wake up and say to you tomorrow morning 'I have had a revelation of the TRUTH it is only to be found in A. Huxley's Yogibogi sect, I shall join it.' You would not unnaturally be a little put out. You might even threaten to leave the old girl should she persist. Well John feels just like that. He thinks ROMAN Catholicism is a foreign religion which has no right to set up in this country, let alone try to make converts from what he regards as the true catholic church of the country. Your letters have brought it out in a remarkable way ....'
[2] Dom Gregory Dix, Anglican Benedictine and high-church theologian.
[3] John Betjeman replied '... It would be far *easier* (but against my conscience) to become R.C. For in this village, which has no Nonconformist Chapel, the only bulwark against complete paganism is the Church and its chief supporters are Penelope and me .... In villages people still follow a lead .... I know that to desert this wounded neglected Church would be to betray our Lord. Really you are quite wrong in thinking that I regard religion as "the source of pleasurable emotions and sensations".'

TO JOHN BETJEMAN   Piers Court.
[28 May 1947]
Postcard

Blind worm, who are you to lead? You should humbly follow. If village life is an occasion of sin, fly from it & mortify yourself in Park West[1] like the fathers in the desert.

I have almost decided to purchase Lisnavagh, a large early Victorian baronial mansion near Rathvilly. I feel a foreigner in Stinchcombe and but for Laura would go further afield to Africa. Hic non habemus manentem civitatem.

E

The physical privations in Ireland are as bad as the English.

[1] Flats in Edgware Road where the Woodruffs and some of the Actons lived.

To Nancy Mitford
Thursday in Whitsun Week [29 May] 1947

Darling Nancy

What exquisite presents you do find for your godchild. The *writing* paper and *on*velopes have been shown to Hattie, causing her to chuckle with pleasure, & then locked away for a few years until she can write and thank you herself. Everything you send her should form her taste and help to make her such a desirable girl as you describe.

At present she refuses her food and yells when handed to the nursery maid.

I expect that your work at the studio will take many months.

Did I tell you I had practically decided on my Irish house – a large prosaic Early Victorian baronial mansion in flat hunting country near Dublin and Ld Fitzwilliam. The romantic castle was condemned by the architect I sent to vet it, as moribund.

I do not think that all my teasing has brought home your beastliness to you. Do you not realise you are the most hated woman in England and the reason is not that you have moved to France but that you voted socialist. Beast. What is more you made a secret socialist cell of your shop in Curzon Street introducing Handycraft who is red too – *next door to Trumpers*[1]

Come soon

Love E

[1] Where Waugh had his hair cut.

To Lady Mary Lygon   Piers Court.
1 June (Glorious 1st) [1947]

Darling

It was very nice to have a letter from you but I couldnt understand a word.

Who has said what about whom going to Ireland?

What Marchioness? Bath, I suppose, it always is.

Then you say you are going to Broads. Do you know what Broads means in American. Something feelthy. Do they make Norfolk flatter?

I too have *Voyages of Destiny*. Very hard to keep from little Laura.

Your G-son goes back to school on Monday. We had his eyes taken out & put back again straight & now he is prettier. Sykes's delinquent child ran away from his school.

Did you see P Rodd's sadistic exposures in *New Statesman*?[1] If you are to be friends with Mrs Attlee[2] you must read that paper & talk about flogging.

This paper is very dirty. It is the last sheet in the house. Soon I will have paper printed with LISNAVAGH Co (County not Company) CARLOW on it. That is to be my Highclere.

Did Poll tell you we found Bob Osmonde alive again exhibiting his good taste engravings at R Academy, so I may get a picture of LISNAVAGH before he pops off.

I have given up smoking cigars except on feasts of the Church except when I have a guest to smoke one with me so please come & do so.

My Highclere has 22 bed rooms 5 baths 12 acres of 'pleasure' grounds – what pleasures, and a 'luggage entrance.' But it is not yet mine as I have not sold this little Sans Souci was that where Col Wigham was he Wigham lived? I mean the man whose R & J Lady S spoiled. Mon Repos? Petit Trianon? What was it called?[3]

I am writing a beautiful tale about corpses. Very seasonable weather for it.

Mrs Sykes came to stay & was terribly sick in the night and in consequence never wrote to thank little Laura for her kind hospitality.

I must soon have my hair cut.

Will you go to Ld FitzWilliam's Derby orgy? I said no on account of my new ascetic life.

Have you explained to Bennett why I will never speak to him again?

Sykes took me to tea with Sir Max Beerbohm. It was a great honour. Would you greatly appreciate it if I gave you a book of his named *Things New and Old*.

Love xxxxxxxx
Bo

[1] Peter Rodd wrote in a letter concerning beating: 'it is not often that its undoubted benefit to the punishers is so frankly stated. Means to sexual stimulus and sexual satisfaction are all too often glossed over.'

[2] Lady Mary had been on a committee with the wife of the Prime Minister.

[3] Colonel Wiggin, MFH, lived at Saint Cloud. Lady Sibell Lygon once surprised him by accepting a Romeo and Juliet cigar.

To Penelope Betjeman [Piers Court.]
4 June [1947]

Dearest Penelope,

I am by nature a bully and a scold and Johns pertinacity in error brings out all that is worst in me. I am very sorry. I will lay off him in future. But really when he says that the truth of the Petrine claims is dependent on his place of residence, the mind boggles. I think there is very clearly a devil at work in him putting him up to all sorts of ideas such as that it is his duty[?] to suffer for his faith while if he had two eyes in his head he would see that it is immensely to his material advantage to remain a protestant. But I will keep silence.

I cant conceive what he means by 'smart' Catholics. All I know, here & abroad, are grotesquely dowdy. Mrs Sweeny[1] I suppose. Well I don't know her & there is really no obligation to, if he doesn't admire her.

I am delighted to hear that you will start lessons in the autumn. Would you like me to hear your first confession? It would be a great help to me in my work.

You never come here. I wish you would, with or without John. Tell John that if he comes I will not broach theological questions.

I WILL KEEP SILENCE. So bring him. Not 11th-15th instant when we shall be away.

Dominicans are sadly socialistic in their opinions.

We make no silage.

Obscure peers – RATHDONNELL[2]. It is his house I am negotiating for. He has a daughter named ALLY PALLY M'CLINTOCK-BUNBURY. It (the house not Ally Pally) is a hundred years old exactly. It looks very English in this picture but its interior is good baronial architect William Robertson.

Please tell John I am sincerely sorry for persecuting him & I won't again.

Sir Max Beerbohm lives near here and I have had an audience with that great master. He was enchanting.

Do come soon[3]

Love & xxx
Evelyn

[1] Margaret Whigham became Mrs Charles Sweeny and was married 1951–63 to the Duke of Argyll.

[2] Lord Rathdonnell (1914–59). Owner of Lisnavagh and father of Alexandra McClintock-Bunbury, born 1940, who married James Doyle in 1960. 'A scatter-brained, slangy rather seedy-looking young man.' *Diaries*. He asked £20,000 for his house.

[3] Penelope Betjeman had postponed instruction because her husband was upset by the idea. She replied to Waugh: 'As far as I can make out John thinks the smart catholic set consists of you, Laura's relatives and Asquiths, the Pakenhams, D. Woodruff, C. Hollis and in fact any English R.C. he knows. He thinks if I go C. and he doesn't you will all persecute him and there will be plots and counterplots and the only thing for him to do is to get right away from it all and go and settle on his own in Swindon for which city he has always had a great liking as you know and where there is an old established Anglo colony. However he saw Crackywilliam clonmorewicklow last night who made him laugh a lot about the whole thing and who told him your patience was at an end which he thought very funny and altogether he seems less antagonistic than he was. . . .'

To A.D.PETERS   White's.
[12 June 1947]

Dear Pete
    No, not for 12 guineas.
    Price for television £50 in a false beard. With the naked face £250.

Yours
Evelyn

To Penelope Betjeman   Piers Court.
13 June [1947]

Darling Penelope

Thank you for John's excellent poem which I here return. What very low company he appears in! How he shines in it!

Talking of low company, I was commanded by Very Rev D'Arcy to accept an invitation from Ben Nicolson[1] to an intellectual dinner, African wine in a South Kensington basement, to discuss 'religion'. P.Toynbee[2] spoke for 20 minutes – absolute balls. I had never seen him sober before & greatly preferred him being sick in Ann Rothermere's lap. He is a pretentious ass. Then a seedy kind of clergyman piped up and I said Who is this and they say Pastor Niemöller[3] and he talked balls too, but not so pretentiously – just flat stupid & boring. There was a young yid who kept snorting contemptuously and I said Who is this young yid who keeps snorting contemptuously and they said it is Mr Ayer[4] but his heart is broken by D.Fellowes's girl[5] and it is tears not derision makes him snort. There was another clergyman there & he never spoke but as we went to pee he said 'Perhaps I am best known as the Vicar of Nottingham (?Northampton?) who has John Betjeman to preach in my church'. Two revolting socialist members of parliament called Crossman[6] who is famous but not to me and Woodrow Williams[7] who is famous to no one talked most. I hardly at all. God it was hell.

The Catholics of Copenhagen greatly need encouragement. You should go & exhort them. I went to early mass & found I was expected to exhort them while they drank coffee.

Did John get a tableau I sent from Copenhagen?

Ed Long[ford]'s prurient interest in protestantism disgusts me.

                                        Love and xxxs from
                                              Evelyn

[1] Benedict Nicolson (1914–78). Editor of the *Burlington Magazine* 1947–78. Son of Sir Harold.

[2] Philip Toynbee (1916–). Novelist and critic. On the *Observer* staff from 1950.

[3] Reverend Dr Martin Niemöller (1892–). Anti-Nazi, in concentration camps 1937–45, a president of the World Council of Churches 1961–8.

[4] Alfred Ayer (1910–). Grote Professor of the Philosophy of Mind and Logic at London 1946–59. Knighted 1970. He writes that it was derision not tears made him snort. Also that Waugh in fact said on entry, 'There seem to be a lot of Jews here. Which one is Freddie Ayer?'

[5] Rosamond Fellowes (1912–). Married 1941–5 to James Gladstone, and in 1952 to Tadeusz Wiszniewski.

[6] Richard Crossman (1907–74). Labour MP 1945–74, editor of the *New Statesman* 1970–72, diarist.

[7] Probably Woodrow Wyatt (1918–). Journalist, newspaper-owner and Labour MP 1945–55, 1959–70.

TO A.D.PETERS
9 July [1947]

Dear Pete,
 ... Then there is the question of whether *The Loved One* should appear at all in USA. It will greatly shock many & I feel comes rather poorly after an article in *Life* in which I declared that I would only write religious books in future. Ought I to concentrate on setting up in USA as a serious (as they mean it) writer or ought I to keep them guessing? It is hard for you to advise without having read the story....

Yours ever
Evelyn

TO THE EDITOR OF THE BELL [1]
[13? July 1947]

'THE PIETIES OF EVELYN WAUGH'

Sir, – I am most grateful for the attention given to my work in your pages and would not intrude in the discussion but for the fear that a hasty reader might conceive the doubt, which your reviewer scrupulously refrains from expressing, of the good faith of my conversion to Catholicism.

I think perhaps your reviewer is right in calling me a snob; that is to say I am happiest in the company of the European upper-classes; but I do not think this preference is necessarily an offence against Charity, still less against Faith. I can assure you it had no influence on my conversion. In England Catholicism is predominantly a religion of the poor. There is a handful of Catholic aristocratic families, but I knew none of them in 1930 when I was received into the Church. My friends were fashionable agnostics and the Faith I then accepted had none of the extraneous glamour which your reviewer imputes to it.

Nor, I think, does this preference unduly influence my writing. Besides Hooper there are two characters in *Brideshead Revisited* whom I represent as worldly – Rex Mottram, a millionaire, and Lady Celia Ryder, a lady of high birth. Why did my reverence for money and rank not sanctify those two?

Your obedient servant,
EVELYN WAUGH

[1] An Irish periodical 1940–54, founded by Sean O'Faolain.

TO PENELOPE BETJEMAN   [Piers Court?]
14 July [1947]

Darling Penelope
  The crocodile [1] serves man in many ways – his hide for note-cases, bags and dago shoes, his name to enrich our literature with metaphor 'crocodile tears', 'as warm &

friendly as an alligator pool' etc. Most especially he is a type & sign for us of our own unredeemed nature.

You must fly dualism like the plague – it is at the root of almost all heresy – just as in psychology schizophrenia is at the root of many insanities. It has never troubled me much so I have no books on the subject, I am afraid. The unaided reason should be able to dispel that nasty dream. John's preposterous theory that Our Lord founded two churches – Roman & Anglican – is of course a form of dualism.

It is impossible for someone like yourself who is in formal heresy to realise the horror which heresy inflames in an orthodox mind. What seems to you a harmless & amusing speculation is, to me, a denial & perversion of God's truth.

I hope John did not resent the parody of his erotic rhapsodies in *Scott-King*.

I did not write & invite him to stay. I will do so after the school holidays.

I think John's irrational horror of Catholicism a very good sign. It is far more promising than the tolerant 'each-worshipping-in-his-own-way' attitude and of course quite insane. As I keep pointing out to him it is impossible for him to be right & me to be wrong. Still more impossible for us both to be right. The alternatives are (a) both wrong or (b) he wrong, me right.

Laura has purchased a French student in the belief that she would need a nursery maid. Now the maid stays on & the student arrives next Monday.

I am writing a singularly unpleasant tale of life in the Hollywood Mortuary.

Ronnie Knox spends next week-end with us. I suppose it would be hopeless proposing you & John came over for dinner? We cant put you up as he has to have the best room and the others are no good. . . .

Love
Evelyn

[1] Penelope Betjeman had written: 'I am just reading an interesting book about dualism. I have always tended to that heresy myself because I could never understand how God could make a crocodile.' Dualism is the doctrine that there are two independent principles, one good, the other evil.

TO NANCY MITFORD   Piers Court.
6 August 1947

Dearest Nancy

. . . I went to London for Daphne's ball which I enjoyed enormously. All old chums making hay and a few pimply & pouting juniors standing about disconsolately. Maureen [Lady Dufferin] gave Randolph a terrific box on the ear. Instead of striking back like a man he tried to pacify her. They stood in the centre of the ball room sweating & arguing for three minutes and then – another more terrific box. I said to her: 'I am all for Randolph being struck but why particularly do you strike him now'. She: 'He never wrote me a letter of condolence when Ava was killed'. So now I keep rather clear of widows. Kick has had the most god awful posthumous portrait made of her Loved One[1]. I saw Debo at the ball & took up a great deal of her time. She was in fine looks but lacking in elegance. The same dress she wore at her own party last year and all her friends look like recently demobilized G.I.s. Should not a girl with her beauty wit and high position make a bit more of herself?

Diana Cooper was in London last week – sane and sweet. I met her quite unexpectedly at dinner at Lady Rothermeres & enjoyed it very much. I spent the week-end at Pam Berrys and was never so sumptuously fed or delicately flattered. Maurice Bowra was there. He greatly lacks frankness, I thought, and I believe all his pretensions to understand foreign poetry an imposture. . . . Then I went to the Betjemans for a night. Penelope just off for a camping holiday in a nearby field. Soon I go for a little jaunt to Scandinavia. You see I am getting about a bit.

Lady Colefax catechised me about your financial stability. I was unable to satisfy but hinted at the worst.

Hatty is indeed eccentric but far from insane.

Love from
Evelyn

Can you give me any details of June Capel's engagement (marriage?)?

Do you prefer 'Mitford' or 'Rodd' in dedication? The former suggests the sister of the pen biter [2].

[1] Presumably the portrait of William Hartington by Oswald Birley which now hangs at Chatsworth.

[2] Probably Unity Mitford (1914–48). A sister who admired Hitler and shot herself, causing injuries from which she never fully recovered, at the outbreak of the Second World War.

To Penelope Betjeman   Piers Court.
8 August [1947] [1]

Dearest Penelope

My heart bleeds for you in your wigwam. I spent many months under canvas at the beginning of the war & never succeeded in getting more than three hours sleep a night however drunk I went to bed.

Do not forget to loose the guys when it comes on to rain and remember that a finger on the tent wall produces a leak. Shallow trench latrines must be filled in daily and the spot marked with pebbles. The night bucket stands in the lines six paces from the nearest tent, one bucket to each thirty men.

God help you all.

It was very kind of you to let me come to stay & to give me such a good dinner & to show me your foal. My children wish to have rabbits and my wife to eat them. Are yours good eaters? If so we will gladly purchase some of those conies.

I go to Scandinavia next week in the hope of finding caviare.

Happy crisis to you & yours
Evelyn

[1] Waugh's diary for Monday 4 August reads: 'To Farnborough to make my peace with the Betjemans. Successful in this. A drive with John looking at 1860 churches. Penelope seems resolved to enter the Church in the autumn.'

To Laura Waugh   Carlton Hotel,
20 August [1947]   Kungsgatan 57,
                                                  Stockholm[1].

Darling

I wish you were here with me. You would find the licensing laws very oppressive but the food is all that you would possibly want and the town is of remarkable beauty – a bourgeois Venice. Sexy Mallet[2] was plainly much loved here and all his friends have been most cordial. Today I lunched with a pansy in a bungalow full of works of art.[3] He gave me great quantities of caviar. Yesterday I took Sexy's girl friend out to dinner. She was very pretty & shy & I should think sexy. My hotel is not very nice. I have worn myself out walking about sight seeing on cobbled streets & when one is worn out there is nothing to do except lie on the bed & stare at the ceiling. I do not know what I shall find to write about this trip for the *Daily Telegraph*. The girls have no make up and lovely figures down to the knees – then their calves are too thick. I asked Hatty to break the news to you that I have decided to live in England for a bit longer. I hope she broke it gently. It was not Mr Churchill's appeal that decided me.

                                                  All my love
                                                     E

[1] Waugh had arrived in Sweden on 18 August.
[2] Sir Victor Mallet, Minister at Stockholm 1940–5.
[3] Vilhelm Assarsson, deputy head of the Swedish Foreign Office 1944–55.

To Laura Waugh   Grand Hotel,
25 August [1947]   Oslo.

Darling

So now I am in Oslo and I shall be glad to leave on Friday. It is a hot, dusty, noisy, shabby, ugly town & the food is as bad as in London. Worse really. I was greeted yesterday by a press conference arranged by my publisher & the Embassy press attaché. Of the journalists one was a girl who was blind drunk, one a communist who walked out in the middle when I answered a question about Tito, only two spoke English. One man drew an offensive caricature of me. The journalist who did all the talking & seemed the most cultured was the representative of a paper devoted to the Merchant Navy. So that was all a bore. Last night I dined with my publisher and agent (female) who became rabidly pro Russian in her cups.

The only thing of interest I have found is the sculpture of a man named Vigeland 1886–1943 – preposterously hideous. There is a whole park devoted to his work & a palace full of it.

... I do hope my ma wasnt too horrible

                                                  All Love
                                                     E

To Graham Greene [Piers Court?]
[September 1947]

It is a great embarrassment. I simply cannot read this signature. Clearly you are a friend & I don't know who. Forgive me.

With regard to your very kind suggestion, I am afraid I shall not be in London for several weeks. Presumably Dr Skoumal is here for some time but I am afraid I am obliged to miss seeing the translator.[1]

Is it possibly Graham Greene? I have tried to read it as Graham but it always spells ENBOR which can't be right. If it *is* Graham – what about your seven-years-overdue visit to me?

E

[1] Greene had written from Eyre & Spottiswoode to ask Waugh to lunch to meet both the new Czech cultural attaché and the translator of Waugh's books into Czech.

To A.D.Peters Piers Court.
14 September [1947]

Dear Pete

I am sorry you don't like *The Loved One*. I have been sweating away at it and it is now more elegant but not less gruesome. I enclose a yank opinion (please return) from a woman of high Boston origins lately become a best seller. But I am not headstrong in this matter & don't want to antagonize future customers. The tale should not be read as a satire on morticians but as a study of the Anglo-American cultural impasse with the mortuary as a jolly setting. This is emphasized in the final version which I here enclose. . . .

Yours ever
Evelyn

To Cyril Connolly Piers Court.
16 September [1947]

Dear Cyril,

I am not going abroad again & am therefore able to dine with you on 28th if your kind invitation still stands.

Are you interested in publishing my latest story in *Horizon*? I think I spoke of it when you were here. It deals with mortuary life in Los Angeles. I like it very much. The final version is now being typed & I could send it to you when I get copy.

It is 30,000 words long & I want it published entire. That would mean devoting a whole issue to it. And I want it out soon. These two stipulations may make the project unfeasible, but I thought I would offer it to you first. I shall not want any payment other than your kind continuance of my 'subscription'. Perhaps you would like to put a guinea or two into Scottie Wilson's begging bowl. [1]

The story would make a very nice Christmas number.

Anyway, let me know if it is worth sending it to you. Clearly you cant decide whether it is worth disturbing your schedule until you have read it. [2]

Love to Lys

Evelyn

[1] Scottie Wilson was a 'naif' painter supported by *Horizon,* often mocked by Waugh, as in the first chapter of *The Loved One.*

[2] Connolly was enthusiastic: 'One of your very best I think. I shall be honoured to publish it.' He made several detailed suggestions, most of which Waugh adopted. *The Loved One* was printed in February 1948 in *Horizon* and in November as a book.

To Nancy Mitford   Piers Court.
[October? 1947]

Darling Nancy

An insoluble problem because of course one always wants to say how one would write the book oneself, not how the chum should.

I am sure you should stick to first person. [1] It suits you perfectly, but the advantage of f.p. is the eye witness account. Can the f.p. you have chosen see enough for herself? Only you can answer that. My fear would be a series of conversations in which other characters come to consult her about their problems so that the readers get the action second hand. Is there no observer nearer the centre of things?

Marriage to deceased aunts husband has always been legal I think. In fact I'm sure.

I am sorry not to be more helpful but at this stage of the story it is an unquickened embryo & the best gynaecologist can do no more than advise temperate habits.

I met a well dressed yank called Paston, Paton, Patton, Patterne? [2] who spoke of you with love.

Connolly and I are bosom friends. I dined twice with him last week.

You heard of course Harry & Nell's tragedy [3]? He is much set down by it.

No doubt you also heard of Ed's Duff-Gordon [4] escape from drowning?

Will you miss your compatriots passing through or be glad [5].

Socialist spies read our letters abroad now so forgive me for saying FUCK THE SOCIALISTS.

Love from

Evelyn

[1] Nancy Mitford had written outlining a plot that was to be much changed before becoming *Love in a Cold Climate,* 1949, and specifically asking Waugh 'Can Fanny tell the story again?'

[2] William (Bill) Patten married Susan Mary Jay in 1939. He worked for the Foreign Service Reserve in Paris 1944–54. She published her correspondence with Marietta Tree, *To Marietta from Paris, 1945–60,* 1976.

[3] Giles Fox-Strangways (1934–47), the son of Lord and Lady Stavordale, had been drowned.

[4] Lord Stanley was an enthusiastic sailor. Sir Cosmo and Lady Duff-Gordon escaped from the *Titanic* rather early in an underloaded boat.

[5] The amount of money the British were allowed to take abroad had been reduced and was now cut off altogether.

TO LAURA WAUGH   Piers Court.
[October 1947]

Darling Laura

I enclose letters from Teresa to you & Bridget. Is this her first communication with Bridget since Eddie's death? If so, rebuke her sharply for not mentioning that event.

I also enclose a letter from Jim Utley [1]. I have written to him to thank him for his trouble. It is now your task to continue operations. I do not know what steps you have taken lately in this matter.

I am grieved but not surprised that Bridget should feel lonely. It was for this reason that I wrote to invite her to stay here.

If it were in fact true that the last few days were the first time in your life you had been of some use to someone, that should be stated in trembling on your knees in the confessional. Let me assure you however that I can recall numerous occasions in the last ten years when you have been of use to your own children & several when you have been of use to me. So shake off these morbid scruples and return to duty as soon as you have effected the introduction of Mrs Anderson [2].

There is of course every reason why Magdalen [3] should be shy of me. She is my junior & knows me very slightly. That is all the more reason why she should conform closely to the conventions. It is precisely for these purposes that civilized society prescribes rules of procedure. There is no question of my not 'doing more for you than for others'. You should be well aware of that.

Trim & Anne [4] come here tonight for a night & I shall probably return with them to Mells for the following night. Henriques lunches here on Thursday. Friday is a day of jubilation for me.

There are now two pigs in your sty. Saunders & Atwood have unearthed some fine looking potatoes.

I want Angela Antrim to make a bust of you. This will entail two weeks at Glenarm [5]. Would the end of November suit you?

All my love. Don't be so bloody wet.
Evelyn

[1] Attaché to the Holy See in Rome.

[2] Mrs Anderson, a French Basque, helped with the evacuee children at Pixton.

[3] Countess of Eldon.

[4] Anne Palairet had married the Earl of Oxford and Asquith that year.

[5] In County Antrim, Northern Ireland.

To Cyril Connolly   Piers Court.
11 December 1947

Dear Cyril

The Loved One is in the hands of [Stuart] Boyle, a draughtsman, who promises to send it direct to you before Xmas.

I would greatly prefer the number of *Horizon* to look like an ordinary issue; except, I beg you, no graphic arts by Watson (Has he found the first draft? I hate to think of it falling into the hands of Lady Cunard & Lord Derwent).

If there is room for more matter, how about putting Knox[1] in then? Would you consider that quite preposterous? I think it would be what the Mitfords used to call 'a good tease' – offensive alike to Catholics who may tend to think I am doing apostolic work by insinuating propaganda in an unlikely place, and to the Dorchester Hotel ladies who may suppose, on reading *Loved One*, that my heart is in the right place after all.

And the majority of readers who just aren't interested in me anyhow would feel that their dose of Waugh was over for the year.

I agree that the crush on VCs is wholly unsuitable to an adult club. We will live to see those hideous paintings moved and ours in their places.[2]

———

I face the Christmas holidays with loathing. I have choked off all US fans and don't get many parcels. Have many of your contributors five children to feed? If not, a little *solid* food – not butter which we have – would be very welcome. I thought the *New Statesman* competition telegrams from you funny. Did you?

———

I am waiting my parcel of *Scott-Kings* to send you one as a seedy Christmas card. They haven't come yet.

———

I suffer much from lack of a pen pal in London now that Nancy has left. If you ever have an idle twenty minutes & a stenographer handy do dictate a page of social gossip. I have no idea what my friends or enemies are doing.[3]

Much love to Lys & yourself
Evelyn

[1] 'Mgr. Ronald Knox' was published in *Horizon*, May 1948.

[2] Connolly had suggested a portrait of Maurice Baring should be hung in White's in place of Carton de Wiart by Simon Elwes.

[3] Connolly replied: 'I have none of the qualifications – I'm not a bachelor girl and professional diner out. I don't find other people's misfortunes uproariously funny, my office is not the hub of the more literate landed gentry on their visits to London.'

To Nancy Mitford   Piers Court.
15 December [1947]

Darling Nancy,

How very kind of you to remember Harriet. I never go to London so I will ask the corporal to send her your presents. She will be delighted. She is a pretty, droll girl.

The airman[1] you speak of is half-American; Dutch on his father's side. (The family owes its prominence to the unnatural affections of William III.) So I do not think that the English services lose their reputation for sodomy by his action. Anyway I never count the R.A.F. as English.

You must have been having a busy time sabotaging trains. Do not repine at the set-back to the Party[2]. Big things will happen in Palestine where the American jews have made it possible for the Red Army to reach its goal in the Mediterranean.

The story proudly dedicated to you appears in *Horizon* in February & later as an illustrated book. I have found a draughtsman who takes down pictures like dictation. It will be a very pretty little book I think.

I was not asked to Cooper's Waterloo Ball[3].

I never go anywhere or see anyone. London is infested by Quennell and Alastair Forbes[4]. I do not repine. It seems to me I am keeping my sanity (if that is a good thing) while everyone else if losing, has lost, his. Also my health & shall live to a great age & see the Restoration.

I long to see your novel. Your projected joke has this weakness that practically none of your admirers read C. Morgan[5]. It is living with Frogs has made you think him important.

Do you mean that Hamish or Taffy is a very evil man?[6]

Osbert has become a Trades Union boss & Lord Kemsley has given him £1000 free of tax.

I think I sent you this Spanish yarn when it came out in a magazine but here it is again with my love for Christmas.

Debo has vanished from my life.

Mrs Betjeman says Desmond Guinness is charming. She is becoming a Catholic. Lady Pakenham is my great new friend.

I am now a Doctor of Letters of Loyola University, Baltimore – not an illustrious seat of learning.   Love from
                                                                    Evelyn

[1] Unnamed, sacked for sleeping with a Wren (WRNS: Woman's Royal Naval Service). 'The French say its the first time they ever heard of an Englishman being normal and he should have been given a prize.'

[2] Nancy Mitford replied: 'I don't know why you think I'm a Communist (must clear this up in your mind) I don't like Communism. I am a Socialist. . . .'

[3] Duff and Lady Diana Cooper gave a farewell ball as he was retiring as Ambassador in Paris. They rented a small château in the park of Chantilly from the French government.

[4] Alastair Forbes (1918–   ). Journalist. Son of American parents, educated in Europe.

[5] Nancy Mitford had thought of borrowing the respectable hero of *The Judge's Story*, 1947, by Charles Morgan, and revealing that when he retires, supposedly to write a book, he is 'doing feelthy things to little girls'.

[6] She meant Taffy Rodd, her brother-in-law. A surprising verdict.

To A.D. PETERS   Piers Court.
[December 1947]

Dear Pete
   I hope you have passed a cheerful & refreshing Christmas. I have not.
   ... To avoid boredom in 1948. *Scott-King* would make a very funny film.
Neutralia should cease to be Spain & become a Soviet satellite, thus giving topical
patriotic point. I would enjoy (or think I would) writing it for Rank. Any good? ...

                                                  Yours
                                                    E

The more I re-read *Loved One* the better content I am with it.

To NANCY MITFORD   [Piers Court.]
26 December [1947]

Darling Nancy
   Your presents to Harriet were a prodigious success. I found it very bitter to part
with the book & not incorporate it in my own library. She had never seen a 'snow-
storm' before & it is a delight to her. So were the delicious trinkets. Thank you very
much indeed for your imaginative generosity.
   Betjeman delivered a Christmas Message on the wireless. First he said that as a
little boy he had been a coward & a liar. Then he said he was sure all his listeners had
been the same. Then he said that he had been convinced of the truth of the
Incarnation the other day by hearing a choir boy sing 'Once in Royal David's City'
in King's College Chapel.
   All the reviews of *Scott-King*, instead of being about the book, have been about
me saying that I am ill-tempered and self-infatuated.
   I wrote in a letter to my great new friend Connolly that I sadly missed you in
London as I heard no gossip now & would he tell me some. He wrote to say he did
not regard the sufferings of his fellow men as the subject for humour.
   The only Christmas presents I have received are the exquisite pen from you and
some wine from Basil Bennett. I love you both. What a pity you & he never married.
   All my most valued books have been eaten by tiny spiders.
   Would you say I was a very ill-tempered & self-infatuated man? It hurts.
   Balfour is back homeless, penniless, without employment, living at Chagford &
trying to write a book – precisely as he was 15 years ago.

                                                  Best love from
                                                    Evelyn

To JOHN BETJEMAN   Piers Court.
[December 1947]
Postcard

One listener at least deeply resented the insinuation in your Christmas Message that your listeners had all been cowards & liars in childhood. Properly brought up little boys are fantastically chivalrous. Later they deteriorate. How would you have felt if instead of a choir boy at Cambridge you had heard a muezzin in Isfahan?

To CYRIL CONNOLLY   Piers Court.
2 January 1948

Dear Cyril

I am in your debt for two delightful letters. I was in London for two days this week & hoped to see you. Perhaps I did see you. I cannot tell, for I got very drunk at once & remained drunk causing, rather than collecting, gossip. I shall be back next week, staying at St James's Club but frequenting White's, remaining over the weekend. Perhaps Lys would let me call on you both one evening?

I was moved by your verdict that the misfortunes of your friends are not the proper subject for humour. I do not know how you can bear to go so much into society if you feel this.

With regard to *The Loved One*: I anticipated ructions & one reason, apart from the predominant one of my affection for yourself, for my seeking publication in *Horizon* was the confidence that its readers were tough stuff.

The Americans embrace the democratic superstition that everything must be equally pleasing to everyone. I think it highly undesirable that the popular papers should get hold of the tale. (After a momentary weakness towards the *New Yorker* which they themselves at once dispelled). Fortunately American law is stricter than ours about quotation. If you insert one of those formal notices about 'reproduction in whole or in part' being 'reserved' they will not be able to say much about it.

For myself I have always found deep comfort in the text: 'Woe unto you when all men shall speak well of you', and rejoice in the stinks [?] & groans [?] of the field dressing station, but I am sympathetic to your own quite different problem as the editor of a magazine which must enjoy goodwill or perish. It might be prudent for you to introduce the story with soft words and I know you will do it brilliantly. I look forward eagerly to seeing the 'Comment' in the February issue but would sooner not see it before or attempt any censorship. It must be your opinion of the tale, not mine

The ideas I had in mind in writing were: 1st & and quite predominantly over-excitement with the scene of Forest Lawn. 2nd the Anglo-American impasse – 'never the twain shall meet, 3rd there is no such thing as an American. They are all exiles uprooted, transplanted & doomed to sterility. The ancestral gods they have abjured get them in the end. I tried to indicate this in Aimée's last hours. 4th the European raiders who come for the spoils & and if they are lucky make for home with them. 5th Memento mori, old style, not specifically Californian.

But there is no reason why any of these should appear in your introduction. I should like to see you treat it as a book for review by a writer unknown to you.

Do you think this post card would make a pretty frontispiece?

———

I disagreed deeply with you about the need for an 'advanced guard' – last months Comment.

Miss Trumper has some fine teats[1] for sale – only £85 a box. Even in my drunkenness I did not buy them.

My plans. I arrive in London Wednesday afternoon and shall be in Whites before dinner, dining out, lunching out Thursday & Friday otherwise not engaged

Could you please, keep me a dozen copies of February *Horizon*?

Yours ever
Evelyn

[1] Cigars at the hairdresser in Curzon Street.

To Rupert Croft-Cooke[1]
20 January 1948

Dear Sir,

You were wrongly informed that I have an aversion to anthologists.

I should be proud to be represented in your forthcoming collection. I don't want any money for myself. Will you take the eight guineas round to the nearest Roman Catholic Church and pop it anonymously in the poor box?

Yours faithfully
Evelyn Waugh

[1] Rupert Croft-Cooke edited *How to Enjoy Travelling Abroad*, 1948.

To the Marchioness of Bath   Piers Court.
27 January [1948]

Dearest Daphne,

It was jolly decent getting a letter from you.

You are lucky in being able to send your children to work in a garage. Mine are a pest. I have managed at last to get rid of two at school, a third is malingering at home & two are permanent squatters. Laura is in agonies of fibrositis. There are paper-hangers doing folk dances in the room over my head. Goodness it is beastly.

My London little season came to end with a party of Pempys[1] where I kissed a great number of strangers irrespective of age & sex. They were surprised & ungrateful. At that party I met the fiend Palffy[2] but did not kiss her much.

Yesterday I went to Oxford to lecture to the Papist undergraduates who were mostly asiatic women. A very polite gentle young man got up at the end and said: 'I should like to ask Mr W. whether it is true, as we are always being told, that we are much stupider & less cultured & amusing than undergraduates were in his day' and I had to say 'Well yes it is' and he said very sadly 'I thought so' and sat down. Sad.

I hope you go regularly to Ronnie Knox at Mells for religious instruction. He greatly needs a new Heloise (Not Lady Ancaster. I refer to a famous figure in history whose brothers castrated Abelard) now that the other Daphne[3] has gone to Africa.

I have just bought a complete set of Max Beerbohm & am re-reading him all day in bed-room slippers with a big fire & a box of Havana cigars sent me from USA so life is not all as beastly as I began this letter by saying.

The paper that is being put up over my head is very remarkable, very dark 1860 Gothic. Betjeman ordered it and it was too much even for him so I took it over. Please come & stay when the room is finished. It will be a nightmare. But I have a nice mechanical organ you could play and a ham you could paint.

Love from
Evelyn

[1] Penelope Dudley Ward (1914–   ). Married to Anthony Pelissier 1930–44, and in 1948 to Carol Reed, the film director.
[2] Louise de Vilmorin.
[3] Lady Acton.

To Penelope Betjeman   Piers Court.
Shrovers 10 February 1948

Dearest Penelope

Here are the twelve shillings I owe you. The paper is hung & looks very well. The dressing-room is still only half-covered as we are reprinting a second edition.

9th March is St Catherine of Bologna's day.[1] She is the only Saint I have ever shaken hands with. She has been dead 500 years but sits bolt upright in a little chair in her nuns habit, face hands & feet bare & rather black but very supple & fragrant. I will pray to her, remind her of our meeting, and commend you to her.

I am greatly impressed & edified by the depth of your studies. I just talked half a dozen times to Father d'Arcy about T.S.Eliot & Havelock Ellis, then popped into Farm Street on the way to dinner one evening & sat up with Driberg in the gallery of the Café de Paris to see a new negress singer. It took me years to begin to glimpse what the Church was like. I was constantly travelling in those days and it was chiefly missionaries who taught me. Of course I was a bit younger than you but not much – 27, how old are you, I suppose 35?[2] Well I shall constantly come to you for advice & instruction.

I suppose in Aquina they always made garlick sausages out of old horses. Here as you know well people sometimes kept decrepit old hunters at grass out of a sentiment of gratitude. [3]

Many things have puzzled me from time to time about the Christian religion but one thing has always been self evident – the bogosity of the Church of England.

Why not come & live in this village. The Manor House is for sale, a paddock, gardens, 1840 Tudor, £9,000.

Tomorrow all the austerities of Lent begin for me. Are catachumens exempt?

Do you get *Horizon*? If not I will send you a copy of my very good new story.

> Your loving brother in St Catherine of Bologna
> Evelyn

[1] Penelope Betjeman was received into the Roman Catholic Church on 9 March 1948 at St Aloysius, Oxford.

[2] Her thirty-eighth birthday was in four days' time.

[3] St Thomas Aquinas says that love of horses is only for what you receive from them.

To Randolph Churchill   Piers Court.
12 February [1948]

My Dear Randolph

I was delighted to receive a letter from you this morning and your kind present of *Grenadine Etching* which will provide welcome Lenten reading.

Your long absence has caused comment. Seymour Berry[1] (who rarely leaves the leatherette fender of White's except to doze fitfully on the bench in the front hall where country members leave their dogs) has put it about that you are entangled with a woman and once more about to become a father. I have loyally maintained that you are doing time in Zing Zing or El Cantara for some minor homicide & that you have chosen to suffer under a pseudonym rather than bring further disgrace on your name. Anyway curiosity about you was rife when last I went to London and I shall now be able to confirm that you are at liberty. ...

I will shortly send you, in care of your father-in-law, a copy of my tale – *The Loved One*, which is re-establishing my popularity in highbrow circles here.

I have seen few of your friends. Angie is thriving; [–][2] is dying painfully – which shows there is justice in this world. Duff fought a man dressed as a policeman at a fancy-dress ball and found out that it was a real policeman. ... While Maimie and her husband were at the races Saccone and Speed[3] rang up their house and said his highness had to leave at once for Scotland and would send a car to collect all his clothes, all Maimie's clothes, and a dozen bottles of champagne. All went according to plan and their highnesses have no clothes at all.

If anyone wants to send me an unsolicited gift say linen pants (short) 39 inch in circumference.

Give my love to any friends you see in USA. There will be none after the publication of *The Loved One*.

> Yours ever
> Evelyn

[1] Seymour Berry (1909–). Conservative MP 1941–5. Succeeded as Viscount Camrose 1954. Chairman of the *Daily Telegraph*.

[2] Manuscript lost. Text taken from Churchill's censored version.

[3] The wine-merchants where Prince Vsevolode worked.

To Penelope Betjeman   Piers Court.
18 February [1948]

Dearest Penelope

I gave nothing to d'Arcy for my instruction[1]. It didn't occur to me & I think word must have got round now among the clergy that there is no immediate financial return from converts. The trouble is we are used to the gentility & endowments of the Church of England & do not at once understand a priesthood of plebeian origin living hand to mouth. But since it *has* occurred to you I think you ought to tip your instructor – a fiver at least, a tenner at most. You may be quite sure he'll have no middle-class qualms about taking it. The Oxford Dominicans are very poor indeed I believe & go days without food or soap[?].

Your parish priest should have a fiver at Easter, a pound at Christmas, half-a-crown every day of obligation. Any masses you *want* to have said should be done by him but there is no need to go out of your way to put work in his way. If he is Irish & goes home for his holidays he would probably welcome a pound pocket money.

I have never had any experience of sacristans. My impression is that they vary greatly in social status and are liable to all forms of English delicacy in these matters. Christmas is safe but I shouldn't tip him at other times.

I thought afterwards perhaps I had suggested that d'Arcy was negligent with instruction. What I meant was that, with me, he saw it was no good hoping for much & the thing to do was just to get the seed in anyhow & hope some of it would come up.

I enclose my article on Forest Lawn. Also my story but please will you return this as I have no other copy. It is odd & rather admirable that you dont take in *Horizon*. Before midsummer I will send you a fine copy of this story with pictures.

A weaver named Hiram Winterbottom[2] talked of John very confidently as 'John'. Is he entitled to do this?

> Love from
> Evelyn

Confirmation is 5/– I think at Westminster. I paid 3,000 lire when the lira was worth quite a lot but that was in Rome by a Cardinal.

[1] Penelope Betjeman had asked: 'When Father D'Arcy had finished his last intruction on Havelock Ellis did you press a few notes into his hand, as to a butler on leaving a country house?'

[2] A neighbour, described in another letter as 'a talkative handsome fellow with a knowledge of Georgian domestic architecture which took me back ten years'.

To John Betjeman   Piers Court.
[February? 1948]

Dear John

It was very kind of you to write about *The Loved One*. I am pleased with it myself but then I was pleased with *Brideshead Revisited* which everyone tells me was a great disgrace. I will send you a beautiful sanguine illustrated edition in the summer.

I say it is good news about your bankruptcy. You will be sold up and I shall get your books.

I have some beautiful acquisitions. Do come & see them. A pair of paintings by Thos Musgrave, Joy of Travel in 1750 & 1850 contrasted. A fine Swoboda (the Viennese Frith) well I suppose you would despise that for being foreign but it's jolly good. An exquisite 1847 Gruel[1] binding velvet & silver gilt and rubies. Do come & see them.

Funny about G.Pike poisoning himself. May all radicals perish so.

Poor Cyril. Do you mean *another* seizure? He had one & was sent to Tring[2] to starve. Lost 1½ stone in 3 weeks. Well that is too much. If he has had another seizure it is really all up with him. I wish I could get Lys as a cook. I have the very worst in England outside the Dorchester Hotel.

Your wall-paper is hung & looks lovely. Like an ass I had the woodwork painted pink. Now I see must be light grained oak but its too late. Damn.

How much do you know about the Eglington Tournament?[3] A wonderful subject for a poem by you. But of course that is an impertinence. Only the poet knows what is his subject.

My taste is receding not advancing. I really only like pre-Great-Exhibition post-Waterloo art.

Curious passage in preface to Balston's *Martin*[4]. 'I thank the Duke of Northumberland, Earl Grey & LORD KINROSS for opening their picture galleries to me'. Patrick comes here on Wednesday.

It may be you are not bankrupt at all. It is a delusion that often afflicts the rich eg. Berners.

I am reading Proust for the first time. Very poor stuff. I think he was mentally defective. I remember how small I used to feel when people talked about him & didn't dare admit I couldnt get through him. Well I can get through him now – in English of course – because I can read anything that isn't about politics. Well the chap was plain barmy. He never tells you the age of the hero and on one page he is being taken to the WC in the Champs Elysées by his nurse & the next page he is going to a brothel. Such a lot of nonsense.

I rather wish I was in Belize[5]. It sounds charming.

Sorry to miss you at Beefsteak[6]. Are you now an habitué? Do come here soon.

                                                        Evelyn

[1] Pierre-Paul Gruel of Paris who was binding books from 1835.
[2] A health clinic housed in the former residence of the second Lord Rothschild.

[3] The Eglinton Tournament was held in 1839 by the 13th Earl of Eglinton at a cost of over £30,000 Knights wearing mediaeval armour jousted in the rain. It is described in Disraeli's *Endymion*.
[4] Tom Balston's *The Life of Jonathan Martin, Incendiary of York Minster*, 1945.
[5] Then capital of British Honduras.
[6] Betjeman had been put up by Waugh and elected to this club on 17 December 1947.

To Cyril Connolly

Piers Court.

[2 March 1948]

Postcard

Poor Scottie.[1] By the way is Mrs L's new consort[2] the rival doodler? I am a little relieved by what you tell me of your regime. But 1½ stone is drastic. What about shirt collars? Yes it was *Partisan Review*[3] – chief subjects Koestler, Proust, Fiedler, Lasky, Hauser. Will you please tell Gallimard to deal direct with Peters. How does Lucian F. get 10/- to give Scottie. Why does Watson not support him properly? I am beset by a local weaver named Hiram Winterbottom who makes very free with the names of my friends. I have written to Maggs[4] asking if they will take my inferior Jones[5]. Your copy is too fine a fish to throw back. You can get gin in Chagford in unlimited quantities – I mean in cases not glasses. Would Lys for a large fee accept post as holiday tutor to my cook (male) a willing boy just out of the army who can't cook at all.

[1] Connolly had written: 'Scottie Wilson has come to London ... only to experience the ingratitude of the dealers and the fickleness of the public. He is now quite destitute and lives on small loans of up to 10/- a time from Lucian Freud. Shall we really give him some guineas from you?'

[2] Robert Kee (1919–   ). Writer and broadcaster. Married 1948–51 to Janetta Woolley, who had changed her name to Loutit by deed-poll when living with Kenneth Sinclair Loutit. During her marriage to Robert Kee they shared a house in Sussex Place with Cyril Connolly. She once opened the door to Waugh in bare feet and so earned the nickname 'Blue Feet'.

[3] Waugh seems to have been sent *Partisan Review* anonymously. Connolly described it as having 'Jewish editors, but the contributors are mostly gentile'.

[4] Maggs Bros, booksellers in Berkeley Square.

[5] Owen Jones (1809–74). Architect and ornamental designer.

To Penelope Betjeman

Piers Court.

St Thos Aquinas [7 March 1948]

Dearest Penelope

Laura & I will be thinking very joyfully about you on Tuesday. May you live happily ever after. I am sure you will. You are coming into the Church with vastly more knowledge than most converts but what you cannot know until Tuesday is the delight of membership of the Household, of having your chair at the table, a place laid, the bed turned down, of the love & trust, whatever their family bickerings, of all

Christendom. It is this family unity which makes the weakest Catholic nearer the angels & saints, than the most earnest outsider.

It is a particular joy for me to be able to welcome you home, who have known you in so many phases. Your prayers will be specially powerful at the moment so please pray for me.

> Yours most affectionately
> Evelyn

To LADY MARY LYGON   Piers Court.
11 March [1948]

My Dear

I have great hopes of little Poll shortly receiving another proposal of marriage. The man is neither wealthy, nor very young, nor of untarnished reputation. His family is not distinguished but he is well connected on his mother's side. He has no fixed employment at present but he has enjoyed responsible positions in journalism, diplomacy, and the Air Force in the past & there is hope of his being engaged on a newspaper. He is healthy, except in the teeth; his head is well covered. He is tall. I refer to your old friend Lord Kinross. He is in search of a wife and I have presented to him all the manifest advantages attaching to your little sister. I invited them to stay here together & sent them for little walks together & left them alone. *He picked her primroses this morning.*

Unhappily there are two widows to whom he must propose first but Poll is third on the list and one of the widows is very fashionable & the other badly pock-marked, insane streaks in her heredity, and too old for child bearing, so I think everything may turn out well.

Poll looked very pretty & girlish & spoke of her cellar with great tact.

Pauper is living in Bayswater attending his dentist. The crazy widow lives in the North; the fashionable widow in London. Perhaps you will be able to intervene & upset their chances in a Chinky way.

> All love
> Bo

To THE MARCHIONESS OF BATH   Piers Court.
12 March [1948]

Dearest Daphne,

. . .ˈAlas Laura cant come on account of cows and kids. She thanks you very much for the kind invitation.

I say it is interesting about your being on the waggon. I am too on account of Lent and I have just read in my paper that there is an unprecedented glut of gin in the West Country in the last few days. Impressive.

Mr Masaryk[1] defenestrating himself would be a good subject for a picture. You could always put a kipper[2] or two in odd corners as the great Masters did well not kippers perhaps but you know what I mean.

I have had Coote to stay and she looked very pretty and I threw her in the way of a friend of mine who is in search of a wife.

... The trouble is that she will probably refuse him too. To my certain knowledge she has turned down three fairly eligible suitors in the last two years. They are all after the white Burgundy in which she prudently invested her little all in 1939.

When I say waggon that doesn't mean Sundays of course & goodness we do get spiflicated then.

Duff is doing communist propaganda I see.

Love from
Evelyn

[1] Jan Masaryk (1886–1948). Foreign Minister of Czechoslovakia. It is uncertain whether his death was suicide or murder.

[2] Lady Bath had written: 'Robin Campbell tells me that you think that we should take to painting contemporary historical subjects, but my muse is more inspired by kippers than by the Queen or Mr Attlee.'

TO NANCY MITFORD   Piers Court.
16 March [1948]

Darling Nancy,

That is a remarkably obtuse letter from the Norwegian[1]. We must get her alone & ply her with snaps schnapps? and questions. Nor do I think it proper for her to refer to her former mistress in those terms. She has made a very bad impression on me.

Did I tell you of Boots' stroke? Not I think paralysis in the full Elwes sense but a definite seizure. His doctor sent him to Tring where he was strapped to his bed for three weeks & treated with enemas & synthetic orange juice. He lost 21 lbs. Well that is a lot for a shortish man. I think it will be the end of him.

Loved One is being well received in intellectual circles. They think my heart is in the right place after all. I'll show them.

I am afraid that when you fall into communist hands you must expect very little gratitude for all your services to the Party. When they were attempting their first coup in Spain, with precisely the same plan as they have employed everywhere since, you applauded ardently. You introduced an entirely false figure into your well known novel simply to suck up to them. But you will get no thanks & no reward.

I am so weary about having been consistently right in all my political predictions for ten years. It is so boring seeing it all happen for the second time after one has gone through it in imagination. For you & Duff & Randolph life must be all one lovely surprise after another.

I am reading Proust for the first time – in English of course – and am surprised to find him a mental defective. No one warned me of that. He has absolutely no sense

of time. He cant remember anyone's age. In the same summer as Gilberte gives him
a marble & Françoise takes him to the public lavatory in the Champs Elysées, Bloch
takes him to a brothel. And as for the jokes – the boredom of Bloch and Cottard.

Osbert Sitwell 3rd volume[2] is out in US. I am reading it. He treads gingerly about
Lady Ida's[3] criminal career. Did you know that the Sitwells only trace their descent
through a female line. The real name of the family is Hurt. They took the Sitwell
quite lately – about 1800.[4] He avoids this very neatly saying that lands of Eckington
were held by Cytwells in the tenth century & then jumping to Sir Sitwell Sitwell first
bart né Hurt. There are precious few Englishmen who could not assume a
mediaeval name if they chose to pick about in their pedigree.

Whenever he writes about Ginger[5] he is splendid but there are some awful drab
panegyrics of Edwardian hostesses.

How Jewish was Proust? I mean like Sutro & Jessel or like Brian Howard? Did
his parents go to synagogue? If he was a real Jew it would surely be quite impossible
for him to know the haute-bourgeoisie, though he might meet the looser
aristocracy?[6]

Patrick Balfour is going to propose marriage to Diana Campbell-Gray[7], then to
Coote, then he cant think to whom. He does want a wife so badly. He has been
staying here & has been very nice. He has £300 in the world & two suitcases of ill-
fitting clothes and no prospects. He is very much nicer in adversity. Well most of his
life has been that. He is trying to write a novel about Angela[8]. It wont be very good.

Henry Yorke is having an affaire with Jenifer Fry.[9]

David Erskine has rewarded (ha ha) the long pursuit of Miss Kelly[10] by marrying
her.

You must have poor Jonathan[11] converted to Catholicism. The only hope for
him.

> Best love from
> Evelyn

[1] Nancy Mitford had sent Waugh a letter from her Norwegian maid, now working for Cyril Connolly,
in which she described her new employer as 'normal'.

[2] *Great Morning*, 1948, the third volume of Osbert Sitwell's autobiography in five volumes.

[3] Lady Ida Sitwell, mother of Edith, Osbert and Sacheverell, had been trapped into borrowing money
and signing papers by a swindler. She was sentenced to three months imprisonment in 1915.

[4] Francis Hurt, a Sitwell on his mother's side, called his son Sitwell. When in 1776 he inherited
Renishaw from an uncle he changed his surname to Sitwell, thus making his son Sitwell Sitwell.

[5] Osbert's father, Sir George Sitwell (1860–1943).

[6] Nancy Mitford replied: 'Proust's mother was a Jewess. . . . Proust himself knew a few aristocrats . . .
but I don't think he was genuinely accepted in society.' Brian Howard thought himself Jewish but it is
probable that he was not.

[7] Diana Cavendish (1909–   ). Married to Robert (later Lord) Boothby 1935–7, to Colonel Campbell-
Gray 1942–6 and to Viscount Gage in 1971.

[8] Angela Culme-Seymour, who was married to Lord Kinross 1938–42. The novel was *The Ruthless
Innocent*, 1950. He did not marry again.

[9] Jennifer Fry (1916–   ). The daughter of Alathea Fry, sister of Evelyn Gardner. She was married to
Robert Heber-Percy 1942–7, and to Alan Ross, editor of the *London Magazine*, in 1949.

[10] David Erskine (1917–   ) was married to Antonia Kelly 1948–65.

[11] Jonathan Guinness, Nancy Mitford's nephew.

To Katharine Asquith   [Piers Court?]
[March 1948]

Dear Katharine

I am delighted & astounded that you like *The Loved One*. I was sure it was much the most offensive work I had done. It shows I simply do not understand about decency at all.

. . . I have read all 3 Fossett books and was *greatly shocked* by them. So much so that I wrote a letter of reproof to Christopher[1] which was not well received.

Love from
Evelyn

My 'Homage to Ronnie' is postponed until May

[1] Christopher Hollis wrote *Death of a Gentleman*, 1943, *Fossett's Memory*, 1944, and *Letters to a Sister*, 1947.

To the Marchioness of Bath   [Piers Court]
[April 1948]

Dearest Daphne

I hope that Henry will be able to read the story I have written for 28th October. It is a little nightmare that troubled me lately. The size of the page limited the horrors.

Low Sunday was high jinks for me. I loved my visit & the gay whirl. The dinner party was just what I like to think my youth was like (and it was not for it was full of melancholy & self-distrust) all light and sweetness. And the pilgrimage to the Greenes & the [teak?] house were melodrama.[1]

My four days in London followed the usual graph of waning popularity. Everyone most welcoming for a few hours & soon tiring of my continued presence.

John de Forrest[2] went to confession and got through 4 years sins in 13 minutes – a record for the Farm Street [course?].

Christopher Sykes has written a most enjoyable novel[3].

Oh, here I am writing to you and of course you are in Ireland. I wish I were there too with lovely Debo. Now I will change plans and send this letter to Lismore & Henry's book to Stamford. Please tell Andrew[4] that yesterday some neighbours telephoned to say they had a young man in the house & couldnt get rid of him so might they bring him to cocktails so they did and who should it be but CAPTAIN BLOW[5]. I dont suppose you know what that means. Andrew does.

Love from
Evelyn

[1] Waugh wrote in his diary 'Olivia ⅓ drunk, ⅓ insane, ⅓ genius.' Olivia Plunket Greene, with whom Waugh had been in love in 1924–5, was living with her mother on the Longleat estate.

[2] John de Forest (1907   ). Inherited Liechtenstein title of Count de Bendern.

[3] Christopher Sykes, *Answer to Question 33*, 1948, dedicated to Evelyn and Laura.

[4] Marquess of Hartington, who has since become Duke of Devonshire and inherited Lismore in County Waterford.

[5] Jonathan Blow, who left the Coldstream Guards under a cloud.

TO NANCY MITFORD   St James' Club.
7 April 1948

Darling Nancy

I have taken refuge here from White's which has become uninhabitable since the budget – all the men who to my certain knowledge have not £100 in the world yelling themselves hoarse (and I think sincerely believing) that they are ruined and the dozen or so really rich men smoking quietly in corners having made themselves registered companies in Costa Rica years ago. The people who really are ruined are the heiresses for Sir Stafford[1] has made it a dead loss (literally out-of-pocket) to have a wife with more than £2000 a year in trust frunds.

I had a long week-end in Somerset. First at the Baths – frightfully noisy & drunken, Daphne keeping me up till 3.30 every night, and the children riding bicycles round the house with loud cries from 6.30. No sleep. Jazz all day. Henry at meals reading the most disgusting pages of Malinowski's *Sexual Life of the Savage* (and goodness they are disgusting) aloud to his 18 year old daughter[2] and 16 year old son[3]. All Longleat park like Surrey – the woods cut, second growth scrub, tank tracks & decaying Nissen huts. Then a great change to Mells – all Pre-Raphaelite paintings & the X-word puzzle with Ronnie Knox.

I visited Olivia Greene – stark mad. She broke her arm writing a letter.

I heard that the Filth-Marine, as Ran calls Palffy, has behaved badly to Diana.

Mrs J Sutro[4] is giving a subscription ball for Diana & Mme Massigli[5]. Proust would have some difficult conundrums about that. I persevere with Proust & still think him insane. Of course I miss all the nuances of language but the structure must be same & that is raving. Eg. 'I' is represented as a chronic invalid of exquisite diffidence etc etc. Then suddenly in order to illustrate Albertine's slang he says: – 'For example talking about the seconds I had chosen for a duel I was engaged in . . .'

I go out shopping after luncheon a bit tight & buy such peculiar things – 3 tie pins, a ½ ton marble 2nd Empire Clock, a solid silver 1830 candelabrum as tall as myself, a pearl grey bowler, six pounds of church candles – they keep appearing in my bed room in the most disconcerting way. Perhaps it is not drink but insanity.

Randolph is back, exactly 3 times as fat as before.

Mrs Loutit has a new look: silk stockings, high heeled shoes, diamond clips everywhere. I dined with Boots [Connolly] last evening in his subterranean dining room superb grub as usual.

I call Handy Handy[6] & he calls me Evelyn now. It is very nice. I had to write & ask him to.

Best love
Evelyn

[1] Sir Stafford Cripps, Chancellor of the Exchequer.
[2] Lady Caroline Thynne (1928–   ). Married David Somerset in 1950.
[3] Viscount Weymouth (1932–   ).
[4] Gillian Sutro was 'a slim shy girl more French than English, who looked as if she had just been let out of a convent . . . the natural grace of a Persian cat.' Harold Acton, *More Memoirs of an Aesthete*, 1970.
[5] Odette Massigli, wife of the French Ambassador to London 1944–55.
[6] Handasyde Buchanan.

To Harold Acton
27 April [1948]

Piers Court.

My Dear Harold

I have spent two enchanted days with your *Memoirs of an Aesthete* – (a most apt title whatever some of your friends may have told you) and must thank you for an experience of rare pleasure.

I expected to find most interest in the Oxford section but, enormously though that did delight me, I found Peking even more enthralling. You have accomplished a great feat in communicating your own tenderness for the place to a bigoted westerner.

The copy of *Aquarium* which you found in the second-hand stall was not the one you inscribed to 'Le faune d'un après-midi ou de plusieurs'. That stands on my shelf next to the bound volume of *Broom*[1] and the manuscript of your lecture on 'English Realism in Early Victorian Art.' My sympathies still stand where you grounded them with Frith & the Pope of Rome as you will see if you ever come to visit us here, where you will also find in the flesh the bouncing progeny which you imagined for me in Canonbury Square.

There is so much to discuss in your book that I regret more than ever that we never meet. It is not yet the time to say so but I greatly disliked Robert[2] in his last years & think he was a dangerous lunatic better dead. Your loyalty to Sachie [Sitwell] does credit to your warm heart. I vastly relished the descriptions of Tchelitchew[3]. Emerald[4] has always given me the shivers but I am glad to see her lauded in her old age. I loved the account of Mr Handforth[5]. Well I could cover pages with an enumeration of all I admired. What a very delightful life you have had and, I hope, are still having!

I hope that the star on the binding means that this is only the first of many volumes.

You give the impression that you went to Eton a Catholic[6]. Surely you were a convert, with Roger Spence[7] as Godfather?

I was delighted that *The Loved One* amused you. It is coming out presently as a pretty book. Please give me an address where I can safely send a copy.

By the way, as one schoolmaster to another, you use the phrase 'inverse ratio' in the opposite to its true sense. The first time you did so I thought it was a misprint but the error recurs.

With homage & affection

Yours ever

Evelyn

[1] 'I had started sweeping away *fin de siècle* cobwebs with a paper called *The Oxford Broom* ... Our editorials assailed the prevalent insipidities ... the pseudo-aesthetes writhed among their willow-pattern teacups, and hastened to change their wardrobes .... Evelyn Waugh ... was my chief support on *The Oxford Broom*, designing the covers and giving us his first, most passionately earnest short story ....' *Memoirs of an Aesthete*, pp. 119, 126.

[2] Robert Byron, who had been killed in 1941.

[3] Pavel Tchelitchew (1898–1957). Painter. His portrait of Acton was not a success. 'By slow degrees I saw myself committed to canvas, an ostrich egg with the mumps....', p. 176.

[4] Lady Cunard.

[5] Tom Handforth (1897–   ). 'An earnest devotee of Picasso ... hot on the trail of self-expression,' p. 324.

[6] Sir Harold Acton was baptised a Roman Catholic but brought up as a Protestant until he complained and was formally received into the Church and confirmed at Eton.

[7] Roger Spence (1904–1964). Business editor of *The Eton Candle*. A regular soldier, he became a brigadier.

To Graham Greene   Piers Court.
3 May [1948]

Dear Graham

I was delighted (so far as I can ever be delighted when speaking on the telephone) to hear your news, which whets my already keen appetite for the book. [1]

It is impossible now to be rich but it is possible to be idle, and this American coup relieves you of work for about fifteen years. What you should do is to have a new contract drawn up with Viking Press for this novel – I presume they had it under the terms of some earlier contract – by which your royalty earnings are paid to you in a salary until they are exhausted. My own experience is that it is simply not worth while earning more than a gross £5000 a year nowadays. I get about £2000 from English sales & odd articles (your price for articles in USA will now be about five times what it was) so I take £3000 a year from my USA publishers in half yearly sums of $6000 each.

There is no way short of domiciling yourself in USA of getting hold of the capital sum, and then you would be subject to American taxation which is not negligible on large amounts.

You will have the most ghastly post-bag for six weeks or so. Then quite abruptly they lose all interest. I read all letters & answered a few rudely. I think this was bad policy. One should either not read any at all or send a post-card photograph of oneself with a scrawl of thanks to everyone.

I should advise you to write out a full (4 page) autobiography & have it printed & circulated. It saves a lot of enquiries. For the six weeks in which you are the chief topic, their curiosity about you is insatiable.

Will your book be taken up by Catholics as specifically popish? If so you will fall in with another great wave of annoyances including a reprimand from the Bishop of London, Ontario, and an honorary doctorate at Loyola College, Baltimore.

I should advise against your going over to enjoy your . . . . [sheet lost]

[1] Graham Greene's *The Heart of the Matter*, 1948, was a Book Society Choice in the United States.

To George Orwell
Piers Court.
21 June [1948]

Dear Mr Orwell

Perhaps in hospital [1] any letters are quite welcome even from a stranger. With this hope I write to tell you of a Wodehouse book which was new to me &, I think, will be new to you: '*The Swoop or How Clarence saved England*' published by Alston Rivers in 1909 with some beastly illustrations by Harrison.

It is extremely pertinent to your essay [2] & to our correspondence about it.

The theme is the simultaneous invasion of England by the armies of Germany, Russia, China, Morocco etc. The population, with the exception of the Boy Scouts are complacent. The worst atrocity is some soldiers marching over a golf links & failing to replace the divots.

'Thus was London bombarded. Fortunately it was August & there was no one in town.'

The boy-scout Clarence muses on 'my country – my England, my fallen, stricken England etc' and is a figure of ridicule.

The book is very much funnier than *The Head of Kays* which preceded it, and in fact forms an important literary link with *Mike* published next year.

If you think of revising your essay this is quite certainly a book you should mention. It reads word for word like the Berlin broadcast which I am told by a friend Wodehouse himself thinks 'one of the best things' he ever did.

Of course don't trouble to answer. I was so excited at being shown this missing link in our argument that I had to pass on the news.

Yours sincerely
Evelyn Waugh

[1] Orwell was in a hospital in Scotland with TB.
[2] George Orwell, 'In Defence of P.G.Wodehouse', *Tribune*, 16 February 1945, which Waugh had reviewed in *The Tablet*.

To GRAHAM GREENE   White's.
[July? 1948]

Dear Graham

   I am delighted that you did not take the review amiss. My admiration for the
book was great – as I hope I made plain.[1]

   It was your putting that quotation from Péguy[2] at the beginning which led me
astray. I think it will lead others astray. Indeed I saw a review by Raymond
Mortimer in which he stated without the hesitation I expressed, that you thought
Scobie a saint.

   I think you will have a great deal of troublesome controversy in USA. The
Bishops there are waiting to jump on decadent European Catholicism – or so it
seemed to me – and I just escaped delation by sending everyone to heaven.

   Do please come whenever you have a spare night or nights.

                                                          Yours ever
                                                          Evelyn

   [1] In his review of *The Heart of the Matter* in *Commonweal*, 16 July, Waugh wrote: 'I believe Mr
Greene thinks him [Scobie] a saint. Perhaps I am wrong in this. . . .' Greene wrote to Waugh, 'A small
point – I did not regard Scobie as a saint, and his offering his damnation up was intended to show how
muddled a man full of goodwill could become once "off the rails".' Waugh wrote a correcting letter to
The Tablet and when the review was translated into French he altered it to read 'Some critics have taken
Scobie to be a saint.'

   [2] The quotation reads: 'Le pêcheur est au coeur même de la chrétienté . . . . Nul n'est aussi compétent
que le pêcheur en matière de chrétienté. Nul, si ce n'est le saint.'

To JOHN BETJEMAN   Piers Court.
[26 July 1948]
Postcard

I lie itchin'
Because of the imperfections of my kitchen
While you are bikin'
Round Berks studying the lichen[1]

   [1] Betjeman insisted: 'Of course it is lityen not lycken'. Presumably he had mispronounced it on the
wireless in a reading of his poem 'Ireland with Emily'.

To NANCY MITFORD   [Piers Court?]
[10 August 1948]

Dearest Nancy

   2000 words a day is very good going. I do congratulate & envy you.

   Nettle-rash is awful. It comes from eating zoned fish. It is just as tho you had been rolling in nettles. It usually lasts a few hours. Mine has lasted over a fortnight & the doctor is so eager to show his appreciation of 'paying patients' (patient is not the right word for me) that he injects me with expensive & dangerous drugs that leave me stupified and morose.

Did you like my great friends the Asquiths.

Lady Lambton[1] was a Miss Jones but no relation to pen pusher[2]. I used to despise p.p. until I went to the Church of the Recessional, Forest Lawn (Whispering Glades) and found that she was queen of the place with a special shrine in the reliquarium. So now I respect her but don't like her.

The extract I sent re dedication was from a long article in an American paper (*Time*) saying how beastly I am – sound in principle no doubt but bang wrong in all facts, like all American journalism. It said that my dedications were not, as I had thought, signs of love for chums, but proclamations of rungs in the social ladder successfully ascended. I must say it gives a very odd order of precedence. Mrs Woodruff (*Scott-King*) is very pleased to be six ahead of Honks [Lady Diana Cooper]. Perry Brownlow is very angry at being four down on Randolph.[3]

So a boring neighbour said would I get a 'celebrity' to judge the beauty competition for the village fête. Not so easy because those who are madly famous in London Paris & New York are unheard of in Stinchcombe. I mean they have heard of Mr Churchill & the Duke of Beaufort and I suppose a number of cricketers whom I haven't heard of, but Sergeant Preston would mean nothing to them. I couldnt think who to ask so I got Osbert Lancaster whom I dont particularly cherish because I thought anyway his name is in the *Daily Express* every day. But no one had heard of him and it poured with rain & I took to my bed & poor Laura was left with O.L. for a week-end. Goodness how sad.

The american article said I had a butler with 'impeccable trousers'. On the man-bites-dog theory of news that is most significant. Do most butlers have peccant trousers – no fly buttons, hole in the seat, one leg shorter than the other – or did they expect him to wear a kilt?

Children are beginning to flock back to the house. Harriet has suddenly become much more agreeable than when you saw her.

The order of precedence again: Honks Mosley[4] bottom but two, well I suppose for a divorced jail bird that is fair but poor Bryan [Lord Moyne], a brewing peer should surely be above Father d'Arcy. I think Bowra must have told them this story.

> All love to Honks
> Evelyn

[1] Belinda Blew-Jones married in 1942 Viscount Lambton who succeeded as Earl of Durham in 1970, but disclaimed his peerage and continued as a Conservative MP until 1973.

[2] Enid Bagnold, who married Sir Roderick Jones in 1920. Nancy Mitford had called her 'a sort of fearfully nice gym mistress'.

[3] Waugh's books written by 1948 are dedicated as follows:

Rossetti	Evelyn Gardner
Decline and Fall	Harold Acton
Vile Bodies	Bryan and Diana Guinness
Labels	Bryan and Diana Guinness

Remote People	Hazel Lavery
Black Mischief	Mary and Dorothy Lygon
Ninety-Two Days	Diana Cooper
Edmund Campion	Martin D'Arcy
Waugh in Abyssinia	Kitty and Perry [Brownlow]
Scoop	Laura
Work Suspended	Alexander Woollcott
Put Out More Flags	Randolph Churchill
Brideshead Revisited	Laura
Scott-King's Modern Europe	Mia Woodruff
The Loved One	Nancy Mitford

A Handful of Dust and *Robbery under Law* are undedicated

[4] Nancy's sister Diana, married to Bryan Guinness 1929–1934 and to Sir Oswald Mosley in 1936. The Mosleys were interned during the Second World War. Bryan Guinness succeeded as Lord Moyne in 1944.

TO A.D. PETERS   Piers Court.
[20 August 1948]
Postcard

Not keen on dramatization of *Loved One* but open to persuasion. Name of dramatist unimportant but he must submit detailed scenario. Then if I approve he can go ahead but I retain right of censorship over all dialogue.

                                                                        E

Sir L. Olivier thinks it will make a film[1]. He must be insane.

[1] Laurence Olivier (1907–   ). Actor. Knighted 1947. Life Peer 1970. *The Loved One* was eventually made into a film in 1965 by Tony Richardson in Hollywood with John Gielgud, Liberace and Rod Steiger – 'an elaborate travesty'.

TO JOHN SHAW BILLINGS   Piers Court.
3 September 1948

Dear Mr Billings
    Thank you for your letter of Aug: 25th. I had already sent you a note under the false impression that you were in London.
    It is certainly true that I am anxious to make a study of the Catholic Church in the United States. It is clear to me (and an increasing number of European Catholics) that the history of the Church for the next few centuries will be determined in America. It is therefore of great importance to us that we understand its local peculiarities. The Church, though essentially the same in every country, offers huge & fascinating superficial variety, which even confuses as sharp an observer as Aldous Huxley who, as I expect you noticed, went woefully astray in Chapter XIII of *Ends & Means* on this very point.[1]

It would not be possible or desirable for me to deal with such questions as the political influence of the Church in USA. What I could hope to do in a few weeks tour is to get the flavour of it. One of the things, for example, which disconcerted us was the way in which your Catholic chaplains conducted protestant & jewish prayers & it seems likely that, though you mention a doubtful 'record of cooperation', your Catholic clergy are very much more cooperative than ours. I should very much like to hear some of your prominent preachers and see the ministry at work among negroes & Mexicans, see how far national differences eg. between Poles, Irish, Spanish stocks created separate Catholic communities within the general body.

Also I am specially interested in American monasticism as the result of reading an intensely moving book shortly to appear by a young man named Thomas Merton[2] who after a disorderly youth has become a Trappist monk in Kentucky. It seems to me likely that American monasticism may help save the world.

Now all this and many other points I want to examine primarily for the purpose of informing European Catholics about the character of their future leaders, but I think it might also interest Americans to know how their Catholics strike a sympathetic & inquisitive foreigner. I cannot think of a more suitable vehicle than *Life* for a special study to be written with this public in view, before I write a fuller study for Europeans. I would be very glad to meet Mr Hughes & could have him to stay here for a day or two during which we could discuss the project in detail.

All commercial questions are in the hands of my agent, Mr Matson of 30 Rockefeller Plaza.[3]

Yours sincerely
Evelyn Waugh

[1] In 'The American Epoch in the Catholic Church' Waugh quoted from Huxley's *Ends and Means*, 1937, at some length, beginning 'Christianity like Hinduism or Buddhism is not one religion but several . . .', and commenting 'Only a very learned man can be quite as hopelessly and articulately wrong as that.' *Life*, September 1949.

[2] Thomas Merton (1915–68). Monk and writer. Waugh edited his *Elected Silence*, 1949, and *Waters of Silence*, 1950. The first 'took a week and resulted in what should be a fine thin volume'. *Diaries* 28 August 1948.

[3] Waugh received $1,000 in payment and was allowed to spend up to $4,000 on expenses.

To Nancy Mitford
4 October 1948

Darling Nancy

. . . Mr Popkin[1] seems to me to be collaborating with the Government. I have had to give him a pep talk. I do not know Ld. Beaverbrook very well but I know Randolphs imitations of him so I did that & Popkin was scared stiff & promised immediate new behaviour.

I went to such an extraordinary house on Wednesday[2]. A side of life I never saw before – very rich, Cambridge, Jewish, socialist, high brow, scientific, farming. There were Picassos on sliding panels & when you pushed them back plate glass & a stable with a stallion looking at one. No servants. Lovely Carolean silver unpolished. Gourmets' wines & cigars. The house a series of wood bungalows, more bathrooms than bedrooms. The hostess at six saying 'I say shall we have dinner tonight as Evelyn's here. Usually we only have Shredded Wheat. I'll see what there is.' Goes to tiny kitchenette & comes back. 'Well theres grouse, partridges, ham, a leg of mutton and half a cold goose' (literally) 'What does anyone want?' Then a children's nannie dining with us called 'Twinkle' dressed with tremendous starched frills & celluloid collars, etc and everyone talking to her about lesbianism & masturbation. House telephone so that generally people dont bother to meet but just telephone from room to room. It made quite a change from Stinkers.

Here is a funny picture of my patriarchal home circle.

Best love
E

[1] Waugh's accountant.

[2] To stay with the Walstons. Catherine Crompton (1916–78) married Henry Walston (1912–) in 1935. He was made a life peer in 1961. She was a close friend of Graham Greene's. On another occasion Waugh wrote to Lady Rothermere: 'She and/or Mr Walston collect some jolly enterprising pictures and objects I must say. Almost nothing in the house I would not be pleased to steal.'

To A.D.Peters   Piers Court.
[Received 4 October 1948]
Postcard

I have heard from my bank & the whole question of opening an account in Rome or giving francs to starving nuns at Grasse[?] seems too complicated. So let us chuck it & collect the money here in pounds in the usual way, before the franc falls further.

But in future if translation rights appear let us make the contract in all cases for all royalties & advances to go straight to Catholic charities in the countries concerned.

E.W.

To Randolph Churchill   Piers Court.
14th October [1948]

My Dear Randolph

I read with intense interest the announcement of your engagement in this morning's *Times* newspaper. Please accept my cordial congratulations.

I do not know the young lady but she must be possessed of magnificent courage. Does the colonel, her father, (also notably courageous I observe[1]) receive you in his house? If so it would not be a laborious journey to call here & give me the opportunity of doing homage to the heroine.

Thanks to your kind offices I am off to USA as soon as the Luce family can get me a cabin. . . . Why not come to New York for your honeymoon?

Yours ever affectionately
Evelyn

[1] The announcement of Randolph Churchill's engagement read 'to June, only daughter of Colonel Rex Osborne DSO MC'. She died in 1980.

TO JUNE OSBORNE
23 October 1948
Postcard

Piers Court.

I lied when I told you that I had sent flowers to you. I meant to order them after luncheon but got delayed in visiting your new spacious & highly convenient house & went straight to the railway station. Please forgive me & please accept my deep good wishes for your happiness with Randolph.

I have known him for a long time; perhaps before you were born, certainly before you could read & write, and have always felt that he had a unique natural capacity for happiness which, one way & another, has never yet been fully developed. I am sure you will be able to do this for him. He is essentially a domestic and home-loving character who has never had a home. My observation has taught me that the best possible guide for choosing a husband is to go for the child of a happy marriage. That has been a huge source of strength to Randolph's father & I am sure it will be so to him.

I am just off to America & can't hope to see you again before Christmas, but please be assured that you will be much in my thoughts & prayers.

Yours affectionately
Evelyn Waugh

TO NANCY MITFORD
24 October 1948

Dearest Nancy

Six months hard I am afraid without remission for good conduct. The manuscript [1] was a delight to read, full of wit & fun & fantasy. Whole passages (eg. Cedrics arrival & first evening) might be used verbatim in a book. The theme is original & promising. There is not a boring sentence (except p.274). But it isn't a book at all yet. No more 40 hour week. Blood, sweat & tears. That is to say if you want to produce a work of art. There is a work of art there, lurking in a hole, occasionally visible by the tip of its whiskers.

The Radletts of course steal the scene again. Jassy & Victoria are intoxicating & real, so real that every other character pales beside them except Cedric who, deplorably, is made to talk in places in exactly their idiom. This is a trick you must look out for. I can just accept Polly speaking exactly like Linda – but Cedric is a Parisian pansy. Oliver Messel doesn't talk like Debo.

Your great failure is 'Boy' who is too important to be left, as he is, a mere collection of attributes. Most of the minor characters are flops. Mrs Corbett begins as though you meant her to be a sort of Jean Norton–Freda Ward but almost at once becomes Erskine-Ogilvie-Grant. She would be greatly strengthened by some of Freda's prudery & shyness. Mrs Cozens is just two or three different people. You start her as a North Oxford dons wife, suddenly enrich & ennoble her and turn her into a hunting girl. There have been rich & sporting dons' homes but not in Banbury Road. They have little manors in the Bicester country (eg. Holland Hibberts & John Beechams).

I don't believe that in a pompous house (not Grace Curzon's anyway) a newly arrived, shy girl would be greeted by gibes about her mother's adultery. I know less of French manners but it is inconceivable to me that Fabrice would talk to a jeune fille as you make him.

Davey was a good foil to Uncle Mathew but he loses point beside Cedric & Boy.

The punctuation is pitiable but it never becomes unintelligible so I just shouldn't try. It is clearly not your subject – like theology.

The narrative doesn't begin until Chapter III and is just developing an intricate & highly enjoyable climax when the siren goes and down tools.

I should mention that (granted the awful failure of Boy to come to life at all) you handle the Polly-Boy relationship admirably everywhere.

Now the book must be saved. So start again. Have no explanations, assume your reader knows *Pursuit of Love*, and plunge him straight into Alconleigh with the Lecturer's first lascivious visit. Then follow him to Montdore and show him as the jagger. Then if you like pack them off to Delhi and start again at your Chapter III. From then on all you have to do is watch the characters & make them speak & behave consistently. Then at the end of Part II Chapter VIII you can get really to work on the serious architectural achievement. It is a Henry James theme, told in a lighter way. Think how James would have developed the final chapters & then write them in your own delicious manner & we shall have a memorable book.

Well I suppose you will hate me now for the rest of our lives. Ms. follows by separate post.

Best love
Evelyn

I was sorry I couldn't dine with Pam [Berry] on Wednesday. That was before I read your notes. Perhaps now it is lucky. [2]

[1] *Love in a Cold Climate*, 1949.

[2] Nancy Mitford had already made changes suggested by Lord Berners and, though expressing gratitude, replied to Waugh: 'I've always known that Boy was too sketchy and that the beginning is clumsy ... but I do feel quite sure that I am incapable of writing the book you want me to – I can't do more really than skate over surfaces, for one thing I am rather insensitive as you know, and for another *not* very *clever*.' She did make several of the suggested alterations.

To Laura Waugh   Cunard White Star,
All Souls [2 November] 1948   RMS *Queen Elizabeth*.

My Darling Laura

It is warm & foggy & fairly calm. I have a little room like a wagon-lit which Miss Case [1] has filled with carnations. Her verdict[?] on the evening at Ann Rothermere's was 'That is the set I should be in if I lived in England'.

I miss you very much – far more than I expected – for every corner of the ship is full of happy memories of you. There is no one on board. I sit in the little private dining room opposite where we sat & the head waiter devotes himself to providing special dishes. He even cooks me a daily loaf of bread. I eat heavily & simply & pass the time in the pleasures I cannot get at home – daily mass & daily Turkish baths and Miss Case's endless encomiums of Mrs Luce [2]. Poor Miss Case, by the way, has to share a cabin with a French Jewess.

. . . Well all this happened on the way to a little party of Sheila Milbanke's [3]. Miss Osborne went there with a temperature of 102°, full of benzedrine given her by Randolph & then proceeded to drink a lot of wine. Randolph took her home to Diana Sandys [4] house & she said she had lost the key & would accordingly commit suicide & legged it for the river pursued by Randolph. He caught her on the embankment where she struck him three times with the clenched fist called the police & gave him in charge for indecent assault. Five police appeared in a flying squad car & Randolph harangued them. Then a strange car drew up to see the fun & Miss Osborne leaped in & was driven away, Randolph thought to death or worse.

. . . So I was taken round to reason with her and was left alone reasoning for hours & she proved quite amenable to reason & I left them both in tears & kisses & Randolph & I went off & got a bit drunk at Bucks, Pratts, Whites.

. . . I will write to you often

All my love
Evelyn

[1] Margaret Case became society editor of *Vogue* in 1926 and was special features editor when she left in 1971.
[2] Clare Booth (1903–   ). Married Henry Luce in 1935. She was a playwright (*The Women*, 1936), journalist, congresswoman and Ambassador to Italy 1953–6.
[3] Sheila Chisholm, an Australian, had married in 1928 Sir John Milbanke. In 1934 she married Prince Dimitri of Russia.
[4] Diana Churchill (1909–63). Randolph's sister. Married 1935–60 to Duncan Sandys, the Conservative minister.

To Laura Waugh   Knickerbocker Club,
9 November [1948]   807 Fifth Avenue.

Darling,

So I have been in great pain. A boil in the small of my back which appeared as I landed & got worse. So I telephoned the hotel doctor who pinched it & poked it &

didn't know what to do. Then next day I said to Miss Perkins who jaggers me at the *Life* Office I have a terrible boil so she sent me to the *Life* doctor who jaggered me & gave me radiant heat & penicillin & then later he sent me to New York Hospital where I first sat ¾ of an hour in an office with a hideous secretary covered in orchids. Then the doctor appeared & sent me to a cellar full of people covered in blood brought in from accidents and no one did anything until someone said 'You want penicillin. Go buy some' so I was sent to a shop to buy a bottle & then I came back to the cellar with my bottle saying 'Will no one inject this penicillin?' But no one would until at last the janitor took pity & injected it. So this morning the doctor from New York Hospital sent a message that I was a surgical case & must come back but I said not on your life and put myself in the hands of the *Life* doctors who have made me much better, but it is a sad way to start my little holiday.

I had some letters from you this morning. I am sorry that your cow is dead particularly as now only one slender horned life stands between us. Why not come to New York by air arriving Dec 6th & staying till 17th? I shall be there all that time. My cabin in *Q. Mary* has two beds.

Please tell Midland Gardens to go ahead without arch to tennis court. You do not say whether carpets have come.

So the last day of the voyage became two days because a fog kept us lying off the harbour & all the Americans became very impatient. It had the worst effect on poor Miss Case who began reading aloud the passages from *Brideshead* about the adultery in the ship saying 'It is Wagnerian' & looking at me in a hungry fashion. Then I ran out of money & had to borrow heavily from her so all my carefully fostered aloofness went to pot.

Well we landed on Saturday afternoon and a jagger from *Life* met me & took me to the Plaza Hotel. Goodness it was decent to see marble & gilding & mahogany & palms again after all the functional decoration of the ship. That evening I dined with Mr & Mrs Luce.[1] It was not a great success; caviar, dover soles flown that day from England etc but neither aware of what they ate or drank. He handsome, well mannered, well dressed, densely stupid. She exquisitely elegant, clever as a monkey, self centred. She came back with me & sat in my suite talking about religion for a long time but complained later that I had no heart. Next day she left on a lecture tour.

On Sunday a lady called Anne Fremantle[2] came to luncheon. I used to know her as a girl. Now she is a leading 'Catholic' intellectual – *very* nice but my boil was already causing me pain. Alec Waugh came to see me at six. He is greatly taken up with some woman, dressed with inappropriate gaiety, talking in an unusual & unbecoming drawl. Then I felt so ill & sad I went to bed without any dinner.

Tomorrow I will write & tell you what else has happened to me.

All my love
E

[1] Henry R.Luce (1898–1967). Founder and editor-in-chief of *Time*, *Life* and *Fortune*.

[2] Anne Huth-Jackson (1909–   ). Proposed to by Cruttwell, Waugh's tutor at Hertford College, Oxford; married Christopher Fremantle in 1930. Journalist and author, she has published thirty books.

including an authobiography, *Three-Cornered Hat*, 1971. At lunch Waugh gave her 'comfortable amounts of Bristol Cream' and caviar, and described her becoming an American citizen as 'with full consent deliberately committing this horrid act'.

To RANDOLPH CHURCHILL   Knickerbocker Club,
9 November [1948]   807 Fifth Avenue.

I am in some doubt whether or no you are married.[1] I received no communication from you at all (except an obscene one) and feared that your heroine's courage had failed or at least that she had faltered more or less in her great task of happiness. But on landing here I am told that the local press has announced your wedding. Pray enlighten me.

I spent my first evening with your friends the Luces. I am afraid it was not a success. I found him ignorant and densely stupid. Her I admired for chic & sharpness but she complained later to others that I lacked heart.

I sit in the local White's pining for the true White's. This is the only place in New York where one can escape running into trash like Sitwell & Beaton. Only yanks & good silent ones – mostly bank managers I believe.

If it is appropriate, my salutations to June.

Yours ever
Evelyn

[1] He was.

To LAURA WAUGH   Boston.
14 November 1948

Darling Laura
... One, half Jew half Irish, novelist called Harry Sylvester[1] lunched with me at the Chambord (best restaurant in the world where I hoped to feed you in December) and denounced the native priesthood. Then I went to a four o'clock cocktail party given by the Jesuits at Fordham University. Then very weary & in pain I went to the Knickerbocker Club of which May's[2] pa (a very dull gentleman) had made me a member & I fell into conversation with a member who turned out to be balmy & he insisted on taking me to his home to drink brandy while he read aloud Anglican hymns. Next day I went to see the head lecture agent who was like a big business man in a film then I went to a fashionable luncheon party at the Rain Club where I sat between Mrs Angier Duke[3] and a lady called Millicent Fenwick who has just written a book on etiquette[4] 650 pages long which I will give you for Christmas

if you like. I hoped it would be funny but it isn't really. Then I went to tea with Miss Case to meet Wolcot Gibbs & then a huge bohemian party in an attic given by Anne Fremantle and one had to go through a child's bed room to get from dining room to parlour & there was another older child making a ship in the bath room so no one could pee & sargent Preston was there among others. A lady spilled wine on my chest so I could not go on to a party that was being given in another part of the town in honour of Alec Waugh. Next day I went to see Andrea[5] (all these engagements were interspersed with medical treatment at the *Life* Office) & went to a tailor & ordered 2 new suits & then to the slums to see Dorothy Day[6] an autocratic ascetic saint who wants us all to be poor, and her young men who are poor already & have a paper called *Catholic Worker* and a soup kitchen. I gave a great party of them luncheon in an Italian restaurant in the district & Mrs Day didn't at all approve of their having cocktails or wine but they had them & we talked till four o'clock & then I went to tea with the leading Catholic lady of New York called Mrs Porter Chandler[7] & Anne Fremantle was there and a deserted Catholic wife, very small & sad, whom I kept meeting, called Mrs Cowles. Then I was $\frac{1}{2}$ an hour late for dinner which was sad because it was meant to be a treat for Miss Case & when I reached 21 she was tight & we went on to the first night of Edna Ferber's play[8] an act and a half late & it was *very* bad & pro Jewish. Then we went to the Gilbert Millers[9] & there was Tony Weldon & the Bussy Shaftels[10] and some fine French pictures & champagne.

Well I was getting healthier but more exhausted so next day I had interviews with *Life* & Matson & lunched with Sargent Preston at Knickerbocker Club & then a Catholic publisher came to see me & stayed all the afternoon & then I had drinks with Cecil Beaton in his splendid suite at the Plaza. Then the chief editors of *Life* gave a dinner party for me & I got a bit tight & teased them but I think it was all right & then an editor & I went to a night club.

All this time the Sitwells were rampaging about New York cutting a terrific splash but I kept clear of them.

I forgot to tell you that I met the notorious poet Auden at Mrs Fremantle's & rather liked him.

... You will think all this time has not been spent much in Catholic enquiries & you will be right really.

All my love

E

[1] Author of *Moon Gaffney*, 1947, *All Your Idols*, 1948. A Roman Catholic, he later left the Church.

[2] May MacDougall, wife of Waugh's publisher, whose father was Samuel A. Welldon (1882–1962).

[3] Angier Biddle Duke (1915–). Diplomat.

[4] *Vogue Book of Etiquette* by Millicent Fenwick (1910–). Congresswoman.

[5] Andrea Cowdin, with whom Waugh stayed in Los Angeles.

[6] Dorothy Day (1897–). A member of the Catholic Labour Movement and co-founder and publisher of the *Catholic Worker*.

[7] Mrs ('Bebo') Porter Chandler's husband had taken a double first at Balliol College, Oxford, and was chairman of the Board of Education of New York City.

[8] *Bravo*, written with George S. Kauffman.

[9] Gilbert Miller (1884–1967). Theatre producer. Married Kathryn Bach in 1927.

[10] Buzzy Shefftel had been at Oxford, but after Waugh.

To NANCY MITFORD   New York.
[November 1948]

Darling Nancy

I think you would wish to hear about Sir O Sitwell. Well he has grown his hair (so carefully kept by Trumper) so that he looks like Einstein. He and Edith (& Mr Horner[1]) are having one hell of a time. Every magazine has six pages of pictures of them headed 'The Fabulous Sitwells'. They have hired the Philharmonic Orchestra which in this town is something very big indeed to play while they recite poetry. Goodness how they are enjoying it. I said 'Is Sachie joining you?' 'Alas. Sachie is High Sheriff of His County and therefore unable to leave the United Kingdom'.

Maureen is here (also Maurice [Bowra] but that is another story) with her bridegroom[2]. They dined with me last night in a fashionable restaurant. The bridegroom wore Wellington boots and a dinner jacket ornamented with gold Grenadier buttons.

I am trying to persuade Sargent Preston to enter a Trappist monastery. I think he will he happier there.

The shops sell an intrument called the 'Beau Alarm' which emits a noise like an air raid siren. It is for girls subjected to passionate & unwelcome advances.

I have made 2 great new friends & many enemies.

Your last novel very popular here among upper classes.

Millicent Fenwick has written a book of Etiquette – 650 pages and not a dull sentence. Would you like a copy for Xmas?

A lady called Miss Case is in love with me – unreciprocated.

Terrible rumours of Randolph's honeymoon spread by Tanis[3].

I meet bad native pansies who all claim to be your close friends.

Love from
Evelyn

[1] David Horner first met Osbert Sitwell in 1921 and was his companion for many years.
[2] Maureen Guinness, widow of the Marquess of Dufferin and Ava, had married Kelpy Buchanan in September.
[3] Tanis Guinness (1908–   ). Married 1937–51 to Howard Dietz.

To LAURA WAUGH   Maryland Club.
20 November [1948]

Darling Laura

No news from you. I hope this means that you are having a time of riotous liberty, not that you have fallen into a melancholy as a result of Victoria's death[1].

I arrived here, Baltimore, late last night. A chain of club membership follows me about the country. It is very convenient. In Boston the Somerset Club was very sedate – like Boodles in 1875. Horrible food, *The Times* two days old flown from England, all the members had been more often to London than to New York.

Boston was charming. You must go there when you come in the late winter. It looks exactly like Highgate, if you can imagine Highgate full of Wren churches. The hotel I stayed in was full of intoxicated bakers. Each wore a cardboard loaf round his neck. I suppose their trade accustoms them to night work. They sang all night & there was no sleep. My hotel here is full of cockroaches which remind me of home. They are much quieter than bakers though equally nocturnal.

I am quite cured of my abscess & in good health except for slight oppression due to unaccustomed heat.

The McIntyres have a charming 1830 house in Louisburg Square. When the city authorities decided to repave the cobble-brick pavements with concrete Mrs McIntyre & all the first ladies of Boston spread carpets outside their houses & sat there until the workmen went away. A good side to American feminism.

Maurice Bowra is lecturing at Harvard which is practically part of Boston. I saw him twice. He was very jolly. We drove through torrential rain to look at Salem, Gloucester, Marble Head and other beauty spots but saw nothing. I went to luncheon with the Jesuits at Loyola College & before you could say 'knife' found myself on a dais addressing undergraduates – just as happened at the convent in California.

Mark Anthony de Wolfe Howe[2], who sent you many messages of love & homage took me to two of his clubs. Boston is all clubs with names like 'The Supper Club of 1776', 'The Ethical Essay Society of 1802' 'The Beacon Hill Literary Institute', etc. Oliver Wendel Holmes, Thomas de Quincey Adams, etc belonged to them all and now the same little high-minded group keep them going meeting twice a day under different auspices. Helen Howe Allen has had her breast removed (cancer) and is distressed about it.

It was all right by the way about the New York dinner with the editorial board of *Life*. I had a letter from the chief of them saying would I please repeat the performance.

The most disturbing event at Boston was a visit to a Father Feeney S.J. at Harvard[3]. Mrs Luce had told me that he was a saint & apostle on no account to be missed. He has a Catholic Center, as it is called, just outside the University campus & has made some showy converts. Well when I asked about him in Boston clergy & laymen alike looked embarrassed & said: 'We haven't seen him for a long time'. I went one morning by appointment & found him surrounded by a court of bemused youths of both sexes & he stark, raving mad. All his converts have chucked their Harvard careers & go to him only for all instruction. He fell into a rambling denunciation of all secular learning which gradually became more & more violent. He shouted that Newman had done irreparable damage to the Church then started on Ronnie Knox's *Mass in Slow Motion* saying 'To think that any innocent girl of 12 could have this blasphemous & obscene book put into her hands' as though it were *Lady Chatterley's Lover*. I asked if he had read it. 'I don't have to eat a rotten egg to know it stinks'. Then I got rather angry & rebuked him in strong words. His court sat absolutely aghast at hearing their holy man addressed like this. And in unbroken silence I walked out of the house. I talked to some Jesuits later & they said that he is disobeying the plain orders of his provincial by staying there. It seemed to

me he needed an exorcist more than an alienist. A case of demoniac possession &
jolly frightening.

I am reviewing an American book of etiquette for the *Atlantic Monthly* for a bit
of fun. Would you like me to arrange for various hostesses to take charge of you here
while I lecture February-March? It could easily be done I think. I have put you into
my lecturing contract – subject Sophocles – in case the Socialist Government
enquire why you travel with me.

All my love
Evelyn

[1] The cow.

[2] Mark Anthony de Wolfe Howe (1864–1960). Writer and editor. Published *Barrett Wendell and his
Letters*, 1924. Married to the Irish writer Mary Manning.

[3] Father Feeney. An unfrocked priest who later made his submission and died in the Church.

To Laura Waugh   [Baltimore]
24 November [1948]
Postcard

Time marches on and no word from the Whisker. I hope this means that you
happily engaged or piously in retreat, not that you are dead. If you are dead please
be buried in the corner of the field adjoining the village cemetery. Have a small piece
cut off & consecrated. I will design the tomb on my return.

Baltimore has been rather boring. I went to one stuffy upper class dinner party on
my first night & I go to another tonight, my last night. Apart from these I have seen
only clergy. Loyola College gave a large, sumptuous, clerical buffet supper for me
yesterday which was both boring & embarrassing.

Today I played a game of pegotty with a pubescent negress in an admiring circle
of black nuns. I won. . . .

All my love
E

To Nancy Mitford   Piers Court.
10 January [1949]

Darling Nancy

Your letter of 4th Jan to hand. I notice it was posted at Marlborough, Wilts. The
socialist underground has slipped up.

The undull book was about Etiquette not Elizabeth. I will send you a copy from
New York where I go in ten days to earn dollars for my unhappy country instead of
spending them on traitors.

Gel-gel[1] be bugbuggered. No sane man could envy Sir Osbert [Sitwell] his ostentatious progress through USA. Nor do the Americans respect him for it. Perhaps I told you that I asked his publisher whether there had been any increase in his sales as the result of all the ballyhoo. 'Yes, 18 copies'. The point is that at last Sir Osbert has found the life that he has groped after all his life, just as you have. So you are both quite happy in your base ways. I suppose you two are the only inhabitants of the Globe (except perhaps the Mountbatten stalking-horse[2]) who can say 'Heavenly 1948'. What an odd idea of heaven. Of course in my country we cannot enjoy the elegant clothes & meals & masquerades which fill your days but Diana has chosen these things also and certainly she is not happy.

I met an expatriate in New York who may be known to you – Anne Fremantle? She too gave her youth to the socialist cause and at once left the sinking ship when her ends were accomplished. But her literary skill is not as gravely impaired by the change – perhaps because she genuinely repented and became a Catholic at the same time. But she would not say: 'Heavenly 1948' of, I suppose, the blackest year in the worlds history since 1793.

But I am forgetting that Coué[3] was a Frenchman, not as one might have thought, an American.

The sounds you hear next door[4] are probably His Eminence doing penance for the frightful sins of yourself & Picasso and that woman Diana took up.[5]

I never go to the theatre now but I believe that there is a great scarcity of tolerable comedies. I have no doubt that given an agreeable collaborator (the just word) you will make a great success of your new career.[6]

Laura is well but hard-driven by the cares of farm & nursery. She is seldom seen heavily veiled in crepe as the Empress Frederick[7]. Harriet is entirely enchanted with the mother of pearl egg which I left in White's & gave her last week. Both send their love.

Mosley[8], I read, is selling up.

If you can find Père A. Gardeil's *La Structure de l'ame et l'expérience mystique* it would be a *great* kindness to send a copy to Thomas Merton, Gethsemani, Kentucky, USA to whom I promised one & have been unable to keep my promise. I will send you in exchange his *Elected Silence* which I am editing (Merton's not Gardeil's).

I pray God you may get a glimpse of Heaven in 1949.

Evelyn

[1] Jealous.
[2] Perhaps Gandhi. Earl Mountbatten had presided over the independence of India in 1947.
[3] Emile Coué (1857–1926). French psychotherapist, famous in the 1920s, who encouraged people to recite: 'Every day, and in every way, I am becoming better and better.'
[4] Nancy Mitford had written: 'I live next door to a Cardinal. There is a curious thumping noise which drives me rather mad, when I asked Marie what it could be she replied reverently "C'est Monseigneur à côté".'
[5] Louise de Vilmorin.
[6] Nancy Mitford had translated *La Petite Hutte* by André Roussin. After success in Paris, it was to open in London in August 1950 and run for 1,261 performances, the thirty-ninth most durable British production of all time, two behind *Annie Get Your Gun*.

[7] Nancy Mitford was going to a fancy-dress ball thus attired.

[8] Sir Oswald Mosley did not move until 1951. Sir Oswald Mosley (1896–1980). Married Lady Cynthia Curzon 1920–33 and Diana Mitford in 1936. Founded British Union of Fascists in 1932.

To A.D.Peters   Piers Court.
[Received 18 January 1949]
Postcard

 . . . Don't want to be published at all by communist countries. If not too late stop all negotiations with them. They might use *Loved One* as anti-American propaganda.

E.W.

To Nancy Mitford   Piers Court.
17 January 1949

Dearest Nancy

Of course I am cross with you for being happy. It is entirely indecent. And of course I am appalled at the blasphemy of writing 'Heavenly 1948'. I assume you wrote it with the intent to be odious.

It would be just tolerable if you had always set up as a porcelain marquise advising the starving to eat more cake. But you were always lecturing us about how much you loved human kind and now with human misery & degradation everywhere at its blackest you talk like a debutante after her first party. It is not that I think your soul in danger but that I doubt if you have a soul at all.

Perhaps Napoleon is not the happiest model to take in your devotion to the French. Think of these things when you reach your St Helena.

I did not know about your being a whore. In fact I thought whoring had been stopped in Paris.

Well I am just off to the hideous round of the Middle West, lecturing to American Catholics who may yet preserve the good things which the French abandoned. But I dont want to be buried among them.

Yes, I am fond of you. Very fond. That is why I write to you in this fashion. Honks [Lady Diana Cooper] long ago gave up the attempt to keep my love.

A Canadian named Dunsmore wrote me a slightly lubricious fan-letter in which he says *The Loved One* formed 'one of the many delightful bonds that *more or less* platonically unite myself [Dunsmore] and young Nancy'. My italics.

Tell your chums they must now read *The Month* [1] instead of *Horizon*.

Deep love
Evelyn

[1] A Roman Catholic periodical edited by Father Philip Caraman SJ. *Helena* was serialized in it in 1950. Father Caraman had persuaded Waugh that he was in competition more with *Horizon* than with *The Tablet*, edited by Douglas Woodruff, to which Waugh felt he owed loyalty.

To John Betjeman   Piers Court.
[18 January 1949]
Postcard

'Jaunty sub-aestheticism' was a villainous phrase. What I meant was that BBC jauntiness of the Tom (Glad he's dead) Handley[1] sort was infecting aesthetics & pushing it below the surface into popular underworld. But how badly I said it. I dont think E. Sitwell a *great* poet; I think Auden a pathetically bad one. Just off to USA. Why not come too. You wouldnt like them but they would like you & you would find many architectural peculiarities. Bowra is there in hideous squalor – perhaps I told you – queuing for his food among students with a plastic tray & no wine. He drinks Spanish brandy before luncheon. Did you tell Hiram WinterBottom to lay off me? If so I am most grateful. He has left me entirely at peace for months. Good about Derwent[2]. E.

[1] Tommy Handley (1896–1949). Comedian, famous for the wartime radio programme ITMA – 'It's That Man Again'.

[2] Lord Derwent (1899–1949). Always called Peter although his name was George. He had left some money to the Georgian Society.

To Nancy Mitford   Piers Court.
12 April [1949]

Darling Nancy

You are kind about the liver pills. I will try & get them from Warwick House[1] without being crossed by the Quennell–Forbes axis. Perhaps if my liver gets better I shall feel forgiving to you for your vile & frivolous panglossisme. Now I am in deep misanthropy. I cant bear anyone else being alive at all & when a man goes past the window with a barrow or a child shuts a door upstairs I fall into an extremity of rage. As for the daily papers ... L'enfer c'est les autres I think your favourite sage says.

One cause for sorrow is that I am bound in honour to write a long article for *Life* magazine whose money I have been spending like a drunken sailor, on the state of the Catholic Church in America, and there is nothing to say except that americans are louts & that Catholic Americans are just a little better than panglossist americans.

So tomorrow I go to Downside taking Frank Pakenham for flaggers no I mean flagers. I have given up cigars & secular reading for Holy Week so I must not read this letter after it is finished so I expect it will have some pretty odd spelling. I gave up wine too but felt so faint at 8 pm last night that I had to mitigate.

My daughter Teresa (age 11) has come back from school with a glowing report by her French mistress, 2nd in class with 82% marks. I asked her to name in French any six objects in the dining-room. After distressed thought she got five, four of them with wrong genders. I know of another girl who came back from another school with a special medal for swimming – a thing like the Garter with a great sash. Her parents put her in the pool and she sank like a stone.

My Gothic fernery, under construction at great expense, is a fiasco. It looks like Lancing College War Memorial 1914–18. So I am making a serpentine walk with a serpents head & eye but you have to go up in a balloon to see it.

I may come to Paris soon for a day or two because I think it might comfort & humanize me a little to see some French paintings – not of course the filthy moderns nor Manet nor Monet nor worst of all Sisley but Fragonard. I had forgotten how cheering he is until I saw the Mellon collection in Washington. Also what do you know about the Jansenist painters you know the Port Royal group Phil Bubbly etc? And are there many in the Louvre & if not there, where? I saw a lovely reproduction in a shop in Sweden of a nun by candle light with a discipline. Very erotic. Not by Bubbly but by one of his chums. . . .

Love from
Evelyn

[1] Ann Charteris was married to Lord Rothermere 1945–52 and lived at Warwick House in London.

To NANCY MITFORD   Piers Court.
[April 1949]

Darling Nancy,

Bubbly was a silly joke. I meant P de Champagne[1]. I must come to Paris for a day or two but I wont invade your flat. It was heavenly of you to offer it. I go to London next week & will make enquiries about Travellers, Ritz etc.

E. Sackville-West has made pansy-high-brow-journalistic history with the phrase 'I seem to feel'. Surely the height of diffidence. First the statement. Then the qualification 'I think'; then the qualification 'I feel'. And now 'I seem to feel'.

I shall think it will be 1st week of May, if I can get tickets & a room.

Harriet has overcome her auto-erotic troubles and is really rather a gay & engaging little girl.

Are you having a good influence on young Pam Berry? I suspect not. I have my eye on her for the Church. Lay off.

Dominic Elwes[2] retailed in appalling detail the story of Prodd's novel[3]. It was about people protecting themselves with mutton fat against an invisible ray which caused panic. I seem to feel that it will be a very juvenile work.

I go to horrible London for a few days next week & will write you to gossip.

Ann must be eating my pills.

Love from
Evelyn

[1] Philippe de Champaigne (1602–74). Painted murals and portraits.
[2] Dominic Elwes (1931–75). Painter. Son of Simon Elwes, and Waugh's godson.
[3] Peter Rodd never published a novel

To William Gerhardie[1]   Piers Court.
[10 May 1949]
Postcard

Very many thanks for speaking about me & for sending me a copy of your address which I read with great interest. As no doubt you recognized I learned a great deal of my trade from your own novels.

My only criticism: would it not be more precise in talking to a foreign audience to avoid the phrase 'English Catholicism'. They might think you meant Anglo-Catholicism.

Warmest regards
Evelyn

[1] William Gerhardie (1895–1977). Novelist.

To Randolph Churchill   St James' Club.
[May 1949?]

Tomorrow, when I have the delight of lunching with you is Friday. I say this, not that you may provide fish but that you may not be disconcerted if you observe me refuse meat.

E

To Nancy Mitford   Piers Court.
2 June [1949]

Darling Nancy

Mrs Piper[1] is famous as the Myfanwy of Betjeman's erotic poetry. She is, in appearance, a mixture of Edith Sitwell & Leslie Jowitt[2], very stout & almost bald.

Have you heard of Sir A. Cooper's very curious conduct. In revenge for our imagined slight on Honks he has vowed to turn my man Sykes & myself out of White's[3]. The method he has chosen is to put Quennell up for the club, abetted by your revolting kinsman, Ed.[4] White's, needless to say, are outraged that he should use the club as an instrument of private spite; they particularly resent the fact that two expatriates should conspire to stop the only earth where those of us who are weathering the storms of our unhappy country, can take refuge from the hounds of modernity. It will end, I hope, with the expulsion of Cooper & Stanley. Meanwhile Quennell shows no reluctance to being used as a directed weapon of destruction.

Really, you and your Beauty.[5]

Connolly comes for Whitsun, not bringing Lys.

The architectural effects in my garden are ruining it & me.
I wrote a deeply touching letter to Honks. No answer.[6]

Love from
Evelyn

The Master of the Air Raid shelter[7] is deeply revered by Picasso lovers in this country. You must send Père Couturier[8] an 'amusing' crucifixion by him.

[1] Myfanwy Evans married in 1935 John Piper. She wrote the libretto for Benjamin Britten's *The Turn of the Screw*, 1955.

[2] Leslie McIntyre married in 1913 William Jowitt, who was Lord Chancellor 1945–51.

[3] There had been a row about politics with Duff Cooper such that, according to Sykes who was present, 'he went red in the face, he shook, his voice rose higher and higher till it was a shriek'.

[4] Lord Stanley proposed Quennell, but had previously signed a letter to the committee urging that he should never be elected.

[5] Anne Murray. Nancy Mitford had written: 'You never saw such a heavenly girl, so good, so beautiful, the daughter, quite incredible as it seems, of Basil Murray.'

[6] Waugh discovered the following January a letter from Lady Diana Cooper which had not been forwarded to him. His 'was the kind of letter that could only be left unanswered by the desire to wound and humiliate', he wrote to Laura.

[7] Henry Moore (1898–). Nancy Mitford had written of his air-raid shelter drawings: 'When one *thinks* of the smart little women in air-raid shelters – if people had arrived draped in towels I'm sure they would have been lynched.'

[8] A celebrated Dominican asked by Nancy Mitford to lunch with Waugh, who disagreed with him over his close friend Picasso. According to Sykes, who was again present, 'The Dominican, versed in the arts of apologetics, triumphed easily.'

To Lady Mary Lygon
Piers Court.

7 June [1949]

Darling Maimie

It was very kind of you to remember me during your foreign tour & to send me pictures of your interesting bed-rooms. I went abroad too to Gay P. and my bed room smelled of cats well rather like the hall in a certain London house[1] I know of no names no pack-drill. It was at Travellers Club where I saw some English Lords drinking and talking smut. Then I went to spend a night with the Coopers in their forest dwelling & that did not smell much but goodness the Coopers were crazy. Both Sir Alfred & Lady Diana fell into the most alarming rages. No self control at all it comes from living with the volatile frogs.

There is beautiful restaurant called 'The Stock Exchange Luncheon Bar'. Mrs Rodd is the height of fashion & knows everything about the frogs their history & habits & language & arts & crafts. Her lover is very thin and has far fewer spots.

Smarty Boots Connolly is staying with me & yesterday we drove to Wolverhampton to see a hideous statue & we were very near the noble line of the

Malvern Hills & we had luncheon at Dumbleton Hall[2], very good young vegetables and a summer pudding and some cream cheese and Beaujolais & too old port.

I am having my garden made much uglier at terrible expense. Do come & see it.

My nettle rash is much better but I suffer from nervous nausea if I go into Society.

I hope you backed the winner of the Derby. Connolly did.

Love
Bo

Monsigneur Knox calls Boaz Booz. Very Dutch

[1] Lady Mary's.
[2] Home of Viscount Monsell (1905–   ).

To Nancy Mitford
Piers Court.

8 June 1949

Darling Nancy

How very odd that the all-knowing colonel does not know the correct form of address of a Dominican Friar. O.P. of course stands for Ordinis Praedicatorum. You are plainly curious about that letter. I was not renewing the attack on Picasso but soliciting help in getting a copy of that book by a French Dominican which I promised an American Trappist and about which I once wrote to you.

Smarty Boots has just left, having spent the week-end in torpor. Needless to say he rushed to the Candidates Book at White's & put his name on Quennell's page. The election will be interesting. Numbers of cuckolds, fearing accusations of jealousy, having subscribed. What a preposterous ass Sir Alfred [Duff Cooper] is. He must know that no one except Ed VII has ever resigned from White's, except Eddie Grant who did so as a love-offering on the day of his marriage to Laura's sister, Bridget. He rejoined as soon as he was back from the honeymoon. I can well understand that the author of *David* is embarrassed in the presence of professional writers. He will now have four instead of three. But it is generally held that his employers at the *Daily Mail* obliged him to do what he has done.

Whenever Cyril woke up it was to tell me of his enduring loyalty to, & dependence on, Lys.

It is a pity that ces messieurs les agents did not make away with Stanley. They would have averted the great Quennell scandal.

Why, pray, did you tell the Porto Finese that I was due there in Mosley's yacht? My children spent many hours scanning the horizon for a sail.

Love from
Evelyn

To NANCY MITFORD   Piers Court.
13 July [1949]

Darling Nancy

Love in a Cold Climate has arrived to temper the heat wave with frigid absence of
inscription. Well I suppose you could hardly have had all the presentation copies
shipped to France & back.

I have re-read the first half already & look forward to a very happy afternoon with
the second half. It is all very much better than I remembered it. I was quite wrong
in advising, as I think I did[1], that you should scrap the first two chapters. They are
very well written. Indeed all the descriptive & narrative passages are *very* good.
Conversations poor. Page 28 is hell. But I was wrong in thinking that publication
would blight your career. The book will be a great success and is appearing at just
the right time when everyone longs for something light.

I cant tell yet whether I shall enjoy the end which I thought so inefficient before.
I think I shall.

I have bought two beautiful pictures. Otherwise nothing to say except
congratulations on the book & your good sense in not being put off by my ill
considered criticism.

But *all* the fashionable talk is awful.

Oh page 28[2].

Love
Evelyn

[1] He did.

[2] On which Fanny, the heroine, is, in the words of Waugh's previous objections, 'greeted by jibes
about her mother's adultery'.

To CYRIL CONNOLLY   Piers Court.
Postcard

Opened by mistake. Very sorry.

Sir A. Cooper, little knowing the complexity of your character, believes that you
too will resign from White's if Quennell gets in. He goes round Paris chuckling '3
for 1'. All he will get is four pairs of literary eyes, rebuking him for *David*.

But I think the plot was cooked in the *Daily Mail* office & poor Coopers infamy
was a condition of his further employment there.

E

P.S. I didn't mean Peter Watson when I referred to your 'semi-literate socialist
colleague'. Think again.

To George Orwell   Piers Court.
17 July [1949]

Dear Orwell – Blair? – which do you prefer?

You must wonder why I never wrote to thank you for *Nineteen Eighty-Four*. The reason is that the publishers never sent it so at last I bought a copy and must thank you all the same, for it is a stimulating experience to read it. I have seen a number of reviews, English & American, all respectful & appreciative. I won't repeat what they say. Please believe that I echo their admiration for your ingenuity & for many parts of the writing eg. the delicious conversation in the pub when Winston tries to pump the old man for memories of pre-revolutionary days.

But the book failed to make my flesh creep as presumably you intended. For one thing I think your metaphysics are wrong. You deny the soul's existence (at least Winston does) and can only contrast matter with reason & will. It is now apparent that matter can control reason and will in certain conditions. So you are left with nothing but matter. But the predicament is not entirely new. We have always accepted the existence of insanity, where reason & will fail to operate, but no one denied that lunatics had souls.

Winston's rebellion was false. His 'Brotherhood' (whether real or imaginary) was simply another gang like the Party. And it was false, to me, that the form of his revolt should simply be fucking in the style of Lady Chatterley – finding reality through a sort of mystical union with the Proles in the sexual act.

I think it possible that in 1984 we shall be living in conditions rather like those you show. But what makes your version spurious to me is the disappearance of the Church. I wrote of you once that you seemed unaware of its existence now when it is everywhere manifest. Disregard all the supernatural implications if you like, but you must admit its unique character as a social & historical institution. I believe it is inextinguishable, though of course it can be extinguished in a certain place for a certain time. Even that is rarer than you might think. The descendants of Xavier's converts in Japan kept their faith going for three hundred years and were found saying 'Ave Marias' & 'Pater Nosters' when the country was opened in the last century.

The Brotherhood which can confound the Party is one of love – not adultery in Berkshire, still less throwing vitriol in children's faces. And men who love a crucified God need never think of torture as all-powerful.

You see how much your book excited me, that I risk preaching a sermon. I do not want to annoy you – for one reason I have promised neighbours of mine Jack & Frankie Donaldson[1] (Etonian socialist farmer & Freddie Lonsdale's daughter) that I will take them to visit you. They are earnest students of all your work and a charming couple and I don't want to deprive them of their treat by my sectarian zeal. Would we be welcome one afternoon?

                                                    Yours sincerely
                                                    Evelyn Waugh

[1] Frances Lonsdale (1907–   ). Married in 1935 John Donaldson (1907–   ) who was created a life peer in 1967. She is a biographer; he has been a farmer and Minister for the Arts.

To Lord David Cecil   Piers Court.
27 July 1949

My Dear David,

Very many thanks for sending me your wise and elegant lecture[1]. All who love Oxford will rejoice in its scoring over Leavis[2] & Richards[3] & Nuffield[4] and the Ministry of Education. I read it straight through before I opened *The Times* and shall reread it often. The peroration is fine.

I am a bigot and a philistine (I fail heavily in your test of sensibility – love of Scott, Hardy and Wordsworth) and I feel you can't *hint* at God. You must either affirm or deny. If affirm, the soul is born with a longing for God and Beauty, Harmony and Order are only desirable as attributes of His. I can't think of a single Saint who attached much importance to Art, tho many enjoyed music and some wrote good poetry.

You will say More but then we don't know at what moment he became a full grown saint – probably in prison, perhaps on the block. He wasn't concerned with music and classical greek then – indeed his voluntary death was a denial of humanism.

There are many people about who claim to love Picasso and Shakespeare and Dante and Mallarmé all at once and equally. I am afraid catholicism is the enemy of Catholicism.

I send you in return a short story of mine as near true as stories ever are, and an American book that may interest you.

Love to Rachel[5],

Yours ever
Evelyn

[1] Lord David had argued in his inaugural lecture as Goldsmiths' Professor of English Literature, Oxford, that 'a true work of art appeals to us because, deliberately or not, it is an image of Divine Perfection and so, in some sort, a revelation of God. This reflects no special credit on the artist; he is a mere vehicle.'
[2] F.R.Leavis (1895–1978). Critic. Fellow of Downing College, Cambridge.
[3] I.A.Richards, (1893–1979). Critic and poet. CH 1964.
[4] William Morris (1877–1963). Created Lord Nuffield 1934. Chairman of Morris Motors 1919–52. Set up a £10 million charitable trust in 1943. None of these is 'scored over' by name in Lord David's lecture.
[5] Rachel MacCarthy (1910–   ). Daughter of the critic and essayist Desmond MacCarthy, she married Lord David in 1932.

To Nancy Mitford   Piers Court.
28 July [1949]

Darling Nancy

Something very odd is happening to the posts. I wrote you a long & rather loving letter when your book first came and a short & less loving card a day or two later. My L and VLL has been stolen. How rude & ungrateful I must seem. Well you all think me that in France I know.

I hope your hostess is not a Jugo-slav woman I met in New York.

Holidays are upon us. Oh the Hellikins! I went on Saturday to the Oratory School to give away the prizes. Sixty years ago it was the leading Catholic public school & everyone like Lords FitzAlan and Rankeillour were there. Now there are 34 boys in a little Queen Anne house smaller than this. All because of the disastrous appointment of an Anglo-Catholic parson, convert & sex-maniac, as headmaster some years ago. Now they have a charming headmaster and all is well but it is Lilliputian. The headmasters speech '. . . The School platoon has been training at so and so . . . last term we had 98% successes in all examinations, five higher certificates, three entrances into Cambridge, two into Oxford etc . . .' And when it came to the prize winners they all had names like Palewski & Radziwill & Couturier.

Then I went to stay with your great new friend Pam [Berry] but she was very weary from dancing all night & I only had glimpses of her. We went to call on Barbara Rothschild who has married a gentile of forbidding appearance named Warner[1], not your old admirer, worse. And there were communists there called Day Lewis[2] (very pretty) and Rosamond Lehmann (not bad looking) and we drank boiling champagne & were bitten by flies.

With enormous goodness of heart I am taking my little boy to the seaside in the Vendée, to a place Pam recommends which sounds quite awful. . . . I remember they behaved well in the Revolution. I imagine it all pine & heather & sand like Surrey, is it?

Osbert's book[3] is queer isn't it. It is extraordinary that a man of his humour can write like that of Lord Wimborne and the general strike & Picasso and G. Stein.

Just got my bill from the garden contractors who have laid down a yard or two of gravel and put up a pillar. A cool thou. Impossible to earn because super tax is always a pace ahead. So I am ruined.

All last week we had the 65 year old *Country Life* photographer staying & pottering round with a camera. His aim in art is to make every room look uninhabited & uninhabitable.[4]

I do hope my warm letter about your book turns up. If not I will write it all again.

Love from
Evelyn

[1] Barbara Hutchinson (1911–), formerly married to Victor Rothschild, married Rex Warner, novelist and classicist, in 1949, and Nicholas Ghika, Greek painter and architect, in 1961.

[2] Cecil Day-Lewis (1904–72). Poet Laureate 1968–72.

[3] Osbert Sitwell, *Laughter in the Next Room*, 1949.

[4] Nothing appeared, but Waugh kept copies of the photographs.

To Lord David Cecil   Piers Court.
7 August 1949

Dear David,

Not in order to lure you into theological debate, but simply to be precise in what I was trying to say, may I add this to my letter?

God's order is manifest everywhere. You and I, as men specially concerned with writing, are entitled to see it specially in writing, so long as we recognise writing as differing not at all from gardening or needlework or any other activity, and so long as we regard all humanism as recreation – a harmless way for fellow[?] men to occupy their leisure and earn their livings.

The danger is to say 'A poet is a lovesome thing, God wot'. I think that opinion came in with the 'Souls' and purists. I can't recall a passage but is not Bridges full of a sort of mysticism of Art? The idea that the great flights of the human spirit, which reconcile man with his unhappy predicament on earth, are embodied in the Everyman's Library? I seem to remember one tag about 'God hath no higher praise and man in his hasty days, is honoured for them'. God hath no higher praise indeed!

Don't please think that I was for a moment trying to impute this view to you. But I did think you were being rather tender towards those who hold it.

Perhaps in the Providence of God the unqualified hideosity of Modern Art has been sent us to scourge us for just this aberration.

That's all I was trying to say.

Yours ever
Evelyn

To A.D. Peters   Piers Court.
[Received 9 August 1949]
Postcard

You grow more like Perry Mason daily. I know no higher praise[1].

E

[1] Perhaps because Peters had suggested offering the film rights of *Scoop* for £5,000; more likely because he was struggling to obtain francs for Waugh in Paris.

To Nancy Mitford   Grand Hotel,
18 August [1949]   La Baule (Loire-Inférieure)
                                                     France.

Darling Nancy

It has been a great pleasure to read your English reviews. I havent seen the American but I expect they are as foolish as possible[1]. You see Americans have discovered about homosexuality from a book called *Kinsey Report* (unreadable) & they take it very seriously. All popular plays in New York are about buggers but they all commit suicide. The idea of a happy pansy[2] is inconceivable to them.

I am in a town of ineffable horror. You might have warned me. There is a strip of sand, a row of hotels and sand-dunes & pines at the back. This is the worst of the many hotels. I came here with my boy Auberon in an aeroplane on Monday to join your great new friend Pamela. I came to the hotel and was told she was too ill to see me & that there was no room for me in the hotel[3]. . . . [My room] has a 'bathroom' – a sandy trough behind a curtain, a broken bidet & no lulu which is all one really needs. The public lulus are balkan.

I found three disconsolate, shifty urchins[4] under the care of a nannie who knew no French at all & had no money. . . . So I dispensed huge sums to relieve the Berries distress & got a room in the hotel to succour them. The hotel is on the main street down which motor bicycles drive all day & night tooting. No sleep. My day is, wake at five & lie with the noise of traffic getting louder & louder dreading the time I must go to the public w.c. Emerge retching & nausea persists all day. From 8 until 12 I sit in a dingy, sandy hall watching the pensionnaires parade in & out in immodest bathing clothes, with bleached hair and blistered navels. Bathe at 12 for five minutes. Water so shallow one has to walk a mile to swim. The deep water full of jelly fish & speed boats. Wait until 1.30 for the Berry family to appear for luncheon. Talk to nannie & provide lemon squash for children. After luncheon drive Berries in hired car to places of interest recommended by corrupt concierge. These places are either (a) gift-shops, open or (b) chateaux, shut. Return for opening of the roulette room at the Casino. Lose 10,000 francs. The only happy moment is seeing the last counter disappear. I make it a rule not to go until I have lost 10,000. Sometimes it take *hours* and the rooms are like one of those Smith[5] drawings of air-raid shelters. Dine with Nanny. Back to Casino & lose another 10,000. Bed. Lie listening to the traffic getting slightly quieter until 5. Doze.

Your great new friend made a brief appearance yesterday to borrow 30,000 and tell me to look out for Prod & Ed who are expected hourly. If Prod comes I shall send him tollgating with Nannie & have some satisfaction. As to Stanley, since his dastardly behaviour about Quennell[6], he is my abomination. One of your reviewers said you 'spring from' Stanley of Alderley. So do I, a mile.

Well I said I was cured of going abroad after the Sykes expedition. The cure is now complete. Never again Never Never Never Never Never Never. NEVER.

My boy behaves beautifully & is very happy. The more I see of other peoples children the less I dislike my own.

Did I tell you about Harriet who came the other day in great excitement to say that the kitchen garden was full of 'white things with horns'. 'Cows?' 'No, smaller than cows'. I thought there must be some visitation of goats & rushed out. It was full of cabbage butterflies. 'You must have seen butterflies before Harriet'. 'Not with horns'. Very odd.

Now it is time to go & lose another 10,000.

Love
Evelyn

---

[1] Nancy Mitford: 'The American reviews are so terrible I have given up reading them – never again will I pay for clippings. No message or meaning – adds up to just nothing is their parrot cry.'

[2] Cedric in *Love in a Cold Climate*.
[3] Lady Pamela Berry, now Lady Hartwell, says she has no recollection of this holiday.
[4] Adrian, Nicholas and Harriet Berry who that year were 12, 7 and 5.
[5] Percy Smith (1882–1948).
[6] Lord Stanley's proposing Peter Quennell for White's.

To Nancy Mitford   Piers Court.
29 August (1949]

Darling Nancy,

It was heaven to get home, to walk into Whites and find Sykes & Dunne & Stavordale all drunk & eating grouse, and to hear a member of committee say that Quennell had 'not a hope in Hell' of election. But Stinkers was depressing, full of daughters & nieces & sleepy wasps and flies and the new buildings in the garden hidden in a jungle of weed and I have been in a melancholy all the week. Stung by a wasp the day before yesterday & swelled like a bolster.

Best news of the week Eddy West's[1] reception into the Church. No surprise to me. I knew he was under instruction and I can never understand why everyone is not a Catholic, but I feel deep joy all the same.

Pam behaved a little better towards the end of our holiday and very well indeed finally by taking my boy Auberon off for ten days cruise in the Camrose Yacht. I am still being told by the way, on your authority, that I am cruising with the Mosleys.

I am very sorry the Americans dislike your book on such frivolous grounds, particularly as it looks as though soon one American reader will be worth ten Europeans. I constantly hear of English invalids who delight in it and the socialists are pleased that you do not suggest any virtue in your marble halls.

Was it Prod & Ed who started the fires in the Landes[2]? I suppose so.

The article I went to America to write is coming out shortly in *Life*. For the last week I have had thousand word cables daily from each member of the editorial board severally & collectively expressing their deep appreciation of a distinguished and notable piece of quality journalism etc etc. As my unhappy servants have to take all these testimonials down on the telephone they have long faces. It is a tremendously boring article anyway. That is what they like you see.

Why not have Toulon as your market-town? I remember liking it very much indeed years ago. But, of course, the Party will insist on your being nearer Headquarters in Marseille. Up the Red Maquis. Come to think of it that is probably why the Americans are being so beastly. You have been denounced for Unamerican Activities.

Why not live in Monte Carlo? Very nice.

... Mrs R. Churchill is said to be treating him slightly more kindly. He is abject.

Best love
E

[1] Edward Sackville-West. His conversion was a considerable surprise to some of his friends.
[2] Forest fires south of Bordeaux in which eighty-two people were killed.

To Thomas Merton
29 August [1949]

Dear Fr. Louis,[1]

I have now read *The Waters of Siloe* and must write to repeat my thanks for the great honour you did me by dedicating it me. Most of the subject matter was entirely new to me and I found it enthralling. It is a fine feat to have distilled such a narrative – continuously exciting – from what must have been a vast body of material, much of it, I suspect, rather monotonous.

If your superiors intend you to go on writing would it not be a valuable work to write a history of Catholicism in the United States. I tried to find such a book when I was there and was disappointed. There are, of course, excellent, full diocesan histories for some parts. What I mean is a comprehensive, middle-brow history four or five volumes emphasizing all the things which protestant and atheist histories have omitted or neglected. The New England histories have established their version of American origins, very much as the Whig historians did in England. I believe you could make an important book of it.

May I, without presumption, make one or two technical criticisms of *The Waters of Siloe*. The arrangements seems to me a little loose. I do not see any need for the *Prólogue* at all which strikes the wrong *artistic* note, smacking of popular journalism in the way you try to catch the attention with an anecdote and I don't really see that the *Note on Contemplative Orders* is required. Everything you say in it, is said better and more fully later on in the book. I have nothing but admiration for the narrative passages, except that there is no consistency of style. Sometimes you write literary English and sometimes slang.

... And in the non-narrative passages, do you not think you tend to be diffuse, saying the same thing more than once. I noticed this in *The Seven Storey Mountain* and the fault persists. It is pattern-bombing instead of precision bombing. You scatter a lot of missiles all round the target instead of concentrating on a single direct hit. It is not art. Your monastery tailor and boot-maker would not waste material. Words are our materials. Also it encourages vice in readers. They will not trouble to study a sentence for its proper meaning if they have learned to expect much the same thing to be said again later on.

Does it seem like looking a gift-horse in the teeth, to criticize like this? You must remember that you caused a great stir with your first book and it is the way of the world to watch enviously for signs of deterioration. I know you have no *personal* pride in your work, but you do not, I take it, want hostile critics to be able to say: 'You see what religion has done for Merton. A promising man ruined by being turned on to make money for the monastery'. That is what many of them will tend to say if you give them the chance.

Anyway they can't say it about this book which is full of vitality and interest. But I wish I saw the faults of *The Seven Storey Mountain* disappearing and I don't.

Yours ever
Evelyn Waugh

I wish you had said more to reconcile the Cistercian vocation with work for the Resistance in France. On the face of it, it seems to offer an excuse to an occupying power to shut monasteries if monks are allowed to house centres of underground movements. [2]

[1] The name taken by Thomas Merton when he became a Cistercian monk.

[2] Thomas Merton replied: 'Your comments on the structure of *Waters* are true . . . . You console me greatly by objecting to the *Prologue* which I had thrown out and which the editor demanded back. The *Note* is my fault . . . . In any case I am glad to get such valuable and stimulating direction, and from one so marvellously qualified to give it. I have no difficulty in accepting you as the delegate of the Holy Ghost in this matter. . . .' Waugh edited and wrote a foreword for the British edition which appeared in 1950 as *The Waters of Silence*.

To KATHARINE ASQUITH   Piers Court.
13 September [1949]

Dear Katharine

Your letter arrived when I literally had pen in hand to tell Tom Burns that I despaired of editing *Waters of Siloe*. I am keenly interested in your opinion. Is it just your old-world courtesy or do you really think it a good book? And do you think it can be published here as it stands.

Elected Silence seemed to me admirable. It (or rather the much longer American version *Seven Storey Mountain*), was a huge success in USA & as a result when the other monks go out to the fields Merton is set down at a typewriter & told to produce books. If that continues he will write two or three a year for the rest of his life. It is for his directors & superiors to decide if that is good for his soul. From a literary point of view the prospect seems depressing. It seemed to me that *Waters of Siloe* had all the defects one would expect from the process. He did not seem to know what he was doing or what he had already done. I thought the historical chapters most interesting but the prologue painful. And his explanations of the contemplative life came in at odd places in no sort of order & were addressed sometimes to people who had never heard of a monk & sometimes to people far advanced in spiritual growth. I do hope I am wrong in this & your letter encourages me.

I had thought of cutting it ruthlessly into a history of American Cistercians with a single preliminary section culled from all over the book giving a description of contemplative prayers. Would it do just to cut out obvious gaucheries & leave the structure as he planned, or failed to plan, it & write a foreword explaining why a Trappist is publishing books at all (which has disconcerted even sympathetic critics)? Or not even that? Publish and be damned? It was my idea not Burn's to edit it & I find I have bitten off more than my failing teeth can chew.

Love from
Evelyn

To Anne Fremantle   Piers Court.
14 September [1949]

Dear Anne

T. Burns sent me your proofs [1] & I read them with zest. I could now suggest several better titles – 'Lost Vocation' or 'Pig in a Poke'. The language, of course, distressed me, as did your sudden introduction of the sexual habits of your adolescent fellow countrywomen, but I thought you had made a rattling good yarn out of Père Mata-Hari.

You want something to print on the cover, not a review. How about 'Hagiography at its sauciest'? or:

$$
a \left\{ \begin{array}{l} \text{highly readable} \\ \text{highly contemporary} \\ \text{modern \& readable} \\ \text{vivacious} \\ \text{vivid} \\ \text{audacious} \\ \text{enjoyable} \end{array} \right\} \text{study of a} \left\{ \begin{array}{l} \text{deeply interesting} \\ \text{deeply significant} \\ \text{very important} \end{array} \right\} \text{life}
$$

Well the best thing in all these cases is to leave it to the author. Put what you like on the cover with my name attached and I shall not complain.

My love to Cathy, Cutting, Claire etc. I get very fond of Americans when I am far away from you all. One came here self-invited to dinner (not Cathy Cutting or Claire) & fell flat on its face drunk & had to be carried out by its chauffeur. No one else was remotely tipsy.

Do write to me whenever you have the inclination & tell me the gossip of New York. My *Life* article is appearing shortly so I suppose that is the end of American trips for me though I filled it with honey & flowers.

My children are all obstreperously well. They are getting up some sort of ghastly theatricals for the end of the holidays.

I write a sentence a week on the Empress Helena. It will be interesting only to the very few people who know exactly as much history as I do. The millions who know more will be disgusted; the few who know less, puzzled. Americans will inevitably fall into these two classes only.

Love from
Evelyn

[1] Anne Fremantle, *Desert Calling*, a biography of Charles de Foucauld, 1949.

To Nancy Mitford   Piers Court.
10 October 1949

Darling Nancy

You can imagine the joy your present has given me. How I wish it were twice the size with all the lovely pictures given a page apiece. It will be the solace of many dark days ahead. It is lucky I dont know French as I fear the written matter would be very offensive to me. From a sentence or two here & there which I managed to construe it seemed plainly to be the work of Père Couturier.

I went to London for a week and hated every minute of it. I saw Cooper walking hand in hand with Palffy[1]. I saw the inside of *Horizon* office full of horrible pictures collected by Watson & Lys & Miss [Sonia] Brownell working away with a dictionary translating some rot from the French. That paper is to end soon. Everyone I met complained bitterly about the injustice of having to earn a living & the peculiar beastliness of his own profession – Cyril about editing, John Sutro about films. I dined with John de Bendern and he was sick three times during dinner. Your publisher H. Hamilton has got into Whites. That augurs ill for the Quennell election.[2] It should be a club for gamblers, lords & heroes.

Handy is absolutely covered with sores.

I went to a dinner given by the *Daily Express* and there was an editor dead lame so I said what happened and he said 'it was my own fault I was foolish enough to go to the first night of a play'. It appears that now the Cinema companies take half the stalls & send actresses whom they want to make famous. Then they inform a circle of adolescents of both sexes who turn up five hundred strong break into the theatre & mob the actresses not reverently asking for autographs but fiercely tearing out lumps of their hair and cutting pieces out of their clothes (literally). This editor got caught in a stampede, knocked down, trampled on & left with a dislocated knee and ankle. Old first-nighters like Eddie Marsh[3] dont dare go near a theatre now. Well it is all part of the century of the common man to make any kind of prominence entirely odious. Think what happened to Harewood.[4] Thank God the People aren't interested in letters. But they, letters I mean, not alas the People are coming to an end anyway. Cyril was offered 1500 dollars to write an article about 'Young writers in Britain swing right' and his mouth watered but he couldnt find one writer under 35 right left or swinging.

We have a 'prison without bars' next door to us. 73 escapes in the last eighteen months. The other day an air force officer walked out into a cottage & bludgeoned three inhabitants, one hovering now as they say between life and death. There are 17 murderers there including the licentious steward who pushed the girl out of her port-hole. All are convicted of crimes of violence. The countryside is terrorised and today indignant to learn that last week-end they performed *Rope* with an all-murderer cast.

Nice Jack McDougall my publisher is publishing no books at all next year. I said why dont you reprint the Stanley letters and he said I long to but the travellers wont let me.

Love in a Cold Climate has become a phrase. I mean when people want to be witty they say I've caught a cold in a cold climate and everyone understands.

I havent said half enough about *L'Art officiel*, it is a joy.

Randolph has contrived a breach between me & your great new friend Pam.

Best love from
Evelyn

---

[1]Presumably Louise de Vilmorin, rather than her husband Count Palffy.

[2] Peter Quennell was elected.

[3]Sir Edward Marsh (1872–1953). Secretary to Winston Churchill, Connoisseur, civil servant, patron of the arts, editor of *Georgian Poetry*.

[4]The Earl of Harewood (1923–   ).

TO NANCY MITFORD   Piers Court.
9 November [1949]

Darling Nancy

.Well why I have not written is that I have just passed the most distressing
fortnight of my life since I left the Royal Marines and I did not want to harrow your
feelings but I long for a sympathetic ear and you have asked for it though goodness
how you dare when you say you cannot read modern depressing books. This is a
chapter from a very depressing modern book. Ready? Teeth gritted? Right.

Well when I came back from USA I made a pious resolution that for a year I
would do everything I was asked to do by Catholic bodies. (I don't mean the late
Lord Tredegar [1]). Luckily I had built up a strong wall of immunity over the years by
constant curt refusals. Now it has begun to leak out and I give ghastly lectures to
ghastly audiences almost once a week. It culminated in a tour of the Northern
Centres of Learning – Edinburgh, St Andrews, Dundee, Aberdeen etc etc. Just
when I was setting out, shaking with misery, I got an SOS from Baby Jungman to
come to Mereworth where Peter Beatty [2] was in despair. I went. His melancholy had
already quite closed in all round him & would have been impenetrable to the Curé
d'Ars [3] (ask Col. [Palewski] if he knows who that was). He had asked a party about as
comforting as a cage of parrots – Freda & Bobby [4], Boofy & Fiona [5], Baby & Zita. [6] We
chattered away & Peter wandered in and out of the room hardly aware of us. Pouring
rain all the time & pretentious rather nasty food. Two days later as you probably
know Peter killed himself [7]. In White's he is talked of as a kind of Captain Oates:
'Good old Peter, game to the last. He did not want to be a burden to others so he
took the best way out'. In fact, of course, he was stark mad. The world is full of
radiantly happy blind men. I was very fond of him in an odd way & the thing upsets
me doubly as showing the huge chasms that separate one from ones friends in all
essential things.

I didn't hear of his death until I opened the newspaper in the train on
Wednesday.

The tour was torture. Hours & hours in dirty, unheated trains. Staying in hotels
where trams always ran under the windows. Modernistic decorations. Revolting
food at unsuitable times. The actual lectures were merely a bore, it was the times in
between. Being greeted by bevies of poverty-stricken adolescents who once they
had said 'Pleased to meet you' lapsed into silence with every sign of displeasure.
Hideous, dead industrial towns. Idiotic questions after the lecture, either from
Catholics 'How do you account for the element of unpleasantness in Mr Graham
Greene's work?', or heathen students of literature 'What Hungarian novelists
influenced you most, Mr Waugh, in writing *Decline & Fall?*'

Nine lectures in nine days. Returned to London worn out and aged to find
everyone talking about Peter's death in the way I have described and Angie saying
to a friend 'I really don't want to meet Evelyn at the moment. He's sure to say
something beastly about Peter'.

Home, now, thank God, and at work again on *Helena* which is to be my
MASTERPIECE. No one will like it at all.

Were you wise to reject American invitation? You would hate it, of course, but you are so tough. They would only want you to sit 12 hours a day in bookshop windows smiling at the customers and you did that during the bombardment of London most bravely. You would find much material for your new life as dramatist.

Next week I give a great party for Clare Luce and after that I give a 'literary week-end', three discourses & organized discussion, at a Convent in Surrey for Catholic writers & librarians. The only person I know is coming is Mrs Chichester: what a life of suffering.

Baby's boy has gone to my sons prep school. I wrote & told him to look after him. He writes: 'It is hard to be nice to Cuthbertson. He is most disagreeable. Very weak and all the boys & masters hate him.' I have written a tremendous homily on the nature of the English gentleman who always protects the weaker & unpopular. Can't say I ever noticed it much myself.

Love from
Evelyn

[1]Lord Tredegar (1893–1949).
[2]He faced total blindness.
[3] Jean-Baptiste Vianney (1786–1859). Parish priest, canonized 1925
[4]Freda Dudley Ward had married in 1937 the Marquis de Casa Maury.
[5]Fiona Colquhoun had married in 1937 Arthur Gore (1910–   ) who succeeded as Earl of Arran in 1958.
[6]Zita Jungman, sister of Teresa ('Baby').
[7]He threw himself from the sixth floor of the Ritz.

TO NANCY MITFORD   Piers Court.
16 November [1949]

Darling Nancy

Tell that flower of the boulevardes Sir A.D. Cooper that in the latest P.G. Wodehouse book[1] when Gussie Fink-Nottle is arrested for bathing in the fountain in Trafalgar Square he gives the name 'Alfred Duff Cooper'.

This is most significant as (a) showing Cooper's fame. Till now Wodehouse characters in these circumstances always call themselves 'Lenin' or 'Aristotle' (b) showing the Master's great ignorance of Cooper's habits. Nothing is more likely than that he would be found wallowing in evening dress at 5 in the morning.

I forgot to say that during the tour of the Northern Centres of Learning I was tormented with tooth-ache and had to visit horrible socialist provincial dentists.

My *Helena* is a great masterpiece. How it will flop.

I wonder if you still correspond with E. Sackville-West. Tomorrow I am having him to dine with the cream of English Catholicism. I shall be interested to hear how he reports on it.

After Pam Chichester's literary retreat I take to chair & speak to Catholic Guild of Artists & Craftsmen. Oh God.

The Midland Gardens I complained to you about are hard at work doing work & worse all round the house.

Love from
Evelyn

Re Suicide. Has it ever occurred to you that bastards are much more inclined to it than those born in wedlock. It has just occurred to me. I can think of so many cases. They know they shouldn't be in the world at all.

[1] *The Mating Season.*

Piers Court.

To Lady Mary Lygon
24 November [1949]

Darling Blondy

Will you ever get this? Who can say? The postmen are so Dutch that I have only just received your tantalizing invitation to luncheon. Too late, too late, the saddest words next to 'it might have been' in the English language. Pray give my deep regrets to your sister Dorothea.

You will find everybody in London very mad and very drunk. I was there last week and was disgusted. Poor R. Churchill cannot survive the year at liberty. The gates of Bedlam gape for him.

Lady Monkton Moncton Muncktoun how? Lady Carlisle Carlyle how? Anyway what they call Bidet [1]. She spoke of you with great love.

I went to a party and I said to the butler I should like another glass of champagne wine if you please and he said Ho would you & picked me up like a doll & carried me downstairs & threw me into a cab where who should be lying asleep but Lord S of A [2]. So he and I went to an underground place with some tarts and we acted them a play & goodness the tarts clapped. So we went home with them and they said Mum will be so pleased to see you & Mum came in & began talking like Mr Connolly about the influence of Gide on Claudel (two horrible frogs) so I went home but Lord S of A talked about Gide-Claudel until 1.30 am, no fucking but some beer at 1 am. So you see London is very tiring. Also unnatural vice is rife.

Bo

[1] Bridget Ruthven (1896–   ). Married 1918–47 to the Earl of Carlisle and 1947–65 to Viscount Monckton. Succeeded as Lady Ruthven in her own right in 1956.

[2] Lord Stanley of Alderley.

To Nancy Mitford   Piers Court.
5 December [1949]

Darling Nancy,

I was delighted to read that 'the most brilliant of the younger writers' has joined the staff of the *Sunday Times*.[1] You should have said 'youngest writers'. We are much younger than Max Beerhohm or E. M. Forster. There are none younger than us.

I have been an invalid for a week recuperating from a brief visit to London. I get so painfully drunk whenever I go there (Champagne, the shortest road out of Welfaria) and nowadays it is not a matter of a headache and an aspirin but of complete collapse, with some clear indications of incipient lunacy. I think I am jolly near being mad & need very careful treatment if I am to survive another decade without the strait straight? jacket.

My great party for Mrs Luce was very expensive & I think a good time was had by most. Eddy chucked.

Then I conducted a meeting of the Catholic Guild of Arts & Crafts where I won their confidence by abuse of Picasso & then lost it with abuse of Catholic Arts & Crafts. I find it most encouraging that everywhere everyone is seeing through Picasso – even old jaggers like R. Mortimer.

Then I had an excruciating week-end in a convent in Surrey conducting a 'Catholic Booklovers Week-End'. The nuns were very attentive with little packets of chocolate and glasses of milk covered with muslin veils weighted with beads do you know what I mean. When I said I never drank milk they quite understood & pursued me from breakfast to bed with a bottle of Burgundy and a medicine glass. The sort of questions are, of course, 'Why does Mr Greene have such a nasty mind?' and 'Is it not the duty of the artist to consider the average reader?' Can you wonder that the mere breath of White's intoxicates?

The backwash of my American jaunt laps all round me. This Sunday a middle-west publisher (middle west is the agricultural part of USA) who was flabbergasted at the proximity of Laura's little farm 'What is hay for?' literally he asked, and 'But where is it pasteurized?' in the dairy. He had a patent nylon shirt which he washed in his bath.

... Everyone who came to the Luce banquet sent Laura a Collins except Luce. Don't you think that odd?

I have deeply enjoyed R.G.Hardy's *Recollections of L.P.Smith*[2]. Have you got it yet? Both of them older than us. Will your Paris articles be about millinery or politics? I long for them.

                                                          Love from
                                                          Evelyn

[1] Ian Fleming had arranged for Nancy Mitford to write a column from Paris – 'my new toy'.
[2] Robert Gathorne-Hardy, *Recollections of Logan Pearsall Smith: The Story of a Friendship*, 1949.

To Anne Fremantle   Piers Court.
3 January 1950

Dear Anne

It was sweet of you to send me a Christmas present. The book was not well chosen for I have no interest in politics, but the thought was kind and I sent the object straight on to my aunt Constance who expressed herself as delighted with it and no doubt passed it on to her vicar.

. . . Quite a number of your fellow countrymen come here from time to time so I hear some news of you all. Clare Luce was in London a month ago. I gave a little party for her to meet papists. At dinner she sat next to Frank Pakenham. I explained beforehand that he was a socialist minister – she thought I meant a non-conformist minister & treated him throughout as though he were a presbyterian Dean of Canterbury.

Laura is well – another baby expected in the summer. I am enveloped in the sloth of the Welfare State & do nothing.

I hope the Foucauld book is having a great success.

                                                    Love to Cathy
                                                    Evelyn W.

To Nancy Mitford   Piers Court.
4 January 1950

Dearest Nancy

I am so glad you enjoyed the Pearsall Smith book. I reviewed it hurriedly & briefly for one of the little magazines no one reads & was so grateful for having enjoyed it that I just said so & nothing more but there was *much* more to be said. I barely know the protagonists but I seem to understand it all.

Smith, I am sure, wanted a Boswell. He felt he was unique & that he was wasting his genius on little private jokes and had left a perfect but minute portrait of himself in *Trivia*. He wanted someone to say about him all the things he couldn't decently say about himself. He was always trying to train Boswells – Connolly, Sergent Preston etc. – but he started much too late. Hardy was his chief protégé but what a disappointment. He is quite unaware of his own deterioration from the pretty young aesthete Smith picked up in the bookshop to the middle-aged plasterer's mate (mot juste) of 1944.

The only way modern books are readable is by reading them between the lines. I see so many unconscious & conscious dishonesties in the book which is two books put together – the Boswell and an apologia for his treatment of the final heir. I don't know anything except what the book suggests, but I suppose Hardy threatened an action to prove Smith insane when he disinherited him. I can just hear the solicitors voice: 'We have two points to prove Mr Hardy. First that Mr Smith definitely promised to leave you the capital sum of your allowance, and that you had amply earned this sum by professional help. Secondly that Mr Smith was definitely insane in Iceland not merely delirious.' Hardy rubs this in all too fiercely.

You must have noticed often in life as I have that however great-souled & delicate-mannered people are, financial obligations between social equals are almost always disastrous. Money runs through the book. Smith was comfortably off but not rich at all. He was alarmed by the rich and he expected the poor to be alarmed by him. He was, of course, a bully & a tease but I suspect Hardy was a bitch & sponge. I am sure he was always digging small sums out of the old boy.

The most moving part, I thought, was the last 50 pages when Hardy seems to have convinced himself that it was all in the cause of sacred friendship that he 'refused to quarrel' with the old man. Really, of course, he felt, 'I can't at the last moment, let him have an excuse to cut me out of the will'. A man of honour would have said: 'You beastly old American cad how dare you talk to me like that. Stick your bloody dollars up your huge arse!' Instead he sends him trout & offers to lend his savings as a plasterer.

Anyway what a delightful story.

The Russell[1] is not, I think, related to the great Whig House. He writes very correct little reviews for one of the Sunday papers. The fashionable view rather well expressed. Sycophantish about O. Sitwell, D. MacCarthy etc.

It was a painful shock to find old Smith being imposed on by Trevor-Roper.[2] I hope he gave that blackguard expectations of a legacy.

> Best love from
> Evelyn

Xmas at Chantilly?

[1] Logan Pearsall Smith's will allowed many of his friends, Robert Gathorne-Hardy among them, to choose books or pictures from his house. The residue, several thousand pounds, was left to John Russell (1919–), a literary critic in the 1940s, now art critic on the *New York Times*. He published *Logan Pearsall Smith*, 1950.

[2] Page 170 of *Recollections of Logan Pearsall Smith*: 'I am reading a scholarly clever witty life of Archbishop Laud by a Merton don named Trevor-Roper. . . . He loved letters, and what pleased me, he loves my writing – and knows a great deal of *Trivia* by heart.' H.R.Trevor-Roper (1914–). Regius Professor of Modern History, Oxford, 1957–80. Created Lord Dacre 1979.

To PENELOPE BETJEMAN   Piers Court.
7 January 1950

Darling Penelope

It was very nice of you to send me a Christmas present. You had aroused the keenest expectations and as the last days of Advent passed without a sign, my heart fell. I do not get so many presents nowadays that I can afford to forgo one. Now it has come & I am delighted. The subject is one on which I am ill informed. I shall read it with great curiosity.

It is nice of you to ask me to visit you but (a) I dont think John likes me (b) I don't think I like your children (c) I know I detest all talk about the varying fads of heretics. I can stomach a traditional, sceptical, formal, Barchester Towers protestantism of the sort my father & grandfathers professed but the nearer these people ape the ways of Catholics the nearer they approach flat blasphemy and it turns me sick (d) I need wine twice a day & you cant bear the smell of it. So we must be pen pals unless you come where I have spent prodigious sums in uglifications.

I have had a year of great suffering because last Easter I made a penitential vow to accept every popish invitation to lecture for a year. At first it was easy because I had built up over the years a fine iron curtain by curt refusals. But it leaked out and I have had an autumn & winter of unspeakable boredom culminating in a 'Book Lovers Week End' at Grayshott. Next Sunday I speak at Middlesbrough and Leicester. There are those who like the sound of their own voices. Not me.

I have done a lot more on the life of St Helena – very good Indeed. I hope to finish before Easter. Would you accept the dedication?

Two suicides[1] among my friends last year. How many to come?

Are you going to Rome for Holy Year. When? We might go together.

Laura has built an all-electric bungalow for her cows. She is £6,420 overdrawn at the end of the year. I have spent £10,000 and not put any aside for taxation (£7,500) so it looks like prison pretty soon, where I am told one has the wireless ceaselessly playing night and day.

It was on account of Aelred Graham's letters in *The Times* newspaper that I removed my boys name from Ampleforth & put him on the Downside list.[2]

. . . On Monday I take my children to London to the circus. Ghastly.

My love to John. Though he doesn't love me I love him.

E

[1]Peter Beatty and Toby Milbanke.

[2]Penelope Betjeman replied: 'That is a real cracker about Dom A Graham (who is as you will have seen under the watchful eye of the Inquisition) because you told me two years ago you were sending your boys to Downside.'

To Nancy Mitford   Piers Court.
11 January 1950

Darling Nancy

Woolgar & Roberts, 3 Dorset Buildings, E.C.4. That is the place for press cuttings. It is a great expense having them and for every one that is interesting fifty are unendurably boring and five are painful, but Popkins will charge it against income tax. Thank you thank you thank you for the picture of Duff.[1] I will take it to White's when I next visit that nest of vipers. I was there yesterday between the Circus & *Peter Pan* and whom should I see but poor Prod. Nothing you told me prepared me for the truth. He had locomotor ataxia and a waistcoat made of an old rug. How you have brought him down. He was such a bright pretty boy. If it were not for his socialism I should have great compassion for him. I thought people like you & he believed in putting the decrepit into gas chambers.

I greatly enjoyed your second article in *Sunday Times*. It has greatly excited the wine lovers. Is the Vigneau '04 not too old? I would dearly like to buy some. Do you know how much one can bring to England without a licence? An excellent feature of your articles is the French. What the English like are phrases of which they easily understand the literal meaning, if possible with words that look like English words, and have quaintness & drollness. That is just what you give them. I mean for instance the warm hampers for the wine. Give us plenty of such phrases, please.

My new Holy Year opens with the prospect of financial ruin. For some time I have been aware that I seemed to be in easier circumstances than most of my friends & accounted for it with saws like 'solvency is a matter of temperament' and by thinking of all the nuns who are praying for me, bringing me in pounds when I give them shillings, and so on.

Well last week I said to Laura 'are you sure you arent over-drawn at the bank?' 'No, I don't think so. I'm sure they'd tell me, if I were'. 'Well do ask'. So she did and, my dear, she had an overdraft of £6,420 which had been quietly mounting up for years. There is no possible way to pay it off, as her capital is in trust and for me to earn that much more, I should have to earn about 150,000 and we cannot possibly spend less although for three years we have been spending 2,000 more than our income (and that 2000 tax free too). Well its a sad prospect isn't it. I shall have to go to prison but that is hell nowadays with wireless & lectures & psychiatry. Oh for the Marshalsea[2].

Please answer my enquiry about Mrs Simpson's Neptune[3].

I do so hate this warm wet winter. We all have colds.

Love
E

[1] Nancy Mitford had written that a friend of hers had been drunk and 'Duff was X though is it for Duff to be X about drunkeness? (I enclose a photograph and you are not to say you have seen it as its really very disloyal of me to send it – loyal to you however.)' On 19 January she began a letter 'You are *not* repeat *not* to show the photograph of Sir Alf to anybody at all. . . .'

[2] Debtors' prison.

[3] Nancy Mitford had written: 'I dined with the Windsors. She has an erotic picture by Boucher in her bedroom of 2 Lesbians at work. I said "Oh, whats that," wondering what she would say. "Well it seems there was some old God called Neptune who could change himself into anything he liked – once he was a swan you know – and this woman liked other women so he changed himself into one."'

TO NANCY MITFORD   Piers Court.
[January 1950]

Darling Nancy

The harm if harm there is has been done. I sent the snapshot of Cooper to Connolly *not* saying it was from you so no embarrassment can result and really it is from the public prints so no secret is revealed so I dont think it matters a button really does it? Only I'm sorry if you do mind.[1]

Gas chambers were not a Nazi invention. All 'Progressives' like Lord Ponsonby[2] believed in them and called it Euthanasia and had a Society all the Fabians belonged to simply to build gas chambers and that is what Health Centres are for besides castrating men and sterilizing women and giving french letters to children. Didn't you know? So take Prod by the hand & lead him to Peckham[3] where the Donaldsons will deal with him in a jiffy.

As a lady in Middlesbrough said 'I see you dedicated a book to Nancy Mitford. Do you really know her?' 'Well, I know one side of her'. 'I do admire her writing so'. 'So do I. I have just been rereading all her books.' '*Books*! D'you mean to say she writes *books*, too? She must be clever. I thought she was only on the *Sunday Times*'.

Everyone is so bored with the General Election. The newspapers have to offer huge cash prizes to get people to write and say that they will vote. The only person excited about it is Maimie who put herself at the disposal of the Central Office and was directed to canvass St Pancras where she claims to have converted 32 proletarian women and heard that the public library is used for orgies after closing time. The only amusing contest is Randolph v. Foot[4] in Devonport. It is nice for the boy to have an opponent just as beastly as himself in just the same way. It is the first time. Up till now he has always stood against decent old buffers.

I woke up in the middle of last night & started worrying about Ed Stanley's brother.[5] Have you ever met him? What is he like?

G. Orwell is dead and Mrs Orwell[6] presumably a rich widow. Will Cyril [Connolly] marry her? He is said to be consorting with Miss Skelton.[7]

Since the recent terrible financial crash I have saved hundreds of pounds in not buying things.

I think P. Popkin is a snake. At least he is helpful to the poor but as soon as one earns more than he does himself envy steps in and he lets one down. Also he lets one overpay and then pretends to be frightfully clever in bringing back some of the money that ought never to have left the pocket. I am obsessed by poverty at the moment. But not so much as multi-millionaire Graham Greene, the socialist, who I gather has been sniffing round Chantilly.

Poor Patrick has written a novel[8] in praise of Angela. Quite good about her but the rest *Forsyte Saga*.

Love
E

[1] She did not.
[2] Arthur Ponsonby (1871–1946). Labour MP. Created baron 1930.
[3] First health centre created after the Labour Government was returned in 1945.
[4] Michael Foot (1913–   ). Politician and writer. Editor of *Tribune* 1948–52. He held the seat for Labour 1945–55, since 1960 has sat for Ebbw Vale. Waugh wrote in March, 'I saw poor Randolph for a minute. "I tell you what the trouble was at Devonport, old boy. There just weren't enough Conservatives."'
[5] Lyulph Henry Stanley (1915–71).
[6] Sonia Brownell had married George Orwell in October 1949. She died in 1980.
[7] Barbara Skelton, the writer, married Cyril Connolly that year.
[8] *Ruthless Innocent*.

To Nancy Mitford   Piers Court.
9 March [1950]

Darling Nancy

Bathe the legs – not yours, the hen's – in warm water & dry thoroughly. Then anoint with a compound of vaseline & paraffin in equal parts. Repeat daily until scales disappear. Another school says: 'kill & boil'.

It is very kind of you to ask me to dinner on April 11th. I look forward to it greatly. Is it 'a few young men' or 'a jew young man' who wants to meet me? If the latter could he not have a cocktail with me at the Gare du Nord?

Another good article. Of course the thing about England *now* – *always* a little bit but *now* particularly – is that there simply is no 'mode' in anything. There is the general, well grounded assumption that anything new is inferior to the old & thats that. There is also no 'monde'. Who should be leading it? Debo? You see it makes no sense. But that is all the less reason why Mrs Gascoigne[1] should be such a beastly bore. She is not missing anything by staying in the country. Some of the most exquisitely entertaining men I have ever known – eg. Conrad Russell – led lives of complete retirement. Boredom is something in people not anything from outside. Look at Juliet[2] who all her life has been surrounded by the most amusing people and remains a crasher. No there was no excuse for Mrs Gascoigne's beastliness.

I have now written the last word of *Helena* and am quite out of work. I would rather like to write a guide book to Gloucester like E.M.Forster's *Alexandria*.

Stick to Mr Peters come what may. Of course Mr Beaumont[3] prefers to deal with a soft lady. Mr Peters will do & say all the things behind your back that you could not bring yourself to do & say and you needn't know and you will greatly profit *and* be more respected by such as Beaumont.

You know the Goller cure for obesity? You take different coloured pills according to what part of the body you wish to make smaller. Anthony Head[4] has been found to be taking breast-pills. I am going to do it for face, neck & stomach and so expect something rather elegant, perhaps unrecognizable, on the 11th.

Honks & Cooper are here honking the French President.[5] You would think they could see him at home without coming abroad for the spectacle.

Love
E

[1]Mary (Midi) O'Neill (1905–) married Derick Gascoigne in 1934.
[2]Lady Juliet Duff.
[3]Hugh (Binkie) Beaumont (1908–73). Theatrical impresario, who was presenting *The Little Hut* in London.
[4]Anthony Head (1906–). Conservative MP 1945–60. Created Viscount Head in 1960.
[5]Vincent Auriol.

To GRAHAM GREENE   Piers Court.
27 March [1950]

Dear Graham,

I am absolutely delighted to receive *The Ministry of Fear* & *Journey without Maps*.
I had lost my copy of the second of these and rather forgotten it. I shall re-read them
both at once. I find I love re-reading now – particularly your books. I am so proud of
my line of signed copies of your work.

You see the Pope has condemned you almost by name? 'Violent & immoral
books cloaked in the glitter of aesthetics.' Hard words.

I long to hear an account of your Boston disasters. I never liked the idea of that
play.

. . . You will not recognize me. I am doing Dr Goller's diet for obesity and am
shrivelling up. I look very like Minty[1] now – a character for whom I have always felt
a very close affinity.

Yours ever
Evelyn

Talking of re-reading, I re-read *Brideshead* and was appalled. I can find many
excuses – that it was the product Consule Bracken[2] of spam, Nissen huts, black-out
– but it wont do for peace-time. The plot seemed to me excellent. I am going to
spend the summer rewriting it.

[1] In *England Made Me*, 1935, by Graham Greene, Minty is described as 'small, wrinkled, dusty'.
[2] As Minister of Information Brendan Bracken gave Waugh time in 1943-4 to write *Brideshead
Revisited*.

To LAURA WAUGH   British Embassy,
15 April 1950   Paris
                                                        [written in Rome][1]

Darling Whiskers

. . . I arived at the empty Embassy & next day lunched with W. Rospigliosi[2] at the
club Sexy Mallet resigned from and then I had cocktails with Mondy & Cécile[3]
(*very* pretty both of them) & they came to dine with me & Angela Antrim & we were
all very jolly. Yesterday I did the basilicas in the rain and a taxi & had my meals with
Peggy [Mallet] who had arrived and goodness the jokes Acton made about her
frugality are not jokes at all. There simply isn't enough to eat. Well dinner last night
was soup and then a very nice little pastry pie like a vol-au-vent with a buttered egg
inside and some peas and a banana. All served on silver plate with three liveried
footmen. Vin très ordinaire. Sexy came back in the evening very sweet. He had had a
little holiday in the north & had enjoyed himself so much it brought tears to the eyes.
He kept saying lets give a party for Evelyn & Peggy looked flint & steel.

. . . Rome is full of boy scouts & girl guides, and they push so to kiss Peters foot
that lots get their teeth knocked out & they have to be swept up afterwards.

All love darling
Evelyn

[1]Waugh went alone to Rome for Holy Year, visiting Nancy Mitford on the way out and on the way back.

[2]William Rospigliosi (1906-   ). Married 1933-58 to Helen Acton, daughter of Daphne Acton. Interned by Mussolini. A friend of Henry Luce, he worked for *Time* magazine in Rome.

[3]Cécile Geoffroy-Dechaume married in 1936 Edmund Howard, second secretary in Rome.

To Nancy Mitford
15 April [1950]

British Embassy,
Rome

Darling Nancy

I cant tell you how much I enjoyed my little visit to you. It was just the kind of entertainment one longs for in the middle of a lonely journey. Blissikins is the mot juste I think.

The reason we were wrong about the Rome Express is that it doesn't exist till May 1st. My train was a rapide and God it was slow stopping at every station except two between Modena & Rome. And a very austere functional diner. All the same I enjoyed the journey & I have enjoyed the last few days here. I have seen mostly English people but that is quite a treat living the life I do.

I am intriguing to get a private chapel at Stinkers behind the back of the Bishop of Clifton who hates private chapels as undemocratic and not contemporary. After seeing a lot of Princes & Cardinals I found the man who really decides such things is a plain Padre Costa, a Brazilian living in the suburbs. I went to him & he received me with great geniality until he learned my name was not Vaughan as he supposed & that I was not a bastard grandson of Cardinal Vaughan. All seemed lost until I found he came from Manaos and by an extraordinary piece of Prodlike scholarship I happened to know that Manaos was the first town in the American continent to have a tramway. After that all was sunny again & I think I may succeed in my pious ambition.

This is a hideous house full of Nazi decorations but with a fine garden. It was the Villa Wolkonsky of which Hare[1] says 'permesso to view may be obtained from your banker.' I have fallen in love with a cousin of Laura's called Cécile Howard (French). . . .

Love
E

[1]Augustus Hare (1834-1903). Painted in water-colours and wrote many guides to Italy.

To Nancy Mitford
26 April [1950]

Pensione Villa Natalia,
Via Bolognese 106,
Firenze.

Darling Nancy,

Let us begin with a little grammar: *Princesse de Clèves* (Mitford's version).[1] Preface. p.1., para 1. 'Allowances have been made for her both by her contemporaries and ever since.' Here you have put two linguistically dissimilar forms into close association. Perhaps it is not absolutely wrong grammatically but it is barbarously inelegant. You must either say: 'both in her own time and ever since' or 'both by her contemporaries and by posterity.'

See?

More next time.

I have come back to Florence after an enchanting festa at Portofino. Say what you like for your snooty frogs, the wops are top nation for simple fun & prettiness. It really was lovely & gay & holy all at the same time. . . . It was frightfully cold all the time & wet most of the time. Johnny Churchill's awful frescoes are all that survived the German occupation. They thought they were Giottos and reverently covered them with six layers of canvas & tarpaulin & ply wood while they were wrecking the rest of the charming Victorian interiors. (Laura's grandfather had all the materials for building shipped out from England).

I met a lively young lady who said she knew you – granddaughter of William Nicholson[2], married to a sort of war correspondent.

She had Osbert Lancaster staying with her. Well say what you will I don't mind him a bit, in fact rather like him.

. . . Harold [Acton] lives a life of great severity. His parents will not permit his going out when they have guests or his staying at home when they are alone, so half his time is spent being polite to aged American marquesas and half eating in poky restaurants. He is not allowed in his fathers car and lives three miles out of town. He will treat me like an aged American marquesa, bows me in & out of doors, holds umbrellas over my head & pays me extravagant compliments. But he knows everything about ART.

We went to see B. Berenson, like Trotsky, in a house[3] which after Harold's is a miserable hole. La Pietra really is very fine. Much more than I ever expected.

I went to see the Master Sir Max Beerbohm at Rapallo. Fatuous Lady B would talk but it was blissikins just to be in a room with him.

Tomorrow I go to Montegufoni[4]. Then with Harold to Verona.

. . . Cécile has passed out of my heart. It was burning passion at the time. Easy come, easy go.

I daresay I'll have something to report of Montegufoni.

Such thinness as you may have observed on my passage through Paris has gone. I am back to normal. The wop food is *not* what one needs really. Nor the wine. . . .

Love

E

[1]Madame de la Fayette, *La Princesse de Clèves* (1678), translated by Nancy Mitford, 1950.
[2]Jenny Nicholson, daughter of the poet Robert Graves though she used her mother's name. She was married to Alex Clifford, who died in 1952, and then to Patrick Cross of Reuters. Died 1962.
[3]I Tatti, at Settignano.
[4]The Sitwells' castle near Florence.

To Laura Waugh   Pensione Villa Natalia,
26 April [1950]   Firenze.

Darling

So I was deeply interested & moved by my visit to Portofino.

The festa was gay & beautiful & holy & [I] thanked God & St George for you with a very full heart.

I found your mother in dire circumstances. Quite penniless, without food, firing or furniture. Gabriel [Dru] had come with the ill considered notion that it would benefit her rheumatics. The cold was intense all the time & it generally rained. I was able to buy a little fire wood to relieve their worst sufferings but they have nothing to eat except vegetables. They will starve at the top of that hill.

The new St George is exactly like the old & when the inside is decorated will be indistinguishable. A damn fool English woman (protestant & middle class) has taken the Castello Brown & thinks herself lady of the manor and goes round saying how important it is to keep the votive plaques out of the church. Well you can imagine the snubs she collects. She is trying very hard & very unsuccessfully to eradicate the name 'Brown'. She said to Osbert Lancaster: 'I expect you know the wonderful novel that was written about this castle?' 'Do you mean A.E.W.Mason's *At the Villa Brown?*' Quick.[1]

On the eve of the festa the Archeprete went round the town with a paste pot sticking posters everywhere which said quite simply 'Arch Priest, we love thee'.

Poor Sexy had a terrible day. He got very drunk before luncheon & promised all the Portofino colony that he would visit them in their homes that afternoon thinking he could whizz round in his car spending ten minutes with each. It was a very weary ambassador who ended up at the Villa Carnarvon.

. . . There was no hot water at Altachiara & Gabriel had not washed any part of herself even her hands since arrival. She ate everything with her fingers including large fried fishes which she held by the tail, clawed the bones out of & swallowed like asparagus. Really a terrible spectacle. But you must not think that I did not love being your mothers guest & that I am not most grateful to her for asking me.

There was a lively young lady who claims to know my children called Mrs Clifford. She has made the Oppenheimer home quite delightful. Mr Clifford has Esmé & Desmond Parsons's disease.[2]

O.Lancaster sat next Gabriel at the Mayor's luncheon & made conversation of what a great friend he was of you & Auberon and all the Herberts and said how like Gabriel was to all her family. 'The only one of your sisters you aren't at all like,' he said, 'is one who married Alick Dru'.

. . . . There was a bearded actor called Clunes[3] (?) who says he is as famous as Olivier & Gielgud.

The procession at Portofino was *much* more beautiful than the one we saw with the original patchy [—] & the fireworks the best I've ever seen.

Your mother was terribly over-excited because the yacht turned its searchlights on the procession & wanted us all to sign a Grand Remonstrance but artful Jenny Clifford calmed her down.

I think your ma thoroughly enjoyed the festa and was quite glad she asked me. I was jolly jaggering all the time & hid my discomfort. The trouble is she simply doesn't realize that the villa is not habitable except in hot weather. It really should be completely furnished & decorated if she ever hopes to get good winter tenants. The echo in all the rooms is beastly.

The garden is well kept up and Sheepers[4] fine solid structure is still sound enough.

When I send you my Verona address telegraph all well and Knox news.

All love
Evelyn

[1]The book referred to was *The Enchanted April* by 'Elizabeth of the German Garden' (Elizabeth Russell), 1922.

[2]Hodgkin's disease.

[3]Alec Clunes (1912–70). That year he directed himself as Macbeth at the Arts Theatre, his hundredth production there.

[4]Henry, fourth Earl of Carnarvon, who built the house. There were many pictures of him in which he was thought to resemble a sheep.

TO NANCY MITFORD   Piers Court.
25 May [1950]

Darling Nancy

Emily Post is not a very gratifying comparison.[1] She was the great American authority on etiquette and a very bad authority too.

I am having great trouble about protagonists. Not only the wild beast of Bloomsbury [Raymond Mortimer] but people as far West as Harley Street write me abusive letters on the subject and Eddy Sackville-West who knows no Greek supports them.[2]

His visit was a heavy responsiblity. I gave him fresh meat at every meal but he took a great number of pills. Were they in order to ameliorate the cooking or reinforce the vitamins? He drinks only whisky in tiny quantities and I generally count on large bumpers of goodish wine dulling my guests' consciousness of their discomforts.

Also he dislikes cross-word puzzles and Ronnie Knox made us do them all the evening in a special way devised by himself to make them more difficult. He (Eddy) looked very elegant, & except for pimples, pretty. He has a dear little dinner jacket with a velvet collar & tiny black suede shoes. I took him for a breathless hot walk and he seemed to enjoy the countryside but he moaned pitifully with the pain of my picture books. He got up at dawn and sat in his overcoat in the drawing room before the fire was lit. Oh dear I dont think he can have enjoyed himself at all. I do like him so. Attempts to make a joke of his tenderness fell very flat. I am afraid Ronnie who thinks only of the Grenfells & Shaw Stewarts thought him rather sissy.

And now I am in great embarrassment because there are some very stiff bold grandees called Guise who have lived quite lost on the banks of the Severn since about 1150 and their daughter is to marry a Catholic (a Fraser to make things worse)[3] so Ronnie wanted her asked so I did so though I hardly know them and they are very haughty about it. Oh dear. She is coming anyway.

Laura is much better, leading a nice lazy life warm in bed in freezing room where I sit most of the day.

Tomorrow I go to stay with Maud Russell.[4] I asked Eddy whom I should find and he said Peter Quennell for certain.

I read that all the French police are on strike. That must be a comfort for all.

I have been invited to spend a Cultural Week at the Hague. Would that be funny or horrible? I've never been there and the only Dutch I know are the Jungman sisters and Henry Yorke's pa. He's rather cultural in a gruesome way but not Jungmans.

Bogey Harris is dead.[5]

Donaldsons went all the way to London for Anthony Mildmay's[6] funeral and their names were omitted from *The Times* list so they are much more socialistic.

I have asked Mr Peters to see that middle-class man with the muffler in Paris.

My garden really looks rather well.

I hope the middle class man's motor car got cured.

Ronnie is sitting saying his rosary over the fire. Is that a good sign? I fear not.

Love from
E

Love to Debo – a faint fragrance of dead romance. H. Hamilton indeed.[7] Why do I dislike him? I don't know him at all & he has done me no injury, but I wish him boiled in oil.

[1] Nancy Mitford had written: 'Who is Emily Post please? The NS and N [*New Statesman and Nation*] says I am the modern she.'

[2] Waugh had used the word in the plural and had written the week before: 'Protagonist. Besides your chum who looks like a Maltese pimp, what is his name, [Raymond] Mortimer, others have written to me about this word.

It is an English word meaning "leading actor". Some dramas, most Greek dramas but not for example Aeschylus, have only one leading actor. Such as *Hamlet*. But other plays eg *Macbeth* 2 protagonists *Julius Caesar* 3 protagonists. If you only allow one protagonist you have to use "deuteragonist" and "tritagonist" which are not English words at all. So balls to the Maltese pimp.'

[3] Philippa Guise (1926–) married Alastair Fraser (1919–), Major in the Lovat Scouts, in 1950.

[4] Maud Nelke married in 1917 Gilbert Russell, brother of Conrad Russell.

[5] Henry Harris, an expert on furniture and painting, died on 20 May. 'I believe no one knows his income, occupation or love affairs.' Cynthia Asquith in *Diaries 1915–18*.

[6] Anthony Mildmay (1909–50). Succeeded as second baron in 1947. Rode over a hundred winners and would have won the National if his reins had not broken.

[7] Hamish (Jamie) Hamilton (1900–). Chairman of Hamish Hamilton since 1931, Nancy Mitford's publisher and friend. She wrote praising him and Waugh replied:

'It is not known why I dislike James Hamish Hamilton. I think perhaps myself being a publisher's son has something to do with it. I grew up with a respect for publishers and don't like to see people fall below my Papa's standards. (Not goodness knows of *flair*. I mean of good behaviour).

Besides I don't like people who are pushful without swagger.

Besides I shouldn't recognise the fellow if I saw him.'

To Nancy Mitford   Piers Court.
28 May [1950]

Darling Nancy

Try & get hold of *New Yorker* for May 13th. It has a gruesome & fascinating description of Mr Ernest Hemingway.[1]

A sad final incident to Eddy's visit. He had an elaborate train journey to Blandford so I sent him all the way to Bath in the village taxi in the hope that it would mitigate his austerities. The taxi-man got him there in nice time, then sat back & lit a pipe to refresh himself. Suddenly he saw a figure like frightened ghost — from the station lugging two suitcases & a medicine-chest, look round wildly, fail to recognize him, leap into another taxi & drive away. There are two stations in Bath & he had been taken to the wrong one. I said at Mottisfont[2] he ate nothing, 'He simply gorges here.'

It was the craving for social life took me to Mottisfont. Well it was all dishevelled war widows playing Canasta (?) One of these widows was Diana Campbell-Grey.

I think nothing of *Nothing*.[3] I began it with the highest expectations & please try & believe me, no tinge of jealousy, and was sharply disappointed. Some lovely lyric flashes, some very funny characters Liz, Penelope the sainted darling, but the idiom rang false everywhere. That idiot paper *New Statesman* of course got the exact opposite of the truth. What Henry never did for a moment was to define his characters social position. Sometimes they spoke 'Mrs Chichesterese',[4] sometimes Air Force, sometimes sheer Gloucester peasant – 'Leave me be': 'Whyever for.' He has just lost his ear through spending so much time with low-class women. All the characters are frightfully common but not consistent in their sort of commonness. Don't you agree. 'I'll take a sherry'. 'Phone me' all the joke-charade vulgarities. Well Etonians of 45 don't talk like that. He might have made a nice contrast with the young, who some of them do, I believe, but not the young men I saw at Mottisfont – Mark Bonham-Carter,[5] Nigel Nicolson[6] etc. They couldn't make out the slang of their generation (in this novel I speak of) but were quite willing to suppose that we talk like John Pomfret & Liz. I daresay Henry never could write dialogue at all & has been bluffing all the time. I mean, we have all said 'How wonderfully Henry has caught real proletarian speech' while all the time it was just as false as his 'Knightsbridge' characters. And anyway what is a Knightsbridge character? I don't regard it as having ever been a defined class, unless he means the royal tarts in the Trevor–Montpelier[7] area. But Maimie wouldn't say 'Lets give a "do"' for a party. Perhaps Sibell might since she moved into Midland industrial circles. I believe thats it. He has got his poor mind all jangled up by Birmingham business chums & Miss Glass. Well its a rotten book, but I'm glad the Americans are lapping it up.

He stole from me the idea of a character having his leg off bit by bit & then dying. I used it about a little boy in my first book, who was shot at the school sports.

Do read the article on Hemingway. If you cant get it, I'll send it grudgingly.

Love from
Evelyn

[1] By Lillian Ross, reprinted in her collection *Reporting*, New York 1964, London 1966.

[2]Home of Maud Russell.
[3]By Henry Green, 1950.
[4]i.e. in a genteel manner.
[5]Mark Bonham-Carter (1922–   ). Director of Collins, the publishers, Liberal MP 1958–9, grandson of Asquith.
[6]Nigel Nicolson (1917–   ). Writer. Director of Weidenfeld & Nicolson from 1947, Conservative MP 1952–9, son of Harold Nicolson and V. Sackville-West.
[7]Squares in Knightsbridge.

To Laura Waugh [1]   Piers Court.
[June 1950]
Postcard

I have answered this in your inimitable hand. Your hay has been 'turned'. People hope to 'pick it up' to morrow. Three glorious peonies struggled through the nettles in your kitchen garden. Much escapism among cattle.

In my loneliness I fell into conversation with Hatty yesterday, she is definitely sub-normal.

Kate Donaldson asks if she can stay here first week in July. As Vera[2] intends to be abroad then, I said, no.

E

[1]At Pixton, before the birth of Septimus on 11 July.
[2]Vera Grover, the nanny.

To Laura Waugh   White's.
4 July [1950]

Darling

I am so very sorry to learn that you are still bearing your great burden. Your condition was surprisingly announced to the peoples of Amsterdam by my chairman who said: 'Mr Waugh's great enthusiasm for the Holland Festival is exemplified by the fact that he has left his wife's side while she is bearing him a seventh child'. But the stolid Dutch showed no surprise.

I am very pleased to be back in London. The trouble was that the Festival organizers billeted me on a very kind family in The Hague suburbs whose house was all tiles & linoleum & huge windows & steel. Ultra-modern 1937 and I cannot be happy for a moment in such conditions. Also they had a number of loutish sons who lay about in the living-room like basking whales. But the host & hostess were so kind. The happiest time was two days in an hotel in Amsterdam. I was also taken to a number of very pretty country houses. Bob Coe[1] is there at the American Embassy. He was very kind. So was Nichols[2] our ambassador – very nice man. Also a Dutch pansy with a monocle. But the rest were dull. My lectures ill-attended as in both The Hague & Amsterdam they chose the same night for me & Redgrave's Hamlet & naturally everyone preferred *Hamlet*.

I have got *much* fatter.

Debo is giving a fancy-dress river party so I must go & get an admirals uniform fitted. She is in *great* looks but I don't love her as I did.

It was very good of you to send me my umbrella. I missed it sorely in Holland.

I have sent you a windmill and a coach & horses by separate post. I think we might experiment with a graver [?] trying to make the coach-and horses better. It looks like nothing much but it is all solid silver and very expensive. So were the lamps – £25. No duty to pay surprisingly enough. They are blue & white. I thought one might do for your bed-room.

The Dutch not only have soup for luncheon but have two helpings of it.

I hope Bridget has forgiven me for being so drunk & your ma for being so sour with hangover.

All love
E

[1]Robert Coe (1902–   ). Diplomat. Magdalen College, Oxford, 1927, Counsellor of American Embassy at the Hague 1948. Ambassador to Denmark 1953–7. 'Inside ensconced cosily behind an embankment of glass, there was a small, dark, cheerful person, looking behind tortoise-shell spectacles, like a determined bee. Mr Robert Coe and his Renault. . . .' An essay in *Cherwell*, June 1927, by Brian Howard.

[2]Sir Philip Nichols (1894–1966).

To P.H. Newby   Hyde Park Hotel.
5 July 1950

Dear Sir,

Thank you for your letter of 3rd July with the kind suggestion that I should make public a conversation between myself and a friend about my writing. I am afraid that this is not practicable because I never mention my writing to my friends.

Yours faithfully,
Evelyn Waugh

An unpublished short story would cost you a great deal more than you can afford.

[1]P.H. Newby (1918–   ). Novelist. Joined the BBC in 1949 and was Controller of the Third Programme 1958–69.

To Laura Waugh   Hyde Park Hotel.
8 July [1950]

Darling

I look eagerly in the columns of *The Times* but every day am disappointed. I am so very sorry for you in this tedious wait, but rejoice you are with your family & with a puppy to keep you amused, and all the coming & going of Pixton to distract you.

. . . The Court Ball was wholly delightful. I dined with the Stavordales for it. We all had a high old time. Full of chums & flowing with champagne, rollicking light heartedness like the last hour of a hunt ball from the first minute and of course the spectacle pure Winterhalter and a delight to the eye.

The Bath wedding[1] was jolly pretty too and Chips[2] had a seizure at the spectacle of the entire royal family in his drawing-room at last.

Between social pleasures I have had a number of business interviews & have more to come. Selznick[3] is trying to buy *Brideshead*. If he does and I get the money into trust & then get it out of trust we may be rescued from our queer street.

Gossip:

Raimund is sacked by Luce.[4]

Murrough O'Brien sacked by Irene.[5]

King of Jugo-Slavia sacked by Queen of J.S.[6]

Maimie has lost all her fortune.

Connolly has lost Miss Skelton.

There is no truth whatever in the story that Fr. Caraman is leaving the *Month*.

Daphne has a new lover called Sam Fielden[7] & wants to learn parachuting to be like him.

. . . Ann Rothermere is giving a rival ball on the same night as Debo.

I dined with Sutro . . . and lovely Natasha Paley[8] was there & she inebriated him so that he acted & sang for three hours with absolute genius.

Fr D'Arcy has nausea.

Well I think that's about all. I will come to Pixton soon. I am longing to see you.[9]

All love
E

[1]Lady Caroline Thynne (1928–   ), daughter of the Marquess of Bath, married David Somerset (1928–   ), heir presumptive to the Duke of Beaufort, on 5 July.

[2]Henry (Chips) Channon (1897–1958). Conservative MP and diarist. Knighted 1957.

[3]David Selznick (1902–65). Producer of *Gone With the Wind*.

[4]Raimund von Hofmannsthal worked for his friend Henry Luce at *Time* 1939–71. There had been a row and he changed his department.

[5]Murrough O'Brien (1910–   ), a major in the Irish Guards, and his wife Irene Richards were divorced, and he remarried in 1952.

[6]Princess Alexandra of Greece divorced King Peter in 1950.

[7]The Marchioness of Bath obtained a divorce and was married to Major Alexander (Xan) Fielding 1953–76.

[8]Princess Natalia Paley, born in 1905. Daughter of Grand Duke Paul of Russia. Married in 1937 John Wilson, theatrical producer.

[9]Waugh was consistently absent at the birth of his children. Laura wrote on this occasion:
'I have been thinking deeply about whether it would be a good thing for you to come and visit me again and though I long for it I don't think it would be if Auberon [Herbert] is going to be here – I don't yet know that he is but it seems to be probable.

I think the mixture of all the children and him would be intolerable to you and even though I know you would be polite to him I know I should be in a fever and miserable, feeling things were not right.'

To GRAHAM GREENE   Piers Court
[15 July 1950]
Postcard

I hear you have consented to write script for film of *Brideshead*. If true, thanks
most awfully. It is more than I ever thought possible.[1]

E

[1] No film was made.

To LAURA WAUGH   [Piers Court]
Wednesday 26 July [1950]

Darling,
It is nice to be out of London. I wish I were at home. There is no home without
you. But I agree that you would do far better to stay away until you are fully well
enough to endure the horrors of the childrens company. I have sent my mother her
instructions; also Teresa. Your barometer-glass is in the hands of Universal Aunts.
When I left you, (still in the great wave of euphoria that began as I escaped from
Holland, mounted at the jolly London parties, mounted still higher at the news of
Septimus's birth and at finding you so well & beautiful) I went straight to Highgate
exhausted by the hot journey & short tempered. I was not at all nice to my poor
mama and left with the first beginnings of bad conscience & melancholy, but I had a
gay, busy day trying to get a sailors uniform and ending up with only bits of one
which I had to go to the East End to find. Then I went to a cocktail party of Graham
Greene's where I was beastly to Father Caraman, Lady Jones and a publisher who
deserves all he gets. Then dinner at Dot's – Loelia Westminster[2], Richard and
Virginia Sykes[3] (who was most loving & sent you many messages) the Hultons[4] (not
very nice), Duchess. Philip Dunn. Odd but jolly party. Then to the boats which
looked lovely. Exquisite young married women in elaborate Edwardian dresses.
The whole party was lyrically pretty & gay. No ugly incidents. Then to breakfast at
Warwick House where Ann's party was just ending sombrely. Next day woke rather
drunk & kept happily drinking all the morning. Burns & Graham Greene came to
luncheon at White's. Burns had been very idle & inept about his organization of
Father D'Arcy's orgy. Jolly drinking in hot afternoon. Went to sleep & woke up sad
& from then on all euphoria departed & melancholy, insomnia, nervous nausea, lack
of appetite, sore eyes, breathlessness and other painful symptoms set in & got worse.
A sad lonely Saturday, a sadder lonelier Sunday, a Monday of despair.
I do hope that your mother and the Drus enjoyed the dinner party. It achieved its
primary end in giving D'Arcy a sense of being surrounded by love & sympathy. I
thought it all pretty beastly but then I was already in general despair. Through
Burns's ineptitude no one seemed to realize that wine was not included in the price

of the dinner and I found myself a grudging host to many thirsty papists. I brought Ann Rothermere & Randolph & June as my guests & put at my table them and Eddy Sackville-West, a pansy I didn't know who was a friend of June's & who was the only chap to offer a contribution towards the wine bill, Mr & Mrs Walston, Graham Greene & Gabriel. She looked quite nice & ate quite cleanly. I put your mother among the big shots. She looked very nice. The dinner was quite good. Frank made a rough, cheerful, sentimental speech. Mr T.S. Eliot was very dull but then he had been shanghaied into the thing believing that it was a small intimate affair. Then Douglas [Woodruff] the funniest & most felicitous speech I have ever heard from anyone. That was a high spot. Poor D'Arcy's reply was not good. He told some footling funny stories & then fell into a rhapsody of self-pity. After that people simply wouldn't go, but hung about cadging drinks while the waiters made off. It was nearly two before I reached my sleepless couch. Yesterday I lunched with Graham Greene, Mrs Walston and Eddy Sackville-West (who complained bitterly about having had to sit next to Randolph the night before). Home on the 4.55. Four servants living in the house looking after no one and the windows filthy. The garden looking pretty horrible. The hedge in front incurably ragged – no fault of Workman's, the grass blotchy & weedy, no Whisker, a pile of tedious American letters to answer. Well it is better than London and soon I shall be healed.

My heart is with you. Take care of yourself. Golly Elwes sent you great love. So did hundreds more whose names escape me

Deepest love
E

[1]Lady Dorothea Ashley-Cooper (1907–   ). Married Viscount Head in 1935.

[2]Loelia Ponsonby (1902–   ). Married to the Duke of Westminster 1930–47 and to Sir Martin Lindsay in 1969.

[3]Virginia Gilliat married Sir Richard Sykes in 1942.

[4]Princess Nika Yourievitch married to Edward Hulton 1941–66. Both wrote books; he owned magazines including *Picture Post* and was knighted in 1957.

TO GRAHAM GREENE   Piers Court
[27 July 1950]
Postcard

I returned to find your very kind present of *the Third Man*. I shall read it with intense curiosity tho I dont expect to enjoy it as much as your real book, or the film. Please don't try & get out of *Brideshead*. I am sure you can make a fine film of it. Don't think I shall be cantankerous. I am cantankerous but not about that sort of thing – about cooking and theology and clothes and grammar and dogs.

E

To Laura Waugh   Piers Court
30 July [1950]

Darling Laura

Harriet and James were not able to give a very coherent account of your condition. They seemed obsessed by the fact that Septimus enjoyed his bath. They also commended Mrs Makey's jelly making.

I miss you unendurably & go whistling about the house & fields never hearing an answer. My health is a little, well much, better. Yesterday I read *Put out more Flags* & thought it *very* amusing. Then Teresa telephoned to me from London to say she was safe. I had not been anxious.

The Donaldsons came to dinner with me on Friday & before that I had gone to the Cinema – very unsteady on pins walking back on golf course – and that night I slept soundly so it was big day. I make fierce sorties into the garden & fall back dizzy bleeding & sweaty after an hours work.

No other news. Let me know if Auberon looks like going and I will come quick. Or if you are going to Bridget.

All love
E

To the Headmistress of St Mary's Convent, Ascot   Piers Court
2 August 1950

Dear Mother Ignatius,

Thank you very much for your letter to my wife about Teresa. I am very glad that you like the child; she certainly loves you all & shows much improvement since she went to you. I am most grateful for all that you are doing.

Her sloth, I fear, may prove incorrigible for she has a very bad heredity on both sides of her family. It is largely for this reason that I lay such stress on the mechanics of charm.

Her chief fault at the moment seems to be an affectation of glibness and boisterousness which would not be offensive if they were genuine, but which are in her case I believe a forced denial of natural shyness. I wish we could persuade her that charm lies in simplicity, naturalness and gentleness. In fact she should take her mother as a model rather than myself.

The letters which she writes weekly are very depraved compositions. I wonder if it would be a good plan to make her show them to her English instructress & to rewrite them if necessary before they are posted?

Her sister Margaret who, I hope, will be coming to you in a year or so is very pretty, very stupid, with abounding charm.

I am so glad that *Scoop* made you smile.

Yours sincerely,
Evelyn Waugh

TO NANCY MITFORD   Piers Court
3 August [1950]

Darling Nancy

Yes it is true that Laura has a son. She is very well & the baby is said to be satisfactory. It is named Michael Septimus. I am not counting in your other god-child to make this my seventh. We have one who died in infancy. How much is a 'quiverful'? Seven I think, or was it nine?

I hope you enjoyed Edinburgh. Betjeman, the silly ass, says without qualification that it is the most beautiful city in Europe. It has some handsome aspects. The Caledonian Hotel used to be excellent but I went there lecturing the other day & found that the State Railways have painted all the beautiful mahogany doors apple-green. Beasts.

Was your obscene play well received?

I am rather back in love with Debo. She gave a party on the river and wore false eye lashes made of sort of Lulu brush bristles stuck on crooked, and I must say my old heart melted.

How I hate the English summer, well any summer for that matter. Weeds everywhere & children & insomnia. Randolph is off to Korea lucky him.[1]

I had a brief London season & enjoyed it in the evenings when there were parties but oh the length of the days sitting in White's or Hyde Park Hotel. Momo[2] gave a really lovely ball. Everyone went round saying 'What d'you suppose its costing her?' Vulgar yes no. I mean of them to ask not of her to spend it. Well she built a great palace for it. I made Boots hire a tail coat and the first thing he saw when he arrived were Henry Bath and the Duke of Marlborough both in dinner jackets so next night he went to Ann Rothermere's in a dinner jacket tho it had 'White tie' rather rudely written on the card. He looked horrible too because his dinner jacket was covered in soup & lipstick. Then I saw him going to the country dressed for St Tropez 1926. That was horrible too.

So there was a great dinner for Fr D'Arcy. Eddy came & how he complained of the placement.

I opened *Life* magazine & what should I see but a full page portrait of Friar Couturier followed by pictures of a disgusting church he has built. Oh for an atom bomb.

I read with interest how the politest people in the world treated the Italian cyclists.

Why no articles in *Sunday Times*? I look every week and am always disappointed.

Laura and I go to New York in Oct. Do come too then.

Debo calls Ran [Lord Antrim] the lavatory chain because he is always flushing. Not kind.

                                            Love from
                                            Evelyn

[1] Randolph Churchill was a war correspondent for the *Daily Telegraph*.
[2] Maud Kahn, daughter of Otto Kahn, the American banker. Married Sir John Marriott in 1920. Died in 1960.

To Nancy Mitford   Piers Court
27 September [1950]

Darling Nancy

That was a most moving letter about Boots. Oh dear I do hope he doesnt settle down with that drab. All my friends seem to marry into the Forbes–Quennell white slave market and it is the end of all friendship. . . . Look at poor Randolph, peppered with Korean socialist shrapnel to get away from the tantrums of his tart. [1] Why cant ones friends marry *nice* girls?

I go to London tomorrow to dispatch copies of *Helena*. One will reach you soon. Dont puzzle your pretty head with it. It will be all Greek – or worse still English – to you. But put it on a shelf & look at its back now & then & think kindly of me.

I wish you had accepted the *Sunday Times* invitation to write the caption for their picture. I dont much mind the papers saying I am beastly, which is true, or that I write badly, which isn't. What enrages me is wrong facts. They always are wrong in these knowing 'profiles'. When they say I went to Cambridge or got the D.S.O. or was converted to Catholicism by the war, I eat the carpet.

It has been a disgusting summer – continuous rain since early June and now nothing to look forward to but winter. I've had a succession of guests to keep me agitated but not amused. The travel agents in America are routing all their Irish tourists via Fishguard now telling them to stop off a night at Stinkers on the way.

Well next week I take Laura to New York for a fortnight. I originally planned the trip as a stimulant for her after childbirth but it is now I who need it the more. It is the most wonderful health resort in the world. I look to it to revivify me. In fact at the moment I am like a patient lying comatose waiting for the doctor to come round with his needle.

Osbert's last volume [2] is very heavy going. One good sentence: 'Although I was already an eminent author, it is a curious fact that I experienced considerable difficulty at this time in getting anything published'. He is already in New York being brought to life.

I hope to go to Jerusalem for Christmas. You can have no idea, living as you do in lively theatrical circles when you come here, [3] of the awful flat dreariness of England under Welfare.

There was a lady here the other day who knows all about the New York theatre. She saw your play in Edinburgh & thought it brilliant but impossible to get past American censors – not because of dirty language but of situation.

I opened my *Times* this morning to read a letter from Prince Bibesco [4] saying how splendid Sybil was. When did she die? [5] I have read my paper daily cover to cover & seen nothing of it. I saw practically nothing of her since she left Argyll House but I had a warm grateful place for her at heart.

Trim Oxford's wife has become a great beauty, tell Honks. It will annoy her and its true.

Come to think of it Henry Yorke married a nice girl but it doesnt save us from *Nothing*

Love from
Evelyn

[1]Churchill was wounded in the knee while crossing the Naktong river behind enemy lines.
[2]*Noble Essences*, the fifth and final volume of Osbert Sitwell's autobiography.
[3]Nancy Mitford had been in Britain touring with *The Little Hut*.
[4]Prince Antoine Bibesco, first secretary at the Romanian Embassy. He was 'as handsome as a Roman coin. Rich in a then rich world, magically generous, gay but dipped in melancholy', according to the autobiography of Enid Bagnold, 1969.
[5]Lady Colefax died 22 September 1950.

To JOHN DONALDSON   Piers Court
28 September 1950
Postcard

Help urgently needed. I am describing two musical chaps leaving a string quartet concert (if such a thing exists, I think I've heard of it). One is critical, the other appreciative, both highly snobbish & technical. Could you very kindly jot down for me the sort of remark discussing the performance that each might make? Not too fantastic. Just straight critics jargon. It is not stated what was played.

                                                                        E

To NANCY MITFORD   Piers Court
[September 1950]

Darling Nancy
    I went to Colefax's Memorial Service. Well attended but only by the old. Everyone looked exactly like Rose Macaulay. None of the young bothered to come except Liz & Raimund who wore a carmine hat and yellow satin tie respectively.
    I had a busy London day despatching *Helena*s, going to confession, seeing the Woburn collection etc. & later dropped into White's to give a final basting to Quennell's goose (quite unnecessary, he is assured of 100% black-balling). Who should I see there but Boots, woolly-headed wild-eyed, costumed as an American college boy. I said: 'I've been hearing about your spree'. He turned pale grey, eyes popped out, lips trembled, no sound. I thought he had not heard so I said much louder: 'I've heard about your SPREE'. Then in a sort of puppy yelp he cried: 'Most inaccurate I'm sure' & bolted out of the house.
    Oh I do look forward to New York.
    Don't try & read *Helena*

                                                                Love
                                                                E

I think Warner kissed you once. Yes? No?

To GRAHAM GREENE   Piers Court
[8 November 1950]
Postcard

Thanks awfully for little fire engine.[1] I agree you are greatest novelist of the century
but am not absolutely sure I should recognise this from the dramatic intensity of the
story, as the blurb promises.

  Come here quick. I have some caviar

                                                                    E

  [1] Graham Greene, *The Little Fire Engine* (for children), 1950.

To NANCY MITFORD   Piers Court
9 November [1950]

Darling Nancy
  Goose. Of course I value your opinion above all others about most things. But
well no not about religion. Your verdict on Mauriac's article in the *Month* struck an
icy stiletto into any hope I ever had that you could enjoy *Helena*. And I genuinely
didn't want you to try because I knew it would be a bore to you. It was love that
prompted me to ward you off it. Don't even open it or cut a page, I implore.
  Six people think it the most beautiful book they ever read and I am first of the six.
Otherwise they all say: 'What was the point?'[1]
  The Admiralty, the War Office, the Secret Service, the Foreign Office have all
tried to suppress Cooper's book on 'Heartbreak'.[2] But since it is being published in
America the irreparable harm is done and they have grudgingly consented to let him
keep his passport and his masonic apron.
  Laura & I are greatly rejuvenated by our few weeks of luxury & make-believe in
New York. It is a great health resort and so cosmopolitan that you can be happy &
busy & never meet an American.
  Do you remember a cold, awkward, ambitious, socialist protégé of Sybil's called
Gladwyn Jebb?[3] You should just see him now. He is the idol of American girlhood
the most sought-after television performer in the country. They can do something
to the face with that apparatus. He looks like Sir Galahad. There are 'Jebb Circles'
in every college. He gets 500 letters a day saying: 'Become an American, stand for
President and we will vote for you'. They pursue him in the street & snip bits off his
coat.
  He has a stately home on Long Island where he entertains lavishly, lolling about
like a Roman patrician and talking, I must say pretty dully, in a lisping fruity tone.
And my word he is enjoying it.
  Poor Osbert [Sitwell] is a tottering corpse. Edith is playing Lady Macbeth at the
Museum of Modern Art on Nov 16th. Glenway Westcott[4] as Banquo, David
Horner in a tartan dinner-jacket as MacDuff. Lady Ribblesdale as the witches.
Cheapest seats £5. I wish I could be there.[5]

Sergeant Preston is as bald as an egg and very watery eyed. I suspect he drinks.

It was very much like being in Paris travelling in the *Ile de France*. Very slovenly, excellent cooking, hideous cheap decorations (Cunarders are hideous but very solid & expensive). The entire ship was manned by a great family of identical multuplets. Short, fat, bald chain-smokers – Captain, pursers, stewards, sailors all indistinguishable.

I hope my nest eggs arrive safely & remain safe.

It is exciting news that you are composing another novel. You are clever to think of plots. Do take care of the grammar and don't introduce communist propaganda. Isn't it time you dedicated a work to me? Or are we estranged.

Much love from
Evelyn

[1]'The indifferent reception given to what Evelyn believed to be by far his best book was the greatest disappointment of his whole literary life as he told me and other friends.' Christopher Sykes, *Evelyn Waugh*.

[2]Duff Cooper, *Operation Heartbreak*, 1950. An account of successful deception by the British who used a dead body to plant false information on the Germans during the war.

[3]Gladwyn Jebb (1900–   ). Permanent Representative of the United Kingdom to the United Nations 1950–4. He because a television star in the debates on Korea. British Ambassador to France 1954–60. Created Baron Gladwyn 1960.

[4]Glenway Westcott (1901–   ). American poet and novelist. He read Macbeth. Among his publications are: *Grandmothers*, 1925, *Apartment in Athens*, 1945.

[5]When asked why she had chosen Lady Macbeth, Edith Sitwell replied, 'Because she amuses me. Because the part suits my voice. And because she was one of my ancestresses.'

To John Betjeman
9 November [1950]

Piers Court

Dear John

Thanks awfully for your letter which I found waiting my return from New York. I am delighted that you liked *Helena*. It is you & six or seven others whom I seek to please in writing.

Credit for typography to a Wykehamist J MacDougall who sits in Bell's chair at Chapman & Hall.

Saints are simply souls in heaven[1]. Some few people have been so sensationally holy in life that we know they went straight to heaven and so put them in the calendar. We all have to become saints before we get to heaven. That is what purgatory is for. And each individual has his own peculiar form of sanctity which he must achieve or perish. It is no good my saying: 'I wish I were like Joan of Arc or St John of the Cross'. I can only be St Evelyn Waugh – after God knows what experiences in purgatory.

I liked Helena's sanctity because it is in contrast to all that moderns think of as sanctity. She wasn't thrown to the lions, she wasn't a contemplative, she wasn't poor & hungry, she didn't look like an El Greco. She just discovered what it was God had chosen for her to do and did it. And she snubbed Aldous Huxley with his perennial fog, by going straight to the essential physical historical fact of the redemption.

Do come here soon

Love from
Evelyn

The only person who hasn't thanked for *Helena* is your wife. Biff her on the boko. How well grounded in faith are the people who spoke of 'My sainted Aunt'.

1 John Betjeman had written: 'What a wonderful book *Helena* is. . . . The only thing that puzzles me in the book is the saintliness of Helena. She doesn't seem to be like a saint.'

To Louis Auchincloss[1]   Piers Court
13 November [1950]

My Dear Auchincloss

As I told you, I saved your book[2] to read on the voyage home. I found my self restraint most repaying. It requires & merits close attention.

I enjoyed it enormously & congratulate you with all my heart. The conception of every story is alarmingly mature and most skilfully achieved. It is hard to believe they are the work of a beginner. I don't like the title – it is not particular apt, it requires explanation (and a title should be immediately recognizable) and it is not easily memorable. Apart from that, and your misuse of 'mutual' (tricky word best left alone if you aren't happy about its precise meaning) I have no criticisms. Only praise for the exact social sense & elegant expression & gratitude to Jack Pierrepoint for telling me about it.

I hope, by the way, Jack is recovering satisfactorily?

It is so encouraging to find an American reverting to the high standards of James, Sturgis, Wharton, Pearsall Smith & disregarding the deep South & the *New Yorker*.

When you come to Europe, please come here.

Yours sincerely
Evelyn Waugh.

[1]Louis Auchincloss (1917–). Lawyer and writer.
[2]*The Injustice Collectors*, 1950.

To Graham Greene   Piers Court
16 November [1950]

Dear Graham

Thanks awfully for writing about *Helena*. I hardly hoped you would like it. I am hugely exhilarant to hear you do. Most of the reviews I have seen have been peculiarly offensive. I don't believe this modern kind of chastisement is really salutary. It is just like being jostled about in a crowd.

Is there any chance of seeing you before your crucifixion among the ants?[1] I am here uninterruptedly until the end of January when I go levanting with Christopher Sykes.

Mrs Luce thinks you do not understand Sartre.

Tonight Edith Sitwell plays Lady Macbeth at the New York Museum of Modern Art. How I wish I could be there.

My younger children speak endlessly about your little fire engine. Have you left the completed ms. of 'The Point of Departure'[2] behind you? I look forward to it feverishly.

> Yours affectionately
> Evelyn

[1]Celia Coplestone was 'crucified very near an ant-hill' in *The Cocktail Party* by T.S.Eliot, 1949.
[2]Greene has no recollection of ever using such a title. *The End of the Affair* was his next novel.

To Maurice Bowra   Piers Court
17 November [1950]

Dear Maurice

I was delighted to find your letter awaiting me on my return from New York.

Of course you are quite right about the Wandering Jew[1] but to have introduced a character of tragedy and mysterious tragedy at that into that stage of the story would have been all wrong so I had to make a mere shadow of him and so spoil the real story. I ought to have thought of some quite other way of getting Helena on the scent.

The Incarnation is no use without the Cross and vice versa. Everyone in the 4th century seems to have been concerned only with the Incarnation, except Helena. That is why in her way she is as important as Athanasius[2].

Ronnie Knox has now published his magnum opus *Enthusiasm*. I expect you have it. Don't you think it is exactly the kind of work that ought to be rewarded with an honorary doctorate? I believe he would rejoice in it and I think he would be more credit to the University than the Egyptian Minister of Education. Do push it through.

Please come here if it ever suits your convenience[?]. It would be a great joy to us.

> Yours ever
> Evelyn

[1]Bowra had written: 'Nor am I quite happy about the Wandering Jew's treatment of Our Lord. Surely he spat in his face, and his punishment is to live with his own hard heart until forgiveness comes to him from God? His doom is that he cannot save himself. Surely a terrible and most important story, which should not be watered down . . . he is more formidable than a mere Jewish tradesman.'
[2]St Athanasius (295–373). Bishop of Alexandria, opposed Arianism.

To Ronald Knox   Piers Court.
18 November [1950]

Dear Ronnie,

The Press have sent *Enthusiasm*. I cant part with it. I am so proud of that dedication that I must have a copy in every room. I feel that if I send a cheque you might destroy it. May I without indelicacy send cash?

I couldnt tell you in the amazement of discovery, and I can't tell you now, how much that dedication means to me. I am sure that you must have chosen me as being the friend who would be most elated. If you had put my name in a pamphlet or a detective story I should have been transfigured with pride. But in your *magnum opus* – it is too much.

Thirty years in the making – twice as long as the time since I first met you. I think I was already a fan of yours thirty years ago for I remember my father's delight when 'Reunion all round'[1] appeared. He read it aloud and I was dazzled as I have been ever since. That must have been 1920? It wasnt I think until you wrote to discourage me from publishing a pamphlet about Oldmeadow that I saw beyond the Max Beerbohm brilliance and the fire works became real illumination. Since then every word you have written and spoken has been pure light to me.

                                                        Well, thanks awfully,
                                                        Evelyn

[1]'This pasquinade in the manner of Swift was written in four days at Eastertide 1914. It satirized the impulse prevalent among certain Anglicans to sink doctrinal differences with the Nonconformist sects in the interest of Christian good fellowship. . . .' Evelyn Waugh, *Ronald Knox*, 1959.

To Nancy Mitford
[December? 1950]

Darling Nancy

There is I believe no doubt that Boots has married. . . .[1] The evidence is conclusive tho it is not known whether he gave her a ring. A Mrs Hulton gave him a wedding breakfast. After the first course Boots had a seizure, fell off his chair frothing & gasping, was carried straight to a waiting van & whisked off to Tring where he spent the first fortnight of married life in a padded cell being starved and hosed and worse. He is now back in London enjoying a precarious tenancy of Sutro's flat in Curzon Street. Their total capital is £5 which Hulton gave him for tips at Tring and he kept, two sacks of sugar and a cottage in Kent . . . . Boots makes alternate proposals that she shall sell it & give him the money to go abroad with and that she shall build on a ball room. He writes daily to Lys begging to see her & saying how wretched he is, but she is adamant. This last titbit from Patrick Balfour who stayed here last week. The rest from my man Sykes and Mrs R.S. Churchill.

I long to read your novel & criticize tho whats the good you never take my advice. My dates are – leave London–Paris Jan 20th return probably via Paris about end of March. So if I can be of any use, tell me. I dont think it would be advisable to risk your manuscript in the souks of Aleppo. I think you ought to devise *some* funny characters. You still have the delicious gift of seeing people as funny which I lost somewhere in the highlands of Scotland circa 1943.

Very sorry about Col. being scalped & blinded.[2] Was it Gen. Moch?

What are your plans for the next war? Do come here only please dont be patriotic again.

Sad about Duke of Devonshire.[3] They might have known it was madness to let him chop wood until the death duties were safe. To read the obituaries in *The Times* you would think that a composite character part Great Duke of Wellington, part Salisbury, part Talleyrand, part Bron Lucas,[4] had left us, instead of that testy alcoholic we knew.

Randolph is in a bad way.

Now I will say happy happy Christmas. No presents for anyone this year on account of the handsome *Helena*'s I gave quite lately. Do you think that will wash?

You spoiled all my efforts to cheer Honks by telling her you instigated them [incomplete]

[1] Barbara Skelton.

[2] Nancy Mitford had written: 'Col. [Palewski] had a horrid motor-accident and nearly lost an eye and was scalped. All right now but it was dreadful at the time.'

[3] The tenth Duke died suddenly at the age of fifty-five.

[4] Lord Lucas (1876–1916). He made a flight over the German lines and did not return.

TO NANCY MITFORD   Piers Court.
6 January 1950 [1951]

Dearest Nancy

No I dont remember the old school chum you mention. If he is a genuine Lancing boy he has a hot potato in the mouth. We all caught it from imitation of a master called Roxburgh whom we greatly revered. Driberg exemplifies it in a marked degree. Pretty little Ali Forbes caught it at Stowe[1] where Mr Roxburgh migrated. Anyway, genuine or spurious, he would be a great pleasure to me. I haven't many admirers left nowadays. Sykes tells me he has engaged a motor car in which he proposes to drive me about Paris surveying the habits of the people between the train from London & the train to Rome. Could we not pick you up & take you to tea with this decent sounding fellow?

I have felt so very feeble in recent weeks that at last I called in a doctor who took my blood-pressure & pronounced it the lowest ever recorded – in fact the pressure of a 6 months foetus. In an access of sudden hope I said: 'Does that mean I shall die quite soon.' 'No. It means you will live absolutely for ever in deeper & deeper melancholy'.

The great news of the New Year is, of course, Maurice's elevation to the Equestrian Order.[2] We are buying him a horse & spurs. As you would expect he takes the subject with deadly seriousness. 'Many of my pupils are now in the key positions. No doubt they wished to show their loyalty. I prefer knighthood to the O.M.'

It is really very odd as he has done nothing to deserve it except be head of the worst College at Oxford and publish a few books no one has ever read. My own explanation is that it was part of a secret treaty made in Washingon between Mr Attlee & Judge Frankfurter[3] but as you don't know the American scene you wont see the point of that. Speculation is rife.

. . . Anyway he takes mockery in poor part.

Ann Rothermere, silly goose, has taken up [Barbara Skelton][4] and asked eight people to meet her at cocktails twenty two of whom came.

Did you hear about Philip Hardwicke[5] & Philip Dunn's opening meet? These two buffoons are Joint Masters[6] of a pack of hounds in the pansy country, insist on hunting the hounds themselves & quarrel of course furiously. The opening meet was at their best subscriber's house, they all sat about having drinks & wrangling who was going to hunt until P.Hardwicke claimed Precedence from rank & decided to move off. No hound was in sight. Tremendous trumpetings & gallopings about, then sinister sounds from the farm quarters where they were at length found in the pig sty devouring a sow with all her litter.

Best love
Evelyn

[1]No, Alistair Forbes was at Winchester.
[2]Maurice Bowra, Warden of Wadham since 1938, had received a knighthood.
[3](1882–1965). A liberal judge of the Supreme Court of the United States 1939–62.
[4]Cyril Connolly's second wife.
[5]Earl of Hardwicke.
[6]Of the Tedworth Hunt.

TO CHRISTOPHER SYKES
Piers Court.

[January 1951?]
Postcard

I know what it is you want to stay where you can have women in your rooms you filthy beast well you wont not with me see we are going somewhere respectable with no goings on except a game of cards with a crook or maybe a bit of buggery but no filthiness with women while I am around please make up your mind to that.[1]

[1]Sykes and Waugh went to Israel, Jordan, Syria and Turkey. Randolph Churchill bought this card from Christopher Sykes.

To Laura Waugh   Jerusalem in the Kingdom of Jordan.
[7 February 1951]

Darling Laura,

Last Friday the consul took us across the no-mans-land into the Kingdom of
Jordan. We are in a solid, simple Arab hotel and the food is delicious compared with
what we were given in Israel. I have had no return of lassitude. We are both well,
busy, happy.

It is very nice to be among people who almost all wear full fancy dress. The
Governor of the city has taken a great fancy to me & keeps filling my pockets with
cigars. Christopher fell in love with a lady called Mrs Wilson[1] in Telaviv. She came
to Jerusalem (Jordan) for the week end to get her daughter christened – no church in
Telaviv of any creed. We saw a lot of her. We were dining on Saturday with a little
English party in the only restaurant when the Governor who loves me said: 'You
must all come downstairs and hear the Lutheran Archpriest play the banjo'. So
down we went & found a *very* peculiar party of all nations I suppose the kind of party
Auberon [Herbert] delights to give. The Governor exercised his authority and had
the place closed so that no one could see him get tight & started opening bottles of
champagne & filling everyones pockets with cigars while a nazi lay preacher played
the guitar and sang English folk-songs.

Then (at a later party at Consul Generals) I took umbrage because I thought the
newly appointed Arab Custos did not treat me with the respect I deserved so the
Governor made him apologise & he said (a) he was deaf (b) drunk (c) did not talk
French well (d) had such a pain in his great toe on the occasion that he had been
obliged to buy a new pair of boots next day. So I forgave him & he promised me a
copy of his edict of appointment in pure gold but that has not yet arrived.

I sent off a parcel of trinkets for the children from Bethlehem but I daresay it will
take many months in reaching them.

Tonight we plan to keep vigil in the Sepulchre which should be an experience to
remember & boast about.

Christopher is being a *fairly* good jagger. He is a little bit over-excited about the
possibility of his writing an article himself and so is fretting to go to Turkey.[2]

. . . Both Jerusalems are full of huge cars flying UNO flags while both countries
starve. Here there are half a million absolutely destitute & hopeless Arab refugees
from Israel. Israel, starving & houseless, is importing 25,000 Jews a month from
Mesopotamia, Abyssinia, the Yemen, everywhere. Neither side has any housing &
both carefully demolish whole villages where enemies have lived. All are stark mad
& beastly & devoid of truth. It is so boring to be the target for endless propaganda all
mutually contradictory.

All love
E

[1] Shirley Harris married in 1948 John Wilson who later succeeded as Lord Moran. Christopher Sykes
writes 'We both rather fell for her . . . an exaggeration.'
[2] Both of them were commissioned by *Life*, Waugh on The Holy Places, Sykes on Turkey.

To Graham Greene   Piers Court.
17 March [1951]

Dear Graham,
    Where are you?
    I am just back from the Levant & find *The Lost Childhood*[1] awaiting me. Thank
you very much indeed for sending it. Almost all the essays are quite new to me & I
am reading them with close attention. The studies of [Henry] James seem to me the
best I ever read on the subject.
    Of course I don't often agree with you. I can never hope to do that this side of
death. As a fellow crank I take umbrage at your treatment of Gill.[2] 'An artist not of
the first rank.' Surely it is first rate to discipline & perfect a single aptitude however
unassuming? Your praise of Lawrence[3] sickens me. Do you sometimes confuse
'genius' & 'artist' as terms?
    I go to that centre of Sadism, Downside, for Holy Week. I suppose I cannot hope
to find you there too?

                                                        Yours ever
                                                        Evelyn

I have just read Marcel Moré on *The Heart of the Matter*[4]. Excellent Yes? No?

[1]Graham Greene, *The Lost Childhood and other Essays*, 1951.
[2]Eric Gill (1882–1940). Sculptor, engraver and writer. Became a Roman Catholic in 1913.
[3]Greene replied, 'I am puzzled by your reference to my praise of Lawrence as I don't like the man
much. . . . It always seems to me Lawrence was ruined as an artist by his genius.'
[4]In *Dieu Vivant*.

To Nancy Mitford   Piers Court.
25 March [1951]

Dearest Nancy
    The Blessing is admirable, deliciously funny, consistent & complete; by far the
best of your writings; I do congratulate you with all my heart & thank you for the
dedication.
    The childrens ball and the visit to Eton are particularly brilliant passages. I didn't
at first see the point of the burglar incident but that became clear at the end. I
confess I wished the children to be victorious and should have liked the happy end
to be the fathers imprisonment but I see that something softer was necessary for the
books consistency. The first act of betrayal, when the father comes to England to
fetch the boy, is brilliantly executed. Nanny throughout is first class – never
overdone. The whole sustained mood of levity is beyond praise.
    Now for one or two criticisms. The Captain doesn't ring true to me. Ed Stanley &
Boots don't mix. The harem is oriental and can only be maintained by flabby,
dependent men. Not brisk men of action. The crew is wonderfully described. Could
you not keep them just as they are but soften & fatten the Captain? And I think it is a

pity to bring in Little Lord Fauntleroy in the open[?]. It is plain to the sharp reader that that is the plot. You might make it a little more obvious for the less sharp by making him suggest lace collar & velvet suit as the costume. But leave the actual name of the book to the last line of the chapter.

2)   Dexter is so richly funny as he stands that it seems a pity to make him a sham. Couldn't he be arrested for homosexuality or embezzlement of Marshall Aid?

3)   Captain again. Should he not alienate Sigismund's affection by something more than a momentary fit of bad temper? The exposure of Hughie at Eton exposed a real awfulness in his character. Couldn't you strike deeper into Ed Spain & make Sigismund detest a real secondrateness?

4)   The grammar is *much* better. 'Nobody' is singular. p.328 l.45.

. . . But these are niggling little complaints just put in to show I've read every word with rapt attention.

The punctuation & misprints you will see for yourself. Several French proper names have gone wrong in the typing. I will return the ms. by ordinary post. It is not marked because there was nothing to mark except what I have mentioned above. It is a most accomplished work. But do please think a bit about Capt. & Dexter.

I notice that you have no idea of the privations of modern English life. It shows how your friends love & fear you that they make a show for your rare visits. In fact we are perishing with malnutrition & boredom.

Oh by the way Bollinger even non-vintage is a good wine. I think you should substitute Ayala or Lanson.

More congratulations. And more deep loving thanks for the dedication. I am immensely proud of it & of you.

Love
Evelyn

To Nancy Mitford   Piers Court.
31 March [1951]

Darling Nancy

Now none of this. No complaints about headaches. Revision is just as important as any other part of writing and must be done con amore.

I don't think H. Hamilton is right about Sigismund's telephone technique. The child constantly varies in age from 5 to 25 and that is a fantasy which the intelligent reader will accept. (It is much odder that he should drive motor cars at high speed.) But I think it might be tactful to insinuate somewhere a reference to his powers of mimicry.

Dexter. Funk is a bad counsellor in art. The audacity always. But I understand your fears.

Capt. No, he wont do as he stands. That breezy, pushful fellow would have had no reluctance in embracing his heiress. Besides he is common and you arent at your best dealing with common people. If you wont fatten & soften him because of your tenderness towards S. Boots (who I think since his marriage deserves no consideration) you should try him as languid & feeble – a sort of David-Cecil-Eddie-West. As he stands he wont wash. Only feeble men inspire that sort of Crew worship.

Fauntleroy. If people are so dull they must just lose a joke. Make Capt., when he is talking about the scenery, say 'Dress him in a velvet suit with a lace collar.' Even, if you must; 'I am sure I have seen a period drawing of something of the sort somewhere.'

You must work hard at this revision despite headaches.

Love
E

To Nancy Mitford   Piers Court.
8 April [1951]

Darling Nancy

Oh dear how awful about the stamps. My man didn't know. He does now. But what I must have cost you in the past. I *am* sorry. How odd the post office is. Why is it more expensive to write to Paris than San Francisco?

I am afraid I must have written far more sharply than I meant. It was your saying you had a headache from correcting & I feared you would think only of French accents & neglect the plot. Of course you are the final & only judge about that. And it's *excellent* as it stands. And it is just officiousness & bossiness that prompts half the suggestions. Writers are the worst advisers because they cant help thinking how they would have written it themselves. Constant readers are the thing. I met Pam Berry who was full of admiration but also full of keys to explain who everyone was. which I always find an infuriating sort of appreciation, don't you?

Mrs Friese-Greene is mad to read it and as you suggested sending it to Heywood Hill as one way of disposal I shall do that unless I get a cable saying Send it Paris at once. You should have seen the genuine schoolgirl delight on *every* face (even Corporal's[1]) when I brought them the news that you had written a masterpiece. Cyril was less pleased. 'Yes' he said 'Yes. She keeps at it. I suppose she is constantly terrified by the thought of poverty in old age.' Goodness he is terrified and rightly so by poverty in middle age. He is in great troubles. Absolutely hates his wife whom he has taken to live at Sussex Place (telephone cut off for non payment & water too by the look of him) with Toynbee, whom he absolutely hates because he has a steady job, and Toynbee's new wife[2] – a juvenile American typist – and Mr Somebody[3] who is the broken hearted last husband of Blue Feet. Mr Hulton sent him first to Tring and then to the Scilly Islands & he is being sued by the Ministry of Health for not sticking stamps on his insurance card and he thinks he is being guided by Fate to a symbolic suicide. I said how d'you mean symbolic but he couldn't explain. Altogether in poor shape. Lys has been adopted by Alice Obolensky[4] and given a suite at the St Regis (2nd best hotel in New York). That makes it much worse for him.

Everyone I met in London was in debt & despair & either much too fat or much too thin. Except I must say Pam [Berry] who is a sort of booster for paganism & Pam Churchill who is a very tasty morsel.

Poor Randolph is in hospital again with his little unhealed wound. No sign of June at the bedside. His legal & financial difficulties are huge. I must say I lead an awfully dull life here but when I see the alternative I am consoled.

Boots said: 'I am going to become a waiter at a fashionable restaurant so as to humiliate & reproach my friends for their ingratitude.' He saw a worried look, I suppose on my face & said: 'Ah, I see now I have touched even your cold heart.' So I said: 'Well no Cyril it isn't quite that. I was thinking of your finger-nails in the soup.'

Frank Pakenham asked me for the night to his new country home in the suburbs.[5] He sent a great government car for me & I settled down to a comfortable drive when what should happen but I was deposited at Cannon Street Station to queue for a one class train.

Love from
E

[1]Heywood Hill.
[2]Frances Smith married Philip Toynbee in 1950.
[3]Robert Kee, who was married to Janetta Woolley in 1948, and to Cynthia Judah in 1960.
[4]Alice Astor married Serge Obolensky in 1924.
[5]Bernhurst, an eighteenth-century house with thirty acres in Sussex.

To Nancy Mitford   Piers Court.
16 May [1951]

Dearest Nancy

All my heart goes out to the gallant Colonel in his lone struggle to salvage the French from themselves.

How very interesting about Jonathan. News to me. Which Miss Wyndham?[1] Not I hope Dick's daughter. In any case she is bound to be a relation of H. Yorke's & that is not a thing to go into light-heartedly. He was here for a very long week-end. In London, where everyone is seedy, he did not appear notable. Here in the country he looked GHASTLY. Very long black dirty hair, one brown tooth, pallid puffy face, trembling hands, stone deaf, smoking continuously throughout meals, picking up books in the middle of conversations & falling into maniac giggles, drinking a lot of raw spirits, hating the country & everything good. If you mention Forthampton[2] to him he shies with embarrassment as business people used to do if their businesses were mentioned.

Poor Dig very cowardly, quite belying her great moustaches, gentle, lost. She has picked up a whole proletarian argot which she employs with an exquisitely ladylike manner. I really think Henry will be locked up soon. Dig's brother is locked up already. It is a poor look out for their wretched son.

I will soon send you a catalogue of 100 best books. I was to broadcast against them but the BBC think my comments in *very* bad taste ha ha.

By the way if you come to England don't wear your new spectacles. Word has got round how you obtained them. Popular fury rages. They would be torn off your nose & stamped into the carpet. This is the review Mrs Hammersley[3] thought offensive.

Love
E

Will start cabling as soon as I know plans for tour.

[1]Ingrid Wyndham, daughter of Richard and a cousin of Henry Yorke's, was married to Jonathan Guinness 1951–63.

[2]Henry Yorke's family home.

[3]Violet Hammersley, a friend of Nancy Mitford's, lost her husband and her money and retired to the Isle of Wight. 'Slight and dark with an olive complexion she had cavernous black eyes over high cheekbones and an expression of sad resignation illumined by Mona Lisa smiles.' Harold Acton, *Nancy Mitford*, 1975.

To Graham Greene   Piers Court.
[21 May 1951]·
Postcard

I *greatly* admire *The End of the Affair* and when I have read it a second time will say so at length for Fr Caraman.[1]

While proof corrections are still possible: is not 'cornice' p 186 a slip for some other word – buttress perhaps?

And p. 206. Could one speak of a 'man' as an 'abortion'?[2]

Don't please bother to answer.

E

[1]Waugh reviewed *The End of the Affair* in *The Month* September 1951 and also in *Commonweal* August 1951.

[2]The sentence on page 186 now reads, 'His nose ran down his face like a buttress'; 'abortion' remains.

To Lady Mary Lygon   Piers Court.
Corpus Christi [May] 1951

Darling Blondie

I was on the point of writing to you when your kind & interesting letter arrived. I wished to report in the gravest terms the behaviour of the B.Y. Yorkes who visited me at Whitsun.

. . . I came to London last week for a night but I did not go near your house because I was disgustingly drunk all the time and I did not want you, whose girlish eyes saw me in my fine prime, to see me in such a condition.

I got to my train d.d. and it was the Cheltenham Flier full of respectable stockbrokers who hunt with the D of Beaufort and I walked down the train picking up all the mens hats & looking inside and saying: 'People who go to such bad hatters shouldn't travel first class'. So I am ashamed to meet any neighbours now.

H. Yorke would not pee in the garden for fear of catching cold in his kok.

I think Swedish Countess was a Sapphist?

Here are pictures of little Laura and her children and my spiritual director.

On Monday I go to Monte Carlo and when I break the bank I will say 'that is for being Dutch to Blondie'.

Randolph is 40 on Sat. Cherish him. His life is a sad pilgrimage. How happy he would be if you had accepted his hand. Saddest words of t[ongue] or p[en] It might have been

XXXXX
Bo

I say are you following the Rev. Box and the Free Masons?

To Laura Waugh
[June 1951]

Hotel du Château,
Rue Connétable,
Chantilly, Oise,
France.

Darling

. . . Yesterday I spent reading all my war diaries & recapturing the atmosphere of those days. Today I began writing & it came easy.[1]

This hotel is *very* modest. No hot water or pillow case. Very simple digestible food. Very quiet & shady. In fact just what was wanted.

Tremendous thunder-storm last night.

All love
E

[1]Waugh was beginning *Men at Arms*, 1952.

To Laura Waugh
ss Peter and Paul [29 June 1951]

Château de St Firmin,
Vineuil, Oise.

Foul Whiskers

No letter from you. Why not?

My book has not gone very well in the last few days. I think it is because I am trying a new method of writing which does not work for me. I hate leaving a trail of unfinished shabby work behind me so I have decided to revert to my old habit of writing each page finally & completely. I will rewrite all I have done & then report progress.

... Your enchanting cousin Virginia Charteris[1] was here & your dreary cousin Lady Wemyss.[2]

I miss your sweet company

All love
E

[1]Virginia Forbes Adam (1922–   ). Married in 1948 the novelist Hugo Charteris, brother of Lady Rothermere (later Mrs Ian Fleming).
[2]Mavis Murray married in 1940 the Earl of Wemyss.

To Tom Driberg
Piers Court.
21 July [1951]

My Dear Tom

Now I am home & can send you a little wedding present.

Nancy & I gloated over the photographs of your wedding.[1] We did not like the expression: 'When the champagne *ran out* . . ' in the *Sunday Express.*

What appalled me in your broadcast was that neither you or Randolph (both gluttons) gave any sign of recognition that food can & should be a source of delight. As for 'nutrition' – that is all balls. Some people can be fully nourished on nuts like Shaw, others need caviar like ourselves. The only test of 'nutrition', I suppose, is the amount of work the fuel produces. I don't see any sign that the lower classes work harder.

I can understand (tho of course I deplore) that politicians may think it makes them popular to restrict the import of exotic delicacies – Havana cigars etc. What is so disgraceful is that under your government (and Churchill's) the simple staples of the poor – kippers, beer, bread, cheese, sausages etc – have deteriorated in quality.

The article on the Festival confirms all my fears.

I am sorry that the Rev. W. Bond[2] did not sing your nuptial mass. Is he dead?

Yours ever
Evelyn

[1]To Mrs Ena Binfield. Not mentioned in his autobiography.
[2]Of Lancing.

To Graham Greene
Piers Court.
18 August 1951

Dear Graham,

Thank you very much indeed for the copy of *The End of the Affair,* which reached me today. I don't know if Caraman showed you the review I wrote for him. It gives a rather stiff expression to the very warm admiration I have for the book. I hope it has a huge success. I am sure it will.

Laura takes my children away at the end of next week & I shall be alone here for nearly a month. Is there any hope of having you for a visit (if with Catherine [Walston], better still) to cheer me up. I am writing an interminable novel about army life, obsessed by memories of military dialogue. I was greatly encouraged, by the way, to read that Bendrix thinks 1000 words a good day's work. I used to write 3000 & can still sometimes do 1200. But I suspect Bendrix writes better than I.

In America when a man is ordained priest he gets a proposal from an insurance company that he should take out a policy against being unfrocked. This apparently is true. Ronnie Knox suggests it as a plot for you – a priest of such charity that he simulates sin in order to help the destitute.

Do come if you can bear the thought

Yours ever
Evelyn

To Graham Greene Piers Court.
21 August [1951]

Dear Graham

You will be most welcome. But I must warn you of certain discomforts. Drink will be abundant, but food not so good. My cook goes on holiday and a village woman takes her place. It you can live on scrambled eggs you will not starve but I fear you will pine for cosmopolitan dishes.

Motor-car. Can you drive? I can't. There will be a decrepit vehicle at our disposal but we may have to walk whenever we want to buy a postage-stamp.

Butler. Gone sick yesterday. All my comforts & yours depend on him. He seems set for a long period in bed.

This is said to suggest that the visit may be uncomfortable for *you*. To me it would be pure delight as I have to endure these sufferings in any case & your presence will mitigate them. If you can face it, please come.

I wear a dinner-jacket in the evenings but there is not the smallest reason why you should do so, if like Henry Yorke you disapprove of such simple garments.

There would be a sitting room for your exclusive use for writing, a bath, a bed. Can't promise constant hot water as the boiler is one of the things my sick butler works. Plenty of coke if you know about fuelling.

It will be Swiss Family Robinson Life.

Connolly has many injuries to revenge.[1] I can't blame him if he takes the opportunity, tho I may have to horse whip him on the steps of his club.

If you can drive the motor car we will call on Knox at Mells.

Yours ever
Evelyn

Catherine of course welcome but warn her of Swiss Family Robinson Life.

[1]Connolly had been commissioned to write a profile of Waugh for *Time*.

To Nancy Mitford   Piers Court
St Bartholomew's Day [24 August] 1951

Darling Nancy

Today is a glorious anniversary in the sad history of your adopted country. I hope
you are keeping it with solemnity & splendour.

I ought to have written before but it has been a dull time for me – none of those
events which make me think: 'I must write & tell Nancy that'. I have been at home
all the time pegging away at my novel & associating with my children whose
interests I do not share – chemical experiments, pony clubs, autograph collections.
Mr Battersby the Master of Chantilly[1] came to stay. He is doing a panel for me. I
quite liked him. An American Professor of Creative Writing also came. He wore a
white dinner jacket with an artificial carnation in the button-hole. Now Laura is
taking the three elder children to Italy and I am having a series of male guests –
Sykes, Pakenham, G. Greene etc. but the cook is on holiday & my man-servant, on
whom I depend for my few comforts, has taken to his bed, so these guests will have
poor entertainment.

I have had a lot of your reviews as they mostly seem to put my name in, and the
press-cutting agent sends them to me (at 3d. a time). I am glad you don't take them
seriously. Reviewers are lazy brutes & hate having to think. They want to say: 'Here
is another Mitford, sparkling & irresponsible in her own inimitable way'. They can't
bear to see a writer grow up. They have no influence at all. Everyone I know
delights in *The Blessing* and I am constantly buoyed up with pride at the
dedication.

Yes, it is true that the Sykeses have destroyed David Herberts pretty house,[2]
which *The Times* newspaper described as 'an ornate bungalow'.

I did not attend Jonathan's wedding. It would have been very expensive in car
hire and present so I took advantage of his failure to write to me, and kept away. But
I wish the young people well.

I came back from France so corpulent that I could not button any of my clothes
and as it would cost about £500 to get a new lot, I took a gruesome course of Dr
Goller's diet so that in two weeks I shrank to the thickness of Eddy West. I am now
swelling gently.

My poverty is very irksome. I notice I have mentioned it twice already. It is often
in my mind. It is sad to have been poor all the time one was allowed to be rich, and
now one is rich it is against the law. I am sued for 3000 dollars which an American
editor once gave me for a story I never wrote. There is no legal means of repaying
him, as I willingly would, so I must go to prison soon. I shall write to Lady Mosley
for advice about what to take.

My novel is unreadable & endless. Nothing but tippling in officers' messes and
drilling on barrack squares. No demon sex. No blood or thunder.

You should now write a shameless & complete autobiography.

All love
Evelyn

Twenty years or so ago Sachie [Sitwell] gave Robert [Byron] & Tony Powell & Harold Acton & me and a few other friends free tickets for a revolting ballet called *Mercure*. Last week he wrote in the *Sunday Times* that he saved Diaghilev from ruin by introducing a claque chosen for their 'wild & fantastic appearance'. How I remember oiling my hair & knotting my little white tie for the occasion. And how I hated *Mercure*. I think we gave a few perfunctory claps out of politeness to our host.

Love to Col. He very kindly wrote to me about bare bosoms but I did a Jonathan & failed to answer. Please try & make him try to forgive me.

[1] Martin Battersby. A painter, particularly of *trompe l'oeil*. He did some murals for Lady Diana Cooper at Chantilly which she transported to London.

[2] In Wilton Park. The fire was caused by defective wiring.

To Catherine Walston   Piers Court
25 August [1951]

Dear Catherine

Of course I wont tell Graham you wrote, but thank you for doing so.

I met you first as a friend of Graham's but I hope I can now look on you as a friend in my own right. I shall love you to come if you can bear the discomforts. It will not even be Swiss Family Robinson – enough servants to keep us behind the baize curtain, not enough to do the things we could easily do for ourselves if they would let us. Laura will be very jealous that she has missed you.

Please believe that I am far too depressed by my own odious, if unromantic, sins to have any concern for other people's. For me, it would be a delight to welcome you here.

But when you say Graham is sometimes happier without you, that is another matter. You know & I don't. I did detect in his letters a hint that he looked forward to a spell of solitude. Only you can decide whether that mood is likely to persist. If you think it a bad time, come later when Laura is home. Anyway please come sooner or later.

Yours affectionately
Evelyn

My socialist neighbours the Donaldsons tell me you live in great magnificence with a domestic chaplain, butlers in black coats and groaning tables of delicatessen. My conservative newspaper tells me you have got away with wads of public money & are starting to grow ground nuts in Cambridge. But, dear Catherine, I don't listen to gossip about you.

To Nancy Mitford
September [1951]

Darling Nancy

There is a first class French Catholic Encyclopaedia called I think the Apologetic Dictionary in numerous volumes.[1] You must keep it at your bedside and consult it rather than poor wayward Col. six times a day. It will save you from howlers. But I am afraid it can never make you *understand* anything supernatural. The fact that you can write of G. Greene's heroine that 'subconsciously she had something' is evidence of worse than defective education.

The habits of G. Greene's characters are *precisely* and in *every detail identical* with those of the Bright Young Yorkes.

G. Greene behaved well & dressed for dinner every night. Mrs Walston had never seen him in a dinner jacket before and was enchanted and will make him wear one always. G. Greene spent his days patrolling the built up areas round Dursley noting the numbers of motor-cars. He takes omens from them.

Not that I would boast but – I put those words into B. Howard's mouth ten years ago in a book about him called *Put Out More Flags*.

Interesting slice of English life. Ever since marriage we have had a piano in the drawing-room which no one ever plays, and a man has come on a bicycle from Cheltenham to 'tune' it every quarter. Last time he came he said it had some internal complaint which it would cost £50 to cure. So I said, give me £50 and you can take it away, which he did. Result. Consternation. A hush over cottage and Hall, the cowman passes me with downcast eyes, the village women who come in sweep in tears. The furniture removers who carried it out treated it like a coffin. Apparently in the lower classes to sell ones piano is the last refuge of the destitute – an irrevocable step down from decency to squalour. Did you know?

Debo sent me an *insane* post card from Capri about the King. Is she really, frankly a bit barmy?

I am scribbling away hard at my maximum opus. I think it is frightfully funny. A bad sign.

Love
E

[1] *Dictionnaire apologétique de la foi catholique* 1911–28 (4 volumes). There had been an exchange of letters on Bremond, the French Jesuit, who offered the last sacraments to an excommunicated man.

To Bruce Cooper[1]   Piers Court
17 October [1951]

Dear Mr Cooper,

As soon as I received your very kind invitation to stand for the Rectorship I wrote to my income-tax accountant to ask whether election expenses were admissable as professional expenses against tax. His answer is: no.

I have also written to my agent & publishers. I have not had their answer. My fear is that they would not be allowed by their accountants to charge these expenses as legitimate advertising. These things are sharply watched.

So it seems that I must pay out of taxed income. This means that for every £10 I give you, I must earn £60. I can therefore only offer a minimum sum. It is plain from Harold Macmillan's experience that money is not an important consideration. What is the least you can manage on? I hope you will understand my parsimony in this matter. I will guarantee £75. Can you do it on that?

I am a little more satisfactory in the question of Scottish descent. The Waughs were unmixed lowland Scot until the late 18th century when they joined the migration South. The last to be born in Scotland, Alexander Waugh, was Doctor of Divinity at Edinburgh. His simple annals may be read in DNB. He was my great, great, grandfather. A rather more illustrious g.g.g. father on my mothers side is Henry Lord Cockburn of Edinburgh, author of *Memorials of His Time*. He was a considerable figure in Edinburgh, is buried there, was painted by Raeburn, has an hotel named after him etc. Indeed his portrait appears on the Commercial Bank of Scotland's One pound note (tho he was no banker).

I have never voted in a general election as I have never found a Tory stern enough to command my respect.

I should think the best election line would be not my worthiness but the conspicuous unworthiness of other candidates.

Compton Mackenzie doesn't know me. David Talbot Rice,[2] a professor of yours, is an old friend. He lives at 33 Moray Place. He might help with some personal impressions.

I suppose the reason for the Catholic students' disapproval is that I went to lecture to them. They know what I am really like.

Please send a questionnaire if there is any more you would like to know about me.

Yours sincerely
Evelyn Waugh

[1]Bruce Cooper (1925–77). Dean of Management Studies at the Polytechnic in Belfast from 1970. A student at Edinburgh University, he persuaded Waugh to stand as candidate in the election for Rector. Other candidates included Jimmy Logan, a comedian, Stephen Potter, the Aga Khan and Sir Alexander Fleming, who won. Chapman and Hall paid Waugh's expenses.

[2]Waugh checked with his old friend who warned that it was a 'tuff and barbarous process' and that there might be anti-Catholic mud slinging. A Waugh supporter did indeed find it 'interestingly uneven and ultimately violent. It was the only time I have been beaten unconscious by a rival firm armed with hockey sticks. . . . ' Waugh himself stayed in the south.

To Nancy Mitford   Piers Court
29 October [1951]

Darling Nancy

You know I think you are going to be the kind of person like Queen Victoria who effortlessly collects legacies. I can see the hoard grow, a cornelian brooch here, a nice sum of money there, chests of linen, a harp – most enviable.

I am cooling down after my popish heat.[1] I think you were wrong about Madrid bookshops unless the place has greatly changed since 1946. Then I found hundreds of Bumpuses all full of Gollancz Left Book Club publications.

It is a long time since I wrote. Honks and party came to luncheon. It was very difficult to get her in or out of the dining room. Physical force was needed in both operations. She wont be led only driven. She admired my moss on unweeded paths. 'You can't grow that in France.' I saw her again in London, full of delight at the politeness of the English lower classes. I went to London for the General Election – just like last time, same parties and same parties in H of C too.[2] Cooper got [veiners] with a jewish hanger-on of Anne's called 'Freud'.[3] I have never seen him assault a jew before. Perhaps he took him for a Spaniard. He has very long black side-whiskers and a thin nose.

Poor Randolph. It was a very difficult seat and he didn't think he could get in. At the count he was so nervous he left the room and returned just as they were finishing. He asked the town-clerk, who presided: 'How am I doing?' 'Thirty something thousand and something.' 'Isn't that rather good?' 'Oh yes you're quite safe. We've only a few more to count and they cant affect the result.' Dazed with joy he rushed out & told his committee. All embraced. Two minutes later the town clerk padded out. 'Oh Mr Churchill I made such a silly mistake. I gave you Mr Foot's figures.'[4] He then had to be protected from the mob by 40 policemen while he went to his train home.

Nothing he has ever done deserves such punishment.

Betjeman has the flu and has retired to the house of the Dowager Duchess of Devonshire where he is waited on ... while the high-church butler reads *The Unlucky Family*[5] aloud to him. Meanwhile he has sold Penelope's house & purchased a villa in the centre of Wantage – 'Oh joy of being back in real suburbia old boy' – and has left Penelope quite unaided to make the move. He *is* Skimpole.[6]

The rival Skimpole, Connolly, has fallen on hard times. He has been hired by *Time* magazine to write a 'profile' of me which always means a collection of damaging lies. He approached me obsequiously with a series of fatuous psycho-analytical questions – did I suffer from jealousy because my father loved him [*sic*] more than me? That sort of rot. I said: 'On the day the article appears I shall horse whip you on the steps of White's'. He turned green white yellow & gray and said: 'What will you pay me not to write it?'

Does the Col. who spends so much thought on religious questions know anything (a) of the number, if any, of apostasies among the priests who have lately been going about disguised as 'workers' (b) of a Dominican Père Perrin who was at Marseilles most of the war and the correspondent of the Great Fraud called Simone Weil? Do please ask and answer.

Are any of my eggs French?[7] If so would you give them to Honks. If they are all American and need my signature it must wait till I come through.

Now that there is a tiny Conservative Majority the persecution of the rich by the politicians will be greatly intensified so that they can display class impartiality.

Love from
Evelyn

[1]Their exchanges after Nancy Mitford had made a mistake in the *Sunday Times* about Roman Catholics in the time of Pius X had been sharp. Waugh had written: 'Would it not be best always to avoid any reference to the Church or to your Creator? Your intrusions into this strange world are always fatuous.' To which Nancy Mitford replied: 'I can't agree that I must be debarred from ever mentioning your Creator. Try and remember that he also created me.'

[2]The Conservatives were returned with a majority of sixteen. The year before Labour had retained office with a majority of six.

[3]Lucian Freud (1922–   ). Painter. Grandson of Sigmund Freud.

[4]Michael Foot's majority was reduced to 2,390.

[5]A children's book by Mrs Henry de la Pasture, 1907.

[6]In *Bleak House*.

[7]Financial nest-eggs in Paris.

To Nancy Mitford   Piers Court
[November 1951]
Two Postcards

If you praise the atheist temples at Vence & Assy it will be the end of a beautiful friendship. I went to a Picasso exhibition last week & looked hard and saw (a) that in youth he drew as well as a *Punch* artist of the period (b) that he had real comic talent & obviously enjoys making fools of his admirers (c) he has a distinct originality in a flibbity-gibbet way. He never repeats himself. Leaves that to his ghastly followers. Altogether a cleverer & more accomplished man than one can guess from reproductions. But as an artist of the fourth rank.

Please it is facts I want about Perrin. Is he still a supporter of Weil? Was he ever? His replies to her beastly letters aren't published in English or, I think, in French. Why did he withdraw his preface to the English edition of *Waiting on God*?[1]

Also whether it is true that some of the priests who disguised themselves as workmen have apostasized. Of course I hope not, but it is being said here that several have. Even if Col. is too busy to think of you or God, there must be someone who can answer.

L.I. of N. MIND *not* MINDS. V. vulgar error. Lovely lovely Cécile Howard is staying here. Now she comes from the French cultural bourgeoise you once spoke of, and she is PERFECT so you are quite right.

E

[1]By Simone Weil (1909–43). Waugh reviewed it in *Catholic Mother*, Christmas 1952, comparing the author unfavourably with Edith Stein whose biography had been written by Sister Teresa de Spiritu Sancto. Reprinted in *A Little Order*, 1977, edited by Donat Gallagher.

To Nancy Mitford   Piers Court
[November 1951]

Darling Nancy

You could write a most amusing & interesting and popular work in this way:
Describe yourself in 1951 taking up *Wigs on The Green*[1] & re-reading it for the first
time since its publication. Print $\frac{2}{3}$ or half of the original text with constant
interruptions from your 1951 self asking: 'Why did I say that?' or saying 'This still
seems funny, why?' So in the easiest & most informal way possible you could write
your reminiscences & the history of the deteriorating world and the improving
authoress.

It would be fun to write & huge fun to read. Do do it that way.

You could produce a magnum opus with minimum of labour and all the critics
would acclaim it as a great 'DOCUMENT'.

I haven't been elected Rector of Edinburgh. It was just a joke that didn't come
off. A really bitter failure has been the loss of 12 greatly over life size busts of the
Caesars on eight foot elaborate pedestals – circa 1800 that were in a house near here
that was being sold up. I asked the auctioneer what they would fetch. 'Ten bob
each,' he said. So I left a bid of £2 each & went away confident I should get them.
For days & nights I have been planning how to erect them, replanning the whole
garden for them. I would willingly have paid £10 each. Now I hear that through
laziness in not going to the sale some other maniac has bought them. It is a crushing
blow at a time when I need a bit of fun.

                                                        Love from
                                                        Evelyn

[1] Novel by Nancy Mitford, 1935.

To Sir Maurice Bowra   Piers Court
29 November 1951

Dear Maurice

I am most grateful for the Harton letter. It is a document I have long wanted. It
was most generous of you to have it copied. Rest assured it will be very carefully
guarded here.

Walker[1] was the great collector who so enriched Liverpool.

I agree that Maclise[2] was a very great painter. I would put him above even Egg[3] &
Mulready.[4] But of course he lacks the picturesque quality of his immediate
successors. There is a very beautiful Maclise – *Love & Poet* – on sale in London at
Bernard's (Ryder Street) but I fear his prices are rising. I remember in 1937 when I
was poor and frugal seeing his masterpiece – the play scene from Hamlet – knocked
down for twenty guineas at Wallis's Rooms. I asked the man who got it, how high he
would have gone and he said to fifty.

I am afraid Vernon Johnson's honour[5] can only be regarded as an honour. It is most unnerving.

I was dead drunk at the Newman meeting. Later I called on [Roy] Harrod who threatened my life because I warned a Belgian financier whom Harrod was sucking up to, that if he sent his son to Christ Church he would fall under the fanatical attention of T. Roper. I did not know such fires inhabited Harrod.

If, as I ardently hope, you find it possible to come here one day I can show you a fine Arthur Hughes.[6]

I have a severe attack of muscular rheumatism. The days pass pleasantly smoking cigars and reading P.G. Wodehouse. My work in progress is going to be a great bore.

Do you think Henry [Yorke] is a communist. Evidence: love of false names and clandestine travel; membership of Fire Brigade; insistence in all his works that social distinctions depend solely on cash; close trade relations, introducing water-closets to the Kremlin; dependence on jazz bands; ostentatious poverty (mulcted for party funds); hatred of architecture, wine and poetry; elaborate code of conventional bad-manners in dress, opening doors to women, etc; obsession with royal family (most disrespectful).

F. Salisbury,[7] like Pugin, has the right ideas but can't execute them.

A well-principalled* [*sic*] young painter who is doing some work for me, ekes out his commissions by teaching in a government art school. He says the students can only qualify for entrance by promising to become teachers of painting in their turn.

> Yours ever
> Evelyn

*I spelt it 'principalled' first. It looked wrong. So does 'principled'. I wish I could spell. I often write angry letters to the headmistresses of my children's schools and after I have posted them realise they are full of mistakes. But they have not used sic on me yet.

[1]William Walker (1856–1933). Supported the Walker Art Gallery, Liverpool. Created Lord Wavertree.

[2]Daniel Maclise (1806–70).

[3]Augustus Egg (1816–63).

[4]William Mulready (1786–1863).

[5]Vernon Johnson had been appointed a Domestic Prelate to the Pope.

[6]*The Lost Child* by Arthur Hughes (1832–1915).

[7]Frank Salisbury (1874–1962). Painter of portraits, historical and ceremonial subjects.

To Professor Jacques Barzun[1]   Piers Court
18 December [1951]

Dear Professor

I wish you had been here at breakfast. I received a postcard from yourself from Germany and a fantastic Christmas card from the Luces called *Life's Picture*

History of Western Man. Some of it is too horrific, but there is much deep laughter in the concluding section.

Thinking it over, I don't really want to do Constantine. He's not a sympathetic figure (to me) and one writes best when one reveres or detests the subject. Of course there's St Helena herself, but I've written a lot about her already. The trouble is that most of the attractive characters of history are quite unimportant.

More is the only man I can think of who (for me) has all the requisite qualities of greatness & charm, so let us persuade Mr Hughes to settle on him. I will tell my New York agent to prepare a contract.

I enjoyed our conversation so much last night. Do come again. Give my warm regards to Helen Howe and to any who remember me on *Life*. Do get hold of a copy of *Life*'s *Picture History*. It must be the work of a parodist.

It's export should be forbidden though. It will do awful harm to American–European relations if it gets seen here.

> Yours very sincerely
> Evelyn Waugh

P.S. I presume you have some expert doing Ignatius Loyola. If not, and if *Life* demands a second choice, I might try him.

> EW

[1]Jacques Barzun(1907–   ). Professor of History at Columbia University, author and editor.

TO NANCY MITFORD   Piers Court
[December 1951]
Postcard

I wrote to you at Rodd palace. Did the letter get stolen by communists? It had all my brief news & boundless good wishes for darling, darling 1952. I consider it most unhealthy & rather alarming that all your recent letters have been full of transformations of sex. I don't believe it will do you any permanent good in the world of letters if you become Lord Redesdale. I suppose it is because you want to get in the Academy & wear that pretty uniform.

I don't quite know what you mean by *Chartreuse de Parme* appeal to Cécile who is pregnant again (still Mondi).

You must get your hands on *Life* Magazine's *History of Western Culture* a thing of horror unexampled since E. West's history of G. Sutherland[1].

I did not find Mrs Taffy a lady.[2]

[1]*Graham Sutherland* by Edward Sackville-West.
[2]Rosemary Dove, married 1948–66 to Taffy Rodd. Now Mrs Baldwin.

To the Editor of the Sunday Times   Piers Court
8 January 1952

Sir – Mr [Robert] Boothby's consternation on reading Mr Wiggin's[1] particular judgement on Mr Maugham must be shared by many readers now that the critic has explained his meaning.

A writer is only important so far as he influences behaviour? What new aberration of philistinism is this?

I can remember that in my early youth I spent many days in attempting to construct a model town from the directions in the *Children's Encyclopaedia*. Those directions, it seems, must be the only piece of important literature I ever read, for I cannot name any book or poem that has influenced my behaviour.

Indeed I can think of only two classes of writing (both of which I eschew) calculated to do so – books of etiquette and of pornography.

It would be interesting if Mr Wiggin would display on television his own behaviour when reading, say, Shakespeare's sonnets.

EVELYN WAUGH

[1]Maurice Wiggin, died 1978. Journalist. Television critic of *The Sunday Times*.

To Clarissa Churchill[1]   Piers Court
8 January 1951 [1952]

Dearest Clarissa

Oh dear. I realize now what an unimaginative present[2] I sent. I chose it from my portfolio for the fatuous reason that I liked it myself. I don't say: 'What will the poor girl do with it? She can't hang it on her wall or stand it on her shelf. She isn't the least interested in calligraphy, and not much interested in minor early-Victorian painters.'

I remember long ago, when I had no home & spent my life globe-trotting, being furious with Hazel Lavery for giving me a glass swan, thinking (rightly) that it is better to be forgotten than so little remembered. Please forgive me. If it hasn't been swept up & burned with your Christmas cards let us swap it for something suitable – bath salts, artificial silk stockings, *Life* Magazine's *History of Western Culture*. What?

1951 wasn't a good year for us beginning & ending with deplorable gaffes – both the fruit of that most dangerous maxim: 'Do as you would be done by'.

It was not a good year for me anyway, mostly spent at work. I have finished a novel – slogging, inelegant, the first volume of four or five, which won't show any shape until the end. Harrassed with arrears of taxation & unpopularity catching me up at last, and with rheumatic hints of old age.

Tell me what you would have liked for Christmas & I will try to make amends.

> Love from
> Evelyn

[1]Clarissa Churchill (1920–   ). Married in 1952 Anthony Eden, Prime Minister 1955–7, created Earl of Avon 1961.
[2]See letter to Nancy Mitford 14 January 1952.

TO NANCY MITFORD   Piers Court
8 January 1952 (the sweet thing)

Darling Nancy,

I liked your Roman letter very much.

. . . I am afraid you are right when you say that there are no ladies & gentlemen now. It was a most important distinction basic to English health & happiness. You see we are the most elaborately stratified people in the world but no one, unless he makes it his special hobby, knows [anything] about the strata except those immediately above & below his own. Everyone was convinced that there was a great impassable line between 'gentlemen' and 'the lower classes' and everyone drew that line immediately below his own feet. 'You're no lady' was the traditional battle cry between two drunken charwomen scratching out each others eyes in a pub.

There are two graves in Stinchcombe church of a father & son, early & middle 16th century, one saying 'Jos. Hinks, Yeoman' and the other 'Jos. Hinks, Gent'. So there must once have been a technical distinction, as between officers and NCOs in the army. Both Hinkses owned the same small property. Can it have been the grant of a coat of arms. In the nineteenth century there was a universal common accent for all the educated. Also a moral code attached which the 18th century knew nothing of, and in the 19th century the high aristocracy seldom observed. The great thing was that *everyone* thought himself a gentleman and closely allied with Dukes, and everyone below him contemptible. So there was a stable, contented society. It never occurred to me to think I wasn't a gentleman until Lady Burghclere pointed it out. I have a friend called Michael Trappes-Lomax[1] who treats me with genial equality but, in fact, regards no one as a gentleman who hasn't 32 quarterings. I think it was the American marriages in the 90s and the lady shopkeepers in the 20s who made all the trouble. It is a fascinating subject. A book on it would be a best seller as it is still the first concern of 80% of the reading public. I think I may write it.

Mrs Taffy was pure Billa[2] to me.

There was a competition in *John O'London's Weekly* to name the most odious books in the language. We were both in the short list.

How I agree about the horrors of the Embassy at Rome. But wasn't 'Reeking' too strong.

You ought to have mentioned the Embassy (Legation?) at the Hague among the good ones. It is Alba's old palace. Splendid. Especially necessary to mention it *now* because the Office of Works want to move.

I can't get on with d'Arcy Osborne[3]. Goodness *he's* a gentleman and a half.

I *must* get abroad at Easter. How many eggs have I?

> Love from
> Evelyn

[1]Michael Trappes-Lomax (1900–72). Somerset Herald 1951–67.

[2]Wilhelmine Cresswell married Roy Harrod in 1938.

[3]Sir D'Arcy Godolphin Osborne (1884–1964). Succeeded as Duke of Leeds 1963. Envoy Extraordinary and Minister Plenipotentiary to the Holy See 1936–47.

To Nancy Mitford   Piers Court
14 January
Sweet 1952 never been kissed.

Darling Nancy

So I have been doing sums for weeks & find I am hopelessly ruined (financially *not* morally). So I have come to a Great Decision to Change my Life entirely. I am sacking all the servants (five does seem a lot to look after Laura & me in a house the size of a boot) and becoming Bohemian. I shall never wear a clean collar again or subscribe to Royal Lifeboat Fund and I shall steal peoples books & sell them & cadge drinks in the Savage Club by pretending to know you. It is no good trying to live decently in modern England. I make £10,000 a year, which used to be thought quite a lot, I live like a mouse in shabby-genteel circumstances, I keep no women or horses or yachts, yet I am bankrupt, simply by the politicians buying votes with my money.

The trouble is getting servants to go. There is no shortage of them now because no one can afford them. And they cannot become harlots because apparently men don't pay women now, they just rape them & take their money. But go they shall, if I have to burn the house down.

The sentence in your last letter about royalty seeing the Airlies & the cooks[1] as equal in rank occurs in the novel I have just sent to be printed. I only mention this in case you accuse me of cribbing later. Goodness that novel is dull and what is worse all falling to bits. But I was going mad trying to set it right so off I sent it.

I don't at all like Florence. Must I come *there*?

Did I ask you to ask Col. (if he was ever in an army) what is the French for 'Halt. Who goes there?' 'Stand or I fire'. 'Take two paces forward & be recognized'. Also do the black French soldiers of Senegal use French for such conversations or some sort of coon talk.

I have read the papers & learned that the Gaullists are collaborating with the Communists. Is this your influence or just a newspaper lie.

I don't think you quite appreciate the great Importance of my Discovery about Gentlemen. It explains all our national greatness 1815–1914 – that everyone felt his natural allies to be those above him (and in his eyes equal) in Social Scale. Perhaps everyone has known this fact for years.

All love

E

I sent three exquisite original early Victorian drawings, joined by exquisite calligraphy to Clarissa whom I love next to Cécile. She thought it was a Christmas card and promptly burned it.

Can you at all explain this? You know I call Honks 'Baby'? Embarrassing but true. Anyway I got a mad letter the other day of the kind one gets most days. No interest. High brow madness typewritten in English. The odd thing was that the address was 'Chez Baby' 16 Rue de Condé, Paris VI. It began 'Dear E. W.' and was signed 'Mary O'Connor'. Is Chez Baby a night club. But one doesn't take a typewriter to a night club – or does one now? I thought it very rum.

[1] The Earl of Airlie (1893–1968) married in 1917 Lady Alexandra Coke. He was Lord Chamberlain to the Queen Mother 1937–65.

To Lady Mary Lygon   Piers Court
23 January [1952]

Darling Maimie

I was on the point of writing to condole with you on your very sad loss. The new year has begun sadly for my friends with the deaths of Colonel Lygon and General Laycock (Sir Joseph).[1] I have had no bereavements. I wish I had. Only the immediate deaths of all my relations can save me from bankruptcy & prison. You remember we used to know a very poor man named Balfour (who later made a fortune & bought a peerage)? Well at his very poorest he was a millionaire in comparison to me. I wish my bankers got drunk. Then they might not know how poor I am.

Little Poll that great snob won't come near me now I am poor.

I have been dismissing servants in such numbers that it looks like a mass eviction – what the socialist call social engineering. I examined household books & found I was spending nearly half as much as I spend on wine, on MILK.

Well this is dull for you. I don't know anything interesting. Mrs Rodd is following the fashion & turned into a man.

Did I tell you that H. Yorke is MAD BAD and DANGEROUS TO KNOW. I wish you would wheedle confidences from poor Dig & pass them on quick.

I have written a book in poor taste, mostly about WCs and very very dull. Well it is a dull subject isnt it. The only exciting moment is when a WC blows up with Capt. Apthorpe sitting on it. The shock & shame drive him mad. He is the hero.

I wish you had a motor bicycle. Then you could come here as general domestic servant. Plenty of MILK.

Bo

[1]Robert Lygon (1879–1952) and Brigadier General Sir Joseph Laycock (1867–1952), father of Robert Laycock.

To Nancy Mitford   Piers Court
27 January 1952

Darling Nancy

I have long recognized your euphoria as a pathological condition as morbid as Honks's melancholy. You each choose minor exterior conditions to explain your states – oddly enough the same one – France.

You have made great friends with a Pole who has introduced you to a number of other Poles. You have found some Jews for yourself, such as your hunting friends and the lady who gave me caviare & pretended to like painting, filling her drawing-room with fine works of art and all the time secretly sipping Picasso in her bed–room. You are the kindest possible hospitaller to your distressed fellow countryman. And you spend long hours with the Harveys[1] talking of socialism. This is not the France of Louis IX or Joan of Arc or Bossuet or the Curé d'Ars. All the great Frenchmen & women repudiate it. Still less is it the real modern France that fills the world with its self-pity.

Your delicate nostrils detected the smell of blood in poor Victor & Peggy's awful house.[2] I retch at the smell of blood all over France – the blood of the hundred thousand massacred in the epuration. What's more I see the guilt of that unexpiated horror in the eyes of all Frenchmen from the hall porter at the Travellers' to Père Couturier.

Of course the French have numerous skills and once had the very purest taste. I am told their music-hall songs are very witty.

Anyway your 'France' is pure fantasy. It may afford you some pleasure but it is transferable.

I have had more mad letters from Paris in different hands. Very rum. Not by Frenchmen but in pure idiomatic English & American. And stark mad.

I get two a week usually from England or USA. Paris is quite a new centre. The letters are not the least personal. I mean they don't accuse me of imaginary injuries or anything like that. They are just drivel which might be addressed to anyone. I should like details of Honks's rumminess [?]. She has seemed desperately unhappy in all her letters lately. She is in London now but I can't go up to see her on account of rheumatism. Is she turning into a man, too? Her crustiness is highly masculine.

Snow & thaw here. Beastly.

Thank you & Col. *very much* indeed for military information of great value.

The wines on the list look tempting but the friendly merchant (a non-French member of your circle I note) doesn't seem to know about rates of exchange. I think

I must make some purchases in Paris when I come over. His English prices are not lower than Peter Thursby's,[3] and he is a friend too.

If you had heard a lecture by an English francophile socialist on the wireless in praise of Corbusier's fiasco at Marseille,[4] I think even you would have been sick. Or did you write it for him?

Lots of love

E

[1] Maud Williams-Wynn married in 1920 Oliver Harvey (1893–1968). He was Ambassador to France 1948–54, created baron 1954.

[2] The British Embassy in Rome.

[3] 'I remember that on the days when I was feeling particularly tired and more than ever plain, I used suddenly to catch sight of Mr Thursby and feel less tired, but far far plainer.' Essay in *Cherwell*, June 1927, by Brian Howard. Peter Thursby was a wine merchant.

[4] Le Corbusier (1887–1965) built a housing estate called Unité d'habitations near Marseilles between 1946 and 1952. '*Dear Sensibility....*' *A Journey through France in the steps of Laurence Sterne*, written and produced by Rayner Heppenstall, was broadcast on the Third Programme, 21 January 1952.

To Nancy Mitford
[15] February [1952]

Piers Court

Darling Nancy,

I have been wretchedly low spirited, plagued by a sort of rheumatism and common cold. I can't get rid of my servants. Three went last week, one is back already saying I *must* employ her because her mother wont let her go to a factory and she *must* stay in the district because she is in love. I say: 'I can't afford you'. She says: 'I'll come without wages'. 'I say: 'It isn't your wages only its the expense of keeping you which is much more'. But she is back with her trunk shovelling down butter & cream and American hampers. Meanwhile two village women who occasionally 'obliged' have permanently ensconced themselves at much higher wages, so my economy campaign has done no good.

While I lay in bed in agony I had to break an engagement in London with Honks – not even an engagement to take her out; merely to meet her at the house of some friends of hers for dinner. Do I get a letter of tender sympathy? Not at all. A scolding saying: 'Never do it again – plan & fail. *I* am too old & easily bruised' (my italics). There is egocentric mania there.

Do your foreign set know that our King [George VI] is dead? Mr Churchill made a dreadful speech on the TSF.[1] Triteness only enlivened by gross blunders. His worst remark was in commending the late King's patriotism. 'During the war I made a point of keeping him fully informed. He understood all I said wonderfully. I even disclosed to him military secrets'. His most inept historical parallel: comparing our present Queen with Elizabeth Tudor: 'Neither grew up in the expectation of the crown.' Elizabeth Tudor had been formally bastardized & declared ineligible by Henry VIII and all three estates of the realm. She survived alive because of the high Christian principles of Mary Tudor, when in any other royal family, she would have been executed. She was jockeyed into place by a gang of party bosses and executed the rightful heir Mary Stuart. All the newspapers are full of glorification of Elizabeth Tudor, the vilest of her sex.

I suppose George VI's reign will go into history as the most disastrous my unhappy country has known since Matilda and Stephen. One interesting point stands out. The King died at the moment when Princess Elizabeth first put on a pair of 'slacks' – within a matter of minutes anyway. The Duke of Windsor lost his throne by his beret much more than by his adultery.

It would be too late for your article I'm afraid for me to add anything to your list of modern buildings spoiling old. The new Bodleian Library you will surely have mentioned. Most of the real dwarfing – such as St James's Street – where two lovely houses Brooks's Club and Boodles are quite ruined was not I think the work of proud architects but simply of shop-keepers who never gave any thought to the matter. There is Soanes elegant obelisk[2] at Reading but that is too minor a work of art for anyone except Betjeman to make a great fuss.

It was decent of you to say the frog-jews like *Helena*. I bet they don't. But thank you for saying so. Yes, I am afraid I must admit to a shade of anti-jew feeling. Not anti-semite. I rather like Arabs. It dates from my visit to Israel this time last year. It was there I realized that all jews are not like John Sutro and Lord Rosebery.

I live so much out of the world that it was a great surprise to me to read in *The Times* that Lord Rothermere had been given a decree nisi against Ann. He must already have filed the suit at the time they gave their Christmas party. I suppose he has found a new girl? I always found him a bore. It is a great thing for Ann, whom I love, to be rid of him & to have the chance of being made an honest woman.[3] I suppose that Christmas party will be remembered as the last private party ever given in a London private house.

Connolly has written this morning about the North Downs thrusting out to sea like a bunched fist. I believe he will soon emerge as a regional poet with ballades about the nutbrown ale of Kent. But his Irish name & Fenian features will haunt him to his death.

Love from
Evelyn

[1] *Télégraphie sans fil*, i.e., wireless.
[2] The Simeon Monument built in 1804 by Sir John Soane.
[3] 'Apparently, since Esmond had a wife, though divorced (or die-vorced as Evelyn always pronounced it), I had been living in sin and was now in a state of grace.' Ann Fleming in *Evelyn Waugh and His World*.

TO GRAHAM GREENE   Piers Court
Ash Wed. [27 February] 1952

Dear Graham
Many thanks for Mrs Luce's humourless joke.
I was sorry our February in Capri did not come off. Aches & pains have been very

severe since Christmas and I am off to warm old joints somewhere else [1]. I was not surprised as I followed in the papers your humiliations at Saigon [2]. I suspected you provoked them by admitting to your red past. Then I read your denunciation of the American spy system. Are we to suppose that those spies uncovered your Cockburn ticket [3]? Surely not?

I have no doubt you have been terribly misquoted. It is madness to say anything before journalists. *Of course* the Americans are cowards. They are almost all the descendants of wretches who deserted their legitimate monarchs for fear of military service. Still it is good to rub it in. But some lunatic reporter said you said that the Catholic Faith forbade a ruler to employ spies to detect & denounce potential rebels. That is actionable. The same reporter said you thought Democracy was reconcilable with Catholicism. I am not sure if that is actionable but it is very damaging.

I finished that book I was writing. *Not* good. Of course all writers write some bad books but it seems a pity at this particular time. It has some excellent farce, but only for a few pages. The rest very dull. Well, the war was like that.

Life sent a smart-alick [4] down here & I think that has ended my profitable connexion with them.

When I heard of N. Douglas's death I began to re-read *South Wind* and to my horror found it very heavy going. I am very sorry indeed not to have met him. I am less sorry to have missed Gracie Fields's wedding [5]. ....

E

[1] Sicily with Harold Acton.
[2] Probably Greene's failure to get a visa for the United States in Hong Kong.
[3] Communist Party membership.
[4] Professor Barzun.
[5] Gracie Fields, the popular singer from the North of England, lived on Capri, as had Norman Douglas. Her marriage to Boris Alperovici excited much popular comment.

To Christopher Sykes   Ethiopia
28 February 1952
Postcard

I shall flit like a beautiful wraith about White's tomorrow & the day after. Then to France 9 pm. There I shall flit in a similar style about Travellers'.

I will leave my article on Holy Plaggers with profane Pearson.

I think my brief marriage with *Life* Magazine has come to a divorce. I wrote to Mrs Luce mocking her history of Western Culture. They at once sent me an apostate frog called professor Smart-Alick Baboon. He stayed here, gave me a viva in history and reported ill.

If you will come with me to Sicily early next week I will support you in modest style fitting my fallen condition.

E.W.

To Laura Waugh   White's.
[?]

Darling

I am very sad to leave you. If you were warm & well I should not feel so badly
about it – but to leave you ill & cold spoils all the exhilaration of departure. Bless
you, darling, and take care of yourself & enjoy yourself. I shall think of you every
hour.

                                                                          E

To Laura Waugh   San Domenico Palace Hotel,
Monday 17 March [1952]   Taormina,
                                                        Sicily.

Darling Laura

My odd illness is momentarily quite cured. Five days ago I was an agonized
cripple; quite suddenly the pain went without any change of weather, place, diet.
Very rum.

I pray your cough and all your business troubles may clear as pleasantly. I fret
about you. It was sad to get no letter at Palermo but posts, I know, are bad.

... Sicily is proving rather a failure (though a change). There is sun here but bitter
cold. What we had not reckoned on was the ant-hill of tourists, North Italians,
Germans, Dutch, Swiss, Scandinavians, all spinning round & round the island in
charabancs & overruning every hotel.

Also I am beginning to feel that every dollar spent now is so much the less for us
when we take a holiday later this year together. The last week has cost more than I
intended.

All the Sicilian nobility is in Rome so we live like tourists.

Taormina is much overrated. A fine view but nothing else.

                                                              All my love
                                                              Evelyn

To Harold Acton   Piers Court
14 April [1952]

Dear Harold

How typical of your benevolence that you should have remembered my little
wish for Neapolitan stationery & have gone to the trouble of procuring some. Thank
you, with all my heart.

I travelled home slowly, delaying in Rome & Siena (my first visit) pursued
everywhere by rain & cold winds.

I spent two nights at Cap Ferat with Mr Maugham (who has lost his fine cook) &

made a great gaffe. The first evening he asked me what someone was like and I said: 'A pansy with a stammer'. All the Picassos on the walls blanched.

Diana joined me in a motor at Nice. We went to visit the Matisse public lavatory cocktail bar chapel at Vence[1] & drove slowly to Paris through snow & hail. Then Easter in retreat at Downside & now home to my ragged, starving, teeming household.

I hope there is sun & light at Naples. Here it is gray & cold & my table is heavy with tax demands. I dread the publication of my new book. I will send you a copy from old affection, not in the hope that you will enjoy much of it.

Laura sends her love

Yours
Evelyn

I greatly enjoyed at second hand your account of my altercation with the American harridan at Verona.[2]

[1]Henri Matisse decorated the chapel of the Dominican convent at Vence between 1948 and 1951.

[2]As recounted by Acton, the scene began with Waugh alluding to an American youth as 'The Ape Man', included his mother volubly regretting that her taxes were being spent on Marshall Aid to Europe, and ended with Waugh turning on Acton and saying, 'This is intolerable. And it's your fault. They spotted you as a fellow Yank. You deliberately enticed them here to annoy me', before he marched out alone. *More Memories of an Aesthete*, 1970, p. 311.

To Laura Waugh White's
28 April [1952]

Darling

Thank you for your forgiving letter. It is a great relief to think I can return not in dire disgrace. I long for Friday.

... I have a dull time on the whole tho I see some chums & witty worm friends. I drink a little too much. I was nice to Auberon & paid for his dinner & Miss Montagu's[1] for a birthday present but I find him horrible. The saddest thing is that he is joining this club. Can you not get Bridget or someone who has influence to dissaude him. Quite apart from his being a trouble to me it is no place for a youth of limited means & intemperate habits. The members are not at all the kind of people he likes & if he uses the club as a place to entertain his own odd friends he will be looked at askance. His proposer & seconder have both been badgered into putting him up by him, & both think him quite unsuitable. But of course he mustn't be black-balled. The only thing for him to do is request withdrawal. ...

All love
E

[1]Judith Montagu (1923–72). Daughter of Venetia Montagu, married Milton Gendel in 1962. Her obituary claimed that she was 'the first person who realized that the war was actually over. To a society numb with austerity she introduced avocado pears, gossip and real Americans....'

To Nancy Mitford   White's
Labour Day [1 May] 1952 Up the
Workers of the World down with
la vie de château

Darling Nancy,

Among the countless blessings I thank God for, my failure to find a house in Ireland comes first. Unless one is mad or fox hunting there is nothing to draw one. The houses, except for half a dozen famous ones, are very shoddy in building and they none of them have servants' bedrooms because at the time they were built Irish servants slept on the kitchen floor. The peasants are malevolent. All their smiles are false as Hell. Their priests are very suitable for them but not for foreigners. No coal at all. Awful incompetence everywhere. No native capable of doing the simplest job properly. No schools for children. Above all the certainty that once one pulls up roots & lives abroad there is no particular reason for living anywhere. Why not Jamaica? Why not Sicily? Why not California? On the move like a jew all ones life.

I have been in London ten days – long empty days & nights. Saw little Pam a bit & the bright young Flemings [1] and Mrs Friese-Greene & Osbert & Sutro & his monkey and witty worm friends here. Home tomorrow gladly. ...

Doting [2] is pitiable but I dont at all rejoice. There are not enough writers for one not to mind one going to seed and there are too many contemporaries in decay.

I dined tonight with Roy Campbell [3] (Dark Horse) a great boastful simple sweet natured savage. I feel quite dizzy from his talking to me.

Kind Mr M Berry [4] will send me to Africa for the childrens next holidays.

Poor Maimie is broke.

All the talk here is of poverty & disease.

B.Y. Yorke's son [5] cannot shake hands. He offers a closed fist.

I am writing a little essay in abuse of Père Couturier.

Tony Powell's new book [6] is said to be excellent.

Boots has dropped writing his psycho-analysis of me.

Henry Bath's health gives grave anxiety.

Met E. Marsh in the Duveen Gallery of the Tate gazing despondently at a new acquisition made of barbed wire & cork. He said: 'I have just realized that I am no longer quite contemporary.'

Mrs Fleming *very* pregnant. It is hoped that Mrs Fleming senior [7] will shortly marry money.

Love
E

[1] Viscountess Rothermere married Ian Fleming (1908–64), creator of James Bond, in March 1952.
[2] By Henry Green (Yorke).
[3] Roy Campbell (1902–57). South African poet.
[4] Michael Berry. Chairman and editor of *The Daily Telegraph*.
[5] Sebastian Yorke.
[6] Anthony Powell, *A Buyer's Market*.
[7] Eve Fleming, Ann's mother-in-law, was engaged in 1951 to the Marquess of Winchester (1862–1962), but he married the daughter of a Parsee high priest. In 1958 the Marchioness sued Eve Fleming, then seventy-three, for enticement and won her case, but the decision was reversed on appeal.

To Nancy Mitford   Piers Court
10 May [1952]

Darling Nancy
    ... More about Ireland. You have no conception of their mole-like malice.
Detraction is their passion. You should have heard the wireless programme
commemorating the centenary of George Moore's birthday. They had been at work
on it for years collecting reports from everyone who had ever known him from the
groom at Moore Park to Dublin literary colleagues. One after another the cracked
old Irish voices took up the tale for nearly two hours, each demolishing bit by bit
every corner of his reputation. That was Ireland all right.
    I have been in London quite a lot. Pam [Berry] is very nettled because I said the
upper classes had all left London. 'Why there's me & Dot [Viscountess Head] and ...
and Dot and me'. So she asked me to a party to launch me in London Society & there
were she & Dot & Honks [Lady Diana Cooper] (not exactly a London figure) & Sir
Laurence & Lady Olivier[1] (the dead spit of Lady Rosse[2]) and Mr Thomas[3], First
Lord of the Admiralty, and a most unarmigerous dancer named Ashton[4] and we
went to a ghastly American play – no attempt to translate it into English & then we
went back to Dot's and that was London Society. But Pam has a very good cook.
Other meals I had in London made me sick – literally.
    How very cleverly Dot paints suddenly.
    Oh I forgot to say that J. J. Cooper[5] obliged with a few songs.
    Page proofs of my fiasco have come, so full of misprints that my eyes dazzle.
Things like 'is' for 'it' on every line. In the old days printers did that sort of thing for
you – did they not?
    I read your play about the sex–change.[6] I expect it is full of *doubles entendres* that I
missed.
    You are taking Col. on a cultural tour of England. Yes? No? ...
                                                        Love
                                                          E

[1]Vivien Leigh (1913–67). Actress. Married 1940–60 to Laurence Olivier.
[2]Anne Messel was married to Ronald Armstrong-Jones and is the mother of Lord Snowdon. In 1935
she married the Earl of Rosse.
[3]J.P.L. Thomas (1903–60). Created Viscount Cilcennin in 1955.
[4]Frederick Ashton (1904–   ). Choreographer. Knighted in 1962, CH 1970.
[5]John Julius Cooper, son of Lady Diana.
[6]Written for a charity revue.

To Nancy Mitford   Piers Court
Whit Sunday [1 June] 1952

Darling Nancy
    I hope your poor noodle has not been battered out of shape by the police. I have
thought of you often during the last few days and pictured you charging at the head
of the communists.

It is very nice of Col. to offer me a young girl.[1] Is the offer reciprocal or do his convenable chums merely want to get rid of their daughter & go on a spree? If they would take Teresa in as an exchange, it is worth thinking about.

I am greatly interested to learn that you know Stuart Gilbert whose work I treasure as a classic example of ingenuity run mad. Have you read his exposition of *Ulysses*?[2] A laugh (not wholly derisive either) on every page.

It is a very terrible truth that modern English – not that I suppose a Lady Myers to be English – *do* tend to omit proper prefixes when addressing the notorious. I am not troubled on the telephone because I dont use the device, but I often get letters from strangers beginning 'Dear Evelyn Waugh'. Perhaps there is some excuse in your case since 'Mitford' is a nom de guerre. One would have written, I suppose 'Dear Saki'; 'Mr Saki' would be absurd. What I most resent is the omission of 'Mr' when other prefixes are retained: 'Sir Maurice Bowra, Dr Edith Sitwell, Lord David Cecil, Brigadier Maclean and Waugh'. My father taught me that the omission of a prefix meant that the man referred to was either a professional cricketer, a convicted felon or else dead.

I am quite sure Boots would never be offended by anything you wrote about him, least of all the portrait as 'the Captain' which is so flattering as to be barely recognizable. I am sure that any coldness he shows, springs from his natural shame of his consort – . . . .

H Buchanan has been here for three days on a professional visit, cataloguing my books. He worked hard & well but in his hours of relaxation was embarrassingly boastful.

I keep seeing Carol Reed[3] (Pempie's husband) who seems to be ready to employ me on a film. What he needs is simply someone to talk to about it. Not very exhilarating work, but he promises good wages.

I have written to Miss Caravaggio[4] in the hope of her finding a home for Teresa. She should be in touch with middle class intellectuals, & I hope, keeps clear of the Paris riots.

Advance copies of my sad little book[5] ought to be ready in a few weeks. I will send you one from my loyal loving heart, but be warned; don't try to read it. If *Pigeon Pie*[6] sells 10,000, it ought to sell 9,000. The great thing is that there is simply no competition these days.

Did you see English newspapers making a scandal of Cadogan Cooper's Academy picture with the entrancing title: *Jealous husband, disguised as a priest, hears his own wife's confession*. I wanted to buy it, wrote to him asking the price, got the answer 700 guineas.[7] I could get a Boucher for that.

'Stone of Insult' to me is the Epstein *Lazarus* just erected in New College Chapel.

You could go to your publisher's ball in a French aeroplane. People are saying he is a Jew and had his nose punched by a boxer instead of cut off by a plastic surgeon. What a pity he did not marry Boots's [wife] instead of poor Boots.

Love

E

[1] Waugh had asked about somewhere for his eldest daughter Teresa to stay in France. 'She does not

need "finishing" – just beginning. The ideal thing would be to find a family who would accept payment in pounds, perhaps for their own child's schooling here.'

²Stuart Gilbert, *James Joyce's Ulysses*, 1930, written at the suggestion of his friend Joyce.

³Carol Reed (1906–). Married Penelope Dudley Ward. Directed *The Third Man* and *Our Man in Havana* by Graham Greene. Knighted 1952.

⁴Waugh's French translator.

⁵*Men at Arms.*

⁶By Nancy Mitford, 1940.

⁷Cadogan Cooper presented the picture to Waugh as a gift.

To Angus Wilson [1]   Hyde Park Hotel
[21 July 1952]
Postcard

I have reached page 143[2] & found Fortt's Bath Olivers. I see I have done you an injustice & that there must be some recondite significance in the brand.

                                                         E.W.

[1] Angus Wilson (1913–). Novelist, critic and biographer.

[2] Of *Hemlock and After*, Angus Wilson's first novel. Wilson replied that they had 'some strange fascination for me connected with the tins and I put the name in by some compulsion'.

To Nancy Mitford   Piers Court
27 July [1952]

Dearest Nancy

I am not greatly troubled by fans nowadays. Less than one a day on the average. No sour grapes when I say they were an infernal nuisance. I divide them into

(a) Humble expressions of admiration. To these a post-card saying: 'I am delighted to learn that you enjoyed my book. E.W.'

(b) Impudent criticism. No answer.

(c) Bores who wish to tell me about themselves. Post-card saying. 'Thank you for interesting letter. E.W.'

(d) Technical criticism. eg. One has made a character go to Salisbury from Paddington. Post-card 'Many thanks for your valuable suggestion E.W.'

(e) Humble aspirations of would-be writers. If attractive a letter of discouragement. If unattractive a post-card.

(f) Requests from University Clubs for a lecture. Printed refusal.

(g) Requests from Catholic Clubs for lecture. Acceptance.

(h) American students of 'Creative Writing' who are writing theses about one & want one, virtually, to write their theses for them. Printed refusal.

(i) Tourists who invite themselves to one's house. Printed refusal.

(j) Manuscript sent for advice. Return without comment.

I also have some post-cards with my photograph on them which I send to nuns.

In case of very impudent letters from married women I write to the husband warning him that his wife is attempting to enter into correspondence with strange men.

Oh and of course

(k) Autograph collectors: no answer.

(l) Indians & Germans asking for free copies of ones books: no answer.

(m) Very rich Americans: polite letter. They are capable of buying 100 copies for Christmas presents.

I think that more or less covers the field.

Love
E

To Nancy Mitford   Piers Court
31 July [1952]

Darling Nancy

Who please is Blaise Cendrars?[1]

Also will you ask Col. whether Fr Leopold Bruckberger is a genuine hero or no. I have been reading his journals[2] and am puzzled.

My work[3] for Carol Reed is over. The story got more infantile & at the same time more incomprehensible every day.

I went to dinner with [Cecil] Beaton. Greatly surprised by invitation & suspicious of the cause – I supposed Miss Case of New York must be the object of the party. But no, there was no object, Beaton was just entertaining his friends & very nice friends they were & very fine the entertainment.

Another little party at the Heads. Dot is preparing to be the Evita Peron of the English military despotism. Antrim, Norwich[4] & Randolph & Head shouted the ceiling down, telling the same stories, full of foul words, over & over again. These people treat stories like songs. They like them to be old & familiar & repetitive. Each in turn told the same anecdote, each louder than the last.

I met poor Frankenstein Monster[5] in London. He is very very balmy and it ill becomes his mad son to mock him.

Frankenstein believes that he is under private instructions from the late King to solve the Ulster problem by having Princess Margaret declared Queen of an independent and united Ireland.

'I have got to go & see de Valera about it next month.'

'Got' is the operative word.

F. sits in White's and whenever a Duke passes he points his stick and says: 'I shall require *you* shortly' (for a picture of the Knights of the Garter).

But he is radiantly happy & pretty & thats more than can be said of me.

Maimie & Vsevolode follow the old, almost abeyant custom, of residing together without speaking. Difficult without servants.

My Battersby trompe l'oeil is up and looks well. What do you think of it?

Children, their cousins, their friends, are all upon me. I am going [to make] a tour of the British armies in Germany at Head's suggestion.

After being very hot it is cold again so all the flies from the garden are now in the house.

You will not guess what the big reliquary contains in Battersby's picture. It is Campion's rope. I have re-read my forthcoming book – awfully bad. But as I have remarked before there is no competition.

Jim Wedderburn has revived the Viscountcy of Dudhope (if we had invented that name customers would complain) so Diana goes down one more place. [6]

Love
E

[1]Blaise Cendrars (1887–1961). French novelist and film director.

[2]*One Sky to Share*: The French and American Journals of Raymond Leopold Bruckberger.

[3]Waugh said he had been working on a treatment of *The Man Who Was*. He wrote to Peters: 'The film as it stands is very silly – the plot all Reed, quite unintelligible and implausible. I don't want my name associated with it. I don't want to hurt Reed's feelings by being snooty. I haven't told him explicitly how bad I think the film. Perhaps the best thing would be to say that they mustn't use my name until I have seen the finished production. They are bound to make radical changes, I think, and those will excuse me.' If this is *The Man Between*, Carol Reed 1953, Waugh's name did not appear.

[4]Duff Cooper had been created Viscount Norwich.

[5]Frank Pakenham. His eldest son Thomas was almost nineteen.

[6]James Scrymgeour-Wedderburn (1902–   ) had his claim to the Viscountcy of Dudhope allowed in 1952, and that to the Earldom of Dundee in 1953. So Lady Diana Cooper, who had already descended from the precedence accorded a Duke's daughter to that of a Viscountess, now had an older creation placed above her. She did not care for her new title, commenting: 'Even Duff or Duff Cooper would have been better than Norwich – better porridge – Man-in-the-Moon better still.' She is now known once more as Lady Diana Cooper.

To Clarissa Churchill   Piers Court
13 August [1952]

Dearest Clarissa

Yesterday was a sad day – gossips confirmed and your dear face smudged across every newspaper.

I mourn the loss of a greatly loved friend & wish I had been gentler at our last meeting, but I fully concede the justice of your not confiding in me.

Can I have Mass said for your marriage[1], or is that impossible?

Yours, with my love
Evelyn

[1]Clarissa Churchill had been brought up as a Roman Catholic in a household that was not fervently religious. On 14 August 1952 she married Anthony Eden, who had been divorced.

To Nancy Mitford
25 August [1952]

Dearest Nancy

A propos of your comment on the French grief when people die: I have just heard from Mlle Caravaggio that her father has succumbed to a long & painful illness at the age of 91. The 'shock' was so great that she fell down in the street injuring her head.

... My plot is this. A man (you might prefer to make him a woman) with a rather unusual name like Gregory Peck. A slightly distinguished but absolutely unknown man such as say the librarian at the House of Lords or permanent head of the Colonial Office – the sort of man who has never had his name in a newspaper except to announce his marriage. One day his wife says: 'How funny, dear, there is a new film actor with your name'. The actor becomes an international hero. At first the man is mildly ragged by his friends & colleagues. Then his life becomes a nightmare. He books rooms for his annual holiday at Scarborough and finds the whole town turned out to greet him, the hotel furious when they find he is not the actor etc. etc. His name comes up for a knighthood and is crossed off because it would look ridiculous etc. Then his wife becomes fan of the actor and he finds her affections vicariously alienated. First ¾ of book is his utter ruin. Last ¼ his revenge. I think he ought to become equally notorious for drugs, communism, unnatural vices etc. so that he consummates the complete ruin of his namesake. They might meet in the end, both down and out, both with their names changed, & become friends without ever knowing one another. Any use?

The late J. Drummond was a poor dietary expert, no millionaire. He slept out because he couldnt afford an hotel.

IMPORTANT PICASSOS indeed. Talk about my becoming nicer! You couldnt write an obscene phrase like that except to offend.

Love
E

To Ann Fleming   Piers Court.
1 September [1952]

Dearest Ann

I am miserable to hear of your sufferings. I pray that your son[1] will make everything worth while. That hospital must have been beastly. I only once entered it when they were torturing Hubert Duggan to death. Did you see anything of a neighbouring mother, Mrs L. Kennedy?[2]

I go to London tomorrow to sign presentation copies of *Men at Arms*. You have had your sneak view but I will send one as a souvenir. Of course don't trouble to acknowledge it. The kindest way to regard it is as the first comic turn of a long musical-hall show, put on to keep the audience quiet as they are taking their seats. If I ever finish writing, and if anyone ever reads, the succession of volumes that I plan to follow it, it will make some sense. It would be very convenient for me if it was a financial success but hardly to be expected – certainly not in America. No competition here except Angus Wilson whose *Hemlock & After* I have read three times & think *awfully* clever, and am reviewing for *The Month*.[3]

Shall I go on writing? Why not. I've nothing to do and letters are quite agreeable in convalescence.

Freddie Lonsdale[4] lunched here on Saturday, the day the papers all accused him of murdering a negress. He looked extremely shifty. I have an aged monk also here. When Freddie left he (monk) said: 'Is that poor man *really* guilty?'

It is a dreary time here with all children at home. Well perhaps you are not exactly the person to complain to about children being a nuisance. My sexual passion for my ten year old daughter[5] is obsessive. I wonder if you'll come to feel like this about your son. I can't keep my hands off her. Her school report was abusive so she is writing daily copies. At the moment she is sprawled with her nose on the paper writing: Picasso is a disgusting beast; Sartre is just an ass.

By the way I heard your [Lucian] Freud on the wireless the other evening. I think he is just an ass, too.

Oh, another good new book, the translation of the Claudel-Gide letters. But perhaps you read them in French.

I went to Cambridge the other day – a dear little town. Why does one not hear more about it? Much nicer than modern Oxford. I went because of one of those upsetting changes of middle life. The bootmaker I have been to for 27 years has fallen into sloth & gone out of business. I was told of a Mr Thrussell who indeed seemed excellent. While I was sitting being measured, in burst Mrs Walston (G. Greene's friend) bare footed. She rampaged round the shop looking in boxes and produced a circular shoe, like the shoes horses used to wear to cut the grass. 'I have never seen anything so chic'. Mr Thrussell 'That, madam, is my own shoe. I regret to say I have a misshapen foot'. Mrs Walston, 'You must make me a pair exactly like them'. Rum. Didn't your Freud's grandad write something on the subject?

I went to her house where she lives with Mr Walston (in whom I discerned a painful physical resemblance to myself) in inelegant profusion. After luncheon he produced one of those absurd boxes of mammoth cigars which wont draw, which people like Korda affect, and said: 'I am not offering you one of these, but I thought you would like to see them'.

Clarissa's apostasy has upset me more than anything that had happened since Kick's [Hartington] death. I cant write about it, or think of anything else.

An American paper asked me to write a profile of Osbert. Poverty compelled me to accept. Though it was all love & praise it is certain to give deathless offence. I was tempted to begin: 'When Sir Osbert's ancestor Mr Hurt adopted the ancient Derbyshire name of Sitwell, he made things doubly plain by naming his son "Sitwell Sitwell".'[6] Perhaps Sir Osbert should have taken the name Hurt Hurt'. But I refrained. It is a shot to keep in the locker in case he turns nasty.

Dear Ann, I love you dearly, and I pray you get well very soon.

Evelyn

[1]Caspar Fleming (1952–75).
[2]Moira Shearer (1926–). Ballerina and actress. Married Ludovic Kennedy in 1950.
[3]October 1952.
[4]Frederick Lonsdale (1881–1954). Playwright, and father of Lady Donaldson.
[5]Margaret.
[6]See note 4 page 274.

To Clarissa Eden
2 September 1952

White's
As from Stinchcombe

Dearest Clarissa

I am too fond of you to shirk the obvious snub: 'mind your own business'.

I have just had a talk with Randolph who, God knows, is not to be trusted, but he has finally snuffed out the hope I was sheltering, that there might have been a secret annulment & a secret marriage in your case. That was the point of the letter I wrote you: when I said 'Can I have Mass said for you?' I take it you have in fact left the Church. If he is wrong, please tell me – simply the word 'wrong' on a postcard. But if he is right, what has it got to do with me?

I have not your shyness about direct questions. Not very long ago I asked you point blank if you were a Catholic & you said that I need not worry. Then as you must know I fell in love with you and so kept away. You simply became a rare treat which now & then came my way. But I trusted in what you said and hoped that if you were seriously tempted to apostasy, you would trust me by asking advice. I see now I was wrong & blame myself because if I had simply sought your friendship I might have had an influence. That is what I meant when I said: 'I concede the justice of your not confiding in me'. Now forget about me. It is because of my love for you that I simply dont mind if you snub me or read this letter over the telephone. Think of yourself. Thousands have died and are dying today in torture for the Faith you have idly thrown aside. I don't suppose you deliberately chose the vigil of the Assumption for your betrayal or deliberately arrived in a Catholic capital on the Feast. But I am sure Our Lady noticed. Anyway, on your jaunt in Portugal did you never go into a church to glance at the Emanuel style? When you found yourself, then, in the presence of Our Lord, what had you to say to him? You must now & then in an *antiquère* have seen a crucifix. Did you never think how you were contributing to the loneliness of Calvary by your desertion?

I have no right to preach to you, except my affection for you. When you read this aloud to your friends please make it clear to them that I claim no right at all but that.

My love to you always
Evelyn

To Clarissa Eden
6 September[1952]

Piers Court

Dearest Clarissa

Don't be alarmed. I am not trying to involve you in a correspondence which would bore you. I just want to clear up everything before the iron curtain falls and it is hard to do that when I am not clear what I wrote in my last letter. The heading, White's, should tell you that the mind was not at its brightest:

If I said anything to suggest that you did not admire & love & respect the man you have set up house with, I am a cad & an ass & most humbly beg your pardon.

I met Randolph at the end of a fortnight or more during which I have been deeply unhappy about you. He seemed to claim the credentials of an ambassador (tho I expect it was my fuddled nut not his that was responsible for this misconception) and his line was: 'What business is it of yours?' You are not the Cardinal Archbishop or the Editor of *The Tablet* or even a cousin'. My letter from White's was an attempt to explain why I minded.

I don't think it presumptuous to believe that I might have influenced you, if I had not fallen in love. We all influence each other every minute. I think you were left in childhood with a conception of the Church as being a sort of club, from which one can resign at any moment if the cooking deteriorates. I don't think you saw it as a complete way of life. As a friend I might have shown you – but I don't like *amitiés amoureuses* with a religious flavour. I can think of several & they stink.

I am haunted by the memories of another not very distant tragedy, when I did give advice, disastrously. An American Catholic girl married outside the Church because she was in love with a man under orders for the front. It caused great scandal. (You haven't heard because only those who knew you in childhood think of you as a Catholic). Then she was widowed, repented & was received back. She asked me what she should have done and I said: 'If you want to commit adultery or fornication & can't resist, do it, but realize what you are doing, and dont give the final insult of apostasy'. Well the girl followed my advice next time & was killed eloping. So my advice isn't, wasn't much help.

If you had chosen a Catholic whom you could marry, I believe you would have married him & gone regularly to the sacraments. Surely you see that the truth of Christ's death cannot be dependent on your own convenience?

But you are in a pickle now. Apart from convenience & pleasure, honour binds you to the man (who, I am sure, is all you think him) whose name you've taken.

I shall never think unkindly of you. (And I know & love Randolph too much ever to think better or worse of him). Please try not to think of me as a prig & fanatic & busybody. I'm not, you know.

Evelyn

To Cyril Connolly   Piers Court
8 September [1952]

Dear Cyril

I thought your review of *Men at Arms* excellent. It is a pity you called 'Apthorpe' 'Atwater'[1] throughout and credited him with two aunts (whereas it was one of my humdrum comic effects that he had only one) because it will make your readers think you did not give full attention to the book. You plainly did, and have clearly defined all that I dislike in the book. 'Beery' is exactly right.

The medal is not, as far as I know, going to play much part in the story, nor will the pace quicken much, but all the subsidiary characters, like 'Trimmer' & 'Chatty Corner' & 'de Souza' will each have a book to himself. Anyway the theme will see me out – that is the humanizing of Guy.

By the way the episode of a senior officer landing secretly & illicitly in a private's uniform did in fact occur, tho later & elsewhere.

If you ever see *The Month* look out for a review of mine of *Hemlock & After*. And if, as I don't think likely, you take in the *Catholic Mother*, read a review at Christmas of *Edith Stein*.

I am so delighted that you admired Hemingway's *Old Man [and the Sea]* as I did. Apart from his skill, it is his piety & chivalry I recognize.

I never go to London but am sometimes to be found in Brighton which I greatly enjoy.

Alf Duggan is engaged to a middle aged spinster.

I think it odd that you did not enjoy the 'thunderbox' incident in what, I fully agree, was a dreary section.

The politicians have reduced me to near penury, but you would be very welcome here if you cared to share our greatly reduced comfort later in the autumn.

> Love from
> Evelyn

Ronnie Knox showed me a letter about your review. I said that if he was simply writing as a reader of the *Sunday Times* rebuking a careless contributor, it was all right; if he was writing as a friend defending me from calumny, I should tell him I thought your criticisms sound. There is a strong affinity between the two characters – tho Atwater was a blackguard, which Apthorpe was not.

Not opened by spies. I had a lunatic fear I had written 'Gertrude' for 'Edith' Stein.

[1]Arthur Atwater is a character in *Work Suspended*.

To Alfred Duggan   Piers Court
8 September 1952

Dear Alfred

The news of your engagement is most exhilarating. My warmest congratulations to both. *Who's Who* is reticent about Sir Quintin [1] – a happy contrast to Sir Osbert Sitwell.

Laura & I will be delighted to come to tea on Sunday 14th.

You know best about the need for regular employment. I find three hours work in a day makes me so weary & so smug that I do nothing else for a week. Your books are much too good – and, I'm glad to see, too famous – to be treated as credentials for an employer. If a wage is *essential*, I should have thought that a schoolmaster's post (the only one I have ever had) was preferable to a publisher's (which my father had, so I know it pretty well). You would of course be worth £100 a week every now & then to a Cinema Company when they were doing a historical film – but that is *most* irregular work and often with rather beastly people.

Anyway one can discuss all this on Saturday, to which I greatly look forward.

Yours ever
Evelyn

If the job is not essential but a guarantee of good character, to hell with it.

[1] Sir Quintin Hill (1889–1963), whose sister Laura married Alfred Duggan in 1953.

To Cyril Connolly   Piers Court
21 September 1952

Dear Cyril

I was sorry to learn that the wording on my gift gave you pain – 'Keep the home fires burning' to me plainly meant what you so clearly expressed in a *Horizon* 'Comment', thanking for a Camembert cheese & saying very justly that the civilians had the worst of the war and further thanking you for making a delightful salon for men on leave, giving them a further choice than Emerald's oven and Sybil's frigidaire.

I will concentrate on the matters of fact in your *Time* article. First I beg you to correct the misstatement that I lectured free. I did so in England, but in America I charged $500 and your magazine is read chiefly by Americans.

2)   My brother was no hero. He was a regular officer who passed through Sandhurst to a line regiment. Without any discredit he was taken prisoner in 1918. If I needed relations to emulate I have many others.

3)   You are all wrong on genealogy but I don't see how this concerns Americans who do not know the names of their grandmothers. If they are curious

(a) The Waughs are not Celts. They populated Berwickshire centuries ago & never knew the English distinctions of squire & tenant. My great great grandfather had no ministry in Scotland. See *Dictionary National Biography*.

(b) The Morgans are of the prehistorical chieftainship of Wales & still hold Tylycoch. Their finances were restored by the mathematician William Morgan my great great grandfather. See *Dictionary of National Biography*.

(c) There are no 'Cockburns of Edinburgh'. My great great grandfather Henry Cockburn, first of Cockburn, was a Cockburn of Langton and simply took the appellation 'of Edinburgh' when made a law-lord. [1] Again, see *D.N.B.*

Rabans were of Staffordshire yeoman stock who went to India at the end of eighteenth century, made a modest fortune there & bought a modest

Somerset property. The last was killed in 1917 fighting in an Indian regiment.

(d) Herberts are not as you suggest West Country squires. They hail from Newbury & thence Wiltshire & Wales. Carnarvon descends direct from Pembroke. My father in law was the brother of the Carnarvon who dug up Tutenkamen. Pixton is an Ailand property which came into Herbert hands about 150 years ago. Laura's brother bought it for him from Porchy (senior) see Burke. ² None of this is of the smallest importance but if you want to write about it, verify. ...

[Incomplete]

¹Henry Cockburn (1771–1845) was a Lord of Session, with the judicial title of Lord Cockburn. He never took, or needed, a territorial appellation; by ancestry he was a Cockburn of Cockpen.

²In fact Laura Waugh's grandmother Elsie, Lady Carnarvon, bought Pixton in 1901 from her stepson the 5th Earl of Carnarvon, for her son Aubrey. Waugh seems confused.

To Nancy Mitford   Royal Crescent Hotel,
Michaelmas [September]1952   Brighton

Darling Nancy

Laura's annual jaunt. A come-down from previous jaunts in *Queen Mary* & Plaza Hotel, New York. But very salubrious.

I was asked to dinner to meet you by the Cambridge Union & refused not for lack of longing to see you, but from the belief we can arrange a happier rendez-vous when/if you come.

Two things. 1) I believe you keep my letters. A month or so ago I wrote a nasty one about Clarissa. Will you be very kind & burn it?¹ 2) I believe Ann is in Paris. How is she? Her letters are very sad. She never mentions her son. Is it all right?

Leave *Men at Arms* until you have read the whole of the national library. I sent it with full preliminary warnings.

Laura & I went to visit the old Belloc² yesterday. Very elaborate prearrangement with children and grand children. I have known him quite well for nearly 20 years. It was slightly disconcerting to be greeted with a deep bow & the words: 'It is a great pleasure to make your acquaintance, sir'.

He was greatly annoyed because 'Nancy' [Astor]³ had not asked his wife, dead these 30 years, to a party 33 years ago. 'Poor woman she has not grasped the European decencies'.

He wore black broad cloth garnished with garbage, enormous labourers' boots and an open collar. I in rather smart & conventional tweeds. He squinted at me for some time & said: 'We all wear exactly the same clothes nowadays'.

But he had a noble look still like an ancient fisherman in a French film.

All love
E

When you have time to write please tell me any *English* gossip you hear.

If you see Dominic Elwes please rub in that he never thanked me for a £10 birthday present & make it your excuse for withholding benefactions. That will learn him.

[1] It has not survived.
[2] Hilaire Belloc died in 1953.
[3] Nancy Langhorne (1879–1964). An American, she married in 1906 Viscount Astor. Unionist MP 1919–45, the first woman to sit in the House of Commons.

To Graham Greene   Piers Court
7 October [1952]

Dear Graham

Your letter warmed me greatly. Thank you very much indeed.

When do you return? It is too long since we met.

I am just completing my 49th year. You are just beginning yours. It is the grand climacteric which sets the course of the rest of ones life, I am told. It has been a year of lost friends for me. Not by death but wear & tear. Our friendship started rather late. Pray God it lasts.

Please keep me seats for your first night.[1] I will clap hard & call 'Author'.

It is no good pretending I wasnt shown your letter about Chaplin in the *New Statesman*.[2]

If Catherine is still in Capri please give her my love.

E

[1] Graham Greene's play *The Living Room*.
[2] Greene had written an open letter 'of welcome ... to one of the greatest liberals of our day'. While on the *Queen Elizabeth* Charlie Chaplin had received a cable telling him that he would not be allowed to return to the United States.

To Graham Greene   Piers Court
12 November [1952]

Dear Graham

How very nice of you to send me the *Little Horse 'Bus* and how clever of you to write it! You really are the most versatile of men (next to Mgr Knox). And a play running in Sweden too! The *Bus* seems very expensive. I dont think any rich children will be able to afford it, but the poor spend huge sums on their children. I expect they will not resent the grammar of the opening sentence.[1] You see how jealous I am of your accomplishments. ...

Yours ever
Evelyn

[1] *The Little Horse Bus* by Graham Greene, 1952, begins: 'Everybody for miles around Goose Lane used to buy their groceries at Mr Potter's shop.'

To ALFRED DUGGAN   Piers Court
5 December [1952]

Dear Alfred
    Very many thanks for *Thomas Becket*. I look forward eagerly to reading it & I am
sure I shall recognize none of the 30 slips jealously noted by Knowles. [1]
    I am off to Goa in ten days time. I have always wanted to see it & now is the time
before it falls down, St Francis crumbles and the Hindus invade. As you know I was
greatly touched & proud as a peacock at being asked to be your best man. I am a man
of my word & I will come. I suppose it is quite impossible for you to postpone the
ceremony for a week or ten days. I should dearly have liked to spend a little more
time in Goa, but of course friendship comes first, and it is plainly a great deal to ask
that you should adjust your plans for the most important event of your life, to suit
my convenience. Did you think of Billy Wicklow as a possible substitute?
    I take it from the arrangements for a nuptial mass that Laura [Hill] has been
received into the Church? Please give her my warmest congratulations.
    I dont know what you would like for a wedding present so send a small gift of
money with my love to you both.

                                                        Evelyn

[1] Alfred Duggan, *Thomas Becket of Canterbury*, 1952. Dom David Knowles had published *The
Episcopal Colleagues of Archbishop Thomas Becket* the year before.

To ALFRED DUGGAN   Piers Court
[December 1952]

Dear Alfred
    I will reach London on January 13th. On 14th early, I will have my old tall [hat]
ironed at Locks. My coat will not button but I have a new waistcoat which will.
    I shall be staying at the Hyde Park Hotel. Let me know where to call for you &
when. Please coach me in the drill. I know it should be the other way about.
    You must have a gold & silver coin. I had a Charles II guinea and Edward the
Confessor 1d. I handed them to my best man – Henry Yorke – while I changed my
trousers and never saw them again.

                                                        Yours
                                                        Evelyn

To LAURA WAUGH   Hotel Mandori,
21 December [1952]   Goa. [1]

Darling Laura,
    A week since we parted. It seems much longer to me. I think of you in your mid
winter & wish you were here. It is not nearly as hot as an Italian summer. A cool

breeze most of the time. The scenery delicious, islands & broad rivers and the ocean and hills. Everything green & red. Outside my verandah the river full of Arab sailing ships from the Persian Gulf. The people very soft & friendly. The Government officials as dull as most officials in most places. I went to cocktails with the Governor General – or rather to whisky. The ladies sat in the centre of the drawing room in a semi circle. One shook hands with each in turn & then was led away to join men on a verandah. Like Hollywood except that the ladies got nothing to drink. Hundreds of baroque churches everywhere – rather like Mexico except that all the sculpture instead of being ferocious is gentle & sweet.

. . . I met a group of pilgrims from Chittagong & told them my grandfather was buried there. They said they would find his grave & pray for his soul.

Indians are full of compliments. On my first morning as I was shaving a government official appeared & said: 'All the peoples of Goa are asking how you slept'. Only one complaint. Fiendish noise in the hotel, which is still under construction. It is impossible even to read a book. But I am out most of the time.

Oh I am sorry for you in your icy house.

Hindus have all your veneration for cows.

All my love
Evelyn

[1] Waugh went to Goa for the celebration of the 400th anniversary of the death of the missionary St Francis Xavier (1506–52).

To Laura Waugh   Goa.
26 December [1952]

Darling Laura & darling children,

Thank you for your telegram of Christmas greetings which reached me at midday today. I see that it was the sloth of the post-offices that delayed it. I had begun to fear that your cold hearts were quite frozen to death.

Christmas was not very cheerful for me. The Goanese keep it strictly as a family feast and strangers are not included in their merry making which consists in exchanging bouquets of paper flowers and eating sweets. I dined & lunched alone at my solitary table here surrounded by Hindus and Jews. The breeze dropped for the day and it was oppressively hot. Midnight mass at Old Goa Cathedral was a moving occasion, the great building crowded to suffocation with pilgrims from all over India & Ceylon. No mistletoe or holly or yule logs or Teutonic nonsense. Simple oriental fervour instead. I feel far closer brotherhood with these people than in France or Dursley or Boston.

. . . I go to dine tonight with the Indian consul. You may imagine my social loneliness when I say that I look forward to it keenly, because he and his wife speak perfect English and it is a great strain talking all the time to people who know very little. But do not think that my loneliness is painful. I am happy alone so long as there are new things to see & think about and I am greatly enjoying the trip. I hope you are all having a joyful time. I think of you all, sweet family, all day long.

My fondest love to each of you severally, Laura, Teresa, Bron, Margaret, Harriet, James and Whats-his-name.

Evelyn

To Laura Waugh Mysore.
5 December [January] 1953

Darling Laura

India is very like Stinkers. There are cows wandering in all the gardens eating the flowers. All the lower orders call me 'master' which I find very familiar.

I spent a dull Sunday in Bangalore. I took out two Italian Jesuits & gave them Chianti. Goodness they did enjoy it. One said: 'When I said mass this morning I little thought I should be drinking Chianti at luncheon'. I should hope not indeed. His thoughts should be elsewhere.

I met an Englishman in the bar. I said I was coming here to look at temples. He said: 'The Hindu religion is nothing but Sex. But mind you they dont look on it as you & I do, as something disgusting. *They* think it is beautiful'.

So today I went to Seringapatam which you will know all about from your historical studies at Albemarle House. Tipu Sultans palace was just like Brighton Pavilion & made me home-sick.

Tomorrow I drive miles & miles to see sculpture. Very exhausting & expensive. Then my plan is to go further south still to Madura & go straight from there to Bombay & home.

An aged babu shaved my moustaches. He also took off nearly all the hair on my head & then took my skull in his hands & tried to crush it, then he tried to break my neck & pinched my arms cruelly. Apparently that is all part of getting ones hair cut in this strange land.

The women here are all charmingly dressed and so feminine they made all European women seem Lesbian. The men are nearly all quite grotesque. The only dignified people are the servants.

I am afraid that I caused offence in Bangalore because an official came to greet me & conduct me to a palatial official guest house but I found it was dry & moved out.

I am sorry not to be with you tomorrow burning furniture. But perhaps you are away from home.

Indian hotels are very sumptuous in some ways. A 'single room' consists of three rooms and a bath-room. Food quite good. Drink prohibitively expensive.

All love
E

To Alfred Duggan   Piers Court
22 January 1952

Dear Alfred

It was an exasperating moment when we landed at Rome in brilliant sunshine for the last stage to London and were told that we could not proceed. You had some presentiment of this disaster I think. It came as a rude shock to me. I was so very eager to see you married & so very grateful to you for postponing the wedding to suit my plans.

I send you again my warmest wishes. I long to hear of your plans & place of employment.[1] I was a schoolmaster once – by no means the least amusing part of my life.

Please give my homage to Laura. Do come here with her whenever you feel inclined. We have no central heating or presentable servants or digestible cookery. But you will be most welcome if you can bear it.

Yours ever
Evelyn

[1] Duggan became archivist of the *Universe*, a Catholic weekly.

To Eric Linklater   Piers Court
22 January 1953

My Dear Eric

A Year of Space[1] has given me the keenest delight. First – for friendship is more than esteem – that you should count me among the favoured thirty to whom it is addressed, and secondly the delight of reading such a workmanlike and continuously beguiling narrative.

I had just finished rereading Aldous Huxley's *Jesting Pilate*[2] when your present arrived. How much wiser you are than Huxley & how much better your write. Your vocabulary drove me twice to the dictionary. When Huxley uses unfamiliar words I am incurious of their meaning.

How I admire your broad charity which embraces Stephen Spender and the youth of Sydney and yet gives so truthful a picture of them that the less charitable shudder.

I have never had much wish to go to the Antipodes. Now I know I never shall.

What a multitude of men you know & like. You see your account of your year has filled me with envy.

May I congratulate you & your publisher on the fine dress of the book? I think there is something awfully wrong with writers who don't care how their books look.

I am just home from a happy Chrismas in Goa & am settling to work without distractions of salmon or deer. Here is a little misprinted Christmas card I meant to send before I went to India.

Please let me know when you next come South.

I have promised to preach against Tito in Glasgow in two months time.

Yours ever

Evelyn

[1]An autobiography by Eric Linklater, 1953.
[2]A collection of travel articles, 1926.

To NANCY MITFORD   Piers Court
18 February [1953]

Darling Nancy

Yes, home from India some time now. Goa was heaven. I wrote a few words about it for your great new friends, *Picture Post*, but what with the black Portuguese telegraphist & Mr Hulton's sub editor, they got sadly buggered. Now I have written a most instructive article no one will print. [1]

I should like to see *Punch* restored to splendour but I am sure you are right to stay with the *Sunday Times*. I think it is a first principle to stay with editors and publishers – and shops and restaurants too – until they are beastly to one. Then to sweep out without remonstrating. Needless to say I dont observe this precept myself but live among brawls.

Dont have anything to do with Ian Fleming's Queen Anne Press. They are dreadful people to deal with. I dont suppose you ever got a Christmas book[2] from them from me, did you? I carefully inscribed two dozen copies & addressed the labels. Only ten acknowledgements. So I thought well people are like that nowadays until I met a chum or two and asked & learned they were mostly lost or astray. But the misprints are so many & glaring that I am quite glad. And the wood engravings by a protégé [Reynolds Stone] of Betjeman's dull as be damned.

Your last article on Paris had an awful howler. 'Each' used in the plural. You really must take care now you are doing a work of scholarship.[3] But I was delighted to read that Col. has grown a beard. No wonder the Director of the Wallace Collection[4] wished to kiss him elsewhere than on the face.

I have had a lovely fortnight making illustrations for a bright young short story.[5] I think in your country they call the work 'collages'? I mean cutting out bits of prints & sticking them together & drawing on them with black & white & changing all the expressions as Lord Berners used to do. When I am paralysed I shall do nothing else.

I have gone stone deaf in one ear which makes all social intercourse impossible. I am stupefied in the presence of more than two people. Still perfectly all right tête à tête.

Surely 'vivant' means 'debauchee'? Could you not legitimately call Falstaff a 'bon vivant'?

After Goa I made a swift tour of the temples of South India. Fascinating & exhilarating. All the lovely sculpture that looks so odd in museums suddenly looking appropriate. The Indians are much more servile than most foreigners. I can only bear intimacy really & after that formality or servility. The horrible thing is familiarity.

At the railway stations the notice 'Gentlemens Waiting Room' has, since the Mountbatten retreat[6], had 'Gentle' painted out and 'Upper Class' substituted.

The famous filthy sculpture of South India is all the invention of poor blind Aldous Huxley.

The Tito tease[7] is the greatest fun to the participants. We are uniformly victorious. No one else bothers about it, of course, but it is all cabled to him I believe, and Mr Eden is said to fret in his bed.

I have had terrible letters from an earnest papist saying how can I praise your books when you make your hero make a sacrilegious communion. Do I praise your books?

My daughter, Margaret, at school in the centre of the storm havoc, wrote. 'There was such a wind the other night that a tree was blown down near the chapel'.

> All love
> Evelyn

[1]'Goa: the home of a Saint' was eventually published in *The Month*, December 1953.

[2]*The Holy Places.*

[3]*Madame de Pompadour*, 1953, her first biography.

[4]Sir James Mann (1897–1962). Director of the Wallace Collection from 1946.

[5]Waugh adapted engravings for *Love Among the Ruins*, 1953. He printed '*A Canova et E Waugh fecerunt*' on the frontispiece but also wrote 'With decorations by various eminent hands including the authors.'

[6]Lord Mountbatten was Viceroy when India became independent in 1947.

[7]Marshal Tito, President of Yugoslavia, was to arrive in England in March and be welcomed by Prince Philip, Churchill and Eden. Waugh wrote letters of protest to the *Spectator*, the *New Statesman* and *The Times*. When Bulganin and Khrushchev came to London in 1956 Waugh wrote to Peters: 'I could write an article (not for the *Express* group) giving reasons why Russian visit is not comparable to Tito's ie. in that case an imposture was being attempted on the British public by representing Tito as a gallant ally when in fact he had been a treacherous enemy and as a liberal statesman when he was in fact a doctrinaire Marxist persecuting the Church in a way of which the general public were kept ignorant. The Russians are open enemies and there is nothing unchivalrous about eating with enemies.'

TO MARGARET WAUGH   Piers Court
19 February [1953]

Darling Margaret

I am glad (and surprised) to hear that you were not washed away in the great storm. Birchington & Ramsgate both seem to have suffered. You must swim very well to have escaped. Were most of the other girls drowned?

I saw Lord Antrim setting off to Westgate to search for his daughter's body. Did you see him?

I am glad you are learning chinese. The ideograms should be written with a brush. In old China calligraphy was regarded as one of the highest of the Arts.

Your mother has given up almost all her pleasures for Lent & looks very proud & sad. I have given up sleeping draughts.

Last Sunday I went to see Bodiam Castle[1] – only just a ruin very fine & lonely standing in swamp and snow. I went to another castle nearby called Sissinghurst.[2] That is quite ruined except for five or six separate towers. It is inhabited and the drawing-room is in one tower & dining-room in another and the bedrooms & bathrooms all far apart in other towers. Very pretty but inconvenient in the rain & snow.

Here is a picture of a Chinese lady for you. It is painted on rice-paper & will fall to pieces at the gentlest touch. So I shall not think ill of you if it does not survive long. But it is a pretty picture 100 years old. I should like you to be able to paint as well as this.

All my love
Papa

Pious Hatty has given up rum & cigars for Lent

[1]Staying with Lady Curzon and Alfred and Laura Duggan.
[2]Home of Sir Harold Nicolson and V. Sackville-West.

To Nancy Mitford   Piers Court
[February 1953]

Darling Nancy

On no account a novel. A popular life like Strachey's *Queen Victoria*, to be enjoyed by Honks & Pam Berry. Plenty of period prettiness. Write for the sort of reader who knows Louis XV furniture when she sees it but thinks Louis XV was son of XIV and had his head cut off. There is no limit to the amount of knowledge *you* must have. The question is how much to impart. Aldous Huxley fails in this matter of taste, particularly in *Devils of Loudun*, he cant resist giving irrelevant information. But I am sure your artistic taste wont fail you.

I write from memory, but I think it is fair to say Mme de Pompadour's influence in politics was disastrous. The defeats of 1759 were her defeats. But I daresay historians have changed their views since I stopped studying.

As far as I remember, the *Parlements* were King's Courts like our royal courts temp. Henry II, designed to break the power of the feudal courts. By Louis XV time I think the feudal courts had not much more power than English J.P.s. *All authority in theory emanated from the throne*, but the *parlements* soon became practically hereditary themselves. The noblesse de la robe, (from whom incidentally most of the best Jansenists came), were a group of wealthy & learned families who shared out the legal appointments among themselves. But Tocqueville will tell you all this, I am sure.

Strachey, in *Q.V.* knew all the politics of the reign inside out and just drew on his knowledge here and there when it was necessary for his portrait. It is like the knowledge of anatomy that is necessary for drawing a clothed figure – but I suppose with your views of art you wont admit that it is necessary.

I imagine Mme de P. as Phillis de Janzé. Phillis did too I think.

Love
E

To Randolph Churchill   Piers Court
13 March 1953
Postcard

Thank you for sending me your interesting review of *Tito Speaks*.[1]

I note she has cost us three aircraft already.

I wonder what relation 'Reg' Butler,[2] the notorious sculptor is to the politician.

The smaller Liddell & Scott does not support your derivation of ποργη [porne].

[1] By Vladimir Dedijer, 1953. Marshal Tito came to Britain as a guest of HMG for five days on 16 March 1953. When Fitzroy Maclean remonstrated with Waugh in 1944 for referring to Tito as a woman, he replied, 'Her face is pretty, but her legs are *very* thick.' *Evelyn Waugh and His World* p. 151.

[2] Reginald Butler (1913–). He won first prize in an international competition for *The Unknown Political Prisoner*.

To Nancy Mitford   Piers Court
14 March [1953]

Darling Nancy

The Tito tease has turned out a great tease for me. All my time & energies in the last month seem to have been spent on it – genuine public spirit fatally combined with the itch to have the last word. Last week I went all the way to Glasgow to address 4000 or less Irish Catholics. The Duke of Norfolk has been prodded into action to present a remonstrance. Everyone, whether pro or anti Tito is sickened by this first excursion of Clarissa into public life. The London police say they cant protect him unless his residence is kept secret, his engagements not announced, a bullet-proof car provided for him; even then they fear assassination. Apart from the Duke of Norfolk and whatever gunmen the Russians send, there are 5,000 Yugoslav refugees in the country, all with scores to settle. So what with one thing and another Clarissa is unpopular and has announced that with brilliant originality she will paint the interior of Stafford House (now called 'Lancaster'. Why?) 'broken white', in a desperate bid to regain the confidence of the party.

The Glasgow visit was very exhausting. I suppose I am a very bad guest. I always complain loudly if I am not offered enough to drink. In Glasgow their one aim seemed to be to intoxicate me. Great goblets of neat whisky thrust into ones hand every ten minutes. And I resented that too.

I am becoming a Russian Imperialist, a reaction to the politicians. What is wrong is not Russia but Communism. Our policy is to bribe all the small states to remain communist but quarrel with Russia. If they are going to be communist its much better Russia should rule them. Great Empires never seek war; all their energies are taken up in administration. Our troubles now come from Clemenceau destroying the Austro-Hungarian Empire. The one certain way to start Third War is to establish half a dozen independent atheist police states, full of fatuous nationalism & power hunger.

Did I tell you that Robin Campbell has abandoned painting & now composes music?[1]

I went to see the apotheosis of Art-nonsense – the International Competition for a statue of an Unknown Political Prisoner. Were the prize winners illustrated in your press? Scottie Wilson is a Velasquez beside them.

Randolph has become an angelic character – hugely fat & jolly. I am sure it was that periodic banting which destroyed his charm. He has a wonderful new idea for a book – English Country Houses. 'Which, Randolph?' 'Well I thought Longleat, Chatsworth, Blenheim etc' 'But haven't they been done rather fully? And what do you know of architecture, genealogy or decoration?' 'Oh, its going to be a *popular* book'.[2] Bless him.

Love to [Hon?] Mme de Pompadour
Evelyn

Simon Elwes sent out an invitation R.S.V.P. The Private Secretary

[1]Not true.
[2]Randolph Churchill, *Fifteen Famous English Homes*, 1954.

TO NANCY MITFORD   Piers Court
[March 1953]

Darling
I am very sorry indeed to hear of your American difficulty.[1] The same thing happened to me – they just printed a few copies of *Handful of Dust*, sent out none for review, and let it flop – but at that time I didn't sell any copies in America anyway. But in your position this could be disastrous. I am sure Peters is doing all he can to rectify his mistake, but it is a very grave mistake indeed.

It has been a lovely week for Art lovers – first Reg's Folly and then Piccasso's eikon of Stalin.

Jesuits it all depends whether you are treating Pomp[adour] purely as a figure of before the deluge or as a symbol of the coming disasters. The expulsion of the Jesuits at the height of their theological triumphs over Jansenism and Quietism, was the first great victory of the Free Masons who were to bedevil Europe & the

Americas for 150 years or more. You'll have to go into Masonry seriously I think. No good asking Norwich. He wont blab even when tight. As *Pomp* is your magnum opus would it be worth while pausing & interpolating a hasty novel to finish your contract with your American publisher.

You could even hire a ghost to produce something unpublishable. That would liberate you.

Tito's visit has been an undisguised fiasco. It has really been a very happy week.

Reg's statue has been taken up in Parliament. His defender – Sir Leslie Plummer, the man who cost us £80,000,000 in ground nuts, who you would have thought would have changed his name and gone to Tasmania.[2]

One can get posterity ink[3] – quite black. The trouble is you have to wash your fountain pen every two days. Would it help your poor failing eyes.

I am quite deaf now. Such a comfort.

I hope you will publish a £3.3 edition of *Pomp* with fine illustrations. Those, incidentally, are the hot cakes today.

Honks is starving at Tring. I expect you knew we have just killed a sheep and gorge.

I long to see your parterre. I may be going to Honks at the end of April. But you'll be at Versailles?

Love
E

[1]Peters told Nancy Mitford's American publisher that she was changing to another firm when she was still contracted to give them one more book. 'I fear he will ruin poor *Pomp*, now out of spite,'

[2]Sir Leslie Plummer (1901–63). Labour MP from 1951; Chairman of the Overseas Food Corporation 1947–50.

[3]Nancy Mitford had written: 'Oh your ink is so pale. Poor posterity.'

To GRAHAM GREENE   Piers Court
[31 March 1953]
Postcard

Thanks awfully for *The Confidential Agent*. It wasn't one of my favourites when it came out but I find when I reread you new excellences appear on every page & I shall fall on it eagerly when I resume secular reading after Holy Week. At the moment I confine myself to the 'Horror Flat' in the *Daily Mail* and *The Man on the Donkey*.[1] You shouldn't have torn up that cheque.[2] When I had a play once I was greatly out of pocket through believing I got seats free at the theatre.

E

[1]H.F.M. Prescott, *The Man on a Donkey*, 1952.

[2]Payment from Waugh for tickets for *The Living Room*, Greene's first play, which opened on 16 April.

To Ann Fleming   Piers Court
Easter Tuesday
[7 April] 1953

Dearest Ann

Welcome home to you both. You have been sadly missed. I am delighted to learn that White Cliffs[1] survived the great storm. I supposed it totally destroyed.

I go to Paris (Golden Arrow) on 17th on the way to Chateau de St Firmin. If you have a minute off from the Spring collections do let us meet. I long to see you. I am too deaf for social life but perfectly sound tête à tête.

Miss Hepburn[2] is terrifying in her ugliness. We stayed in the same hotel in Brighton last year. Her face was then mottled brown & yellow in huge irregular patches like a circus pony.

Graham Greene's life is as mysterious to me as to you. Ivor[3], Perry[4], etc must be Mrs Walston's choice, I am sure. She found him very lonely and morose & thought it her duty to enliven him with new acquaintances. Indeed it is thanks to her that I have seen so much more of him during the last three years.

... Surely you cannot have a telephone exchange at the Tate Gallery? It is full at the moment of preposterous objects called prisoners of war. You have missed a heap of artistic fun. This exhibition the chief [of] them. When I saw the English selection six months ago I thought: 'This is the end of modern art God be praised'. But the result has been odder than that. There is now an ideologic division. 'Abstract Art' is Tory, Capitalist, Bourgeois etc. 'Realistic Art' is communist, proletarian, progressive etc. Robin Campbell in despair has abandoned painting and now composes music.

The other treat was Picasso's eikon of Stalin, published by Aragon and denounced by *L'Humanité*.[5]

I have bought an exquisite Augustus Egg since I saw you last.

The news from Ye Oaken Cottage is welcome.[6] It will be a happy day for us who love him when Cyril is emancipated.... At present I gather he is under the illusion that he is the reincarnation of Coleridge. I heard a good old story of him last week. Someone met him about six months ago and he, Cyril, said: 'People think I have no sense of loyalty & honour. I admit that now & then poverty has obliged me to do things I regret. But I have some standards of decency. I was offered a large sum of money by a Sunday newspaper to write personal revelations of two friends who had become notorious. One with a wife & children in this country. Of course I refused with disgust. That at least I could not sink to'. This was a fortnight before the appearance of the Burgess–Maclean articles.[7]

I have had a tedious time since I returned from India (which was heaven) engaged in teasing Tito. It was fun at first but soon palled. It has been a sharp lesson to me never again to write to the newspapers about anything.

In two months time you will receive a pretty copy of a silly little story[8] of mine – the one Ian saw, slightly embellished.

Please ask Ian to look up the file at Queen Anne's Press about the second issue of *Holy Places* and, when he has a moment to spare, to stir them to action.

Mr Alfred Duggan is happily married & fully employed. Lady Curzon is behaving rather well.

Laura joins me in love for you

Evelyn

[1] White Cliffs, near Dover, had been bought by Ian Fleming from Noel Coward.
[2] Katharine Hepburn (1909–   ). Actress.
[3] Viscount Wimborne (1903–67).
[4] Lord Brownlow. Ann Fleming had written of meeting Greene in Jamaica, 'Can he like such people? Is he living in sin? Is he tortured? He remained remote from all, totally polite and holding the cocktail shaker as a kind of defensive weapon.'
[5] Louis Aragon (1897–   ) as editor of Les Lettres françaises published the drawing which was denounced by the French communists.
[6] Cyril Connolly had been bitten twice by Barbara Connolly's female coati. Her comment had been 'This house is full of unsatisfied women.'
[7] Collected as The Missing Diplomats, 1952.
[8] Love Among the Ruins.

To Nancy Mitford
[1953]

Darling Nancy

It is shocking that you have taken employment under Lulu[1] rather than enjoy the social conditions you have striven so hard to create in your own country. You were full of patriotic claptrap when it meant the destruction of Italy & Central Europe. Now that it means paying taxes in order to establish your egalitarian world, you prefer to write advertisements for poppy seeds or whatever it is that earns you French nationality. You cannot conceive how much I despise you.

I long to see you however. But I dont come to London any more. B. Bennett like all jaggers turned on his master so that I no longer care to patronize the Hyde Park Hotel & all other hotels are full of industrial crooks going to exhibitions. Will you not spare a few nights to come here? Surely the seedsmen & the film studio neither work at Whitsun. You know the disadvantages of coming here but it would be a great treat to us if you could bear it.

Hatty has become the despair of all. Would you like to take her to Paris with you? She wont eat. Well I cant blame [her but she] wont let either of two quite pretty nursery maids touch her which is less excusable. She yells. In her rare moments of self-command she is extremely droll. Do adopt her.

Sykes has been here for Sunday. Camilla was sick. His son Mark is being expelled from school.[2] We too have a ham. Nothing else. Bet you cant read this. The trouble is that I brought this *writing* paper in Hollywood & ink runs on it so I have to use a kind of stylo.

It is all Yorke's fault. No one wrote about the poor before him. Greek thought defined tragedy as dealing with people of the highest rank only. In Shakespeare the low born are always buffoons. Connolly thinks I spoke of Lys when I spoke of Loutit[3]. It is all too difficult.

If Auberon Herbert marries Elizabeth Cavendish will my love for Debo be incestuous?[4]

I hear ghastly accounts of Antrim.

This paper is called 'Greylawn Baronial Letter Sheets'. How does Connolly like that?

I have lost all interest in book-collecting.

Love to Mark.[5]

Love. Come soon

Evelyn

[1]Waugh's name for Louise de Vilmorin, hence also for Vilmorin, the French seed and plant firm.
[2]Mark Sykes (1937–   ). Transferred from Eton to Downside.
[3]Janetta Woolley.
[4]Waugh's brother-in-law did not marry the Duchess of Devonshire's sister-in-law.
[5]Mark Ogilvie-Grant.

To Christopher Sykes   Piers Court
10 April [1953]

My Dear Christopher

Please convey to your son my warmest congratulations on his resuming his Christian education which was so rudely interrupted. I am sure that St Henry in heaven constantly prays for the rescue of the unhappy little victims of his perverted foundation, and that he is to be thanked for this triumph of Grace.

Did the boy get a leaving book?[1] If not I will repair the omission.

I hope he will come under the influence of Father Aelred Watkin.

I was glad also to learn that your brother Daniel[2] made his Easter devotions at Ampleforth with exemplary fervour.

You should have made the full Wednesday-Sunday stay at Downside. You would have seen Abbot Lucius[3] fall dead singing a ribald song and also met a convert man of letters[4] whose wife threw first his children & then herself out of a window.

I sought you in White's on Tuesday but found only Berners.

I see your forthcoming book announced as 'Two studies ...' Did Lady Chrysanthemum Paget lose her virtue?[5]

Your pretty young wife proposed herself to luncheon some months ago. We awaited her daily. Now the visit must be postponed until May when peace will be reestablished.

I go to Graham Greene's fourth first night on 16th. If you and p.y.w. are there, pray dine with Laura & me afterwards.

My cousin Agnes [Holmes] sends you her love (the lodging-house keeper of Stratton-on-the-Fosse).

Lord Revelstoke, whom I have never met, keeps sending me abusive & illiterate letters. Odd?

> Yours affec.
> E. Waugh

P.S. I have been elected an honorary Gregorian. [6] What is the tie? I must assume it as soon as I am out of mourning.

[1] Yes, he received the traditional parting gift from the school.
[2] Daniel Sykes (1916–67). An interior decorator.
[3] Abbot Lucius Graham died during dinner.
[4] Milton Waldman, historical writer.
[5] Sykes's *Two Studies in Virtue* (1953) was originally planned to include Lady Muriel Paget.
[6] Society of Old Downside boys.

To GRAHAM GREENE   The Travellers',
21 April [1953]   25 Avenue des Champs-Élysées,
       Paris

My Dear Graham
The play held me breathless. Your hospitality before & during the performance dulled my old nut a bit and I must return in very cold blood to enjoy much that I missed. All I was able to realize was that you had written a first class play & had been well advised in your choice of performers (except perhaps the priest – but no one can act priests). [1]

My warmest thanks & congratulations. There is a heat wave here. I am unsuitably dressed & feel swollen footed.

Do come & visit me whenever it suits you. I don't mean here – in England.

Messrs Mortimer & Sackville-West after the show were most enthusiastic. We vied in your praises.

> Yours ever affectionately
> Evelyn

[1] *The Living Room* was a success. Dorothy Tutin made her name, Eric Portman played the priest, and a lavatory was heard, but not seen.

To FATHER AELRED WATKIN [1]   Piers Court
1 May [1953]

Dear Fr Aelred
I am very sorry to say that my publisher does not think that your mother's charming memoir constitutes a publishable book. He will be writing to tell her so shortly. He let me read the manuscript and I am bound to say that I agree with him, though the tale is of haunting beauty & pathos. The character of Mme de Noailles is fascinating. I had the feeling that much more could have been made of your

grandfather. Perhaps pietas forbade it. His conversion alone is so odd & unexplained. Have you ever thought of rewriting it yourself? It needs so little to make it a work of the highest interest.

Alternatively, why does your mother not send it to Fr Caraman for publication as it stands in *The Month*?

Your mother writes charmingly but there is a lack of orderly structure which, in a very small book, is essential. The visual scene is not always precise. Jalabert [2] etc. need revivifying with a little research into their studios. I was unable to *see* the Yorkshire [3] house as I wished. The story falls between an autobiography of your mother & a biography of your grandmother in places. These are a few of the defects which I think could easily be altered by a male hand.

I read the manuscript aloud to Lady Diana Cooper (a good judge) who was fascinated but, like me, a little frustrated by it.

Yours very sincerely,
Evelyn Waugh

[1]Dom Aelred Watkin (1918–   ). Headmaster of Downside 1962–75. See note 1, page 461.
[2]Charles-François Jalabert (1819–1901). Painted Father Watkin's grandmother in Paris.
[3]Mistake for Norfolk.

To Alfred Duggan   Piers Court
7 May [1953]

Dear Alfred

I am greatly relieved by your letter. I feared that you had unearthed in the arcana of the *Universe* some damning evidence against me. [1]

I am very sorry to hear that your mother has had to undergo an operation. I did not see the announcement. I hope the burglars did not despoil Bodiam of all its treasures.

Much as I delight in *Lady for Ransome*, I shant be able to lecture on it in Buenos Aires. When I heard that they had destroyed their Jockey Club, I cancelled my lectures. [2]

The Coronation is indeed a great affliction. In our case particularly bitter. Having just got all the children off to school we expect them back in a few days, each with a schoolfellow whose parents live abroad.

... What a good idea to live in Hastings.

Love from
Evelyn

Your seconder at St James's, besides Lyttelton is Gabriels husband Alick Dru. He has attested that he has known you intimately for ten years. Please dont expose him.

[1]Duggan had inscribed his latest book, *The Lady for Ransom*, 'With the compliments of the author', which Waugh found cold.
[2]Plans for these lectures had been going on for six months. Waugh suggested 'Catholicism in England with special reference to Catholic writers', to be paid for by 'pocket money, wine and cigars'. They wanted several lectures and too much travelling.

To Margaret Waugh   [Piers Court.]
Whit Sunday [24 May] 1953

My Darling Margaret

Your last letter was a disgrace in many ways but I am not going to scold you at a distance. We will talk about it this time next week.

Meanwhile believe me I am very unhappy that you should be unhappy. I will try & find you another school. That will perhaps give you a new interest in school life.

I have given permission for you & Hatty to come back for the Coronation though this will mean a great deal of extra work here particularly for your mother who may have to go to London to meet you. I consider it very lazy of the nuns to have a holiday at all. The monks at Downside are more conscientious. The Ascot nuns are as lazy as yours. Teresa will be here with Annabel Hennessy.[1]

When we meet you must tell me whether you are really unhappy or merely giving way to a silly mood. I love you & will not let you be really unhappy if I can prevent it.

I had to go to London last week. The decorations are hideous, common and feeble. Perhaps they will be pretty at night when lit up. By day they are beastly.

I went yesterday to look at a school at Lechlade for you. It seemed less attractive than Les Oiseaux.

I really am very worried you should be unhappy, darling little girl.[2]

All my love
Papa

[1] Annabel Hennessy (1937–   ). Married Ian Chisholm in 1963. A school friend of Teresa's.
[2] Margaret stayed at home and was taught by Waugh for the rest of the term. Then she and Harriet were sent to St Mary's Convent, Ascot.

To Nancy Mitford   Piers Court
30 May [1953]

Darling Nancy

I dont believe I have written to you since our day at Versailles. I did enjoy that. It began my recuperation which was nearly completed by a day in bed overlooking the garden quad at the Ritz. Then the Norwiches returned & I have not been quite well since. Norwich was clearly heading for a breakdown. Poor Diana was morbidly restless and irascible. It is very odd her coming here for the Coronation. All the letters I get from London are written in despair. I spent a day there to sign the copies of my silly little story & took a cab down the main streets to see the decorations. They were abominable. The politicians have contrived to be both common & feeble in a unique degree.[1]

Dear dotty Debo tells me you are making her learn to read. Is that kind?

I read long articles about French politics. Pray tell me why I never see Col.'s name mentioned? I think he is pulling your leg when he tells you that he is a leading politician.

Even here the coronation has its horrors. I am giving a garden party to the Dursley Dramatic Society whose president I have been for 15 years without ever meeting one of them. The Stinchcombe Silver band will play throughout the afternoon. My fear is that they will think '5.30–7.30' means they are expected to stay two hours. There is not a single flower in the garden & the lawn-mower has developed engine trouble. I have asked the Vicar too. Oh God. Also I have all my daughters (& various friends of theirs whose parents live in Africa) on my hands again. We have killed a sheep & will eat roast mutton at every meal. I have Susan Mary[2] coming, which is nice for us – Gloucester Cathedral, Stanway, Stratford-on-Avon. I think you *should* go to New York. All I hate about it – the hot rooms, geniality etc. you would enjoy.

I always knew you were a Communist.[3] I do wish McCarthy would start his good work here on the Mountbattens and Day Lewis. Poor Frank Pakenham's book[4] is falling flat. They can't get anyone to review it because everyone loves him too much. I do hope your diagnosis of Diana[5] is correct. I feared real barminess.

I wish you had said you liked the illustrations of *Love Among The Ruins*. Perhaps you didn't.

I visited the Jungman sisters. Their condition of destitution & privation. though serious, has been greatly exaggerated. Very pretty little cottage, clean & sweet smelling, two sorts of jam (Tiptree) hot scones, plum cake, China tea, lilies-of-the-valley.

J.MacDougall is an Oxford chum who is now head of Chapman & Hall. The dedication[6] is a little joke on account of his now occupying my late father's chair. 'Nostri' may have foxed you. In that sense it means 'in our days'.

H.Buchanan has been most disloyal about *Love Among The Ruins*. McCarthy will get him soon if he doesnt watch out.

Love
E

[1]Lord Eccles was Minister of Works.

[2]Susan Mary Patten. Waugh met her in a Rolls Royce and wore white tie and decorations for dinner. Then he said she would make a speech: 'Mrs Patten was in Westminster Abbey watching the Queen's liege lords drop to one knee as they rendered homage to her.' She had not been in the Abbey but managed with what she had seen on television.

[3]Nancy had written: 'They wanted me to go to America with *The Little Hut* but I said I was a Communist before the war and that made it quite all right not to go. Wasn't it a brainwave, Prod thought of it.'

[4]*Born to Believe,* an autobiography, 1953.

[5]Nancy Mitford had described Lady Diana Cooper as 'worried out of her mind'.

[6]Johanni McDougall
    Amico
  Qui nostri sedet in
    loco parentis

To Graham Greene   Piers Court
5 June [1953]

Dear Graham

My greetings to you in Albany. You & Mr Priestly & Miss Sterne[1] should have some profound talks in the rope walk.

My great thanks for *The Living Room*. I bought a copy & have read it with close attention reliving the excitement of the first night. The suicide is much more real to me now. In my champagne-dulled mind I got the impression that the young lady took two pills & fell dead like Goering.

I am dazzled but not a bit surprised by your mastery of your new art.

May I make one criticism. The old ladies did not seem to me Catholic. Of course the Church abounds in dotty & disagreeable spinsters, but I thought that pair much more like Christian Scientists or members of some odd sect. The atmosphere was more that of Strindberg or Ibsen. Is it possible that you conceived of them as protestant & then thought it would be rather unsporting to hold up protestants to odium & contempt? I don't see how one could be a Catholic, however dotty, and nurse that fear of death.

Love among the Ruins was a bit of nonsense begun 3 years ago & hastily finished & injudiciously published. But I don't think it quite as bad as most reviewers do.

Love from
Evelyn

[1]Probably G.B. Stern (1890–1973). Novelist and Hollywood script writer.

TO CHRISTOPHER SYKES   Piers Court
[11 June 1953]
Postcard

Did the well-chosen, perfectly spelt words in the Pryce-Jones Gazette fall from your golden pen?[1] If so pray accept my thanks. I have been much upset by violent & inaccurate abuse in the Beaverbrook press and it is balm where balm was needed, to read the *Literary Supplement*. I passed through London yesterday. No sign of Quennell but [Alastair] Forbes literarily everywhere.

E

[1]Christopher Sykes had written a friendly review of *Love Among the Ruins* in *The Times Literary Supplement*, edited 1948–59 by Alan Pryce-Jones.

TO RANDOLPH CHURCHILL   Piers Court
4 July 1953

Dear Randolph

I do not think you have chosen a subject[1] well suited to your genius. You have no appreciation of architectural beauty or of the paintings & decorations & treasures which enhance it.

The only family with whose history I have any familiarity is the Herberts and I have supplied a few corrections to your account of them.

I do not know what reader you seek to interest. Certainly not the specialist or the amateur.

Forgive my bluntness. This is not your proper work. You need hot, whisky-laden, contemporary breath, the telephone, the latest gossip, the tang of the New World, to bring out what is lively in you. History & Culture are for gentler creatures.

It is most kind of you to invite me to your new home. If my preceding comments have not caused deathless offence, I will come with great pleasure. Would early August be suitable?

Momo [Marriott] gave me the best dinner I ever ate on the evening of Lord Kinross's party. The company later was varied, distinguished, gay, elderly. The only undesirable intellectual I saw was Henry Yorke.

My regards to June & my condolences at the shame she must feel at seeing her daughter's photograph in the papers.

> Yours ever affectionately
> Evelyn

[1] *Fifteen Famous English Homes.*

To Christopher Sykes
[6 July 1953]
Postcard

I don't know this Quennell personally. I am told he is a very deserving young man with a ginger beard and one leg. He lost the other parachuting into France with Basil Bennett. Were you at pauper's party? A great number of people were there such as General Sir J. Marriott,[1] Lord Faringdon, T. Driberg and all that set. Next day I saw the most extraordinary man named SYLVESTER[2] and cannot get him out of my dreams night or day. He was an art-critic & looked like an American soldier of the most alarming kind.

[1] Major General Sir John Marriott, born in 1895. Served in Middle East 1940–2, when his house in Cairo was a social centre for, among others, Waugh and Christopher Sykes.

[2] David Sylvester, the art critic. At this time he used to wear a US army combat jacket bought at a surplus store in Paris.

To Nancy Mitford   Piers Court
8 July [1953]

Darling Nancy

You do not understand the meaning of the word 'eke'. It means to make something last longer by adding something else to it. Eg. eke out butter with margarine. When you write: 'I might as well eke out the month in London as anywhere else', you commit a gross vulgarism. But I am glad you are coming to

England to polish up your English. You may fall into poor Harolds[1] pit of having no language. Of course we will meet. You would be very welcome here if you can bear a host of children. I have no summer plans, have been in a lethargy, no work done & publisher fretting. Soon I must concentrate if I still can.

Susan Mary was a tough & appreciative little guest on whom I spend great trouble & money. She enjoyed herself no end.

I do congratulate you on having finished your work. Mine is all before me.

Old Driberg came here last Sunday, very fat & sinister & gave me a repulsive book he has written in praise of himself named (believe it or not) *The Best of Both Worlds*. Much worse than Pakenham's.

Patrick Balfour gave a party last week – real old Bohemia & everywhere I moved I found rakes & wantons of the 20s gravely discussing child welfare & education.

I am sorry but not surprised to learn that your campaign to teach Debo to read has come to nothing. I am engaged on the same task with my daughter Margaret. They should be caught young.

I forget, are you obsessed by Ruskin as I am? There is a beautiful little book of his last (unpublished hitherto) love letters, just out.

You should safeguard your investments with Cpl Hill[2] by forbidding his assistant from advising customers *not* to buy books. He is doing this with my last novelette. Great cheek and bad business.

> Love from
> Evelyn

[1] Acton.
[2] Nancy Mitford had put £3,000 into Heywood Hill's bookshop in 1945.

To RANDOLPH CHURCHILL   Piers Court.
21 July 1953
Postcard

I have just learned the alarming news that Norwich is to be of your party next Sunday. Please believe that it is not only fear of infection that makes me ask you to excuse me. I find him so impolite that I really can't sit at table with him.

May we revert to our original plan – an outing for Bron & Winston & bring them together after the 19th August.

To RANDOLPH CHURCHILL   Piers Court.
27 July [1953]

Dear Randolph

I am sincerely sorry if my defection has disturbed your plans for the week-end. I cannot think that your other guests will be sorry. Cooper I have never tolerated except for his enchanting wife. In later years he has given up any pretence of tolerating me. My last visit to him was the occasion of his going too far. The Polish nobleman I barely know.

I must go to London on August 5th for Belloc's Requiem – shall console myself at the bar of White's (if open). If by any chance you happen to be in London that day, please give me the chance of seeing you.[1]

Yours ever affec.

Evelyn

[1]Churchill showed this letter to Lord Norwich, who wrote to Waugh. Lady Diana, uninformed, wrote on 29 July: 'Duff has a well known weakness of uncontrolled rudeness. We all have grave weaknesses – Baby's [i.e., her own] is melancholia and cowardice. You have some too. ... But since recriminations are the note neither B nor D would have told all and sundry that their hosts were trying to poison them in both town and country. She will not write again – it's too painful to face the leaden answers devoid of understanding and love.' On 2 August she wrote: 'What is this I hear that you chucked Randy because Duff was of the company? It's hard to believe. ... You must not lose friends so deliberately. You'll find it hard to lose me — you've tried – but it's possible to succeed, tho' I should be miserable.'

TO DAPHNE FIELDING[1]   Piers Court
30 July [1953]

Sweet Mrs Fry-me or Fritter-my-wig,

I shall love you till death under whatever name you choose & whatever colour you paint yourself. I must admit to a preference for the red blotches on white as that is my own colour scheme after half a glass of welfare gin. I will try & get one of those electric freckling machines to prepare for our next meeting.

Thirteen years ago to the day I was busy making Cornwall safe for democracy. A beast called Capt. Digby-Bell, Royal Marines, had Looe & destroyed most of its amenities. I dug up the Armada beacon near the Eliots' bathing hut. They minded *awfully*. I lived in a hideous brick hotel half way down the cliffs – cant remember its name – and found eight pairs of scissors under the sofa cushions. A great bomb fell quite near. Can't remember Plaidy. There was a very pretty derelict Gothic house on my company front. Is that it?

The beard[2] was designed for Mrs Eden.

All love

Evelyn

[1]Daphne Vivian's marriage to the Marquess of Bath had been dissolved and she had married Xan Fielding that year.

[2]In an illustration to *Love Among The Ruins*.

TO ANN FLEMING   Piers Court
[August? 1953]

Dearest Ann

What fun your luncheon was. Ronnie Knox was greatly exhilarated by his dip into a strange world & loved you all, you especially.

For the last three weeks I have been undergoing a cure for obesity (plain starvation without medical or pharmaceutical aid) and am now light as a feather and feeble as tissue paper. My clothes hang round me like classical draperies.

The day after your party I met R.S. Churchill and was so full of kind feeling and self-reproach for ever being such an ass as to write to *him* indiscreetly, that I greeted him with my old affection. He replied with hectoring complaints of my chucking his party. That was too much for my rare mood of charity. Every year, I suppose, for uncounted years I have resolved to avoid him. I always made it up, so I suppose I shall do so again. At the moment I dont feel like it.

A propos of that incident, I don't think I made it clear that 'never tolerated Norwich' was used in a second letter, replying to his idiotic complaint that his party had been arranged 'for' me. I didn't say N was intolerable. Merely that he was only tolerable for his wife. And God knows I have had to tolerate a lot in the last 23 years. I have never been alone with him for 5 minutes by my own wish.

My nose is very out of joint with little Margaret. She shows a marked preference for the company of her brothers, sisters & cousins. So I have sent her to Pixton and am alone & loveless & cheerless here.

What a queer treat Ian has had underground. [1] I was obsessed by the *Journey to the Centre of the Earth* when I was younger and was always being hauled out of rabbit holes by my heels.

I made it up with two old cronies – Yorke & Woodruff, (neither, I think in your life at all) – while I was in London, so I am one up on the year so far.

I do hope, tho I suppose it is past hoping, that the *Kinsey Report* on American women's nasty ways is a complete flop over here. I shouldn't be surprised if it does not draw off the McCarthy hounds into pursuit of female masturbators and a great new purge of the State Department and of all their recent fiction.

Never an hour passes but I think of Sylvester. My hunger makes it worse.

Do write me a consoling & informative letter.

Love from
Evelyn

[1] The Flemings had been to the Pyrenees where Ian had explored caves.

To J. Weltman   Piers Court
2 September 1953

Dear Sir,

In answer to your letter 04/SB/JW:

I have instructed my agent to discuss with you the fee for my appearance in *Frankly Speaking*.

I have not had the pleasure of hearing any of these performances. Could you be so kind as to tell me the next date when I can do so? This would give me a clearer idea of the services you require. I am prepared, provided the fee is adequate, to answer any number of reasonable questions on general subjects. I do not think I have the necessary talents to give the impression that I am taking part in a three-cornered intimate chat with personal friends, with the bandying about of Christian names and so forth, of the kind which deeply shocks me in some of the performances I have sometimes begun to hear.

Two or three years ago I spoke on the wireless in London and the fee for 'expenses' fell short of the money actually spent on the expedition. I was then told that this fee was decided by some unalterable law. I trust this has now been changed?[1]

I am,

Yours faithfully,
Evelyn Waugh

[1]Waugh appeared on *Frankly Speaking* on 16 November 1953. Christopher Sykes found it 'like watching inexperienced toreadors taking on a bull who knew all the tricks of the ring. They were gravely horned.'

TO NANCY MITFORD   Piers Court
17 September 1953

Darling Nancy

What a strange girl you are. Your magnum opus finished and you are not elated? Would to God mine were. No need of money? My children starve & my clothes fall in rags about me. You should be dancing in the streets not sprawling in the sun. The sun is the great enemy of the human race. In civilized times everyone hid from it. O yes, I know, you will tell me that Louis XIV lay naked on the roof of Versailles surrounded by naked cardinals & duchesses and I shan't believe you.

I cant think what you mean by my 'quarrel with Duff'. I am on terms of tender intimacy with him.[1]

What do you know of Belgium? I am thinking of taking Laura there for her harvest-home treat. Am I right in thinking that the Belgians are still well disposed to the English? There are few places where an Englishman can now set foot without being stoned. It is true that the Belgians behaved disgracefully to their King. Apart from that I know nothing against them. They have some fine pictures have they not?

I am reading an enormous life of Dickens[2], by an American professor of course, which gives details of every chop he ever ate & every speech at every public banquet. Did you know that he was a perfectly awful man?

School holidays have been agonising but are at last bit by bit coming to an end.

I am *much* thinner than when you last saw me. Really rather pretty.

Love
E

[1]The row had ended. Lord Norwich wrote an icy letter on 4 September in answer to Waugh who had apparently written that he had only regarded himself as a guest of his when staying at the embassy in Paris; elsewhere presumably he felt himself to be the guest of Lady Diana. On 14 September Lord Norwich wrote a friendly letter thanking Waugh for and accepting his apology – 'I shall not mention it to any of those who have enjoyed our quarrel more, I suspect, than we have.'

[2]Edgar Johnson, *Charles Dickens*, 1953.

To John Betjeman   Piers Court
17 September 1953
Postcard

Thanks awfully for telegram. I was reading a book by a professor which said that
Dickens stood dazzled by the gorgeous colours of the W sisters[1] and I remembered
them whitish but I remember everything wrong these days so I thought now I have
lost my reason indeed but your kind reply has comforted me. My memory is not at
all hazy – just sharp, detailed & dead wrong. This affliction leads me into countless
humiliations. Love E.

[1] Anna and Christiana Weller. Anna married Charles Dickens's brother.

To Teresa and Margaret Waugh   70 Rue Royale,
8 October [1953]   Bruxelles.

My Darling Daughters,
    Your mother and I are now staying with Mme Bisch[1] and the Donaldsons have
gone home. Mme Bisch's house is a fine example of the architecture of the epoch of
the Empress Maria Teresa; interior decoration by the Prince de Ligne 1806.
Unhappily since those days a tramway has been laid under its windows and the
noise is awful. But the cooking is splendid. Monsieur Bisch is a large, shy man.
    We had a very tiring day when we first crossed from Dover to Ostend, having left
home that morning. At the end of it we left the casino at about 1 o'clock & found that
a sea fog had come up & blotted out the lights. No taxis about. No one about. Mr
Donaldson confidently offered to show us the way. It was only about 500 yards from
the casino to our hotel but we wandered round & round in the fog for an hour, with
fog warnings of all kinds – bells, maroons, hooters coming from the sea – until I very
cleverly found a doctor who had a light in his house, and he directed us to our hotel.
It was almost next door to him.
    The Donaldsons ate enormously. I never saw a man (except Randolph Churchill)
eat so much as Mr Donaldson – all the richest dishes, but with no ill effects.
    We stayed at Bruges to see the Flemish paintings & sent you postcards from there.
Then we had a night in an hotel in Brussels & your mother was robbed by a hairdresser of her purse and a large sum of money.
    Mme Bisch sends her regards to Tess.
    We shall soon return home as everything is so expensive here that we shall run
out of money.

                                                                    Your loving papa
                                                                         E.W.

[1] Madame Bisch writes novels, admired by Waugh, under the name Edith de Born.

To NANCY MITFORD   Piers Court
22 October 1953

Darling Nancy,

I find Lord Montgomery's courtship[1] very odd & rather nasty. I have always heard the worst accounts of him. I suppose that his charm for you is the contempt of the Americans. We thought him a whipper snapper who did down good Lord Alexander[2] by sucking up to journalists & politicians. There must be some secret & disgusting reason for his washing his own shirts. How, pray, did you come to see his bedside?

God alone (literally) knows what is happening in the French Church. The Dominicans all seem mad bad & dangerous to know. All this devotion to Miss [Simone] Weil. As far as I can make out there are two quite different kinds of prêtre ouvrier. There are simple missionaries who sometimes go native and contemplatives who find the conveyer belt conducive to prayer. *Tablet* address is 128 Sloane Street. Subscription 42/- at home or abroad. There is usually at least one readable article a week. The literary part is bad because no publishers send them books to review. It is not a sin to cheat over taxes in most modern states. Don't worry your head about the theology of this. Just take it from the theologians. It is not true that any Catholic thinks the poor go to a servants' hall in heaven. Read Bossuet's great sermon on the Eminent Dignity of the Poor. Also Gospels. Dives & Lazarus. It shows the sort of pipsqueak Ld Montgomery is that he puts these ideas into your puzzled nut. I wish Senator McCarthy would grill Lord Montgomery and expose his communism.

Belgium was very restful for Laura after harvest & holidays and very expensive for me. Much worse than France. Cheapest wine £1 a bottle in restaurants. The natives talk a queer gibberish but look *good*. I dont mean pretty, but virtuous. Brussels was full of undesirable Britons such as Gaitskell[3] and Hugh Fraser.[4] There was a man called Peter Ustinov[5] who was *very* funny – like John Sutro at his old best. Magnificent pictures everywhere. We spent most of the time in Antwerp. Excellent cooking. Half a dozen splendid churches all oddly enough in the quartier toléré. I have never seen a quarter like it in Europe. The girls are exposed in shop windows and leap about like monkeys to attract attention. And all the good middle-class families troop to church through these streets with their eyes downcast.

Wiertz[6] was rather a disappointment. I had heard so much about him but his painting isn't good enough. Better in photographs. Younger Breughel stupendously good. Oh how bored one gets with Temptations of St Anthony with devils blowing trumpets from their behinds.

Have you heard of the lady who writes under the name of Edith de Born – an austrian-hungarian-jewess I suspect – married to a French banker called Bisch? She writes in English quite beautifully. *Daughter of the House* etc. We stayed with her in a fine house in their Park Lane in Brussels. I thought Bisch was Belgian until the last day and dropped brick after brick. No possible way out & back from a gaffe as big as that. Telling him patronizingly how well the Congo was run compared with Algeria – that sort of brick.

What has happened to Prod? I never hear of him now.

Poor Sir John Gielgud has had trouble with the police. Is a reception being arranged in Paris for Lord Montagu?[7]

Cooper's memoirs[8] in *Sunday Times* are all an enemy could ask. But I am his friend now so I weep for him.

Now I put on my woollen underclothes & settle in for the winter to finish second vol of war novel.

If you listen to BBC *New Reading* on 25th you will hear a bit cribbed from *Highland Fling.*[9]

Do you *dread* the publication of *Pompadour*?

Reviewers wont let you change subjects except T.S. Eliot whose subjects were so obscure. But no one pays attention to reviewers now – which is rather a bad thing really.

Much love
E

[1]Nancy Mitford had lunched with Field Marshal Montgomery and reported: 'All my books by his bed and when he gets to a daring passage he washes it down with Deuteronomy.'

[2]Field Marshal Alexander (1891–1969). Commander-in-Chief in North Africa, when Montgomery, who was in command of the 8th Army, received more acclaim.

[3]Hugh Gaitskell (1906–63). Leader of the Labour Party 1955–63.

[4]Hugh Fraser (1918–   ). Brother of Lord Lovat. Conservative MP since 1945. Married Lady Antonia Pakenham in 1956.

[5]Peter Ustinov (1921–   ). Actor and writer.

[6]Antoine Wiertz (1805–65). Portrait painter.

[7]Lord Montagu went to prison for homosexual offences. Sir John Gielgud was fined for importuning.

[8]*Old Men Forget* by Duff Cooper, 1953.

[9]The scenes on the Isle of Mugg from *Men at Arms*.

To F. Leon Shipley — Piers Court
7 November 1953

Dear Sir,

Thank you for your letter 08/SE/FLS of 5th November.

I find it difficult to believe that a 'profile' of myself, however rosy, would calm the anti-English frenzy of the Italian people. However you are the judge of that.

In the last month I have recorded an interview for your colleagues in Baker Street to be used, I believe, on Orientals; also an interview at Broadcasting House to be used on the English. Would these records not suffice?

If however, you need more information, send a young man with three five pound notes in his hand to the Hyde Park Hotel at 11 o'clock on Wednesday morning next, 11th November.

Please confirm this appointment by letter to that hotel not later than Tuesday afternoon. [1]

Yours faithfully,
Evelyn Waugh

[1]On the letter is written: 'Fee unusual. 10 guineas for an hour, not in notes. No good.'

To Graham Greene   Piers Court
[12 November 1953]
Postcard

Personal & urgent. Please forward

I have just learned a most disturbing thing. Perry Mason is a Free Mason (*Case of the Dangerous Dowager*). [1]

E

[1]By Erle Stanley Gardner, 1937.

To Reynolds Stone [1]   Piers Court
24 November [1953]

Dear Reynolds

I am very sorry you were 'dismayed' when I found the letter heading too small. I had given you the desired dimensions, you know, in writing, with the request, also, that the block should include a scroll of lettering. I think the block prettier than ever since you have worked on it, but I am afraid it does not fulfil specifications. I had in mind something like the hotel and tradesmen's (and occasional private house) headings in common use in happier days.

It is very nice of you to suggest coming here. You (and of course your wife too if she can come) will be very welcome. But don't come now. The house is deadly cold and the aspect depressing. Do come in the Spring. I hope Dorchester is softer.

I have been given a superb washhandstand designed by William Burges for Lord Bute 1865 with painted panels by Poynter, which I believe you would enjoy.

Yours sincerely
Evelyn Waugh

[1]Reynolds Stone (1909–79). Designer and engraver, responsible for the £5 and £10 notes of 1956. He had been working on a letterhead from Waugh's detailed instruction from before April 1953.

To the Editor of the Daily Mail   St James's Club
Tuesday 24 November 1953

P.G. WODEHOUSE

Mr Iddon asks the question: "Remember Wodehouse?" (*Daily Mail*, November 11). The answer from all lovers of fine writing is: Yes. We await each new book with eagerness and constantly re-read the splendid collection of his life's work.

Mr Iddon further says: "I still have a letter of 'explanation' from him in my files." I presume this refers to his completely satisfactory answer to the attacks made on his honour during the war. Mr Iddon's use of inverted commas seems to suggest that the explanation is in some way suspect, but since it has now been made public and is no longer hidden in Mr Iddon's files, this sneer, if sneer is intended, is worthless.

Now that Mr Wodehouse has at last published the true facts of the case, it would be seemly if the B.B.C. invited the originator of their war-time attack to make an apology to one of the most brilliant of living English stylists. [1]

Evelyn Waugh

[1] P.G.Wodehouse thanked Waugh for writing this letter.

To Cyril Connolly   Piers Court
9 December [1953]

My Dear Cyril

Thank you very much for my fiftieth birthday present. [1] It was too self-effacing of you to refrain from inscribing it. No doubt you thought I would pass it on as a handsome Christmas present to an aunt. Not at all. I have stuck a book-plate in it & put it in my shelves to read on my 60th birthday when I hope a golden haze will cover its decade. 'Golden' I am sure was Mr Weidenfeld's [2] epithet not yours. Pink, grey, yellow occasionally silver, yes but not then or now golden surely?

I always enjoyed the magazine & was grateful to you for printing my work in it, but there was an ugly accent – RAF pansy – which kept breaking in; not indeed from you but from your artless colleagues. That spoiled the enterprise for me. I see from the 'contents' that you have bravely retained the full flavour: By 1963 I daresay it will have become hallowed. Not yet. 'Modern' has always had a pejorative sense in English. *Horizon* was the last (and first considerable) attempt to give it attraction.

I deeply wish that I saw you more often. Why are you always in such a bustle in White's, the last refuge of leisure? Is it because you have given up cigars? Those teats compel an hours repose. They change the pace of one's breathing too and act as a yoga exercise producing calm.

I work away at my brewery. Another cask of. ... [incomplete]

[1] *The Golden Horizon*, edited and introduced by Cyril Connolly.
[2] George Weidenfeld (1919–   ). Publisher. Chairman of Weidenfeld and Nicolson from 1948. Created life peer 1976.

To Nancy Mitford   Piers Court
11 December [1953]

Darling Nancy

.... Christopher [Sykes] is a mystery. I haven't seen him for more than a year
though I have made repeated loving attempts to meet him. Always rebuffed or
chucked at the last moment. I fear something is amiss. I daresay connected with that
son whom he adores & the shadow of Daniel.[1] But I am more alarmed still by
Randolph who I fear will be in a strait-jacket quite soon.

My broadcast was pretty dull. They tried to make a fool of me & I don't believe
they entirely succeeded.

I am stuck in my book from sheer boredom. I know what to write but just cant
make the effort to write it.

Best news of the week is that Trevor-Roper, the demon don, has written an article
with four historical errors in the first three lines[2].

Curious case of 'Experiment with Time'. I sat next to Maurice [Bowra] at dinner.
He (and I) praised the Ashmolean. He raised subject of Arthur Hughes's *Return
from Sea*. He said: 'I hear there is a version of it with a second figure, a sister's,
sitting by the boy's side.' Self: 'That's the only version I know. Isn't that the one in
the Ashmolean?' 'No, no, old boy. Do find out for me where the other is'. I looked it
up in my library. Sure enough, Ashmolean version contains sister. I investigate
further & learn that when first exhibited the picture contained only boy. It failed to
sell so Hughes painted in sister to add pathos. No living human eye, except Sir
Maurice, has seen original version. It may be prevision of what will happen when
Sir K. Clark[3] gets to work with his vitriol & wire brush removing what he calls 'over-
painting'.

See how *I* praise Sykes[4].

Love
E

[1]Christopher Sykes's brother.
[2]The resulting correspondence is in the Appendix on page 641.
[3]Kenneth Clark (1903–   ). Art historian. Created life peer 1969. Director of National Gallery
1934–45, presenter of television series *Civilization*, 1969.
[4]Waugh had reviewed Sykes's *A Song of a Shirt* warmly in *Time and Tide* December 1953.

To Christopher Sykes
11 December [1953]

Dear Miss Quennell

Would you be so kind as to put this in Mr Sykes's Christmas stocking.

What a sad season this must be for your cousin Peter! – but I suppose all seasons
are sad for him really. At any rate they fucking well ought to be.

Yours truly
Evelyn Waugh

To Lord Kinross   Piers Court
[1953]
Postcard

Sorry to be a bore. The Betjeman Benefaction [1] has arrived minus an essential organ
– the serpentine bronze pipe which led from the dragons mouth to the basin. I am
making a row with Pickfords. Can you testify that it left your house intact? Oh the
hell of Christmas cards. How lucky to be genuinely Scottish – or has this beastly
custom spread north?

Happy hogmanay
E

[1] The Burges wash-hand stand.

To Cyril Connolly   Piers Court
20 December [1953]

Dear Cyril

I saw the parcel with Chapman & Hall's label & thought 'Six copies of *Vile Bodies*
in Finnish'. It was a huge delight to uncover the rare & lovely edition of Prudentius.
Jesuit edited, too. He is not a poet they taught me to read at Lancing. Lately I have
been remotely aware of his existence as someone who was a natural friend whom I
had never met. Now I shall start the new year with the firm intention of doing a
regular construe, with the certainty of enjoyment. I am deeply touched by the gift.

I have been pleased to see from the reviews that few people shared my slight
distaste for *Horizon*. You must be pleased, are you not, by the high praise in high
quarters which your anthology has won. I am sure it must be a fault in me, not in
the book – yet when I see 'greatness' applied to Klee I am dumbfounded.

I liked your article on restaurants. I think you put too much blame on the
Americans. For example in furniture & decorations the French have the lowest
taste. Those old fashioned restaurants were agreeable only because of their
proprietors' parsimony. When the French decide to 'do over' a restaurant they
make a hell of it, while the Bel Air in Holywood, Pavilion in New York, Colony etc
are very pretty & comfortable.

I wish you would write something which Michelin would notice, about the need
for listing restaurants which play wireless. Two thirds of the best provincial
restaurants (I don't mean the celebrated international ones but the three star houses
which were so fine in our youth) have a continuous blare. And that is from the
French taste, not the Americans. I have had constant rows with native motorists
when I have turned it off.

All Christmas goodwill to you

Evelyn

To John Betjeman   Piers Court
29 December [1953]

Dear John

The trouble with [Reynolds] Stone is he cant draw. He engraves & writes very prettily.

I am very sorry to learn of Penelopes accidents & diseases.

Re your Great Benefaction. Patrick has kindly torn out part of his water closet & sent it to me. The missing organ is something quite other – either a hallucination of mine or an act of theft on the part of one of his bohemian friends. As I remember the G.B. there was an ornamental bronze pipe which led from the dragons mouth to the bowl below.

See over page [Drawing].

Did I dream this or did it exist.[1] The hydraulics of the piece are fascinating. The tank now empties itself into the bowl from an aperture (mouth of bearded face – a wind?) in the bowl itself. The cistern shows an aperture which should lead to dragons mouth. Was there some division of hot & cold?

The piece looks very splendid against the green red & gold wall paper (discovered by you).

Sad about Haselden's death.[2] I thought he would see us out.

Oh yes go to the Holy Land. It is lovely. The American treasury has fine 18th century objets d'art which many pilgrims miss. The Church of the Holy Sepulchre is bound to fall down in a few days so go there quick.

Love
Evelyn

[1] It did not exist, it *was* an hallucination – the first sign of his impending ordeal.
[2] W.K. Haselden (1872–1953). He did humorous drawings for *Punch* and the *Daily Mirror*.

To Margaret Waugh   Piers Court
[January 1954]

Sweet Meg

Oh I have been ill since you left. First a cold & then agonising rheumatism. So I am jumping into the first available ship. She goes to Ceylon. I shant come back until I have finished my book[1] but I hope I shall do that on the voyage. The sad thing is that I booked my passage before I realised that I should be arriving there during the Queen's visit when everything will be noisy & expensive. I will see the Buddha's tooth which she isn't allowed to see.

It is no good hoping for a letter for a long time as I shall be going away & the letter will have to come all the way back.

All my love to you
Papa

[1] *Officers and Gentlemen*, 1955.

To LAURA WAUGH   Cape St Vincent.
3 February [1954]

Darling, I wish you were with me. I think I shall come quickly when I reach
Kandy. My rheumatism is much better – quite tolerable. It is Feb 3rd and we are
not yet in the Mediterranean. My nut is clearing but feeble. It is plain that I had
been accumulatively poisoning myself with chloral[1] in the last six months and
might easily have had a much longer spell of idleness than my present little trouble
will cause. I will come home and lead a luny bin life for a bit. It was at 50 that
Rossettis chloral taking involved him in attempted suicide, part blindness & part
paralysis. We will avoid all that. I find it hard to keep sentences connected even in a
letter like this. It is 3 nights now since I had the last dose of sleepers & have had little
continuous sleep as a result. That is why it is fortunate that I am absolutely alone I
mean alone from everyone & thing except you. When I wake up which I do 20 or 30
times a night I always turn to the other bed and am wretched you aren't there &
puzzled that you are not – odd since we usually have different rooms.

The ship is not luxurious & the diet would be meagre if one were hungrier. Pretty
empty and the passengers pleasant. The chief trouble is the noise of my cabin. All
the pipes and air shafts in the ship seem to run through them. To add to my
balminess there are intermittent bits of 3rd Programme talks played in private cabin
and two mentioned me very faintly and my p.m. [persecution mania] took it for
other passengers whispering about me. If a regular rural life out of doors doesn't
work the trick I'll see an alienist. But I want to be back with you now.

                                                        Evelyn

[1] For insomnia.

To LAURA WAUGH   Continental-Savoy Hotel,
8 February [1954]   Cairo.

Darling Laura

I got your two letters yesterday at Port Said. I cant express the elation I felt. I
have missed you terribly daily and am resolved never to go anywhere without you
again. Your prayers have been a great help in a difficult time. I must have been more
poisoned than I knew. Then when I was beginning to rally I found myself the victim
of an experiment in telepathy which made me think I really was going crazy. I will
tell you about it when I get home. It has made me more credulous about Tanker's
box.[1]

Now I am here waiting an aeroplane to Colombo. I am not going to attempt any
work there. The thing now is to recover health. We are not pressed for money & I
wont get in a fuss about work. Natural health first.

My heart bleeds for you in the bitter cold. I will come & share it with you soon. I
don't know what I wrote to you on the ship or even if I wrote at all. I was semi-
delirious most of the time so disregard whatever I wrote except my deep love. I am
sleeping rather better & quite naturally. Eating a little too which I couldn't do on the

ship. Hand is steady today and the malevolent telepathy broken for the first time – perhaps not permanently. Please don't be alarmed about the references to telepathy. I know it sounds like acute p.m. but it is real & true. A trick the existentialists invented – half mesmerism – which is most alarming when applied without warning or explanation to a sick man.

All my dearest love to you darling Laura. I will write from Colombo. Explain to the children that I haven't been well enough to write to them.

I shall fly back as soon as conditions sound better at home.

E

[1]Diana Oldridge, a neighbour, nicknamed 'Tanker' because she once said 'I just come tanking in'. She believed in 'the black box', a contraption which was supposed to cure both men and beasts from a distance if a sample of blood or hair were submitted. Many successes were reported.

To John Lehmann[1]   Continental-Savoy Hotel,
9 February 1954   Cairo.

Dear Mr Lehmann

Please forgive my delay in answering your letter of 27th.

Probably Peters has told you that I have been ill. I meant to congratulate you on your first number of the *London Magazine* which I enjoyed enormously.

I am hung up with the novel I was working on. I am delighted to hear that the opening amused you. The Mugg scenes have already been read on the wireless. I think this precludes printing. If you like to use the opening, you are welcome to it.[2] I think it should be prefaced by a note indicating that the book is held up & no date of publication certain.

I have not been well but hope to complete it in the summer.

Yours sincerely
Evelyn Waugh

[1]John Lehmann (1907–   ). Poet, publisher, and editor of the *London Magazine* 1954–61.
[2]'Apthorpe Placatus' appeared in the *London Magazine* in June.

To Laura Waugh   Galle Face Hotel,
12 February [1954]   Colombo.

My Darling

It is rather difficult to write to you because everything I say or think or read is read aloud by the group of psychologists whom I met in the ship. I hoped that they would lose this art after I went ashore but the artful creatures can communicate from many hundreds of miles away. Please don't think this is balmy. I should certainly have thought so three weeks ago, but it is a fact & therefore doesn't worry me particularly. All it means is that this trip has been a complete failure as far as settling down to work as we hoped. Also a failure as far as getting any pleasure from it. But it is a huge relief to realize that I am merely the victim of the malice of others, not mad myself as I really feared for a few days.

I must stay on at this island for a week or so & then will come back & no doubt I shall be able to find some rival telepathist who will teach me how to ward these people off.

It is really a very rum predicament. Dont worry darling & tell Tanker I now believe in her box

All love
E

To Laura Waugh   [Ceylon.]
16 February [1954]

Dearest

I passed through Kandy yesterday & got your letter telling me of the floods. My heart bled for you as the weather here is delicious. I will soon come home to share your hardships. As I explained work is impossible here.

I have had great fun sightseeing. Do you remember a nice little American who is director of the Museum of Modern Art in New York, called Monroe Wheeler. [1] We met him at Minnie Astor's. [2] I ran into him in Colombo & we went off together for a few days looking at ruins & calling on a most eccentric local painter who lived in a very clean house with dozens of cheerful pictures by himself – half folk-art, half Picasso. He had nothing in the house & had to send out for three cigarettes and a box of matches.

Now Wheeler & I have separated and I am in a cool hill resort, rather too cool, until Sunday when I return to Colombo.

The British Council for once have been most helpful and instead of cadging for cultural lectures have done practical acts of charity such as meeting me & getting me rooms & so forth.

I have written to the children today. The address I gave you in Colombo was a telegraphic code address. Use it in case of emergency. I dont think it is worth your while writing in answer to this as I hope to leave shortly.

As I write this I hear the odious voices of the psychologists repeating every word in my ear. As they are in Aden & I am here it is a more remarkable feat than Tanker's box. It is most putting off. You must realize that this is the reason for the rather cold tone of this letter.

All my love
E

[1] Monroe Wheeler (1900–   ). Director of Exhibitions at the Museum of Modern Art 1946–67.
[2] Mary Cushing married Vincent Astor in 1940 and later James Fosburgh.

To LAURA WAUGH   Grand Hotel,
18 February [1954]   Nuwara,
                                                        Eliya.

Darling Laura

I have just got your cable urging me to return.[1] I need no urging & will start for
home as soon as I can make arrangements. At the moment I am exiled from
Colombo on account of all the hotels being full. I go there the day after tomorrow.
Then I shall have to make arrangements about luggage & I think it would be civil to
stay a day or two after all the trouble the British Council have taken over me. I will
return by air. Of course the times of arrival are uncertain at this season but I will
cable the probable date as soon as I know it.

This is a chilly hill station – the only hotel where I can find rooms. Last night I
went to an Indian cinema. I saw the same film as I saw in Madura last year. Very odd
as these two cinemas are the only Indian ones I have ever been to.

I am still grossly afflicted by the psychologists. I think they can be better dealt
with from England.

All my love
Evelyn

[1]Laura had grown increasingly worried and had arranged to fly out with Jack Donaldson. Frances ·
Donaldson has written a detailed account of the episode in *Portrait of a Country Neighbour*, 1968. Waugh
flew home safely, still hearing voices. When Laura pointed out inconsistencies in his delusions, he
accepted them and saw first Father Caraman and then E.B. Strauss, a Roman Catholic psychoanalyst.
Chloral was banned and paraldchyde substituted. Waugh recovered immediately.

To NANCY MITFORD   Piers Court.
5 March 1954

Darling Nancy

Pompadour arrived yesterday morning & I have spent two days of enchantment
in reading it. Thank you so very much for such a lovely present. It is very seldom
that I have been so sorry to come to the end of a book.

I think you have managed your vast mass of material brilliantly. Never a dull page
& never a page that is not unmistakably your own. The quotations all fit into the
narrative most naturally & you bring a real sense of intimacy with the complicated
scene. I am sure you need have no fears about its success. It is very clever of your Mr
Hamish [Hamilton] to produce it so well at so modest a price. Beaton's drawings
always give me goose flesh but the wrapper is easily disposed of. Everything else
admirable.

It is very long since I wrote to you. I have been suffering from a sharp but brief
attack of insanity. My alienist thinks that it was due to excess of drugs not to any
constitutional defect. But it was alarming at the time. It caught me in solitude on
board ship going to Ceylon. A disastrous expedition.

So Père Couturier has joined Norwich[1] in purgatory. Which do you miss the more? Again, deepest thanks & deepest congratulations on Poisson[2].

Love
E

[1] Lord Norwich had died at the beginning of the year.
[2] *Madame de Pompadour* was née Poisson.

To Margaret Waugh   Piers Court
1st Sunday in Lent [7 March] 1954

Darling Meg

Thank you very much indeed for the charming poem which was delivered to me by the proud prefect Teresa. I hope she will not be too proud to take this letter back to you.

I am quite well now but it was sad being ill alone in a foreign country and I will never travel again without company. Perhaps when you are a proud prefect you will travel with me.

I was greatly amused to hear of the success of your play. I also hear that you used the most ruthless means to compel attendence at rehearsals. The plot seems to have changed a good deal during dramatization.

I bought an elephant's foot in Ceylon. It is coming back by sea. I had great difficulty in getting permission to export it. The Ministry of Wild Life wanted to know where the other three feet were. If it ever arrives I am going to use it as a waste paper basket.

Miss Hooper is very much upset to learn that she was mocked in the Ascot play. I wonder who told her. She says she will never allow you inside her great village hall.

I hope that you have given up swearing & smoking & drinking for Lent.

Your writing is much better. Mine is worse – trembling hand through old age.

All my love to you darling child
Papa

To Graham Greene   Piers Court
2 May 1954

Dear Graham

Since you showed me the Grand Inquisitors letter my indignation has waxed. It was as fatuous as unjust – a vile misreading of a noble book.[1]

Do you want any demonstration by the admirers of *The Power & The Glory?* I shall be delighted to take any part in it. I dont think that in your position I should (shall?) want anything of the kind. I know you have the best ecclesiastical advice. It seems to me, as a layman, that it is the business of the Inquisitors to make every move. You have not asked for an *imprimatur*. It is their business to propose detailed alterations & to make themselves ridiculous in doing so. They have taken 14 years to write their first letter. You should take 14 years to answer it.

But if you do feel that any public protest is needed, please count on me.

Yours ever
Evelyn

[1] *The Power and The Glory* had been condemned by Cardinal Pizzardo of the Holy Office. Greene made no changes, 'on the casuistical grounds that the affair was in the hands of my publisher'. It was allowed to drop.

To Nancy Mitford   Piers Court.
5 May 1954

Darling Nancy

My news are the great news that all my children have at last disappeared to their various places of education. My unhealthy affection for my second daughter has waned. I now dislike them all equally. Of children as of procreation – the pleasure momentary, the posture ridiculous, the expense damnable.

It is sad to read that Larue is shut. My newspaper this morning says you could eat eight courses there for 2,500 francs. I did not find it so on my last visit.

Your mad chums reference to U-address = P.Q.R.[1] must be a tease of Osbert [Sitwell] who has had to change his NOTE Paper from 'Renishaw Hall, Derbyshire' to R.H., Renishaw, Nr Sheffield'.

U speech is fast disappearing. An officer in the Blues was lately heard to order: 'Two beers,' in the anteroom at Windsor.

I look forward to the film of *Pompadour* with her & Louis going hand in hand to the guillotine.

I don't think you will find Moscow at all like New York. You will at any rate be safe from the impertinences of the natives. No telephones, invitations, philosophic speculation by taxi drivers and lift-men, interviewers, autograph collectors etc. which make New York hideous. You are being invited there simply to cheer up the isolation of the diplomats & to tell them the gossip of the Free ha ha World.

What news of Honks? I hear the Sunday galas are in full swing again.

You know that poor Maureens daughter[2] made a runaway match with a terrible Yid? Well this T.Y. has painted a portrait of Ann Fleming with a tiara all askew obviously a memory of his mother in law. It is a very careful, detailed, neat picture not like some I could mention & that makes the tiara funnier.

So I had a very happy day in London with Cyril Boots (It is so unfair they have taken to calling a dreary politician 'Smarty Boots'[3]). He was in the uttermost abyss of melancholy. His Animal[4] has been sacked from the Zoo & sent home to Oak Cottage in disgrace. Not for the usual offence. She chewed her tail. Mrs Boots refuses to cook for him. He bought a silver knife, fork & spoon in a leather case to send to Lys.

Poignant. We went from shop to shop where Boots examined silk shirts & antique silver & complained bitterly that he could not afford to buy all he saw. I asked him why he always wears such horrible clothes and he said it was to spite Molly MacCarthy[5] who ruined his life 30 years ago by telling an admiral he (C.B.) was a bugger. 'I *had* a bowler hat,' he said, 'and an umbrella, and a top hat. I resolved never to use them again'. Later we were joined by Mrs Boots who had been changing her clothes in the loo at the Ritz. Suddenly Cyril could only talk classical Greek.

Have you heard about the 'Edwardians'?[6] They are gangs of proletarian louts who dress like Beaton with braided trousers & velvet collars & murder one another in 'Youth Centres'. Poor Cecil is always being stopped now by the police and searched for knuckle-dusters.

I hope you wont travel alone to Moscow. Since I lost my reason on the way to Ceylon I have a resolve never to move without an escort.

I saw Simon Elwes a lot at Downside at Easter. He lectured me on the importance of the artist representing the Zeitgeist. Hard words coming from him. Poor Christopher [Sykes] has Lady Russell[7] quartered on him for life.

All love
E

[1] A.S.C. Ross, Professor of Linguistics at the University of Birmingham, had told Nancy Mitford that the ideal upper-class address was 'P Q R where P is a place-name, Q a describer (manor, court, house etc). and R the name of a county'.

[2] Caroline Blackwood, daughter of the Marchioness of Dufferin and Ava, was married to the painter Lucian Freud 1953–7.

[3] Viscount Eccles (1904–   ). Conservative MP, then Minister of Education.

[4] A coati.

[5] Mary Warre-Cornish (1882–1953) married Desmond MacCarthy in 1906.

[6] More usually 'Teddy-boys'.

[7] His mother-in-law.

To Ann Fleming   Piers Court
Whit Monday [7 June 1954]

Dearest Ann

I am sorry you have lost your voice. It was a very agreeable one.

I read Ian's new book[1] & was moved to notice how fully he shares your marine interests.

How dare Mr Freud lecture to the young about 'Art' when he can't even put a tiara straight on a lay figure?

Was Sylvester the fat man dressed like an American soldier lunching in the Cromwell Road?

Bill Deakin is a very lovable & complicated man. He can't decide whether to be proud or ashamed of his collaboration with Tito. Quite right of Sir Maurice to give him a hint.

Randolph & June turned up here yesterday in a decrepit taxi. (Has Randolph done a Bevan & lost his licence?) & whisked us off to Bath where they are buying an exquisite miniature palace. A fine staircase, a really splendid ball-room, a good secondary ball-room, two attics, terraces leading to a public cemetery. It will cost at least £5,000 each to furnish the ball-rooms at all adequately. JUNE MADE A JOKE very quick & to the point. After that she felt poorly.

I should love to lunch with you next week. I can't fix a day now because it depends on an Archbishop when I come to London. May I please telegraph to you soon and say either 15th, 16th or 17th?

What heaven for Mrs Eden to cancel her ghastly engagements. I hope it means she is cosseting an embryo.

> Love
> Evelyn

[1]Ian Fleming, *Live and Let Die*.

To Nancy Mitford   Piers Court
18 June 1954

Darling Nancy

I do hope that you are going to publish an essay telling us all about your experiences in Russia. Or are your lips sealed by your obligations to the Ambassador?[1] If so, please write for me and posterity in a long full letter.

Our news is that Lord Camrose has kicked the bucket.... There is much speculation about who will control the *Daily Telegraph*,[2] who will live at Hackwood, which Berries will at once divorce, which will bring into the open unsuitable wives and husbands hitherto kept in cellars & garrets. Lord C.'s last act was to give Pam the house he had taken for Randolph. Randolph has been peremptorily evicted & Pam is tearing out fine Queen Anne woodwork. Randolph is buying a palace in the outskirts of Bath. It comprises one really magnificent ball-room which cannot be suitably furnished for less than £10,000 one very fine secondary ball-room, which might be done for £5,000 and two attic bed-rooms which lack room for a pot. There is a noble terraced garden leading directly to a public cemetery.

Cecil Beaton has produced a curiously incompetent book.[3] You will be surprised to learn that you and I and Harold Acton & Oliver Messel[4] came from Oxford together & thenceforward lived in close intimacy with Loelia Ponsonby for whom we provided dance-bands, cabarets and practical-joke Art Exhibitions. You may also be surprised to learn that the great leaders of fashion were Alice Obolensky, Phillis de Janzé, Diana Vreeland[5] and Cecil's Aunt Effi[6] (a new character). There are gross historical misstatements on every page. I was asked to review it. It shows how I have softened since my lunacy, that I have refused. Ten years ago I should have romped into it.

Will you be coming to England at all? Perhaps for Fionn O'Neill's ball?[7] I like to go to one party a year and shall go to that. Do come. It will be all old fogies.

I long to write to *The Times* newspaper, which is full of laments for the dispersal of the Chatsworth treasure, to tell of Debo's aspirations with the india-rubber.[8] But I don't. Soft again you see.

Much love from
Evelyn

[1]William Hayter (1906–   ). Ambassador to USSR 1953–7. Warden of New College, Oxford, 1958–76. He asked Nancy Mitford not to publish anything. Her diary of the visit eventually appeared in *The Water Beetle*, 1962.

[2]Seymour Berry (1909–   ) succeeded as Viscount Camrose and became deputy chairman at the *Daily Telegraph*. His brother Michael Berry, later Lord Hartwell, succeeded Lord Camrose as chairman and editor-in-chief.

[3]Cecil Beaton, *The Glass of Fashion*.

[4]Oliver Messel (1904–78). Painter, decorator and theatrical designer. He was at the Slade School of Fine Art, not Oxford.

[5]Diana Vreeland (1924–   ). Fashion editor of *Harper's Bazaar* 1937–62, editor-in-chief of *Vogue* 1962–71.

[6]Jessie, the sister of Cecil Beaton's mother, married Colonel Pedro Suarez, Bolivian minister in London.

[7]Fionn O'Neill (1936–   ). The daughter of Ann Fleming by her first husband.

[8]Nancy pretended to think her sister emended the drawings at Chatsworth.

To Lady Mary Lygon   Piers Court
28 June [1954]

Darling Blondy

I am most distressed to hear you are ill. Is it your brilliant mind or your beautiful body that is affected? I lost my reason in February but got some of it back in March. I am terribly afraid that the coming eclipse of the sun may drive me mad again. You are too young to remember the previous occasions in 1652, 1715, 1724 and 1927. They were most alarming, particularly 1724, and my mother tells me 1598 was worse and that her mother had a miscarriage in 1424. Draw your curtains and on no account look out of the window.

Mr Beaton's book is a veritable congeries of factual error – Mme de Janzé's white colonel described as an Arabian Pasha[1], your aunt Loelia confused with her cousin Elizabeth Ponsonby[2], 'Lady Ripon, later Lady de Grey'[3], Oliver Messel at Oxford etc. etc. etc. A disgrace. He gave two balls in its honour. Most appropriate ha ha ha. I suppose he is unhinged by sexual excess.

Rose Cotterell's[4] wedding day is one of deep emotion for me. I was touched to learn she has taken the name of Evelyn. I shall cry a lot in solitude here.

I go to London for the day tomorrow to take an ArchBishop (RC) to luncheon with Dot [Viscountess Head]. Rum you will say. Well he wants Anthony to be his jagger. I wish I could come & see you with grapes & flowers & filthy stories but, alas,

I know I can't as it is SS. Peter & Paul so I have to go straight from Paddington to church, then straight to luncheon & then as straight as Dot's hospitality allows straight to Paddington again. But I think I shall be in London a week later for longer. May I come then?

Is it not very expensive in your bin?

E[dward] Tatham has stolen P. Thursby's wine shop. I am trying to write a book but the spelling is so difficult.

How very badly Sexy Beaton draws. Not like little Poll. I suppose his hand trembles from fucking so much.

I am very sorry you should have seen Mr Isherwood's book.[5] It deals with a very nasty subject. Your dear father would not have approved.

So Lady Curzon gave a guest luncheon to impress Alfred's [Duggan] American publisher and all she asked were old ladies who talked of nothing but what had Queen Mary done with the vase they gave her at Christmas 1915 and the publisher would have preferred young tarts I think. I was late, well 1.30 sharp, and cruelly beaten.

I planted 100 bulbs advertised in *The Times* newspaper as looking like an orchid, smelling like a tuberose and growing five feet high. 6 I have begun to come up. It is interesting because rabbits eat anything else & they will not touch these exotic blooms.

Now do not forget about this dangerous eclipse at lunch time on Wednesday. Try to be calm. Tell yourself it is all quite natural & that it will pass & that if you can get over this one you are safe until 1999 (August 11th). Let us spend that day together. I shall be rather old & therefore very nervous.

Fondest love
Bo

[1]Phillis de Janzé is said to have fallen in love with a pasha in Arabia.

[2]Loelia Duchess of Westminster is not necessarily confused with Waugh's friend, who became Mrs Dennis Pelly. Each has been described as a 'bright young thing'.

[3]Lady de Grey became Lady Ripon when her husband succeeded as marquess.

[4]Rose Evelyn Cotterell (1932–   ). Daughter of Lady Mary's sister Lady Lettice, she married Charles Hambro in 1954.

[5]*The World in the Evening.*

TO CHRISTOPHER SYKES   Piers Court
30 June [1954]
75% Eclipse of Sun.

Sir or Madam,

My Mr Peters has sold the broadcasting rights of one of my books to Mrs Bray. She says: 'Christopher Sykes will prepare the scripts himself and he does not anticipate that you will find it necessary to do any writing on them.'

I used to know this Mr Sykes. Indeed I held him in high esteem and tender affection. I introduced him to my wife and even asked him to stand sponsor at the baptism of my penultimate son. But of recent years this man has spurned all my friendly advances and eschewed my society in a manner which can only be explained by personal dislike. He is a capable fellow & quite able to do his work of adaptation without assistance. I know it would be highly embarrassing for him to renew an acquaintance he has been at pains to sever. He would fear that the reconciliation might be attributed to avarice and sloth – two qualities of which he was innocent in the years I knew him.

I am, Sir or Madam,

> Your obedient servant
> Obediah Catchieside
> (Late Maj. Gen.)

TO EDWARD SHEEHAN   Piers Court
6 August 1954

Dear Sir,

Thank you for your kind interest in me.

I suggest you change your plans slightly and come here on the fourteenth for the fête. You would find material for an article on a typically English rural event and you could be of great help to us.

We need men of resource to manage traffic, detect thieves, 'bark' at side shows, spend money, and judge children's sports. Also in the morning to help erect booths.

Have you any accomplishments other than writing – conjuring, ventriloquism, contortionism – that you would be willing to display? Can you draw lightning portraits? We can offer you a bed on the night of the fête and the remains of the refreshment tent. There will not be much luncheon or dinner for us that day. Plenty of wine, however, for willing helpers.

Perhaps you play the trumpet? The Stinchcombe Silver Band would welcome a solo while they rest.

Have you a motorcar or do you wish to be met at Stroud?

> Yours faithfully,
> Evelyn Waugh

Please post attached poster[1] in Grosvenor Square.

[1] Illustrated in *Evelyn Waugh and his World*, p. 212.

TO CHRISTOPHER SYKES   The Egyptian Hotels Ltd,
18 August 1954   Mena House Hotel Pyramids, Cairo.
                                  [Probably Piers Court]

Sir,

A lady calling herself Mrs Bray lately arrived at my hotel with an introduction from you in which, unless I misread it, you described her as a person of means.

She spent some time examining the bedrooms and the menu before deciding that she was unable to afford to stay here. Such enquiries are not uncommon in my trade. Usually the customer modestly leaves. This lady is still sitting in the vestibule loudly demanding to interview the proprietor.

Will you be so good as to direct her to a Youth Hostel where she will be more at home.

> Your Obedient servant,
> Obediah Wildblood (Proprietor)

TO NANCY MITFORD   [Piers Court]
15 September 1954

Darling Nancy

I have just returned home from a week in London where, – need I tell you? – ill-informed reports of your Balearic adventures are rife.[1]

I spent almost all the week sitting in White's with decrepit old cronies drinking too hard but it was a necessary relief from the endless school holidays. Now Downside has gone back and I have only my affectionate younger daughters at home so I can creep into convalescence.

Fond farewells with the Laycocks just off to Malta.[2] One dinner at Ann Fleming's where she had asked a great booby called Darwin[3] whom we mocked. Otherwise just Ed and Harry Stavordale and Ran & Randolph & Ali Mackintosh and Jack McDougall. I get no feminine company these days since poor Clarissa's awful misalliance and I miss it.

Sir Maurice Bowra has transferred his patronage from Pam to Ann. 'Mrs Fleming is aristocratic & corrupt. Lady Pamela is neither'.

You will have read Ed on Prod[4] no doubt. Not very good.

I long for you in November. I am sure you would not be comfortable here. I will come to London to see you.

It is not the English who make messes on the floor. It is their dogs. It is not always easy to distinguish I know but you must remember their habits from the days of your youth.

Graham Greene's letter[5] was fatuous and impertinent. He was tipsy when he wrote it at luncheon with some frogs & left it to them to translate & despatch. He is dead to shame in these matters. You will go to his play[6] in Paris?

> All love
> E.

[1] Nancy Mitford had been cruising on a yacht with Daisy Fellowes.
[2] Robert Laycock was Governor and Commander-in-Chief of Malta 1954–9.
[3] Sir Robin Darwin (1910–74). Painter and principal of the Royal College of Art 1948–67.
[4] *Sea Peace*, 1954, by Lord Stanley contains a chapter on Peter Rodd.
[5] An open letter to the Archbishop of Paris in *Le Figaro* attacking him for refusing to allow a priest to say prayers at the funeral of Colette. Greene comments: 'I was not tipsy with alcohol when I wrote the letter but tipsy with rage.'
[6] *The Living Room*.

To Teresa, Margaret and Harriet Waugh   Royal Crescent Hotel,
6 October [1954]   Brighton.

Darling Meg (and Tess & Hatty)

Thank you very much for your letter.

The congress of dipsomaniacs at Rheims was rather fatiguing.[1] They *were* fat. I was about the slimmest. Perhaps for that reason our kind French hosts (one of whom Princesse de Caraman-Chimay[2] is a cousin of sweet Annabel) thought we needed exercise. They took us for ten mile walks underground through the cellars. The finest is Pommery et Greno (*not* the finest wine) which consists of huge quarries made by the Romans and now linked together by passages, all cut deep in the chalk. A hundred years ago when M. Pommery married Miss Greno no one dared go near these caves as they were full of brigands & reputed witches.

Here is a programme of our jaunt and a list of guests. My friends marked with a cross.

Lord Sempill caused great surprise and pleasure (to the French) by arriving at the Cathedral for the dedication of the window in a kilt. When asked what he was he declared he was the ArchBishop's 'Gentiluomo' (Italian, I think, for valet). He insisted on standing with the ArchBishop throughout the ceremonies, taking snuff from a large gold snuff box with a great flourish of a lace handkerchief.

One day we had luncheon and the menu said 'Potée Champagnoise, Salade, Fromages, Dessert'. We did not know what 'Potée meant. We thought perhaps it was a misprint for 'Patée'. We sat down and were given a delicious soup. 'Oh, alas,' thought all the fat men, 'it is a misprint for "potage". We are going to have only soup & salad'. Goodness they were sad. Then the soup was removed and a second dish appeared consisting of all the ingredients of the soup – beef and pork & chicken & bacon & sausage.

Lord Wicklow looked more disreputable than ever. It was lucky that Lord Sempill was there in his kilt to restore the prestige of the British nobility.

I am sorry you are 7th in form. I am sorry you are a trouble to the Head Girl. I hope you are severely flogged.

Your affec. papa,
E.W.

[1]Waugh had attended celebrations to mark the restoration of Rheims Cathedral by the champagne manufacturers.
[2]The daughter of Lord Ernest Hennessy married in 1922 Prince Alphonse de Chimay.

To Graham Greene   Piers Court.
[October 1954]

Dear Graham

I am delighted about White's. It shows how high you stand that you have overcome the awful handicap of being proposed by Stokes[1] & me. I hope you have ordered high white collars, a hard hat, an umbrella, a tie pin, black brogues and all the other requisites.

It is a rule that letters to the newspapers may not be written on the club writing paper.

I wish we were to be in Jamaica together. I go in January for a month.

Punch has been banned at my daughters' school as a result of your harmful contribution.[2]

I was at Cambridge the other day and told some Catholic girls about your letter from the Inquisition condemning *Power & Glory*. I hope you don't think that this was a betrayal. *I think* you told me that you didn't mind as long as nothing appeared in print. Now I have cold feet. Was I all right?

Love
Evelyn

Need I say that the Cambridge Catholic girls were indignant?

[1]Richard Stokes (1897–1957). Labour MP 1938–57. Lord Privy Seal 1951.

[2]'Special Duties', in which a businessman discovers that his secretary, instead of visiting churches to gain indulgences on his behalf, has been spending her time with a lover.

To Joan Saunders[1]   Piers Court.
23 October 1954

Dear Mrs Saunders,

I come to you for medical advice.

My hero escapes from Crete (as many did) on June 1st 1941 in an open boat in company with a dozen others. They drift for a week before landing in Egypt suffering great privation, thirst, hunger, exposure. The hero is unconscious by the time he is brought ashore.

Could you please tell me in non-technical language what particular ills he would be suffering and what treatment (diet etc.) he would be given in hospital.

For the purpose of the story I wish him to receive a visitor within ten days of his reception and to be able to talk intelligently though feebly. His condition should be such that it is possible, by pulling strings, to have him invalided back to England leaving Egypt on or before June 23rd and to be fully recovered & passed fit for active service again after the six weeks circuitous voyage home.

Can you make this plausable for me? I would welcome details of hospital routine as seen by a patient in his condition.

Could you also, please, send me a copy of the *words* of Cole Porter's 'Night & Day'.

Yours sincerely
Evelyn Waugh

[1]This is an example of the sort of research Mrs Saunders often undertook for Waugh.

To Nancy Mitford   Piers Court.
23 October 1954

Darling Nancy
    ... More instruction please. What is the force of 'Cher Ami' as the start of a letter?
Is it more or less intimate than the use of a Christian name?
    Are the following expressions colloquial frog:— 'Comme vous êtes complètement
film star aujourd'hui'.
'Je crois bien' (I bet) 'que vous n'avez pas trouvé cela en Egypte'. 'Quel drôle de
panier' (What an amusing shopping basket). 'Enfin, madame, c'est génial'. (Well
that's brilliant of you.) Spoken by a smart Levantine woman – not high Parisian.
    Here is the *Punch* parody.[1] No good really.
    I do not think communists half-witted – merely very very wicked. The fact that
you approve the communist organised massacres after the 'Liberation' is plain
evidence of party direction, if not membership. I have in my possession a
photograph of you with Driberg in the days of the popular front. I am not sending it
to McCarthy bcause I love you. All your lovely dollars will stop flowing if the truth
comes out.
    It is indeed hard to think of novel plots for novels. You see nothing that happens
to one after the age of 40 makes any impression. My life ceased with the war. When I
have squeezed the last thousand words out of that period I shall have to cast back to
my still unravished boyhood.
    What do correct French catholics think of the Index? I was asked the other day &
couldn't answer. My impression is that those who are scrupulous at all are very
scrupulous. Right?
    I long for your visit to London. Don't spend every minute with Pam. I hope to
have finished my work in progress and to be in a jolly leisurely mood by mid
November.

                                                                Fondest love
                                                                     E.

    [1]'Pursuit of Fame', a parody of Nancy Mitford's writing by Julian Maclaren-Ross, *Punch*, 13 October
1954.

To Graham Greene   Piers Court.
SS Simon and Jude [28 October] 1954

Dear Graham
    Twenty One[1] came on my 51st birthday. I wish I had been able to give you half
as fine a present on yours. Thank you very much indeed.
    I am sorry you have dropped the West African beginning, which I thought had
some beautiful work in it. I'm glad you have introduced 'The Hint'. A fine story.

'Blue Film' is brilliant & beastly. I wish you didn't think 'destruction is a sort of creation'.

It is a great relief to hear you don't mind my mentioning you & the Inquisition at Cambridge. It was not part of my lecture. In question time a girl asked if I had ever had any trouble with Holy Office. I said no, but a friend had, and then blurted out your name. I wish you had heard the gasp of incredulous indignation from all those unpainted young persons. No 'passionate disloyalty' there.

I say, buy the White's uniform in one go. Otherwise you will be like that sad self-portrait of S.Butler – never the shoes and the shirt and the trousers all together. [2]

Love from
Evelyn

[1]Collection of stories by Graham Greene.
[2]In *The Way of All Flesh* by Samuel Butler.

To NANCY MITFORD   Piers Court.
16 November 1954

Darling Nancy

Very many thanks for your kind help with my frog dialogue. This book [*Officers and Gentlemen*] is done at last, posted off to the printer and not to be seen again until June. You will be able to sympathise with my sense of elation. It is short and funny & completes the story I began in *Men at Arms* which threatened to drag out to the grave.

Poor Prod is plainly awfully barmy. The only disquieting feature is that he can, I believe, sue as a pauper at the public expense, lose his case & leave Ed and me to pay our lawyers. It may be necessary to have him certified. Do you mind particularly? [1]

Lady Birkenhead [2] was here on Sunday full of the delights of Rue Monsieur. Have you been seeing Auberon Herbert, do I gather? How did you find him.

Daphne has written her memoirs. [3] Contrary to what one would have expected they are marred by discretion and good taste. The childhood part is admirable. The adult part is rather as though Lord Montgomery were to write his life and omit to mention that he ever served in the army.

When oh when do you come to London. Please let me know in good time.

All love
Evelyn

[1]Waugh had reviewed Lord Stanley's *Sea Peace*, an account of sailing expeditions on one of which Peter Rodd accompanied him. The main criticism of Rodd was that he was a bore.
[2]Sheila Berry (1913–   ). Writer. Sister of Michael Berry, later Lord Hartwell. Married the Earl of Birkenhead in 1935.
[3]Daphne Fielding, *Mercury Presides*, 1954.

To MARGARET WAUGH   Piers Court.
11 December 1954

Darling Meg

You have suffered under a grave injustice. I thought you had neglected to write to me. I find that the infamous Head Girl has been destroying your letters in the hope of supplanting you in my affections and inheriting a larger share of my fortune. Why, pray, do you not put your own letters into a separate envelope?

On Tuesday night your mother & I went to Mells for James's first communion. He looked very nice with a large white flower in his button-hole. We had a breakfast-feast. The little boy next to me, I could see from the corner of my eye, had a pile of loving letters from his brothers and sisters. Not so poor James. He came out to Mells for the day and cheated at Solitaire. It was an awfully cold wet day. That evening your mother & I went to London and next day to Granny Waugh's funeral. The day after, home.

Granny Waugh has left all of you a little token of her love, to you the Greek eikon (Greek for picture) of Our Lady that hung in her drawing-room. Do you remember it? To Harriet a cameo brooch and a needle work picture.

Granny Waugh's death was very peaceful. Mrs Yaxley found her dead in her chair after tea. I am afraid you will always remember her as very old & feeble. I wish you had known her when she was young and active. She loved all you children very much. You six were her chief interest in her last years.

I look forward greatly to your return, darling Meg.

                                                Your loving papa
                                                E.W.

To NANCY MITFORD   Piers Court.
18 December 1954

Dearest Nancy

A happy Christmas, wherever you may be.

How about January 7th for us to meet? I will come up for luncheon – Ritz Hotel 1.15 – if that suits you. We might go again to the pictures at Burlington House. I was dazed by delight at my first visit. Fragonard in full splendour for the first time in my experience, a fine Tiepolo, a delicious Oudry[1] still life. You must tell me more of this painter. I think Poor Pam had a deplorable Pug by him. Otherwise I know nothing.

Allan Ramsay[2] was a revelation too.

Did I tell you that David Cecil, having pretended to be at work for 15 years on a life of Lord Melbourne, dashed it off suddenly in emulation indeed in exact stylistic immitation of *Pompadour* & that the Americans bought an edition thinking *Lord M*. meant Lord Montagu?

I have had a grave week as my mother has just died, aged 84. You say the English always say 'Happy release' at a death. It was really so in her case. Not that she was in pain, but bitterly weary and irked at her dependent state. She was found by her maid dead in her arm chair. So for her it was happy, but it fills me with regret for a lifetime of failure in affection & attention. And of course there has been a lot of uncongenial work with relations & lawyers.

Children come flooding in by every train. It is rather exhilarating to see their simple excitement & curiosity about every Christmas card. 'Look, papa, the Hyde Park Hotel has sent a coloured picture of its new cocktail bar'.

When I reviewed that Victorian book[3] I took the writer to be a bumptious young puppy. I hear he is an aged and wealthy pansy. What astounds me is the standard of reviewing. The book was a congeries of platitude & misstatement produced like a prep-school examination paper on 'jellygraph'. I keep opening papers which say 'Mr Dutton's scholarly & penetrating work – impeccable taste – sumptuous production' etc.

I went to Oxford & visited my first homosexual love, Richard Pares,[4] a don at All Souls. At 50 he is quite paralysed except his mind & voice and awaiting deterioration and death – more dignified than John Hayward,[5] no lolling tongue, but more helpless. A wife and four daughters, no private fortune. He would have been Master of Balliol if he had not been struck down. No Christian faith to support him. A very harrowing visit.

Debo's face in the *Daily Mail* this morning from the wop painter whose work gives me the creeps.[6]

Until 7th

> Much love
> Evelyn

How disgusting about the frogs all getting drunk. Is it a lie put about by the CocoColo [*sic*] makers?

[1] Jean-Baptise Oudry (1686–1755). Painter largely of still lives and animals.
[2] Allan Ramsay (1713–84). Scottish portrait painter.
[3] Ralph Dutton, *The Victorian Home*, reviewed by Waugh in *The Sunday Times* 28 November 1954.
[4] Richard Pares (1902–58). Professor of History at Edinburgh University. He married the daughter of Sir Maurice Powicke, also an historian.
[5] Man of letters and close friend of T.S. Eliot. He suffered from muscular dystrophy.
[6] The Duchess of Devonshire was painted by Annigoni.

To P.G. Wodehouse   Piers Court
29 December 1954

Dear Dr Wodehouse[1]

There was an awful moment about 25 years ago when Edith Sitwell leant towards me like a benevolent eagle and said: 'Mr Waugh, you may call me Edith'. I did not dare address her for five years. I can't write, to my revered master, 'Dear Plum' but I am most exhilarated by your very kind card.

I hope you had a more cheerful Christmas than we. Influenza, mild but vexatious, swept the house. Only *Jeeves & the Feudal Spirit* passed from sick bed to sick bed relieved the gloom.

I don't expect to come to America this year. It is a place to visit when one is successful and the book I have just finished is of purely insular interest. Is there no hope of seeing you in England?

Yours with deep respect
Evelyn Waugh

I don't know whether the address you gave in *Punch* is genuine so send this to your publisher.

[1] Wodehouse was an honorary D.Litt. of Oxford University, 1939.

To CYRIL CONNOLLY   Piers Court.
9 January 1955

Dear Cyril

I procured a copy of *Encounter*. Golly what a paper. Never again. But I read your reminiscence[1] with keen enjoyment. I notice a silk hat, no bowler. I greatly doubt whether you sported one even before Miss Stein took command.

The thing about Nina [Countess of Seafield] was that she was entirely invented by buggers. She didn't exist at all outside Mark's [Ogilvie-Grant] imagination. Have you seen her lately? I have. Non existent. That is a theme for a book – the way buggers in our day created characters for heirs & heiresses – Brian [Howard] & Robert [Byron] etc etc etc.

I can't see the Knightsbridge mews vision. What on earth had the pseudo Cyril been doing with the baby while Miss Fisher had her bath? Who paid her for what in the night club?[2]

I enjoyed seeing your refugee standing drinks in your club but I am afraid I shall have to resign soon.

The floor was covered with loose calico at the ballet so the poor girls couldn't dance. They just stood and stroked one another. In Ashton's ballet[3] I mean.

I hope to find you when I return from Jamaica. Write if you feel inclined care Perry [Lord Brownlow] 'Roaring River'.

Love,
Evelyn

[1] 'One of My Londons' by Cyril Connolly.
[2] Connolly wrote 'a tall well-dressed young man with a baby in his arms stands on the darkening step, the door is opened by a laughing girl in nothing but a bath towel', and imagined their evening out together.
[3] *Rinaldo and Armida*, choreography by Frederick Ashton, had its first night on 6 January 1955.

To Margaret and Harriet Waugh   [On boat to Bermuda]
[January 1955]

Darling Meg & Hatty (and when I say 'Hatty' I mean that you, Meg, are not to behave like the infamous Head Girl & keep this letter to yourself).

I was very sorry to leave without saying goodbye to you. I read the news of the English weather daily with great anxiety. I fear you must be still enclosed in snow in Devon and nearing starvation. The weather has been awfully bad at sea too but we have not been starved – caviar every night. It has been so rough that most of the passengers have lain in their cabins groaning. Not so your sturdy old papa, who has sauntered about blowing cigar smoke in everyone's face and eating a lot. There are three or four men from White's on board so we drink a lot too and laugh loudly in our coarse way.

There is a poor old journalist named Beverley Nichols on board who cares more about his personal appearance than the vainest of ladies and he has come on to this ship purely in the hope of sun-bathing and acquiring a becoming sun-tan. It has been far too stormy for him to venture out on deck and he is in tears of disappointment.

We have mass every day (and I go) said by a black priest with a great beard just like a Father Christmas dipped in ink.

Tomorrow I land at Bermuda (find it on the map) and then fly to Jamaica. That is where the Rum is made that is such a problem at South Ascot. I will write you instructive letters about the geography, manners & customs of these interesting islands.

On board we have a cinema every afternoon and games every evening. I have learned to play Scrabble. We will get a set & play at Easter. I play with poor weeping Mr Beverley Nichols.

All my love to you two darling girls and to the great Head Girl too.

                                                                    Papa

Whose handwriting is affected by the roughness of the ocean not by debauches with wild men of White's

To Auberon Waugh   Roaring River,
27 January 1955   St Anne's Bay,
                                                   Jamaica BWI.

Dear Bron,

I was sorry not to see you before your return to Downside. Had I done so I would have offered you sage advice. I got the impression that last term you were going a bit far in your defiance of school rules. I should hate you to be low spirited and submissive, but don't become an anarchist. Don't above all things put on side. It is an excellent thing to see through the side of others – particularly of youths who think they are young Gods because they are good at games. But they at least are good at something. There is no superiority in shirking things and doing things badly. Be superior by cultivating your intellect and your taste. Enough of this, but pay attention to it.

We had a very stormy voyage as far as Bermuda but I enjoyed it greatly. Many friends from White's on board and delicious food. In this degraded decade the comfort of a Cunard liner is the most congenial in existence. By constrast BOAC which brought me here was squalidly incompetent.

Lord Brownlow has a fine airy house on a hill over-looking the sea in a park from which he has cut away all the palms, leaving only forest trees. It is rather like Pixton if you can imagine the sea starting at the gates & running to the horizon brilliant blue. Poor Lord Brownlow suffers greatly from accidents to all his gadgets – the electric cocktail shaker wont work, the Jaguar has broken its back axle, both jeeps are lacking essential parts. He takes all these mishaps very hard. He has just married a new wife.[1] She has a pain in the neck but she takes it lightly. We bathe sometimes in the sea sometimes in a fresh water pool and drink rum and sleep and I do two hours work every morning in a pavilion. I haven't seen much of Jamaica yet. It is an odd island. The whole north coast where Roaring River stands has quite lately become the resort of millionaires, mostly American. Ten years ago the coast was an empty coral strand with a few negro fishing villages. Now it is all Hollywood style villas and huge hotels charging 40 dollars a day for their smallest rooms and the poor negroes cannot now find a yard of beach to paddle in. The interior of the island where I hope to go soon is all wild hill country inhabited by very poor negroes. Land on the coast which ten years ago could be bought for £20 an acre now costs 2000. Great fortunes have been made in land speculation but no benefit goes to the people. Perhaps they will massacre the whites one day. At present they seem too lethargic.

I wish your mother was here with me. She would not like the bats which fly about the verandahs in the evening in hundreds. I left her very cold & sad. I hope she is now at Pixton recuperating.

Lord Brownlow's son[2] has just failed to get a commission in the Grenadiers – a sad warning to boys who give themselves airs. Take warning.

Tiny humming birds are hovering round the flowering trees. It is really most agreeable here.

Your affec. papa
E Waugh

[1] Dorothy Power an American, had married Lord Brownlow in 1954. She died in 1966.
[2] Edward Cust (1936–   ). Succeeded as Lord Brownlow 1978.

To GRAHAM GREENE   Piers Court.
11 March 1955

Dear Graham

I have just come home to find *Loser Takes All* awaiting me. Thank you very much for giving it to me. I had read fragments in a nasty paper I picked up and feared at first that they might have spoiled it for me. But not at all. When I got it compact and complete and elegant I read straight through with keen enjoyment & admiration. The characters are so real that they have set me fretting. How they are going to regret their renunciation of wealth when the transports of the honeymoon have abated! I see that idiot girl now shivering at the bus-stop and gnawing her pub sausage & fairly bursting with homesickness for Monte Carlo. Whats more of course she wont stay faithful to her ageing clerk for ten months. I suspect that even in the yacht she developed a crush on Korda.

I missed all the reviews. I hope they appreciated the masterly skill of the story.

Why by the way do you suppose that papists are more prone than heathens to identify characters in fiction with their author? It seems to be a universal nuisance among the unimaginative.

I found Jamaica awfully dull, but an effective health resort. I found your footsteps in Noel [Coward's] bungalow and at Tower Isle, where at this moment Cardinal Spellman is spending his Lent. That finally ends any loose talk of his being *papabile* I think.

If you are in London let us keep our postponed festival at White's.

Yours ever
Evelyn

To T.W. GADD   Piers Court.
Easter Monday [11 April] 1955

Dear Mr Gadd
Thank you for sending me this poem. I wish I could give an opinion on it. The trouble is that I simply don't understand anything later than Tennyson. You must go to Spender or Lehmann for appreciation.

I am glad you find 'Sebastian'[1] an interesting character. I don't think he had any egotism. He was a contemplative without the necessary grace of fortitude.

Yours sincerely
Evelyn Waugh

[1] Sebastian Flyte of *Brideshead Revisited*.

To T.W. GADD   Piers Court.
April 1955
Postcard

Thank you for your letter. Pray do not suppose that my inability to enjoy modern art is a source of pride to me. I deplore it. Nor is it the fruit of affluent circumstances. I know many richer & better educated than myself, who rejoice in Picasso.

E.W.

To ANTHONY POWELL   Piers Court.
25 April 1955

My Dear Tony

I have now read *Acceptance World* slowly and with great relish. I think it even better done than its predecessor and congratulate you with all my heart. I prefer Mrs Erdleigh to Mr Deacon as a piece of apparatus and the climax of Le Bas's seizure to the cascade of sugar. The whole Old Boy dinner is superb. The plot seems to me altogether denser and I prefer the economy in comment. In fact it is an admirable book. I am glad I haven't to review it. I don't quite know how I would define my admiration. I feel each volume of this series is like a great sustaining slice of Melton Pie. [1] I can go on eating it with the recurring seasons until I drop.

Yours ever
Evelyn

[1] Elaborate cold meat pie, speciality of Melton Mowbray, Leicestershire.

To JOHN BETJEMAN   Piers Court.
3 May 1955

My Dear John

I am sorry that Penelope forbade our reunion after the Hollis wedding. I wanted to confer with you about (among other things) Charles D'Costa [1] a very nice Jamaican jew with whom I stayed in that island. He boasts (a) that Cyril Connolly was his tutor (b) that you flogged him at Marlborough. [2] These high claims have raised him to the intellectual leadership of the Caribbean and N. Coward and I. (Bond) Fleming do him homage.

You will shortly receive an invitation from the Head Girl of St Mary's Ascot (my daughter Teresa) to amuse the girls there. They are *very* pretty. I know, less well than you, but pretty well, horrors of such invitations. But if you accept I will try and provide a jolly dinner afterwards for you & Penelope, Laura, Head Girl etc. We might perhaps do an effortless humiliating comic debate together? It is the H.G.'s last term of office and it would end in a glow if she got hold of you, to whom all the senior girls are deeply devoted. Please think seriously of this.

Do you possess, do you want, the *Architectural Review*, bound, 1895–1905 (circa)? I am offered it and would give it to you if acceptable.

Anyway it is far too long since you were here. After your duties to the party are fulfilled on May 26th do please try & find a time to visit us.

Yours
Evelyn

[1] Charles D'Costa (1910–74). His family had been in Jamaica since the seventeenth century and had prospered in sugar and later in commerce generally.
[2] Betjeman replied that he was never in a position at Marlborough to beat anyone.

To JOHN BETJEMAN   Piers Court.
13 May 1955

Dear John

D'Costa says you flogged him for not blacking your boots correctly. I must say it doesn't sound like you. But all Jamaica, Jew Christian black & white believes him. Actionable? I doubt it.

Mother Mercedes suggests Ascension Day for your kind visit to Ascot. That suits me. Any day suits me. You fix it with her and I will roll up. We wont on any account dine with the nuns. There is a Trust House at the gates where we can get tight after the tomfoolery.

Do you think a debate between us, 'Girls have a better time at school than boys' 'Girls should have university educations – careers in shops', 'Art is a bore'. Any sort of nonsense like that.

The *Architectural Review*s have come 5 vols not consecutive but I should think full of useful reference material for you. I will bring them to South Ascot.

Was that secretary an Ascot girl – or just in your mind at the time of writing.

I bought Plomer's poems[1] on your recommendation & think I was a sucker rather.

                                                              Love
                                                              Evelyn

[1]William Plomer, *A Shot in the Park*, 1955.

To AUBERON WAUGH   Piers Court.
23 May 1955

My Dear Bron

Dont write in that silly tone. No one has any motive with regard to you except your own welfare. No decision is absolute yet. If you have a better suggestion to make I shall be pleased to hear it.

I warned you at the beginning of last term that you were heading for trouble. You paid no attention. I need not repeat what I said to you at the end of this holidays. I could not tell you then what I had in mind for your future, as I had left the Headmaster to make his own arrangements in his own time with the house-masters. I fully realise that it is a most unusual kindness of the Headmaster's to allow you to change houses. My first idea was to send you to another school. It is possible that Stonyhurst might take you, but I should have to ask them to do so as a favour, and I cannot do this unless I am confident that you intend to behave yourself. If you go there as Psmith & Mike[1] went to Sedleigh, determined to sulk, it would be hopeless.

You have made a mess of things. At your age that is not a disaster, but you must help yourself. Your future, temporal and spiritual, is your own making. I can only provide opportunities for your achievements.

                                                   Your affectionate papa
                                                   E.W.

[1]P.G. Wodehouse characters.

•

To Auberon Waugh   Piers Court.
14 June 1955

My Dear Bron
I congratulate you with all my heart on your success with your story. You do not
name the discerning magazine – *Everybody's*[1] perhaps? Anyway it is an agreeable
thing to see ones work professionally recognized. I look forward greatly to seeing the
issue. They won't pay you until the end of the month in which it appears. That is the
usual practice.

Your hairless uncle Alec Waugh has also had a success at last. His latest book[2] has
been taken by the American 'Book of the Month', serialized, filmed – in fact the
jack-pot. It is very nice for him after so many years of disappointment & obscurity.
He has not drawn a sober breath since he heard the news.

Your Uncle Auberon's hopes are less rosy,[3] but your mother, grandmother,
aunts and pig-walloper[4] have had and are still having a highly enjoyable time in
Sunderland. Your mother still believes she has been in Sutherland.

I am glad the Headmaster is paying attention to you. His aim, I think, is to find
whether it is better to continue your education or to send you with a changed name
and £5 to Australia.

I trust your Empire League is not under the auspices of Sir Oswald Mosley? If it
is you will end in prison like my old friend Diana Mitford.

Think of all lonely schoolboys on Ascension Day in memory of your father in
1916.

Your affec. papa
E.W.

[1] Auberon Waugh's story 'Caligula' was published in *Lilliput*.
[2] *Island in the Sun*.
[3] Auberon Herbert stood as a Conservative and lost by 3,000 votes.
[4] Alick Dru.

To Graham Greene   Piers Court.
[4 July 1955]
Postcard

Mystified by your predilection for son-in-law. If it is really a CAMEL OWNER you
seek, you should – surely? – try further East. If CANAL OWNER, I think John
Betjeman can fix you up in England.

E

To Messrs Knight, Frank and Rutley[1]   Piers Court.
4 July 1955

Dear Oldfield

You may remember that you came here about nine years ago when I had an idea of moving to Ireland.

Now I have the idea of moving anywhere. I am sick of the district.

I would like to sell out. I realise that prices have dropped a great deal. We have built various farm buildings & made the garden better but I believe that £10,000 is the most I could ask. I would not want to sell for less. I am in no hurry to go. I don't want the house advertised. But if you happen to meet a lunatic who wants to live in this ghastly area, please tell him.

Have you still got photographs? *Country Life* & various other journals have photographed us rather often. I could send prints.

If you would like to look at us again, you would, of course, be very welcome any day.

                                        Yours sincerely
                                        Evelyn Waugh.

I don't want frivolous sight-seers. Only serious lunatics who want to live near here.

[1] Estate agents and auctioneers.

To Anthony Powell   Piers Court.
[5 July 1955]
Postcard

'Crouchback'[1] (junior: not so his admirable father) is a prig. But he is a virtuous, brave prig. If he had funked, the defection of 'Ivor Claire' could not have had the necessary impact on him.

I wonder what you made of T. Pakenham[2] who was on his way to you from me. Not *sortable*, I thought, but likely to grow up agreeable. Spots & hair horrible & awkward with his hands. See next *Spectator* for fine essay rejected by *Punch*.

Do pop over one day soon.

                                        E

[1] In *Officers and Gentlemen*.
[2] Thomas Pakenham (1933-   ). Writer. Eldest son of Frank Pakenham.

To Sir Maurice Bowra   Piers Court.
14 July 1955

Dear Maurice

Very many thanks for your letter. I had the pen poised to send you a copy of my novel and then I thought: no, it is cheek sending stuff like this to a panjandrum. ▶

am horrified to think of you buying it. Thank you and please forgive me for not giving it to you. Next time I will, if there is a next time. I have lots more to tell about the characters: how Tony Box Bender developed a monastic vocation in jug and broke his father's heart. (Ivo the mad dead brother who died before the story began is a key character. Guy's silence in the hospital is all part of the strain that works out variously in the members of the family). Then of course Mrs Troy remarried Guy because she found herself in the shit, without money and pregnant by Trimmer. Trimmer's son becomes the heir of the family and Old Crouchback died happy. Da Costa was really a communist all the time and behaves horribly in Jugo-Slavia. Lots to tell, but my poor mind may go again before I tell it.

I have not spoken to Cyril for a long time. I see his blue quivering face peer round the door at White's sometimes but he scuttles away if – as there nearly always is – there is a hearty mob with me. Do I gather he has shed the châtelaine of the Oak Cottage?[1] Good for him.

I suppose your vacation plans would not include a visit here? Late September is a pleasant season sometimes. The cook is awful but the cellar all right, and some objets d'art I should like to display.

It is a sorrow to me that I got the hymn wrong.[2] I have not heard it since Lancing Chapel. I consulted the head housemaid who sings in the protestant parish choir. She gave me the wrong words. I must look up *Hymns A & M* and see if they are on the Index. If they are not, I will get a copy and avoid sad mistakes in future.

As from today Stinchcombe is without a vicar. Isaac Williams built the Vicarage and Keble, his brother-in-law, often preached here.

Betjeman very kindly came to entertain the girls at St. Mary's, Ascot. Goodness he gave them a good time in real Ensa[3] style. I am awfully encouraged that you like *Officers & Gentlemen*. The reviewers don't, fuck them.

Lady Pamela has faded from my life like a little pat of melting butter. But I see and correspond with Ann. I go to her at Dorn for the first of August. Couldn't you invite yourself too? Ian will be in America then I fear.

Yours ever
Evelyn

[1]Barbara Connolly.

[2]Waugh had published an article in the *Spectator* 8 July 1955 entitled 'Awake My Soul! It is a Lord,' confusing the first lines of two hymns 'Awake, my Soul, and with the sun,' and 'Hark, my soul, it is the Lord.' The article mocked Nancy Spain (1917–64), the hostile literary critic of the *Daily Express*, and Lord Noel-Buxton (1917–   ) who had called at Piers Court uninvited and been sent packing.

[3]Acronym for Entertainments National Services Association.

To Edith Sitwell   Piers Court.
14 July 1955

Dearest Edith

'Desiderata' is disgusting. I have destroyed it. *Desiderata* indeed!

It is delightful to know that you & Osbert are amused by my exhibition of Spain &

Buxton and by my book. As you must know there is no one whose opinions I value more than yours & his. It was good of you to get to the fag of writing.

But the real joy of your letter is in the last paragraph.[1] Welcome. Welcome. Will you be very kind and send me a postcard when the thing is fixed so that Laura and I may make our communions for you? I know of many people who will want to thank God for you and many priests who will want to remember you in their masses. But I presume you don't want the matter spoken of, so shall mention it to no one until you give the word.

Is it exorbitant to hope that your example & prayers may bring Osbert to the Faith? I have often thought I saw in his writing (tho not as plain as in yours) that he was near the truth.

I take it you will be received at Mount St Mary's, where I have so often heard mass & prayed for you all?

My love to Father Caraman. You must be a deep joy to him.

Evelyn

[1]Edith Sitwell became a convert to Roman Catholicism. She was taking instruction from Fr Caraman sj.

To Christopher Sykes   Piers Court.
15 July 1955

My Dear Christopher

The Press Agent has at last sent me your review of *Officers & Gentlemen*. I am delighted to note that Spender has not corrupted your grammar or your taste. It is a most discerning & lucid review. Thank you very much.

It was good news this morning that Jehovah has struck at the divorcés of Ascot. A pity he missed.

The Director of the Spoken Word says he has no authority to order *The Critics* to observe polite conventions.[1] I have reported him & them to the Director General.

Rumours reach Stinchcombe that Boots has shed the chatelaine of Oak Cottage. That too is good news.

I have a theory about the modern Teddy-boy school of novelist & critic – [John] Wain, [Kingsley] Ames, [*sic*] etc. It is that they all read English Literature for schools[2] and so take against it, while good critics & writers read as a treat and a relaxation from Latin & Greek.

It is very cool & fragrant here and I shall not go to London until the fine weather ends. I hope to see you in the sleet & drizzle. Have you taken your name off the Rockingham?[3] It is full of men called Forbes[4] now, a worse man still in the same trade called O'Brien.[5] Randolph roars obscene gossip about Sir A. Eden.

Have the Jews a club of their own which you frequent in preference? St James's used to be their hide out. Did it hurt being circumcised? I was done in infancy owing to connexions with British India. Clonmore was done late in life to stop him frigging. So was Hobhouse for other reasons – not ritualistic.

Did you read a beautiful book named *Picnic at Sakkara*?[6]

Betjeman doesnt know it is forbidden to wear a straw hat in London before Goodwood.

I go to Folkestone in August. If you are taking ship there, stop & see me.

Did you know that the family who owned this house were close connexions of Wingate?[7]

Your affectionate brother-officer, fellow Gregorian & rival in the art of letters

E. Waugh

[1]Waugh had objected to being referred to as 'Waugh' and not 'Mr Waugh' on the BBC radio programme *The Critics*.

[2]Final examinations at Oxford for the B.A. degree.

[3]The Rockingham was a club based on White's invented by Sykes in *The Song of a Shirt*. It also turned out to be the name of an existing homosexual meeting place.

[4]Probably Alastair Forbes.

[5]Alan Brien, a journalist but not a member, was introduced to Waugh in White's by Randolph Churchill. He decided to be in his own phrase 'tediously pushy', and questioning Waugh about a profile in *Truth*, received the reply: 'I assume that you are the author of that miserable and ill-informed piece. It is scarcely likely that anyone else would either remember or care about its contents.' Waugh assumed rightly. Further insults were exchanged through Churchill.

[6]By P.H. Newby.

[7]Christopher Sykes was to publish a biography of Orde Wingate in 1959.

To NANCY MITFORD   Piers Court.
18 July 1955

Darling Nancy

I hope you and Col. danced about the streets like mad things on 14th to celebrate the liberation of M. de Sade.

I am surprised & delighted that you managed to get through *Officers & Gentlemen*. Mrs Stitch threw away Guy's letter because she thought it contained the incriminating War Diary of Hookforce in Crete. War Diaries had to be sent to C.H.Q. Records by Intelligence Officers.

Here is Miss Spain's article. Please return. I gather you see the *Spectator* so you will have read Lord Noel-Buxton's infamous attempt to put the blame on the woman. Only a socialist and a quaker could be quite so caddish. I know nothing of either of the pilgrims except for that one incident. I don't think Miss Spain can be very nice, whatever her grandmother's horticultural gifts,[1] as I have had a mountainous mail from people as different as Edith Sitwell and Violet Bonham-Carter, telling me of sufferings at her hand in the past. Nor do I think Mr Raymond[2] can be very nice. I have read some very common articles by him. Are you getting into the wrong set?

I look forward to seeing the final draft of your letter in the *Spectator*. I don't think journalists are any better than tourists. The difference is that there are lots of idle tourists in Paris and none in Stinchcombe while the journalists are fairly respectable people like Mr Giles.[3] In England there are beastly journalists who can only get into print if they are offensive. I don't take any Beaverbrook papers but I gather they specialize in beastliness. The *Spectator* has been running a very effective campaign against them. Mr Gilmour seems a high minded young man. He has a *very* attractive wife.[4]

I find about journalists that even when one has been hospitable to them and quite liked them & thought they quite liked one, they invariably put some awful statement into ones mouth. Politicians have to face the risk because they live on popular votes, but for novelists it would not affect the sale of a single copy if we were never mentioned in the Beaverbrook press. The editors know this and it riles them.

It is so long since I wrote that I forget what I last told you. Did I say that Desmond Guinness[5] came here with a wife like Tilly Losch who has learned English solely from your books? An enjoyable couple.

Cnossos is a wonderful fake is it not? I particularly relished the 'reconstructions' of the frescoes. A whole school of design contrived out of bits of plaster the size of a thumb nail.

It has been so hot that I haven't been to London at all & missed Debo's water gala which I gather was highly enjoyed by all.

... On Saturday I saw *Murder in the Cathedral*[6] at Gloucester. I went not expecting to like it much & was deeply moved.

Lady Jones got Honks right in the cemetery.[7]

Love
E

[1]Nancy Mitford had written that the garden of Nancy Spain's grandmother 'was the pride of the Redewater valley. She's a funny rough creature (Nancy) but I rather like her. ...'

[2]John Raymond (1923–77). Critic and author.

[3]Frank Giles (1919–   ). *The Times* correspondent in Rome and later Paris. Deputy Editor of *The Sunday Times* 1967. In 1946 he married Lady Kitty Sackville.

[4]Lady Caroline Montagu-Douglas-Scott (1927–   )married in 1951 Ian Gilmour (1926–   ), editor of the *Spectator* 1954–9 and Conservative MP since 1962, succeeded as baronet 1977.

[5]Desmond Guinness (1931–   ), son of Lord Moyne (Bryan Guinness) and Diana Mitford, brother of Jonathan, married Princess Marie-Gabrielle (Mariga) of Württenburg in 1954.

[6]By T.S. Eliot.

[7]In *The Loved and Envied*, 1951, a novel by Enid Bagnold (Lady Jones).

TO FATHER PHILIP CARAMAN   Piers Court.
19 July 1955

Dear Fr Caraman

Edith Sitwell has told me that she is under your instruction and will be received into the Church next month. I need not say how much I rejoice with you in this & how much I admire your delicacy in the matter.

Don't please think me impertinent. I am an old friend of Edith's & love her. She is liable to make herself a little conspicuous at times. This morning I have had another letter from her. She says she will be received in London. Am I being over-fastidious in thinking Mount St Mary's much more suitable. What I fear is that the popular papers may take her up as a kind of Garbo-Queen-Christina. I was incomparably less notorious when I was received and I know that I suffered from the publicity which I foolishly allowed them. There are so many malicious people out to make a booby of a Sitwell. It would be tragic if this greatest occasion in her life were in any way sullied. Can you not persuade her to emulate St Helena in this matter?[1]

What, by the way, has happened to *Weston*?[2]

Yours ever
Evelyn

[1] The ceremony was held in London but publicity avoided.

[2] *The Autobiography of an Elizabethan* by William Weston, translated by Philip Caraman, foreward by Evelyn Waugh, June 1955; published in New York as *An Autobiography from the Jesuit Underground*.

To the Editor of the Spectator
Published 22 July 1955

Piers Court.

MEN OF WAUGH

Sir, – Mr. Carlisle's[1] testimonial to Lord Noel-Buxton's sensitive scholarship and intrepid paddling would be more impressive if it did not appear in conjunction with that nobleman's own letter. Finding he has made an ass of himself, he turns on the lady whom he chose to escort, and publicly calls her a liar. Has Miss Spain no brother? Has the editor of the *Daily Express* no horse-whip?

But I am more concerned with my own narrow squeak. If I accept the unchivalrous repudiation and believe that the words which have caused so much innocent fun during the last three weeks – 'I am not on business, I am a member of the House of Lords' – were invented and put into Lord Noel-Buxton's mouth by Miss Spain, I may ask: if this is how she treats an old and valued friend, what would she have done to me? What monstrous infelicities would she have fathered on her reluctant host, if I had let her in to dinner.

Yours faithfully
EVELYN WAUGH

[1] Anthony Carlisle had written to the *Spectator* describing Lord Noel-Buxton as 'a sensitive student of history prepared to test his theories about Roman fords at considerable discomfort and even risk.' Lord Noel-Buxton when he failed to walk across the Thames explained, 'It must be all that rain up in the Cotswolds.' He wrote himself to say Nancy Spain had misquoted him.

To Nancy Mitford
23 July 1955

Piers Court.

Dearest Nancy,

In the last two days two separate parties from Paris have passed through Stinchcombe.[1] One told me and the other confirmed the terrible story of your social ostracism. If I had known, I would not have made untimely jibes about your frequenting the wrong set. I *am* sorry for my heavy footedness. You must be lonely & chill sitting with Mr Raymond & Miss Spain.

Of course I was as shocked as any frog by your attack on Marie Antoinette but since we once had an estrangement after Mosley's Albert Hall Meeting, I had resolved never to let your subversive opinions influence my love. [2]

Some of my informants say you may be readmitted to the fringes of Society. Others that you will have to change your name & go to Dakar. Well it is warm there and you will like that.

Love from
Evelyn

[1]Lady Diana Cooper, Frank and Lady Kitty Giles.

[2]"Even in her cherished France she could not resist writing an article which infuriated many whose opinion she cared for. This was more than a tease for she sought to justify the execution of Marie-Antoinette as a traitress. Prince Pierre of Monaco cut her dead and as her dear friend Princess Dolly Radziwill remarked "Some doors will for ever be closed against her."' Harold Acton, *Nancy Mitford*. p. 100. But Nancy Mitford wrote, 'However now I'm back they can't resist me and empty though Paris is I dont have many meals alone with Miss Spain.'

To the Editor of The Times Piers Court.
24 July 1955

STATUES IN LONDON

Sir, – Would not the House of Lords be the most appropriate place for a statue of the first Earl Lloyd George? He first made his mark by eloquent denunciations of that House. In his years of power he did more than any Prime Minister to embellish it with new names. In his wise old age he entered it himself.

I am, Sir, your obedient servant,

EVELYN WAUGH

To Nancy Mitford Grand Hotel,
5 August 1955 Folkestone.

Dearest Nancy

Mrs Arthur[1] sounds splendid. I hope she exercises wide influence.

I met another traveller from Paris. I said: 'I hear Mrs Rodd is entirely ostracized.' 'Oh not at all. I saw her with' – and then a string of names. But all those names were jewish american or English. Dur parmesan. Mrs Arthur, despite her brilliant literary acumen, doesnt sound like the Faubourg. Well perhaps Hollywood will bring some comfort. Lots of the people there have taken very august names. 'Guermantes' in every studio cafeteria speaking with strong Danubian accents.

I have come to live here for a bit, everything nice except the cooking and the customers. I see Ann [Fleming] and Bettine Davison[2] – Noel Coward and I dont do any work which was the object of my coming.

Yesterday I went to London to stand godfather to Edith Sitwell who has submitted to the Pope of Rome. She looked fine – like a 16th century infanta and spoke her renunciation of heresy in silver bell like tones. Afterwards a gargantuan feast at her Sesame Club. I had heard gruesome accounts of that place but she gave us a rich blow-out. Very odd company none of whom I had seen before, only one I had heard of – the actor Alec Guinness,[3] very shy & bald. He is turning papist too, so there is something to balance the loss of Miss Clifford[4] who is marrying a man with no legs & two wives. Think of *choosing* to be named Atalanta Fairey! No sense of propriety. Ed Stanley has written a first rate essay on Belloc as preface to the *Cruise of the Nona*.[5] Ann says he is impotent and greatly depressed about it.

Honks has had a tooth out and gone to starve with Loelia. The tooth drawing was sudden. Ann telephoned to Loelia to say she would be arriving in a weakened state and would need some nourishing broth. Loelia replied: 'I have sent my cook on a holiday. I made it quite clear that there would be *no* meals'.

I keep sending notes to the chef 'Don't put cornflour in the sauce' etc. Now he comes up and glowers at me in his white hat from behind a screen in the dining room.

I am sorry you thought the *Observer* 'profile' good. I found it grossly impertinent.[6]

How impatient I am with the rot in the papers about science. Really, to spend millions of pounds of public money in letting off invisible fireworks! A football 200 miles away, travelling at 18,000 miles an hour. They are howling mad.

Love
Evelyn

[1]Nancy Mitford had written: 'She places Os and Gs [*Officers and Gentlemen*] among the great novels of the world.'

[2]Bettine Russell (1905–). Married in 1929 Patrick Davison who succeeded as Lord Broughshane in 1953.

[3]Alec Guinness (1914–). Roman Catholic convert. Knighted in 1959.

[4]Atalanta Clifford (1932–) married 1955–60 to Richard Fairey, the son of the founder of the Fairey Aviation Company.

[5]1925, reissued 1955.

[6]The profile ends: 'Embittered romantic, over-deliberate squire and recluse, popular comedian, catholic father of a family, Evelyn Waugh is one of the oddest figures of our time.' *Observer*, 31 July 1955.

To Edith Sitwell
As from Piers Court.

9 August 1955

Dearest Edith

I have left St Margaret's Bay so only got your charming letter last night when I was on the point of writing to you to thank you again for choosing me as sponsor, for your present of your poems and for the delightful luncheon party. I thought your circle of friends round the table remarkably typical of the Church in its variety and goodwill. August 4th will now mean 1955 to me, as well as 1914.

It is 25 years all but a few weeks since Fr D'Arcy received me into the Church. I am aghast now when I think how frivolously I approached (though it seemed grave enough at the time) for every year since has been one of exploration into the mind & heart of the Church. You have come with much deeper insight. Should I as Godfather warn you of probable shocks in the human aspect of Catholicism? Not all priests are as clever and kind as Fr D'Arcy and Fr Caraman. (The incident in my book of going to confession to a spy is a genuine experience.) But I am sure you know the world well enough to expect Catholic bores and prigs and crooks and cads. I always think of myself: 'I know I am awful. But how much more awful I should be without the Faith'. One of the joys of Catholic life is to recognise the little sparks of good everywhere, as well as the fires of the saints.

I am greatly cheered by what you say of Osbert. Suffering is by nature bad, but it is the work of the redemption that it can be turned to good. I am very hopeful that with your help he too will find the truth.

I liked Alec Guinness so much and will try to see more of him. I have long admired his art. How one welcomes converts. One great sadness in Catholic life is year by year to count the apostasies – seldom from reason, almost always through marrying outside the Church. I can think of more than a handful of close friends lost – temporarily, it is reasonable to hope. But each leaves an open wound. Then one hears of and sees the Grace of God steadily reinforcing the ranks. It is a great consolation.

I heard a rousing sermon on Sunday against the dangers of immodest bathing-dresses and thought that you and I were innocent of that offence at least.

With love from
Evelyn

To Nancy Mitford   Piers Court.
1 September 1955

Dearest Nancy

Thank you very much for sending me *Encounter*. I read your essay[1] with keen relish. I wish it had been much longer.

The exposition of Fortinbras[2] is first class; also all your rebuke to upper class for their capitulations. I think you are less sound on the economic position of the rich. You say there are a few great houses still kept in style, but their owners once kept half a dozen houses apiece going full blast. It is simply that a few families were so awfully rich that a reduction of 90% in their position still leaves them fairly imposing. And even they are not escaping tax, they are spending capital and despair of their heirs having anything eg. the Duke of Beaufort.

I am sure you have worked earnestly at your facts but are you correct in saying that 382 peers have coat armour *in the male line* from pre-Tudor times? Surely not. I should have thought fewer than 100 and of them half Scottish who did not regularize heraldry (or legitimacy) until late. I am no genealogist but almost every august family I can think of had a female succession at least once & surname & arms granted to an outsider.

I wish in your Upper-class Usage you had touched on a point that has long intrigued me. Almost everyone I know has some personal antipathy which they condemn as middle class quite irrationally. My mother-in-law believes it middle-class to decant claret. Lord Beauchamp thought it m.c. not to decant champagne (into jugs). Your 'note-paper' is another example. I always say 'luncheon' but you will find 'lunch' used in every generation for the last 80 years [by?] unimpeachable sources. There are very illiterate people like Perry Brownlow who regard all correct grammar as a middle-class affectation. Ronnie Knox blanches if one says 'docile' with a long o. I correct my children if they say 'bike' for 'bicycle'. I think everyone has certain fixed ideas that have no relation to observed usage. The curious thing is that, as you say, an upper class voice is always unmistakable though it may have every deviation of accent and vocabulary. Compare for instance the late Lords Westmoreland, Salisbury, Curzon. A phonetician would find no point of resemblence in their speech.

Herbaceous borders came in as an economy. The first drawing in of horns when potting & bedding-out became too expensive.

Oh I have forgotten your poor eyes. I should have written large as I do to Honks. Must not Miss Maxwell's[3] cruise be hell?

I have committed an inexcusable solecism in the *Spectator* 'Anadyomene' for 'Anadyomenos'. What can be more ignominious than to use a rather recondite word and to use it wrong? I am hiding my head in shame – a bourgeois quality, you tell me.

All love
Evelyn

[1]'The English Aristocracy', later included in *Noblesse Oblige*.
[2]An imaginary peer used as an example.
[3]Elsa Maxwell (1883–1963). A frequent organizer of parties, she had this time arranged for 128 people, including Lady Diana Cooper, to sail from Venice to the Greek islands on a cultural cruise aboard a ship loaned by Stavros Niarchos.

To Nancy Mitford
19 October 1955

Piers Court
Stinchcombe
Nr Dursley
Glos.

Dearest Nancy

Thank you for sending Hamilton's letter. I can't deal direct with a man who, not knowing me at all, refers to me by my Christian name, but I will send *you* a proof of my letter when I get one. At present only a manuscript exists which I have sent to *the Encounter.*[1] It is about 4,000 words long. Except that I expose you as a hallucinated communist agent there is nothing in it to hurt. I deal with heraldry, genealogy, precedence, conception of 'gentleman', the finances of aristocracy and such important topics. Very little about verbal usage. That was a minor issue in your article and I think it very morbid of your readers to attach such importance to it. Professor Ross did not seem to me to do much except borrow from Uncle Matthew and the old Society for Pure English Tracts and to invent the expression 'non U' which I regard as vulgar in the extreme – like VD for venereal disease and PC for postcard. 'U Book' would be a dreadful title.

This is writing paper or letter paper. Single sheets are note paper. Pray note 'Glos' on the engraving (and always write the departments of France in full in future. No 'S et O'.[2])

All love
Evelyn

[1]'An open letter to the Honble Mrs Peter Rodd (Nancy Mitford) on a Very Serious Subject' appeared in *Encounter*, December 1955.

[2]For 'Seine et Oise'. Nancy Mitford replied: 'I've NEVER in my LIFE put S and O or A and M on letters – what an awful idea. As bad as U – quite.'

To A. D. Peters   Piers Court.
20 October [1955]

Dear Pete

The 'Aristocracy' article has gone to *Encounter*.

I think as a matter of prestige that if it is used in an anthology of snobbery by H. Hamilton it should somehow be made plain that it was a book by Nancy & me with a few press cuttings thrown in. Please dont quote the foregoing sentence to Hamilton or it will be repeated to my discredit. Can you convey the sense of it, as coming from *you*? In fact Nancy's article & mine together, alone, would make an excellent pamphlet. I answer her at every point. Prof. Ross is a bore. ...

Yours ever
Evelyn

To Nancy Mitford   Piers Court.
21 October 1955

Darling Nancy

The editor of the *Encounter* has mistakenly sent me a letter written to Mr Weidenfeld. He says: 'I have looked through our correspondence and I find that we have not promised the aristocracy series to anyone else. So you have first call – though, as I say, it is going to be many months before the series is anything like complete. ... When we have the other articles in, we can then write to authors and tell them of our plans'.

It is a strange underworld you have led me into.

I have instructed Peters to make it plain that the *Encounter* have only first serial rights and are not empowered to make any arrangements about book publication. Perhaps you will do the same & also warn your friend Hamilton of these subversive jewish plots. Or is Hamilton also a Jew? I have heard it suggested.

Love
E

To Nancy Mitford   Piers Court
21 October [1955]   Nr Dursley
         Gloucestershire

Darling

Look. I have found some old note-paper with Glos. in full.

You will now have found my letter exposing the Kristol-Weidenfeld plot.[1] I thought it great impudence of Kristol to think he can arrange our publishing for us.

I think the book should have a pompous name 'An enquiry into the identifiable characteristics of the English Aristocracy'[2] or 'The Patrician Anatomy'. Something like that.

Your letter of reply is not very honest about your red sympathies, is it? You call the *New Statesman* your 'Mag' and rejoice in every noxious word. Of course everyone will think that it is The Party which restrained you from publishing your Moscow travel-diary. Are you sure it is a good plan to print a reply? If there is anything in my article you think impolite, say and of course I will change it.[3] I think you miss the point about putative parentage. I merely meant pedigrees were not infallible in attributing character, eg. noses. There are only about four shapes of nose. People say 'look there is the Fortinbras nose'. Rot, really.

I grieve deeply to learn that you like Priestley, but I am happy to say that your other new literary friend John Raymond has written well about Belloc in 'The Mag'.

Fond love
Evelyn

I say do you think it proper when writing to me in public to refer to Spender as Stephen? I should never call him that. 'The Editor' or 'Stephen Spender' or Messrs Spender & Kristol. No?

[1] Irving Kristol (1920–   ). Founder and editor with Stephen Spender of *Encounter*. He returned to the United States in 1958.

[2] The subtitle of *Noblesse Oblige*, 1956.

[3] Nancy Mitford replied: 'How I've been shrieking! The PLOT.... I've withdrawn the reply but you must also change your piece. You know I'm not a Communist Evelyn, now dont you? ... Think of me as a Christian – *early* if you like.'

To NANCY MITFORD   Piers Court.
All Souls [2 November] 1955

Dearest Nancy

I have cut out all reference to communism & attributed your class-war battle cry
to your admiration for Lloyd George.

I haven't changed the 'Hon' bit because after all it was you who made the Hon
joke public property, even if you didn't originate it. It will always be linked with
your name, not with the Duchess or the Communist. [1]

Is that satisfactory? [2]

Fond love
Evelyn

[1] Her sisters Deborah and Jessica.
[2] Nancy Mitford replied: 'Yes thats perfect. I know you can't tell the difference between Lloyd George
and Stalin but other people can.'

To GRAHAM GREENE   Piers Court.
5 December [1955]

Dear Graham

Thank you very much for sending me a copy of *The Quiet American*. [1] I have
already read it with deep admiration & wrote a review which should soon be among
your press-cuttings. I am afraid I let my dislike of Fowler run away with me. What a
shit he is! But I hope I made it apparent that the book is first rate.

I saw Stokes the other evening. We both lamented that you never come to our
club. ...

[1] 'A masterly but base work'. *Diaries*.

To GRAHAM GREENE   Piers Court.
7 December 1955
Postcard

I am very sorry your secretary should have read a letter so full of indelicate
expressions as mine.

Let us meet at White's at 7.30 on Friday 16th.

E

To Graham Greene   Piers Court.
22 December 1955

Dear Graham

Thank you for a most delightful Christmas present. It appals me to think of the peasantry being so luxuriously accommodated. It is a comfort to know that any cottages that were built from these designs are now occupied by best-selling novelists. It is just the sort of book I love, and it is one I don't possess.

I wish I had a present for you. I haven't and now it is too late, but I will set all my children praying that your theatrical ventures bring you all the recreation you require.

I wish we had not had Cyril when we dined together. He is a man of moods. We met next day & he was bright & funny. I cant pretend to any sympathy with him in his present troubles and I find it indecent in him to proclaim them so widely. But I am a prig. He said you comforted and strengthened him greatly.

I wish we met more often. I am deeply fond of you.

                                                                    Evelyn

To Nancy Mitford   Piers Court.
29 December [1955]

Darling Nancy

My poor spastic Hatty is not able to express herself. I can assure you that the copy of *Uncle Tom's Cabin* which Handy sent her at your order, caused deep joy. Also the cards you sent Margaret. Thank you thank you.

I don't suppose you see *Punch*. I enclose an example[1] of the banal byproducts of your communist tract. We have scotched the jewish plot, but we must watch out for 'Hamish Hamilton' who may wish to adulterate our contributions with trash of this kind.

Scotch, Scottish, Scots – you really must look up the history of these terms in the Oxford dictionary (incidentally scholars like Ronnie Knox think it barbarous to speak of that work other than as 'Murray's').

'Britain' can only be used of these islands in Roman times. 'Great Britain' or 'the United Kingdom' in modern age. 'British' is the only possible adjective in certain rare cases. You cant say 'Great British' or 'United-Kingdomly'.

But have a care you do not step outside the limits of polite conversation into those of the King's English. That is the study of a life time and it is too late for you to start. The charm of your writing depends on your refusal to recognize a distinction between girlish chatter & literary language. You will be lost if you fall into pedantry. Stick to pillow cases v. pillow slips.

Have you seen Eric Siepmann's autobiography?[2] I roared. He thinks Col. is a jew. Is *he*? I mean Siepmann.

Fond love
Evelyn

[1]'A Woman of a Certain Class' by Paul Dehn, who used the *Oxford English Dictionary* to show that some words Nancy Mitford designated as U were not as old as Non-U alternatives.
[2]*Confessions of a Nihilist*, 1955.

To Nancy Mitford   Piers Court.
11 January [1956]

Dearest Nancy

I am sorry to learn that Col. has lost his seat but I am glad that it should be in such a good cause. Where will he wear his beautiful dark suit now, unless at mass on Sundays?[1] My brother-in-law has been turned down at Taunton for his Faith.

O.P. = Ordinis predicatorum = of the Order of Preachers = the correct address of a Dominican friar. Col. revealed his ignorance in the case of Couturier.

I notice Carlyle wrote 'Scotchmen'. It was neither upper nor lower class, simply a period use. Of course Scotchmen nowadays make a thing of it – part of the regional revival we find so tiresome.

You must try & love me again.

I have collected a great deal of interesting information about fish-knives for inclusion in your book. Please insist that there is no note thanking Kristol & Co for 'permission' to reprint. Their permission is not required and we caught them trying to sell what was not their property to another Jew. Remember?

Saw Honks at Mells last Sunday – in high spirits. I played Scrabble much against my will with Ronnie Knox & much to my surprise won all the time. He kept the score. Every hand it was 50 to me, 12 to him. At the end, totting up, he said with feigned surprise 'You seem to have beaten me.' 'I had all the luck'. 'Yes, you are 7 ahead'. Dont tell Col. It may shake his faith.

Teresa, my eldest daughter, is coming out in London this summer. Expense ghastly. How can I save £40,000?

Graham Greene recommended a pornographic book[2] in the *Sunday Times*. I mean the sort of book you go to jug for.

… I am glad you have not heard of Mr Kingsley Amis.[3] *Not* a worthy man.

Love
E

[1]Gaston Palewski, who had been Vice-President of the National Assembly, was made French Ambassador to Italy the following year.
[2]Vladimir Nabokov, *Lolita*, 1955.
[3]Kingsley Amis (1922–   ). Poet and novelist. *Lucky Jim* was published in 1954, *That Uncertain Feeling* in 1955.

To ANTHONY POWELL   Piers Court.
[13 January 1956]
Postcard

Ref today's *Punch*.

Sir Brian Robertson[1] was DSO,MC and despatches 1914–18. How could he conceivably be 'belittled' by Mr Muggeridge who, on the only occasion I met him, was attending picnic parties in Algiers in a civilian capacity 1944?[2]

                                                            E

[1]General Sir Brian Robertson (1896–1974). Created Baron Robertson 1961. There had been a paragraph about him in *Punch*, of which Muggeridge was editor, which could be thought slighting.

[2]Malcolm Muggeridge (1903–   ). Journalist. In the Intelligence Corps 1939–45.

To ANTHONY POWELL   Piers Court.
[19 January 1956]
Postcard

You tell me Mr Muggeridge has got into Pratts. It is perfectly true. I have consulted the list. He describes himself there as 'Major'. Curiouser & curiouser.

                                                            E.W.

To MARGARET WAUGH   Royal Crescent Hotel,
27 January 1956   Brighton.

Darling Meg

I am delighted that you enjoyed your London treat. It is very nice to know what you want more than anything in the world, to get it, and to find it comes up to expectation.

Your mother wanted to come to Brighton more than anything in the world. It seemed impossible. Then Derrick[1] fell too ill for his other work but not too ill for milking & Mrs Donaldson's mother fell ill so that she had to leave Rose,[2] so Rose came to look after Teresa and your mother & I came here and she is leading a dizzy life of theatricals & shopping.

Not so dizzy as your London visit. The young Catholic gentlemen sound very wild. I am sure you need not have felt ill-dressed at luncheon. Everyone saw you as a soldier in uniform among a lot of cowardly civilians.

I wonder how many of the Ascot girls at Lady Phipps's told the truth & how many said they were late back at school for reasons of health.

Your mother goes home on Tuesday I go to London for a night. No other treats until February 9th when I go to Dublin for a party given by that sinister Lord Wicklow who took your fancy in the photograph.

I had a splendid bonfire of all the property left in the drawing-room. There was an album of picture post-cards that burned well. Was it yours or Hatty's, I wonder? Do you believe that? If so you are a donkey.

All love sweet Meg

papa

[1] The cowman.
[2] The Donaldsons' daughter, aged nineteen.

To Ann Fleming
30 January 1956

Royal Crescent Hotel,
Brighton.

Dearest Ann

Very many thanks for your letter, card and press cutting. I got into touch with Walkers at once but fear the Rebecca Solomon has been snapped up. I have two pictures of hers which I greatly enjoy. She led a life sadly at variance with the teachings of your new guru, Mr Riddell. [1]

I have brooded darkly about your description of Enton Hall. Then came yesterday's (Septuagesima) epistle which is a direct commentary on it. While it was read I thought of you & Diana & Judy and all the poor waifs who are subject to these attacks of lay ascetism. I decided that Enton Hall was a far graver danger to the soul than White's & that I must pass on St Pauls words to you. He wrote: 'Every athlete must keep his appetites under control; and he does it to win a crown that fades, whereas ours is imperishable. So I do not run my course like a man who is in doubt of his goal .. I buffet my own body and make it my slave; or I, who have preached to others, may myself be rejected as worthless'.

His goal, of course, is God & through God charity. Drink is not bad because it gives one a hangover or a bleary eye, but because it keeps the soul from God. There is a God-implanted instinct in man towards asceticism. All religions practice it. Its object is to turn man's soul *outward* from himself. Mr Riddell perverts this high instinct & turns it *inward* so that people think of their livers & joints & how to make them more comfortable. It is healthier to suffer drunken remorse than be inflated with a spurious sense of well-being.

Laura & I are buffeting our bodies in Brighton (where I should greatly like to return with you for Mogs's [2] ball if she asks me & Teresa).

An opportunity came for temporary relief for Laura at the milking stool so I seized it & whisked her away and she flowers hourly like a parched garden in the rain. Rain in fact is very much with us but we go to the play & do cross-word puzzles. She is taking her ball [3] with rather alarming calm. She has been in desultory correspondence with Margot Howard for some time. Today I have propelled her to London for the day to lunch with her & transcribe her List.

Tomorrow night (Tuesday) I have to make a speech to sailors at Greenwich (why do I do these things?). I shall arrive at White's in the morning. If you can lunch then or on Wednesday could you leave a message at White's? I would continue my sermon.

I take it that the 'Atticus'[4] who admires Auden is not Ian?

Much love from
Evelyn

[1] Mr Riddell was in command of the health farm, Enton Hall.
[2] Imogen Grenfell (1905-69). Married Viscount Gage in 1931.
[3] The Waughs were arranging a coming-out ball for Teresa, to be shared with Lady Christina MacDonnell, daughter of the Earl of Antrim, and Susan Baring, daughter of Lady Rose Baring. It was held in a marquee in Kensington Square.
[4] The *Sunday Times* column to which Ian Fleming was a contributor.

To Father Aelred Watkin   [London.]
7 February 1956

Dear Father Aelred

Thank you very much for sending me the second version of Maria Pasqua's Life,[1] which I have read with deep interest. I wish I had the first draft to compare with it. It is much more informative & authoritative but it seems to me that something has vanished during the rewriting – that peculiar poetic quality which made the first version so haunting. This is a highly interesting piece of family history – but the other promised much more. Perhaps it is the novelist in me that wishes to defeat the historian. As a novel there were three characters only, Maria Pasqua, her husband, the Countess and three atmospheres the Abruzzi, the eccentric luxury of the Countess's milieu, the flat gloom of Norfolk; three acts of gross selfishness, the original 'sale' by her father, the domineering will to keep a human being as a toy, and the boredom inflicted by the squire, and together these trinities could & should comprise a work of art. In this version there is much distraction about uncles & brothers and unless my memory deludes me, some omission of bizarre elements. Was not much more made originally of the countess's peremptory, benevolent demands on the married couple? Did she not ask to have partridges sent her out of season? Wasn't your grandfather's parsimony more grim? Surely he kept his household in the dark for an hour after sunset? Or have I imagined this? Was there not some incident when he grudged her a visit to the theatre? Was there not the hint that he put up with what would seem intolerable interferences, because of his expectations of a legacy?

Perhaps I have played with the idea of Maria Pasqua so long in my mind that I have added inventions of my own.

Please don't misunderstand. I think this a charming book of reminiscences. But there is a unique & poignant story somehow lost in it. It is as though the Norfolk atmosphere had obliterated something very rare.

It ought to be a tragedy of imprisonment. The beginning & end point this, but in between is so much that is prosaic and in a few cases commonplace.

Oh dear. Can't you take a deep breath & invoke Virginia Woolf and Max Beerbohm and start again with the single aim of creating a literary masterpiece? Even at the price of exaggeration & fancy?

Yours very sincerely
Evelyn Waugh

[1]Maria Pasqua was born the beautiful daughter of poor Italians in 1856. Her father took her to Paris where she had great success as a child model, until a portrait of her was seen by a rich and childless Englishwoman, the Comtesse de Noailles. Failing to buy the picture, she bought the child for the price of a vineyard. After an eccentric upbringing Maria Pasqua met and married an English doctor twenty years older than herself. Though he loved her he shared none of her interests, and she lived as a lonely captive in Norfolk until he died at the age of ninety-four. Her daughter had tried to write her life; now her grandson, Father Watkin, was working on it. Eventually *Maria Pasqua* appeared in 1979 written by Father Watkin's sister, Magdalen Goffin.

To the Editor of the Observer   Brighton.
[Printed 12 February 1956]

P.G. WODEHOUSE

Sir, – Your reviewer[1] of Mr P.G. Wodehouse's *French Leave* remarks on "the absence of any mention of England." Had he read attentively, he would have been rewarded by a delightful sketch of the English Civil Servant, Sir Percy Blunt.

He further says of Mr Wodehouse's previous works: "The heroes and heroines always take their leave of us at the moment when the real story begins, i.e., at the altar. (Doesn't Mr Wodehouse ever wonder how they got on after they were married?)"

Mr Wodehouse's novels abound in studies of the complexities of married life. Of the heroes whose subsequent married life is revealed, Mike and Bingo Little may be named as two of many.

But these are blots common in modern criticism. What prompts me to write to you is his final judgement: "But I cannot quite get rid of the feeling that the needle is scratching rather badly and that sooner or later the record will have to be taken off."

Mr Wodehouse has been writing for more than fifty years with a fecundity unrivalled among living novelists of comparable distinction. To use these terms about a man of his age strikes me as singularly infelicitous. – I am, Sir, your obedient servant.

EVELYN WAUGH

[1]John Wain (1925–   ). Author and critic. He had published two novels and a book of poems. He replied:'My sympathies are very easily enlisted in favour of Mr Wodehouse, who has given me so much pleasure, and I rather approve of Mr Waugh's springing to his defence. It is not *criticism*, of course, to defend a poor book by pointing out that the author is an elderly man, or to maintain that anyone who has written a lot of books must be a great author, but then Mr Waugh is not a critic, however much he may generalise about "modern criticism".'

To Father Aelred Watkin   Piers Court.
11 February 1956

Dear Fr Aelred

No, not a novel. I wrote hastily using, I think, the words 'fancy' and 'exaggeration'. I realize now that that was a mistake. The authenticity of the book is essential to its charm and all the corroborative evidence should be preserved, perhaps in footnotes. The personal form of narrative should be preserved. It must be your mother's memories of her mother. What is needed is a rearrangement by which the dramatic theme – beauty in captivity – is kept predominant.

The early part and the very end are excellent. I think without anywhere straying from the evidence, they could be a little more pictorial – the frightened child in the gilded salon could be more richly represented. Then I think more could be done about her early Catholic life, the church being the one place where Madame did not follow her, the sea-side Catholic set her only independent friends and the husband emerging in that set. But up to the marriage the present version is very good. What I think needs dramatizing is the contrast between the drab Norfolk captivity and the peremptory, bizarre eruptions of Madame. The orders to cut trees, erect shelters, inhale chemicals etc. – could these not have been inserted as they occurred – or as they presumably occurred – in the flat routine? The arrival of a letter in Madame's handwriting – what is she going to demand or give now?

I think it is artistically rather a mistake to mention the later estrangement of mother & daughter.

Could not the fading of beauty be more delicately and insistently stressed?

Should not a time sequence be more observed – even though there may be some doubts in your mother's mind about precise dates?

One needs a single, diversified, culminating narrative.

I am sorry I did not notice the partridges. Negligent reading on my part, but a sign perhaps that the incident was unaccented.

These are just a few ideas that occur to me.

But please don't let me discourage you. I am sure that in its present form the story will delight many. It is just that I feel it could be so much better with a little revision.

Your father is a better critic than I. What does he think?

                                                    Yours very sincerely
                                                    Evelyn Waugh

To Auberon Waugh   Piers Court.
11 February 1956

Dear Bron

I have written to enquire at what age apprentices are taken in the hotel-trade. I think you are still too young, but I don't know.

Meanwhile think & *pray* about your future. This is an occasion that will affect your entire life.

I have much sympathy with your restlessness with school life. I felt as you do at your age, asked my father to remove me, was resentful at the time when he refused. Now I am grateful to him.

If there was anything you ardently wished to do – go to sea, learn a skilled trade etc – because you felt a real vocation for it, I would not stand in your way. I believe you think of hotel-keeping simply as a means of leaving school. That is a very poor motive for taking a job and hotel-keeping is not a craft which fits you for anything else. If you fail in that, you will be further from starting anything else. 'Previous experience: two years as kitchen-boy, waiter, liftman, book-keeper' is not a high recommendation for any other appointment.

If you leave school now you will not get a commission in a good regiment. Perhaps you will not get a commission at all.

Most of the interest and amusement of life comes from ones friends. All my friends are those I made at Oxford and in the army. You are condemning yourself either to a lonely manhood or one among second-rate associates. All because you lack the will-power and self-control to make a success of the next eighteen months by cooperating with those who have only your own best interests at heart, throwing yourself into the life of the school & doing your work and obeying the rules. At your age, wherever you go, you will find yourself under discipline much less humane & benevolent than that of the monks.

You have a sense of humour and a good gift of self expression. On the other hand you are singularly imprudent and you have a defective sense of honour. These bad qualities can lead to disaster.

My financial interests have no bearing on my wish for your welfare. I am sorry you should suggest that they might.

Your affectionate papa
E. Waugh

To Brian Franks[1]   Piers Court.
11 February 1956

Dear Brian

This is not to negotiate about the ball but to consult you on a personal problem.

My boy, aged 16, is very restless at school. He has not been sacked and he passes his various exams with credit but he is anxious to get away from school. I have some sympathy with him. He is thinking seriously of the hotel trade. I think either you or Basil[2] told me that there was a system by which boys were taken on & trained in all the departments for eventual management. At what age do they take them? Could he do his basic training before his military service?

He is taller and better mannered than his father. Do you think it a good opening for him?[2]

Yours ever
Evelyn

[1]Managing director of the Hyde Park Hotel.
[2]Basil Bennett, chairman of the Hyde Park Hotel.

To Alec Waugh   Piers Court.
11 February 1956

Dear Alec

Thank you very much for sending me *Island in the Sun* which I have read with keen pleasure. It is very encouraging that you have the powers to complete so large a composition. I must soon get the name of your rejuvenating injections.

I have no surprise that the book has been a success. It is a remarkable portrayal of a community and I greatly admire the intricate chain-reaction of small causes & large effects. Carson is a first class piece of character drawing.

Terence [Greenidge] will be pleased to find himself named as one of the ornaments of the 20s. I am sorry to learn that there is a rival to Mrs Postlethwaite-Cobb in providing comforts for literary men.

One passage puzzled me. What is the significance of the small cut under the thumb of the adventuress which so excited the ADC on the morrow of their fornication? I have thought about it and consulted worldly friends & can't understand.

I think I have told you already, have I not, how elated I am by your great success with this book? Now I know how well you deserve it.

Your affec. brother
Evelyn

Please explain about the cut thumb?[1]

[1]Alec Waugh replied: 'Margot dabbed the blood on the ADC's back with her handkerchief, later cut her finger, mixed her blood with his and took it to the obeah man.'

To Father Aelred Watkin   Piers Court.
Quinquagesima [12 February] 1956

Dear Fr Aelred,

Another thought. Could you not conceive of Maria Pasqua's life as a film? I don't mean – Heaven forfend – that it should be filmed, or that you should attempt to give it any of the character of a Hollywood script. I mean in the *mechanics* of the *imagination*. Instead of seeing it as an historical document, imagine yourself watching a film – each incident as precise and authentic as in the present version, but with the *continuity* (in the technical cinematographic sense) and selective dramatic emphasis and scenery of a film. And then write as though describing the experience. Does this help at all? Or make matters confused?

Yours ever
E.W.

To Terence Kilmartin[1]   Piers Court.
12 February [1956]

Dear Sir

I see you have printed my protest about Mr Wain's review of P.G. Wodehouse & I have read his note with interest.

I was, of course, rebuking his manners. To tell a man of, I think, 76 that he won't be able to go on much longer, seems to me the acme of caddishness.

But what interests me is Mr Wain's use of the word 'critic'. 'So-and-so isn't a *critic*' (his italics). When I was young everyone was a critic. Those who were paid to write reviews were neither the best nor the most influential critics. (Incidentally I began reviewing for the *Observer* nearly 30 years ago).

But Mr Wain seems to mean that nowadays there is a specialized trade, entrance to which comes from having taken a diploma in English Literature at some 'University'. This links up with Mr Maugham's recent attack on the new state-educated graduates.

There is an amusing essay to be made of this, taking Mr Wain's note as the text, but I am unwilling to give it free to the correspondence column. I would write you 1000–1200 words on this for 30 guineas, preferably in the Correspondence Column. That is the form it would most conveniently take. But if you *greatly* prefer, as a literary essay.

Yours faithfully
E. Waugh

P.S. Could you be so kind as to let me have an immediate answer as I should like to write on this topic elsewhere if you are not interested. [2]

[1] Literary editor of the *Observer* from 1952.
[2] 'Dr Wodehouse and Mr Wain' appeared in the *Spectator*, 24 February 1956.

To Father Aelred Watkin   Piers Court.
Ash Wednesday [15 February] 1956

Dear Fr Aelred

I should not leave out anything about Madame – rather amplify it. Nor about your grandfather. Uncles & aunts to be kept in the background. It is rather a question of emphasis than omission.

I think you might allow yourself some freedom of conjecture where nothing is known. Also freedom to insert undated letters, or extracts from them, where they best suit the dramatic sequence.

Surely some Betjemanesque evocation of late Victorian Catholic Bournemouth would be legitimate. No need to scan parish registers. Create the atmosphere.

Please don't bother to answer unless there is any other point you would like to discuss – in which case please don't hesitate.

I think that after all I may be able to get to Downside for the triduum. We might talk of it then.

Thank you very much for remembering me at your Mass.

> Yours very sincerely
> Evelyn Waugh

To Auberon Waugh   Piers Court.
20 February 1956

Dear Bron,

I am delighted to hear from Tusky[1] that, unaccustomed as you are to public speaking, you have won the debating prize and are going to Sherborne with the team. You will not, I think, hear your cousin Peter[2] speak there.

The only honest answer to your letter is this: growing up is a disagreeable process for most men. You have to grow up somewhere. Downside seems to me the best place, but I am always open to other suggestions. If you leave prematurely everyone will always think you were sacked. To be sacked from school is not absolutely fatal but it is a grave disadvantage for the early years of whatever career you decide on. I am pretty sure it will prevent your getting a commission in any Household regiment and would make entry into Oxford more difficult.

I could probably get you into Stonyhurst, but as it is school itself, rather than Downside, that you dislike, I don't see the advantage unless it enabled you to shake off undesirable friends. But one can make undesirable friends anywhere if one has the taste for them.

I don't suppose you want to go to Dartmouth?

I see no reason why, once you have passed into Oxford, you shall not spend the last two terms before going up at a foreign school learning a language.

In the hope of understanding you better I have been reading the diaries I kept at your age. I am appalled at what an odious prig I was. Debating, boxing, ragging the OTC, intriguing for advancement, atheism and over-eating seem to have been my consolations at Lancing. One great advantage you have on me is the contact with a place of prayer. Don't neglect that advantage. Your spiritual and moral welfare is the main thing of absolute importance.

> Your affec. papa
> E.W.

[1]Father Ralph Russell, master at Downside.
[2]Alec Waugh's son.

To Tom Driberg   Piers Court.
23 February 1956

Dear Tom

I am touched and most grateful to you for your present of *Beaverbrook*.[1] I opened
it with eagerness as I had seen it advertised as a 'hostile' biography. What do I find?
A honeyed eulogy. You mention a few of Beaverbrook's more notorious public
aberrations but you give little impression of the deep malevolence of the man.
Instead you exalt him to the dignity of a St John – a brilliant statesman who just
failed. Was all the story of your tiff with him a 'publicity stunt' devised by the pair of
you. If Beaverbrook really thinks your book hostile, he must have singularly little
sense of his true position. It is not only crusted Tories and 'Roman Catholic
intellectuals' who hold him in contempt, but illiterate protestants, too, and radical
free-thinkers. I was disappointed to find so little of your own writing in the book. It
is a bunch of press-cuttings – and cuttings from the basest sources.

It is a pity you wrote before the appearance of Bloggs Baldwin's life of his father,
and were obliged to rely on G.M. Young. To prefer Hannen Swaffer's word to
Baldwin's (on the *Globe* interview) seems to me to be carrying professional loyalty to
a preposterous extreme.[2]

While you fail to give the full villainy of the man, you fail to give his superficial
charm. He is, or was, at his best among women. Yours is an all male caste.

I was shocked to find you falling into the popular misuse of *expertise*. In France
this word does not mean 'skill' but the judgement by an expert on the authenticity of
a work of art.

All this sounds ungrateful. Please believe it is not unfriendly.

Yours ever
Evelyn

[1]Tom Driberg, *Beaverbrook, a Study in Power and Frustration*, 1956.
[2]In May 1924 Stanley Baldwin gave an interview to the political correspondent of the *People*, whose
editor was Hannen Swaffer. When published it contained a savage attack on the Lords Birkenhead.
Beaverbrook and Rothermere, the last two described as 'men I would not have in my home'. Baldwin
denied that he had said the words attributed to him. Driberg believed that he did. G.M. Young's *Stanley
Baldwin* appeared in 1952, *My Father, the True Story* by A.W. Baldwin in 1955.

To the Earl Baldwin   Piers Court.
24 February [1956]

Dear Bloggs

I dont suppose Driberg's life of Beaverbrook would normally come your way. It
has a picture of your father which you have already demolished but I think you
should read pp. 178–185 and, if you think fit, answer them in a letter to *The Times*.[1]

Yours ever
Boaz

[1]Lord Baldwin does not mention the incident in his book, nor did he write to *The Times*.

To Ann Fleming   Piers Court.
25 February 1956

Dearest Ann

What has become of you? I am sure that in your emaciated condition you cannot withstand the frost and have fled to Golden Eye.[1] This is the first February I have spent in England since 1944. Never again. I meant to write a great work of literary art but I am numb. Never again.

I last saw you in London. Well after that my life followed what Cyril would call the manic-depressive curve – what I call going on a bust and sobering up. I had a lovely two or three days in London – mostly with Daphne and her Mr Zan [Xan Fielding] to whom I took a fancy. Then everyone went away and I did not dare to go home for fear of the cold so I sat about in lonely clubs. Then I went to Dublin for a night to see my old crony Lord Wicklow. I had meant to stay longer but the cold was worse there so home I came and here I have been ever since, stultified by frost.

Laura and I went through blizzards to Bristol to see Mrs Kennedy in *King Lear*.[2] She was awfully bad and King Lear's sufferings seemed no sharper than mine. But, I say, what a film *Lear* would make! The only Shakespeare play obviously designed for the Cinema....

I have read an awfully bad life of Lord Beaverbrook and a jolly one of Lady Mendl.[3] Most of the time I keep rereading *Lear* and thinking what a good film it would make. I also read Alec Waugh's best-seller. Well its rather good if you think of it as being by an American which he is really. It is extraordinary to notice in the reviews of the *Archbishop and the Lady*[4] how few people have read Ronnie Knox's *Enthusiasm*, one of the great books of our life-time. In 50 pages he tells one all one needs to know of Mme Guyon. When people say there is no anti-clericalism in England I think of the huge reputation Ronnie would have if he were a heathen.

Love from
Evelyn

[1]The Flemings' house in Jamaica.
[2]Moira Shearer (Mrs Ludovic Kennedy) played Cordelia.
[3]L. Berrelmans, *To the One I Love the Best*, 1955. Lady Mendl was 'a sort of eighteenth century

To A.D.Peters   Piers Court.
17 March 1956

Dear Pete

I have waited a long time to catch the *Express* in libel. I think they have done it this time. Miss Spain's statement that I complain the *Express* sold only 300 copies of my novel is entirely false. I enclose the article[1] she has misread.

Also the figures of my sales are, as you know, wildly wrong.

There should be no difficulty in proving malice.

Will you please take legal opinion and if that is favourable bring in a writ. Perhaps Chapman & Hall might like to come in too.

Yours ever

Evelyn

[1]The *Spectator* article, 'Dr Wodehouse and Mr Wain'. Waugh had said that the critics of the Beaverbrook press no longer had any influence at all, which provoked Nancy Spain's attack in the *Daily Express*.

To Margaret Waugh   Piers Court.
17 March [1956]

Darling Meg,

I went to London to take Teresa to a debutantes' cocktail party given by a friend of mine.[1] There were 250 pimply youths and 250 hideous girls packed so tight together they could not move hand or foot. So I sat with the butler in the hall and that is the last anyone has seen of Teresa. I suppose she was crushed to death & the corpse too flat to be recognized. About 100 dead girls were carried out & buried in a common pit. R.I.P. I shall never let you, my ewe lamb, become a debutante.

I have great hopes that Miss Spain has libelled me in the *Daily Express*. I am taking legal advice. If I win some fine tax-free damages I will give you a treat. What? Well I don't know. Something edifying & instructive.

Poor Lady Diana Abdy, who painted the portrait of me in Hatty's room, has been unconscious for 15 days after a motor accident.[2] Her only son is delirious with skull, thigh, jaw & pelvis all broken in another hospital. The husband/father came to luncheon today. He was bright as a cricket.

At Paddington I saw Lady Hylton[3] & Sweet Alice[4] staggering under a load of luggage. There were hundreds of porters about but Lord Hylton is so strict they dare not employ one. I carried some of their luggage for them but they did not give me a tip.

We have a very pretty pale cook who cooks very well. She is a girl guide. You may join her troop.

All love

Papa

[1]Lady Ravensdale.
[2]Lady Diana never recovered and died in 1967. Her son Valentine recovered completely.
[3]Perdita Asquith (1910–   ). Married William Jolliffe, later Lord Hylton, in 1931.
[4]Their daughter Alice (1937–   ). Married John Chancellor 1959–69, Richard Windsor-Clive in 1969.

To LADY MARY LYGON   Piers Court.
[March 1956]

Darling
    So my great new friend Mr Donaldson went to call at 19 Boltons during the frost
and he saw the disfigured motor-car and he said: What happened to your beautiful
car? That, said the socialist,[1] is the work of a Russian Countess.
    I am glad to hear of your great social progress but still gladder to know that you
have not discarded your humble friends and are to dine with Pauper [Lord
Kinross]. He asked me to share his modest fare but alas I am here and cant come.
    Am I right to address you by your virgin name?[2]
    That sex maniac Sir Robert Abdy was here on Saturday. His pretty wife is
unconscious & at death's door and his son is delirious in Truro. He talked a lot about
his KOK.
    Little Laura has to go to London to show her daughter off to the Queen so I shall
be all alone frigging to keep my spirits up.
    I wish they would cart off Randolph to the Seychelles. A merciful release for all of
us and a very suitable torture for the traitor Makarios.[3]
    I was in London for a day last week. O I hated it. Never again never never never

                                                    All love
                                                    Bo

[1]Anthony Crosland (1918–77). Labour MP and Foreign Secretary. He lived in a flat above Lady Mary.
[2]Lady Mary's marriage to Prince Vsevolode was dissolved that year.
[3]Archbishop Makarios of Cyprus had been arrested and sent into exile in the Seychelles.

To NANCY MITFORD   Piers Court.
22 March 1956

Dearest Nancy
    I am hugely grateful to you for sending me *A Legacy*.[1] I read it straight through
with intense pleasure. For the first half – up to the marriage of Jules & Melanie – I
was in full agreement 'one of the best novels I ever read' as you say. After that I
found a slight falling off, as though the writer had suddenly taken a stiff dose of
Henry James, particularly in the long talks between Sarah & Caroline. Also I think it
was clumsy to have any of the narrative in the first person. The daughter relates
things she cannot possibly ever have known as though she were an eye witness. But
these are small blemishes. What a brilliant plot! How grim the military school
incident! How intensely funny the Jewish household & Gottlieb and the monkeys
and the christenings! Clara is a failure half the time, I think. The writer doesn't
know much about Catholicism. 'Is it not insisting on error, this making images of
what is itself illusion' could only be said by a sort of bogus theosophist, (p 188) and

(p354) 'It is presumption even to talk of being saved' by a despairing Calvinist. The English is slightly odd in places. 'Merz's' is always written instead of 'Merzes' as the plural of Merz.

I wondered for a time who this brilliant 'Mrs Bedford' could be. A cosmopolitan military man, plainly, with a knowledge of parliamentary government and popular journalism, a dislike for Prussians, a liking for Jews, a belief that everyone speaks French in the home ... Then, of course, it came to me. Good old Col. He *has* employed his retirement well. Do give him my genuine homage.

Best Love
Evelyn

[1]By Sybille Bedford, 1956.

To Alec Waugh   Piers Court.
24 April 1956

Dear Alec
Thank you for your letter.

It is typical of Miss Spain that she should say you asked her to luncheon when it was she who asked you.

I wrote to you several weeks ago to the Savile, marked 'please forward'. I expect my letter is far away.

The facts of the libel spring from a senile aberration of Lord Beaverbrook's who believes that you and I are consumed with mutual jealousy which he wishes to aggravate.

In the course of this he set Miss Spain on to libel me. I hope to earn a tax free sum which will pay for Teresa's coming-out. It is all very satisfactory. I think I can't lose. It is simply a question of how little or how much damages I get.

In the course of the libel on me she wrote: '*Island in the Sun* foretold by me as this years runaway Best Seller has now topped 60,000 copies as a direct result of my *Daily Express* notice. So the publishers told me yesterday.'

This is not libellous. On the other hand it cannot be agreeable to you or Cassells to have it declared that your great success is due to Miss Spain. It is plainly false that Cassells said so.

Would a representative of Cassell care to go into the box and repudiate the statement? Such a repudiation would further emphasise the irresponsibile malice of the *Express*.

I enclose a shameful little book [1]

Evelyn

[1]*Noblesse Oblige*, edited by Nancy Mitford, with a contribution by Waugh.

To ANTHONY POWELL   Piers Court.
[31 May 1956]
Postcard

Delighted to read of your decoration.[1] I should rather like something of the sort
myself. How does one set about it? I hope it doesn't block you from a knighthood.
That's what one really needs. Is Major Muggeridge suprised at being passed over?
Hot Lunch Rt. Hon![2] I went over Abbotsford with Mr R.A. Butler.[3] Will that
help?

Curzon preferred 'Marquis'. Laura's grandfather refused a marquisate on the
grounds that it was a French title.

[1]CBE.
[2]Hugh Molson had been made a Privy Councillor.
[3]R.A. Butler (1902–   ). The Conservative statesman. Then Lord Privy Seal and Leader of the House
of Commons. Created life peer 1965.

To NANCY MITFORD   Piers Court.
7 June [1956]

Darling Nancy
O the horrors of U. In this morning's *Times* the entire Burmese cabinet have
adopted this damnable prefix.

It is clever of you to be able to work. My life is greatly disturbed by Teresa's
London début and Laura's waiting attendance on her. Also by people coming to see
the house, which I have put up for sale. But I look forward greatly to finding a new
one if I sell this. Castle preferred, 50 rooms, 50 acres a water fall £5000. It should
not be difficult to find.

I can't blame Debo for falling in love with Mr Xan [Fielding]. I am a little in love
with him myself. But it will make her very unpopular if she robs Daphne.

I say do you in your large literary circle know of a Maurice Baring, male or
female? Have Honks and I ever spoken to you of Maria Pasqua, the grandmother of
a Downside monk who in the 1860s was the most popular child model (Trilby[1] not
mannequin) in Paris and was purchased from her father by an eccentric English
Countess of Noailles, married to an aged, dull Norfolk squireen, a cousin of
Coopers? It is a most moving story of Beauty in captivity, very sad & full of
authentic, bizarre detail. Not a plot for you or me, but it could be made a great work
of art by someone. Who? All the documents are available & the daughter's (monk's
mother) not quite good enough attempt at writing them up. If you think of
anyone, do tell me.

Your Mr. Raymond has been behaving very oddly, trying to pick up my 17 year
old niece[2] in London and telephoning to her from a neighbouring public house.
He also wrote improperly of John Evelyn. Is he a friend of Mr. Beachcomber? I bet
he is.

Tony Powell has accepted a CBE. No sour grapes but I think it very WRONG that politicians should treat writers as second grade civil servants. Osbert Sitwell opened the breach by accepting this degrading decoration. I trust you will stand out for CH or Dame. [3]

I went to stay in the lowlands of Scotland – *very* beautiful. They talked of U there. I stopped on the road home with socialist jews at Cambridge. U again. There was a song, do you remember 'And you know darn well that its U again?'

Laura and Teresa are here for a few days playing a kind of patience with debutantes names fitting them into dinner parties for balls.

Love
Evelyn

[1] Trilby was an artists' model and the eponymous heroine in a novel by George du Maurier.

[2] Anne Grant.

[3] Waugh refused the CBE in 1959. Nancy Mitford accepted it in 1972 and wrote to Robin McDouall, 'I suppose it's what Evelyn said is an insult and refused. But I accepted with pleasure as a mark that it is not thought unpatriotic of me to live abroad.'

To PENELOPE BETJEMAN
Piers Court.
[3 July 1956]
Postcard

Warn Hungerford CWL [1] of dreadful influence of French Dominicans. I wish you would come to our ball. I have sold this house, [2] have to get out quick. Advertised in *Times* for Victorian Castle, got answers from owners of Lutyens mansions, Tudor manors etc. It is not only long hair it is sweat and cricket shirts and woollen socks the young men have. Would I were ashes like your pa and did not see it. Army always queer in best regiments, hence decent appearance.

[1] Catholic Women's League.

[2] For £9,500 to Mrs Gadsden.

To BRIAN FRANKS
Piers Court.
[3 July 1956]
Postcard

Cant remember how many I ordered dinner for on Tuesday. Number should be 18 eighteen. Cold Madrilène, Lobster Newburg, Vol-au-Vent of chicken, Salade, Strawberry & ice. Non Vintage champagne for all but me

E

Hope you are coming to the ball

To Margaret and Harriet Waugh   Piers Court.
8 July [1956]

Darling Meg & Hatty

It is very vulgar of you (Meg) to want to see press cuttings about your sister's ball. We kept out photographers, of course, and tried to keep out journalists but some nasty guest must have gossiped and there were some silly paragraphs in one or two of the commoner papers.

However it was a great success. Teresa wore a dress of emerald green calico trimmed with zebra skin and a straw hat, button boots of patent leather and woollen gloves & was greatly admired. Unfortunately she was given a black eye by Alice Jolliffe but we bandaged her up & she managed well with one eye.

We had the Stinchcombe Silvular band to play and Miss Mildmay crooned. For supper there was plenty of stout and kippers and bread & margarine and blancmange and plum jam for those who came early but it soon ran out.

Your mother insisted on bringing all 14 cows and they took up most of the ball room but there was a little tent in the garden. Christina McDonnell[1] and Susan Baring[2] smoked clay pipes all the time & the tent grew rather stuffy. A lot of criminals came uninvited and began robbing everyone so the police charged with truncheons and, I am sorry to say, arrested Alec Waugh and Alick Dru by mistake. They are still in prison but we hope to get them out on bail in a day or two. To make things difficult Alick Dru had five watches, six diamond rings and some silver spoons in his pocket when arrested so he may get sent to prison for a year or two.

One of the cows escaped from the ball room into the Kensington Square Convent. The nuns have been milking her ever since & feeding her on sun-flower seeds.

Polly Grant was murdered by a black man whom your uncle Auberon brought.

Otherwise the ball was a great success.

Your affec. papa
E.W.

[1]Lady Christina McDonnell (1938–   ) married in 1963 Joseph Hoare.
[2]Susan Baring (1938–   ) married in 1962 Joseph Rogaly.

To Harriet Waugh   Piers Court.
16 July [1956]

Darling Harriet,

This enormous sum is not all to be spent before the end of term.

We look forward greatly to your return for your last holidays here.

We have seen an attractive house near Taunton called Combe Florey with an Elizabethan gate-house. There is an asylum for half witted men (not dangerous lunatics) next door and they work in the garden for very low wages.

Your sister Teresa is very much occupied with the London season. I gave a dinner party for her last week for the Duchess of Norfolk's ball.

Your god-father Basil Bennett is going mad. He was heard at Ascot Races complaining that there was a bird in his top-hat pecking his head.

> Your affec. papa
> E. Waugh

To Ann Fleming   Piers Court.
26 September [1956]

Dearest Ann

... You ask what I thought of Miss Macaulay's book.[1] Well, it was an Anglican lady's *Brighton Rock*, the grim story of une âme damnée. The reviewers thought it a whimsical travel book. Miss Macaulay has always had a tender interest in waifs and orphans. Lady Eden is the waif and orphan of the age.

Lady Pamela's interior – I speak of her bijou residence not of her bowels – is a triumph of self-expression and to be admired accordingly. I am being greatly frustrated in expressing myself in my new hide-out because the vendor is a crazy colonel straight from facetious popular fiction who wont let me or my architect or plumber come near the place until he moves out. I shall be homeless for many months. The colonels sister lets me in when the colonel is away. Yesterday he was at a wedding – not Antonia Pakenham's[2] – so I was able to skulk round for a few hours.

On the way there I left my son James in charge of the Hollises to send with their boy to Stonyhurst. They were on the platform at Bath dressed for Antonia's misalliance and Mr Hollis had no hat and though I say it who loved him looking more like a friend of yours than of mine. Laura lost her platform ticket but the man at the gate said: 'Don't trouble, madam, we can trust *you*' adding 'That *was* Mr Aneurin Bevan you were talking to wasn't it?'

Teresa made a good soup three days ago & seems slightly more composed in her mind. The bills for her ball keep coming up – the total is crippling.[3] Never again....

I have done several days hard work in the last few weeks. The mad book is going to be very funny, I believe.

> Love from
> Evelyn

[1]Rose Macaulay, *The Towers of Trebizond*, 1956.
[2]Antonia Pakenham (1932–   ) married Hugh Fraser, the Conservative MP, in 1956.
[3]£2,271; Waugh's share presumably £757.

To Daphne Fielding   Piers Court.
2 October [1956]

Darling Daphne

How are you? Where are you? Well I will send this to Cornwall with fourpence in stamps in the hope someone sends it on. Several things to say. First, I met your boy

Weymouth[1], he came to a sad little dinner at Captain Bennett's hotel before a ball and I think he is the most enchanting creature of either sex I have met for twenty years. I didn't know who he was but a lot of dreadful looking young men with long hair were saying how do you do to me and then I saw his mothers lovely mad eyes and I said what cocktail and he said gin & tonic. That really was all I saw of him but goodness I fell in love. Then two or three nights later I met him in Hill Street and he told me a story I could not follow about having his overcoat stolen. Goodness he is a beauty. I say, talking of mad, I am full in the middle of writing an account of my going off my rocker. It seems funny to me. Would you think it awful cheek if I dedicated it to you? So I have sold this house to a very decent old girl who has paid too much for it and I am on the move to a house near Taunton. Go West Old Man. Dull, square, sand stone, secluded, nice for Laura near all her relations. I nearly bought a bishops palace at Exeter but was outbid by a government office. So this new house is where I shall die and it will be a long lifes work to make it pretty, but it can be done. Goodness, have you seen what Lady Pamela Berry has done in her house? Well she is richer than me and more full of zeal and zip. But I hope I don't quite do that. So Ran & I gave a ball and you didn't come and the bills keep coming in and are crippling. And no one has heard of Coote[3] for six months. If you get this letter please answer to this address where I shall be for a week or two. I can't tell you my new address for fear Lord Noel-Buxton discovers it.

All love
Evelyn

[1]Daphne Fielding's son Viscount Weymouth (1932–   ). Painter.
[2]*The Ordeal of Gilbert Pinfold* is dedicated 'To Daphne in the confidence that her abounding sympathy will extend even to poor Pinfold'.
[3]Lady Dorothy Lygon was in Istanbul working as a governess.

TO NANCY MITFORD   Piers Court.
23 October [1956]

Dearest Nancy
    Thank you very much indeed for the French translations. I wish I could make a suggestion for your title but I don't know nearly enough about the subject. Is there not perhaps some luminous key-phrase used by Voltaire himself. How about 'Sense & Sentiment', 'Brain & Heart' 'The credulous sceptic', 'Voltaire in Love' 'Emily's thorny bed'?[1]
    ... Beaton slipped a disc carrying Garbo's jewel case.

Love
E

[1]Nancy Mitford, *Voltaire in Love*, 1957.

To Ann Fleming   Piers Court.
23 October [1956]

Dearest Ann

The Duggan Memorial Luncheon was a great deal better than I expected. Last time I sat between Ladies Milner[1] and Howe.[2] But I was sorry not to see you. Alfred is a saint. Lady Violet Powell[3] is a pillar of the Church of England. Powell I suspect of agnosticism.

This is the last day in the old home. At least the last day of peace. Tomorrow the furniture vans begin coming. Poor Laura is beginning to mope. I am entirely delighted, elated, exhilarated. My only sorrow that I shant quite finish the barmy book, which is going to be quite long but I believe funny. I shall probably go to Brighton – shabby genteelers – to finish it....

Love from
Evelyn

[1] Lois Brown married in 1917 James Milner, a Labour MP created Baron Milner in 1951.
[2] Sybil Johnson, who married in 1944 the fifth Earl Howe.
[3] Lady Violet Pakenham married Anthony Powell in 1934.

To Gabriel Fielding[1]   Piers Court.
29 October [1956]

Dear Mr Fielding

Thank you for sending me Mrs Spark's remarkable book.[2]

The first half, up to the motor accident, is brilliant. The second half rather diffuse. The mechanics of the hallucinations are well managed. These particularly interested me as I am myself engaged on a similar subject.

Mrs Spark no doubt wants a phrase to quote on the wrapper and in advertisements. She can report me as saying: 'brilliantly original and fascinating.'

Please do not trouble to acknowledge this.

Yours sincerely
E. Waugh

[1] Gabriel Fielding (1916–   ). Pseudonym of Alan Barnsley, doctor and novelist.
[2] *The Comforters*, 1956, Muriel Spark's first novel.

To Ann Fleming   Pixton Park
7 November [1956]   Dulverton.

Dearest Ann

I have studied the Suez expedition with interest. These are the important facts (a) it cannot be justified on moral or legal grounds (b) practically no recent action of any

British government can be justified morally. e.g. Death duties (c) Any troup of Boy Scouts can defeat the Egyptian army (d) No one can govern Egypt now that Nasser has armed the school children (e) No one can manage the canal without governing Egypt (f) if Jerk[1] really wants to increase the traffic in this country by importing more petrol through the canal, he must depopulate Egypt. This can very simply be done by destroying the Nile barrages. The wogs would starve to death in six months (g) a more humane solution is to stop motor traffic – particularly buses & charabancs. in England (h) Our long occupation of Cyprus proves fatuous since its justification was to keep a holding force ready for immediate police action in just this situation.

No doubt everyone has said all this a hundred times to you. I don't talk to anyone about it. I have great satisfaction in seeing the crypto-radical in Maurice Bowra peep out of its hole. He did just the same in 1926 when you were a little girl in the General Strike. It was the socialists, you will remember, who gave him his spurs.

I have had a gruesome week of duty. Left Stinkers for good & drove to Lancashire to entertain my dreadful little boy[2] at Stonyhurst. Then to Ascot to entertain my little girls[3] there. They gave me a severe cold. Since then I have lain in bed here.

Teresa I am glad to say is being very aloof from undergraduate excitements over politics.[4] She gave a whisky party – like Mrs Rodd.

I have been sent proofs of a very clever first novel by a lady named Muriel Sparks [*sic*]. The theme is a Catholic novelist suffering from hallucinations, hearing voices – rather disconcerting. It will appear quite soon. I am sure people will think it is by me. Please contradict such assertions.

Love from
Evelyn

[1] Sir Anthony Eden (1897–77). Prime Minister 1955–January 1957. Created Earl of Avon 1961.
[2] James, aged ten.
[3] Margaret, fourteen, and Harriet, twelve.
[4] Teresa was in her first year at Somerville College, Oxford.

6 Decline and Fall
1956-1966

COMBE FLOREY HOUSE
TAUNTON

16ᵗʰ March 65

Dearest Elizabeth

Don't answer.

It was jolly decent of you to forward Gerhardi's pathetic appeal. He has, according to my 'Who's Who' an O.B.E. Goodness knows why he wants to heighten his rank. He is not a friend of mine tho' I greatly enjoyed his early books. I think he is bit dotty probably.

You ask what I thought of of Pope John's spiritual diary. It was exactly what a thousand priests in search of perfection might have kept (and indeed do keep). It's chief interest was that it exploded all that air balloon about 'the Johannine Revival'. He was a good old man who got better. He had no conception of the Pandora's box which his Council would open. This comes out most clearly in the French book of anecdotes I reviewed at the same time. The best (which I can't at the moment find) when asked about that Jesuit archaeologist whom the Americans admire. 'He is French. Why worry about such things. Teach the Pater, the Ave, the Credo. Basta.' That was Pope John whom the

Introduction

Waugh spent the last ten years of his life at Combe Florey in Somerset, twenty miles from Pixton where Laura's family lived. Though he wrote four books and had as many planned his energy gradually ran out. Gilbert Pinfold did not return. The three eldest children left home, got married and had children of their own. The raids on London grew less frequent and more exhausting. His teeth hurt and his friends died. He grew old and died before his time.

This waning was gradual not immediate. *The Life of Ronald Knox*, 1959, is a major work entailing much research and a trip to Rhodesia. The resulting travel book, *Tourist in Africa*, 1960, he dismissed as a 'pot-boiler'. The final volume of the war trilogy, *Unconditional Surrender*, 1961, shows no falling off, and the next year he returned to British Guiana with his daughter Margaret to see the changes brought by thirty years. The writing of *Basil Seal Rides Again*, 1963, a story 'in my earlier manner', and *A Little Learning*, 1964, planned as the first of three volumes of autobiography, were interspersed with trips to Europe.

More letters have been omitted from the last years than from any other period. He wrote many, more survive; but his life was uneventful, repetition was inevitable and for the first time widespread.

To John McDougall   Combe Florey House,
Postcard   Combe Florey,
                                               Nr Taunton.

Here is the new end.

I think I should read galleys.

For wrapper – could we get permission to reproduce one of Francis Bacon's paintings? It would be out of the question of course to commission one, but he might let us have 'serial rights' of an existing horror.

How about large paper edition, 50 copies at my expense? We aren't lucky with hand made paper. How much would large paper & buckram cost me?

                                                               E

To Margaret Waugh   Easton Court Hotel,
[November? 1956]   Chagford,
                                               Devon.

Darling Meg

I had just written to you at Ascot when a nun telephoned to say you had taken poison[1]. Silly ass. I hope it has not given you a very severe pain. I hope you will not take poison again. I hope the hospital is comfortable and the nurses polite. Write to me here and tell me you are well.

                                                          All love
                                                           Papa

[1] An accident. Margaret sucked mercury through a pipette.

To Margaret Waugh   Tetton House,
[November 1956]   Taunton.

Darling Pig

I went to Combe Florey today to see the first load of furniture in & found it a very much larger & pleasanter house than I remembered. We hope to sleep there for the first time on Wednesday.

I do not understand what Sister John the Baptist means by saying she 'must have your travelling arrangements'. You & your sister simply take the most convenient train to Taunton, informing me in good time of the *date* & *hour* of your arrival. Your second class railway fares should not exceed £2. I enclose £3 & expect a detailed account & change.

I have chosen you a very nice room at Combe Florey. It faces West by South and is next to the Pinfold bathroom which you may use when there are no visitors. I am having a bottle of quicksilver put on your wash hand stand. The stomach pump will be kept in the cellar.

I met a nice couple named Addington. They said: 'Are you the father of the famous girl who attempted suicide?'

> All love
> Papa

To Margaret Waugh

> Combe Florey House,
> Combe Florey,
> Nr Taunton.

Sweet Pig

Of course I am not angry with you.

I hope you will be the belle of the ball in your garland of sausages.

You might combine spiritual with physical exercise by making your Stations of the Cross with a bucket of water balanced on your nut.

> All love
> Papa

To Ann Fleming
28 November 1956

> The Manor House,
> Mells,
> Frome.

... Pixton was overrun by a golden horde of Magyar[1] defeated freedom-fighters, so I have taken refuge here. I spent one evening in London where everyone was much madder than ever I was.

Today I went to the sale of furniture at Ston Easton. The prices were enormous – a plain mahogany dining-room table which I wanted and was prepared to pay £150 for, made 1000 guineas. But I bought a huge, elaborate oak 1860 side-board for £3 and the two massive accompanying pedestal cupboards for £1. At first the auctioneer refused to take my bid saying, truthfully, there was £20 worth of fire-wood in it, but all the dealers started shouting 'Go on give it to the little gent for his quid' so with bad grace he yielded. Flimsy little coffee tables were going at £40 each. A very pretty Chinese-Chippendale overmantel £1400. . . . [incomplete]

¹ The uprising in Hungary had been quashed by the Russians.

TO THE DUCHESS OF DEVONSHIRE   Combe Florey House.
Midwinter 1956

Darling Debo

They are *very* pretty – like M. Angelo's Moses but I dont suppose you have seen him – also like cuckold's horns. I don't think I hear any better for them, but I look more dignified. Thank you, thank you for your kindness in sending them. Perhaps you have forgotten what you sent. It was snails in tin.

It is very kind of you to ask me to visit you. I should love to come. I am rather good with pregnant ladies. I take them for short walks which is good for them & dont let them jump off stiles. If there is ever a day when you are not full up with alien race gangs, call for me I don't mean by carriage or telephone. I mean send a post card.

I saw a lot of your husband in London. Haven't seen your wife¹ since our one beautiful meeting. Spent an evening with Mrs (U for unEnglish) Rodd but didn't get any intimate gossip owing to stage folk.

This house is not appreciably smaller than Chatsworth but golly it is uncomfortable, dozens of artisans in every room beating it with hammers. No loo and very cold in the laurels.

Lavatory chain² says your daughter Emma³ is exciting. L.C. got very drunk last week at a ball (where I wasn't) and people came up to my daughter Teresa and said: 'You ought to look after your father. He's fallen down again'.

I.T.A.L.Y. (Know what that means?)⁴

                                                            Evelyn

¹ An ancient joke: Lady Katherine Fitzmaurice (1912–   ) married Viscount Mersey in 1933.
² The Earl of Antrim (because he used to flush).
³ Lady Emma Cavendish (1943–   ) married Tobias Tennant in 1963.
⁴ I trust (or treasure) and love you.

TO ANN FLEMING   Combe Florey House.
28 January [1957]

Dearest Ann

Showy paper, don't you think?

I enjoyed your letter very much tho I cant sympathise with your distress in the *Britannic*¹. I envy you every hour of your journey. I should not have sought the company of O'Neill² or Old Caspar³ but I suppose you have some natural affection for these fruits of your womb which is not stirred by my remote cousinship. They all say that Sir Anthony [Eden] is dying. Clarissa will be left penniless & friendless in the Antipodes. It is the part for which she is naturally cast but my heart bleeds for her.

Also said to be dying is Ronnie Knox. I went to visit him at a hospital in the City Road, E.C.1, which had without compromise painted across the front in enormous letters *St Mark's Hospital for Diseases of the Rectum.*

Dead. Your mad chum Minton[4]. Poisoned himself.

I hope to take Laura to Monte Carlo soon for a weeks relaxation. The house, after weeks of chaos, has quite suddenly begun to look rather decent. I have been buying objects like a drunken sailor – candelabra, carpets, fire places. The prodigious sideboard which I bought at Ston Easton has been erected with an infinity of skilled labour and is very splendid.

Bron sits about all day smoking cheroots & reading P.G.Wodehouse. At dusk he slinks out with a gun & sometimes brings in a pheasant. I am seeking to transport him to Florence.

Please give my regards to Mr & Mrs Da Costa.

Ed Stanley, a disappointed candidate for the task of writing Belloc's life, has very magnanimously reviewed his rival – whose book[5] is not as good as Ed might have written.

I overheard Randolph saying huskily: 'All I try to do is bring a little happiness into the lives of others'.

He is shedding many crocodile tears over Eden's illness.

Fond love
Evelyn

[1] *Caronia*, in fact, going to Jamaica.
[2] Raymond O'Neill (1933–). Ann Fleming's son by her first marriage. Succeeded as Baron O'Neill in 1944.
[3] Caspar Fleming. Ann's son.
[4] John Minton (1917–57). Painter and illustrator.
[5] By Robert Speaight, 1957.

To NANCY MITFORD   Combe Florey House.
Shrove Tuesday [5 March] 1957

Darling Nancy,

I saw Debo last week. I feel it my duty to tell you that she is spreading a very damaging story about you: that you have allowed yourself to be photographed by the Television. Of course I don't believe it, nor does anyone who knows & loves you, but I think you should scotch this slander before it spreads to people who might do so. It would entirely destroy your reputation as U governess.

Col. sent me such a pretty drawing at Christmas. What was it?

I had an exhilarating expedition into the law courts[1] and came out two thousand pounds (tax-free) to the good. But there were anxious moments. At the end of the first day I would have settled for a fiver. A disgusting looking man called Russell[2] from the *Sunday Times*, not the pretty [John] Russell I met with you, gave evidence against me. The judge was a buffoon who invited the jury to laugh me out of court. But I had taken the precaution of telling the Dursley parish priest that he should have 10% of the damages. His prayers were answered in dramatic, Old Testament style. A series of Egyptian plagues fell on Sir Hartley Shawcross from the moment he took up the case, culminating in a well-nigh fatal motor accident to his mother-in-law at the very moment when he had me under cross-examination & was making me feel rather an ass. He had to chuck the case & leave it to an understrapper, whose heart was in the court next door where a Bolivian millionaire was suing Lord Kemsley for saying he buggered his wife (the Bolivian's wife, not Lady Kemsley). I had a fine solid jury who were out to fine the *Express* for their impertinence to the Royal Family, quite irrespective of any rights and wrongs. They were not at all amused by the judge. All the £300 a day barristers rocked with laughter at his sallies. They glowered. That was not what they paid a judge for, they thought.

So Father Collins got £200 and a lot of chaps in White's got pop[3]. But there has been some retribution. I was all set for Monte Carlo when an appeal came to take Ronnie Knox, who has had a cancer operation to the sea side. He couldn't face the journey to Monte Carlo. He wouldn't even accept Brighton. Torquay it has to be. So I am off there tomorrow for three weeks. I love and revere Ronnie but –

Write to me there at the Imperial Hotel putting my mind at rest about this terrible Television scandal.

Did you know Sir Oswald Mosley had mumps? And that Debo doesn't at all like jokes about it. She has a Dutch follower & looks very large & pretty.

Love
Evelyn

[1] The libel case against Nancy Spain and the *Daily Express* for the article published on 17 March 1956. Nancy Spain had said, among other things, that Waugh's sales were dwarfed by those of his brother and had got the supporting figures wrong. Waugh was now claiming that he had been represented as 'an unsuccessful writer who had made a false and malicious attack upon Miss Spain in the *Spectator* by reason of personal spite against her; that he was a writer whose name carried insignificant weight with the general public, the film rights and options in whose books were not worthy of purchase, and who was not worthy of consideration for the writing of articles'.

[2] Leonard Russell, literary editor of *The Sunday Times*.

[3] A second case against Nancy Spain was settled out of court for £3,000. Waugh received a telegram from Anthony Powell: 'Congratulations on Burning Sappho' and from Graham Greene: 'Congratulations on singeing Spains Whiskers.'

TO MARGARET WAUGH   Combe Florey House.
March 1957

A Sad Story

Once upon a time there was a hideous little girl. She had flat feet, round shoulders and she bit her nails. Many observers mistook her for a pig. But her good father loved her dearly and when he was enjoying himself at White's, he received a letter from her asking him to return home. So he did so. But when he reached his home, which was full of workmen and very uncomfortable, this pig-like girl said she would sooner be with her aunts & grandmother & cousins than with this unselfish father. He was bitterly hurt but he still loved her.

Then there came a time when this odious child had no aunt or grandmother or cousin to play with – only girls as pig-like as herself. So she wrote a beautiful poem asking her father to visit her. He was very much pleased with the poem & longed to come but by that time he had found a poor, sick clergyman who was all alone and he had promised to take this holy man to the seaside at the opposite end of England. He goes there on Ash Wednesday to the Imperial Hotel, Torquay; miles from Ascot where he would much sooner be with his beloved daughters.

Moral. See all you can of Papa while he is available. Other people who have no aunts, grandmothers or cousins alive need his company more than pigs do.

To Margaret Waugh   Imperial Hotel,
10 March [1957]   Torquay.

Darling Meg
   This is the way to write :–
   Take a pot of ink and a pen – either a goose or turkey quill or, failing them, a wooden pen-holder with a metal nib. Hold it so that your fingers are at least $\frac{3}{4}$ inch from the point. Dip the point $\frac{1}{4}$ inch in the ink. If you keep the point downwards there is no possibility of the ink flowing up to the fingers. Do not wipe the nib in your hair or on your face. Do not suck it. You will find that you remain perfectly clean.
   If you balance a basket of eggs on your head while writing it will help cure the curvature of your spine.
   Poor Mgr Knox is not in a cheerful mood. He does not enjoy his food or wine. It rains so much that he cannot sit out or say his office in the garden. He wants to move but cant make up his mind where.
   Your mother goes home on Wednesday to induct the sacred cows. I shall be alone with sorrowful Ronald. I do not succeed in cheering him up.

                                    All love greedy pig
                                    papa

To Ann Fleming   Belmont Hotel,
19 March [1957]   Sidmouth,
                                                  Devon.

Dearest Ann
   A beautiful letter. Thank you very much.
   This is plainly the hotel which served as a model for *Separate Tables*.[1] My life

here is ghastly. Tomorrow I escape & take Ronnie to Combe Florey. Magdalen[2], who was supposed to take charge of him, shirks all responsibility & behaves as basely as you did in the case of Lord Brownlow's hat[3]. All she has done is to come & dine with us once.

I am by many years the youngest boarder here. There is a disgusting old man who sits next to me every day in the tiny smoking-room and grunts & snuffles like an old dog.

There is another Monsignor, also dying, in the town. He comes to see us occasionally. Poor Ronnie cannot read for long. All he likes is to smoke a stinking pipe and to make desultory comments on the news in the paper. *The Times* crossword, done on a peculiarly laborious system, (not reading the lights for the downs at all until we have filled them in conjecturally) lasts us from nine to ten in the evening. Sometimes I walk up & down the front for half an hour.

I have teased Randolph in the next *Spectator*.[4]

Home tomorrow. I have been very home sick.

Love
Evelyn

[1] Play by Terence Rattigan, 1954.
[2] Countess of Eldon.
[3] In Jamaica Ann Fleming refused to swim out beyond the reef to rescue Lord Brownlow's hat and so was accused by Waugh of cowardice and dereliction of social duty.
[4] 'Randolph's Finest Hour' by Evelyn Waugh is a review of *What I Said About the Press* by R.S.Churchill, 1957.

To A.D.PETERS   Combe Florey House.
[April 1957]

Dear Pete

Where are my cigars? What explanation do the americans give of their beastly conduct. Have cigars been dispatched? When?

I do not mind the americans putting this blurb on my book but they must send cigars.

I do not mind the Poles publishing short stories. My mind is on cigars.

I have no recent photograph of myself. Nor have I cigars.[1]

Yours ever
Evelyn

[1] One of many letters about cigars.

To ANN FLEMING   Hotel de Paris,
26 May 1957   Monte Carlo.

My Dear Ann

I have composed a poem on the subject of Ed's change of name.[1]

Trusty as steel,[1] more valuable than plate,[2]
Aspiring Sheffield knocked at heaven's gate.
Peter[3] (who read *The Times*) pronounced his doom
Simply remarking: 'Stanley, I presume'.[4]

Notes

(1) Sheffield was famous for steel and for silver-   (2) plated copper
(3) The Peter referred to is the first pope who is popularly believed to hold the keys of heaven.
(4) An American journalist named Stanley pursued an English missionary into central Africa and greeted him with the words 'Livingstone, I presume'.

When all that is understood you will see it is neat

My idea of heaven is a Marble Hall out of season. This is the best Marble Hall I know anywhere and is quite empty. Ali Mackintosh sits all day in the bar.

We sometimes see Sir Winston (at a respectful distance) gorging vast quantities of rich food. His face is elephant gray and quite expressionless. His moll sits by him coaxing him and he sometimes turns a pink little eye towards her without moving his head. Poor Sarah[2] sits silent and eats sparingly.

My brother Alec is at Villefranche with a ferocious lady who is in love with C. Connolly.

Charabancs of *dopo lavoro* wops arrive in the afternoons and sit in the outer rooms of the casino. No Americans in sight except a few tipsy old ladies talking about their dentists. Otherwise a great desert. The sun is under cloud most of the day. I stroll in the gardens while your cousin Laura plays roulette. An idyllic life.

Sorry to read that O'Neill has jived himself into a decline – but not surprised.

Keeping Ascension at Chantilly.

Love
Evelyn

[1] Lord Stanley's family had also an older Irish barony, so he was in full Baron Sheffield and Stanley of Alderley.
[2] Sarah Churchill's husband, Anthony Beauchamp, had died that year.

TO MARGARET WAUGH   Combe Florey House.
3 June [1957]

Darling Meg

A sad and saddening letter from you. I am sorry you are in hot water. You do not have to tell me that you have not done anything really wicked. I know my pig. I am absolutely confident that you will never never be dishonourable, impure or cruel. That is all that matters.

I think it is a weakness of girls' schools that they have no adequate punishments. When a boy is naughty he is beaten and that is the end of it. All this admonition makes for resentment and the part of your letter that I don't like at all is when you say the nuns 'hate' you. That is rubbish. And when you run down girls who behave better than you. That is mean. Chuck it, Meg.

It is only three weeks since Mother Bridget was writing warmly of your 'great efforts' to reconcile yourself to school. If you have lapsed in the meantime it is only a naughty mood. Don't whine about it.

As to your leaving early – we can discuss that next holidays. I was miserable at Lancing and kept asking my father to take me away. I am very glad now that he did not. The same with Bron. The whole of our life is a test & preparation for heaven – most of it irksome. So each part of our life is an irksome test & preparation for something better. I think you would greatly enjoy Oxford and get the best out of it. But you can't get there without much boring labour and discipline.

Don't get into your silly head the idea that anyone hates you or is unfair to you. You are loved far beyond your deserts, especially by your

                                                                 Papa

To Margaret Waugh   Combe Florey House.
7 June [1957]

Darling Meg

I send you all my love for your birthday. I hope it is a very happy day despite the savage persecution of Mother Bridget.

You have certainly made a resourceful & implacable enemy in that holy lady. She has written to both Colonel Batchelor[1] and Mrs Critchley-Salmonson strong denunciations of your moral character and behaviour. I have sent these documents to my solicitors and hope you will soon appear in the courts suing her for libel. Damages will be so heavy that no doubt the school will have to close down.

She has done more than that. She has written to the committee of the St James's Club warning them not to admit you to luncheon on 23rd. I have had a letter from the Chairman asking whether it is true that you steal the silver when asked to luncheon. She also told them that you are invariably drunk & disorderly. I call that a bit thick.

But her most cruel move has been to circularize all the London fishmongers warning them under pain of mortal sin not to have any white-bait during your visit to London. The poor men are so frightened of her that they have forbidden the fishermen to catch any for the next fortnight.

Her powers are infinite. She has agents everywhere. I fear you have got yourself into an appalling predicament.

I have just received a letter from Lady Diana who writes: 'Since learning from Mother Bridget of Margaret's terrible wickedness I wish you to destroy the photograph of her and me which was taken last year. I do not want there to be any evidence of my ever having met the odious girl.'

All this malevolent campaign must, I am afraid, rather over-cloud your birthday.

Nevertheless I hope you have some pleasure in eating the cakes which, I know, the other girls will refuse to share with you.

Sweet Meg, don't be a donkey. Everyone loves you – particularly I – me? which I wonder is grammatical.[2]

Your loving
Papa

[1] Colonel Batchelor and his sister sold Combe Florey to Waugh.
[2] Margaret left St Mary's Convent, Ascot, at the end of the term.

To Ann Fleming

Combe Florey House.
17 June 1957

Dearest Ann

Very many thanks for your kind invitation to eat fish & chips in the Festival Gardens[1]. Alas, I am too old for such excitements. Try Ian Fleming.

I wish I could come & help you entertain Clarissa[2]. I am as opposed to the Egyptians as she could wish and I have been thinking of her with deep compassion during recent months. But then she had herself photographed going to a protestant church so all my kindness was turned to despair again. I hope she enjoys the Portuguese Chianti. You could show her Hugo's[3] dirty pictures after dinner.

We spent two nights with Diana on the way home. A sad little household of Oggie[4], a universal aunt (literally) Miss Faye and a poor waif of a grandchild[5] – brotherless, friendless, Godless, obsessed by the fear of hypodermic injections. 'Has he come to prick me?' is her greeting to all new arrivals.

We came home to find Septimus in hospital without his appendix & Margaret involved in a crime wave at her convent, and a cinema company impatient for some work I promised them. I have now finished the work and very tedious I found it. The peacocks still hate us. The cart horse ran away and was missing for a week. A great number of Muscovy ducklings appeared briefly from their eggs, swam about as fast as water beetles & then vanished – eaten by rats the peasants say.

Minnie Fosberg[6] told me something of the horrors of Mr Todd[7].

What has happened to the *Sunday Times*? Atticus unreadable. An illiterate and profoundly vulgar biography of an Armenian businessman of no conceivable interest[8]. Half a page of passport photographs of nonentities who were at Oxford together. A spurious postal address for the Cross Word.

I am going to one of Miss Foyle's Literary Luncheons in July in aid of Mr Pinfold. I despise myself but Mr McDougall (who, did I tell you? fell deep in love with you) besought me with tears and I have been so beastly to him lately because he has made such an ugly book of poor Pinfold, that I consented. I shall not have a song. I don't imagine you wish to come? Date is 19th. If it has grown cold again I might come to London for that week. Can't bear London when it's hot.

I am reading *Chartreuse de Parme* (in translation) for the first time. Why is it called the first 'psychological' novel. It seems to me that nothing any character thinks or says or does has any relation to human nature as I know it.

This Saturday & Sunday I have to take my daughters out in London. Next week we visit Mells where Ronnie is slowly weakening. He got through his Romanes lecture. If he had been an atheist he would have got the OM this birthday.

I hear Aunt Cynthia[9] is off to compete in Television in New York.

The plumbers & electricians are finally out. The painters move in again next week. I have some fine gilt candelabra from the Holborn Restaurant. Sad about Crowther[10] popping off in jug.

Your affec. cousin
Evelyn

All today the house has been full of small birds. They fly in like bees and beat at the windows. Why?

[1] The premiere of the film *Around the World in 80 Days*, followed by a party in the Festival Gardens arranged by Lady Pamela Berry.

[2] Ann Fleming had written that Lady Eden 'only wishes to meet non-appeasers. This limits the field to John Sparrow, who cannot come.'

[3] Hugo Charteris (1922–70). Novelist and brother of Ann Fleming, had taken some slides of female circumcision in Africa.

[4] Olga Lynn, died 1957. Singer and teacher.

[5] Artemis Cooper (1953–   ), daughter of the second Viscount Norwich (John Julius Cooper) and Anne Clifford, whom he married in 1952.

[6] Mary Astor married James Fosburgh, the painter.

[7] Mike Todd (1907–58). Producer of *Around the World in 80 Days*, married to Elizabeth Taylor.

[8] An extract from *Mr Five Per Cent*, a biography of Calouste S. Gulbenkian by Ralph Hewin.

[9] Cynthia Charteris (1887–1960). Married in 1910 Henry Asquith, son of the Prime Minister. She had a success on a television quiz show with Jane Austen as her subject.

[10] The prominent antique dealer.

To John MacDougall   Combe Florey House.
[June 1957]

Oh no John no John no John no.

I won't appear on the television. If I was willing & able, like Randolph, to do such things, I should have no need of an advertising agent. He must make others do these disgraceful things for him and preserve my privacy.

Pinfolds the friend, not Waugh.

He should 'plug' (if that is the word) 'Waugh the recluse.' He must not reveal my new address. Literary Garbo.

I have 70 labels addressed. I will bring them to London when you give the word.

Would it be a good thing to have the gist of my speech to Miss Foyle's ladies printed and issued to the press at their table?

It continues very agreeable here. Do some soon.

E

To John Montgomery[1]   Combe Florey House.
[30 July 1957]
Postcard

I find with alarm that the Polish firm publishing my books is PAX, a proscribed and excommunicate body of renegade priests. This must cease. How deeply am I committed to them? Have I signed for other books? If not, pray tell them that I cannot, on religious grounds, allow them to publish any more.

                                                              E.W.

  [1] Journalist, author, sometime literary agent and egocentric.

To the Duchess of Devonshire

10 August [1957]   Derbyshire.

Dearest Debo

   You were sorely missed at the tea-party which was not as well attended as our host hoped and between you & me was rather dismal.

   This household of aged bachelors makes a sombre contrast to you and your handsome wife & impeccable children – no television, no telephone in the public rooms, no bonfires, no gin before half past seven. The talk is mostly of medicines. I can just keep my end up on sleeping draughts but Mr Hartley[1] has us all beat by a great bite in the left foot over which he has consulted two doctors and a chemist.

   I did love staying with you and meeting your little ones and getting a glimpse of the treasures of Chatsworth. Thank you. Thank you.

   I hope you have a glorious 12th & 13th & 14th ad infinitum with plump young birds falling like confetti. May the fresh air of the moors disperse all the vapours of the arts and waft you back to manly English philistinism.

   No one has shown any curiosity about the strange Trove of Edensor. They wot not of the pot.[2]

                              Love & gratitude & more love from
                                          Evelyn

  [1] L.P.Hartley (1895–1972). Novelist.
  [2] Waugh had found an unemptied chamberpot in the cupboard by his bed. The Devonshires lived in Edensor House until 1959 when they returned to Chatsworth.

To Robert Henriques   Combe Florey House.
15 August 1957

Dear Robert,

   Mr Pinfold's experiences were almost exactly my own. In turning them into a novel I had to summarize them. I heard 'voices' such as I describe almost continuously night and day for three weeks. They were tediously repetitive and sometimes obscene and blasphemous. I have given the gist of them. I have had no recurrence of the trouble. Since my book came out I have had a number of letters from fellow-sufferers. I am greatly grieved to hear that you have been experiencing something of the sort. I don't know what to advise. My voices ceased as soon as I was intellectually convinced that they were imaginary. I do not absolutely exclude the possibility of diabolic possession as the source of them.

I am very sorry to hear that you have abjured the realm. I abjured Glos but find Somerset very agreeable. It would be a great pleasure to Laura and myself if you came for a night but it will be no pleasure to you until the end of next month when the school holidays are over.

Have you seen *The Comforters* by Mrs Muriel Spark – an admirable study of hallucinations. I am told she was very dotty and got over it.

Yrs ever,
Evelyn

To Ann Fleming   Combe Florey House.
20 August [1957]

Dearest Ann

You will be most welcome on Monday. I have no great faith in any of Laura's relations keeping strictly to plans, but if I don't hear to contrary I will meet you at Taunton. I will try & get some Portuguese claret. Failing that can you drink French? My children ask: will she put her tongue out through her cheek? Do not disappoint them.

I felt very old at Debo's. Television in the dining-room, telephone in the drawing-room, charming children talking a secret language but I enjoyed wandering at will & alone about the treasures of Chatsworth.

I felt very young at Renishaw – a bachelor group of Osbert, [David] Horner and Hartley. Osbert supporting with great gallantry his gruesome illness, the other two *malades imaginaires* talking only of pills and diets. Leslie was bitten on the ankle by a midge, saw two doctors & a chemist, smelled of disinfectant and consumed huge doses of a specific to prevent blood-poisoning. Osbert has introduced electric light into some of the bed-rooms. Delicious food & wine but no gin before 7.30. Thirty years ago Georgia [Sitwell] & Willie Walton[1] & I used to escape Sir George & drink cocktails in the golf-club. Under Osbert's reign I found Leslie & myself similarly occupied.

Freud came to luncheon looking very horrible. Osbert loudly quoted: 'Je n'aime pas le. Jamais encore'.

You are dead right about Alfred Duggan's sanctity.

Love
Evelyn

[1] Sir William Walton (1902–   ). Composer. Knighted 1951. A close friend of the Sitwells since 1920.

TO BRIAN FRANKS   Hyde Park Hotel.
[September 1957]

Dear Brian

Have you ever, when inspecting your premises, been shown a lightless and airless
cell numbered 315, with walls so thin that every fart can be heard from the next-
door prisoner and a bed so narrow that if one dozes one falls out? I am sure not. It is
the kind of thing that is hidden from commanding officers. It was in this cell that in
your absence your henchmen sought to confine your old comrade in arms.

                                                    E. Waugh

Even Harry[1], who is constantly and cruelly persecuted has never, he says, seen
anything like the horror of 315.

[1] Lord Stavordale.

TO FATHER HUBERT VAN ZELLER   Combe Florey House.
25 September 1957

Dear Father Hubert,

Ronnie Knox[1] entrusted me with his biography – a task for which I have no
qualification except love. I am going through the papers he left at Mells. Among
them are a large number of letters written to him by Daphne Acton in 1937, '38 and
'39. I have had her permission to read these. There are many references to a monk
who, I think, must be you whose advice they sought about regulating their
friendship.

More than once Daphne refers to your opinion (if you it was) that she was a good
influence on Ronnie in making him 'less intellectual'. Could you give me some light
on your meaning? Did you simply mean that in a human, social way he was in
danger of becoming donnish, or was their a spiritual sense in which his Faith was too
much a matter of reason and that she helped give it life?

Daphne's letters are extremely intimate. Now that I have read them I am rather
surprised that she let me, and I am much touched by her confidence.

If you are not the Downside monk refered to, can you suggest who he is? She calls
him simply 'the Holy Man.'

                                                    Yours ever
                                                    Evelyn

[1] He had died on 24 August.

To A.D.PETERS   Combe Florey House.
[28 September 1957]
Postcard

I have not made any contract for Knox's life and would sooner not do so until I know how long it is going to be. It looks like being at least a years work & a hefty volume – perhaps 2 years & 2 volumes. I am busy 7 hours a day answering letters from his admirers & reading his letters – most of them in Greek verse which I can't read. It will be a magnum opus.

To ANN FLEMING   Combe Florey House.
30 September 1957

Dearest Ann

May I, in the interests of future historians, urge you to date your letters with the year? I am engaged in sorting some hundreds of letters to and from Ronnie Knox & all of them are merely dated 'Friday evening'. This and the fact that most of them are in Greek verse makes my task very laborious.

I enclose my repartee to Mr Priestley[1]. I would rather like to have it back if it would not be too much trouble. An example of the great strain of gentlemanly behaviour has been keeping silent about Debo's pot. It shows how little the young trust the honour of their friends that she has herself revealed the gross scandal.

I have not left home since you were here but soon I go to Edinburgh to cross examine Ronnie's surviving sister, Lady Peck[2]. Later to Rhodesia to grill Daphne Acton. I am busier with Ronald's affairs than I have ever been over my own.

Trooper Waugh[3] is at Caterham in a sort of daze – not particularly unhappy I think, too weary for that.

... Is Mr Macmillan[4] a pious anglican? I know he goes to church but is he pi? This is pertinent to my Ronnie excavations. It is clever of him to put up the postage to America by 150%. There will now be no temptation to answer American fan letters.

Your visit here was much enjoyed by all. Do come again when you feel the need of a long sleep.

                                                 Love from
                                                 Evelyn

[1] 'Anything wrong with Priestley?', Waugh's reply to J.B.Priestley's review 'What was Wrong with Pinfold', which had argued that the attempt to ape the manners of a country gentleman had driven him mad. *Spectator*, 13 September 1957.
[2] Winifred Knox (1882–1962). Married in 1911 Sir James Peck.
[3] Auberon Waugh was doing his national service in his father's regiment, the Royal Horse Guards.
[4] Harold Macmillan (1894–   ). The Conservative statesman, then Prime Minister. Chancellor of the University of Oxford since 1960. Tutored by Ronald Knox.

TO LADY ACTON   Combe Florey House.
2 October [1957]

Dearest Daphne

I am awfully glad to know that Ronald really wanted me to write his life. He would have found it difficult to say no, when I suggested it. Do I detect a rebuke in your 'I thought you would spend a year or two on the early years'? I have no intention of rushing out a *Time* magazine 'profile' but I have an itch to collect all the material I can as soon as possible. There may be another war to stop all communications. Or you might go dotty like poor Pinfold. So I'll come early next year while the going is still good.

I have read all your letters to Ronnie. They aren't a bit soppy. They only made me think what an enchanting girl you were and what a (literal) Godsend to Ronnie. You gave him just the tenderness and hero-worship which he had from the 1912 undergraduates; which he needed and didn't find anywhere else. It was jolly trusting of you to let me read them. I shant abuse your trust.

Don't please trouble to answer this.

Love from
Evelyn

TO JOHN MCDOUGALL   Combe Florey House.
19 October [1957]

Dear Jack

... The visit to Edinburgh was rather pleasant – the town empty & bright & warm and the natives friendly. Poor Lady Peck nearly died of the strain of talking to me. She had read Pinfold and concluded that I must be given Crême de Menthe at all hours.

I told Peters that you didn't at all like another publisher having *Knox* & that you were to have it unless anyone made an absurd offer. He tells me that a highly respectable firm (whose name he asks me to conceal) has offered £2500 and will go up to £3000[1]. This is enormously more than Speaight's *Belloc* earned and more than I should like you to pay. I am tied to C & H [Chapman and Hall] by every bond of gratitude & friendship, but it doesn't seem grateful or friendly to make you pay three times what a book is worth. Anyway I shant be signing anything for many months and shan't sign anything without telling you first. There's no sort of hurry to decide. I thought you would like to know how things stood.

I saw Oliver Chandos[2] yesterday. He is literary executor to Anthony Eden, with [Brendan] Bracken & Birkett[3]. He says they have already been offered more than £100,000 for Eden's memoirs. Publishers must be soft on the crumpet.

Please give my love to May and tell her how tantalizing we found the brief glimpse of her.

Yours ever
Evelyn

[1] McDougall replied that he was delighted to pay £3,000.

[2] Oliver Lyttelton (1893–1972). Created Lord Chandos in 1954. Conservative MP, Secretary of State for Colonies 1951–4.

[3] Norman Birkett (1883–1962). Lord Justice of Appeal 1950. Created baron 1958.

To Anthony Powell   Combe Florey House.
20 October [1957]

Dear Tony

It was awfully good of you to send me *Lady Molly*.[1] I had been looking forward to it like seven days leave and read it without interruption. It is delightful – every bit up to the predecessors. What a fine work it is going to be when it is complete and the whole scheme revealed. In the opening pages I felt the void of Widmerpool really aching – I could not have borne another page's delay of his entry. Did you intend him to dominate the series when you introduced him in the first volume? Erridge is a magnificent creation and the evening at his house masterly. Lady Molly herself remained a bit vague to me. It was genius to put the tale of Widmerpool's discomfiture into the general's mouth. It was no surprise to me, nor was Erridge's elopement.

Thank you very much for a real rare treat.

Is there any hope of you & Violet coming to see us? It isn't far. Do. I sit home all day reading Knoxiana.

Your galloping Major[2] is *not* to be expelled from Pratt's. It is thought he would get the club talked about in undesirable quarters.

Yours ever
Evelyn

[1] Anthony Powell, *At Lady Molly's*, 1957.

[2] Malcolm Muggeridge.

To Nancy Mitford   Combe Florey House.
24 October [1957]

Darling Nancy

I feel great guilt about yesterday. I was so dazed & worn with travel that I didn't show the welcome or the gratitude I felt. I resolve in future always to sleep in London before going out to luncheon.

I have read a third of *Voltaire*[1] with keen pleasure. The characters are as alien to me and as vivid as those of *Lucky Jim*.[2] You have a unique gift of making your reader feel physically in the presence of your characters. What horrors they were! The book should correct two popular heresies 1) Cinema-born, that only beautiful people enjoy fucking 2) Spender-born, that the arts flourish best in a liberal society.

I am only waiting to finish this letter & throw myself back into Voltaire.

Laura is delighted at the prospect of your winter visit to us. Come whenever you can for as long as you can bear it.

I feel I was grumpy too about Debo and her wife[3]. It is affection for her that makes me censorious.

Pam has very kindly asked me to dine with her and you on Monday. Alas my feeble frame simply cannot support another journey.

Fond love
Evelyn

[1] Nancy Mitford, *Voltaire in Love*, 1957.
[2] First novel by Kingsley Amis, 1954.
[3] Viscountess Mersey.

TO JOHN MCDOUGALL   Combe Florey House.
29 October [1957]

Dear Jack

Thank you for letting me see this[1]. I have made a few corrections on matters of fact and a few suggestions. There are numberless misprints.

I think it is too long. It suffers from having been written off and on instead of straight off – Stopp doesnt always remember what he had already said. He makes the same points sometimes more than once. Can you persuade him, do you think, to revise it and condense it? A third could go without loss. Then you would have an interesting book – interesting at any rate to me. He has an original method of criticism which I find attractive. I don't think he need summarize all the plots except so far as they support his thesis. And I don't think all the extracts from my occasional journalism very valuable.

Very sorry to hear you have had a cold. I start my 55th year in good health and have composed the opening sentences of *Knox*.

Did you leave a pair of vermilion stockings here? It is beastly to have a house where visitors are not packed for.

I hope to spend the first week of December in London. Let us eat & drink together then.

Yours ever
Evelyn

[1]The manuscript of *Evelyn Waugh, Portrait of an Artist* by Frederick J. Stopp, a Caius don at Cambridge, published by Chapman and Hall 1958. It is said that Ronald Knox sent Waugh a telegram 'Stop Stopp Stop'. 15,000 words were cut as Waugh suggested.

To Brian Franks   Combe Florey House.
11 December 1957

Dear Brian

That was another memorable banquet.[1] Thank you very much indeed for asking me. Every year the faces round the table look grosser & madder – but how we enjoy it. I made my train successfully and was deeply shocked to find a man in the carriage who had plainly been drinking. I scowled at him till he fell asleep & then fell asleep myself.

Has Harold Acton sent orchids?

Yours ever
Evelyn

[1] Annual gathering of the proprietor's friends at the Hyde Park Hotel.

To Father Hubert van Zeller   Combe Florey House.
30 December [1957]

Dear Father Hubert

As soon as you left I fell upon the notes you left me. Every word is golden. It was extraordinarily kind of you to take so much trouble in producing so full & valuable an account.

When the autumn comes and I start on Ronald's life as a priest I shall be much out of my depth. I knew him as a literary man, never went to confession to him or consulted him on spiritual or moral questions. I wonder whether I ought to have a chapter by another hand on Ronald's spirituality or leave it for someone to produce a separate book. Perhaps we can discuss this at Easter.

It was most delightful seeing you & Father Vincent[1] yesterday.

Yours ever
Evelyn

[1] Father Vincent Cavanagh, bursar of Downside, who died in 1975.

To Graham Greene   Combe Florey House.
10 January 1958

Dear Graham

It is good news that you are in England.

I go to Rhodesia early next month. I shall sleep the night of the 6th in London. Could we dine then? Or lunch that day?

'Pax', I understand, is run by renegade priests[1]. I don't blame Polish laymen for dealing with them since it is their only means of livelihood, but it is all humbug about 'keeping Catholic culture alive'. The books of mine that 'Pax' want show Americans and Europeans as decadent & thats why they want them.

They make very free with your name as evidence of bona fides. I had a long letter from your friend in much the same terms as the letter you quote. He said he was a Catholic writer who published with Pax but had no other connexion with them. He wrote from his private address. But there was a rubber stamp of 'Pax' on the envelope. He is plainly employed as their advertising agent. God knows I don't blame Poles for any shifts they have to resort to. But, as I told him, I have the undeserved privilege of living in a country where compromise is unnecessary.

I don't think the English countryside attracts you much. If for any reason you feel like coming here for a night or two before Feb 6th you would be welcomed with open arms & bottles.

Yours ever affectionately
Evelyn

[1] Greene, after some doubts, allowed Pax, a Roman Catholic organization, to publish his books, though he attacked it in the *Sunday Times* after a visit to Poland.

To Graham Greene   White's.
6 February 1958

Dear Graham

It was jolly decent of you to include me among the host of your friends clamouring for admission last night[1]. It was an enthralling evening. It seemed to me that all the audience was enthralled. I do hope it will have a prosperous run.

I am not theologian enough to understand the theological basis. I wish you would write it as a novel explaining more fully to simple people like me. I should like details of James's life in his school holidays, the circumstances of his courtship and so on.

I thought the wife (both wives) excellent, also the man who played the priest[2]. Admirable scenery. Sir John [Gielgud] seemed a bit seedy.

It was a memorable evening

Thanks awfully
Evelyn

[1] To Graham Greene's play *The Potting Shed*.
[1] Gwen Ffrangcon-Davies, Irene Worth and Redmond Phillips.

To Laura Waugh   White's.
6 February 1958

Darling Laura

You will be relieved to hear that I have examined the Trust deed & Septimus *is* included. It was so drawn up as to include all subsequent children. Furthermore by a provision I had entirely forgotten boys get more than girls (in the proportion 10:15) in the final division. So there is no need for you to leave Septimus your jewels.

Graham Greene had not sought to insult me in giving me a seat at the back. I was next to Dr Strauss[1] who sent you extravagant sentiments of esteem. Other friends were at the back of the dress-circle. He had not been treated generously in the matter of tickets.

Perhaps it was because I was so far away, the play seemed very much under acted to me. John Gielgud had a pain & was very poor. The play is great nonsense theologically & will puzzle people needlessly. Afterwards I had supper with John Sutro & his wife at a night club in Belgravia.

I will write from Rhodesia, if I get there. All love to you you & the little girls.

Evelyn

[1] Dr Eric Strauss, head of the psychiatric department at St Bartholomew's, who had seen Waugh on his return from Ceylon.

To Laura Waugh   M'Bebi,
[9 February] 1958   Mazoe,
                                                 S. Rhodesia.

Darling Laura,

I am afraid you have lost your first chance in the £50,000 draw. I arrived weary but alive & safe. As usual with aeroplanes we set off seven hours late. It was fortunate that the delay was in London & White's not in some African aerodrome. I sat about all Friday looking at the snow in St James's Street. We left at 7 in the evening. Mrs Stirling (senior)[1] was the only friend in the aeroplane. A good dinner with masses of free drink but no cigar smoking allowed. Midnight stop in Rome. Then on again, practically no sleep, breakfast at dawn in Khartoum. All day the stewards are at ones elbow with sweets, sandwiches, canapés, drinks, cigarettes, fans, towels soaked in eau de Cologne. Almost too many attentions. Arrived at Salisbury at six. Andrew Waugh[2] & Daphne [Acton] on the tarmac to greet me. Andrew *very* helpful taking me out of a back door without having to wait for customs and passport officers. He presented me with a box of 50 fine cigars each sealed in glass tube to withstand the tropics. A very civil boy. Daphne thin and austere looking but very friendly. A long drive in the dark. John Acton[3] thin & ill, diabetes, not allowed wine, deaf but genial. Host of pretty & polite children. The house hideous surrounded by the roughest rough grass you could want with a few gaudy flowers emerging. Tin roofs, concrete walls, large bare rooms, everything painted white and awfully dirty. They have a chaplain[4] and a jewish looking sick South African[5] living here and people popping in and out quite a lot. Invitations awaiting me from Simon Dalhousie, Andrew's Governor[6], the Campion Society of Salisbury, the chief bookshop to a Literary Luncheon. The last I have said no to. I don't think there is anything to keep me here more than 3 weeks or so. The name of this house is pronounced MeBaby. Daphne has built a mission school on the farm. We had mass there this morning She has converted all her serfs. A Somerset lady, cousin of Rothwells, came to luncheon. She had seen me buy the side board at Ston Easton. Her husband is a professor called Fletcher[7]. Everyone except Daphne talks of nothing except local politics.

It isn't hot. Just as Ronnie said a wet English August. 5000 feet up. Insignificant country so far as I've seen it. No fine trees, no tropical birds or flowers, scrubby hills, wire fences, bungalows. The staple dish at all meals is corn on the cob, tell Meg.

All love to you all
E

[1] Margaret Fraser born 1881. Married in 1910 Brigadier-General Archibald Stirling and had five children, including William (Bill), who commanded the SAS regiment which Waugh joined in 1943, David, and Margaret who married the Earl of Dalhousie.

[2] Son of Alec Waugh, ADC to the Governor General.

[3] Lord Acton (1907–   ). Grandson of the historian. Left Rhodesia after the Unilateral Declaration of Independence.

[4] Father Maxwell.

[5] John Michael Kalmanson, who started a paper-bag and cardboard-box factory in South Africa. Lord Acton was a director.

[6] Earl of Dalhousie (1914–   ). Married Margaret Stirling in 1940. Governor General of the Federation of Rhodesia and Nyasaland 1957–63.

[7] Professor Basil Fletcher. Vice-Principal of the University College of Rhodesia and Nyasaland 1956–60. He married Gerrardine Daly in 1928, a cousin of Mrs Frank (Boobla) Rothwell.

To John McDougall   Combe Florey House.
[March? 1958]
Postcard

Yes, I am back like a midget refreshed. Rhodesia was a rich mine of Knoxiana but no holiday resort. One ancient monument – no one knows who built it or why or when or how. Natives drab. Whites drabber. No sun. Rain continuously. Re-reading what I wrote about Knox I see all the Oxford part needs re-writing to enliven and embellish it. Thing is to get all facts down while they are in my poor nut and then spread myself being elegant. I will let you know when I come to London. Do come here with the spring.

E

To Ann Fleming   Combe Florey House.
10 March 1958

Dearest Ann

I think your letter must have travelled with me in the aeroplane from Salisbury. I had left M'Bebi when it arrived and was at the Dalhousies' (whose genial and lavish hospitality was slightly clouded by the presence of Princess Pat and husband[1]). It was a jolly good letter. Thanks awfully.

I went to Graham's play before I left. I thought he knew how to write it but that

Sir John [Gielgud] couldn't act. The theme is great balls theologically. The reviews next day all said: 'only Roman Catholics will understand it'. We are just the people who don't.

Rhodesia is not an interesting country. The natives are as drab as Jamaicans – no dressing-up or undressing – no wild life, no trees; one ancient monument which I toiled through floods to see, called Zimbabwe. No one knows who built it, or why, or when. The whites are (a) Old Rhodesians – that is to say families dating from 1890, survivors and descendants of the riff-raff who came up from the Cape with Jameson & Rhodes. Dreadful people rather stuck up (b) English county families who came there in 1946 to escape the Welfare State. They are rapidly becoming middle-class (c) Displaced persons – Hungarians etc. very poor & rather gay (d) Jesuits & other missionaries. Black Americans who come to the Federation are labelled 'foreign natives'; white Americans are 'Europeans'. Sky scrapers in the city, bungalows in the country. Every white man has a motor-car and a dinner-jacket and goes to bed at 9. The women drink tea all day long. A huge Art Gallery presented by Sir Somebody Courtauld with nothing to put in it. On my last day an exhibition of photographs was opened called 'the Family of Man', which has been touring the world and was said to have had a success in London. It was flagrant anti-American propaganda. Oddly enough arranged by the Museum of Modern Art in New York and circulated by the American office of culture. Simon Dalhousie insisted on the removal of some of the most obscene items before he would open it.

Daphne Acton is no Anglo-Catholic; genuine Roman and what is more a saint. Not as succulent as she was as a girl – rather gaunt. Mother of ten and grandmother of 3⅓. It was funny to hear yells of rage from a little girl in the grips of a larger boy: 'Mummy, mummy stop Danash taking my Teddy' – an aunt complaining of her nephew[2]. Children were everywhere, no semblance of a nursery or a nanny, the spectacle at meals gruesome, a party-line telephone ringing all day, dreadful food, an ever present tremendously boring ex-naval chaplain, broken aluminium cutlery, plastic crockery, ants in the beds, totally untrained black servants (all converted by Daphne to Christianity, taught to serve Mass but not to empty ash trays). In fact everything that normally makes Hell but Daphne's serene sanctity radiating supernatural peace. She is the most remarkable woman I know. She has been an immense help with my life of R.A.K.

You are wrong in thinking A. Crawley[3] was back in England. I saw him distinctly in Salisbury.

I was cruelly persecuted by Catholics – made to attend a Catholic businessmans luncheon (where I only got wine by roaring for it), lecture to the Campion Society and to the Jesuit white public-school. On the latter occasion I was saved by the rain. I was to speak in 'the Alfred Beit Hall', a showy classical building. Luckily Alfred[4] had economised on the roof and made it of tin. After I had spoken for ten minutes there was a cloud-burst and everyone was deafened and the ordeal curtailed. It rained continually. I am like a pit pony in the English sun. It rained away the Kariba dam – or bits of it. This caused great local excitement. I flew over it & saw the flood – very impressive. All the niggers are laughing like mad saying the Gods of the Zambesi will ruin the expensive project.

I came home to find the family unaccountably pleased to see me. The morning-room has now been papered and looks very sombre & old fashioned.

... Many Stirlings in Salisbury. David far from well.

Love from
Evelyn

[1] Admiral Sir Alexander Ramsay (1881–1972), uncle of Lord Dalhousie, married in 1919 Princess Patricia (1886–1974), daughter of the first Duke of Connaught.

[2] The Acton children were born between 1932 and 1954. 'Danash' was Denès Marffy, son of the eldest daughter Pelline, then three years old with aunts of four and seven.

[3] Aidan Crawley (1908–   ). Married Virginia Cowles in 1945. Labour MP 1945–51, Conservative MP 1962–7.

[4] Sir Alfred Beit (1903–   ). His family had made a fortune in Southern Africa.

To Lord Baldwin   Combe Florey House.
14 March [1958]

Dear Frisky

I can't recommend Miekle's Hotel, Fort Victoria, S.Rhodesia where I lately spent a night.

I hope you go to Caldey from Tenby and tease the Trappists into talking.

I used to know Brian Howard well – a dazzling young man to my innocent eyes. In later life he became very dangerous – constantly attacking people with his fists in public places – so I kept clear of him. He was consumptive but the immediate cause of his death was a broken heart. His boy friend gassed himself in his house[1]. There is an aesthetic bugger who sometimes turns up in my novels under various names – that was $\frac{2}{3}$ Brian $\frac{1}{3}$ Harold Acton. People think it was all Harold, who is a much sweeter & saner man.

I have been staying with a saint, whom you knew, Daphne Acton, collecting items of information about Ronnie Knox. Writing his life takes me into unfamiliar places, mostly among aged High Church clergymen.

I wish you would come and visit us here. It is not very far out of your way if you take a steamer from Tenby to Weston-super-Mare but perhaps they only run in the summer.

I hope Edward[2] is enjoying the army. Bron is at the last hurdle of getting a commission. If he scrambles over he goes to Cyprus to be stoned by school-girls.

Very decent obituary of Diana in the *Sunday Times*[3]. Who by? Rupert Hart-Davis?

Yours ever
Boaz

[1] Waugh wrote a postcard on 3 May: 'I learn that I misinformed you about the circumstances of Brian Howard's death. His American boy died suddenly but naturally in his bath. Brian poisoned himself some days later.' In fact 'Sam' was gassed in his bath because the exhaust pipe had been removed.

[2] Viscount Corvedale, his son, since 1976 Earl Baldwin.

[3] A note on Lady Diana Cooper announcing that in the next issue there would be an extract from *The Rainbow Comes and Goes*, the first volume of her autobiography, published by her nephew Rupert Hart-Davis.

To Ann Fleming   Combe Florey House.
21 May 1958

My Dear Ann

Thank you for the pretty picture of Canterbury Cathedral. I hope you sit under Dr Hewlet-Johnson there and pray for the conversion of Freud, Quennell etc.

I think the report of my happiness must derive from the fact that I got tight one afternoon lately in London. That evening I had a Monsignore (whom I had not met before) to dinner. The last thing I remember saying is: 'Vodka, with your caviare, Monsignore'. We talked for hours. He told me numberless scandals about seminary life. All is a blank. Two days later I got a letter from him apologising for being tight.

I am a manic-depressive about money. At the moment I am depressive & think myself destitute. I find I spent over £17,000 last year. This year I shall make 5 and pay tax on 17 – so I have reasons for depression.

I have tooth ache.

Mr Peters, my man of business, says he can't understand a word of my life of Knox.

My pea-hen lays eggs all over the place & wont sit on them.

Meg is fat as butter.

Come & see us again soon.

Cornet Waugh is enjoying Cyprus top-hole.

Diana's book is first class – except for Cooper's terrible interpolations. [1]

                                                            Love
                                                            Evelyn

[1] Several letters from Duff Cooper are included in *The Rainbow Comes and Goes*.

To Anthony Powell   Combe Florey House.
[9 April 1958]
Postcard

Delicious dinner, jolly meeting, thanks awfully. Proud to have had chance of praising *Molly* to Yanks. I say, read *Flash & Filigree* and see if you dont think 'Terry Southern' is a pseudonym of Henry's. It reads as straight Green.

Mrs Muggeridge [1] came here on Monday. I saw her from a window.

                                                            E

[1] Katherine Dobbs married Malcolm Muggeridge in 1927.

To John McDougall   Combe Florey House.
18 April 1958

Dear Jack

Thank you most awfully for the boiled beef and wines. I do so enjoy our luncheons together. I hope I don't seem to take them for granted. They are a real treat.

I have written to Peters turning down the 'Cities of Enchantment' proposal. I did not scold him, but I think he should not have intruded on what was a purely personal question between us. You were most magnanimous and I would have taken you at your generous word if I had really wanted to write the book, but I decided on reflection that I had only a year or two ahead in which I was capable of original work and I shouldn't waste that time in hack-work. Soon I shall have to jump at every chance of writing the history of insurance companies or prefaces to school text-books. Squire & Belloc warn us of the horrors of longevity. But meanwhile while I have any vestige of imagination left, I must write novels.

I am very sorry you have the accidie. I don't think the cure really is new & varied activities. I think God sends these times to remind us that there is no rest except in Him. He takes away all zest in human affairs to give us the chance of seeing our immortal destiny.

A curious incident. When I reached the Hyde Park Hotel after lunching with you I found they had failed me & my luggage was not in the hall. Seven minutes delay with no time to spare, and myself raging. Who should be standing there grinning but John Sutro & John Sparrow[1]. I got to the train in the end with whistles blowing & flags waving. Standing on the platform grinning John Sutro & John Sparrow. They had come all the way to Paddington expressly for the fun of seeing me miss the train. This was *not* a Pinfold.

Yours ever
Evelyn

[1] John Sparrow (1906–). Barrister, Warden of All Souls College, Oxford, 1952–77.

To A.D.Peters   Combe Florey House.
17 June 1958

Dear Pete

... The news of Bron is fairly hopeful[1]. He was hit by three bullets – has had his lung and his spleen removed and his left hand is shattered. They thought he could not live, but every day he grows a little stronger and if no infection occurs there is a good chance of his survival. Laura is with him.

Thank you very much for your sympathy

Yours ever
Evelyn

[1] On 9 June Auberon Waugh, doing his national service in Cyprus, had been very seriously wounded. In his own words: 'I had noticed an impediment in the elevation of the Browning machine-gun in the

turret of my particular armoured car, and, having nothing else to do, resolved to investigate it. Seizing hold of the end with quiet efficiency, I was wiggling it up and down when I noticed it had started firing. Six bullets later I was alarmed to observe that it was firing through my chest and got out of the way pretty sharpish.' Auberon Waugh 'The Ghastly Truth', *In the Lion's Den*, 1978. He received the last sacraments.

To LADY ACTON   Combe Florey House.
23 June 1958

Dearest Daphne,

Thanks awfully for your letter of enquiry about my son Bron. It has been an alarming business and is not yet over. According to the official account a machine gun suddenly opened fire on him from an empty armoured car. It sounds rum. Anyway he stopped six bullets. He could not possibly have lived on a battle field but medical help was handy and the notices in the press set off all the nuns & monks & clergy & laity praying like mad. As the result he began to make a miraculous recovery. The latest news is not quite so good. I think they must have slacked in their prayers. So I have sent out further demands to Poor Clares etc. He has had his spleen, a lung, two ribs and a part of a hand removed. He edified the regimental surgeon (a Papist) by quietly saying the De Profundis on his way to hospital. Laura is with him, staying in reasonable comfort at Government House but confined to it except for a twice daily journey to the hospital under armed escort. It is very dull & lonely & anxious for her. Please pray for her too. Please thank Fr Maxwell awfully for saying Mass for Bron.

If I could say Mass I would do so for Father Maxwell. He must be having a ghastly life on that stoep with all those children.

Magdalen's boy Encombe has grown a beard and been sent down for shooting a deer in Magdalen Park.[1]

Did you see the letter in *The Times* signed by the Prime Minister & the Duke of Norfolk and a lot of nobs asking for money for the Knox Memorial? I am having copies printed and will send you some to press on those Popish Rotarians who made me lunch with them and on the Dalhousies and all Rhodesians black & white. Money is not yet rolling in. The plan is to have Arthur Pollen's excellent bust cast in bronze & stuck up in Trinity. The younger dons insist we must also endow a scholarship to send them abroad in the Long Vac. Elizabeth Wansbrough[2] a deaf convert Jewess is in charge of the funds but she doesn't understand that no one ever parts with money unless badgered.

Do you want any copies of *A Spiritual Aeneid*[3] for yourself or anyone else. I have a superfluity.

I am now describing Ronald's life at St Edmund's – very discreetly with dark hints of unspeakable scandals. I went there for a night lately. It is a barbarous place. I also went for two nights to Ampleforth to see Laurence Eyres[4] whom I have grown to love. I was dazzled by the luxury of the school hospitality – most unlike Downside where the guest-master thinks he has done his duty by sticking his head in at the door and saying: 'Finished with *The Times*?'

Henry Esmond reads aloud well. Also *Bleak House* but your children would not understand about London fogs I suppose & the best parts are all fog-scapes.

Please don't stop praying for Bron & Laura.

Love to you all
Evelyn

[1] Viscount Encombe (1937–   ). An undergraduate at Trinity College, Oxford, he shot the deer with a bow and arrow and gave a party. 'It tasted more like kipper', said one of the guests. Succeeded as Earl of Eldon 1976.

[2] Elizabeth Lewis, from a Jewish family of lawyers, became a Roman Catholic in 1919 and married George Wansbrough in 1928.

[3] By Ronald Knox, 1918, republished 1950.

[4] Laurence Eyres (1892–1966). At Trinity College, Oxford, with Knox, and his friend and disciple. He followed Knox into the Roman Catholic Church, collected his writings and edited his posthumous *In Three Tongues*, 1959.

To Auberon Waugh
Combe Florey House.
8 July 1958

My Dear Bron

Welcome home. I am delighted that you have escaped from the torrid & treacherous island of Cyprus. I wish I could come and greet you but I have a long-standing and very tedious engagement in Germany. It started as a treat for your mother, who now can't come with me. I am being paid to stand up in a theatre in Munich and read aloud for an hour to an audience of Huns who think that such a performance will somehow help celebrate the 800th anniversary of the foundation of their city. I am sure neither the Huns nor I will enjoy it.

Teresa who, insanely, means to spend August in Turkey will visit you, then your mother, finally I. I cannot tell you when dear little Septimus will arrive. Your grandmother has dashed off to persecute Lord de Vesci[1] but no doubt she will soon be at your bedside. She is well known to raise all invalid's temperatures five degrees.

I hope you get a decent room to yourself overlooking the river. If the walls seem bare tell your neighbour Sir John Rothenstein[2] to bring round a few of the fine paintings he keeps hidden in the cellars of the Tate.

For spiritual comfort summon Mgr John Barton, 43 Palace Street, Victoria 7635. A learned, very tall, slightly bawdy prelate who has been praying for you.

The pea-hen has layed two more eggs and is sitting. The pea cock is so bored we can't keep him out of the house.

Yours ever affec.
E.W.

[1] Viscount de Vesci (1881–1958). A cousin of Mary Herbert, Waugh's mother-in-law.

[2] Sir John Rothenstein (1901–   ). Director of the Tate Gallery 1938–64.

[3] Mgr John Barton (1898–   ). Priest in charge SS Peter and Edward's, Palace Street, 1950–75. Author of many religious works.

To CHRISTOPHER SYKES   Combe Florey House.
16 July 1958

Dear Kitty

You are a good little chap to find me all that valuable information about the late R.A.Knox. It exposes many respected clergymen as liars or at least as hallucinated. All the staff at St Edmund's think they remember his returning from London on the evening of 16th January 1926. Now I can put all that right. Thank you thank you.

I expect that in your great work on Wingate you met many untruthful and deluded soldiers. I look forward to your book and to its great success. When you are a best seller like Boots [Connolly] perhaps you will show your pretty nose in the Rockingham [White's] again.

I went to Germany for the first time last week. The Germans are not at all as you & Randolph used to describe them to me. They are a slow gentle inefficient inoffensive people, soberly dressed, their children well brought up. Their architecture and decoration is of the Pompadour style. They excel in making wooden painted angels. They live on white, fresh water fish. Their women look like Mr A.D.Peters. You and Randolph fairly led me up the garden path urging me to shoot these simple creatures.

Oh, listen there is one more very important point about R.A.Knox's broadcast. You say it happened in Edinburgh. Does this mean that it was heard only by the Scotch or could they in 1926, as they do now, 'relay' his voice from London? Was it done from Edinburgh simply because he happened to be there or was the idea Scotch in origin?

I am having my wounded son, Bron, moved to Sister Agnes' Home which I think is near your Broadcasting House. It would be kind to visit him. He cannot read easily yet but he likes long playing records of light Italian opera, melons and opium (and its derivatives).

Do not eat the caviar on the Dover–Ostend packet.

A large number of those Germans you spoke so ill of are Roman Catholic.

Pray come & stay with me soon.

                                              Yours ever
                                              Evelyn

To A.D.PETERS   Combe Florey House.
[6 August 1958]
Postcard

Could you very kindly make a discreet enquiry for me? A Mr Eric Newby has written an excellent book about a trip to Afghanistan called *A Short Walk in the Hindu Kush* to be published by Secker & Warburg. He tells me that Doubleday in

USA will only publish it if it has an introduction by someone else. If this is true, I am willing to do it, but if he is pulling my leg & merely wanting an extra puff for his book, I won't. Terms don't matter. I should be doing it as a kindness.[1]

E

[1] The book appeared as *A Short Walk* in the United States with a preface by Waugh in 1959.

To EDITH SITWELL   Combe Florey House
6 August 1958

Dearest Edith

Of course I should not have dreamed of sending you the appeal for Ronnie Knox's Memorial if I had had any idea you would not welcome it. I am very sorry he should have offended you. . . .

What I guess must have happened was that he was invited to join the Sitwell Society himself or to [go] to a dinner or something of the kind. He had a horror of press stunts and he may have thought the young men involved were seeking advertisement and he refused rather sharply. It was, if I remember right, about the time when one of his flock was making an ass of himself by being photographed in a balloon with Tallulah Bankhead. . . .

I say all this not to urge you to subscribe but to clear Ronald's name of the imputation of officiousness and bad judgement.

Yours ever affectionately
Evelyn

To LADY ACTON   Combe Florey House.
21 August 1958

Dearest Daphne

The Novena has worked. My son has taken a turn for the better. Thanks awfully. It was most obliging of you. He is now fattening up in Sister Agnes' home for butchery in October and is greatly enjoying himself being much pampered by all.

No second parcel of letters has yet arrived, full or empty. I live in hope that it will come.

I have come to you in the book. Now what would you like, to censure [sic] what I wrote or not? Can you trust to my undoubted goodwill and more doubtful good taste not to offend? As I see it your difficulty will be that if you read & approve the portrait of yourself before publication you will be in some embarrassment about giving your imprimatur to the nice things I shall say about you. While if you haven't seen it first you can put all the blame squarely on me for anything spinal.[1]

I will draw up with professional aid an appendix on Ronald's confirmation and submit *that* to you. If you have kept Fr Caraman's criticism of my version, could you send it back? Do you think it scandalous if I mention your 'face value'? It cannot be denied that if you had been plain Ronald would not have been so keen on you. But perhaps the clergy are supposed to be free of all such susceptibilities. I don't know.

I'll write again soon. This is primarily to say stop praying for Bron. I am sure there are more urgent cases waiting for your attention.

Love
Evelyn

[1] A word used by Ronald Knox to mean 'something that gave him the creeps', p. 229, *Ronald Knox*.

TO ANN FLEMING   Combe Florey House.
28 August 1958   Taunton

Dear Ann

Pray note change of address as above.

Your life is indeed a many splendoured thing. I would far sooner read of it than participate.

I wonder how I missed the Fragonard obscenity [1].

The attempt to starve me was twofold – first by a florid man named Levita who runs a travel agency. I took a ticket via Ostend and Taverne Express. Ship reaches Ostend at 8 pm. I said: 'Can I dine on train?' 'Oh, yes'. 'Make sure'. So Levita talked gibberish to a telephone and said Yes there was certainly a diner. When I got to Ostend I found it was put on at 7 next morning at Stuttgart. Next evening I was due to recite my works in a theatre from 8–9. A tricky time. I said to Consul 'Ought I to dine first?' 'No. There is a civic banquet afterwards for you to which I have been asked'. Arrived at theatre at 8 having drunk a few cocktails alone in my hotel. A horrible Hun said 'I am afraid that in Bavaria we are not very punctual'. We sat in a dressing room which unlike the auditorium was severely 'functional'. At 8.30 other horrible Huns joined us. One said he would 'say a few words' of introduction. We sat on the stage behind the curtain. The h.h. went in front and talked & talked in gibberish and the audience laughed and laughed. At 8.45 I was pushed through the curtains. Charming spectacle of chandeliers and tiers of h.h.s. Read for an hour. Bowed. Horrible Huns clapped. I retired behind curtain expecting to be greeted, thanked & congratulated. Not a soul. Sat down on the stage in Rex Whistler opera setting. Sat till 10. Then two proletarian Huns in overalls came & began turning out the lights. So I went to my hotel which wasn't far and was beetling across the hall to Walterspiel when a horrible hun seized me & said 'No. No. You are expected this way'. Was led into a dingy parlour where sat in a monoglot circle 10 h.hs and consul. After a long time in which they talked gibberish and no refreshment appeared I said to consul 'What about my dinner?' 'Oh, haven't you had it? Everyone dines early in Munich'. Then he consulted in gibberish with chief Hun and said: 'You can get nothing hot in this part of the hotel'. 'Then tell him to get something cold'. More gibberish. 'What do you want cold?' 'Oh anything – some consommé, a salmon trout, duck and a peach'. More gibberish. 'He says you cannot get those things in this part of the hotel'. 'Then for Christ's sake bring whatever I can get'. 'Would you like something to drink too?' 'Yes.' 'What' In despair 'Beer'. So after a long pause a claret glass of lager was brought. Also a tin tray with two pieces of black bread covered with some sort of bloater. This was put, not before me, but on a little table by two female Huns who eagerly devoured it. Consul said 'You see these are middle class people'. So I went up to my room where I found I had been robbed of £17 in my absence.

The Herberts have been a great bore during Bron's lying in. Luckily they have been distracted first by Ivo de Vesci's death, then by the engagement of Anne Grant[2] to an elderly & penniless bachelor of good family.

Douglas & Mia Woodruff came last Saturday. Mia slept till Monday. Douglas gave me much information about Knox which I have since proved to be false.

Love from
Evelyn

[1] Ann Fleming had written 'a nymphet with a lap dog's tail between her legs shocked me more', of an exhibition in Munich.

[2]Anne Grant married Ian Fraser (1923–   ), chairman of Rolls Royce Motors since 1971.

TO AUBERON WAUGH   Combe Florey House.
13 October 1958

Dear Auberon Alexander

The man who calls on you purporting to be my brother Alec is plainly an impostor. Your true uncle does not know your whereabouts & supposes you to be here convalescent – as witness this card which came with a volume of his describing the more obvious & picturesque features of the West Indies. Did your visitor offer any identification other than baldness – not an uncommon phenomenon? Had he a voice like your half great uncle George? Did he wear a little silk scarf round his neck? Was he tipsy? These are the tests.

Your sister Harriet tells me you are to be operated on this week – the ponderous & intricate machinery of Sir Clement's[1] mind having at last come to movement. I hope you enjoy the anaesthetic and that your awakening is not too disagreeable. Your mother told the Jesuits that you were to be operated on last week and they all prayed hard. I daresay God can postpone the effects. He must anyway be awfully bored at the moment with all the prayers for Pius XII who is already sitting pretty. Much better to pray for Chips Channon whose case is more precarious.[2]

Your aunt Gabriel is obsessed by the need to lend you a relic of the true cross. Contrary to all experience she thinks it safer to send it by hand of Herbert than by post.

Your sister Margaret had a sharp attack of alcoholic poisoning, as the consequence of having been put in charge of the wine last week-end.

I resolutely deny myself butter potatoes bread etc. and am shrinking in girth in a most encouraging way. My life otherwise is without interest.

If you would like your uncle Alec's treatise on the West Indies tell your mama and I will send it.

The Monks of Prinknash have started a rival Ronald Knox Memorial. I am having pleasure in supplying them with the names of those who have shirked subscribing to ours – Ladies Eldon, Hylton, Hardwicke etc.[3]

Would you like an absolutely gruesome novel about people dying of senility?[4] It might lighten the weight of your own sufferings to think what far worse things are in store 50 years ahead.

The proletarian major[5] at the gates has paid his rent in advance and has so far caused no trouble.

Mr Coggins[6] broods about your condition perpetually.

> Yours affec.
> E.W.

[1] Sir Clement Price Thomas, the surgeon.
[2] Both Pope Pius XII and Sir Henry Channon had died the week before.
[3] Knox left his books to the Benedictine Abbey of Prinknash which needed money to create a special Knox Library. 'Ours' was the bust by Arthur Pollen which is in Trinity College, Oxford.
[4] *Memento Mori* by Muriel Spark.
[5] Major Austin.
[6] The gardener.

To LADY ACTON   Combe Florey House.
All Souls [2 November] 1958

Dearest Daphne,

This wont reach you in time for your birthday I am afraid. Sorry. I meant to send a high brow book too. Can't find one high enough. There is a gruesome novel out in which all the characters are over 80. Very clever. The book I mean not the ancient characters. Shall I send that? I sent Ronnie's last book *Literary Distractions* round by sea. That wont reach you much before Christmas I expect. With it I sent theological matter and gossip for Mrs Rous about her new sister in law[1]. The wedding has left me very shaken. With your large hospitable heart you will not be able to conceive the suffering I endure when there are people staying here – particularly young people. The ceremony was all right but Ian Frasers chum Fr Hollings[2] preached the most spinal sermon I ever heard. He was deeply resented by all, Catholic and Protestant alike. I soaked gin in the hope of keeping in a good temper and instead got in an awfully bad temper. Then I went to London & saw your headmistress from Aldenham who gave me a photograph of you & Lady Baden Powell. Not as good as the one of us with the gorilla. I had the Macaskie twins[3] out to dinner with their husbands. Claudia is much the prettier but Nicola has the prettier husband. I loved all four. I also saw David Stirling who says he is going to introduce Television into Rhodesia. I hope you'll stop that. I have a crush on the new Pope. A most trustworthy looking man and good for 25 years placid inactivity.[4] Someone called Davenport[5] says he was a chum of yours. True?

I do hope you have a jolly birthday. I suppose it is spring in your garden.

Love
Evelyn

Did you get my version of your version of Ronald's version of his Confirmation and Fr Caraman's comments?

I have just had a letter from Fr Martindale telling a damaging anecdote about Ronald which is in fact a garbled account of something that happened to me.

I am getting the historian's scepticism of 'contemporary sources' – not, I hasten to say, yours.

I say pray a bit for my son. He thrived while his name was in the papers & people prayed. Now they have forgotten and he is going downhill a bit.

Love to Ticky[6] & you all
Evelyn

[1] Anne Grant's husband is the brother of Mrs Peter Rous.
[2] Father Michael Hollings, Chaplain of Westminster Cathedral 1954–8.
[3] Claudia de Lotbinière and Nicola Roberts.
[4] John XXIII, who died five years later.
[5] John Davenport. Literary journalist.
[6] Jill (Ticky) Acton (1947–). Her daughter. Married Nicholas Lampert.

To John Donaldson
[18 November 1958]
Postcard

Combe Florey House.

Laura says she 'half invited' you & Frankie for Monday night next, Nov 24th. May I wholly invite you? *Lolita*[1]. I only remember the smut. The Yankee edition is full of very high-brow allusions. It set me wondering whether there was a modern counterpart of Bowdler (who excised smut from works of literary merit) whose office is to introduce 'literary merit' into smut. If in your corrupt Court circles you know anyone who has a copy of the Paris edition, do get it for me. It may be a mare's nest but if I have hit on a truth it will be jolly funny.[2]

[1] By Vladimir Nabokov.
[2] It was a mare's nest.

To Lady Acton
[1958]

Dearest Daphne

I say, what a photograph! I have been telling my family how pretty you all are & now you send them this very disillusioning group. Not like human beings at all. But thank you for the kind thought.

If you're going to be at home in March I could easily drop in, I think, for a night. ... 28 years ago I travelled by lake & river & train from Nairobi to the Cape through the Congo. It was awfully boring and uncomfortable. It might be interesting to see how communications have deteriorated since then, but anyhow M'bebi seems on the route more or less.

... I want, please, to dedicate my book on Ronnie to you & Katharine Asquith. She says she doesn't mind. Do you?[1]

Last Sunday the *Express* newspaper said that John [Lord Acton] had broken a herd of wild elephants to the plough. I didn't believe it.

Love to you all
Evelyn

Another Downside boy – head–boy twelve years ago – went to prison today for 'false pretences'.

[1] *Ronald Knox* is dedicated 'to Katharine Asquith and Daphne Acton'.

To LORD KINROSS   Combe Florey House.
31 December 1958

Dear Patrick

I hope you have a rollicking Hogmanay.

The major humiliations suffered by Yorke after your luncheon do not directly involve Dame Rose [Macaulay]. She, you may remember, was without water at her flat. Yorke claimed intimate acquaintance with a dignitary called 'Stop Cock' or 'Turn Cock' whom we pursued through a number of fire stations at each of which Yorke's efforts to pass himself off as a proletarian met ludicrous rebuffs. Yorke then reverted from fireman to engineer & said he would mend Dame Rose's cistern himself. (He had been telling some pretty tall stories of his intrepidity on roofs during the 'blitz'.) When we got to Dame Rose's flat we found the cistern was on the roof approached by a rather steep iron ladder. Dame R. shinned up it like a monkey. Yorke trembled below. Only my taunts made him climb. He got to the top, panting & groaning, clung to the tank for a few moments then came down. He had some sort of spasm, seizure or collapse at the foot.

All the obituaries of Dame R. which I read (including Betjeman's) spoke of her as a Cambridge girl. She was in fact at Somerville, Oxford[1]. They also spoke of her piety. She was, I think, quite devoid of the gift of faith.

Off to East Africa soon. God knows why.

Yours ever
Evelyn

[1] She was at Somerville College, Oxford, but her father lectured at Cambridge from 1905.

To Laura Waugh   Tanga,
4 March [1959]   Tanganyika.[1]

Darling,

It is only 5 weeks today that I said goodbye. It seems much longer. I am a very different creature – all melancholia gone. In 5 weeks & three days we meet again. This is the last letter I shall be able to write for a week as I return to the coast tomorrow where it is too hot to move a pen. I am on a motor tour with Jack's [Donaldson] jolly sapper friend and an aged brigadier. They go from government post to post interviewing worried officials. I go sight seeing. There are not many sights to see except giraffes & ostriches & blackamoors & worried officials. I spent one day with the Masai. They are a people who like the whisker are mad about cows tobacco & south african sherry. Unlike W. they paint themselves with ochre & spend all day doing their hair & bedizening themselves. They all carry spears & shields & clubs & live in mud bird-nests and are only waiting for the declaration of independence to massacre their neighbours. They had a lovely time during the Mau Mau rising. They were enlisted & told to bring in all the Kikuyus' arms & back they proudly came with baskets of severed limbs. Yesterday I spent with the Chagga, the neighbours they particularly want to massacre as they are rich & civilized. So civilized indeed that a coon came out to greet me – believe it or not – carrying a copy of Stopp's magnum opus[2]. I dined with the paramount chief, who said: 'Don't dress. Come in your tatters & rags'. He was born in a mud hut but has a brand new villa with five lavatories, all of which he showed me. Also an extensive collection of neck-ties in a specially constructed cabinet, six wireless sets and many bottles of spirits and an album of souvenirs of the English coronation. He was very jolly – much more lively than Ann Grant's Basuto[3].

Tonight we are stopping in the hills in a little German hotel at the head of a valley over a waterfall. It is coolish & very pretty. I wish you were here. I rather dread returning to the heat of the coast. This time next week I go to the Southern hills & take an aeroplane from a place called M'Beya to Salisbury to the Actons. I fear all the Rhodesians will be in a state of great over excitement about politics and the rising in Nyasaland. Who should I meet in Dar es Salaam but the young lady who used to live at Bencombe & married & then left Sir Somebody Stamer. She is married to someone else now, pretty & jolly.[4]

Please tell Bron how elated I am to hear of his progress. I wonder whether you will be at Teresa's 21st birthday party & whether Meg will be there. I grieve about your condition of health. Would it be fun for you to go straight to Brighton with Bron when he comes out of hospital?

I am having great difficulties in getting anything to smoke. Everyone has a pipe here. The Brigadier smokes one under the shower-bath.

All love
E

---

[1] Waugh was in Africa from the end of January to the beginning of April.

[2] *Evelyn Waugh; Portrait of an Artist.*

[3] Constantine Bereng (1938–   ). King Moshoeshoe of Lesotho since 1966. He had been at school at Ampleforth and stayed at Pixton.

[4] Stella Binnie was married to Sir Anthony Stamer 1948–53 and they lived near Stinchcombe. In 1953 she married Charles M. Barrow who was attached to the emigration department in Dar-es-Salaam.

To Ann Fleming   Combe Florey House.
21 April 1959

My Dear Ann

I returned home ten days ago greatly rejuvenated and have spent most of the time answering letters, correcting proofs and unveiling statuary. I was not at all massacred in Africa. The report in the newspapers about cars being stoned arose from the Public Works Department in Rhodesia making a traffic check. A black man was found with a basket full of stones at the side of the road and, asked what they were for, said 'For cars, sir'. He couldn't count so had been told to put a stone into his basket for every car that passed.

Thank you for reminding me of Debo's plight. Those Devonshires don't get enough to eat. I must send them a leg of pork.[1]

Thank you, too, for asking me to treats. I have set the builders at work again here so cant afford to come to London – unless they make so much noise & dust that I have to leave. Even then it would not be for [Lucian] Freud & Harling[2] and your socialist friends.

Margaret has grown rather plain in my absence. Her nose has coarsened. She eats & drinks too much. She looks rather like Sir Ronald Graham[3] now. Bron has made a remarkable recovery – hardly an invalid at all.

The captain of the *Pendennis Castle* said: 'It's a funny thing – this is the first voyage I've had without a passenger going mad. Coming out I had two stewards sitting on a man all the way to stop him going overboard'.

I went to a great feast at Trinity, Oxford, on Saturday. Delicious wines. My deaf ear was given to a Jew called Wind[4] whose lectures are so popular that he gives them each twice in the [Playhouse] theatre. My good ear was vexed by an awful bore called Sir Somebody Luke[5]. I slept in college & had quite forgotten the horror of Oxford bed rooms.

Meg Dalhousie has become much grander since last year. When she leaves the dining room now she stands in the doorway with all the ladies round her and then they all curtsey together to Simon like altar boys.

If you read the next number of *The Tablet* you will see the report of a speech of mine[6] which made Tommy Lascelles blub.

I was asked to dinner by the Paramount Chief of the Chagga tribe. He said: 'Don't dress. Come in your tatters and rags'. It is sad to see the bohemian fashions of Victoria Square spreading to central Africa.

Read *Memento Mori* by Muriel Spark.

Perhaps Debo has no one to cook a joint for her. I had better send bananas, which are very sustaining.

I take Margaret sight seeing in Oxford on 30th and 31st of May. Why don't you go & stay with Maurice Bowra then?

Ever yours affec.
Evelyn

[1] Ann Fleming had written: 'I had a letter from Debo saying you had gone mad again, apparently she was receiving honey and cauliflowers from various African ports.'
[2] Robert Harling. Typographer and novelist. Editor of *House and Garden* since 1957.
[3] Sir Ronald Graham (1870–1949). Ambassador in Rome in 1921. He had a red face.

⁴ Professor Edgar Wind (1900–71). Lectured on the history of art.

⁵ Sir Harry Luke (1884–1969). Traveller and author.

⁶ 'The Quintessence of Oxford', Waugh's address at the unveiling of Arthur Pollen's bust of Ronald Knox.

To LADY ACTON
22 April 1959

Combe Florey House.

Dearest Daphne

It was jolly decent of you to send me those letters of thanks for the ball and it was jolly decent of Catherine to write too.

I had a very dull voyage home. I was the youngest & prettiest first class passenger. No priest on board. A Godless Easter for the first time since I became a Catholic. Since I got home I have acquired a rosary and I peg away. No result.

The unveiling of Ronald's bust at Trinity last Saturday went all right. Lots of his friends came from great distances and the portrait was acclaimed a good likeness. I don't like it in bronze nearly as much as in terra cotta. I told the President how lucky he was to be getting a promising scholar like Richard[1]. He said: 'Yes, I hope very much he gets in'. Not an absolutely satisfactory answer. But he (President) is a very well disposed man. The dons are awfully above themselves nowadays with so many people clamouring for admittance.

Soon I will send you a photograph of Bron to whet Jill's appetite. He is hardly an invalid at all now. Did you know Sir Ronald Graham? Margaret is growing just like him. I think it must be the drink.

The Woodruffs, having refused to subscribe to Ronald's memorial and having done their utmost to prevent others doing so, had the effrontery to turn up on Saturday. Also mean Lady Hylton. Katharine [Asquith] was there – very spry.

I sent you Ronald's *Priestly Life*[2] last week. It is having a brisk sale to people who think it is the biography of J.B.Priestley.

Lady Peck has moved to a nursing home. There will be no killing her there for years so I have sent her the proofs of masterpiece. I dread her reply.[3]

It is very difficult explaining to your English admirers why you are building a swimming-pool before a church.

Fr Caraman is taking all the work of editing Ronald's sermons off my hands and is smoothing down all the publishers I have offended and is doing wonders.

Laurence Eyres found so many mistakes in masterpiece that the publishers are in despair.

Isn't this clever of Speaight?[4]

Love to you all
Evelyn

A young lady near here named Stukely[5] says she spent the winter with you. Was she at the ball?

¹ Richard Acton (1941–   ). Lady Acton's eldest son. A banker and later a barrister.

² Ronald Knox, *The Priestly Life: A Retreat*, 1959.

³ It was enthusiastic.

⁴ Robert Speaight, *A Modern Virgilian*, 1959.

⁵ Christine Stucley (1940–   ). Married in 1961 David Lytton-Cobbold.

To LADY MARY LYGON   Combe Florey House.
Labour Day [1 May] 1959

Darling Blondie

Please do not be too proud to accept a little Easter present from me with my deep love.

I am very sad to hear you are sad. Loss of faith is the saddest thing that can happen to one. Do you positively disbelieve in the Christian revelation – I mean think the gospels are false – or are you simply in the mood when it doesn't seem to matter whether they are true or false?

Do you think that perhaps the religion taught you by the Rev. Drunken Jones was all right for a pretty little girl but not enough for an adult woman? If that's the case, as seems likely, would you let me introduce you to a real beast[1] who would dispel your clouds? I think Anglicanism gets a lot of English people to heaven as long as they don't put too much strain on it. But a time comes for others when they need something stronger & deeper

I think you don't like travel much, but if you ever thought of paying us a visit it would be a great joy to one & all.

                                        All love
                                        Bo

[1] Priest, in their private language.

To LADY MARY LYGON   Combe Florey House.
Monday before Ascension [4 May 1959]

Darling Blondy

Holidays? From what? What is it that you do with this blind doctor? Quelquechose aussi?

Listen. There is a beast in your neighbourhood who was a friend – well anyway an acquaintance – of Hughie's at Oxford; a Spanish beast called Alfonso de Zulueta (of highly respectable family, dear Lady Mary). Would you like to meet him? Or I can offer a very clever Jesuit who says he is French but is really I think a Turk, called Fr Caraman of 114 Mount Street. Or would you like a simple English gentleman? I can supply that too. Or a hell-fire Irishman? I believe that everyone once in his (or her) life has the moment when he is open to Divine Grace. Its there, of course, for the asking all the time, but human lives are so planned that usually there's a particular time – sometimes, like Hubert, on his death bed – when all resistance is down and Grace can come flooding in. I don't know, darling Blondy, whether that is your condition now, but if it is, it's not a thing to dilly-dally about.

If you aren't troubled by intellectual doubts – Dead Sea Scrolls and all that balls

– I think it is just your soul opening up to God. I'd awfully like to pimp for you in that affair.

Did you read Lady Curzon's untruthful memoirs?[1] I found them in a ship the other day. She plainly accuses Alfred & me of buggery. After a long list of Hubert's young ladies she says: 'Alfred preferred bachelors – Gavin Henderson[2], Robert Byron, Evelyn Waugh'.

All love
Bo

[1] The Marchioness Curzon of Kedleston, *Reminiscences*, 1955.
[2] Gavin Henderson (1902–1979). In 1927 on the eve of his marriage he took eight two-gallon tins of petrol and literally set the Thames on fire. Succeeded as Baron Faringdon in 1934.

To NANCY MITFORD   Combe Florey House.
19 May 1959

Darling Nancy

This is a fan letter. I've just re-read *Voltaire in Love* and must tell you how much I admire it. I enjoyed it hugely at the first reading but I didn't appreciate it. You write so deceptively frivolously that one races on chuckling from page to page without noticing the solid structure. Perhaps because I've just finished writing a biography myself (an easy one, with all sources accessible – personal knowledge of the subject) I can now realize what an achievement of research, selection & arrangement you apparently effortlessly performed. It is a masterly book.

You wouldnt have enjoyed my African tour at all. I covered miles of featureless country and met thousands of featureless people and ate drab food. . . . But it was a blank two months and just what I needed to invigorate me.

Did you see Boots's very discreditable review of Honks[1]. The booby calls those adventurous & wildly unconventional men, Maurice Baring & Belloc, 'tame' and the exquisitely candid Conrad Russell 'Pawky'. Someone must have been tickling his class consciousness again.

. . . But I am wandering from the point, which is to say Hurrah for *Voltaire in Love*. What's next?

Love
Evelyn

Andrew Devonshire in his cups called me a sponger. It rankles.

[1] *The Light of Common Day* by Diana Cooper, 1959, her second volume of autobiography, was reviewed by Cyril Connolly in *The Sunday Times*. He found it 'less of a book and more of a scrapbook than the first . . .'.

To Graham Greene   Combe Florey House.
29 June 1959

Dear Graham

My guess is that the Lord Chamberlain took umbrage at the phallic joke with the cigar. I can't find any indecent adjectives.

What a clever play[1] it is. I have read with great delight the high praise it has won in all the papers I read and I hope very much to get to London to see it. Reading it I am dazzled at the cleverness. I congratulate you with all my heart & thank you for sending me a copy. I hoped by now to have sent you a copy of my life of Knox but the binders have struck to show their sympathy with the manufacturers of printers ink or some such nonsense. But I don't think you thought as highly of Ronald as I did.

On the rare occasions I go to London I always ask for you and am always told you are far away. I am always here and it would be a great treat to see you if you ever felt the need to hide.

Just read with fascination the life of Edward Johnston[2].

Are you sure Clive shot himself?[3] I always thought it was the razor. I looked in DNB but it just says 'died by his own hand'. That's the kind of ambiguity I hate.

Love from
Evelyn

[1] Graham Greene's *The Complaisant Lover*. Ralph Richardson flourished an exploding cigar, but with no phallic reference.

[2] Priscilla Johnston, *Edward Johnston*, 1959. Johnston (1872–1944) was an eminent calligrapher. He had shown Waugh, aged fourteen, how to cut a turkey-quill into a chisel-pointed pen.

[3] Michael Edwardes in *Clive: The Heaven-born General*, 1977, asserts that he stabbed himself with a penknife in a lavatory in Berkeley Square.

To Nancy Mitford   Combe Florey House.
29 June 1959

Darling Nancy

Is it persecution mania or was your interview in the *Daily Express*[1] deliberately aimed at me, to make me gobble like a turkey with baffled rage? That was certainly the effect. I had to loosen my collar & lie in a darkened room for an hour after reading it.

Where is your new house? Burgundy or still in Paris? It is very invigorating, I found, to move in middle age – also crippling in expense.

... I hoped by now to have sent you a copy of my *Knox* but the socialists have made a strike against the literary world.

Boots bought smut from Corporal Hill. They have had trouble before with smut buyers who refuse to pay because they know the Corporal daren't sue. I said Boots was much more frightened of the police than they were, and I am right. Boots has coughed up.

Deka's (?) Dekka's (?) Decker's autobiography[2] will just be socialist propaganda. No spicey bits about you & Honks, I bet. . . .

She [Lady Diana Cooper] had a great crush at Hatchard's bookshop when she sat there to sign copies. Devonshire took six but none of her buggers turned up.

No, I didn't think *Lolita* any good except as smut. As that it was highly exciting to me.

Tell me about your new house[3] and your summer (any chance of your coming here) and your winter. Jan & Feb loom up. We shouldn't quarrel you know if we were together.[4] Where will you be?

Love from
Evelyn

[1] Entitled 'Your morals, money and men'.
[2] Jessica Mitford, *Hons & Rebels*, 1960.
[3] Nancy Mitford wanted a house in Versailles and did move there in 1967.
[4] She had said they would quarrel if they went to China together.

To John McDougall   Combe Florey House.
8 July 1959

Dear Jack

. . . Decent of Hatchards to make *Knox* book of the month. I think I know why. I was rather tight & very jolly when Diana was signing there* but not so tight that I didn't notice that 80% of the copies signed were presented to her by shop-girls not by individual customers. Moreover some of these copies were on sale that evening in other shops e.g. Rees.[1] Diana has better looks & better manners than I. What do you estimate the sale would be if I exposed myself? Would they guarantee 250 copies? How would it do if I did the signing in comfort & privacy in Essex Street?[2] How would our former friends in Curzon Street[3] take this defection? I think we should consider such things before accepting. But I want to do all I can to alleviate your losses on this book.[4]

Let us cadge from a college when we go up. Sparrow?

Yours ever
Evelyn

*There is ambiguity here. I mean because I was jolly that day they think I am jolly every day. I was shameless in accosting strangers & drawing them up to the table for Diana's book. Wouldn't for my own.

[1] Hugh Rees Limited.
[2] The offices of Chapman and Hall.
[3] Heywood Hill's bookshop.
[4] Waugh did not sign copies at Hatchard's.

To ANNE FREMANTLE   Combe Florey House.
14th July to Hell with the Revolution 1959

Dear Anne
    Do you know, or can you discover from your diverse sources of information,
anything about a fellow countryman of yours named John d'Armes, D'Armes,
Darmes, a Rhodes scholar from Princeton now in his last year at Oxford? His father,
I understand, has academic connexions and is employed by the Rockefeller
Foundation whatever that may be; not, I hope, connected with that building near St
Patrick's Cathedral. Any information you can supply about his antecedents &
present position would greatly interest me. My eldest daughter expresses a
romantic interest in him. [1]

                                        Yours ever
                                        Evelyn Waugh
Love to Kathie Cowles

    [1] Teresa met John D'Arms (1934–   ) as a student in Oxford. He became a professor of Latin and
Greek at the University of Michigan and since 1977 has been the director of the American School of
Archaeology in Rome.

To ANN FLEMING   Combe Florey House.
28 July [1959]

My Dear Ann,
    Thank you very much for your letter. It is very agreeable to have the duty of
answering it instead of writing about my days in Africa – a work of ineffable tedium
and triviality.
    I am sorry Thunderbird[1] has left the *Sunday Times*. As long as his fastidious
mind brooded over its pages I felt that the spirit of Edmund Gosse was still with it.
Now there will only be the *Observer* and that has become purely a black man's
paper. How painfully slangy the Devlin report[2] was. Judicial summings up used to
be models of English prose. De Quincey, by the way, says that the custodians of
good prose are well-born spinsters who forego marriage rather than pollute their
blood with plebeian strains and console themselves for the loss of family life by
writing letters to men of culture. Tell Fionn.
    Did you observe that at Eckington (next village to Renishaw) natural, explosive
gas was bursting through the stones of Pinfold Street? I speak literally. It was
reported in yesterday's paper.
    Even if I had (which I had not) filled the Devonshire pot before dinner Debo's
housewifery is condemned. An old fashioned, well trained housemaid empties pots
when she turns down the beds.
    I hope this Canadian[3] (why did you want to meet him?) will not sack poor

Connolly, dreary as he has been lately. I am sure he is not a Trades Unionist.

What honourable motive can you have for lunching on television? ...
[incomplete]

[1] Ian Fleming.

[2] Patrick Devlin (1905–   ). Justice of the High Court 1948–60, life peer 1961, had chaired a committee which recommended the formation of the Central African Federation.

[3] Roy Thomson (1894–1977). Created Baron Thomson of Fleet 1964. The Thomson organization bought *The Times* and the *Sunday Times*.

JOHN MONTGOMERY   Combe Florey House.
29 July 1959
Postcard

As you know better than I, most film projects come to nothing. I should think the Americans would make an absolutely awful film of *Men at Arms* & *Officers & Gentlemen* but I should not want to co operate with them or censor them provided they paid enough. One stipulation – no use of my name in publicity until the money is actually paid. We have had trouble with that before.

                                                          E.W.

TO JOHN MCDOUGALL   Combe Florey House.
[1959]
Postcard

Yes, of course, I will sign copies for Heywood Hill. I say I have been thinking – David Cuthbert has kicked the bucket. You say his widow has some family materials about Holman Hunt. I bet she can't write. I should awfully like to write a full biography of Hunt *if important information not in his autobiography* is available. Could we do a deal with her?[1]

                                                          E

[1] She used the material herself and published under her maiden name Diana Holman Hunt *My Grandmothers and I*, 1960, which enjoyed great success and was admired by her cousin Waugh.

TO AUBERON WAUGH   Combe Florey House.
26 August 1959

Dear Bron
    ... I enclose a catechism. Your grandmother (on Harriet's authority, I think) has told the monks of Downside that you are composing a diatribe against them. I am confident you are incapable of ingratitude to these patient and magnanimous men.

Pray bear in mind that until you are 21 you cannot legally publish a book without my consent as you are incapable as a minor of signing a contract. I do not anticipate having to withhold an imprimatur. Your best course, I think, will be to have it typed and send it to Peters asking him to find a publisher without disclosing your name[1]. It will be more gratifying to have it accepted on its own merits than on my or my brother's notoriety. As soon as it is accepted you can claim it & publish under your name.

The best restaurant in Genoa is named Pichen.

Your affec. papa
E Waugh

[1] Auberon Waugh did nothing with the manuscript until after he was concussed in a car accident the following year. Then he reread it, had it typed and sent to John MacDougall, who published it: *The Foxglove Saga*, 1960.

To Ann Fleming   Combe Florey House.
2 September 1959

Dear Ann

My heart bleeds for you on your Mr Pooter holiday but I rejoice to hear you have found a house.[1] There are few pleasures to touch those of embellishing a building and I am delighted that the grubby banknotes of pornography should be so transformed. Have you any idea of the cost of building these days. Five plain stone steps have cost me £200. Simple balustrading is now £20 a yard. You are one of the very few women I have met who have positive good taste in visual things. When a woman has taste it is quite different from a man's and still more from a bugger's. I am sure you will make something fine. Given £10,000 or £15,000 I could do much here, but my children devour my substance and I have to content myself with tinkering. There is pleasant country round Faringdon and the sort of neighbours whom you entertain in Victoria Square, so I am sure you will be happy. Perhaps you will hunt with Heber-Percy[2]. Gavin Henderson[3] will be most sympathetic politically. Betjeman, I am told, is seldom at home.

The summer here is entirely delicious. I stand at the window at 3.30 before my second swig of paraldehyde and snuff the air & thank God I am in England.

Margaret has procured two adhesive glass discs which she applies to her eye-balls instead of giglamps. They give her a mournful but appealing expression.

I think I told you of my terrible losses of peacocks. I now have a grey budgerigar, very delicately marked with four black spots on his white beard and a nose like a pugilist's quite flat on his face.

Fionn's low tastes are distressing. What I fear for her is that she will marry a proletarian and in two years become a howling snob. I have seen it happen before.

It is the season when American tourists persecute me. They have fallen in numbers with my fall from fame but there are still too many of them – priests mostly. In retaliation I am sending Teresa to Boston for the autumn. She got a second like all girls.

You would not, I think, be interested to hear of my social life with my neighbours. You will not, I am sure, be interested in my treatise on East Africa. *Knox* will reach you on 8th October.

I knew a Rouge Dragon Pursuivant once[4]. Then he was promoted Somerset Herald and now when he tells anyone what he is they think he is correspondent of a provincial newspaper. All heralds stammer. Your chum will not rise above pursuivant if he has the full use of his tongue.

You will be wise to keep the billiard-room for old Caspar's friends. You might use the ball room for Fionn. Bring her out again under a new name and give her a second chance in life.

> Yours ever affec.
> E.W.

[1] Sevenhampton Manor, near Swindon.
[2] Robert Heber-Percy (1911–   ). Inherited Faringdon House from Lord Berners.
[3] Gavin Henderson (Lord Faringdon) was a socialist, which Ann Fleming was not.
[4] Michael Trappes-Lomax.

TO THE EDITOR OF THE TIMES
17 September [1959]

10 Buckingham Street, WC2.

SOCIAL DISTINCTIONS

Sir, – Your reviewer of Miss Compton-Burnett's new novel[1] describes its characters as 'upper-middle-class.' They are in fact large landowners, baronets, inhabiting the ancient seat that has been theirs for centuries. At this season when we are celebrating the quinquennial recrudescence of the class war, is it not desirable to be more accurate in drawing social distinctions?

> I am, Sir, your obedient servant,
> EVELYN WAUGH

[1] *A House and its Head.*

TO MARGARET WAUGH
2 October 1959

Combe Florey House.

Sweet Pig,

I enclose my election address. I think it is funny to hold up Trevor-Roper[1] as Macmillan's great folly instead of Suez or Cyprus or Hola like all the other chaps.

You wrote a very ignoble letter to your brother Auberon but since it was not addressed to me I will not tell you how much I despise you for your discontent self-pity detraction of others etc. etc.

Smuts was a South African general who fought against us in the Boer War and then became a friend and as long as he was alive stopped the Boers being so beastly.

He came to stay in the Hyde Park Hotel during the war and I had his room after he left and when I picked up the telephone and ordered breakfast I found I was speaking on a private line to the War Cabinet Office.

We have been greatly puzzled by the behaviour of Fr Walsh. He was due to come on Monday. That morning we got a telegram from Munich saying 'Arrival delayed will write from Rome'. Yesterday we got a telegram from Vienna saying 'Regret delay arriving Birmingham 2nd' (today). I think he must find the complexities of European travel too much for him. *How* did he get to Vienna if he was on the way to Rome?

Lord Hylton came to present Combe Florey with its beauty prize. Bron & Teresa went to the ceremony in the village hall. He chucked her under the chin and said 'What are you doing here, you naughty little thing?' Then he went to Bishops Lydeard & returned here & said: 'I never eat anything' and ate a whole cold chicken pie at 9 o'clock. He tells me that what we have built at the front door is known as a PERRON and that no gentleman's house is complete without one and that Claud Russell[2] would not go to Ammerdown[3] because there was no perron there.

If you drive here alone from Oxford you are not to give lifts to hitch-hikers because they might turn out to be sexual maniacs & rape you.

There has been a great deal of telephoning. Your mother & Bron go to tipple with Mrs Vernon tonight, to tea with Miss Batchelor[4] on Monday. We have had to give back the comfortable car to your grandmother.

Now that priest says he is coming here tomorrow & gives the time of the London train not the Birmingham train. Holy, but soft on the crumpet.

I go to London on Tuesday to send you a copy of *Knox*. Also to lunch with Mrs Fleming, dine with Maimie Lygon and lunch with MacDougall. Not much work on my dull African book you will say and you will be right.

Teresa has gone to Tresham[5]. She hates her home. Billy Hylton was very flirtatious with her – like Mr Hale and you. How convenient it would be if Per [Lady Hylton] fell down dead & she married him instead of her yank. She has asked her only respectable friend to stay to impress us – called Miss Rimmington[6] – but Miss Rimmington won't answer.

They are scratching paint off the stone of the doorway and it looks very Italian. By they I mean Clifford[7] & Manfredi[8]. Stansells' men have run away leaving me sore at heart.

Did I tell you we went to luncheon at Dunster on Sunday? It was to meet a reformed socialist fellow of All Souls named Rowse[9]. Also an aged man who said he was the grandfather of that girl at Ascot whom Teresa deserted at Oxford – what was her name? Her father died suddenly.

It may be you will meet respectable Rimmington when you come home – may be not.

All love
Papa.

[1] As Prime Minister, Harold Macmillan had in 1957 appointed Hugh Trevor-Roper Regius Professor of Modern History. The election for the Oxford Chancellorship was being contested.

[2] Sir Claud Russell (1871–1959). Ambassador to Portugal 1931–5.
[3] The family house of Lord Hylton.
[4] Miss Batchelor had lived at Combe Florey before the Waughs.
[5] The Donaldsons' house.
[6] Clare Rimmington, an Oxford friend.
[7] Clifford Bracker was handyman at Combe Florey for about a year. Everyone else called him Terry.
[8] Giovanni Manfredi, butler, cowman and, occasionally, builder. His wife Tina was the cook.
[9] A.L.Rowse (1903–   ). Elizabethan historian.

To Graham Greene
Combe Florey House.
13 October 1959
Postcard

I thought your review of *Knox*[1] jolly decent. I knew you did not revere him. I wish you did. I was never a 'Sliggerite'.[2]

E

[1] In the *Observer*.
[2] F.F.Urquhart (1863–1934). Modern historian. Nicknamed Sligger. Fellow of Balliol 1896–1934, a strong influence on generations of undergraduates.

To Lady Acton
Combe Florey House.
20 October 1959

Dearest Daphne

... The reviews have been jolly decent to me. A few beasts, notably Graham Greene, have been beastly about Ronnie. It is selling like warm cakes & being broadcast about. Which reminds me: an American Oratorian came to stay here & he said he had seen a television film in his country purporting to show life at Aldenham with an actor acting Ronnie and an actress acting you, and twin girls and Ronnie reading his bible aloud to you & preaching to twins. I can't think of anything more outrageous to Ronnie's sense of decency. Do you want me to punish them? I can, I think, because they have used copyright material. Would you like me to get a copy of the film to show to your blackamoors? It might be jolly funny.

My mother-in-law, like an ass, told the most evilly – no damn it evily – no evilly was right – disposed journalist Malcolm Muggeridge that 'C' was Macmillan & Muggeridge has written in the *New Statesman* that I was persuaded to suppress the name in order to secure electoral advantage for the Conservative Party.[1]

It is nice for you that Jill is becoming a nun – sad for Bron. He has gone up to Oxford and says he is starving there. His Logic tutor gassed himself fatally[2] after his second tutorial so he is left without instruction. He is fairly well for a man lacking so many essential parts. He had never been athletic so doesn't feel his incapacities as he might. Margaret (whom I miss) is being crammed for her scholarship in Oxford.

Poor half baked Hatty is back at Ascot, the boys at school, so Laura & I are alone for the first time for years and greatly enjoying it. The other Daphne [Fielding] came to England last week and I was struck with a hangover without seeing her or drinking myself. Just her presence is enough.

An absolutely ghastly vin d'honneur was given for *Knox* under the Old Palace, what used to be the wireless shop, now a bookshop. It was black with clergymen and I was deafened & asphyxiated.

... I am trying to write about my African jaunt. It is hard going because I can only be funny when I am complaining about something and everyone was so decent to me. Have you met a very jolly bounder called Rogers who has gone to Salisbury as agent of Tanganyika. He was the Brummell of Dar es Salaam. I think you are all too gentlemanly for him in Rhodesia.

Teresa has formed an attachment to a respectable but utterly dreary American and has pursued him to Harvard. Don't miss her.

Love to you all
Evelyn

[1] Harold Macmillan had been tutored by Knox, who referred to him in his *Spiritual Aeneid* as 'C'. Waugh followed this example. Knox had left after Mrs Macmillan, a Nonconformist, had asked him not to mention religion to the boy and he had refused. He was much upset. Malcolm Muggeridge suspected the identity of 'C', then Prime Minister, and surprised Mary Herbert with a direct question on the telephone.

[2] Michael Foster (1903–59). Though he taught philosophy at Christ Church he was not to tutor Auberon, who was therefore not left uninstructed.

TO SIR MAURICE BOWRA   Combe Florey House.
22 October 1959

Dear Maurice

The Christian Dictionary has just come. What a source it is going to be! I have dipped into it and each time struck something valuable. You could not have made me a more welcome present. I do thank you.

It was most agreeable in Oxford last week. Laura and I enjoyed dining with you enormously.

We went to see Ann's house. It is no beauty; nor yet an eyesore. A typical English country house that has been buggered about for 350 years. Rather large. She talks of demolition. I urge that it is almost as expensive to destroy as to build and that (except for carpets) large rooms are much cheaper to furnish well than small.

By the way I thought the Lodge at the Queen's College as ungrammatical as Lord David [Cecil] himself.

The question you asked me about the identity of 'C' in *Knox* has been answered in the newspapers by prize shit Muggeridge, who bluffed the truth out of my aged mother-in-law.

I say, when you have five minutes to spare could you be very kind and answer this question. Suppose per impossibile that all the governing body of a college – not, of course, the House[1], nor the new foundations like Keble and Hertford, but a mediaeval college like New College – were to be converted to Roman Catholicism is there any legal impediment to their turning over the chapel to popish worship?

You very kindly promised me a copy of the Betjeman-Princess Margaret poem[2]. I hope you have not repented.

Yours ever
Evelyn

[1] Christ Church.
[2] One of many unpublished scurrilous verses which Bowra wrote to amuse his friends.

TO THE EDITOR OF THE SPECTATOR

10 Buckingham Street,
WC2.

[Printed 24 October 1959]

MR 'C'

Sir, – It is of the essence of Grub Street to impute base motives to reticence. In your 'London Diary' Mr Muggeridge seeks to identify a minor character in my *Life of Ronald Knox* with a major character in public life and suggests that I suppressed his name in order to further the electoral advantage of the Conservative Party. I am not concerned either to gratify or titillate his curiosity. The truth is simpler than (I suppose) Mr Muggeridge can conceive. I was guided solely by what I believed to be Ronald Knox's wishes and by my own sense of literary manners.

In his *Spiritual Aeneid*, written in 1917, Ronald Knox referred to two friends, both then alive, as 'B' and 'C', saying: 'Their names are no business of anybody's'. 'B' has been dead for 41 years and I saw no objection to naming him. 'C' is alive and I have preserved his anonymity. The decision was mine alone.

EVELYN WAUGH

TO FATHER HUBERT VAN ZELLER

Combe Florey House.

[November 1959]
Postcard

Yes, indeed. 'The Beerbohm of the Cloister', 'the Michelangelo of the Abbey Church', 'the Demosthenes of the Chapter House' 'the Francis Xavier of the Middle West' or whatever sobriquet you like.

E

To John McDougall   Combe Florey House.
[November 1959]

Dear Jack

I think this (rather jealous?) passage from a letter of Margaret's may amuse you.

'Mary MacDougal (sic) is already a sort of Zuleaka (sic) Dobson. She wears black velvet dresses and pearls and comes into the room amid an awed silence with a regal wave and a "my people, my people" nod.' [1]

DONT PLEASE ANSWER
Evelyn

[1] Mary McDougall (1941–   ). Daughter of John McDougall. Married in 1976 Ian Dunlop.

To John McDougall   Combe Florey House.
Postcard

TOURIST IN AFRICA // TOURIST'S DIARY // DIARY OF A TOURIST IN AFRICA // AFRICAN DIARY // A TOURIST IN AFRICA //

I think any of these titles would be better than '*Africa Revisited*' – Perhaps you will consult Spottiswoode Houston & Methuen. [1]

Bron has a cracked skull & he's in the hospital at Winchester. He wasn't driving, I am glad to say, but he's much the worst hurt of the party.

E

[1] *Tourist in Africa*, 1960.

To Joan Saunders   Combe Florey House.
[Acknowledged 31 December 1959]

Dear Mrs Saunders

May I once more avail myself of your services? I am shortly starting another war novel[1]. I wish to open with the scene in London when 'the Sword of Stalingrad' was exhibited before being sent to Stalin at Yalta. I have vague memories of the event (the exhibition) causing great enthusiasm, crowds queuing etc. Could you provide an account taken from contemporary newspapers? The actual spectacle – dates, time, weather etc. – is of first importance but I shall also welcome any comments, the more bizarre the better, by the public & public persons in speeches and letters to the papers.

Yours sincerely
Evelyn Waugh

The above is now my permanent address

[1] *Unconditional Surrender*, 1961.

To Ann Fleming   Combe Florey House.
17 February 1960

Dear Ann

I hope this reaches you before you leave. I have only just got your jolly letter. I have been having a ripping time at the expense of the *Daily Mail*. Three weeks with Laura, first in Venice which I have never seen in January – exquisitely melancholy, misty, empty, silent, not an American in sight. Far lovelier than in summer. Then to Monte Carlo, cool, sunny, again no yanks but a full season of decent Europeans. Esmond[1] met me twice a day and ran like a rabbit. He looks exactly like Coward in *Our Man in Havana*.[2] Boofy & Fiona[3] in servitude. Randolph turned up. What are you doing here? Covering the insurrection in Algiers.

He was very much on his best behaviour, feeling I think the weight of paternal authority six floors up. Laura bought a book called *The Pitfalls of Gambling and How to Avoid Them* and followed it with the result that every evening she made small sums of money which turned out to be 'New Francs' and quite valuable. Then she had to go back to her cows. I went on to Rome where no one talks of anything except the film *La Dolce Vita*[4]. I don't normally call at embassies but as I was going to luncheon with Gaston[5] I observed protocol & wrote my name in our ambassadors book. He entertained us by singing love songs in Portuguese & Hungarian for two hours, explaining first: 'This little song says "The moon loves the stars, the stars love the earth, the earth loves the sun and I love you." Tumpty tumpty tum'.

Then I came home because the papers said there was to be a strike and I didn't want to end my days at Calais like Beau Brummell. It wasn't till I reached Dover that I heard the strike was off. So now I am continuing my tour to Athens, taking Margaret with me.

The Pope is in rollicking form. I had a nice day of Judy[6]. Then she went off to St Moritz. Gaston was highly over excited about politics and longs to die for his general.

I don't envy you Jamaica a bit.

Did you see a very funny parody of Thunderbird in the *Spectator?*[7].

Love from
Evelyn

[1] Viscount Rothermere, Ann Fleming's ex-husband.
[2] Noel Coward was in Carol Reed's film of Graham Greene's book.
[3] Earl and Countess of Arran.
[4] Directed by Federico Fellini, 1959.
[5] Gaston Palewski was French Ambassador in Rome.
[6] Judy Montagu, who lived in Rome.
[7] A review by Bernard Levin of Ian Fleming's *The Thrilling Cities*, 1960, entitled 'Queen of the North West'.

To Nancy Mitford   Combe Florey House.
24 March 1960

Dearest Nancy

How very nice to see your writing again and how bitter to have to say that I don't see any hope of our meeting in London. Does your English tour include a visit to Crichel?[1] You would there be half way here. Can't we coax you to adventure as far as this? London is a dreadful place full of demonstrating students. No friends left there. I hope the reason for your visit is the delivery of your new novel[2] to your funny looking publisher. I look forward to it and to Tony Powell's 'Pagoda of the Amber Moon'[3] (I think it is called) as the only readable books of the year.

I had a very enjoyable little winter tour, first with Laura then with my daughter Margaret. I have had to pay for it by writing some very uncongenial articles for the *Daily Mail*. Venice in January was damp & cold but empty & silent and mysterious. I had never been there in mists before. Monte Carlo was delicious – no Americans within hearing. Homburg was hell but we stayed only one night. A great mistake. I saw a lot of Mark [Ogilvie-Grant] in Athens. He is going to Delphi to greet Debo. He broke the news of the Armstrong-Jones[4] fiasco with great glee.

Colonel Gaston's affection is gratifying & inexplicable. He has grown much prettier but is very restless in his fine house. The footmen literally run behind him as he darts from one saloon to another. He eats his food too fast. It is very good and deserves lingering attention. I think he has the death-wish strongly.

I saw Mrs Taffy Rodd[5] acting ludicrously badly in a film.

If you have a minute to spare in Chelsea do call on Maimie who is lonely and sad working at a shop called Sloane Gallery, 277 Kings Road.

I was very sorry indeed to hear that the sale of your Versailles house has fallen through. I hope this will induce you to return & live in England.

I am told Chatsworth is kept at stupefying heat. You must like that.

Everybody who has read my life of Ronald Knox has written to point out horrible mistakes & misprints.

The Oxford Chancellorship was a great conflict of loyalty – hatred of socialists against hatred of Trevor-Roper[7]. Anyway I am not a MA and couldn't vote.

Since you saw this house the porch has come down and a balustraded perron gone up – much improved.

My family are well but inordinately expensive.

                                                  Much love
                                                  Evelyn

Is *Hons & Rebels* any good?

[1] The house in Dorset which Raymond Mortimer shared with friends.
[2] *Don't Tell Alfred*, 1960.
[3] *Casanova's Chinese Restaurant*, 1960.
[4] Princess Margaret married in May 1960 Antony Armstrong-Jones, who was created Earl of Snowdon in 1961.
[5] *La Dolce Vita*. Rosie Rodd was paid £10 a day, and her dog, which also appeared, £5.
[7] Harold Macmillan, backed by Professor Hugh Trevor-Roper, was made Chancellor.

To Lady Acton   Combe Florey House.
25 March 1960

Dearest Daphne

Here is another Knox[1]. Perhaps you are getting bored by this steady rain of Knoxes. But this is all right – edited by clever Fr Caraman not by me. I hear his – Knox's not Caraman's – voice in every sentence. Well perhaps you are bored by hearing his voice. I'll go on sending them to you until told to stop. I am afraid it will arrive too late for Lenten reading – but it is always Lent in a way at M'Bebi. How impolite that sounds. I mean it is always 'spiritual reading' there, not that the cooking is not fine.

Douglas [Woodruff] came here last week with Mia. His vitality for a man of his great age is stupendous. He is spending Easter in conducting the 600 readers of *The Universe* to Rome. Mia was a bad colour.

I had a lovely winter at the expense of the *Daily Mail* in Venice – Rome & Monte Carlo & Athens. First with Laura, then with my daughter Margaret in grande luxe. My daughter Margaret (whom I love) has failed Oxford and is to canonise Campion instead at Caraman's expense.[2] I sent John a picture post card of the casino at Monte Carlo.

I keep the triduum (goodness knows how many days it is now) at Downside & hope to visit Mells. There are *no* services in Holy Week under the new regime. One just sits twiddling ones thumbs & despising the Old Boys.

Young Corbett[3] had a photograph of his brother's wedding showing dear Jill in a very bad light. Young Auberon is not so keen & wants a nautch girl instead. I say not elder n.g. but younger o.k.[4]

I hope you don't see English papers much. They are all about Africa now & calculated to offend.

So I went to a public audience of the Pope's. You know how it used to be – a series of drawing-rooms all the people segregated according to how they were dressed and ring kissing. Well now its quite different. You all fight for places in a hall like a cinema & then Papa is carried in on his chair and sits on a throne & cracks jokes in Venetian patois for half an hour and those who understand fall about laughing and then an american monsignor says through the microphone 'His Holiness blesses you and your families and any pious objects in your possession.'

Athenians very gay – wouldn't go to bed.

Where is Richard?[5] You said he was coming here in January.

I hope none of you are blood-bathed. If any, Peter[6].

Much love
Evelyn

[1] *Occasional Sermons*, 1960.

[2] Margaret Waugh went to work with the Society of Jesus at Farm Street on the canonization of the English and Welsh martyrs.

[3] Robert Corbett (1940–   ). Oxford friend of Auberon Waugh. His brother Joseph married Catherine Acton, Daphne's daughter, in 1960.

[4] Mary Anne and Jane Acton had danced round the swimming pool.

[5] Richard Acton.

[6] Peter Acton (1950–   ). The youngest son, now a farmer.

To WILLIAM F. BUCKLEY [1]   Combe Florey House.
4 April 1960

Dear Mr Buckley

I have to thank you for a) *Up from Liberalism* [2] (b) *McCarthy and his Enemies* [3] and c) *The National Review* [4] containing Colm Brogan's description of 'British hysteria'. I don't think you must take the last too seriously. McCarthy is certainly regarded by most Englishmen as a regrettable figure and your *McCarthy and his Enemies*, being written before his later extravagances, will not go far to clear his reputation. I have no doubt that we were sent a lot of prejudiced information six years ago. Your book makes plain that there was a need for investigation ten years ago. It does not, I am afraid, supply the information that would convince me that McCarthy was a suitable man to undertake it. Rovere [5] makes a number of precise charges against his personal honour. Until these are rebutted those who sympathise with his cause much deplore his championship of it.

                                        Yours sincerely
                                        Evelyn Waugh

[1] William F. Buckley (1925–   ). Conservative American writer, editor, critic and television personality.
[2] 1959.
[3] 1954.
[4] Buckley has edited *The National Review* since 1955.
[5] Richard Rovere (1915–   ). Liberal writer, editor and critic. Published *Senator Joe McCarthy*, 1959, which Waugh reviewed in the *Spectator*.

To DAVID WRIGHT   Combe Florey House.
21 April 1960

Dear Mr Wright

Thank you for the new issue of *X* [1] and for your accompanying letter which is so polite & appealing that some explanation is required when, as I reluctantly do, I refuse your kind invitation to contribute.

I have not seen the article you mention in *Critical Quarterly*; nor have I heard of the magazine. Worse than this in studying your own pages I find that the great majority of the names which are quoted as those of important young writers are wholly unfamiliar to me. That will demonstrate how ignorant I am of recent literary movements. I don't think this is a particularly unhealthy condition for an elderly writer. There are flibbertigibbets who in middle age attend international cultural congresses and busy themselves with the latest fashions. Few of these are notable for their literary production. A writer should have found his *métier* before he is 50. After that he reads only for pleasure; not for curiosity about what others are doing. Please do not interpret this as scorn or jealousy of the young. It is simply that their tastes and achievements are irrelevant to his work.

A lot is said about the 'predicament' of the young writer. Perhaps you would like to hear of the 'predicament' of the old (and if you think it would interest your readers you are at liberty to publish this letter). In middle age a writer knows his capacities & limitations and he has a general conspectus of his future work. Besides that he sometimes writes topical articles for the press. He can contribute either to popular papers or to those of small circulation. In the first case he will find his work mutilated by sub-editors and scrawled over with inappropriate titles, but he will be paid 20 times as much as by a more humane employer. The choice is between vanity and avarice. The avarice is not always selfish. Elderly men have many dependants. They are not to be blamed severely if they choose to sacrifice their vanity.

Remember also that most writers have interests other than artistic – political, local, religious and so forth – which they are importuned to serve occasionally by giving their work.

Now & then he is moved to express an opinion on some general topic; then he writes to *The Times*. If he wants to give his opinion on a book, he will review it in one of the weekly papers which is read by his friends & acquaintance because it is they primarily with whom he wishes to communicate.

So that when I wished your venture well, I was entirely sincere, but I do not think my cooperation would be a benefit. If you search your heart, will you not find that when you wrote to me you were not really much interested in anything I might say, but had the hope that the *name* of someone who has been writing for more than thirty years and is therefore known to people who would not normally buy *X*, might attract attention on the cover?

Yours truly
Evelyn Waugh

[1] A review of literature and the arts, edited by David Wright and Patrick Swift.

To Ann Fleming   Combe Florey House.
28 April 1960

My Dear Ann
It is kind of you to invite me to your house on 6th May. I regret that I shall not be in London on that day. Like all loyal subjects of the monarchy I am appalled by the proposed mesalliance. [1] The happiest solution would be for the press photographer (who I read is constant in his attendance at church) to be ordained a Protestant clergyman & made Archbishop of Canterbury. This would give him precedence immediately below the royal family. It confers no precedence on his wife, but she might be granted the style of a duke's daughter. They can then rock and roll about Lambeth Palace. I understand Jones likes the smell of the lower Thames. There are several other surviving Anglicans – David Cecil, Betjeman, Lancaster, Piper, Elizabeth Cavendish and two (I think Lesbian) spinsters in Combe Florey who could compose their court.

I did not know Lady Norwich had borne an heir[2]. She is on the list of apostates with Clarissa, Mary Dunn[3] etc. for whom I pray. Hers is the worst case as she had no motive except wrong headedness to leave the Church.

Before your time L<u>d</u> Haddington had a delightful and woebegone younger brother Charlie whom I loved.[4] It is very odd he should be staying with Honks. Well, nothing is odd there.

I shall be coming to London fairly often this summer but only from Saturdays to Mondays to visit Margaret whom I have sent to work for the Jesuits. It is a very nice time when all the fuddy duddies are sponging in the country, but I can hardly hope to find you at home then. I shall take Maimie out too.

I am much in Thunderbird's debt for his telling us it is not necessary to dry our razor.

I am shortly embarking on a third volume of the Crouchback saga[5]. Tony Powell's latest volume[6], which I've had for review, is a sad disappointment – only three pages of Widmerpool.

You tell me nothing of your house in Oxfordshire.

I rejoice at Bridget's acquittal and at her courage in fighting the case. I still can't understand why the German Embassy has taken the place of Vine Street as a lock up.[7]

Will you not come & visit us here soon? Preferably in the middle of the week.

Plovers' eggs are on sale at White's. Gulls' are clearly good enough for the fuddy-duddies. Why do you not make a little hamper of the remnants of your Jones banquet and a bottle of Portuguese claret and take it next day to Margaret (who has an hour for luncheon) and regale her in Mount Street garden? Bringing with you, of course, no delinquent friends. You will find her fat but jolly. She lives with her cousin Anne Fraser. But don't, in mistaken kindness, ask her to your house of ill fame.

I went to London for a day last week & earned 1000 dollars by reading my works aloud with an American gramophone. Then Maimie came to dinner in marble halls. She works in Sloane Galleries, King's Road, Chelsea. You should visit her. She is lonely and not averse to delinquents.

> Yours ever affec.
> Evelyn

[1] Princess Margaret's marriage.

[2] Viscountess Norwich, whose son Jason was born in October 1959, had been brought up as a Roman Catholic.

[3] Lady Mary Dunn had been divorced and remarried.

[4] The Earl of Haddington (1894–   ), was the brother of Charles Baillie-Hamilton (1900–39), Conservative MP 1929–31.

[5] *Unconditional Surrender*.

[6] *Casanova's Chinese Restaurant*.

[7] Lady Bridget Parsons had been arrested for drunken driving in Belgrave Square and taken into the German Embassy until a police car arrived. The Duke of Devonshire and Lord Kinross gave evidence as to how little she had drunk at dinner.

To Joan Saunders   Combe Florey House.
Postcard

Many thanks for your valuable information about Sword of Stalingrad. October
29–31st are the important dates. Clearly a change of popular sentiment occurred
between the exhibition of an object of craftsmanship at Goldsmiths' Hall and V & A
and the veneration at Westminster Abbey. Provincial exhibitions not important. I
think Hansard would have something in Question Time. I don't suppose the then
Dean of Westminster is still alive but there should be surviving Canons who have
some memory of how the sword came to be exposed there and of the circumstances
in which it was laid in state and removed. I am not much interested in the
appearance of the sword. It is the (spontaneous?) wave of popular sentiment
culminating in its ecclesiastical status that interest me. E.g. was it blessed?
    Weather Oct 29th–31st desired. Also was London then free of all air raids

                                                             E.W.

To Father Philip Caraman   Combe Florey House.
17 May 1960

Dear Philip
    I owe you a word of explanation about Friday's dinner. Mary Lygon is an old &
dear friend of mine whom I always try to see when I come to London. She is in
distressed circumstances. ... She knows no Catholic priest and her Anglican–
Orthodox faith is dim. I think it is very important that people like her should at least
know the name of a priest to turn to if they feel desperate (as she may well do). I
don't suggest you should do anything about her. Simply that if the moment comes
she should turn to you.
2)   Margaret is awfully happy in her work. I am enormously grateful to you.
3)   Alec Guinness was admirable in his work. I thought Rattigan's play & most of
the other actors fraudulent.[1]
4)   Do you receive and have you kept the reviews of Ronald's sermons?[2] I should
like in a few weeks to write a review of the reviews. I can get them from Burns &
Oates no doubt. If you have them, I should like one day to borrow them. I want to
demonstrate in a secular paper the neglect of religious literary work.
5)   Bad soles at Hyde Park Hotel I thought

                                                        Yours ever
                                                        Evelyn

    [1] Alec Guinness portrayed T.E.Lawrence in *Ross* by Terence Rattigan.
    [2] Waugh reviewed Knox's sermons under the heading 'An Important Publication' in the *Spectator*
25 November 1960.

To Nancy Mitford   Combe Florey House.
18 May 1960

Dearest Nancy

I bought a copy of Decca's book[1] & read it with keen attention. I can well understand that it is wounding and I was able to detect numerous errors of fact, but it has filled me with curiosity. Someone told me you reviewed it. Is this true?[2] If so where can I find your review? What surprised me was that she not only gives a nasty impression of the people against whom she has conceived grievances, but about those she presumably loves. I dont think I ever met Esmond Romilly[3]. Certainly I didn't know him at all. She makes him quite detestable. What did he do in the Canadian Air Force? She describes him as sub-humanly incompetent with every sort of mechanism. What became of her second child by him?[4] It must be grown up. Is it simply an American like all the rest of them? Did Decca write all the book herself? It seems by two hands, half fresh & funny if false and half trite & stodgy – the first page of the last chapter, for instance, can she have written that? Is she not now married to a sort of jewish don. Can he have put in the sticky bits. All that cheating & stealing & lying combined with sermons on socialism seems very odd.[5] Do you think it true that the captain of the English ship, intent on abducting her, gave his word not to?[6] Didn't she come to Europe last year? Did you see her?

Margaret now works in London canonising 40 martyrs at £10 a week. No London season for her. Can't afford it and Teresa collected the most awful friends at great expense. She is very happy canonising. I went up to London to entertain her. I shall never go to that city again. I can't eat anything they cook there. Had to live on caviar at £1 a teaspoonful. She made me go to a play about Lawrence of Arabia. All the actors except Sir Alec Guinness were comic buggers & the plot was all buggery – as far as I can gather false to history. We went to the Soane Museum which is still very empty & pleasant. Poor Maimie came to dine with us. She could only talk of the hardships & humiliations of her life which are indeed gruesome. We also had the Jesuit [Father Caraman] who is Margaret's employer. It was not a happy combination. She told him she always read the psalms for the day which I am sure is an illusion derived from memories of the schoolroom at Madresfield. The poor Jesuit thought his leg was being pulled.

Our asparagus is abundant & delicious – far better than anything you can get in France. I wish you were here to eat it.

Is Decca still a communist?[7] Jolly uncomfortable for her in U.S.A. I should have thought. She doesn't seem to have done anything to help the 'Loyalists' in Spain. Just sponged on them.

You see her book has upset & puzzled me a great deal. I barely knew her. Odd that it should. You see you made her so amusing & sweet in your novels it is very disconcerting.

I am toiling away at third volume of war novel. There have been no good new books except an unfinished posthumous one by a Sicilian duke[8] – not Fulco[9]. Tony Powell's forthcoming volume of his polylogy is a disappointment, but I don't think you admire him anyway, do you?

There are no English left in London.

Is it true Momo is very ill?

Do write & tell me your news and explain Decca more fully.

Love from

Evelyn

[1] Jessica Mitford, *Hons and Rebels*.

[2] No.

[3] Esmond Romilly eloped with Jessica Mitford to the Spanish Civil War. He became a navigator in the Royal Canadian Air Force.

[4] Constancia Romilly (1941–   ). Worked for the Student Non-Violent Co-ordinating Committee and later became a nurse.

[5] Jessica Mitford married Robert Treuhaft, a Jewish lawyer, in 1943. She wrote all of *Hons and Rebels* herself but worked with her husband on *The American Way of Death*, 1963. Waugh, reviewing the latter book in *The Sunday Times*, wrote: 'It is easy to guess the nature of their collaboration; here is little Decca teasing on the telephone, there is solid Bob at his desk doing his sums.' To which Jessica Mitford added in her second volume of autobiography, 'In fact we each wrote half the book.'

[6] A destroyer turned up off the coast of Bilbao when Jessica Mitford and Esmond Romilly were in Spain. Nancy Mitford is quoted in *Hons and Rebels* as saying, 'Everything was all arranged for the captain to lure you on board by promising delicious things to eat, but he said you wouldn't be lured.'

[7] The Treuhafts had resigned from the Party in 1958.

[8] Giuseppe Tomasi, Prince di Lampedusa, *The Leopard*, translated by Archibald Colquhoun.

[9] The Duke of Verdura (1907–78). Designed materials for Chanel and became a successful jeweller in New York.

To Ann Fleming

Combe Florey House.

26 May 1960

My dear Ann

What pray has become of you? It is time you wrote me a long detailed gossip sheet. You must think of me as living in Tasmania eager for news of fuddy-duddies etc. I am slowly composing a third volume of war novels – not bad so far – all about the 'Sword of Stalingrad'. Do you remember that? Does anyone? It is the theme of the first part of the book and it will fall pretty flat if it is quite forgotten. Ask representative younger people such as O'Neill if they have heard of it. Well I suppose the young don't read my books anyhow.

Did I tell you Bron has a bizarre book[1] appearing shortly? Very funny, I thought when I read it but I can't remember anything about it now. It is very pleasant losing ones memory. One can read old favourites with breathless curiosity. I have just reread all G. Greene and A. Powell.

I spent a week-end in London with Margaret and came near death from exhaustion – Soane Museum, St Paul's Cathedral, a play about buggery called *Ross*, (visit to A. Guinness in dressing-room) much champagne with Maimie, Royal Academy to see Stanley Spencers, huge very expensive meals in marble halls of which I could eat nothing. An odd attack of Pinfold. I had planned to come home on Sunday. On Saturday, dead sober, I told hall porter to look up a train for me to Gloucester – a station I have never used in my life. I had the time firm in my mind.

Margaret came to see me off and I went to the booking office and asked for a ticket to Gloucester. She corrected me. Dazed I asked for Taunton. Last train had gone. Had to spend another night in London and give Margaret another enormous dinner (St James' Club). Why in heavens name Gloucester? It was always Kemble or Stroud when I lived at Stinkers.

Margaret now spends long evenings in Maimie's basement rooms studying her scrap-books of the '30s.

I have read with extreme disgust in the *Daily Express* that the young shits who go to balls keep a directory of accessible debutantes. I am confirmed in my refusal to give Margaret a season. Instead she has composed a pamphlet about 40 Martyrs which is having a first printing of 100,000 – more than her poor father or (I should guess) Thunderbird. What's more she's been paid £30 for it.

I was deeply shocked by Decca's book.

Now I have nothing to tell you. You must tell me. Think back to before Easter and write all.

I don't expect you know today is Ascension Day. This day 1917 was the most unhappy of my life. My first term, first month at Lancing. I had never heard about Ascension Day before. It was not observed in my home or at my prep school. Well, I overheard boys talking of this mysterious day and when it came they all disappeared. It was a whole holiday. I had nowhere to go and no friends. The steward gave me some ghastly galantine (first war food worse than second) and I ate it alone in the rain on the downs near Chanctonbury Ring. So every Ascension Day since I have felt that things can never be as bad as that.

Cynthia, I suppose, has taken the secret of *The Young Visiters* to the grave?[2] Now say you are out and don't take telephone calls and write me a letter.

> Yours affec.
> Evelyn

[1] Auberon Waugh, *The Foxglove Saga*, 1960.
[2] *The Young Visiters*, 1919, was written by Daisy Ashford at the age of nine. James Barrie wrote an introduction and it was widely suggested that he had in fact written the whole book. Cynthia Asquith as his secretary and close friend would have known if this had been true.

To William F. Buckley   Combe Florey House.
3 June 1960

Dear Mr Buckley,

Thank you for your letter of 31st May.

It is most gratifying that you would like me to contribute to the *National Review* & I appreciate that in the circumstances your offer is a generous one[1], but until you get much richer (which I hope will be soon) or I get much poorer (which I fear may be sooner) I am unable to accept it.

> Yours truly
> Evelyn Waugh

[1] '5,000 dollars a year for a piece every few weeks, of 2,000 words.'

To Tom Driberg   Combe Florey House.
[6 June 1900]
Postcard

Dear Tom,

I read with great interest your article on the new Buchmanism[1] in *New Statesman & Nation*. Can you tell me: did you in your researches come across the name of Wm F. Buckley Jr, editor of a New York, neo-McCarthy magazine named *National Review*? He has been showing me great & unsought attention lately & your article made me curious. Has he been supernaturally 'guided' to bore me? It would explain him.

Yours ever,
Evelyn

[1] Moral Re-armament. Driberg's article was entitled 'MRA, The New Offensive'.

To Tom Driberg   Combe Florey House.
11 June 1960

Dear Tom

Thank you for your kind judgment of *Knox*. The misprints in the first edition were ghastly. I have never taken so much trouble about spelling, getting the proofs read by numerous hawk-eyed Wykehamists and monks, but they sprang up everywhere. The fourth edition, which may some day appear, should be free of them. I am told that printers' readers no longer exist because clergymen are no longer unfrocked for sodomy. There were also errors of fact. I was obliged to rely a great deal on the memories of septuagenarians & they misinformed me.

I have thrown away all copies of *National Review*. These are the directors. Only one familiar name, Chambers[1] (who kept secret documents in a pumpkin). Buckley wrote *Up from Liberalism* (unreadable); his magazine is mostly devoted to attacks on American 'Liberals'. I don't think he is a Papist. He would have told me, I think, if he were. Chambers certainly espoused some form of Christianity – Quaker? It would be interesting to know if this was a nest of Buchmanites.

You mustn't blame Arnold Lunn[2]. He is honest at heart. He is awfully hard up, likes Switzerland, and I think his praise of Caux is comparable to the situation – per impossible – that I should be offered long hospitality at the Hotel de Paris by the Prince of Monaco and in gratitude attested (truthfully) that I found the devotions at Ste Devote edifying.

I wish someone (not I) would examine Buchmanism. Its connexion with pacifism in 1939 is significant. Also I believe many of the Quisling party in Norway were Buchmanite – no, when I say 'believe' I mean I was told at the time, and goodness knows one cant *believe* anything one was told then.

Won't it rather spoil the Mrs Proudie side of the Church of England if you admit women to Holy Orders? If Slope had been her husband & she Bishop, no joke.

I did not hear the wireless *Pinfold*. I have let myself in for cross-examination on Television by a man named Major Freeman [3] who I am told was a colleague of yours in the Working Class Movement. Do you know anything damaging about him that I can introduce into our conversation if he becomes insolent?

I met Maurice Child [4] once with you; you took me to a roomful of buggers. He was very civil. I could not find it in me to be uncivil about him though I think his leadership in 1913 makes all Ronald's set of that time questionable in their sincerity. Ronald never uttered a word of criticism of Child or of any of his associates except (very mildly) of the 'Abbot' of Caldey [5].

It is good of you to ask me to dine in the House of Commons. I hardly ever come to London. I hope you may come to Somerset.

Yours ever
Evelyn

[1] Whittaker Chambers confessed to having been a communist agent and was the main prosecution witness at the trial of Alger Hiss in 1950. Hiss was held to have been an agent, which he constantly denied.

[2] Sir Arnold Lunn (1886–1974). Author, skier and supporter of MRA. He wrote in response to Driberg's article. His controversy with Knox, published as *Difficulties*, 1932, preceded his reception into the Roman Catholic Church.

[3] John Freeman (1915–   ). Labour MP 1945–55, editor of the *New Statesman* 1961–5, British Ambassador in Washington 1969–71, chairman and chief executive London Weekend Television 1971–1979. Waugh was to be the subject of one of his *Face to Face* series of television interviews.

[4] The Reverend Maurice Child, a high-spirited Anglo-Catholic friend of Knox's, who influenced him in his decision to become a Roman Catholic.

[5] There was an unorthodox Anglican Benedictine Abbey on Caldey Island visited by Knox who described the Abbot (Benjamin Carlyle) as 'a man of dynamic energy . . . . What held you was the brightness of his eyes. They were not (as I saw them then) the eyes of a mystic . . . . It was rather some trick of hypnotism they had.' *Pax*, Spring 1956.

To ANTHONY POWELL

Hyde Park Hotel.

18 June 1960

Dear Tony

Thanks awfully for sending me a copy of *Casanova*. I have put it very proudly among its companion volumes.

I had in fact read it in proof and have reviewed it for the *Spectator* where I gave the opinion that your admirers will regard it as an essential link in a fine series. The scene in the third part of Stringham's drunken appearance is as good as anything in any of the books. I can't say I liked the new musical characters – I mean I didn't like them personally, not that they were not excellently portrayed. I hope you wont think my review captious. In a work as large as yours no reader can enjoy all parts equally. *Lady Molly* remains my favourite.

Yours ever
Evelyn

TO NANCY MITFORD   Combe Florey House.
21 June 1960

Darling Nancy

What good news that you have finished your novel both for your avid public &
yourself. I long to read it. Printers are so lazy nowadays that there is a huge period of
gestation.

I am very sorry you should have been bothered by Chas E. Linck, Jr.[1] I have no
memory of him. I always throw away letters from Americans unread. I am sure no
one will publish his book & that it is simply a ruse to make himself a bore.

I did not find Debo's Emma at all forthcoming when I once met her but I hear
good accounts of her on all sides. Mark Grant tried to have her devoured by wolves
on Mount Parnasus.[2]

Last week I was driven by poverty to the humiliating experience of appearing on
the television[3]. The man who asked the questions simply couldn't believe I had had
a happy childhood. 'Surely you suffered from the lack of a sister?'

My daughter Margaret publishes a book today *Forty Martyrs* – a work of
research for the Jesuits. First printing 100,000. More than I have ever had or I
daresay you either.

Debo was seen hopping in a London street with Freud holding up a foot calling
the attention of passers-by to her new shoes.

I saw a sickeningly silly play about people turning into Rhinoceroses.[4]

I rather long to go to the London Library sale but shan't. I think the prices will
cause much jealousy among our confrères & consocurs.[5]

What a rum time to go to Venice. You will find it full of trippers.

Love from
Evelyn

[1] Charles E. Linck Jr (1923–   ) had written to Nancy Mitford for information about Waugh's social
life. He is the author of *The Development of Evelyn Waugh's Career 1903-39*, 1963, one of four authors of
Evelyn Waugh: A Checklist of Primary and Secondary Material, 1972, and a frequent contributor to the
Evelyn Waugh News Letter. None of these has been published in England.

[2] Mark Ogilvie-Grant had acted as guide to a party that included the Duke of Devonshire and his
daughter Lady Emma Cavendish. They were lost for several hours while darkness fell.

[3] The *Face to Face* interview with John Freeman was shown on 26 June.

[4] *Rhinoceros* by Eugene Ionesco with Laurence Olivier, directed by Orson Welles.

[5] A sale at Christie's of manuscripts and pictures on behalf of the London Library. The manuscript of
A Passage to India by E.M.Forster fetched £6,500, then a record T.S.Eliot copied out *The Waste Land*
which went for £2,800. The manuscript of Waugh's *Scott-King's Modern Europe* fetched £160.

TO JOHN DONALDSON   Combe Florey House.
28 June 1960
Postcard

Thanks awfully for your card. The BBC people were very silly but civil. Over 30
were employed in recording that conversation. One of them[1] had been in the party

who came to Stinkers & set Pinfold on the run. I asked what had become of the questioner. He has become a professional hypnotist. Significant? Now Tanker's Box[2] is under investigation in the courts as perhaps you have seen. I hear of you from Mrs Fleming. Meg Dalhousie used to have the King Kong death song played at Government House Salisbury to clear her dinner parties.

E

[1] Dr Stephen Black, the model for Angel in *The Ordeal of Gilbert Pinfold*.
[2] The contraption that cured from a distance, at which Waugh had scoffed until he heard voices.

To Erle Stanley Gardner   Combe Florey House.
21 July 1960

Dear Mr Gardner,
    May I, as one of the keenest admirers of your work, correct what I at first took for a slip but now realise must be genuine misconception?
    You seem to think that a 'davenport' is some kind of sofa. It is, and can only be, a small writing desk.
    Are you, perhaps, confusing it with a 'chesterfield'?[1]

Yours truly
Evelyn Waugh

[1] An editor at Gardner's publishers answered that 'davenport' was used for a kind of sofa in the United States. Gardner sent a supplementary reply informing Waugh that if he was 'the Evelyn Waugh who wrote that wonderful exposé of Hollywood and apparently you are . . . you have the greatest gift of satire I have ever encountered and that means philosophical perspective and writing ability of a high order.'

To Charles E. Linck Junior   Combe Florey House [crossed out]
August 1960
Postcard

Read *Evelyn Waugh* by F. Stopp published by Little, Brown in USA or Chapman & Hall in England.
    The answers to your specific questions are: (1) No (2) Impossible (3) Not understood. I travelled where I wanted to go & wrote about it afterwards.[1]
    You must not attempt to see me when you come to England.

E.W.

[1] The questions concerned Waugh's social life in the 1920s, models for the characters in his novels and his journalistic arrangements for travelling.

To Lady Mary Lygon   Combe Florey House.
17 August 1960

Darling Blondie

How lovely to hear from you. It was very wrong of you not to come & visit me here. You promised you would when you steeled yourself to leave London. But no you prefer Elmley & Mona [1] who don't love you as I do just because they are an Earl and a Countess. Kind hearts, it has been wittily said, are more than coronets.

It is kind of you to recommend Ede's cars. Alas, I am too poor to drive anywhere. I walk the streets with bleeding feet like P. Balfour. If Mr Ede has a hearse and you are allowed to drive it I will engage it for my funeral – which cannot now long be delayed.

Misled by jaggering reviewers I *bought* a book about Rome [2] by Miss Elizabeth Bowen (the widow Cameron in real life). Would you like me to give it to you. It is all about the Forum & Palatine & Vestal Virgins instead of the Holy Roman Catholic Church. It is not as well written as Augustus Hare or as appreciative of porphyry as Boom [Lady Mary's father].

I gave Little Margaret a beautiful pork pie to take to you. She put it in the Jesuits' refrigerator and forgot about it and it grew moss & she was ashamed to tell you. Goodness how sad.

Did you know that Tim Ebrington's grandfather before the days of the telephone wrote a book about a deer [3] which reduces L. Margaret to tears.

I am writing a novel. It is all about a funeral. Ought to be popular.

People keep writing to say they are coming to stay with me and I get very excited & have my hair cut in Taunton and buy smoked salmon & then they chuck at the last moment. It has been happening all this summer and is very bad for me. It makes me what Connolly would call 'manic-depressive'.

Love xxx
Bo

[1] Her brother, who had succeeded as Earl Beauchamp in 1938, married Else Schiwe in 1936.
[2] *A Time in Rome*, 1960.
[3] Sir John Fortescue, *The Story of a Red Deer*, 1897.

To Ann Fleming   Combe Florey House.
5 September 1960

My Dear Ann

It is sad for you to leave Porto Fino on the 9th. That is the date of Little Margaret's arrival. She is covered with spots, breakfasts off sloe gin and has taken to smoking cigarettes, but she could hardly fail to be an inspiration to you.

I have read Thunderbird's articles with interest. [1] He cribbed all that account of the Neapolitan urchins kidnapping niggers straight from an admirable film called *Paisa* [2]. His advice about sitting to gamble is not in accordance with the experts.

There is the well known, perhaps true, story of the American millionaire (usually identified as Pierpont Morgan) who stopped for a night in his yacht at Monte Carlo in the days of Le Blanc fils (or was it beau fils?) Anyway he had never seen roulette before and in a few minutes his financial mind mastered the principles. He sent a message to the management that he would play if the limit was removed for the evening. Le Blanc asked only one question: 'Is he sitting or standing?' 'Sitting'. 'Then he may play' and he lost prodigiously. What the casino could not risk was a single huge even chance stake. Or so I used to be told.

Many men like large beds even if they sleep alone. I do myself & Graham Greene is much taller than I am [3]. There is no evidence of adultery in his preference. There is indeed an element of ostentation. . . . He is a great one for practical jokes. I think also he is secret agent on our side and all his buttering up of the Russians is 'cover'.

I am busily & happily at work on a sequel to those two war novels I wrote. The trouble is that it is quite unintelligible to anyone who doesn't know them by heart. I have to keep dipping into them to find what I wrote seven or eight years ago. Otherwise it is a gripping tale.

Laura brought back from her Boots Library a novel [4] by your brother, Hugo, about diamond mines in West Africa. It confirms my fears that he has no literary talent. Literature is simply the appropriate use of language. He has no feeling for English and goes at it slap dash hitting the wrong word on almost every page. He has a narrator, unidentified, who pops up here & there in the first person & gives detailed descriptions of scenes he never witnessed. I think he should go into partnership with Fuddy Duddy Fish Face [Peter Quennell], who has nothing to say but has in his dry, vacuous way a mastery of the language.

I hope poor torpid O'Neill is a little more lively. Do they have grouse in Ireland? If so pray send us some. No one has done so from Scotland.

A few days ago I fell into despair with our cook, said I was starving and had to go to London to get a square meal. I was punished for this outburst by being struck, as my feet touched Paddington platform, with a kind of impotence – I could swallow nothing and during three days consumed only six snails and two spoonfuls of caviare. As I arrived back at Taunton my appetite quickened and I laid in heartily to the pasta.

My niece, Anne, chose your brother, Hugo, as godfather to her new daughter. Do you not think that rum?

I am distressed to hear that you have disregarded my advice and are demolishing your house. In domestic life space is all.

I am glad to hear that Rome is absolutely empty. No one has gone to their ridiculous sports [5]. The Grand Hotel has not let a room and the Roman householders who thought they were ging to make fortunes are left penniless.

'Stuart Hampshire' [6] must be an assumed name.

Yours ever affec.
Evelyn

[1] Collected in a book, *The Thrilling Cities* by Ian Fleming, 1960.
[2] *Paisa* by Rossellini, 1946.
[3] Waugh was 5 foot 7 inches tall.

[4] Hugh Charteris, *Picnic at Porokorro*, 1958.

[5] The Olympic Games.

[6] Stuart Hampshire (1914–   ). Philosopher, Warden of Wadham since 1970.

TO ANN FLEMING   Combe Florey House.
22 September 1960

My Dear Ann

I am not sending you or any of my honoured friends a copy of my African pot boiler because I despise it.

I hope that you are rejoicing in having Caspar off your hands as much as I rejoice as the wheels on the gravel bear my many little ones to their expensive schools. There is a remarkably life like portrait of old Caspar, under the name of Tarquin, in my son's forthcoming novel[1]; all the more remarkable for the fact of their having never met.

C. Connolly wrote last Sunday that G. Greene, I and another man I had never heard of[2] were enabled to continue writing in spite of prosperity by 'internal tensions'. What can the booby mean? Perhaps it is your duty to introduce internal tensions into your coterie of fuddy duddies who don't seem awfully productive. Boofy[3], now that's a man who I should say had internal tensions but he doesn't write.

No game reached us from Shane's Castle[4].

My son Auberon has formed a close friendship with Alan Lennox-Boyd[5]. Is that healthy?

It is possible that I may have a months employment in London. If that should come about I hope to meet you.

A shocking accident befell Master Dru[6]. He was mounted on his little pony setting out to hunt cubs in the early morning. A horse ridden by his sister Mary came up behind, seized him with its jaws by the buttocks, lifted him from the saddle and threw him across the stable yard.

Margaret's glass eyes were washed away at Porto Fino so she was spared the sight of Muggeridge.

Have you read the jolly book by my cousin Mrs Cuthbert (Diana Holman Hunt)[7]

Yours ever affec.
Evelyn

Lord Boyd gives Bron privately printed works of Guinness family history. Odd?

[1] Tarquin is the repellent child in Auberon Waugh's *The Foxglove Saga*.

[2] William Golding (1911–   ) whose novels include *The Lord of the Flies*, 1954, and *Pincher Martin*, 1956.

[3] Earl of Arran, prolific journalist.

[4] The Irish house of Lord O'Neill, Ann Fleming's son.

[5] Simon Lennox-Boyd, eldest son of Viscount Boyd (1904–   ), has been a close friend of Auberon Waugh since they were at Christ Church together.

[6] Bernard Dru (1951–   ), Laura's nephew.

[7] *My Grandmothers and I*.

To Ann Fleming   Combe Florey House.
5 October 1960

Dear Ann

I shall not be going to London. There was a talk of my doing an English version of *La Dolce Vita* but I wanted too much money. It is a good thing, really, as the novel I am working on is going very nicely and I should like to get it finished by Christmas. Then India – so much to see before the Chinks take over. If you came too you might be able to study the Yogis at their pleasure. If what you tell me is true, they seem to have discovered a method of contraception that does not outrage the moral law.

Do I really stink of paraldehyde or is it simply that you know I like it & were warned by your medical adviser that it stank & therefore suppose I stink? I have consulted Margaret on the subject and she says she has noticed nothing. Laura has noticed an occasional whiff before breakfast. [1]

Why did you not heed my advice about your house? I warned you that any building, except in prefabricated units, is beyond any purse private or public. You have a plain, spacious house; why bugger it up? Buildings condemned as unsafe by architects stand for centuries. If the rain comes into one room move out the furniture & keep poultry in it. Live like the Irish. In the lonely winter evenings you can write your reminiscences. Diana's third volume arrived by the same post as your letter. So far I have only read the references to myself – *not* very nice. [2]

You must remember Bron was only 19 when he wrote his novel. Douglas Woodruff, also, was dismayed at the brutality of little Caspar.

Have you read the widow Cuthbert's [Diana Holman Hunt] reminiscences. Very funny about my cousin Mrs H.H. You had a Fuddy-duddy called Ironmonger or Ironsides who wrote disrespectfully of H.H. [3] whose *Shadow of Death*, now hidden in the vaults at Birmingham is one of the great paintings of the century. He was under 30 when he made it.

Do you know Betty Asquith [4] (Clovelly. Ock's widow)? She came here yesterday & was literally imbecile. Poor martyred Mary Rous [5] leads her about. She has no idea where she is or whom she is speaking to.

I am preparing a panegyric for P.G.Wodehouse's 80th birthday which falls next year. To aid me I got hold of a copy of the broadcast Cooper had made denouncing him as a Nazi collaborator. It was more vile than I knew. Cooper's blackest hour.

No, I never see *Encounter*. I have an idea that Fuddy-duddy Spender edits it. It can't be much good. But he did publish the text of Wodehouse's innocuous and witty broadcasts from Berlin. That was a good act. Also Muggeridge, I find, behaved well when Cooper had him (P.G.W.) arrested in Paris. Cooper as a writer manqué had a peculiar hatred for good writers. The only men he really liked were Eddie Grant and Rufus Clark & Tommy McDougall (before your time). I suppose it is seeing so many photographs of Cooper in Diana's book that has turned my thoughts towards him. Has it been arranged, by the way, who gets this year's Cooper prize? Powell I hope. [6]

Any time you feel like slipping into Paddington & taking the train to Taunton look it up first. They have all been changed, to the great inconvenience of our rare visitors.

Do you know anything of Gerald Yorke's boy, Vincent?[7] His father was a sorcerer. Margaret brought him here the other day. He is tall & stammers. Is he as sinister as Gerald?

I am glad you are chums with Connolly. He has botulism but it is not contagious. A man of great worth. Give him some tensions so that he can write books.

> Your affec. coz.
> E Waugh

There was, if you remember, a very horrible road-house-club near your Banbury seat. Would that not satisfy Thunderbird's appetite for pink gin & low company?

[1] 'He indignantly denied that he smelled of it, until he was sharing a sofa with Evangeline Bruce in my house when she asked, "Should we tell Ann the gas is escaping?"' Ann Fleming, 'Yours affec: Evelyn', in *Evelyn Waugh and his World*, p.237.

[2] In *Trumpets from the Steep* Lady Diana Cooper refers to Waugh sitting in 'a gray dejected heap without a word a smile or a nod . . . he said that he was never so happy in his life', on his way to Yugoslavia in 1945. Ann Fleming found the references to him 'dull but kind'.

[3] Robin Ironside, *Pre-Raphaelite Painting*, 1948.

[4] Betty Manners (1889–1962) married in 1918 Brigadier General Arthur Asquith, son of the Prime Minister. They lived at Clovelly Court in Devonshire.

[5] Mary Asquith (1919–   ). Daughter of Betty Asquith, had married in 1943 Keith Rous, an eccentric.

[6] The Duff Cooper Memorial Prize went to Andrew Young for his *Collected Poems*. It is not awarded for novels.

[7] Gerald Yorke, brother of Henry, was a close friend of Aleister Crowley. He has three sons. Vincent (1942–   ) is a painter.

To Muriel Spark   Combe Florey House.
11 October 1960

Dear Miss Spark

How do you do it? I am dazzled by *The Bachelors*. Most novelists find there is one kind of book they can write (particularly humorous novelists) and go on doing it with variations until death. You seem to have an inexhaustible source. *Bachelors* is the cleverest & most elegant of all your clever & elegant books. I have no idea how wide your success has been up to date. I suspect that you are still the sort of writer whom people rejoice to introduce to their friends; *Bachelors* should take you clear through that phase into full fame. May you enjoy it.

If your publisher wants a puff for you before the reviews appear he can quote 'I am dazzled by *The Bachelors*' and anything else in the foregoing note of homage.

> Yours sincerely
> Evelyn Waugh

I have gushed so about my delight in reading the book that I have neglected to thank you for the gift of it. Thank you.

To Ann Fleming   Combe Florey House.
10 November 1960

Dear Ann
    A shameful week for English justice – Randolph declared brave, Lawrence
declared a great writer. How I wish I had been called as witness in both cases; to
describe Randolph's countless acts of cowardice beginning with his knocking out
Margaret Birkenhead at the opening night of the San Carlo Restaurant[1]; to explain
to the bemused jury that Lawrence's reputation has been made by an illiterate
clique at Cambridge. He couldn't write for toffee. He is right down in the Spender
class. I knew Mervyn Jones[2] quite well in the war. His brain must have softened.
Why did he not call expert evidence for the prosecution? Well, I suppose that topic
is dead as mutton in London. It frets Combe Florey.
    I went to London for a night to see a civil young man who says he is the editor of
the *Sunday Telegraph*. He signed his letters 'Peregrine Worsthorne'. I said 'an
unusual name'. He said: 'Yes, my father chose it when he stood for parliament. I
should be called Koch de Gooreynd'. Then to make it quite simple added: 'He
called my brother Towneley'. 'Like the Towneley marbles?' 'Yes, he owns them'.
Confusion of elderly party.[3] Well, this man of mystery proposed to send me abroad
for a treat. We drank heavy and I behaved rather like Randolph in his braver
moments, calling for more & better wine, until I said: 'I presume Michael Berry is
paying for this?' 'No, indeed, I am, out of my wages'. So then I felt I had behaved
badly & could only atone by giving a lot of wine to the mystery man, so I took him up
the street to my club and we drank heavy and I woke next day with the vague but
persistent impression that I have promised to go to the war in Algiers for him.[4] Not
at all what I wanted. My French is not up to jolly evenings in paratroop messes nor
are my stiff old limbs in any condition to dodge terrorists.
    Nancy comes this afternoon. I have every fire stoked but I fear she will not be
comfortable. I gather that high French Society drinks whisky. That I can provide
but much else is lacking. No cheval glass in her room and lights so placed that she
can't see to paint her face.
    I took Margaret to luncheon in marble halls after my night with the mystery man.
Bill £15 odd. Wind of change is blowing very cold in my bank.
    You are an ass to knock down your house. I have said it before and will say it
again.
    Poor Bron has become involved in a very common paper called *Queen*[5]. Not, as
you'd think, about buggery. A sort of whining *Tatler*.
    I go to London again for Hyde Park Hotel vomitorium on Dec 14th. Would you
care to spend evening of 13th with me?
    An American named Mr D'Arms has proposed marriage to my daughter Teresa
& been accepted. She is coming to England 'to arrange a wedding'. He has no money
but is said to be kind.
    When you say 'St Edmund's Chapel' do you mean the chapel of Teddy Hall?
    I despair of Oxford &, if I can afford to send them anywhere, shall send my
younger sons to Cambridge.

Is your new property in the area they propose to devastate for iron works? Serves you right, if so.

Yours ever affec.

E. Waugh

[1] Before the war, at the opening of a restaurant, possibly the Malmaison, Lord Castlerosse threw a vase at Randolph Churchill and narrowly missed Lady Birkenhead.

[2] Mervyn Griffith-Jones (1909–). Prosecuting counsel in the *Lady Chatterley's Lover* case.

[3] Broadly correct. Colonel Koch de Gooreynd took the name of a local village, Worsthorne, in 1921, thinking that a Belgian name would be a disadvantage to a Parliamentary candidate. One son, Simon, called himself Towneley on inheriting part of the Towneley estate. The other, Peregrine Worsthorne (1923–), became deputy editor of the *Sunday Telegraph* in 1961. He remembers Waugh betraying prior knowledge by asking for him by his father's name at Boodle's. When such a member was denied, Waugh complained, 'Is it not the custom when one gentleman invites another to dine with him in his club, for the host to take the elementary precaution of joining the club in the first place?'

[4] Worsthorne's version: 'After dinner I offered Waugh a glass of port. When it arrived he complained that "this is not the kind of port which Lady Pamela Berry would wish you to offer me." To this I replied rather frostily: "But it is not Lady Pamela offering it to you." On hearing this Waugh pulled out his wallet and began sprinkling fivers all round him. ...' He had promised to go to Algiers, but Peters got him out of it.

[5] Auberon Waugh had left Oxford after one year and started his career in journalism.

To the Editor of the Spectator   Combe Florey House.
[Published 18 November 1960]

LADY CHATTERLEY

Sir – Mr Levin[1] admits to a failure of memory about the fate of Lawrence's paintings. Is he also forgetful of their appearance, or did he perhaps never see them?

I remember some of them fairly well. I remember the exhibition clearly, because it was there that I realised Lawrence's incapacity as an artist. I had never found his books readable, but I was more respectful of fashion in those days than I am now, and was ready to admit that I was obtuse in my judgment. Then I saw the miserable pictures. The poor fellow couldn't paint at all and had no idea that he couldn't, and the people who applauded his books were equally enthusiastic about the paintings. I began then to understand that a work of art is not a matter of thinking beautiful thoughts or experiencing tender emotions (though those are its raw materials), but of intelligence, skill, taste, proportion, knowledge, discipline and industry; especially discipline. No number of disciples compensate for lack of that.

Yours faithfully

EVELYN WAUGH

[1] Bernard Levin had written an article in the *Spectator* entitled 'The Lady's Not for Burning'.

To A.D.Peters   Combe Florey House.
25 November [1960]

Dear Pete

It sounds as if no one wishes to send me to India in February.

Ghana was a random shot. I would like Siam or Borneo or Tierra del Fuego just as much.

Yours ever
Evelyn

To the Editor of the Spectator   10 Buckingham Street,
[Published 9 December 1960]   WC2.

THE DEATH PENALTY

Sir, – This, as most modern English disputes, reveals a sharp division between the heathen, who believe that physical survival, even in conditions of degradation, is preferable to extinction, and Christians who regard life on earth as a time of probation leading to an eternity of heaven or hell.

'Depend upon it, Sir, when a man knows he is to be hanged in a fortnight, it concentrates his mind wonderfully.'

It would be a great convenience to know well in advance the hour of one's death so that one could 'concentrate' on practical and spiritual matters. Most of us have the irksome and discouraging duty of living each hour as though it were our last. Only to the very wicked does a merciful society grant this final boon. The issue has been muddled in the last hundred years by the supposition that only murderers are so wicked as to deserve this dramatic chance to 'concentrate'. There are few of us who would not benefit from a fortnight's 'concentration' ending on the gallows. –

Yours faithfully,
EVELYN WAUGH

To Viscount Asquith[1]   Combe Florey House.
15 December 1960

My Dear Asquith

I hope that you insist on being addressed by your courtesy title by your sisters and younger brother. That was always the custom in noble families until very lately when the use of baptismal names has deplorably crept in.

I repeat:

My Dear Asquith,

Thank you very much for your interesting letter. 'Mistral' is not only the name of your ship and of a wind but of a very tedious Provençal poet. I hope you will never be made to read him.

I have never been to St Lucia or to Rat Island or Pigeon Island. I went once to Martinique but that was after the volcano spoilt it. Rat Island must be very jolly if you have a terrier to worry the inhabitants. I read in a book that your house has a tree planted by the Duke of Windsor. Do you climb it?

I met a general [Robert Laycock] who had been to visit you who was deeply impressed by your & your sisters' knowledge of classical Greek. He said your younger brother had been bitten by bugs. Younger sons are always cruelly neglected in noble families.

I have a son who has written a novel and a daughter who has written pamphlets about the 40 martyrs and another daughter who, alas, is to marry a very poor American.

I cannot give your love to everybody because I know so few people. I have given it to all I know and they reciprocate gratefully.

Your handsome cousin Alice [Jolliffe] came to stay a night with us & was taken ill & stayed a week which was nice for us but sad for her.

Your affec Godfather
E. Waugh

[1] Raymond Asquith (1952–   ). Son of the Earl of Oxford and Asquith.

To Lady Diana Cooper
24 December 1960

Combe Florey House.

Darling Pug

It was nice of you to think of your faithful old friend amid all your worries of moving house. You are never long from my mind and never for a moment from my heart. I sometimes hear strange travellers tales such as that your butler has been assassinated by Algerian terrorists and that you have given your literary prize to an octogenarian clergyman.

I have been indoors all the summer writing the final volume of war novels. Nothing to tempt me into the rain. As soon as the book is finished I shall make tracks for foreign parts – but where? The Queen is opening up India as a tourist resort and everywhere else is being shut down by politicians.

My daughter Teresa is to marry a studious, penniless American. My son, Bron, has had an undeserved but gratifying success with a novel and is a dandy with rooms in Clarges Street and a thousand cards of invitation & is enjoying himself top hole. Margaret is my darling still – much prettier again after a time of looking like a toad. Laura has at last had to give up her herd of cows and mourns them. They cost as much to keep as a troupe of ballet girls and the horrible politicians made a law that one can no longer charge them against income tax.

. . . Mrs Fleming's health gives cause for alarm.

All love
Bo

To Christopher Sykes   Combe Florey House.
2 January 1961

Dear Jew

We greatly enjoyed our visit to your luxurious palace. Does your PYW[1] always wear trousers at luncheon or did she do so on that occasion in order to put the Japanese lady[2] at ease? I wrote that day ordering a copy of *Brideshead Revisited* to be sent to me so that I could inscribe it facetiously & forward it to you. It has not come yet. I greatly hope it comes in time for your Epiphany.

Thank you for your noble efforts on behalf of Dr Wodehouse's exculpation[3]. I have not heard of or from 'Lindsay Wellington'[4] (an assumed name I presume) but I shall be very happy to discuss the matter with him though I should naturally prefer to do so with you.

July 15th this year is a Saturday. Is that a good day to catch the ear of the populace? I would sooner not show them my face.

Mr Wellington should communicate with Mr Peters in arranging for payment. My primary motive is altruistic to pluck up Plum's drowned honour by the locks.

M. Grisjambon Vert has written a very sorrowful novel[5].

Now here is a bit for PYW
Dearest Camilla

It was revealed that you buy furniture professionally. May I engage your services? I want 2 very comfortable drawing-room chairs. Not just fauteuils (if that is the word) for witty frogs to crack jokes in, but pieces in which corpulent novelists can doze. But they must go with drawing-room furniture. Not chintz or modern. I bet you know someone called Alan Pryce-Jones. Well, I was taken to his rooms in Albany and sat in just such a chair as I want. Would it be called Bergère? But also what Earl [*sic*] Stanley Gardner calls 'over-stuffed'. Leather is too hard for my delicate frame. Needlework would be best. It would be rash to say 'expense no object' but I don't mind going to £300 for a suitable pair.

Back to Jew.

No I am not interested in fox hunting. I suspect that the dogs on the whole rather enjoy it and I hate dogs.

Thanking you again, dear Jew and agnostress for your kind entertainment

I am dear J and A
Your ever affec. servant
Mrs Broadbent[6]

[1] Pretty young wife.

[2] Helen Homewood, the Australian fiancée of Mark Sykes.

[3] Waugh wished to record a tribute to P.G.Wodehouse, establishing the innocence of his war-time broadcasts. Sykes, employed by the BBC, was overcoming considerable internal opposition. See his *Evelyn Waugh* p.410.

[4] Lindsay Wellington, then a director of Sound Broadcasting at the BBC.

[5] Graham Greene, *A Burnt-Out Case*, 1961.

[6] He had called Miss Homewood 'Mrs Broadbent' throughout lunch on Boxing Day, as well as pretending to think she was Japanese.

To GRAHAM GREENE   Combe Florey House.
3 January 1961

Dear Graham

I have been sent an advance copy of *A Burnt-Out Case* and read it with deep interest. I could write much of my admiration for your superb description of the leper-village and for the brilliance with which you handle the problems of dialogue in four languages. I particularly admired the sermon of the Father Superior. But I am not reviewing it and I want to write a personal letter of apology.

I know, of course, how mischievous it is to identify fictional characters with their authors, but, taken in conjunction with your Christmas story, this novel makes it plain that you are exasperated by the reputation which has come to you unsought of a 'Catholic' writer. I realise that I have some guilt in this matter. Twelve years ago I gave a number of lectures here and in America presumptuously seeking to interpret what I genuinely believed was an apostolic mission in danger of being neglected by people who were shocked by the sexuality of some of your themes. In fact in a small way I behaved like Rycker[1]. I am deeply sorry for the annoyance I helped to cause & pray that it is only annoyance, and that the desperate conclusions of Morin[1] & Querry[1] are purely fictional.

Yours ever affectionately
Evelyn

[1] Graham Greene characters. Greene replied that, foreseeing hostility in the Catholic press, he had asked Father Caraman, as editor of *The Month*, to give *A Burnt-Out Case* to Waugh whose criticism, if severe, would be founded on unemotional principles. 'I have always found our points of disagreement – as in the case of *The Heart of the Matter* refreshing or enlightening and miles away from the suburbia of the *Catholic Herald* or *The Universe*. I do really assure you that never once have you behaved like Rycker.' Some of Querry's reactions had indeed been his, but he had wanted 'to give expression to various states or moods of belief or unbelief. The doctor . . . represents a settled and easy atheism . . . .' He ended the letter with expressions of affection.

To ELIZABETH PAKENHAM   Combe Florey House.
4 January 1960 [1961]

Dearest Elizabeth

Thank you for your charming letter & the promise of your Party Book[1] which I have seen much commended in the papers. It hasn't come yet but I have learned to bear with the sloth of publishers & postmen & shall enjoy it when it comes all the more. Laura has never given a childrens party in her life. Pray God it does not move her to do so.

As you saw Teresa has become engaged to marry an American. He is dim & studious but she seems to have taken a great liking to him and is having him instructed in the faith.

Bron's book has had an undeserved success which he is thoroughly enjoying and does not expect to repeat. It was nice of you & Frank to go to his party. I feared press photographers – apparently there were none & I could have gone safely.

It is very interesting that you are sending a boy[2] to Cambridge. I should never have conceived such a thing possible 20 years ago but now I believe it is the better place. Oxford has gone wrong. Do you know what the young call Maurice [Bowra]? – 'Old Tragic'.

It has been a bad year for the old literary hacks – Elizabeth Bowen, John Betjeman, Leslie Hartley down & out of the race; Tony Powell & Nancy Mitford just clinging to their saddles but out of control.[3] And now Graham Greene has written a most distressing work.

Did you know that Archbishop Roberts had an audience with the Pope a week after Dr Fisher had gone charging in crying: 'Your Holiness, we are making History'?[4] The Pope said to Roberts, 'There was another Archbishop from your country here the other day. Now who was he?'

I am sure that your recension of Queen Victoria's journals[5] will have a huge success.

I suppose that all your leisure is now taken up with the banking families. If you ever have time for old friends do come & see Laura & me.

My love to Frank
Evelyn

Now I see a damn fool letter in this morning's paper from Graham about Laos[6]. He seems in a shocking bad way.

Does Edward read the *Spectator*? He must have been surprised to see Frank described as the head of his family[7].

[1] *The Pakenham Party Book*, 1960.
[2] Michael Pakenham (1943–   ).
[3] *A Time in Rome* by Elizabeth Bowen, *Summoned by Bells* by John Betjeman, *Facial Justice* by L.P.Hartley, *Casanova's Chinese Restaurant* by Anthony Powell, *Don't Tell Alfred* by Nancy Mitford. All published in 1960.
[4] The 'courtesy call' paid by Lord Fisher of Lambeth (1887–1972) on John XXIII was the first by an Archbishop of Canterbury on a Pope since 1397. Waugh told the story many times.
[5] Elizabeth Longford, *Victoria RI*, 1964.
[6] Headed 'Lessons that were not learnt', Greene's letter protested against American intervention in Laos and drew a parallel with German and Italian behaviour in the Spanish Civil War.
[7] In a review of her book by Bernard Levin. Frank Pakenham succeeded his brother Edward as Earl of Longford later that year.

TO NANCY MITFORD   Combe Florey House.
4 January 1961

Darling Nancy

No, no, no. You must not think of giving up the novel. As I said in all sincerity *Alfred* positively clamours for a sequel.[1] Handy has all the concealed malice of the underdog. Don't believe a word he says. Reviewers are a paltry lot.

... I have just been editing a little life of La Veuve Clicquot-Ponsardin – very interesting.[2] I had always vaguely supposed her a woman of the Second Empire. Did you realise she was born 12 years before the Revolution & widowed in year of Trafalgar (Austerlitz to you), the daughter of a Jacobin deputy, ancestress of three dukes? Wine was at first a minor concern; her husband liked trotting round on a horse so he paid more attention to his vines than the banking & cloth-weaving which were the source of a very modest fortune. But I expect you knew all this.

I have not yet had my teeth out. The day cannot, I suppose, be far off. You can get them drawn free here but not replaced. I don't much care for Uncle Matthew 'dentures'. I believe one can rub ones gums with a preparation which hardens them well enough to chew most things. Anyway I like soft food & prefer pâtés & mousses to hunks of meat.

What do you suppose 'nouvelle vague' VAGUE means? According to my dictionary either 'vague news' or 'new wasteland'. Idiot English reviewers are always using it.

I bet you can't say 'Lovely, lovely 1960'.

All love
Evelyn

[1] Waugh had written: 'Yes your communist manifesto, *Alfred* [*Don't Tell Alfred*], is your best novel. I have reviewed it for a funny little paper run by Evelyn Gardner's niece and a beaver whose name escapes me – Rosse? Rose? He calls me Evelyn.' Alan Ross, editor of the *London Magazine*, had a beard at the time.

[2] Waugh rewrote the translation as well and wrote a preface for *The Life and Times of Madame Veuve Clicquot-Ponsardin*, by Princesse Jacqueline de Caraman Chimay, 1961.

TO GRAHAM GREENE   Combe Florey House.
5 January 1961

My Dear Graham

I fear your secretariate must be working full-blast on Laos but I must interrupt them to thank you for the many kind things in your letter & to make clear a few points. No answer required.

I was not so dotty as to take Rycker as a portrait of myself. I saw him as the caricature of a number of your admirers (among whom I counted myself) who have tried to force on you a position which you found obnoxious. You have given many broad hints which we refused to recognise. Now you have made a plain repudiation. You will find not so much 'hostility' among your former fellowship as the regrets of Browning for his 'Lost Leader' – except, of course, that no one will impute mercenary motives.

It was not the *Month* who wanted me to review *A Burnt-Out Case*, but the *Daily Mail*. They intend to make a splash of it. No doubt many papers will do the same. I don't think you can blame people who read the book as a recantation of faith. To my mind the expression 'settled and easy atheism' is meaningless, for an atheist denies his whole purpose as a man – to love & serve God. Only in the most superficial way can atheists appear 'settled & easy'. Their waste land is much more foreign to me than 'the suburbia of *The Universe*'.

I cannot wish your book success and I will not make a sensational attack on it, such as the *Mail* would relish. (At least I suppose they would. There was no specific invitation to do so in their proposal.)

God forbid I should pry into the secrets of your soul. It is simply your public performance which grieves me.

Yours ever affectionately
Evelyn

To Lady Diana Cooper Combe Florey House.
21 January 1961

Darling Pug

It was exhilarating to get a letter from you after how many years of post cards. Of course I will proudly give you another Pot-Boiler to replace stolen copy, but I imagine you don't want to accumulate any more possessions in France. I will bring it to Red Light District when you are settled there.[1]

I heard rumours of Susan Mary's engagement.[2] Was there not an American journalist named Alsop whom Miss Judy [Montagu] pursued hotly. Is it the same? I heard of the engagement because a reporter rang up, of all people, little Meg to ask what S.M. was like. Meg drawing on childhood memories said her main interest was acting charades.

The death of Mrs Fleming seems to have been postponed. She dined with [me?] the other evening & ate voraciously, drank moderately and talked lucidly.

You may well ask, what about Graham Greene's Christmas story? Is he Morin? He has now produced a novel with a precisely similar character – distinguished Papist who has lost his Faith and is disgusted with those who still look to him as a leader. I have had a sharp little Claudel-Gide correspondence with him which ended by my saying 'Mud in your mild & magnificent eye'. His alienist Dr Strauss kicked the bucket last week. No one to keep an eye on him now.

I long for India but am chained to my desk till I have finished novel.

All love
Wu

[1] Lady Diana Cooper was moving to Warwick Avenue.
[2] Susan Mary Patten married Joseph Alsop in 1961.

To Ann Fleming   Combe Florey House.
St Valentine [14 February] 1961

My Dear Ann

You are my Valentine. You have been described in the newspapers as 'a Tory Egeria' by Muggeridge. I have consulted all available dictionaries & find that Egeria is (1) a stream 2) the tutelary deity of childbirth. Is this actionable? I have never met anyone except socialists in your house.

I always thought Thunderbird was keen on Coward. I am glad the passion is reciprocated.[1]

It is very good news that Perry's farm bailiff has been raped. I don't think it can be Perry's work. The burnt cork would have left traces. Our best news is Edward Longford's death. Before the body was cold Frank was telephoning all over the United Kingdom trying to promote publicity. He persuaded me to write a panegyric in the *Observer*. It was a model of how such a thing should be done so as not to offend the family and at the same time reveal the essential absurdity of the deceased. Young Lord Silchester says he wishes to be known as plain Mr [Thomas] Pakenham. Not so Mrs Fraser who has leapt out as Lady Antonia.

If Col. Donaldson is still with you, pray tell him that at Magdalene College, Cambridge, which was refounded & reendowed by his father, a socialist canvasser was yesterday soaked in water.

My mind still runs on the late Lord Longford. It is not known how he has disposed his (once considerable) fortune.

It is very painful to me to be in England at this season. I am tied to my desk by my novel. I can't leave until it is finished. I am killing off the characters fast with 'flying bombs' & hope to take Margaret to Monte Carlo by the end of the month. . . .

Ever your affec. coz.
E. Waugh

[1] Noël Coward had bathed Ian Fleming when he was ill.

To John McDougall   Combe Florey House.
[28 February 1961]
Postcard

Our friend Louis Auchincloss (who is very much like what I conceive my character 'the Loot'[1] to be) uses the expression 'visit with' in his latest novel. It is said by a third generation New York millionairess who was brought up in the highest society of Newport.

E

[1] In *Sword of Honour* trilogy.

To Christopher Sykes   Combe Florey House.
4 March 1961

Bonjour Tristesse

Tout va bien chez vous? Votre jeune jolie marie a envoye mes chaises a Wincanton en place de Taunton. Elle a envie de me chasser fou sans dout?

A nos moutons.

Look here, I don't at all like the arrangement you have made for the Wodehouse panegyric. It should not be fitted into a space called 'the World of Books'. It should be a STUNT with a place of its own – not 'Mr Waugh is here as guest understudy for Mr Snooks who has a stomach ache' but 'Here for the first time in its history the BBC is making an *amende* for ancient injustice inflicted on a great artist by a low politician. Mr W. has unworthily been chosen to express the deep contrition of all English writers and to tell you what a magnificent fellow Dr Wodehouse is.'

I suspect that rats have been at work behind Sir Carleton's[1] back. Perhaps I ought to have gratified his generous wish to give me dinner. If this is absolutely necessary I could dine with him on 16th or 17th when I come to bid for Holman Hunts at Christie's.

Le corps de Lumumba[2] est pourri dans sa sepulchre mais son esprit marche en avance.

Le journal *Times* refuse a publier une lettre de moi disant que les professeurs d'histoire moderne à two les deux universities manque l'importance des censeurs de Westminster.

J'espère que votre sex-life est en bonne condition.

Acceptez, cher juif, mes sentiments les plus distingués.

E.W.

[1] Sir Hugh Carleton Greene (1910–   ). Director General of the BBC 1960–9. Brother of Graham.
[2] Patrice Lumumba (1925–61). First premier of the independent Congo. He had been killed the month before.

To Ann Fleming   Combe Florey House.
27 March 1961

Dear Ann

I am just off to the monks at Downside for my Holy Week retreat. I will pray for you & for poor Thunderbird in prison.

D. Jackson[1] is not a friend of mine. Nor for that matter is his sister in law Debo. Gaitskell[2] is no friend either, nor of my children. I think Donaldson took him to a party of Bron's. I did not mention Bron's engagement when I came to call because I was on my way to interview Lady Onslow[3]. I regard it as a highly imprudent undertaking but I have no authority to forbid it as I have no money to settle. The girl is pretty and seems sharp. I served at Windsor for a short time with Mick Dillon[4], her uncle, & liked him very much indeed. A P.G.Wodehouse character who has lately become a fervent Catholic. This has not softened Lady Onslow's heart towards the Church. You may judge Mick's intellect by the following anecdote. An order came that we were to have the numbers of our vehicles painted on the rim of the wheels. Mick fell into a rage with his corporal-of-horse saying:

'The man has not only painted the numbers at the bottom instead of the top but he has done it upside down.'

Mary Herbert thought the Evan Charteris caricature[5] unrecognisable. I know the James[6] one well but not who has it. I think it was in Guedalla's collection – if so its at Oxford.

Meg is making herself obnoxious in London by moving about with a train of riff-raff who break into people's houses & eat all the food in their larders & drink all their whisky.

I am glad you are reconciling yourself to Esmond before his death.

It will be a convenience to little Old Kaspar to inherit, now that T. Bird is on the rocks.

My daughter Teresa has returned from Massachusetts very lean & spotty. I too had envisaged a card:

The Earl & Countess of Onslow
&
Mr & Mrs Waugh
request the pleasure of your company
at the marriages of their daughters
Teresa,
to Mr A. Waugh and Mr J. D'Arms respectively

but, alas, it seems T. Onslow will not become Catholic so she & Bron would not be admitted to the sanctuary but would have to stand outside the rails. This would cause offense to Lady Onslow. Both weddings fill me with gloom.

I have been reading the report of the *Lady Chatterley* trial. What rot was talked! It is odd that both sides thought decency a Victorian invention. In the 18th century 'damn' was printed 'd--n' and Wilkes was turned out of the House of Commons for privately circulating an erotic poem. Perhaps you were abroad when it occurred. (I mean *Chatterley* trial not Wilkes's expulsion). If so get the Penguin report.

I thought O'Neill much prettier when I saw him in your house. . . .

I got the two Holman Hunts – cheap & nasty.

Ever yours affec.

E

[1] Professor Derek Jackson (1906–   ). Scientist. Married to Pamela Mitford 1936–51, to Janetta Woolley 1951–6.

[2] Hugh Gaitskell (1906–63). Leader of the Labour Party from 1955.

[3] Pamela Dillon (1915–   ). Married 1936–62 to the Earl of Onslow. Auberon Waugh was engaged to their daughter Lady Teresa.

[4] Viscount Dillon (1911–   ).

[5] A drawing of Ann Fleming's uncle by Max Beerbohm.

[6] Henry James, shown listening at a door.

To A.D.PETERS   Combe Florey House.
4 April 1961

Dear Pete

I have finished the novel – now called, did I tell you? *Unconditional Surrender*. I hope to send you a typescript by the end of the week. I don't think the last $\frac{1}{3}$ as good as the first $\frac{2}{3}$. I shall be interested to hear your opinion. I am sending a carbon direct to Jack McDougall. I have had, as you know, £1500 advance. How much more can I hope for? £1,000? Will you please send your copy to Little Brown?

I am sure that the three war books together would make a film with Alec Guinness as lead. I know A.G. would like to act in a book of mine. If you think it desirable, will you have a typescript made of your copy & send it to A.G.? He clearly has to make plans in advance & I don't suppose proof copies will be available before August at the earliest.

I don't think I shall write another novel for five or six years. Jack McD. has practically retired from C & H and I feel no loyalty towards his successors. I am therefore open to offers & still more, to suggestions for non-fiction work. I understand C & H have been taken over by a Jew.[1] Could he be induced to make an extravagant bid to take me over? I might write a 3 volume autobiography over ten years.

I think it would be useful (I know it would be pleasant) if we met. If I come to London next week or at the week-end, should I find you there?

                                                Yours ever
                                                Evelyn

[1] A Mr Samuel had made an unsuccessful attempt to take over Associated Book Publishers into which Chapman & Hall had been absorbed.

To FATHER PHILIP CARAMAN[1]   Combe Florey House.
5 April 1961

Your Reverence,

I am happy to report a signal favour granted me by the intercession of the XL Martyrs.

I have a daughter to whom I was tenderly attached and who in her youth seemed to reciprocate my affection. I obtained highly respectable employment for her in London & highly respectable lodging with a Catholic family. In spite of these advantages she soon gave me cause for anxiety. She took to the use of tobacco & spirits, fell into low company and despite generous wages has repeatedly had to be rescued from debt. Her appearance is slatternly. She gave up writing to me, though she had solemnly promised to do so frequently.

I took my sorrow to the XL Martyrs asking for a change of heart in this girl but without result.

I then changed my prayer & asked that I might become detached from her and indifferent to her ingratitude & lack of natural affection. This petition has been answered. I no longer care how dirty her finger nails are or how disorderly her habits. I no longer have the wish to visit her. I hope you will see fit to include this favour in your bulletin.

I am your reverence's obedient servant
Teresa Pinfold

[1] Written in the knowledge that his daughter Margaret, as Father Caraman's secretary, could and would intercept the letter.

To A.D.Peters   Combe Florey House.
[19 April 1961]
Postcard

Titles for Bradford to choose from:
'Depths and Shoals of Honour', 'Shoals of Honour', 'Peace without Honour', 'Honour comes a pilgrim grey'. 'Guy Crouchback', 'The End of the Battle'. 'Peace'. 'The Sword'. 'A Sword'. 'Quixote in Modern Dress'. Or if he prefers it 'Uncle Tom's Cabin & the Seven Dwarfs.'

E

Also: 'It was a Famous Victory'[1]

[1] *Unconditional Surrender* is called *The End of the Battle* in the United States because Bradford of Little, Brown had pointed out that the English title had been used there that year. Waugh had suggested *Chivalry* and *Conventional Weapons* earlier. 'Which will help the poor reviewers to understand better? That's really all that matters.'

To Daphne Fielding   Combe Florey House.
22 May 1961

Darling Daphne
How decent of you to send me your lovely novel[1]. I have read it with delight & admiration. Thank you, thank you.

Its a painter's book, isn't it? Like Giles's? All those fine visual impressions. Also a cook's – all that luscious food. As for writing it is as though Norman Douglas and Nancy Mitford and Ernest Hemingway had sat down tight to a paper game. Two particular jewels I envied – the girl sticking the straws from her drinks in her hair and the student arguing to himself about incest on a tape recorder. Three objections. It is a vulgar error to suppose that Jesuits are unscrupulous as to 'means'. (2) Chap couldnt knock head off a clay bust. There is always an elaborate wire structure (armature?) inside. (3) Men don't hunt in caps with rat-catcher –

bowlers or what my hatter calls 'reinforced Cokes'. Minor point: a thing can't be 'soporific making', 'soporific' includes the 'making'.

I was delighted when the dog perished in agony. What do you mean, he was the only one? There was a whole pack of fox hounds enjoying themselves top hole. I wish Sheridan had been stung to death by wasps. I like a book in which justice is seen to be done & the bad are punished. It was very perverse of you to give him a young, pretty, docile, rich bride.

What leaves an old pro like me aghast is your prodigality. In your bounteous way you have squandered six books in one. You have used almost everything that has happened in the last twelve years. Its lovely for us but what will you do when you come to write another? And we shall all clamour for another.

I have written to the *Spectator* asking to be allowed to review it but there has been a change of management and I don't know the new young gentlemen. I should like to give public utterance to my appreciation.

My life at the moment is hideously overshadowed & agitated by weddings. I have a daughter marrying a studious & penniless yank in a fortnight and hard on that a son marrying a pretty, well endowed English girl. But the turmoil & expense are damnable.

Love to Xan
Evelyn

Do you think Smarty Boots Connolly will think he is 'Sheridan'. No wasps on Boots. He is selling all his private correspondence to d'Avigdor Goldsmid[2].

Diana is very low spirited. Lost not only all her furniture en route from Chantilly but the new radiators in her new house taken out by burglars. But I expect you know.

Its awfully touching how Bog Rose is only happy leading her daughters hunting. Brought tears to my dry old eyes.

Yesterday's *Express* said you learned writing on Max's knee. You write much better than his other pupils. But, you know, you do need a tutor. There are technical imperfections which any old hack would put right in exchange for a kiss on the brow.

[1] *The Adonis Garden.*

[2] Not true. But Sir Henry d'Avigdor-Goldsmid did help Connolly financially from time to time and paid for his treatment during his last prolonged illness, observing 'Cyril is dying beyond my means.' Connolly sold his manuscripts, but the bulk of his letters was in his library when he died. Waugh asked if he could buy his own letters at market-price.

To Christopher Sykes

Combe Florey House.

9 June [1961]

Dear Genocide,

I enclose the fair copy of my oration.

Thank you for your letter. It is not clear to me that you are fully aware of the obligations you have incurred by summoning me to London. I will come by the train you recommend & look out for you at Paddington. If you are not there I will return to Taunton. It was not on this train that I wished you to engage a seat for me but on the return journey, now postponed a day through the ambition of St Regis Greene.[1] You have to book spacious & quiet rooms for me for the nights of 19th & 20th. You will have to fetch me from these rooms on the morning of 20th; also in the evening. How will you entertain me during the rest of my visit? No strip tease please. I am told there are some facetious university graduates named 'the Fringe'[2]. You might get a box for them on 19th. You will have and draw a large special grant for my entertainment. I have lately been put to grievous expense by the marriage of my daughter[3] and I cannot let myself be out of pocket as the result of my visit to B.B.C.

Mrs Rodd is meditating about death.

Your obedient servant
Bernard Waley-Cohen[4]

[1] Sir Hugh Carleton Greene had asked Waugh and Sykes to dinner after the recording.

[2] *Beyond the Fringe* with Alan Bennett, Peter Cook, Jonathan Miller and Dudley Moore had opened in May. Tickets were not available.

[3] Teresa had married John D'Arms the week before.

[4] Bernard Waley-Cohen (1914–). A neighbour. Lord Mayor of London 1960–1.

To NANCY MITFORD   Combe Florey House.
9 June 1961

Darling Nancy

At the moment of death each individual soul is judged and sent to its appropriate place – the saints straight to heaven, unrepentent sinners to Hell, most (one hopes) to Purgatory where in extreme discomfort but confident hope we shall be prepared for the presence of God. Our bodies remain on earth & decay. Only Our Lord's & Our Lady's bodies were assumed into a different order of existence. All this is quite straightforward. It is called 'the Particular Judgment'. You will remember that Our Lord said to the penitent thief '*This day* thou shalt be with me in paradise'. It has never been suggested that his body did not follow the normal course of mortality.

The Last or General Judgment is something quite different & very mysterious. It is the end of the world and of time. It may happen at any moment now or in the remote future. The Christians of the first century seem to have expected it momentarily. At the Last Judgment those still living will be judged there & then. There is no appeal for us who have died earlier from our particular sentences. The change will be our reunion with our bodies. What comprises these bodies no one claims to know. They will be individual, recognizable and free from the defects of our present bodies. In 13th century it was generally held that these bodies would have full physical existence – position, weight etc. Modern theologians think these terms poetic & metaphorical. No one pretends to understand the mechanics of the change. The essential principle is that we are *not*, as most orientals believe, spiritual beings temporarily encumbered with a body which we gladly shed & then lose our personalities in some all embracing soul. God had to become man & take a body to show us this. The body is not simply a source of sensation, temptation, pain & decrepitude. It is us.

Besides heaven, hell & purgatory there is generally believed (though not dogmatically defined) [to be] limbo where the unbaptised noble savages go. They never enjoy the beatific vision. Neither do they suffer the pains of hell.

It is generally believed that children under 7 are incapable of mortal sin. The Curé d'Ars said of a child of 5 'Its lucky she died when she did. She will have a long time in purgatory. Had she lived she would have been damned. She was far gone in sin.'

Bossuet's death[1] was indeed a sad loss to the Church. I am surprised you have only lately heard of it.

I am having a grievous time with weddings. A daughter last week, a son at the end of the month. Most fatiguing and costly.

Love from
Evelyn

If you are gravely concerned about the problem of the reunion of soul & body I will look up a sermon of Ronald's which makes as much sense of it as reason can.

[1] In 1704.

To Nancy Mitford·   Combe Florey House.
19 June 1961

Darling Nancy

No, you haven't got it quite right. The body is an essential part of us. That doesn't mean we must pamper it. St Paul says 'bring it into subjection' like schooling a horse. There are two contrasting heresies – Boots who thinks his beautiful body is made to be crammed with rich food and covered with kisses & lady Astor[1] who thinks her body is an illusion. Good people (not I) whack themselves with chains & wear hair shirts, just to remind themselves forcibly that they are not all soul.

If the Col. you speak of is Col. Bill Stirling & he remembers he is Hatty's godfather, remind him he has not yet sent her a christening present still less any tokens of affection at Christmas. He was a rich man when I asked him to stand sponsor. Now I fear he has ruined himself at cards. He was a very indulgent commander to me at one stage of the war.

Can't advise anything to read – I am fortunate in having such a bad memory that I can read the same detective story every six weeks and still wonder who the murderer will be.

Bron's young lady is pretty and has a little money. Alas she is one of the most tiresome kinds of protestant – she can't see the difference between her Church & the Popes and has to be restrained from making sacrilegious communions in foreign churches.

Try *Pauvre et Saint* (Editions du Seuil) by D.Pezeril. That will show how good people look after the bad.

Honor Guinness[2] was received in the Church. It is rumoured that Eric Dudley[3] is under instruction.

Oh dear I have to go to London today. Horrible place in the summer.

Love
E

[1] Nancy Astor was a Christian Scientist.

[2] Lady Honor Guinness (1909–76) was married 1933–45 to Henry (Chips) Channon and in 1946 to Flight Lieutenant Frantisek Svejdar.

[3] The Earl of Dudley (1894–1969) married Princess Grace Radziwill in 1961.

To W.J.Igoe   Combe Florey House.
4 August [1961]
Postcard

Thank you for your letter. May I commend two points to your attention 1) The character of all the Crouchback family of withdrawal from the world, at its lowest in mad Ivo, at its highest in the father. This explains much of Guy's failure to re-enter the world in the army 2) The idea that God creates no man without a special purpose. Guy's was to rescue Trimmer's son from a disastrous upbringing.

Thank you again for your kind interest.

E.W.

To Nina Bourne[1]   Combe Florey House.
6 September 1961

Dear Miss Bourne

Thank you for sending me *Catch 22*. I am sorry that the book fascinates you so much. It has many passages quite unsuitable to a lady's reading. It suffers not only from indelicacy but from prolixity. It should be cut by about a half. In particular the activities of 'Milo' should be eliminated or greatly reduced.

You are mistaken in calling it a novel. It is a collection of sketches – often repetitious – totally without structure.

Much of the dialogue is funny.

You may quote me as saying: 'This exposure of corruption, cowardice and incivility of American officers will outrage all friends of your country (such as myself) and greatly comfort your enemies.'

Yours truly,
Evelyn Waugh

[1] Nina Bourne of Simon and Schuster had sent Joseph Heller's first novel to Waugh for comment.

To Ann Fleming   Combe Florey House.
[September 1961?]

Dearest Ann

Thank you for your letter.

I think your new friend (like so many of them) must be an impostor. Praed died in 1839 leaving 2 daughters (from one of whom Douglas Woodruff descends)[1]. It is possible, I suppose, that the younger daughter bore a son at the age of 45 and that he took his mother's name for reasons of social advantage and is now botanizing in Switzerland at the age of 78 – but it sounds fishy. Whatever his origin he is correct on the subject of the Loch Ness Monster. It was seen by the late Abbot of Fort Augustus.

Oddly enough I knew that Poor Louis[2] had tacked himself on to Chaplin. I was smoked out of my hole last week by the Pixton junketings and heard the news in London from Diana who was proud that her loyal boy should have made so good. We (Diana and I) went to the theatre and saw a brilliant new (to me) actress named Maggie Smith.[3] We couldn't get seats and then said 'How about a box?' 'Oh, yes, of course there's always a box. Do you really want one?' So we sat cheek by jowl with Maggie Smith and admired her feverishly. A stage box is the ideal place for a party of two. The trouble is that people think that when they have paid four or five guineas they must pack it and then no one can see or stretch his legs. Well Miss Smith is a fair treat and the two little plays she is in give her a chance to show it. She will become famous. Perhaps she is already and it is like my saying: 'Keep your eye on a clever young American called T.S.Eliot?'

From London I went to visit Pam Berry. She had an American picture dealer there and socialists came to dinner. No sign of Michael. Pam complained a great deal that everyone was dull, dirty, drunk. She wishes to overturn the monarchy and set Lady Harewood up as First Lady. Her condemnations, so vehement as to be scarcely rational, ranged from the Knights of the Garter to the Marylebone Cricket Club. I said 'You are like Philip Egalité', 'My favourite man' but I found that all she knew of him was his portrait as a child at Waddesdon. Have you been there? Very oppressive. It is like being Alice, after she shrank, in the Wallace Collection. Everything superb but twice its proper size. Pam, 'We ought to give all these back to Versailles'. E. 'If the frogs have no king, they have no right to have a palace.' P. 'Oh, how can you be so reactionary?'. From there to Claydon where the English rococo seemed light as down.

From Pam to Penelope Betjeman. A sharp contrast. All the time I was with her

Penelope never said a disagreeable thing about anyone. We went with the Woodruffs to Lyford (the house where Campion was taken prisoner). It belonged to the Woodruffs for 30 years but always let to a farmer. Now two rich pious spinsters have bought it, laid parquet flooring, exposed oak beams, smothered the place with white paint and attempting to make a popish pilgrimage centre have made a Maidenhead villa. But all the time Mia was saying 'Just what Douglas and I always wanted to do if we could have afforded it'. When the spinsters rebuilt the roof they found a unique relic, an Agnus Dei (wax medallions cast and blessed by the Pope) of Campion's date still wrapped in the paper in which it had been tucked away when the pursuivants searched the house. An object, to me, of greater interest than anything at Waddesdon. It was sad for the Woodruffs to know that they had owned it for 30 years unawares.

Paul Betjeman[4] is in a third class jazz band touring American bases in France. His great ambition is to become a second class bandsman. This can only be attained by a three year course of study in U.S.A. A strange grandson for a Field Marshal.

Penelope drove me home, stopping often for ginger beer on the road, and she could not utter the words 'kiss' or 'feet'. Yesterday she ran through the crowded gallery crying 'Oh look, Bo, here's another cunt'.

My morning paper tells me poor Ed is to marry again.[5] His bride seems to be famous – not to me.

Your account of Pakenham fascinated me. It was very well farmed when I used to stay there. Until his marriage Frank used to be allowed to give a party there once a year. Edward and Christine used to hate us all but we gave them subjects for conversation for the ensuing year. I wrote an obituary of Edward in the *Observer* recalling these jolly days. That barge was always a death trap; so were the horses. I daresay the stables are empty now. Mr Paul Johnson[6] is a Stonyhurst boy, reclaimed to the Faith. Frank has a hero worship of him. Perhaps he discerns prison fodder.

Janet Kidd (Aitken-Campbell-Montagu)[7] has a ball on Saturday – we have a house full for it. I have bought Laura an engine for washing plates. It's arrival here has been like one of those early Bolshevist films when a tractor came to a primitive village. All worship it. Since our last servants left washing-up has been a great bore.

Picasso will celebrate his 80th birthday by giving £2,000,000 worth of daubs to Barcellona Barcelona? That should draw the criminal classes and offend the communists. Your Australian buffoon, Cooper[8], has been writing letters to *The Times*.

I was boasting that the whole tourist season had passed without a single American fan intruding on us. I spoke too soon. Today a Californian judge and his wife will barge in. I shall talk to him of Erle Stanley Gardner.

Yours ever affec
E

[1] Ann Fleming had described an acquaintance as 'grandson of the poet'.
[2] Paul-Louis Weiller.
[3] Maggie Smith, whom Waugh had not remarked in a small part in *Rhinoceros*, had succeeded in revue

and was now succeeding in comedy. The play was Peter Schaffer's *The Private Ear and The Public Eye* with Kenneth Williams.

[4] Paul Betjeman (1937–   ). He had gone to America and become a Mormon for a time.

[5] Lord Stanley married Kathleen Wright, then Lady Crane, that year. Her fortune derived from the manufacture of bicycles.

[6] Paul Johnson (1928–   ). Editor of the *New Statesman* 1965–70.

[7] Janet Aitken (1908–   ). Daughter of Lord Beaverbrook, married 1927–34 to Ian Campbell, later Duke of Argyll, 1935–40 to William Montagu, and in 1942 to Major Edward Kidd.

[8] Douglas Cooper (1911–   ). Art critic and historian.

To Ann Fleming   Combe Florey House.
23 September [1961]

My Dear Ann

You say 'R.S.V.P.' but give no address. Perhaps someone will forward this.

It is very kind of you to ask me & red nose[1] to Golden Eye. Alas, I fear we shall be on our way home by the time you arrive there. Esmond's bounty [*Daily Mail*] is good for two months rum drinking – not more.

Mrs Kidd's ball was very lavish – nothing remarkable if it had been in Surrey but sensational in Somerset. Two bands, one of niggers & one of buggers, a cabaret, an oyster bar in the harness room, stables flood lit, much to discomfort of the horses. One bit an American pornographer[2] who tried to give it vodka.

Mrs Kidd (calling herself the Hon. Mrs Edward Kidd, which of course she isn't) announced in *The Times* the names of those who gave dinner parties. She included Lord Hinchingbrooke[3] who came with one daughter & a young man, Lady Colyton[4] who wasn't there, and a man named Duncan[5] who was complaining bitterly that he had had no dinner at all having just arrived by train to stay with Mrs Kidd. A neighbouring prep school master had put up 12 total strangers but his name was not included. There was a great surplus of women. At one stage of the evening I found myself like the jeune premier of an old fashioned musical comedy with ten rather pretty girls surrounding me.

I had never before met Lady Jean Campbell[6] and was fascinated. She came to us next day bringing the bitten pornographer. He might have stepped straight from your salon – a swarthy gangster just out of a mad house where he had been sent after the attempt to cut his wife's throat.[7] It is his first visit to England. His tour is Janet Kidd, Randolph, Ian Argyll. He will be able to write a revealing pornogram of English life.

Your protégé Angus Wilson has written an admirable novel[8] which the reviewers have all abused.

I was faced with having to abandon writing because the people who made Relief nibs have taken to making them in a new way. But I have found a cache of nearly 500 of the old stock which should last me ten years. After that time I shall be blind and palsied & reduced to dictation.

Mrs Whistler Morgan[9] wrote me a jolly decent letter.

Harriet has returned from Beirut and is now on our hands. Rather pretty, full of energy, quite mindless. What can be done with her? I wish you could find a solution. In happier days she could have been sent to Malta to marry a sailor. Diana has weakened in her readiness to accept a companion. She (Hatty) is a good girl with no aptitudes.

Meg is here completing the biography of her sainted ancestor Philip Howard.[10] I am beginning to frighten her with tales of snakes, stingray, pirai, bêtes rouges and other denizens of the Guianas.

Your affec. cousin
Evelyn

[1] Margaret.

[2] Norman Mailer (1923–). American writer. Married to Lady Jeanne Campbell 1962–3. His books at this time included *The Naked and the Dead*, 1948, and *Advertisements for Myself*, 1959.

[3] Viscount Hinchingbrooke (1906–). Succeeded as Earl of Sandwich in 1962, disclaimed the title in 1964.

[4] Barbara Bart married first Charles Addams, the *New Yorker* cartoonist, and in 1956 Lord Colyton, who as Henry Hopkinson had been Conservative MP for Taunton, Waugh's constituency, 1950–6.

[5] Ronald Duncan (1914–). Writer.

[6] Lady Jeanne Campbell (1928–). Daughter of Mrs Kidd and her first husband, the Duke of Argyll.

[7] Norman Mailer comments: 'The horse did bite me on the finger but I was not feeding him vodka, just patting his nose .... I did not cut my wife's throat .... Jean Campbell asked me what I thought of him [Waugh] and I said "Lots of fun. Much sweeter to me than I expected".'

[8] *The Old Men at the Zoo*, 1961.

[9] Fionn O'Neill married John Morgan, a diplomat, that year.

[10] Philip Howard, died 1595 in the Tower of London. The pamphlet was published by the office of vice-postulation.

To the Editor of the Spectator

Combe Florey House.

13 October [1961]

OLD MEN AT THE ZOO

Sir, – Can you find space for a second opinion on Mr Angus Wilson's latest novel, *Old Men at the Zoo?* I read the book with keen delight and admiration and have since been dismayed by the reviews I have seen, of which Mr. John Mortimer's[1] in your columns is typical. I have only the most shadowy personal acquaintance with Mr. Wilson and none at all with his publishers. My only motive in writing to you is the fear that the public may be discouraged from reading what seems to me a very fine book.

Your readers have already been given some indication of the plot. Few critics, including your own, seem to have appreciated the technical achievement of its intricate structure. There are not so many master craftsmen among the post-war novelists that we can afford to neglect them. I have always admired Mr. Wilson's skill, but hitherto with certain reservations of sympathy and suspensions of credulity. As Mr. Mortimer remarks, he has described 'a small and creepy world.' It should be an occasion for rejoicing that he has now chosen a larger and (to me) more plausible milieu. All his new characters, major and minor alike, seem to me brilliantly observed and drawn. Nothing in the narrative is haphazard. Every incident has significance. The least successful scene is the one which some critics (not Mr. Mortimer) have singled out for praise – the party after the young keeper's funeral – which is most like Mr. Wilson's earlier work. Reviewers should welcome variety and development in a writer.

Mr. Mortimer opens his review by deploring the tendency to regard writers as authorities on questions of morals, politics and philosophy. I think he confuses two issues. On one I agree with him. Some days ago there appeared in *The Times* a letter signed by a number of well-known writers (Mr. Wilson among them) protesting against the arrest of an Angolan poet. Injustice, if injustice has been committed, is equally deplorable whether the victim is a poet or a peasant. I do not believe that all the signatories were familiar with this poet's work or had even heard his name before being invited to subscribe. I do not believe they all had *personal* knowledge of the circumstances of his arrest. This seems to me an example of 'pressure' being brought on them 'to pontificate'. But Mr. Mortimer's condemnation is wider. 'Many writers,' he says, 'are not very good at anything except writing and the value of their work is often not to be judged by the quality of their thoughts.' But writing is the expression of thought. There is no abstract writing. All literature implies moral standards and criticisms – the less explicit the better.

Mr. Mortimer's second confusion is in his use of 'symbolism.' In a novel the symbols are merely the furniture of the story. They are not to be taken allegorically as in *Pilgrim's Progress*. They are not devised consciously but arise spontaneously in the mood of composition.

Thirdly, and this is most important, Mr. Mortimer and all the critics I have read have been trapped by the date – 1970. It was audacious of Mr. Wilson to put his story into the near future and, as things turn out, injudicious, for *Old Men at the Zoo* is not a novel like *Brave New World* or *1984* in which a warning is offered of the dangers to posterity if existing social tendencies fructify. Mr. Wilson postulates no new scientific devices. His characters live and speak in the present or in the recent past.

A novelist has a difficult task in fixing his characters in historical time. Many – I think if one counted them up one would find most – good novels are set in the past. Public events intrude on private lives. It is very difficult to write a novel about 1961 which can give any indication of the final destiny of the characters, and it is with their final destiny that their creator is primarily, if unobtrusively, concerned. Mr. Wilson informs us that he does not think the public events of his book are likely to occur. If I read him right, he is concerned with what might have happened, rather than with what will happen. Consciously or unconsciously he has written a study of 1938–42. The causes of his war are deliberately made absurd. He required *a* war for his plot and the war he has given us is what many Englishmen feared at the time of Munich. They were given wildly exaggerated notions of the impending disaster. Gas, microbes and high explosive would devastate the kingdom. Communications would cease. Famine would ensue. We should capitulate and the victors would impose a Nazi regime. The young may find it hard to believe, but that was in fact the belief of many intelligent people. Mr. Wilson has accepted all that body of – as it happened – quite false assumptions and has used it in the machinery of his story. What he is concerned with, and what he so brilliantly portrays, is the working of the machinery on the lives of his characters.

EVELYN WAUGH

[1] John Mortimer (1923–   ). QC and playwright.

To the Editor of The Times   Combe Florey House.
13 October 1961

INDEXES

Sir, – You say in your leading article today, "No one has ever suggested that novels should have indexes".

I possess a translation of Tolstoy's *Resurrection*, published by Messrs. Grosset and Dunlap of New York and "illustrated from the photoplay produced by Inspiration Pictures Inc.", which has a particularly felicitous index. The first entry is: "Adultery, 13, 53, 68, 70"; the last is: "Why do people punish? 358". Between them occur such items as: Cannibalism, Dogs, Good breeding, Justification of one's position, Seduction, Smoking, Spies, and Vegetarianism.

I am, Sir, your obedient servant,
EVELYN WAUGH

To Graham Greene   Combe Florey House.
26 October [1961]

Dear Graham

Thank you very much indeed for your note book.[1] I have already read it with intense interest (which I have lamely tried to express in the *Spectator*). As you know *Burnt-Out Case* shocked me. It is very interesting to note that none of the shocking features were in your mind when you began your search for a character & did not come to you in the Congo.

I wish you had been at the dinner for Harold Acton. He was exuberantly malicious & the food & wine (chosen by John Sutro) were splendid. There were some very sinister smiling strangers at the table but the old gang silenced them.

I am sorry you are not going to Abyssinia. No sex there certainly in my time – hideous women – but plenty of odd religion. Why not come with me & my daughter Margaret to British Guiana? Sailing Nov 26th in *Stella Polaris*. Communist agents rife there I believe.

Miss no Dame Rose Macaulay's 'faith' seems as shaky as Querry's. I always thought of her as the last spinster. Do you think her adultery was an hallucination?[2]

I am delighted that your protégée M. Spark is doing so well.

Do come to Guiana. We could keep Christmas on Devil's Island.

Love from
Evelyn

[1] Graham Greene, *In Search of a Character: Two African Journals*, 1961.

[2] Rose Macaulay, *Letters to a Friend*, edited by Constance Babington Smith, 1961, told of an affair and of Dame Rose's difficulty in reconciling it with her religious beliefs.

TOM DRIBERG   Combe Florey House.
SS Simon and Jude [28 October] 1961

Dear Tom

I am deeply touched by your remembering my birthday. It is an appalling thought that I may live as long again as the time since I wrote my first novel and then be no older than that disgusting old Picasso. (How enjoyable that his Australian clown[1] got stabbed. Johnny Rothenstein I presume).

No umbrage at the *New Statesman* article.[2] How could I mind anything so largely composed of my own words? The last two sentences are silly but no doubt written by your understrapper. I have never sought to disguise my parents' circumstances. As I remember it the television fellow was asking me about my childhood not my adolescence. When my father built his little house at North End it was almost as rural as Combe Florey – much more rural than Stinchcombe when you visited me. The tube had not reached Golders Green & there were fields all round us. Not that it matters.

If you have had the patience to read my last book & have, as you promised, noted misprints & mistakes, I should be most grateful for a list of them.

Was any biography of J.F.Roxburgh[3] ever written?

I go to British Guiana in a months time to retread old steps. Is Mr Jagan[4] a crony of yours? I hear he is coming to London to borrow money. I can't lend him any but I should like to meet him if you are on terms to ask him to luncheon, I could come up. Warn him I am no socialist & shall be writing articles for the *Daily Mail*. In fact, from what I remember of 29 years ago, the coastal belt of B. Guiana might benefit from socialism, not the interior where my interests lie.

Roger Fulford was guest of honour at an Old Boys' dinner. A general called Evitts wrote to me to ask who he was. Who was Evitts?[5]

I am very glad you employed that 'Vicky'[6] to caricature me. No danger of being accosted in trains by strangers who recognize it. Why are there no caricaturists nowadays?

Yours ever
Evelyn

[1] Douglas Cooper was found stabbed outside Nîmes. John Rothenstein had once struck Cooper at a party at the Tate Gallery of which he was director.

² 'Stout Party', unsigned, partly by Tom Driberg. He disowned the last two sentences which are: 'Some years after he [Waugh] had thus piously resuscitated her, the Vatican discovered that the legend of Helena's finding the true Cross was baseless and abolished the feast that commemorated it. Collapse, one might suppose, of Stout Party.'

³ Noel Annan, *Roxburgh of Stowe*, 1965.

⁴ Cheddi Jagan (1918–   ). First premier of British Guiana 1961–4.

⁵ Sir John Evetts, born in 1891. In India, and then Senior Military Adviser to Ministry of Supply in the war. Knighted in 1951.

⁶ Victor Weisz (1913–66). *Evening Standard* cartoonist from 1954.

To Nancy Mitford   Combe Florey House.
[October 1961]

Darling Nancy

You killed a heroine in child-birth.[1] That is a very rare occurrence. Several chaps I knew were bombed in the chapel at Wellington Barracks.

Only Box-Bender thought the ending happy.

Nabokov[2] may make an opera of *Pinfold* if I may sing in it & design the scenery.

I was in London for V2s and agree they were not at all alarming, but I passed through during V1s and got the impression people were nervous. Wasn't it then the lower orders jeered at Sir Winston? I certainly heard two upper class ladies discussing whether they ought to pray for V1s not to fall on them.

I made bourgeois Box Bender and Elderbury bugger[3] – if by that term you mean decamp.

Love from
Evelyn

And especial love to your poor eyes. Have you no one to read to you? In England everyone would. The French are such selfish hogs. Think how we all read to Peter Beatty.

[1] Nancy Mitford had written of Virginia Troy's death in *Unconditional Surrender*: 'But in fact people one knew were never killed in raids – I mean no human being of any sort that I knew was except Myrtle [Myrtle Farquharson, who married Robin d'Erlanger]. So there is an unreality about this you would be the first to point out in the work of another. Still I'm glad about the happy ending.'

[2] Nicholas Nabokov (1904–78). Composer. Cousin of Vladimir.

[3] Nancy Mitford had written: 'I've never despised the English bourgeoisie so much as during the air-raids – they were lamentable – they used to come into the shop, buy huge armfuls of books and bugger.'

To Cyril Connolly   Combe Florey House.
23 October 1961

Dear Cyril

I hope this reaches you. They are very slack at White's in forwarding letters. But I don't know your other addresses.

A mischievous woman in London tells me that you identify a character, named 'Spruce', in a book I lately sent you, with yourself.[1] I hope this is pure mischief. If not, it is persecution mania. Just count the points of resemblance & difference between yourself & that character & see what the score is.

There are of course asses in London, who don't understand the processes of the imagination, whose hobby it is to treat fiction as a gossip column. You must appreciate their asinityty (ASININITY).

But what distresses me (if true) is that you should suppose I would publicly caricature a cherished friend.

Yours ever
Evelyn

[1] Everard Spruce, editor of a war-time magazine in *Unconditional Surrender*, bears a definite resemblance to Connolly, who had telephoned to Ann Fleming and then reported to Waugh that 'though she was perfectly tactful, it irritated me that she took it so much for granted that it was me'. Waugh wrote to Sykes: 'Gossip tells me poor Boots has persecution mania thinking he is that editor. Silly ass.' He also wrote to Nancy Mitford light-heartedly that Connolly appeared as the proletarian aphorist and murderer Ludovic, and again to Sykes that all the characters male and female were based on Teresa Jungman.

To Cyril Connolly
Combe Florey House.
29 October 1961

Dear Cyril

I am delighted to have your country address. It is very kind of you to ask me there. May I come in the spring? I am shortly off to the tropics.

Thank you for your review in the *Sunday Times*. I am glad you liked *Officers & Gentlemen* more on a second reading.

It is very proper that you should have proud memories of *Horizon*. It was the outstanding publication of its decade. I am greatly annoyed to see that two reviewers have attempted to identify it with my invention *Survival*. That magazine was the creature of the Ministry of Information. *Horizon*, of course, was Watson's benefaction. It is true that you had a semi-literate socialist colleague but he was not 'Spruce'; still less you. As for secretaries, Lys was beautifully neat and, as I remember her, Miss Brownell was quite presentable. Some time later you had a bare footed landlady but (surely?) she had no part in *Horizon* and very little part in the delightful parties you gave. The whole identification is a fantasy.

I hope you enjoyed your Senegalese luncheon.

Don't let Mrs Fleming drive you into persecution mania. It is an aptitude of hers.[1]

Love from
Evelyn

[1] On 20 November Waugh wrote: 'I have told that mischievous London woman to look nearer her own hearth for "Spruce" and she is busy now identifying him with the late editor of the Cornhill [Peter Quennell].'

To Anthony Powell   Combe Florey House.
31 October 1961

Dear Tony

Thanks awfully for your letter.

I am disconcerted to find I have given the general impression of a 'happy ending'. This was far from my intention. The mistake was allowing Guy legitimate offspring. They shall be deleted in any subsequent edition. I thought it more ironical that there should be real heirs of the Blessed Gervase Crouchback dispossessed by Trimmer but I plainly failed to make that clear. So no nippers for Guy & Domenica in Penguin.

The law of sepulture was changed (largely I think by a fascist beast named Arnold Wilson) but not retrospectively. My father was buried in Hampstead parish churchyard in 1944 in a plot he had bought freehold forty years earlier. Peregrine went into a Crouchback plot. There is a popish cemetery at Mortlake (where Lady Burton rather dubiously planted her husband). Bentley is there and quite a number of illustrious papists. I am pretty sure they sold freehold plots until about 1900.

There is also a Broome[1] in, I think, the midlands which is now a seminary.

You must be glad to be back in Somerset after the horrors of U.S.A. I am off shortly for the equator taking a daughter as decoy for mosquitoes.

I forgot about Chatty when naming Mrs Corner[2]. That should be changed too. Thank you for pointing out the ambiguity.

Violet does not seem to have completed her civilizing mission with young K. Amis.

                                                        Yours ever
                                                        Evelyn

[1] The home of the Crouchbacks in *Sword of Honour*.
[2] Two unconnected characters, Apthorpe's legatee and Uncle Peregrine's housekeeper, have the name.

To Harold Acton   Combe Florey House.
31 October [1961]

Dear Harold

Thank you very much for the kind things you say about my novel. It has had a mixed reception exciting some class warfare among the younger reviewers. A mischievous cousin of Laura's called Mrs Fleming told Cyril Connolly that he was caricatured in the book & has upset a long but always precarious friendship.

I have not done more than dip delightedly into the Bourbons.[1] I am keeping it for my sea voyage. A work of that kind, so rich & learned, must be studied with proper reverence. The South Atlantic is the place & I long for the uninterrupted days in the deck chair. That, of course, is what has discomforted the critics. They like a little book they can skip through & be smart about. A serious big work like yours takes too much time. They don't know the subject and are too impatient to learn so they have been civil to you and dredged up a few memories of their history lessons at school and given no proper impression of the gaiety – is that how it is spelt or is there an e somewhere? – that, a sampling shows, runs through & illuminates the patient research. It and its predecessor will, I am sure, steadily grow in reputation & become classics when *Lucky Jim* is totally forgotten.

It was a delight to see you in London. John recovered from his ague, he tells me.

I hear disappointing reports of Guiana – full of motor cars & aeroplanes where I went laboriously on foot 30 years ago. But I can only go where I am paid to go. I think there might be amusing secret societies still. The food will be awful. I shall be still more emaciated when I return. Good for my daughter, too. You kindly describe her as PreRaphaelite but she is too robust.

I have another daughter married to an american named D'Arms. They are in Rome. If they turn up in Florence, please be kind to them. He is a respectful, respectable 'student' – what of, heaven knows.

I was 58 the other day. Longevity is one of the greatest curses introduced by the scientists. Look at Maugham & that brute Picasso and the Carbonaro Churchill.

Love from
Evelyn

[1] Harold Acton, *The Last Bourbons of Naples*, 1961. Waugh described it in his diary as 'unreadable'.

To Laura Waugh
12 January [1962]

Hotel Tower,
74 & 75 Main Street,
Georgetown,
British Guiana.

Darling Laura

A very amusing & welcome (undated) letter from you describing the beagle ball. I am sure it was a tearing success. My heart bleeds for you in the intense cold. I am delighted to hear you have found employment & lodging for Hatty[1]. Now, I trust, you will be free to pursue your social career until Feb 15th (St Valentine?) when I return to you.

Meg & I have got into the Portuguese set – all old Stonyhurst boys, the nearest thing to an upper crust in Georgetown. We have also been taken up by the public relations officers of the commercial firms. We flit about in private aeroplanes & launches and live in luxurious guest houses but I am awfully bored at seeing welfare activities. It is like being Princess Margaret. This week we have been for two nights up the Demerara to a Canadian company who mine bauxite in a most efficient way. They have a new engine they are very proud of. It digs 1000 tons of sand an hour. It cost £850,000 and takes seven men only to work it.

After that we went to New Amsterdam & saw sugar & rice plantations. Meg has collapsed at so much movement and I have ordered her to bed for 24 hours.

We have had tea with Dr Jagan & his sinister communist adviser and we drank a lot of rum with Mr D'Aguiar the leader of the minute conservative party.

There is an amusing but interminable law action about a disputed parliamentary election in a constituency consisting of illiterate Amerindians – as the Indian aborigines are now called. The succesful candidate – ½ Amerindian – is accused of saying that if his rival was elected black men would come up from the coast and eat all the Amerindian babies.

I am very well. Meg is exhausted. Her chief interest is sun tan – most unbecoming to her. . . .

All love
E

[1] With Father Caraman at Farm Street.

TO NANCY MITFORD   Combe Florey House.
7 March 1962

Dearest Nancy

Have you been plastiquée? As a notorious socialist you must be in great danger. They missed Graham Greene by inches and he is much less forthright in his subversive utterances. Do come to England where it is safe.

I have been away for months taking my daughter Margaret in my footsteps in British Guiana. We missed the riots there by several days – also those in Caracas. We also just missed two domestic murders. All very disappointing for Meg. Golly the food was horrible in the Caribbean. Oh the joy of getting on board a French ship. We joined her midway in a cruise which included H. Nicolson & Vita[1], Sillitoe the policeman[2] not the proletarian novelist and a new Jewish chum named Sir Philip Sebag-Montefiore-Magnus-Allcroft[3]. There were also a lot of frogs on board who never stopped shaking hands with one another. H Nicolson is quite senile. He awoke for a few minutes a day to tell very old English stories in French. Lady N. was accompanied by a lady who kept saying: 'Where's Vita?. I *must* get at her hair'. There were also Letty Cotterell[4] in a poor way – diabetic, cataracted eyes & a bit alcoholic – terrible shakes before her third gin – and a lot of noisy elderly English women who talked all the voyage of what tips they should give at the end. But the cooking was splendid. The frogs seem able to unfreeze frozen food so that it still has a taste – fruit & cheese always au point, delicious bread, plenty of caviare. The ship is named *Antilles*, should you ever think of taking a cruise.

Do you remember Patrick Buchan-Hepburn?[5] He is a lord now & lives in unexampled splendour in Trinidad. There is a portrait of him in every room.

I climbed precipices in Guiana & did not die.

Saw Daphne [Fielding] in Lisbon. It is all rot about her leaving. A story put about by Diana who now wants to collect everyone in the smoke of Paddington Station.

Have you read Isherwood's new publication?[6] Awfully clever & amusing. No change at all since his Berlin days. He makes himself out to be very young & rather nasty. Perhaps he is.

A propos of buggery – what about J Sparrow's exposure of Lady Chatterley.[7] It was all new to me tho everyone else says he knew about it all along.

Same subject. Poor Boots can't show his face in White's. Apparently Cecil Beaton was interviewed on the television and the fellow said, 'But have you no *men* friends, Mr Beaton.' 'One. Cyril Connolly.'

Daphne tells me Debo is now installed in White House Washington. You can't approve of that much. Worse than Freud.

Did you ever know an old spinster called Rose Macaulay? It appears she was no spinster but had a lover (hallucination?) and she wrote a lot of disagreeable letters to a protestant clergyman in America. The publishers said did I mind references to myself in them. There were all kinds of strictures on 'Evelyn'. I didn't know her, so I said, yes I minded.[8] I met her at Mrs Fleming's once & thought her sharp but ladylike. Not at all the kind of person to gush to a parson.

I expect you will recognize characters in Isherwood's book. I couldn't.

Is it normal for frogs to shake hands so much or have they picked it up from the Americans? All the sailors, even, shook hands whenever they passed one another on deck.

Love from
Evelyn

[1] Victoria Sackville-West (1892–1962), writer, married Harold Nicolson in 1913. Nicolson noted: 'I talk to Margaret Waugh – a charming girl intelligent and lovely'. 8 February 1962, *Diaries and Letters*, 1968.

[2] Sir Percy Sillitoe (1888–1962). Director general of the Security Services 1946–53.

[3] Sir Philip Magnus-Allcroft (1906–   ). Historian as Philip Magnus.

[4] Lady Lettice Lygon (1906–   ). Married to Sir Richard Cotterell 1930–58.

[5] Lord Hailes (1901–74). Conservative MP, created Baron Hailes 1957, Governor General of West Indies 1957–62.

[6] Christopher Isherwood, *Down There on a Visit*, 1962.

[7] John Sparrow, Warden of All Souls College, Oxford, 1952–77, wrote an article in *Encounter* which showed from internal evidence that Mellors had sodomized Lady Chatterley.

[8] Four references to Waugh remain in *Letters to a Friend*.

To NANCY MITFORD   Combe Florey House.
27 March 1962

Darling Nancy,

I must agree – Pam's party was a disappointment. Not her fault or yours. Partly mine – I had come to London too late or too early. Either one should have a bath & change or rush straight from the station. I had sat 6 hours in White's drinking too much – indeed I was tight. Also I had had a shock there. I can't remember if I told you. I was sitting in the hall at 7 pm being no trouble to anyone, when a man I know by sight but not by name – older than I, the same build, better dressed, commoner –

came up & said : 'Why are you alone?' 'Because no one wants to speak to me'. 'I can tell you exactly why. Because you sit there on your arse looking like a stuck pig'.

That, added to a letter from Clarissa to Ann saying that the Haileses in Trinidad, whom I thought I charmed, found me a frightful bore, and Debo's idea that I am a counter-hon have worked to produce strong Pinfold feelings of persecution.

Why, I wonder, does H. Hamilton suppose I shall not rejoice in your essays? – Pinfold himself. C Sykes lunched with me the day after Pam's fiasco. He has got involved in the idea you first mentioned to me, that I should sing in an operatic version of *Lolita*. Rum.

I got back in time to receive a socialist – Lord Walston – who was conducting an agitation in Taunton. Without his wife he is very jolly.

Cambridge, to purge the shame of Snow-Leavis, are giving Graham Greene a doctorate. Jolly good. When [Ivy] Compton Burnett was proposed for a doctorate at Oxford, the council merely asked : 'What has she given to the building fund?'

Poor Hatty is not fit for employment. The Jesuits in their charity have taken her into Farm Street & allow her to make cocoa for the secretaries. She is 'coming out' in a very modest way. Laura's mother is giving a ball for her at Pixton. I presume you would hate to come?

I think Tony Powell suffers frightfully from all human contact. Violet is no more painful to him than you and I. There is an affinity between him & Henry Yorke which, no doubt, the Cambridge School of Literature will eventually investigate.

I am reading *Middlemarch* for the first time, with enjoyment.

Perhaps I might come to Paris for the week-end of Hatty's ball here.

I say, Michelin guide have, I see, introduced a sign marking restaurants where there is no wireless. I suggested this in a letter to *The Times* five or six years ago. Do you think it conceivable that they ' paid attention? I should be proud and dePinfolded if I thought I had started this great reform.

Love from
Evelyn

To Lady Diana Cooper   Combe Florey House.
30 March 1962

Sweet Pug

Your letters are not as frequent, full & fond as those which Conrad [Russell] sent you. Nevertheless I thank you for your picture post card and rejoice that you are home. Swapping yarns is best done in writing. Who knows who might interrupt us in Paddington – [Alastair] Forbes, the widow Hemingway[1], A. Herbert or worse. I went to London last week & did not enjoy it at all.

. . . Another thing: I went to B. Guiana at the *Daily Mail*'s (generous) expense to write travel articles. I came back to find that the editor had changed. New one said: Why do you want to write about Guiana? Well I had made myself a great nuisance to everyone there & said I was a foreign correspondent and been given private aeroplanes etc. to get about and had interviews with politicians of all colours. Now *Daily Mail* says: 'write us instead some hard-hitting articles about modern social usage'. What does a man of honour do? Repay £2,000 already spent (tax free)? The truth is never never to have any truck with popular press. Too late to learn. I am caught every time. Damn. So you see my pecker is down too. Sorry about your pecker all the same.[2]...

All love & xxxxx
Bo

[1] Martha Gellhorn.

[2] He had received a reassuring telegram from the *Daily Mail* beginning 'Desolate my silence has been misunderstood'. An article, 'Here they are, the English Lotus Eaters', appeared on 20 March.

To A.D.PETERS   Combe Florey House.
4 April 1962

Dear Pete
    I am afraid I am being a great bore about the *Daily Mail* & British Guiana. Please forgive me.
    Today I got (with difficulty) their galley-proof of the article I wrote for them. They have cut it down to insignificance, removing almost every personal note. It was not a very good article before. Now it is contemptible & calculated to injure my reputation.
    I have sent them a long 'hard-hitting' article on modern etiquette.[1] Goodness knows what they will do with that, & I don't greatly care. But Guiana is different. I spent weeks there ostensibly as their correspondent, accepting hospitality & privileges in that capacity. I can quite understand that they don't think it hot news. But I owe an obligation to the unhappy Guianese. Do you think it is still possible to get back from the *Mail* all I have written about Guiana, and to get a respectable paper e.g. *Telegraph, Sunday Times* to take a long article *Portrait of a Distressed Dependency. Mail*, for a consideration to surrender all rights on my voyage?

Yours ever
Evelyn

[1] 'Manners and Morals', 12 and 13 April. 'Return to Eldorado' appeared in the *Sunday Times* magazine in August.

To NANCY MITFORD   Combe Florey House.
April 1962

Darling Nancy
    My writing again. How you will groan. It comes from our frustrated meeting. No need to answer. But I must explain about boring the Haileses because it has been

what young people call 'traumatic'. Hailes was a pretty young politician you may
have known as Patrick Buchan-Hepburn. I knew him slightly years ago. He is now
Governor General of the now defunct Federation of the West Indies. I had never
met his wife but took a liking to her, and they were jolly hospitable to Meg & me.
The crucial point is that I was confident they both enjoyed my visit. It made a lovely
change, I thought, from most of their official visitors. When I briefly returned to
Trinidad they sent ADCs to drag me back. I talked loud & long & they laughed like
anything. Now I find I bored them. Well of course everyone is a bore to someone.
One recognizes that. But it is a ghastly thing if one loses the consciousness of being a
bore. You do see it means I can never go out again.

Same in a lesser degree with Debo but I knew I was being a bore there because she
turned on the television at dinner. It is not knowing that is fatal. 'Your best friends
will not tell you' like those American advertisements.

Don't please strain your poor eyes & waste your valuable time in answering.

Love
E

I have written an article to say it is absolutely unforgivable to arrive at dinner drunk.
Middlemarch wasn't any good really.

To Brian Franks   Combe Florey House.
[June? 1962]

Dear Brian

I am most interested in M. Harben's[1] letter. I would answer him direct if I was
sure of my facts. A. Bennett's omelette was certainly flat & dry; of that I am
confident. I can't remember if there was another ingredient besides eggs & haddock.
I seem to remember something red – tomato or paprika perhaps, – but the dominant
flavour was haddock.

That, with a delicious soup called Tasse du Prince de Galle – turtle & egg with a
cheese pastry – was Λ. Bennett's after theatre supper at the Savoy Grill, on the left
near the door, circa 1927.

I celebrated my bunk from Crete – 21st anniversary – without pomp.

Yours ever
Evelyn

Mme de Caraman Chimay said to me: 'je trouve que vous n'êtes pas du tout
mondain'. I consulted a scholar as to her meaning. 'Just that you aren't a gentleman
old boy'.

[1] Probably Philip Harben, the television cook.

To Ann Fleming
Combe Florey House.
16 June 1962

Dear Ann

You must have forgotten me entirely if you think that I need warning against the horrors of speed-boats on the lagoon. The people who like such things should be confined to the ghastly Excelsior and never allowed on the main islands. The only way to appreciate Venice is on foot.

Window cleaners at work keep popping their faces up in the most disconcerting manner.

An American general – unknown & unintroduced – wrote & asked if I would write a preface to his philosophic reflections. I answered that I was too expensive for him but that (wishing to do a good turn to a distressed friend of yours) I could recommend a sound, cheap writer named Quennell. He cabled 2000 dollars by return so now I suppose I must write it. [1]

The mounting horror of my mother-in-law's ball shows no abatement. Laura & her sisters spend all day juggling with house parties. Now they are consumed by a passion for aspic and comb the slaughter houses for veal bones.

God, there's that window cleaner again.

Why did you stay at ugly Bauer? [2] The proximity to the Moser[?], I suppose, and its good concierge.

I was very sorry to see that turn-coat Aidan [3] got elected to parliament. It shows there is no justice in this world & that one must look to a life beyond the grave to regulate the accounts.

New Nabokov [4] a stunt – but a clever one. New Tony Powell [5] very good. J. Sparrow's reply to his critics re *Chatterley* wipes the floor with them.

I shall never go to London again except to take the train to Dover or Southampton. Local barber is good enough for my old grey nut.

I look for the announcement of Fionn's delivery [6] with affectionate anxiety.

Yours ever
E. Waugh

[1] T.A.McInerny, *The Private Man*, New York 1962.
[2] Hotel Bauer Grunwald in Venice.
[3] Aidan Crawley, formerly a Labour MP, had been elected as a Conservative.
[4] *Pale Fire*.
[5] *The Kindly Ones*.
[6] Fionn Morgan's daughter Mary was not born until October.

To Nancy Mitford
Combe Florey House.
4 July 1962

Dearest Nancy

I was titillated by your publisher's appeal for identification of the water beetle rhyme. I had never heard and when you said you were to call your collected pensées 'water beetle' I did not see the point. Now all is plain. An excellent, disarming title making everything easy for reviewers. How I look forward to the book. I hope you have expunged all the profanity that sometimes taints your occasional papers.

I think you find an unwholesome pleasure in observing the decay of English decorum. How about this. Ten days ago Pam Berry asked me to stay for the night. I found her in an ugly mood railing against all her social superiors. To stop the flow of vilification I led her to politics, said I thought U Thant an enemy and added: 'The government must be pretty hard up to get people to meet him. They even asked Laura and me'.

... My summer has been much disturbed by Harriet's 'coming out'. My mother in law who never gave a ball for Laura or her sister decided she must give a ball for Harriet, here in Somerset. Our lives have been made hideous plotting house-parties. All the young scrupulously and often superfluously write to thank for parties. They can't bring themselves to answer invitations. My mother in law insisted on matriarchal style. No caterers. All our kitchens have been filled with veal bones stewing to make aspic; all our poultry were slaughtered. Unlike Uncle Matthew's aged peers, our 'young men' were all 30 year old alcoholics. It was from this ball that I imprudently fled to Pam.

After Pam I went to Penelope Betjeman. Now there is a jewel for you. Mad as a hatter and overflowing with pure kindness. All the time I was with her she never said one disagreeable word about anyone. A most cleansing experience after Pam's unending gush of denigration, detraction and calumny.

Hatty is pretty from the crown of her head to her collar-bone – hideous below and half baked in mind. But she seems to be enjoying her season. Do you go to Venice this summer. Diana has been lent a little house and has engaged a pansy attendant but isn't looking forward to it. Do cherish her. She is not happy.

Reading the Wilde letters.[1] The saddest thing is his euphoria in the first few days after leaving prison, all turning to dust immediately. The reviewers complain there are too many pleas for money, but the poor beast was penniless.

I toil away at autobiography. What a dull life I seem to have had.

Love from
Evelyn

[1] *Letters of Oscar Wilde*, edited by Rupert Hart-Davis, 1962.

To ANTHONY CURTIS[1]   Combe Florey House.
4 July 1962
Postcard

I am sorry to say that your kind invitation to review *The New Rhythm*[2] reaches me 30 years late. In youth I was fascinated by Firbank. Now I can't abide him.

E.W.

[1] Literary editor of the *Sunday Telegraph*.
[2] Ronald Firbank, *The New Rythum and other Pieces*, 1962.

To Nancy Mitford   Combe Florey House.
[July 1962]
Postcard

Why not adapt it, saying 'after Belloc', to:
　'Titillates the human race (or British race)'
　'By gliding on the water's face'
　'Assigning each to each his place'?
or　'Incorrigibly out of place'?
or　'Contemptuous of power and grace'?
or　'A bit of arsenic and old lace'?
or　'Superior to time's dull pace?'[1]
　Or something like that which you can easily better.

                                                              E

[1] Nancy Mitford did adapt Belloc's *The Moral Alphabet* so that the poem that precedes and gives its
name to her collection of essays *The Water Beetle* (1962) runs:
　'The water beetle here shall teach
　A lesson far beyond your reach.
　She aggravates the human race
　By gliding on the water's face
　Assigning each to each its place.
　But if she ever stopped to think
　Of how she did it, she would sink.
　　　　　Moral
　Don't ask questions.'
The changes are in the direction of modesty. 'Lesson' replaces 'sermon', 'aggravates' is for 'flabbergasts'
and Waugh's third suggestion is adopted instead of 'With ease, celerity and grace'.

To Daphne Fielding   Combe Florey House.
30 July [1962]

Darling Daphne,
　It has always seemed to me as unnatural for two people to write a book together as
for three people to have a baby. I am very sorry to hear that your collaborator has
lost his reason. Can't you get him put away and carry on alone?[1]
　Of course use anything you want from *Vile Bodies*. The difficulty of further
contributions is that I really put all I knew about her into that sketch. I was never
allowed back. The last time I set foot in the Cavendish was after dinner before
Henry Yorke's wedding. We all went on to the Cavendish. Rosa[2] was having some
trouble at the time over a cheque with a man called Lulu Water-Welch (not of our
party). She fixed me with fierce eyes and said: 'Lulu Waters-Waugh take your arse
off my chair' and waved L.W.W.'s stumer. I was never a real habitué. Most of my
knowledge was second-hand from Teddy St. Aubyn[3] and Alastair Graham.
Alastair, as I told you, would be a most valuable source. He has become a recluse in
Wales. I haven't seen him for 25 years. My closest chum once.

As you know Rosa had no liking for writers. Thornton Wilder once had one of the flats at the back; as also did Aldous Huxley, Cyril Connolly and his first wife stayed there but, I think, got persecution mania. There is some unhappy memory there that Cyril is loath to speak of. You might be able to coax it out. I think Cyril used to mind not looking exactly like a cornet of the Blues (and, as you know, c of Bs were what Rosa really accepted). Apart from those three, I can't think of any writers who went there much. Not, as you might have expected, Maurice Baring unless 1914–18. My awful brother in law, about whom Xan spoke so kindly; lived at the Cavendish in 1945 and kept in close touch. Have you tried Raymond de Trafford? I don't know how far gone he is, but if his memory is at all intact he should be useful.

Shane Leslie's[4] memory is *not* to be trusted.

I blush to say it, but I think it was after *Vile Bodies* that writers started to try to get into the Cavendish. They were driven out at once unless they were Americans. I don't remember ever seeing a foreigner of any other nationality there, tho I believe Auberon [Herbert] introduced some Poles.

All the articles I saw when the Cavendish closed were very skimpy.

I should awfully like to visit you at Brighton, but I don't think I can really contribute much to your work.

If Elizabeth Eliot is the one I suppose, she is pock-marked like a Turk.

There was an elderly woman circa 1926 called Lady Cook who used to be a crony of Rosa's. 'Now don't you go out after those street women. Why don't you have Lady Cook here?' My peerage is antiquated. She seems to have been alive in 1947 at Villa des Pyrénées, Pau but I daresay she is a gonner now.

Rupert Bellville[5] died last week. There arent many of her middle-period set and, of course, none of her first. Has Martin Wilson any Ribblesdale relics that wld be relevant? Alfred Duggan (Hubert's reformed brother) Old Court House, Ross on Wye might have memories.

I fear I haven't been much help.

Love and xxxx
Evelyn

[1] Daphne Fielding was writing *The Duchess of Jermyn Street*. Her collaborator George Kinnaird was getting divorced from Lady Elizabeth Eliot and withdrew.

[2] Rosa Lewis (1867–1952). She ran the Cavendish Hotel in Jermyn Street, and had not been pleased by Waugh's version of it and her in *Vile Bodies*.

[3] Edward St Aubyn (1880–1960).

[4] Sir Shane Leslie (1885–1971). Anglo-Irish poet and author.

[5] Rupert Belleville (1905–62). Flew to Russia with Venetia Montagu before the war. Best backgammon player in White's. Imprisoned by the Left in the Spanish Civil War.

To DAPHNE FIELDING   Combe Florey House.
10 August 1962
Postcard

P.S. Rosa often called the penis 'the WINKLE', a term I have not heard on other lips.

When chaps refused to avail themselves of Lady Cook and sought pleasure outside, Rosa pounced on them on their return and said:'I'll get a doctor in to look at your winkle.'

I imagine Lady Cook's visits were intermittent. The period when I remember her in attendance was 1925.

She can't be alive, can she?

To LADY DIANA COOPER   Combe Florey House.
16 August [1962]

Darling Lady Ismay[1],

You are in Venice & I don't know where. I hope someone will forward this letter for it is the announcement of our Meg's engagement. She has fallen head over heels for an Irishman, 27 years old, short, rather oriental in face, raffish, penniless, a stock-broker's clerk of ten days' experience, but a gentleman and a Catholic – name Giles FitzHerbert[2]. I have not the heart to keep them apart. They will soon be spliced. I told Meg I consented to a marriage not to a wedding. She said: 'But I must have Lady Diana there.' FitzHerbert, before meeting me to ask for her hand *bought* Baby's book to see how Duff tackled the Duke of Rutland and was greatly discouraged.[3] You should find these two episodes sympathetic. Meg is bird happy about her affair. Let her enjoy it quick before the Light of Common Day.

Who should turn up to breakfast on Monday but Bloggs [Baldwin]. Said he and Elspeth had been 'bickering' & he needed male company. Stayed an hour. Then off with Elspeth to Amsterdam. Stone deaf.

Venice means so many things to you. To me it means you and Hubert & Maimie and Sykes branding the yankee[4] and Rosse deafening Tug boat Annie[5] and James marooning Tilly[6] . . . – how long ago? Twenty years?

All love
E

No damn it nearer 30

[1] Lord Ismay, like Lady Diana, was nicknamed Pug.
[2] Giles FitzHerbert (1935–   ). In 1966 he joined the Foreign Office.
[3] There were two interviews between Duff Cooper and his future father-in-law. At the first the Duke was exquisitely polite, but forbade the match. Before the second he gave his consent to Lady Diana, adding: 'Don't go upstairs for a little. I don't want your mother to think I gave in at once.' Then he talked to Duff Cooper for ten minutes about money and for ten minutes about the growth of Bolshevism and the future of the Territorials. Recorded by Lady Diana in *The Light of Common Day*.
[4] Sir Richard Sykes (1905–78). He had stubbed out a cigarette on the hand of the tobacco heiress Doris Duke. She screamed. Public sympathy was with her and Sykes was attacked. Lady Diana's birthday party was spoiled. When he sent long-stemmed tuberoses in apology they were returned.
[5] The Countess of Rosse (then Anne Messel) stepped innocently on to a balcony with another man. Though they were not yet married, the jealous Earl of Rosse boxed her ears with some violence. When he sent long-stemmed tuberoses in apology they too were returned.
[6] Edward James, patron of the arts, and Tilly Losch, the dancer, who were married 1931–4.

To Nancy Mitford   Combe Florey House.
[Received 22 August 1962]

Dearest Nancy,

I am excited to read that next Sunday we shall have a sample of your reminiscences. A very nice change from Cyril's grand tour which fizzled out in Sicily – I daresay through bad editing. The *Sunday Times* is ruining itself with Lord Snowdon's blindingly ugly & banal coloured supplement.

Aggravate – of course *you* can use it to mean what nanny meant, but Belloc would not have done so and if it is meant as an adaptation of him it rings false. Never mind. I am just a retired schoolmaster. Fewer than a thousand readers will notice and of them most will be pleased because it will give them a momentary sense of superiority.

I write to give you news more important to me than to you. You remember my daughter Margaret to whom you showed such kindness in Paris? Well, she has fallen head over heels in love and I can't find it in my heart to forbid consummation. 'Young love satisfied' was what Belloc put beside 'broad lands to leave' as the desiderata of a happy life. There are no broad lands to leave. He is a penniless Irish stock broker's clerk named FitzHerbert of good family but rather caddish & raffish appearance. 27 years old and has not done a hands turn – his stock-broker's clerkship began on the day of his engagement. A Catholic of not very pious disposition, father killed honourably in the war, a brother I haven't been allowed to see, whom I suspect is a skeleton in cupboard (as is mine, and also Laura's for that matter). She had a number of suitors of the kind an old fashioned father would have preferred, but she must have FitzHerbert, & so she shall. She wants children & that is a thing I can't decently provide for her. I expect that in ten years time she will be back on my doorstep with a brood.

Bloggs Baldwin says he never met you. Rum. He came here the other day & my son, James, said: 'At last I have met a P. G. Wodehouse character in the flesh.'

I am told that this Common Market will make good French wine prohibitively expensive here. As you know we can buy it in London much cheaper than in Paris. The cellar, whose poverty you remarked, is being rapidly filled in panic.

Love from
Evelyn

To Nancy Mitford   Combe Florey House.
[Received 28 August 1962]

Darling Nancy,

The Oxford Dictionary was not planned like the French to exclude misuses of words and establish what is correct. Its readers hunt for misuses & proudly display them. Your 'aggravate' is 7th of the meanings & and the authorities are negligible except when it is used conversationally in fiction by people of low education. Fowler: 'Aggravate, aggravation – The use of these in the sense *annoy, vex, annoyance, vexation* should be left to the uneducated. It is for the most part a feminine or childish colloquialism, but intrudes occasionally into the newspapers.'

Warn Decca before she goes all out in mocking the Americans that almost all the features of their funerals that strike us as gruesome can be traced to papal, royal & noble rites of the last five centuries.[1] What is unique & deplorable would probably not strike her – the theological vaccuum, the assumption that the purpose of a funeral service is to console the bereaved not to pray for the soul of the dead.

Years ago, I vaguely remember, there was a vogue for yankee undertakers journals among Gerald Berners, G. Wellesley[2], Malcolm Bullock & Co. A fellow socialist of hers called Cedric Belfrage[3] wrote a book about undertakers in U.S.A. Not very good.

When her book is published I shall get all her press cuttings – bother.

You may congratulate me on my great beauty of character in surrendering my daughter to Fitz Giles – not on the acquisition of him as a son-in-law. On no account send a present.

I look forward to a time when wedding celebrations will be outré as funeral celebrations now are.

Dr Eaton of Forest Lawn (the 'Dreamer' not 'Joyboy') wrote to me about a year ago asking me to sign a document disclaiming any intention of mocking him. Of course I refused and have heard no more. But I think Decca should take advice from lawyers before publishing. Please tell her I did not believe her story that an English naval officer attempted to shanghai her from Spain giving his word of honour for her safe return.[4]

Love from
Evelyn

[1] Jessica Mitford was researching *The American Way of Death*.
[2] The Duke of Wellington (1885–1972).
[3] Author of *The Frightened Giant*, 1957, and *My Unfinished Affair with America*, 1961. It was alleged in 1954 that he had been a communist in 1937–8.
[4] An exaggeration of the story in *Hons and Rebels*.

TO LADY DIANA COOPER   Combe Florey House.
28 August [1962]

Darling Stitch Pug Baby,

Your letter full of understanding. It is, to me, a bitter pill and ungilded. I would forbid the marriage if I had any other cause than jealousy & snobbery. As it is, I pretend to be complaisant. Little Meg is ripe for the kind of love I can't give her. So I am surrendering with the honours of war – without war indeed. The wedding will be at the end of October. I think in London. They will make all arrangements. I have given them a meagre sum of money & said spend it on trousseau or linen or festifications with bad champagne & photographers, just as you please. I will, of course, go to the church – not, I think, to any subsequent party. I haven't met FitzHerbert's widowed ma.

Your Venice sounds sad. What does 'two Freuds'[1] mean? One is ghastly. I thought his pretty wife escaped to America.

... Winter plans? Any? Shall we sail to Madagascar with Mrs Rodd & Raymond Mortimer? I don't care about sun. Just to escape Christmas.

Do you remember books I wrote about a character called 'Basil Seal' – a mixture of Basil Murray & Peter Rodd. I suddenly yesterday began a story about Basil Seal at 60. Jolly good so far.[2]

How long since you read Max Beerbohm's essay on Venice. His best. And, did you know?, commissioned by Northcliffe for *Daily Mail*. Rum.

You see I feel that with Meg I have exhausted my capacity for finding objects of love. How does one exist without them? I haven't got the Gaiety euphoria that makes old men chase tarts. My ghastly brother calls them 'pipe lines' through which he is refuelled with youth. Not for me. Did I tell you my brother has written an autobiography in which he says: 'Venus has been kind to me'?

Meg and FitzHerbert have found a lodging in Westbourne Grove, not very far from the canal zone. I suspect him of being a crook but I cannot doubt the sincerity of his love for Meg – nothing to be got from her or me. When I said 'gentleman', I meant of respectable ancestry. He has rather a common way with him.

Please tell me about week-end of 15th Sept. Oysters & grouse. We might have fun of a subdued sort.

Last time we met – at least not last time, that was when the spectre Auberon buggered everything – we talked of books in which you appeared as character. I forgot one by a man who was shot in Mexico – can't remember his name. Title something like 'Way of Contrition – Revelation?' Does that suggest anything.

Pray for me at the tombs of St Mark and Giustiniani.

All love
Bo

[1] The first was Lucian Freud whose wife Caroline had married Israel Citkovitz in New York in 1959; the second was his brother Clement Freud (1924–   ), Liberal MP 1973–   , writer, broadcaster and caterer.

[2] *Basil Seal Rides Again or The Rake's Progress*, 1963.

To Randolph Churchill   Combe Florey House.
18 September 1962

Dear Randolph,

I have lately visited London where I was told that you are speculating in the book market and that your wish to obtain 'association copies'[1] is commercial rather than sentimental.

If this is so, you must observe the customs of the trade and enclose stamps for the return of volumes which you send soliciting autographs.

Yours ever
Evelyn

[1] Churchill had asked for a signed copy of *Scoop* and mentioned that he had not got a *Rossetti*.

TO RANDOLPH CHURCHILL   Combe Florey House.
20 September 1962
Postcard

Your bibliomaniac ghost has overreached itself.[1] You were given *Brideshead Revisited* and *The Ordeal of Gilbert Pinfold* in the hand-made paper editions. I have your letter of 21st July 1957 acknowledging receipt of the latter.

[1] The 'ghost' was Churchill's secretary, whom Waugh pretended to believe to be the author of Churchill's books.
[2] Churchill had sent five of Waugh's books to be signed on 18 September. Next day he received Waugh's letter of the eighteenth and wrote protesting that he wanted a complete set for sentimental reasons only. On 23 September he wrote explaining that he wanted both first and limited editions, so could he have *Brideshead* in the latter and *Pinfold* in the former?

TO ANN FLEMING   Combe Florey House.
11 October 1962

Dear Ann
    ... Yesterday was a very proud day for me – at last after quarter of a century's waiting I appeared in *The Times* Crossword.[1] Better than a doctorate at Reading, an MBE or a concert in Festival Hall.

Yours ever affec.
E.W.

[1] The clue was 'Place revisited in literature (9)'. Waugh had written to Penelope Betjeman in 1939: 'J [John] was mentioned in *Times* light leader today. Gratters. X-word next, then Tussaud.'

TO NANCY MITFORD   Combe Florey House
27 October [1962]   Combe Florey
                                      Nr Taunton

Darling Nancy
    'Flayed' indeed! I annointed your carapace with spikenard.[1] There were no mistakes of syntax in *Beetle*. I was enumerating your general excellencies & defects.

It was what a publisher calls a 'good selling notice'. Not so Comrade Laski's.[2]

If you had had a Christian upbringing you would know that suicide is very wicked. Scott & Co may have been tempted to this sin but they resisted. Oates just went for a walk in the snow. There was a very high probability that he would not come back but that is not the same as taking poison or shooting oneself the nature of which acts is lethal. There is nothing lethal in the nature of going for a walk any more, say, than in swimming among sharks or crocodiles. By the way, was his body found? I have always thought Scott may have eaten him as the Italians ate Amundsen.

The [Second Vatican] Council is of the highest importance. As in 1869–70 the French & Germans are full of mischief but, as then, the truth of God will prevail. The spirit of that wicked Père Couturier still lives on in France & must be destroyed. I hope your hostess and her Curé agree.

The redundant Combe Florey is for the benefit of motorists not postmen. It tells them to look for an outlying hamlet not for a town house. New York is a huge state extending to the Canadian border.

My daughter, Margaret, was married in a tea gown of her great-grandmother's out of the acting cupboard, used in countless charades, and looked very pretty. High lace collar. All male guests (except one)[3] looked absolutely horrible. They had hired tail coats but neglected to provide themselves with starched collars.

Daphne Weymouth [Fielding] has suddenly become a very old woman with long white hair.

The wedding was a ghastly expense. I wish I were richer.

Did I tell you how poor Boots got on the wrong table at Mrs Fleming's party & was given no caviar & was still in tears the next day? Boots is up to something rather fishy in collecting letters, I think for sale in America. Be wary. There is a nice nest egg for us all in our senility in our correspondence. American Universities are buying them at extravagant prices.

My daughter saw a book on furniture in which a circular pedestal table was described as a 'loo table'. 'What big lavatories they must have had'.

Fondest love
E

[1] Nancy Mitford replied: 'Of course I was delighted with the "spikenard". Only teasing.'

[2] Marghanita Laski had written in the *New Statesman:* 'What we get here [in *The Water Beetle*] is mostly not caprice but its shabby relative, impudence.'

[3] Lord Reay (1937–   ).

To Nancy Mitford   Combe Florey House.
[December? 1962]

Darling Nancy

Oh dear alas no I can't be in London now. Damn.

I suppose you will go to the Cooper Memorial celebrations. Monty![1]

I enjoyed *Pale Fire* awfully & thought the poem no parody or pastiche but a jolly good composition in its own right. *Much* better than *Lolita*. But a show-off. Too clever by half. But a pleasure.

Now Madagascar's off where will you be Jan–Feb? I have no plans, don't particularly want sun, just change. India? Must see it quick before the Chinks take over.

Can it be true that ladies of fashion now wear tweed skirts at night?

Was Miss —— the American journalist who made advances to my daughter, Margaret? I greatly enjoyed funeral story. Don't know 'Frauders'.

Much love
Evelyn

[1] Field Marshal Viscount Montgomery presented the Duff Cooper Memorial Prize to Michael Howard for *The Franco-Prussian War*.

To Terence Kilmartin   Combe Florey House.
Postcard

Thank you for *Private Eye on London*. It exposes me as a hopeless old fogy. Not one of the objects of its jokes was known to me & the drawings seemed incompetent scrawls. So it is no good my trying to review it.

Try my son A.A.Waugh of 44 Chester Row, s.w.1. He is in touch with modern London.

E.W.

To Ann Fleming   Combe Florey House.
3 January 1963

Dear Ann

I am deeply sorry to hear of your sister's distressing death.[1] You must pray for her soul. This is best done by going to a chapel where the Blessed Sacrament is reserved. The most convenient for you is Westminster Cathedral; go up the far left aisle under the screen. Kneel. Dispel from your mind all other considerations. Say, not out loud but in your mind: 'I have no right to ask you anything. Please don't consider my merits or my sister's. You made her and me what we are. But you sent Jesus to die for us. Accept his sacrifice. With luck I have a few years left to me to make amends. She hasn't. So please accept anything good I have ever done as a negligible contribution to the immeasurable sacrifice of the incarnation, and let my sister into heaven.' Easy? Yes, really, particularly for you who have no pride. Try it anyway.

I will proudly dedicate my little story to you. Thank you for allowing it. Would you like your full name on the page or just 'A.F.'?[2]

We are almost totally cut-off. Only H.M. mails plod through. I cleverly ordered a regular supply of tasty little pies from Fortnum & Mason during Meg's caviar season. These arrive stale but regularly, so I am not hungry. The rest of the family live on tinned beans.

I don't suppose you remember this house. The back part is a glass roofed courtyard. This is now quite dark with accumulated snow. Local wiseacres say that when the snow falls off the roof the whole glass house will collapse. It holds a hogshead of Burgundy (French not Portuguese) waiting to be bottled. Disaster is certain. . . .

Yours ever affec.
Evelyn

[1] Mary-Rose Charteris (1919–62). She married in 1940 Roderick Thesiger and in 1949 Francis Egerton Grey.

[2] *Basil Seal Rides Again* is prefaced with an explanatory note in the form of a letter to 'Mrs Ian Fleming', beginning:

'Dear Ann

In this senile attempt to recapture the manner of my youth I have resurrected characters from earlier stories which, if you ever read them, you will have forgotten.'

To Alec Waugh
16 January 1963

Combe Florey House.

My Dear Alex

I have sad news to give you of our uncle, George, & aunt Emmie.[1] We received a message from one of their neighbours during the recent (and present) frosts to say that they were in a grave condition. Yesterday Laura was able to get through the snow to Keinton Mandeville & found things far worse than was expected. George is senile, paralysed, bed-ridden & incontinent (I speak of excretions, not sexually). Emma is senile but still mobile. They live in the utmost squalour. A few neighbours have taken pity on them from time to time but they, reasonably, are unwilling to take permanent charge.

George is unable to express an opinion but certain animal sounds are interpreted by Emmie as meaning a reluctance to move. Emma has so exhausted herself with caring for him as to be almost incapable of forming or expressing an opinion. All that is clear is that she will not be parted from George.

I have found a nursing-home which is willing to take them in temporarily, during my absence abroad. If they can be induced to move I will tell you the address. George may die any minute or live for some years. He cannot live without constant attention.

I will send you further particulars as soon as I know them. This is merely a warning that devoted & expensive attention will be required of both of us shortly.

Yours ever affec.
Evelyn

[1] George and Emma Raban were half-brother and half-sister to Catherine Waugh.

To Nancy Mitford   Hotel Royal Westminster,
2 February 1963   Menton A.M.

Darling Nancy,

'Damn' you will say, or in your cosmopolitan way: 'Merde. *He's* writing again. The man who bored the Haileses out of Trinidad'.

But it's all right. This doesn't need an answer. I write from the extremity of loneliness which will be relieved by the time you get this by Laura's return. I have spoken to no one since she went to Naples.

I was never much of a one for parlez-vousing, as you know, but 30 years ago I could often catch on to what the frogs said and even make a few intelligible noises myself. Now I might be among Chinese. Words fail me more & more. I find it with English too – a shrinking vocabulary.

About Quennell's bun shop. We must remember Q is aging. It is alarmingly possible that he has got in an apprentice baker who is taking a nibble. Quennell I am sure would not pick at a currant. When I get back to England I will make discreet enquiries. The awful thing is that I am totally dependent on him both for bread & cakes.

Did you know that the frog priests who have taken to trousers call them their 'clergymans'?

This is a *very* nice hotel but I am dying of boredom and infertility. I went to the cinema & understood what you meant by 'sitting in a box like an old pew'. I read it as 'jew' & was puzzled. I couldn't understand a word of the film, named *Ophelia*[1]. The heroine was hideous.

My treat today is to visit the Salle des Mariages in the town hall decorated by Cocteau.

One can never get a chair in the casino. I like to sit down & play away for hours for minimum stakes. I hate having to shout to the croupiers over rows of old women.

DONT ANSWER

Lots of love
E

[1] By Claude Chabrol, 1962.

To Nancy Mitford   Combe Florey House.
9 [19?] February 1963

Darling

Your tomb. You can get a slap up angel for £4000 – do you really mean that sum or was it a slip of the pen for N.F.? But where will you set it up? Protestant parsons are tigers in this one matter in which they retain authority. Lately a poor widow put 'for ever in my thoughts' on her husband's grave & was made to remove it. The

Church of England does not believe in angels any more. I presume you want to be planted at Swinbrook[1]. Unless the parson there is exceptionally venal & snobbish you haven't a chance of an angel. Also the French customs are very strict about exporting corpses. Your best plan would be to die in Genoa – very comfortable hotel called, I think, Columbus – where every licence is given to sculpture. Or you could buy a plot at Brookwood – near the foot guards but not really very nice.

I am engaged at the moment in trying to get permission to build a 12 bedder vault here. Bishop of Bath & Wells not forthcoming at all. Perhaps Mrs Hamish Hamilton could get you into a Jewish sanctuary – they believe in angels. So do Mohamedans but they aren't allowed to make statues of them.

There is a very nice cemetery at Mentone full of the English who were sent there to die of consumption. I cheered up a lot there after Laura joined me. There was a lovely bus full of Lolitas which collected them from school at 11.30 and eventually went, shedding them alas, to Monte Carlo.

My life here is embittered by the presence of a senile aunt. She described a friend as 'rather poorly with cancer'. The Pope is said to be in that condition too. I have just written his obituary for the Yanks.[2]

I saw Peters in London. He shone with simple honesty. But there is some delay in getting money from America. I wonder if his Yank agent is as honourable as he.

Love
E

[1] Nancy Mitford is buried in the churchyard at Swinbrook in Oxfordshire, near the house built by her father in 1927.

[2] 'An appreciation of Pope John', *Saturday Evening Post*, 27 July 1963.

To Ann Fleming   Combe Florey House.
20 February 1963

Dear Ann
Just home, to find your letter of 22nd January. I am writing to Goldeneye in the hope that you are still there, tho I do not at all envy you the tropic sun or the local society.

When I read of [Hugh] Gaitskell's death I thought sadly of your loss of a cherished friend. That, coming so soon on your sister's, must have brought death very close. I always feel the breath on my neck. You don't normally, I think; you will lose someone you love every year now for the rest of your life. It is a condition one has to accept & prepare for.

Mentone was very agreeable. I went there to work but did not write a single word. Instead I read pre 1914 English best-sellers in the hotel library. I was awfully bored for ten days while Laura was visiting the D'Armses in Naples. When she rejoined me I got quite jolly. We went to rich meals at Vence & Monte Carlo & very simple ones in local fish restaurants. There is a Casino at Mentone with very low stakes & continual quarrels. Every turn of the wheel produced an altercation. Spender-like Italian youths come on motor bicycles & snatch the winnings of bemused English widows & the croupiers make no attempt to maintain order or justice.

The French do not drink paraldehyde. I spent a lot of time crawling from chemist to chemist explaining that I was held up by snow & had my doctor's prescriptions in England 'Vous savez que je suis habitué a quelquechose assez forte'. It always worked & I have returned with a large & varied collection of narcotics. I put them in aspirin bottles.in case the customs noticed so there is likely to be a death here soon of the next person who has a headache & looks in my room for a remedy. . . .

> Yours ever affec.
> Evelyn

To Ann Fleming   Combe Florey House.
13 March [1963]

My Dear Ann

It is not true that I come to London weekly. Were it so, you would be constantly plagued by invitations to marble halls. I don't know what can have put this into the von Hofmanstahls heads but I was tight when I last saw them & may have told them anything.

Jack Donaldson is correct in saying that if you & any of your friends get to heaven you will rejoice individually in one anothers company but he is pulling your leg if he suggests a continuation of common pleasures. Only the Mohamedans expect fucking in heaven. As for jokes, you may remember that it was one of Ronald Knox's problems (a) all humour springs from imperfection (b) how can we conceive of Thomas More & Philip Neri devoid of humour? What is certain is that we should be jolly different, beatified and perfect & united in the love of God & one another; each retaining individuality; not like Buddhists mingled into an eternal, undifferentiated unity. But no one knows or can imagine what our condition will be. Jack will go to heaven, I think. It is hard to conceive of a beatified & perfected Randolph who was recognizable at all.

I hope your 'flu' has passed.

Mary Herbert says that it was impossible that your grandmother ever feared divorce.[1] Why don't you put the horse whip into the hand of that tipsy buffoon don who married Mary Strickland's girl? Carr? Ker? Kerr?[2]

The young FitzHerberts are back at 15 Westbourne Terrace. He is making a slow recovery from jaundice. She is out of work but busy buying bric-a-brac instead of furniture.

Oakeshott aspires to commit hypergamy.

Please don't ask me to O'Neill's wedding. I can't afford a present. Will Quennell be best man in his blue shirt?

Greatly enjoying *Rosebery*.[3]

Nancy Rodd has left £4,000 in her will to purchase a marble angel for her grave. Very hard to get parsons to put up angels these days. She must go to Genoa to die. I am negotiating for a 12 bedder vault here for all my immediate family.

I read in a newspaper (not *The Times*) that Frank would write the life of Gaitskell[4]. He won't do it well, you know.

Do you think it very plebeian to tuck ones table napkin into ones collar? The Pope does so. So do I often – not in London because in private houses the napkins are either made of loo paper or covered in old lipstick.

Your story wont be out till autumn. I will send you proofs as soon as they are ready. Then you can refuse the dedication if you don't like it. Its final version is slightly better than what the *Telegraph* printed.

Who killed Rodney Berry?[5]

Why is Perry [Brownlow] selling his fine silver?

I am very lame. Carrying too much weight. Can't get down the weight walking because of the lameness. A vicious circle. I think I must go to that place in Surrey. Douglas Woodruff lost 2 stone there. But I don't play cards. What should I do between baths & douches?

I am surprised that old Kaspar thinks James Bond highly sexed. In the film you took me to I saw no evidence of this – rather the reverse. Gaming & homicide seemed his weaknesses.

Fr Caraman is still with us – a gentle, uncomplaining visitor.

> Your affec. coz.
> E.W.

[1] *Arthur James Balfour* by Kenneth Young, published that year, suggested that Viscountess Elcho, later Countess of Wemyss, feared that her husband might bring legal action because of her relationship with Balfour. It is far from certain that they had an affair.

[2] Sara Strickland (1926–) granddaughter of the Countess of Wemyss, married in 1950 Raymond Carr, historian, and Warden of St Antony's College, Oxford since 1968.

[3] Robert Rhodes James, *Rosebery*, 1963.

[4] Lord Longford never considered doing so.

[5] Rodney Berry (1917–63). Director of the Iliffe Press. Died under surgery.

TO LADY ACTON   Combe Florey House.
15 March 1963

Dearest Daphne

I am returning the tract you kindly lent me with some very cross marginalia. I didn't like it at all. Apart from objecting to much of the theme, I thought it common

602 THE LETTERS OF EVELYN WAUGH

& cocksure in expression, sometimes asserting as fact what it had to prove & sometimes lapsing into commonplace.

Some people, like Penelope Betjeman, like making a row in church and I don't see why they shouldn't; just as the Abyssinians dance & wave rattles. I should feel jolly shy dancing & I feel shy praying out loud. Every parish might have one rowdy Mass a Sunday for those who like it. But there should be silent ones for those who like quiet.

The Uniate Churches are highly relevant. They are allowed to keep their ancient habits of devotion and to have a ritual in languages like Syriac, Byzantine Greek, Ghiz, Slavonic which are much deader than Latin. Why should we not have a Uniate Roman Church & let the Germans have their own knockabout performances?

I think it great cheek of the Germans to try & teach the rest of the world anything about religion. They should be in perpetual sackcloth & ashes for all their enormities from Luther to Hitler.

The worst mistake of your Fr Davis is his almost blasphemous degradation of the conception of the Mystical Body into a parish meeting. You & I & the dancing Abyssinians & the saints in glory are, as you well know integral parts of the Mystical Body. We don't have to be shouting one another down in the next pew.

When Fr Davis says that the new, impoverished Holy Week is a good thing because it teaches people the Old Testament, he is raving. There was six times as much Old Testament in the old services than the new.

The word 'vernacular' is almost meaningless. If they intend to have versions of the liturgy in the everyday speech of everyone, they will have to have some hundreds of thousands of versions. In civilized countries Norway has 2 languages, Spain 3, Milanese can't understand Sicilian etc. When you get to Asia & Africa it is Babel. As you know most African languages are quite incapable of conveying theological meanings & some haven't even a word for 'virgin' I am told – simply two words for girls before and after puberty.

I have had a great scolding from Penelope Betjeman about my article.[1] She admits she just wants to make a noise – also to teach half baked children.

Surely it is one of the signs of the Holy Ghost that the half-baked and illiterate do somehow grasp the truths of the Church without understanding the words?

The decision actually taken at the Council, I gather, will be that all the introduction to the canon of the Mass will be in vernacular on days of obligation. They also say that we must have the same version as the Americans, heaven help us.

I shall have to come to M'Bebi to perform my duties in Mashona.

Love from
Evelyn

[1] 'The Same Again Please', *Spectator*, 23 November 1962.

TO ANN FLEMING   Combe Florey House.
28 March 1963

Dear Ann

 ... My Sunday papers said that all England had been agog with rumours that the Minister for War had shot a nigger at Cliveden.[1] No ripple reached us.

I am very glad that O'Neill's father-in-law-to-be[2] believes in evening dress. I have seen O'N after dark in *most* unsuitable costume. You may have noticed that on the rare occasions I dine with you I always dress – precisely like the proverbial Englishman in the jungle.

I have been reading (for my autobiography) my diaries at the age 16–17. I was a ghastly boy.

Bond's passions. I have not studied the texts but you showed me a film and I thought he looked very temperate, despite your interesting enclosure which showed he had impregnated a girl at a great distance. The real satyromaniac doesn't care what women look like – old, young, deformed, all are the same. That wish to be seen about with notably pretty girls suggests Beaton and Kaetchen Kommer. In the film I think he dallied during a sweaty siesta with a half caste and then went off in a boat with a prize cock-drop – a sort of Swedish games-mistress.[3] But I was not very attentive. Anyway there was nothing there to excite Old Kaspar.

                                        Ever your affec. coz.
                                        Evelyn

Is Randolph running a second-hand book-shop? He keeps sending me volumes to sign.

[1] John Profumo, Secretary of State for War, told the House of Commons on 22 March that there had been no impropriety between himself and Christine Keeler, whom he had met at Cliveden. She was having an affair with a negro.

[2] Ann Fleming's son Lord O'Neill married in 1963 Georgina, daughter of Lord George Montagu-Douglas-Scott, brother of the Duke of Buccleuch.

[3] Ursula Andress in *Dr No*, directed by Terence Young.

TO RANDOLPH CHURCHILL   Combe Florey House.
2 April 1963

Dear Randolph

 No gift could have given me greater delight than your discovery of Francis Crease's *Designs*.[1] Will you not let me repay you for the purchase? If you insist on being munificent, I can only redouble my thanks. The book comes most opportunely as I am at the moment writing of Crease in my autobiography.

A handsome leather case has arrived with copies of books of mine for inscription. I am gratified that you should want a complete set for your own library. It is not clear why you require duplicates, unless you are going into trade. Your generosity in the matter of Crease's *Designs* disarms me, but I must point out that I gave you a copy of *Men at Arms* on publication. What happened to that? And why *two* more copies?[2] Do you make frequent bonfires of fiction?

If you wish me to register the return parcel ghost must send sealing-wax. I never register anything. Delivery is delayed, compensation for loss (except in the case of special insurance) is negligible. It is always the registered bags that are stolen *en route*.

Unless I hear that you wish the parcel registered I will send it by ordinary post.

I hope you are not finding the privations of Lent enervating.

> Yours ever
> Evelyn

[1] Waugh had written a preface for *Thirty-Four Decorative Designs*, privately printed in 1927, for Francis Crease, who lived near Lancing.

[2] Churchill said he wanted a set for each of his children.

TO RANDOLPH CHURCHILL   Combe Florey House.
7 April 1963
Postcard

I should perpetrate a fraud if I inscribed to you personally books intended for the market. I have therefore signed duplicates on the title page as I do for charitable bazaars.

TO LADY DIANA COOPER   Combe Florey House.
25 April 1963

Darling Pug

Here is a little picture to remind you of our happy days in Rome. How happy you made them. It was years since I saw so much of you. Time fell away & I was back on tour with *The Miracle*.

My Florentine excursion was very different – all palaces full of white gloved footmen & colossal statuary. At Harold's I had a bed room as big as the throne room at the Vatican & not unlike it. Light switches indistinguishable from bells concealed behind tapestries. Whenever I woke in the night to take my poison I rang by mistake & troups of servants of all ages & sexes charged in crying 'Il bagno adesso?'[1] We visited many American millionaires in neighbouring palaces & I pined for Piazza S.Bartolomeo & even the rough grass of Pogson's park.[2] The grass here, by the way, is very brilliant and succulent & offers rich grazing for you all the summer. Do come & browse.

Admiralty House has gone down hill since baby's [Lady Diana Cooper's] time. The fine dining room is transformed into offices, the dolphin furniture banished with the Capt. Cook paintings. White paint everywhere. Baby's bedroom is the drawing-room, but the luncheon party was very cosy. I think the Prime Minister[3] wanted to escape the cares of state by recreating Balliol 1912. The only discordant voice was that of Thomson the Canadian newspaper-owner, a pathetic oaf. I said to him: 'We met at the first night of *Dr No*. I couldn't understand it, could you?' Thomson: 'There were girls without much clothing. I liked that.' E.W. 'You must be very over-excitable sexually'. That made the wop ambassador split his sides.

Home to find piles of letters to answer & Lady Onslow in residence.

I shan't come to London for a long time. If you come here (not in easy reach of Stratford or Bath) I promise you shall never enter the dining-room but have all meals on the grass wet or fine.

All love
Bo

[1] At La Pietra, Harold Acton's house.
[2] Commander Frank Pogson married the Princess Doria.
[3] Harold Macmillan, who was living at Admiralty House while 10 Downing Street was renovated.

To Ann Fleming
7 May 1963

Combe Florey House.

My Dear Ann

I received no letter from you in Rome. No doubt it was stolen by Mrs Henley[1] who was in occupation of Mother Judy's mortuary. It is sad as I should dearly have liked to see you & do not expect to be in London again for many weeks.

Easter in Rome was (for me) vividly social. Except for seasonal attendance at church I was with Diana all the time. She was buggerless[2], eating ravenously between meals, shying away from dining room tables & demanding picnics on coarse grass in full sunshine. A minute modern bar in the Via Condotte is her new haunt – a great improvement on the odious California. The chief interest among Romans was the incident of Doria-Pamphili-Pogson calling Princess Isabella Orsini an 'old bitch'. People said: 'In Ronnie Graham's day he would have been officially reprimanded. Ward is useless.'[3]

I had expected tourists & pilgrims in Rome. No one warned me of the elections – every building obscured by hoardings, helicopters showering leaflets overhead and worst of all loud-speaker vans in every street at all hours. Most unnerving. In Florence I was given a beribboned plastic bag of earth with the statement: 'This is the sacred soil of your country which the socialists seek to take from you.'

Tony Powell knows a lot about painting. In youth he drew Lovat-Fraser-like decorations of military subjects. He slept with Nina Hamnett[4] and attended the L.C.C. School of Arts & Crafts in Southampton Row.

I cannot judge his musical tastes. He was a friend of Constant Lambert[5] and the musical conversations in what was it called? 'The pagoda of the Amber Moon'? No, something like that. *Casanova's Chinese Restaurant* perhaps – anyway those conversations impressed me with his inside knowledge. I don't think you appreciate Tony as you should. Of course everyone is at his worst at Grubstreet's[6] table.

Do you know Miss Kathleen Hale's drawings – *Orlando, The Marmalade Cat* series? She has done a very pretty frontispiece for the story I am dedicating to you.

. . . Is Sutton, Surrey in London? A great-nephew of Hughes has a painting of his for sale there which I should like to see. 11 Laburnum Avenue. Would you like to make a reconnaissance if it is near your asylum?[7] The address on your letter doesn't seem adequate so I am sending this to Victoria Square in the hope that it will be forwarded.

Ever your affec. coz.

E.W.

[1] Sylvia Stanley (1882–   ). Married in 1906 Brigadier-General Anthony Henley who died in 1926. Lord Stanley's aunt.

[2] Not a sexual reference. It means she was without companions.

[3] Sir Ronald Graham was British Ambassador in Rome 1921–33; Sir John Ward (1909–   ) was British Ambassador in Rome 1962–6.

[4] Nina Hamnett (1890–1956). Portrait and landscape painter.

[5] Constant Lambert (1905–51). Composer, conductor and critic. At twenty-one he was the first British composer to be asked to write a ballet for Diaghilev.

[6] Lady Pamela Berry.

Forest Mere, a health farm.

To Nancy Mitford   Combe Florey House.
24 May 1963

Darling Nancy

I was in London yesterday & heard from Mrs Freeze G[1] the news of your mother's illness and of your sad vigil on Mull. She told me you wanted letters. It is a long time since I wrote, but my life is so dull that there is little to tell.

I have been made a new-fangled thing called a 'Companion of Literature',[2] the invention of Freddy Birkenhead, no emoluments, no adornments, no precedence, no duties – average age 78. I am by far the youngest. They live scattered between Cap Ferat, California & Hong Kong so I don't think I shall enjoy much companionship. But I thought it would be stuck up & unfriendly to Freddy if I refused. I have to go to a banquet which I dread.

Prince Richard of Gloucester is being sent to stay with Harold Acton to broaden his (H.R.H's) mind. Harold was examined by the Duke and pronounced most suitable.

Daphne [Fielding] has finished her treatise on Rosa[3]. It is jolly good but I think full of inaccuracies. My friend B. Bennett (Hyde Park Hotel) has bought the Cavendish & proposes to rebuild it & retain the name. Daphne mentions you as an habituée. Surely not true?

My daughter Margaret attends a 'Pre-natal clinic' in Paddington where she is the only patient who is both white & married & is treated as a rare bird.

Your lunatic cousin Randolph has set up as proof corrector.

Mrs Fleming has spent £5,000 on a gorilla by Nolan[4]; £200 on a touching scene by Arthur Hughes – *The Convent Boat* portraying grim nuns rowing a novice away from her mourning family. Mr Fleming is very jealous of the Duchess of Argyll who has been paid £60,000 for [her story].[5] The Duke is getting only 40 thou. Peters refused to handle her affairs. I spent most of yesterday with him & am convinced of his high honesty and devotion to our interests.

Birds fall dead all round us poisoned by farmers. Our asparagus, usually our one good crop, has failed – a few stunted purple stumps.

Harold Acton has also written a novel[6] – did I tell you? Very odd & funny. He has forgotten the English language – a warning to all expatriates.

Do they talk Gaelic on Mull? I couldn't understand John Betjeman's last Celtic joke book.[7]

Darling Nancy, I haven't said a word of sympathy about your mother's illness, but I feel it keenly.[8]

Love from
Evelyn

[1] Mrs Friese Greene.
[2] An award from the Royal Society of Literature.
[3] *The Duchess of Jermyn Street.*
[4] Sidney Nolan (1917–). Australian painter.
[5] The Duke of Argyll had been granted a divorce for adultery on 8 May. In the event the Duchess brought an action to prevent his publishing two of six articles in the *People* in 1964.
[6] *Old Lamps for New.*
[7] *A Wealth of Poetry.*
[8] Lady Redesdale was dead by the time Waugh's letter arrived.

TO BRIAN FRANKS   Combe Florey House.
28 May [1963]

Dear Brian

Cavendish

It is essential that the Jermyn Street stucco façade & the lamps remain undisturbed by whatever you do behind them.

It is highly desirable that Rosa's [Lewis] parlour remain intact. What has happened to the portraits of her? Edith[1] & Daphne [Fielding] would know. This should be a champagne parlour presided over (under strict surveillance) by someone like Daphne or, better, Maimie Lygon.

The value of your property is 4/5 the prestige (?) Rosa gave it. You should attract English customers of the right (?) sort – i.e. old Rosa types. *They* will draw in the Yanks more than any new-fangled shower-baths etc. They can wash anywhere. If they come to Cavendish, it will be for unique atmosphere, associations etc.

Seriously suggest M. Lygon as your 'hostess'.

Yours ever
Evelyn

When you re-open Cavendish you could re-issue Daphne's book[2] with an epilogue saying that you were carrying on old traditions etc.

Centenary of Rosa's birth is in about three years. Suitable time for re-opening.[3]

[1] Edith Jeffrey, friend and lady-in-waiting to Rosa Lewis for forty years. She continued to run the hotel for ten years after Rosa's death.

[2] Daphne Fielding, *The Duchess of Jermyn Street*, 1964.

[3] The hotel was rebuilt completely, retaining no links with Rosa Lewis.

To Lady Acton   Combe Florey House.
10 June 1963

Dearest Daphne

I was much relieved to get your letter. I feared I had been too uppish in criticising that paper-back on the liturgy & that you had taken umbrage. I should have known you better.

My crush on Pope John became less fervent when all the newspapers took him up. Of course I revered him to the end but there is an instinctive and (I find) uncontrollable antipathy towards anyone whose photograph one sees twice a day. You can bet that all this fever of praise is the preliminary for a very cold welcome to his successor. Pray God not the Austrian. Milan or Palermo for me.[1] No danger at all of Spellman.

Woodruff has developed a senile infatuation for a very dangerous clergyman called Kung[2] – not Chinese, central European; a heresiarch who in happier days would be roasted.

You are jolly calm about the Wind of Change in Africa. I daresay it is much calmer on the spot. If you see English newspapers you would suppose we are all in ferment over 'the Profumo affair'. We aren't. They call it 'the greatest scandal of the century'. To my knowledge in my life time three Prime Ministers have been adulterers and almost every cabinet has had an addict of almost every sexual vice. Poor Profumo – an Italian, jew, freemason – had an affair with a prostitute. Every paper pretends to be horrified. He did wrong to lie about it, but Rufus Isaacs lied to the House of Commons in a 'personal statement' about the Marconi contract, and ascended to great honours. So I daresay that when I read in these same papers that Rhodesia is in a ferment, it looks calm in Mazoe as it does in Combe Florey. The trouble is that disastrous political events (in Mazoe and in C-F) can happen without us bothering.

Don't take seriously Richard's fuss about Schools. No one ever fails unless, like A. Lunn, he deliberately insults the examiners. This nervous excitement about schools is something quite new since my time. My nephew, [Robin] Grant, came here the other day twittering about his schools. It is a hysteria entirely novel, introduced by the undergraduates with whom they now associate. Anyway one's class in schools makes no difference to ones subsequent prosperity. E.g. Gerald Gardiner,[3] the present top barrister, went down without a degree. Also Robert Byron, dead but famous, J. Betjeman alive & famous and thousands of others.

... I should be much interested to know whether the antiquarian – what was his name?[4] – has fled Uhuru.

The polite boy A. Waugh[5] has command of a ship.

> Much love
> Evelyn

Are you being persecuted by a lame French girl who is writing a thesis on R. Knox?[6] Beware.

[1] The Cardinal Archbishop of Milan became Pope Paul VI.
[2] Professor Hans Küng (1928–). Professor of Theology at Tübingen. A reformer.
[3] Gerald Gardiner (1900–) took a Fourth Class degree. Created Lord Gardiner 1963, Lord Chancellor 1964–70.
[4] Alastair Goldsworthy.
[5] Waugh's nephew Andrew.
[6] Solange Dayras.

To ALFRED DUGGAN   Combe Florey House.
19 June 1963

Dear Alfred

I am at work on an autobiography[1] and am asking various friends how much they mind being mentioned. Of course, if they object, they will be left nameless. I asked 'Lord' Hot-lunch Molson if I might say he was tight at Lancing on Ascension Day 1921. He replied that he did not mind but that the revelation would cause great grief in the High Peak Division of Derbyshire.

Do you mind my mentioning you as a notably debauched undergraduate – hunters, night-chauffeur, the empty chair at your table (in case you had asked a forgotten guest the night before) etc?

If you do object, I shall, of course, exclude all this. You may well think it would embarrass your adopted son and I should well understand.

> Yours ever
> Evelyn

[1] *A Little Learning*, 1964.

To ANN FLEMING   Combe Florey House.
18 July 1963
Lord Broughshane's 60th birthday[1]

Dear Ann

It is very kind of you to ask us to Sevenhampton. Alas, we have no car except our old bus which is too uncomfortable for long journeys. We ordered a new car months ago but the makers are always on strike & have not sent it yet. If it ever comes, and if there is any day when you are alone, we will visit you with pleasure. I read in the papers that Ian has a new car and that it is a great happiness & consolation to him.

Yesterday I sent you what our betters used to call 'a Wimborne'[2] for explanation of this term see my life of Knox.

The Grub Street gang had another go at my watch[3] – stole it from my bedside. Fortunately the controlling minds were distracted & their agent popped it in Taunton for 1/10 of the value, so he is in prison & the watch back in my pocket.

You must remember that the Prime Minister, like Sir Winston & Lord Hailsham, is ½ American & cannot be judged by English standards, but I can well understand that, confronted by Quennell, his thoughts strayed wistfully to dukes. All his friends were killed in the war. . . . Worst of all he saw the light & rejected it. If he had made his submission to the Church in 1916 when he momentarily decided to, he would not be prime minister nor married to a Cavendish but he would have been a happy & virtuous publisher. His gravest crimes have been (a) destroying the Clarendon Hotel to build a Woolworth stores in the Corn [Cornmarket Street] at Oxford (b) appointing Trevor-Roper Regius Professor. The former was symbolic of his break with his undergraduate life – the Clarendon was the meeting place of his friends & the scene e.g. of the 21st-er which caused Charles Lister[4] to be sent down (though P.M. was a junior generation); the latter appointment showed malice to the Church. I was staying with him in Naples in 1944 when he got the news that Churchill & Roosevelt had consented to the destruction of (Catholic) Lithuania. He showed obvious satisfaction saying: 'Well, that's one problem the less'. I think he has grown a carapace of cynicism to protect a tender conscience. Perhaps he may find his soul in retirement.

Butler[5], of course, is sub-human.

I think you said you never saw the story I am dedicating to you. You will receive a handsome copy with a frontispiece by Marmalade Cat Miss Hale. Meanwhile here are some proofs.

Fuddy Duddy Spender caused deathless offence to all the other Fuddy Duddies.[6] It is not becoming in him to show scorn of anything, least of all at a literary gathering. Such things are his life's work. He must not pose as a Rimbaud.

It took me many days to recover from the strain of 2 days in London.

If in arranging your furniture you wish to get rid of that mahogany (rose wood?) & ormolu fluted column to which I have a pair, please remember I shall be a willing purchaser.

Ever your affec coz
Evelyn

The Charterises held a family council the other day about the Balfour adultery. Were you not invited?

[1] No. Lord Broughshane was born 18 June 1903.

[2] 'A "Wimborne" (taking its name from the photograph of a footballer which appeared in a newspaper over the title "Lady Wimborne, who has adopted the new wind-swept style of hairdressing") was a picture cut from a newspaper with which was included from an adjoining column a particularly inappropriate caption.' *Ronald Knox* p.223.

[3] Previously Stephen Spender had been taking Waugh's watch to be mended, when, much to his embarrassment, it was stolen from him. It was recovered, slightly damaged, and he had it repaired.

[4] Charles Lister (1887–1915). Son of Lord Ribblesdale. Killed at Gallipoli.

[5] Then First Secretary of State and Deputy Prime Minister.

[6] At a meeting of the Royal Society of Literature, Spender came in wearing a dinner-jacket and an order and smoked his cigar before the loyal toast.

To ANN FLEMING   Combe Florey House.
7 August 1963

Dear Ann

. . . I distil a few daily drops of exquisite boredom about my early life. I am also writing a preface for an American edition of Galsworthy's *Man of Property*. Ever read it? Don't. He was the last English novelist to be granted general reverence. He is really shockingly dull. I had the hope that it was youthful snobbery which made me despise him. But no. He's no good.

I gave you sage advice about your country seat. You disregarded it. Now you will be ruined financially and a prey to claustrophobia.

You read of Maurice's defeat in his project of building a sky-scraper zoo opposite Keble. A don here yesterday said it was not a defeat. Maurice did not want a zoo and insisted on seconding the motion so that he could antagonise the congregation.

The plumbers, plasterers and painters of Somerset are skilled and respectful. You are building too near the midland cities.

> Yours affec.
> Evelyn

To JOHN McDOUGALL   Combe Florey House.
22 September 1963

Dear Jack

It is a very beautiful thought of Spotty's to give me a birthday present.[1] I have already had a fine clock and a trompe l'oeil (no, that must mean to cuckold a goose. How is it spelt?) from Chapman & Hall. Still if Spotty feels munificent keep him up to it. Perhaps we can discuss it on Saturday. My preference would be for a more permanent pledge of Spotty's love e.g. an umbrella or an air tight mahogany cigar box or some decanters. The last of a crested set of my great grandfathers was broken the other day & I mourn them.

The great thing about the Tring-Enton-Liphook cure is that it does not cure one of drink but confers the benefits anew. Forty years ago I was deliriously happy on two cocktails, half a bottle of champagne & a glass of brandy. Now I drink $\frac{1}{2}$ bottle of whisky without the smallest sense of inebriation.[2]

Laura & I look forward so much to seeing you & May again.

Pray do not reply.

> Yours ever
> Evelyn

[1] For Waugh's sixtieth birthday on 28 October.
[2] Waugh wrote on 14 October: 'Lost 15lb in 14 days. No euphoria until first dinner of grouse pie and burgundy.'

To Margaret FitzHerbert   Combe Florey House.
S.S. Simon and Jude [28 October] 1963

Darling Pig,

What a lovely present. It is most generous of you and Giles to part with these exquisite drawings which you cleverly found and acquired for your own delight. I will leave them back to you in my will. Hicks[1] did not use the postmen in the painting, which makes it the more interesting. It is clearly a study for it. The female figure, I think, was for his *Billingsgate Market*. I shall have them mounted together and put in one frame and hung near the big Hicks in the morning-room. I shall *not* send the bill to you. You have too many calls on your purse at the moment. Your letter was enchanting.

You will be constantly in my thoughts and prayers during the tedious time ahead of you and I look forward tenderly and eagerly to your visit with the piglet.

Your mother and I have just returned from a visit to the Flemings at their new edifice in Berkshire. They have spent prodigious sums in destroying a large house and building a very small one in a narrow strip of swamp which they have had to drain, excavate and fill with acres of soil imported from afar. Their drawing-room can only be reached through the dining-room. They have larger quarters for themselves. The spare rooms are minute and divided by paper-thin partitions through which every sneeze is plainly audible. The company (not staying but coming from the neighbourhood) was comprised of former loves of mine – Clarissa, Teresa Cuthbertson, Virginia Charteris[2] (in that case a mere romantic interest which never developed).

Lord Avon kept his distance. Penelope Cuthbertson was greatly admired by Ian Fleming – not by me. I thought she needed a hair-cut and elocution lessons. She was impolite to her mother. She told me you had been to a party of hers. I hope you exercise a good influence on her.

I am not noticeably thinner for my sufferings at Forest Mere but am very much healthier and much rejuvenated. Poor Ian ten years my junior is very decrepit.

Nancy Mitford says that no young girl would be put off marrying by the supposed discovery that she was engaged to her brother. True? Ask some of your wilder, irreligious friends so that I can refute her. I should have thought it was a deep-rooted taboo.[3]

The wall on the terrace opposite the morning-room window is up and the sphynxes hoisted into place. It looks very well to my eyes.

Here is the hundred pounds I promised. Don't bother to acknowledge.

Fr Caraman's present is charming. Found by you? Is he abroad or merely immersed in social life. I sent him my little book but got no answer. He is normally very punctilious. Can Aitken[4] have failed to send it? Do enquire tactfully.

The little Waughs come tonight for a week.

All love sweet Hog
Papa

[1] George Elgar Hicks (1824–1914).
[2] Virginia Forbes Adam (1922–   ). Married Hugo Charteris in 1948.

³ The plot of *Basil Seal Rides Again* depends on Seal preventing his daughter marrying by revealing, falsely, that he is her fiancé's father. Nancy Mitford had written: 'Now Evelyn seriously do you think being brother and sister would really have stopped them marrying? I call this rather naif ... but the trouble is Prod has turned into you and this falsifies everything.'

⁴ Gillon Aitken (1938–   ), then general editor of Chapman & Hall.

To ANN FLEMING   Combe Florey House.
28 October 1963

Dear Ann

Laura says I teased you too much about your edifice and on reflection I believe she is right. Please forgive me. It is my ugly nature to pick holes. I should have said much more in congratulation for what you have achieved and much less in complaining where our tastes differ. Here is a suggestion for remedying the unsightly slope [drawing]. You could find the voluted stone-work by diligently searching masons' yards and the vendors of garden ornaments. It would cost a lot to get them cut new.

What you have achieved is a house absolutely suited to your own & Ian's needs. If you had bought an old house it would have imposed its habits on you. You have made something where there is no predecessor breathing down your neck and you have insured a happy twenty years in watching it mature & filling it with treasures.

We enjoyed our visit enormously – such beef, such grouse, such Taittinger such Bollinger, so many old loves for me, so many kinsfolk for Laura. We think we must be very dull company for you in comparison with your bizarre habitués. I never *feel* the need of pep pills. Perhaps my friends wish I took them.

I wish you would come here. You would find it as restful & austere as Forest Mere.

I have verified that 'lunette' is what Battersby is making for your door.

You must put ink, pens, blotting paper etc in drawing-room & main bed rooms. Also matches (preferably in heavy silver cases engraved with the name of the room) and clocks. Superfluous beds to be kept in store room when not in use.

... I still have a nagging fear (apart from Laura's rebuke) that I was not a good guest. Sorry.

Ever your affec. coz.
E.W.

To ALFRED DUGGAN   Combe Florey House.
[29 October 1963]
Postcard

Thanks awfully for your telegram. I feel greatly rejuvenated at reaching the age when I can decently refuse to carry logs.

E

To Randolph Churchill   Combe Florey House.
29 October 1963
Postcard

   Thank you for your telegram. It is agreeable to be exempt from jury service.
   Some time ago I sent you a valuable little book. Search ghost's trunk. He may
have appropriated it.

                                              E.W.

To Nancy Mitford   Combe Florey House.
29 October 1963

Dearest Nancy
   Your odious letter was on my breakfast table on the morning of my 60th birthday.
Ah, at least one old friend has written to congratulate me on reaching the age when I
am exempt from jury service and can no longer decently be expected to carry
anything. Not at all. A sharp reminder that my powers are fading and that I am a
bore.
   All you say, I refute. The story is too short, not too long. It would have made a
novel. Old people are more interesting than young. One of the particular points of
interest is to observe how after 50 they revert to the habits, mannerisms and
opinions of their parents, however wild they were in youth. I see it on all sides as
well as in myself. B. Seal had highly conventional parents. His change & recovery of
his youth are the theme of the story.
   I hope it is clear that the claim to have fathered Albright was totally false – a
device to save his daughter whom he loves from marrying a beatnik.
   Your family, if reports at the time were true, were peculiarly tolerant of incest. It
is a taboo deeply rooted in the most heathen. I do not think that morals have
declined much since the age when Byron was driven from the country. As for that
girl's heart, it will mend quickly. Of course Basil was fiercely jealous. That should
be apparent.
   The only fault I admit to is the misspelling of Clicquot.
   We have just returned from a visit to Ann Fleming's edifice. She has spent as
much as the government have on the reconstruction of Downing Street, pulled
down a large commodious house & put up a cottage.
   . . . The few bedrooms are tiny cubicles with paper thin walls through which
every cough & snore is audible.
   My own house, though better than Ann's, is invaded by son, daughter-in-law,
granddaughter and a swarthy monoglot nannie[1], second generation Spanish
communist refugee to south of France.

                                              Love from
                                              Evelyn

[1] Lolita Gordo.

TO SIR MAURICE BOWRA
Combe Florey House.
All Souls' [2 November] 1963

Dear Maurice

I loved Maurice Baring. Nothing will be better chosen for my birthday than his holograph translation. It must be almost the last thing he wrote. Interesting it should have come into the market. Laura Lovat?[1]

I wish I had had the opportunity to conduct you round Ann's edifice pointing out its deplorable qualities. She has spent on it as much as the rebuilders of Downing Street. It has almost every deficiency.

Old Thunderbird perked up a little on Saturday night when he had a young girl to show off to. He wishes to end his life and is determined to have his final seizure on the golf course or at the card table. Ann will be disconsolate.

How John Sparrow must be praying today, *toties quoties* for the soldiers of Agincourt.[2]

Yours ever
Evelyn

[1] Laura Lister (1892–1965). Married Lord Lovat in 1910. Benefactress of Maurice Baring in his long final illness.

[2] As Warden of All Souls, which college was founded in 1438 for (among other things) 'the offering of prayers for . . . the souls of . . . faithful subjects of the realm who died in the French wars', Sparrow would read a prayer referring to them on All Souls Day.

TO ALFRED DUGGAN
Combe Florey House.
18 November 1963

Dear Alfred

Very many thanks for *The Story of the Crusades*. I am delighted to possess a copy with your inscription. I had in fact already seen it & thought it was precisely the sort of lucid account which I needed to supplement my meagre education. I hope it will be adopted in all the schools.

Last week I went to London for an assembly of ghosts of our past – the 40th anniversary of the foundation of the Oxford Railway Club. John Sutro quite unchanged, also Harold Acton. Terence Greenidge, whom I had not seen for 25 years, has had large parts of his brain removed by a surgeon. It has made him very cheerful but removed most of the idiosyncrasies which used to endear him. It was, of course, a hard-drinking occasion so I do not think you would have got much amusement from it. Roy Harrod brought 2 sons[1], I a son & a son-in-law[2]. A young Guinness[3] represented Bryan. These young people looked rather bewildered at our sexagenarian levity.

Terence is one of the majority of my old cronies who, like you, say 'publish & be damned' about my reminiscences of their youth. The exceptions are Hot-lunch Molson & Matthew Ponsonby[4].

By the way could you very kindly send me a post card to put me right on one point? Did you keep your own motor-car & chauffeur at Oxford or rely on hiring from Morris's Garage?

> Yours ever affec.
> Evelyn

[1] Henry and Dominic.
[2] Auberon, and Giles FitzHerbert.
[3] Desmond Guinness, son of Lord Moyne.
[4] Matthew Ponsonby (1904–   ). Friend of Waugh's in the 1920s. Brother of Elizabeth. Succeeded as Lord Ponsonby in 1946.

TO JOHN McDOUGALL   Combe Florey House.
3 December 1963

Dear Jack

I have completed the first volume of my memoirs. Should it go to you or to Spotty? There are points to discuss – with you or Spotty?

Captain Grimes[1] had third thoughts about his vicious past and has given me written licence to print what ten years ago could not have been printed about the dead let alone the living.

. . . Want to call Vol 1 of memoir *Little Learning*. It must have been used often before. I have asked Aitken to investigate.

> Yours ever
> Evelyn

[1] Richard (Dick) Young matriculated at Keble in 1912 and took a BA, in absence, in 1918. He was the model for Captain Grimes in *Decline and Fall*. Waugh had traced him through a cousin to the Saint Cross Alms Houses of noble poverty at Winchester, where he was living 'owing to some unfortunate speculations'. He felt that 'It might be an ideal place for you [Waugh] if you were not married and were a trifle older'. He had written a detective story, *A Preparatory School Murder*, in 1934 under the name Richard Macnaughton, using Arnold House as a background. Then he was a solicitor, 'but I was then too old to start a learned profession and took little interest in it'. He died in 1972, leaving £58,000 and a collection of German and Chelsea porcelain to the Ashmolean Museum.

TO MIA WOODRUFF   Combe Florey House.
[Typed postcard]

Your aged but incontinent husband maintains a separate establishment at Bourne Mansions[1] (a peculiarly offensive nomenclature for those who remember the Cardinal). Verb. Sap.

> A Well wisher

[1] Douglas Woodruff had recognized a description of his flat in *Unconditional Surrender*, and had headed his most recent letter to Waugh 'Bourne Mansions', the address it had been given in the book.

To Lady Acton   Combe Florey House.
7 January 1964

Dearest Daphne

. . . I was much amused to see that the Queen had decorated John [Acton] for 'services to Rhodesian agriculture'. As I remember it he served a Jewish-South-African company manufacturing bags out of imported materials[1]. Surely someone has been pulling the royal leg? I am jealous, though I want the spurs of knighthood like Galahad.

It is very enterprising of you to send your boy to the blackamoors' school. It is gratifying that it should be two members of the English nobility[2] who should set an example to those loutish 'pioneers'.

Thank God the 12 days of Christmas are over. I spent them at home for the first time for many years & had to numb myself with heavy private drinking. You think I may be 'sour & crusty'. My word, I am.

I have finished the first volume of an autobiography. No 'masterpiece', but it has some comic bits, ending with an unsuccessful attempt at suicide at the age of 21.

I have 3 grandchildren now including, to my satisfaction, a grandson in the male line. There will be a 4th in May but it will be American so doesn't count.

If you haven't done so, read Mary McCarthy's *The Group*. Not for Jill but brilliantly illuminating. Miss McCarthy is an apostate Catholic. It is very interesting to see how the good sense of Catholic teaching has survived the loss of all faith & devotion.

It has been a sad disappointment to me that the Pope escaped from Palestine with a buffeting. I hoped for assassination. He has two very fine houses of his own in Italy. I think it very vulgar of him to go touring with the television. All this talk of ecumenicism is exceedingly painful to my sour & crusty nerves. In a happier age Küng would have been burned at the stake.

Jill wrote me a fan letter. I hoped she would develop into a pen pal but silence has fallen.

Beware Mlle Dayras a French cripple who is writing a treatise on Ronnie & is a great bore.

I wonder if you answer your voices back, as I did, or just listen in silence. Are you trying great swigs of paraldehyde? – very nasty but good for voices.

My daughter Harriet (19) is a great trial to me – quite pretty, very good & affectionate but stupid & dull & incompetent. My son James (17) is also a thorn. Won't go into the church or the army, smokes cigarettes & can't take his hands out his pockets. My youngest son is a jewel but I suspect he will grow up homosexual.

All love to you & Jill & the CMG and the nautch girls.

They say Douglas [Woodruff] is still alive but I haven't seen him. The tone of *The Tablet* is *very* low these days.

Evelyn

[1] True; but he received the CMG as chairman of the Salisbury Agricultural Show and director of the Gwebi Agricultural College.

[2] Peter Acton and Simon Rous were the only white boarders at St Ignatius, a Jesuit school.

To Lady Mary Lygon   Combe Florey House.
20 February 1964
Postcard

I was abroad (& ill) for the Captains [Hance] funeral. I would have polished my top
hat with Guinness had I been in England and well. I wrote to Jackie & had a deeply
touching answer. Trumpets over the grave – quite right. But how did Capt G.B.H.
rise to rank of Lt.Col?

                                                        OXO
                                                         BO

To Ann Fleming   Combe Florey House.
3 March 1964

Dear Ann

My heart bleeds for you, as for the Unbearable Bassington, in your tropic exile. I
am glad you have a toad to sit to you.

Toads thrive on burning cigarette ends & human milk. Some 40 years ago I had to
read the *Letters of Junius*. All I remember is that one of the royal family was 'subject
to the hideous suction of toads'. No doubt erudite Quennell will be able to place the
passage exactly.

I have recovered my health & chucked going to Sister Agnes where Randolph has
taken up his quarters. I have been a fellow patient with him before.

When I saw the doctor he asked about my habits. I said 'I have practically given
up drinking – only about 7 bottles of wine & 3 of spirits a week' 'A week? Surely you
mean a month?' 'No, and I smoke 30 cigars a week & take 40 grains of sodium
amytal'. He looked graver & graver. 'Oh, yes, a bottle of paraldehyde a week'. He
brightened greatly & said: 'Now *that* is an excellent thing. Far too few people use it'.

I go to Rome for Easter (Grand Hotel) to avoid the horrors of the English liturgy.
Come too.

Thunderbeatle has been very much in our thoughts lately. The *Daily Express* has
written of nothing else for ten days. What a gruesome luncheon Mr McColl got. I
knew his father.

I have seen no one except children & grandchildren and done nothing except
answer letters from people I once knew very slightly (and some I have never met)
commenting on a dreary exhibition I made of myself on the television.[1]

Come to Rome 25th

                                                   Your affec coz
                                                        E

[1] Waugh appeared on *Monitor*, 16 February 1964.

To LADY DIANA COOPER   Combe Florey House.
[April 1964]

Darling Pug

I cannot & will not attempt to say that your illness in Rome was anything but a deep sorrow – perhaps deeper to me than to you as you were asleep so much of the time. I rejoice that you are safe home – but *are* you safe? Have you seen an English physician? You don't cosset yourself. You were in no condition for that awful return journey which would have killed me, tough old soldier as I am. You should hire a pansy as permanent guard & guide. Why don't you marry — ? *Much* better than Beaton.

Alfred Duggan kicked the bucket [1] and Laura & I had to go to the Welsh marches for his requiem.

Daphne's book on Rosa Lewis very amusing but frightfully common title. Did you ever hear her referred to as 'the Duchess of Jermyn Street'? I certainly did not.

Take care of yourself, Pug. Don't go in for wild austerities like sleeping in cellars & fasting & flying in crowded night aeroplanes.

                                        All love
                                          Bo

I have become reconciled with Randolph. He looked so pathetically thin & feeble and when he tried to shout a whisper came. So 12 years enmity are expunged.

[1] On 4 April 1964.

To GRAHAM GREENE   Combe Florey House.
7 May 1964
Feast of Ascension

Dear Graham,

I have been asked by the Council of the R. Literary Society to ask you to think again about your refusal to become one of their 'Companions'. So I ask you, with little hope of moving you.

The appointment involves no effort on your part, no obligations, no emoluments, no adornment, no precedence. You need not (though they would like it) be present to accept your scroll of honour. Until they very kindly elected me I knew nothing of the R.S. of Literature. They seem to comprise decent, simple people with a liking for books. No commercial interests. They instituted this 'Companionship' quite lately on recognizing that few active writers were members of their society. They are not a clique, they do not elect one another. The existing (& diminishing) 'Companions' have nothing in common except the exercise of their trade. There would be no question of your having 'to feel at home' in 'a literary institution'. You need never meet any of them. I have not – except at a quite pleasant dinner when I was given a *very* well inscribed scroll of membership. The other members are not disgraceful.

The point is that a lot of well-intentioned people have offered what they think is an honour. I was in doubt whether to accept (on the grounds that it was too recent an establishment). I don't regret it.

Some years back I refused the C.B.E. from side (not good enough, I thought) and am now ashamed.

If you refuse, you snub not only the Council but all the quite respectable people who have accepted. A sin against courtesy is a sin against charity.

Come on; be a sport; tell old R.A.B.[1] that you submit.

You saw that Alfred Duggan kicked the bucket? We may all fall downstairs any day. Pocket pride & accept 'C.Lit'.

Love
Evelyn

[1] R.A.Butler was president of the Royal Society of Literature.

TO GRAHAM GREENE
Combe Florey House.
[May 1964]
Postcard

I knew it wouldn't work. I wrote reluctantly, because a decent old buffer[1] asked me to (not R.A.Butler). Forgive me for having been a bore. Greatly shocked at your acquittal of church robbers.

May I congratulate you on the increased legibility of your handwriting. Is this because purchasers of your manuscripts can't tell what they have bought.

Unamuno[2] (Junior Prefect)

[1] Lord Birkenhead, chairman.
[2] Miguel de Unamuno (1864-1930). Spanish philosopher and novelist mentioned by Greene in his introduction to *A Burnt-Out Case*.

TO RANDOLPH CHURCHILL
Combe Florey House.
15 June 1964
Postcard

Very many thanks for *Marlborough*[1] which I shall study with attention.

Thank you also for calling off Lord Snowdon. I can now remove the false beard I have worn since I got Mr Russell's alarming letter.[2]

E

[1] Winston S.Churchill, *Marlborough, his Life and Times*, 1933.
[2] Leonard Russell, associate editor of the *Sunday Times*, had written on 10 June: 'I hear vaguely of a proposal to photograph you with your tulip tree, in connection with Randolph Churchill's piece.'

To Ann Fleming   Combe Florey House.
18 June 1964

Dear Ann

I anxiously await news of Thunderbeatle. When we last met he was in Sister Agnes. I hope he is now at liberty and at ease.

I trust you have not gone to that disgusting Biennale.

You spoke of coming here. Do. You will find the house in a peculiar condition because an ancient aunt of mine who lived alone with the accumulated possessions of a poor family in a cottage not far off, caught fire & asphyxiated herself. We have had to take all her possessions into safe custody for eventual distribution so that we are like a junk shop. Luckily both Bron & Margaret are moving into larger quarters and are eager for the furniture – all falling to pieces. Would you like any bracelets made of human hair? I have dozens.

The dangers of reconciliation with Randolph! I heard indirectly that he wanted to send Lord Snowdon here to photograph a very shabby tulip tree. I have succeeded in convincing him that they are as common as laburnums in the West country. I think if you went from Tewkesbury to Exeter you would find one every five miles. The poor booby thinks them a great rarity.

I now have an American grandson[1]. In my copy of *The Times* the announcement was illegible so I made a fuss and they wont charge for it.

Our asparagus is plentiful, green peas delicious, strawberries just ripening. Do come.

Your affec. coz.
E.W.

[1] Justin D'Arms had been born on 31 May.

To Randolph Churchill   Combe Florey House.
19 June 1964
Postcard

For Ghost's (not Snowdon's) information my tulip trees are now in full flower.

I am enjoying *Marlborough*. The author has no specifically literary talent but a gift of lucid self expression in words – lost when least excited. His military reports are in the same class (though lower) as Belloc & Duggan.

E

To Nancy Mitford   Combe Florey House.
6 August 1964

Dearest Nancy,

Jolly decent of you to write. No, I am not at all busy, just senile. Since we last met (when?) I have become an old man, not diseased but enfeebled. I read my letters &

work at *The Times* cross-word & never set foot out of doors. I was mildly ill in Mentone in February & so spoiled Laura's hols. I am making up for it by taking her to Spain in October. I don't like the food & can't speak the lingo & dont much look forward to it, especially as I must write an article at the end.

In a few weeks you will receive a copy of my interminable autobiography. I look forward to your studies of Louis XIV. I lately read Sir Winston's *Marlborough*. How he alienates all sympathy. I found myself on every page praying 'Oh God, do defeat the Grand Alliance'.

Living as I do, seeing no one & reading only *The Times* newspaper I am quite bewildered by Bob Boothby's case.[1] £40,000 paid out of court when they had not mentioned his name. If one is incapacitated for life by the negligence of a motorist one is lucky to get £4,000. Perhaps in Constantinople you missed it all. One curious point – the unnamed peer was said to have gone to an 'all male' party of licentious clergymen at Brighton. Now in November last John Sutro & I organized a party to Brighton to celebrate the 40th anniversary of the foundation of the Oxford Railway Club. Bob was there. Clerical dress was not worn but I remember thinking how very clerical most of our voices sounded – impotent grandfathers to a man. Can that have been the origin of the rumour?

Seldom a week passes but I read of a contemporary acquaintance falling downstairs, usually fatally.

Best love
E

[1] A story on the front page of the *Sunday Mirror* said that a peer 'whose name was a household word' had been consorting with gangsters and homosexual clergymen in Brighton. Lord Boothby wrote to *The Times* who published his denial. Though no libel action was suggested, the *Sunday Mirror* sent him £40,000.

TO MARGARET FITZHERBERT   Combe Florey House.
9 August 1964

Darling Pig

. . . I have only read Proust in translation. I thought he began well but went dotty half way through like J Joyce in *Ulysses*. No plan. Nancy says it is uproariously funny throughout & only English & Americans treat it as anything superior to P. G. Wodehouse.

Pray for me
E.W.

To Ann Fleming   Combe Florey House.
20 August 1964

Dearest Ann

I did not write immediately when I heard the news of Ian's death because I knew that it was something you daily dreaded & prepared yourself for & that you would be overwhelmed with condolences & the business of rearranging your life.

I hope that the event was not too harrowing for Caspar. His is a bad age for bereavement. My prayers are for him.

The papers, such as I see, have been uniformly just & generous to Ian. One said I was his best friend. As you know that is not true but I liked him & fully realise the deep loss his will be to you.

For Caspar's sake don't marry again. Widowhood is a dignified estate & one specially blessed by the Church. It would be disastrous for Caspar, now, if you produced Ali Forbes or Quennell as a stepfather. You will suffer the particular loneliness which only widows know. But half the most admirable women I have known have been widows.

I enclose a much misprinted copy of my autobiography. Don't dream of acknowledging it. It is a little better than the extracts in the *Sunday Times* might make you think.

Laura & I go to Spain for the first three weeks of October to avoid the English elections. Any hope of seeing you there? If so, I will give you our itinerary.

Love from
Evelyn

To Katharine Asquith   Combe Florey House.
14 September 1964

Dearest Katharine,

There is no one whose opinion I value more than yours. I assure you that I do not introduce obscene passages in my work with the motive of offending you. I rightly feared that there was an anecdote in my memoirs which would offend you & therefore was in two minds about sending you a copy. But affection overcame discretion.

How can I explain? It is a question, surely?, of manners rather than morals and manners change not only from age to age but from individual to individual. There are many subjects I would discuss & expressions I would use in talking to my children & to Alice &, indeed, to Diana, for it is not a question of date, which I should think inconceivable to employ in talking to you or Helen. I should not in your presence use a mild oath like 'bloody'. I don't think it is a question of reticence or civilization; merely of what is suitable to the person you are addressing.

In writing it is rather different. I certainly should not have taken advantage of modern loose standards to recount that incident of Grimes 30 years ago. Why do I do so now? Simply because I find it a richly comic incident. Forget the moral implications of Grimes's vicious life. I may have told it badly but the point was that here was a new, senior master more or less in command of all of us who had given no hint of his sexual proclivities nor had any indication that any of us would have any sympathy with them. He suddenly electrified us with an unsought & unexpected confession told with complete aplomb. The grotesque details make the point. If I had written: 'He confessed to sexual irregularity', there would be no point. I still find it an enormously comic moment but I know there are fastidious people who won't like it & I am sorry to offend them.

I was shanghaied from the train on Friday by Violet Powell[1] & spent the night at Chantry. It was tantalising to be so near & not to see you. I had been summoned to London to dine tête-à-tête with Archbishop Heenan to discuss the attitude of the laity to the liturgical innovations. He showed himself as deeply conservative and sympathetic to those of us who are scared of the new movement. He thinks that 'the intellectuals' are all against him. 'They regard us as mitred peasants', he said. I think I was able to encourage him a little.[2]

Laura & I go to Spain to avoid the General Elections.

Love to Helen
Evelyn

[1] Anthony Powell was present and in fact extended the invitation.
[2] Cardinal Heenan (1905–75) was Archbishop of Westminster. In his diary for Easter 1965, Waugh wrote: 'Cardinal Heenan has been double-faced in the matter. I had dinner with him *à deux* in which he confessed complete sympathy with the conservatives and, as I understood him, promised resistance to the innovations, which he is now pressing forward.'

To Lady Diana Cooper   Combe Florey House.
17 September 1964

Darling Diana

That was a sorrowful letter.

... Prayer is not asking but giving. Giving your love to God asking for nothing in return. Accepting whatever he sends as his will for you. Not 'Please God give me a happy day' but 'Please God accept all my sufferings today in your honour'. He doesn't want sugar-babies. Have you ever experienced penitence? I doubt it. No wonder you are in the dumps. Do you believe in the Incarnation & Redemption in the full historical sense in which you believe in the battle of El Alamein? That's important. Faith is not a mood.

I got such a wigging from Katharine for the smutty bit in *A Little Learning*. I don't care about reviewers. You & she are the people whose opinion I value.

All love
Bo

To Sir Maurice Bowra   Combe Florey House.
Michaelmas 1964

Dear Maurice

Thanks awfully for your kind corrections to my book. There was a confusion at
the office of the firm now calling itself 'Chapman & Hall', which resulted in the book
going to press before I had read final proofs. Even so there is a multitude of mistakes
which prevented me from sending the book to critical friends like you and
J.Sparrow. If a second edition is ever needed, I will send you the less imperfect
version.

I think, in fact, Chapt 1 is lucid and logically arranged but I can well understand
the reader losing interest. It was the only part Tony Powell enjoyed.

The Manor House Hospital, North End Road, is in some way the preserver of
socialists. They all go there to die.

I greatly regret that you should think I imputed 'tuft-hunting' to you. There is no
reason why I should have made any impression on you. When sober I was
inconspicuous, when drunk I avoided senior members of the university. In fact we
did meet several times and as our ways from Balliol led together to the corner of the
Broad we walked back together, but I am sure there was nothing I said to attract
your notice.

. . . Just off to Spain to avoid the parliamentary elections.

I was greatly cheered to read yesterday of the rebuffs given to Cardinal Bea at
Patras. That should put off ecumenism for a millennium.

                                                    Yours ever
                                                    Evelyn

To Ann Fleming   Combe Florey House.
10 November 1964

Dear Ann

It is a long time since I heard of or from you. How are you? Are you still beset
with legal affairs? Have you remarried? I read with alarm that Mrs Osbert
Lancaster[1] had kicked the bucket. *He* would not make a good stepfather. I once saw
a photograph of his own son. It was highly alarming.

Spain was most exhausting for me but invigorating for Laura. I really have no
wish to travel ever again. I am too old for adventures with camels & canoes and the
organized tourist trade has made all civilized places uniform. Of course Spain is full
of splendid works of art & architecture but *life* there for one who doesn't speak their
language is very flat. And one work of art a day is all the human mind can
comprehend. The food is no longer pungent & poisonous. It is, in the tourist resorts
anyway, as hygienic & tasteless as those trays of cellophane wrapped horrors they
put in ones lap on aeroplanes.

The British Consul-General in Seville (father of two) has a voice quite indistinguishable from step-father Beaton's.

My son-in-law FitzHerbert stood for parliament in Co. Fermanagh and had his clothes literally torn off him by your brother-in-law's[2] gangsters. Meg was stoned.

My dud son James has passed into Sandhurst so need not go to Australia.

My dud daughter Hatty divides her time rather oddly – by day she works in the College of Arms, by night she is lavatory attendant at an expensive homosexual restaurant in Beauchamp Place where, she says, she is often given tips of £1.

Do you remember Bailey, Mary's [Herbert] maid? She lost her sight. Now she has lost the use of her legs. Laura's day is largely occupied in taking her brandy & bananas.

I wrote a review in great haste for *Sunday Times* saying 'please please correct mistakes'. They left '*marriage blanche*' for '*mariage blanc*'. Very humiliating particularly as the point of the review was mocking D. Cecil's bad grammar.

Letter post up to 4d. Too much. But I shall never again leave this house & you won't come here, so write we must.

I see 3 beneficiaries of Ian's got £500 each. Make them give it to you to emend the sloping wall at your edifice.

Try not to marry Quennell or Forbes.

Are you selling Golden Eye? Are you left rich or poor?

Please write & tell me all that has been happening to you in the last two months – and to my acquaintances. Will lack of government employment ruin Andrew?[3]

On a *Friday*, passing through London, I was feeding Meg on caviar when what should I see at the next table but Antonia Fraser eating *grouse*. But she gave birth[4] next day so, I suppose, was free of abstinence. Her mama's book on Queen Victoria was jolly good.[5] It is a great relief her papa [Lord Longford] is not Home Secretary – else we should all be murdered by sexual maniacs.

Ever your affec. coz.

E.W.

[1] Karen Harris, who had married Osbert Lancaster in 1934. He married Anne Scott-James in 1967.
[2] Captain Terence O'Neill (1914–   ). Prime Minister of Northern Ireland 1963–9. Life peer 1970.
[3] The Duke of Devonshire had been Minister of State, Commonwealth Relations Office, 1962–4.
[4] Damian Stafford Fraser was born on 26 October.
[5] Elizabeth Longford, *Victoria R.I.*, 1964.

To DAPHNE FIELDING
Postcard

Combe Florey House.

I detested Emerald. What will you call her?

'The Duchess of Covent Garden Opera'?[1]

I am toothless & despondent.

I don't know what a 'Mas' is. I hope it is something agreeable.

E

[1] Daphne Fielding was working on *Emerald and Nancy; Lady Cunard and her Daughter*, 1968.

To Randolph Churchill   Combe Florey House.
Postcard

Here is a corrected copy of my book. I hope the corrections will give it some interest.

I read *Marlborough* throughout. Were I reviewing the work of a novice I should fall on it furiously but in the case of a man of your father's distinction, I think it would be impertinent. I was everywhere outraged by his partisanship & naive assumption of superior virtue. It is a shifty barrister's case not a work of literature.

I learn you are to be vicariously decorated by the Jews.[1] Send Ghost.

[1] Churchill accepted the Theodor Herzl Gold Medal on behalf of his father in December.

To Brian Franks   Combe Florey House.
14 November 1964

Dear Brian

It is very good of you to remember your old comrade in arms. I shall think of you all with envy on December 14th but, alas, I can't be there. The truth is that I am no longer sortable – deaf, toothless, without appetite, reduced to extreme exhaustion by travel. I should only be a bore and a burden. But thanks awfully for asking me. My love to Bennett & all old friends.

I enclose a book I wrote which won't amuse you but will stand as a token of affection.

                                             Yours ever
                                             Evelyn

To Brian Franks   Combe Florey House.
20 November 1964

Dear Brian

I am deeply touched by your wish to have me at your banquet and by the offer of rooms on 13th & 14th to rest my decayed body. I accept with gratitude & the repeated warning that I can only be regarded as ghost. People get a macabre pleasure in observing the decay of their contemporaries. That is the only pleasure I can hope to give the assembled company. I shall have great pleasure in *seeing* you all. I can't hope to hear you.

                                             Yours ever
                                             Evelyn

To Lady Diana Cooper   Combe Florey House.
28 November 1964

Darling Pug

What do you mean: 'no admirers'. My admiration is undeviating & increasing.

Now how about the evening of Sunday Dec 13th? I shall be at Hyde Park Hotel but you would not be subject to the vulgar glare in the public dining-room; have private parlour. Do dine alone or are you staying with buggers? Failing that there is the next evening but I have suggested Annie for that & I would prefer you tête-à-tête. Also I shall be crapulous on the Monday as the result of Brian Franks's orgy-luncheon.

It is very sad about Annie. She has always been one for the fashion & we shall all be dirt poor very soon. You rode out the storm of the Cripps-Attlee terror without knowing how we under-privileged people suffered. So did she. Now it will be 1964 [*sic*] again with nobs on.

I fear it may be true about Lord Corvedale's defection.[1] It was published in the papers & not denied. Bloggs has always seemed to me the backbone of the old country. Betjeman's son has become a Mormon. Ghastly but B is Dutch. But think of Lord Chetwode turning & turning in his grave.

Should a loyal friend & cousin dispose of Old Kaspar?[2] It should be easy in that Swindon swamp.

I knew no good would come of Mrs Judy's joining that place in Berkeley Square. She was altogether too cock a hoop about it.[3]

Now please send me a post card saying you will dine on Sunday 13th.

14th is rather a gloomy day. It is an annual luncheon which was a huge treat when instituted in 1946 when there was no food or wine in England. Now we are all old, deaf and on regimes.

All love
Bo Wu etc.

What peculiar people win Cooper's prize these days.[4]

[1] Lord Baldwin's son, Viscount Corvedale, became an American citizen for a time when working in San Francisco in 1964.
[2] Lady Diana Cooper had said that Ann Fleming was going to have no money as it all went to her son.
[3] Judy Montagu, now Mrs Gendel, had joined Aspinalls and lost £17,000 gambling.
[4] Aileen Ward for *John Keats – The Making of a Poet*, 1963; Ivan Morris for *The World of the Shining Prince*, 1964.

To Margaret FitzHerbert   Combe Florey House.
16 December 1964

Darling Pig

It was a treat to find a letter from you on my return. I needed a treat.

... I have been seedy for days & the London journey made me worse. In fact I could eat & drink practically nothing of what was manifestly a superb banquet. Here is the menu. The placement was careless. I found myself far from Ran & Bob & Christopher between two business associates of Bennett's who were like the bad man in *The Pumpkin Eater* [1].

I dropped into Edith Sitwell's requiem late & dropped out early. It was sparsely attended.

... Darling Pig I am sorry for all the annoyances & anxieties of your last few days. I wish my love could help. It is all yours

Papa

[1] Jack Clayton's film (1963) of the novel by Penelope Mortimer. Waugh 'could not understand it. I went again two days later and still could not understand it. The last 20 minutes was pure BONKERS.'

To Constantine Fitzgibbon [1]   Combe Florey House.
24 December 1964

Dear Mr FitzGibbon

My memory of Cyril's dinner-party are vague. I had not then heard of Dylan Thomas & thought his presence there rather odd. I am sure Grigson [2] was not present. Robert Byron was (or came in later) for it was he who discovered the resemblance between Thomas and myself & twitted me on it. It is certainly untrue that Thomas insulted Desmond [MacCarthy]. He embarrassed him slightly as Desmond did not like talking smut [3] to a man of a different age & class but it was a momentary embarrassment.

I may be confusing two parties in the same flat but I *think* the dominant & discordant figure was a gross American novelist named Joseph Hergesheimer who boasted painfully. If it was the same evening Deirdre Hart-Davis [4] & the Richard Elweses [5] were there.

Thomas made no particular impression on me. He seemed sober & subdued. I never met him again. Nor have I ever, so far as I know, met Grigson.

I fear this will not help much

Yours sincerely
E. Waugh

[1] Constantine Fitzgibbon (1919–   ). Writer. His *Life of Dylan Thomas* was published in 1965.
[2] Geoffrey Grigson (1905–   ). Poet and critic. He helped tidy Thomas up for dinner, but did not attend himself.
[3] About Swinburne's addiction to flagellation.
[4] Deirdre Hart-Davis, sister of the publisher, married Anthony Bland.
[5] Freya Sykes (1904–   ) married in 1926 Sir Richard Elwes.

To Ann Fleming   Combe Florey House.
27 January 1965

Dear Ann

Our last letters crossed.

I own a tooth-brush but since I have no teeth it is a superfluous possession – like the tiaras of ladies who are never asked out. But I have the name of a man in London who makes false teeth and I have written to order some. I don't imagine the process can be complete in a single visit so I shall probably be in London often in the near future and hope to see you. This is the time I normally go abroad but there is nowhere I want to go. Perhaps with my new snappers I will go for a gastronomic tour. I once knew an old man who at the end of dinner buried his face in his napkin and made retching sounds and then raised a toothless face saying he could not taste port with false teeth. I have a deep horror of them.

For the past fortnight my drive has been worn into pot-holes by telegraph boys bearing extravagant offers from newspapers to describe Sir Winston's obsequies.[1] I have of course refused. He is not a man for whom I ever had esteem. Always in the wrong, always surrounded by crooks, a most unsuccessful father – simply a 'Radio Personality' who outlived his prime. 'Rallied the nation' indeed! I was a serving soldier in 1940. How we despised his orations.

I see that you and/or Ran who pierced my canvas at the Hyde Park Hotel have been at work in the Uffizi now. I suppose you and/or he have the shoes used in Ian's recent film[2].

Did I tell you that I had got a lady-in-waiting to send a letter of condolence in the Queen's name to Mary's one time maid in hospital. The effect has been startling. Not only has she become the tyrant of the ward but she has now convinced herself that she is a near relation of the Queen's.

Giles FitzHerbert who gets more like P.G.Wodehouse's 'Ukridge' daily, believes that he can make his fortune by importing tropical fish.

I suppose the editors who solicited my help in describing Sir Winston's funeral had vaguely heard I once wrote a book about funerals in California.

My health has improved since we last met. If you would like a chilly journey to a servantless, unheated house you would be warmly welcome.

I hope you have not yet made an imprudent marriage.

Ever your affec. coz.
E.W.

[1] Sir Winston Churchill had died on 24 January.
[2] In *From Russia With Love*, James Bond was attacked by a lesbian from whose shoes sprang poisoned daggers.

To Monsignor McReavy [1]   Combe Florey House.
15 April 1965

Rt Rev. Monsignor,

Pray forgive me for troubling you. I do so because I am told you are often kind enough to give expert advice to troubled laymen.

When I was instructed in the Faith some 35 years ago I was told of the obligation to hear mass on the appointed days (a) that it applied only to those living within three miles of a church and that the invention of the motor-car had not modified this ruling and (b) that the obligation applied only from the Offertory to the Priest's Communion.

Is this still the law?[2]

I do not ask what is best for me; merely what is the least I am obliged to do without grave sin. I find the new liturgy a temptation against Faith, Hope and Charity but I shall never, pray God, apostatise.

I enclose an envelope for your kind reply.

Your obedient servant,
E. Waugh

[1] Monsignor McReavy answered queries in the *Clergy Review*.
[2] Waugh was told that on the first point he was technically correct but that obligation referred to the whole Mass.

To NANCY MITFORD   Combe Florey House.
29 May 1965

Dearest Nancy,

You praised Mr Rainbird[1] highly. He came here and I thought him a dull dog and a great snob.

What do you know of a Mrs Lancaster[2] who gives you as reference in soliciting help in writing a treatise on Brian Howard? I can't believe he will be subject of many biographies. It would be a pity if some hack who didn't know him or see his point, should take him in hand. Is she American? What age? Except you and Nancy Cunard there are few women who knew him.

It has been a year of deaths beginning with Alfred Duggan, then Baby Jungman's boy[3], then Harry[4]; the other day Phil Dunne[5]. There has not been a fortnight without a funeral. Ian Fleming is being posthumously canonized by the intelligensia. Very rum.

Honks [Lady Diana Cooper] tells everyone I am dying. I don't think it's true. But I suffer in dignity & pleasure from my new snappers and I do no work.

Love,
Evelyn

[1] George Rainbird (1905–   ). Founded George Rainbird Ltd in 1951, a publishing firm which had enormous success with *The Sun King* by Nancy Mitford in 1966.
[2] Marie-Jaqueline Lancaster edited *Brian Howard: Portrait of a Failure*, 1968.
[3] Richard Cuthbertson was killed in a car accident.
[4] The Earl of Ilchester, previously Lord Stavordale.
[5] The MP and sportsman, not the Canadian baronet.

To Margaret FitzHerbert   Combe Florey House.
30 July 1965

Darling Pig,

I quite understand that you are housebound at present. I do hope you get a good
nanny soon.

I saw *The Knack*[1] and couldn't follow it at all. I thought the heroine hideous and
the scoffers very common but I did laugh once, when she mistook Buckingham
Palace for the Y.W.C.A. hostel. There was no continuity between the incidents.
Now Wilson, though subversive, writes very well. His plot must be taken not as a
forecast of the future but as representing the apprehensions of the British Museum
staff in 1939.[2]

D'Arms's epileptic brother is engaged in the War on Poverty. Perhaps he can
help you.

The William Burges furniture has arrived. The settle looks very well between the
windows of the morning-room. The wardrobe, not so beautiful, but quite suitable
opposite the washhand stand. The gilt gothic whatever-it-is has had to go the attics.
It will take a highly skilled cabinet-maker many weeks to mend.

I have been to communion 3 times since you told me I should. Did I tell you that
Daphne Acton thinks I shall go to heaven?

I wrote to Fr Caraman to suggest a farewell meeting either here or in London but
his secretary tells me he has left without an address. Hatty seems to be collecting
subscriptions for a joint present with Auberon. Your mother will subscribe to this. I
should prefer to give him something on my own. Can you suggest anything suitable
within my means? He has been so very munificent to me.

Are the Jesuits closing Beaumont[3] simply to develop the site as villas? It seems a
most shady transaction.

You would have seen a rum mixture of people if you had gone to Eddy Sackville's
Requiem. Perhaps you read the list.

Your ever loving papa,
E.W.

[1] Richard Lester's film starring Rita Tushingham, 1964.
[2] Angus Wilson's *The Old Men at the Zoo*. Wilson had worked in the Reading Room at the British
Museum.
[3] The Jesuit public school near Windsor, now defunct.

To Nancy Mitford   Combe Florey House.
5 September 1965

Darling Nancy

It was *very* nice to hear from you. I have not written because the last 10 months
have been ineffably dreary – my only excursions to dentist and to funerals and my
house perpetually full of grandchildren.

I read in a paper that you had gone into the musical comedy world.[1] I hope it is rewarding. I find I can't follow the plot of any plays or films nowadays, whether it is my decay or theirs I don't know.[2] The girls all seem hideous and the men common. Diana Honks says I am dying of drugs. Don't believe it, but my loss of teeth has deprived me of all pleasure in food.

No one in this house wears unsuitable clothes but, like you, I hear alarming accounts from more fashionable resorts.

... The film of *Loved One*[3] is a great annoyance to me – one of the few occasions when Peters has let me down. He sold it years ago to a mad Mexican for a paltry sum with the assurance that it would never be produced but that Alec Guinness and I might have an agreeable jaunt together in Mexico. The next thing I heard was that an American company had bought the rights from the Mexican and were producing an elaborate travesty. No redress.

I've never heard of Wells play[4]. Shows how I am out of the swim.

The buggering up of the Church is a deep sorrow to me and to all I know. We write letters to the paper. A fat lot of good that does.

I enjoyed Hemingway's Parisian memoirs[5]; did you? Laura finds consolation in horticulture. I am a dreary companion for her these days.

Oh the hell of people who write theses. I get them from two sides – Ronnie Knox's works and my own.

La Pietra is grand but very uncomfortable. Have you stayed there before? Better stick to the hotel and see Harold [Acton] when convenient.

I remember men dressed as women – Beaton, Byron etc – at parties in 1927 but they did not call it 'drag'. What an odd name. Dragging the skirts?

I pray that your poor eyes are clearer.

> With much love,
> E

[1] *The Pursuit of Love* with music by Julian Slade ran for four weeks at the Bristol Old Vic from 24 May 1967.
[2] In a letter to John MacDougall: 'Diana took me to *Who's Afraid of Virginia Woolf*. Most confusing.'
[3] Directed by Tony Richardson, 1965.
[4] He misread 'Redl' in a reference to *A Patriot for Me* by John Osborne.
[5] *A Moveable Feast*.

TO LADY DIANA COOPER   Combe Florey House.
23 September 1965

Darling Pug,

My peacock died last night. He was in fine feather and voice all the summer, ailed for two days (it is thought from a surfeit of melon seeds) lost the use of his legs and then turned up his toes. The latest of a 12 month long series of bereavements. Fortunately he leaves progeny. He was 11 years of age – early middle-age for his breed.

... No, there's no 'reward' in this world. Perhaps retribution hereafter.
A propos, can you give me the text and provenance of

> La vie est brêve   (wish it were)
> Un peu d'espoir
> Un peu de rêve
> Et puis bonsoir

I have read a new good book about Swift by a man called Nigel Dennis. I found many affinities with the temperament (not of course the talent) of the master. Except his bossiness. That doesn't trouble me, thank God.

Little Meg has grown peevish. Not up to the struggle of life.

All love always
Bo

TO A.J.P.TAYLOR[1]   Combe Florey House.
28 October 1965

Dear Mr Taylor

Many thanks for your kind letter.

I asked my publishers to send you a copy of my war novel[2] because I heard you had commended the last volume in a Sunday newspaper and it occurred to me that it might amuse you to see the whole if you ever had a period of convalescence.

Trimmer married a Johannesburg jewess and is now greatly scared about his safety and fortune.

I am not surprised to learn that the late Lord Beaverbrook had read nothing of mine. I used to meet him quite often in the late 30s and I noticed that though he went out of his way to be civil, he always got the names and titles wrong. He liked to get information at second-hand from his hangers-on – e.g. Valentine Castlerosse, Venetia Montagu, Perry Brownlow etc. But I don't think he had the patience to plough through a new novel. I believe he was much disappointed by his failure to promote the success of William Gerhardi (who deserved it). I think it made him realize the impotence of the press – like the *Daily Mail* Hat which only survives on the heads of the outside porters at the Berkeley Hotel.[3]

No doubt you are in touch with Gerhardi. It was a significant incident. Incidentally he is old, ill, and poor and longs for a knighthood. Perhaps you can help him?

Yours sincerely,
Evelyn Waugh

[1] A.J.P.Taylor (1906–   ). Historian and journalist.
[2] *Sword of Honour*, the war trilogy in one volume.
[3] Lord Northcliffe, inspired by a photograph of Clemenceau in an unusual hat, offered in 1920 a prize of £100 for one of a new design. In spite of a campaign in the *Daily Mail* and Winston Churchill being among the first to wear it, the new hat failed.

To Margaret FitzHerbert   Combe Florey House.
6 December 1965

Darling,

Thank you for your loving letter. You must not worry about my condition. I am growing old and old men suffer from aberrations of one kind or another. Dope is less harmful and less sinful than, say, drink or chasing young girls or boys. It would of course be better to be a saint. God chooses his own. The awful prospect is that I may have more than 20 years ahead. Pray that I 'make my soul' in this period. I shall just become more and more boring I fear. Don't let me in my dotage oppress you.

Just back from the funeral of Gaffer Prater [1] – not well attended.

. . . It seems to me quite likely that another world war will break out soon. In that case stock-broking will cease to be profitable. It would be much more convenient for Giles to be already settled in government service.

All love darling Pig,
E.W.

[1] Prater worked in the garden and was the father-in-law of Brown, the official gardener.

To Graham Greene   Combe Florey House.
Midwinter [January 1966]

Dear Graham

I was on the point of writing to congratulate you on *The Comedians*, and to thank you for your loyal friendship in sending me a copy, when I opened the newspaper to see the exhilarating news of your having been made a Companion of Honour. Am I not right in thinking that one of your characters remarks that it is the only public recognition worth having? I fear this letter will be one of a huge pile of congratulations. If it slips through the mesh of the secretariat please accept it as a real expression of joy.

I greatly admire *The Comedians*. What staying power you have. It might have been written 30 years ago and could be by no one but you.

1965 was a bad year for me in a number of ways – dentistry, deaths of friends, the 'aggiornamento'. I try to face the new wars with resignation.

Of course don't answer,

Love,
Evelyn

To Ann Fleming   Combe Florey House.
[January 1966]

Dear Ann,

As you can see, this was a good luncheon but I had little heart for it. So many friends dead in the last year and my snappers very uncomfortable. I am glad you did not send demon lover Driberg to me. I went to bed at 9 o'clock and brooded about Buchan-Hepburn finding me a bore. I have not been the same since that revelation.

Christmas was not as painful as most years. No young children. I could not have danced with you in the snow.

1965 was a bitter year for me. Many bereavements. No work. Feeble health. Those who love me tell me I am dying but professional opinion does not confirm them. Fr Hubert van Zeller, *One Foot in the Cradle* pp70–71 expresses beautifully what I feel. 'Dying is just growing up. I am not unhappy. I just do not much like being alive.'

Graham Greene has fled the country with the CH and a work of communist propaganda. Margaret forces me to church.

What do you mean by 'snap'? The family group was carefully posed by the Fuddy Duddy Beaton in Taunton.

If I read your letter rightly you and Andrew must have drunk £400 worth of whisky. I call that going it.

The Solomon family[1] were very odd. I have never admired him. He came to a bad end. So did Rebecca. The eldest was highly respectable. All children of a rabbi.

Never get involved in a controversy. The boredom of it. . . . [incomplete]

[1] Abraham, Rebecca and Simeon, all nineteenth-century painters.

TO NANCY MITFORD   Combe Florey House.
28 February 1966

Dearest Nancy,

It is a long time since I wrote to you; so long that I do not know when. If I repeat myself, pray forgive me.

Graham Greene's address is 130 Boulevarde Malesherbes Paris 17. I cannot tell you if he is alone there. I suspect not. But he is more social than his books would give one to think.

The attack on Diana[1] was (to me) terribly shocking. Not the loss of her fur coat and whatever else the ruffians took but the loss of dignity. I think it is coming home to her. She has been deserted by servants and that Iris (whom I have never liked or trusted). When Lord Noel Buxton and your friend Miss Spain intruded in my house I put it in the market next day because I felt it was polluted. That was a mere impertinence, not a physical outrage. There should be a Praetorian Guard of Pansies (we know from the war how brave they are) to keep a standing 24 piquet on all these widows like Ann.

My health is slightly better. I keep getting the news that I am dying and drug soaked. Not true. But I am very idle because taxation in my country removes what the newspapers call 'incentives'.

Your dud goddaughter Harriet spends her days in the College of Arms and her evenings as cloak-room attendant in an expensive restaurant but she still costs me a great deal. My finances are embarrassed by a trust fund invented years ago by Peters which now appears to be invalid.

I have escaped from my Rainbird contract[2] (clever Peters) and shall now slog away at autobiography. M. Bowra's autobiography[3] will be a great disappointment to people ... who read only for malicious gossip. It is really very soft and dull. He said you and I had sexual connexions. I explained to him that it was not so and he expunged the offending passage.

Love
E

[1] Burglars broke into Lady Diana Cooper's house and tied her and Iris Tree up. She wrote to Waugh: 'I was less frightened than I am in aeroplanes .... The funniest moment was stooping to pick up a leather belt for them to handcuff me with and the thug saying "Thank you".' Iris Tree quoted from *Othello*: 'Who steals my purse steals trash'.

[2] To write about the Crusades.

[3] Maurice Bowra, *Memories 1898–1939*, 1966.

To Alec Waugh   Combe Florey House.
6 March 1966

Dear Alec,

It was kind of you to write. As usual the newspapers had got their facts wrong. It is true that all last year I was idle and low spirited but I was free from hallucinations. I had foolishly contracted to write 4 books[1] (not one) and could not face the task. Also I had a lot of teeth drawn and find that the false snappers ruin my appetite for solid food. Also the universal tourism makes me reluctant to go out of the village. But I have not been insane or really ill.

We shall all end teaching the Yanks. I think I once saw a play about Oklahoma.[2] They did not seem a very critical people. But I understand that American undergraduates are in a perpetual state of mutinous ferment.

Please give my regard to Franky Filleul and to David Herbert.[3] It is said here that he has ennobled himself and goes under the name of Lord David. As far as I know there has never been a warrant out for him in this country.

Yours ever affec
E.W.

[1] On the Crusades, the Popes, American history and Volume 2 of his autobiography.

[2] Alec Waugh was going to Oklahoma as writer-in-residence.

[3] Francis Filleul, a contemporary of Waugh's at Oxford, and David Herbert (1908–   ), brother of the Earl of Pembroke. Both lived in Tangier, as did Alec.

To Lady Mosley   Combe Florey House.
9 March 1966

Dearest Diana,

It was a delight to get a letter from you and to hear that you sometimes think of me.

It is not clear whether you have completed your memoirs and published them and that I somehow missed them or whether you are still working on them.[1] I long to read them. My *Little Learning* dealt with adolescence, before I knew you. It is truthful in the sense of stating nothing false but, of course, it omits a good deal. My brother's memoirs were embarrassingly revealing. I am now at work in a desultory way on a second volume which presents graver problems because I must mention several living people.

You ask why our friendship petered out. The explanation is very discreditable to me. Pure jealousy. You (and Bryan) were immensely kind to me at a time when I greatly needed kindness, after my desertion by my first wife. I was infatuated with you. Not of course that I aspired to your bed but I wanted you to myself as especial confidante and comrade. After Jonathan's birth you began to enlarge your circle. I felt lower in your affections than Harold Acton and Robert Byron and I couldn't compete or take a humbler place. That is the sad and sordid truth. Politics had not then raised their ugly head.

I took my then 15 year old daughter to the Musée Grevin some years ago. It was all clean and handsome with a splendid 'transformation' room.

I have become very old in the last two years. Not diseased but enfeebled. There is nowhere I want to go and nothing I want to do and I am conscious of being an utter bore. The Vatican Council has knocked the guts out of me. But you would find most of your English friends in a bad way. Bright young Henry Yorke I hear is quite decrepit. . . .

All you Mitfords seem to have great stamina.

                                                    All love
                                                    Evelyn

Alec Waugh was sacked from school for what was then called 'the usual thing'.

[1] Diana Mosley, *A Life of Contrasts*, 1977.

To Lady Mosley   Combe Florey House.
30 March 1966

Dearest Diana,

Beware of writing to me. I always answer. It is part of my great boringness, never going out or telephoning. An inherited weakness. My father spent the last 20 years of his life writing letters. If someone thanked him for a wedding present, he thanked them for thanking him and there was no end to the exchange but death. Nancy pretended she was going blind to choke me off.

But I must not leave you with the delusion that *Work Suspended* was a cruel portrait of you[1]. It was perhaps to some extent a portrait of me in love with you, but there is not a single point in common between you and the heroine except pregnancy. Yours was the first pregnancy I observed.

I sent you a copy when you were in jug. Surely you remember me well enough to know I should not have done such a thing at such a time if I thought it a 'cruel portrait'?

You speak kindly of my war books. Do you possess them all in the single, final version? If not, I should like to send it to you as an Easter present in case you ever thought of looking at it again. It is not much different but slightly pulled together.

John Sutro had hallucinations of poverty and was cured by electric shock.

Easter used to mean so much to me. Before Pope John and his Council – they destroyed the beauty of the liturgy. I have not yet soaked myself in petrol and gone up in flames, but I now cling to the Faith doggedly without joy. Church going is a pure duty parade. I shall not live to see it restored. It is worse in many countries.

Please don't answer, unless to say you would like the *Sword of Honour* omnibus.

All love,
Evelyn

[1] Lady Mosley explains that she did not really believe herself lampooned as 'Lucy' but thought it might 'do him good (I mean make him happier) if he thought I thought he'd got his own back a bit'.

Waugh died on Easter Day, 10 April 1966. He attended Mass, said in the form he preferred by Father Caraman, returned to Combe Florey and had a sudden heart attack during the morning.

Appendix

Hugh Trevor-Roper, then Student of Christ Church, published an essay in the *New Statesman* in December 1953 entitled 'Sir Thomas More and the English Lay Recusants' (reprinted in his *Historical Essays*, 1957). Waugh, who considered Trevor-Roper anti-Catholic, wrote to attack it. The ensuing correspondence is set apart from the main text because it is of specialized interest and because it is hard to follow unless the letters are read consecutively, though not of course as hard as it was for readers who had to wait a week between replies. Waugh had written publicly to criticize Trevor-Roper when he published *The Last Days of Hitler* in 1947, and there was a further exchange when he reviewed *The Life of Robert Southwell* in 1956.

TO FATHER PHILIP CARAMAN   Piers Court.
[7 December 1953]

P.S. Have you read Roper in this weeks *New Stateman*? I spotted four errors in the
first 3 lines & have written about them. I seemed to find a dozen others. I am sure
that someone better educated than I am could find a hundred. Would it not be a
good thing to employ one of your learned friends to go through the articles with a
fine comb & expose them all in a long article. It is time Roper was called to order &
this article seems a happy opportunity.

                                                                    E

TO THE EDITOR OF THE   Piers Court.
NEW STATESMAN AND NATION
[12 December 1953]

Sir, – Since Mr. Trevor-Roper has introduced my name, rudely and irrelevantly,
into his article, "Books in General," may I offer two reflections?

Why does this contributor write so very often about the Catholic Church, a
subject on which he is conspicuously ill-informed? Sometimes one has to read three
or four paragraphs before striking the howler which reveals the quality of his
scholarship. This week three lines suffice. "On July 6, 1535," he begins, "Sir
Thomas More went, with Bishop Fisher, to the block. They were the first English
recusants."

St. John Fisher was a Cardinal at the time of his execution. This occurred on
June 22, not on July 6.

Among men of education "recusant" has a limited and useful meaning. It has
nothing to do with high treason and the denial of the monarch's spiritual
supremacy; it simply means refusing to attend Anglican Church services. But even
in Mr. Roper's loose employment, he has got his facts wrong. The protomartyrs of
the English Reformation suffered on May 4 of that year – the Brigettine monk,
Richard Reynolds, and the three Carthusian Priors, John Houghton of London,
Robert Lawrence of Beauvue and Augustus Webster of Axholme.

Later, among the strange jumble of speculations and mis-statements, Mr. Roper

                                    642

truly remarks that in the last century the English Catholic Bishops were chary of encouraging men of their faith to take University degrees. Can he wonder at this when he himself presents the spectacle of a tutor in Modern History who clumsily and offensively attacks the Catholic religion?

EVELYN WAUGH

Sir, – Being abroad, I have only just seen Mr. Waugh's letter, in which he says that I am "conspicuously ill-informed," that my work is a "strange jumble of speculations and mis-statements," and that its abundant 'howlers' sufficiently reveal the quality of my scholarship. The actual howlers which he cites in evidence are: (1) That I carelessly extended the date of More's execution to cover that of Fisher, who actually suffered a fortnight earlier. This is an error which I acknowledge. (2) That I called Fisher a Bishop when in fact he was a Cardinal. In England, where his Cardinalate, being in defiance of the law, was not recognised, he was Bishop of Rochester. (3) That, unlike "men of education," I apply to More that term "recusant," which properly "has nothing to do with high treason and the denial of the monarch's spiritual supremacy," but simply means one who refuses to attend Anglican church services. I am far from my books, but I think that if Mr. Waugh will take a little trouble before screaming about my "howlers," he will find that before 1570 the word "recusant" was generally applied to those who refused the oath of supremacy; it was only later that it acquired its meaning of non-attendance at church.

My general point in referring to More as the first recusant is that he was the first *layman* to refuse the oath of supremacy, and thus became the hero of the later *lay* recusants whose recusancy was defined by their refusal to attend the national church. To this point, earlier clerical recusants are immaterial.

Mr Waugh asks why "this contributor" writes "so very often" on this subject. In the ten years during which I have contributed articles to THE NEW STATESMAN, I have written three times on the English Catholics – *i.e.*, as often as on the English Quakers and a good deal less often than upon the English Protestants. This seems to me to show a sense of proportion.

H. R. TREVOR-ROPER

TO THE EDITOR OF THE   Piers Court.
NEW STATESMAN AND NATION
2 January 1954

Sir, – I accused Mr Trevor-Roper of having made four howlers in the first three lines of his essay. To these (a) he pleads guilty, (b) he excuses himself on the grounds that "Cardinal" is not a legally recognised title in this country. Yet in the same essay he refers to "Cardinals" Wiseman and Manning. The plain inference is that he forgot, if he ever knew, that St John Fisher had an equal right to the title. (c) Mr Trevor-Roper is "away from his books." When he returns and consults the dictionary he will see that "recusant" is defined as: "One, especially a Roman Catholic *(Popish recusant)* who refused to attend the services of the Church of England." (d) He excuses his omission of the protomartyrs on the grounds that he was writing exclusively of laymen. But he wrote: "They" (More and Fisher) "were the first recusants." Did he "away from his books" suppose that Fisher was a layman?

One honourable course is open to Mr Trevor-Roper. He should change his name and seek a livelihood at Cambridge.

I am sorry if I exaggerated the number of his attacks on the Church in your columns. My impression is that, whatever the ostensible subject of his contribution, he makes a hobby of introducing opprobrious references to the Church. I have kept no count. If I am wrong, I readily apologise.

But even if I am wrong, Mr Trevor-Roper's position as a tutor to Christian undergraduates seems to me dubious. In the essay under discussion he wrote: "In the intellectual emptiness of modern English Catholicism only the snob-appeal" (where do young dons pick up their vocabulary?) "is left."

This is to insult not only Roman Catholicism, but all forms of Christianity. No one can doubt that we possess the Scriptures, the Creeds and the Fathers. We claim much else beside. The sane Christian criticism of Roman Catholicism is that we are too full and have enriched the original deposit of faith with legends and opinions. If we are empty what does Christendom contain?

EVELYN WAUGH.

Sir, – In reply to his first letter, I advised Mr. Waugh to take a little trouble before screaming about my howlers. In reply to his second I can only repeat this advice.

First, Bishop Fisher. Mr. Waugh now accuses me of having written, in extenuation of my use of this title, that the title of Cardinal "is not a legally recognised title in this country"; and on the basis of this accusation he proceeds to find me culpably inconsistent in referring to "Cardinal Wiseman." If Mr. Waugh will look at my letter he will see that I made no such foolish evasion. What I stated, with perfect clarity, was the historical fact that *Bishop Fisher's* Cardinalate – announced by the Pope when Fisher was already deposed and attainted of treason – was not recognised in England. Mr Waugh has thus falsified my words, and the generalisations which he bases on such falsification are, in his own words, "rude and irrelevant."

Still on the basis of this falsification, Mr Waugh presumes that I am ignorant of Fisher's Cardinalate. Every schoolboy has been told how Fisher, on the eve of his execution, was declared a Cardinal in Rome, and how Henry VIII promptly (and accurately) replied that if the red hat came there would be no head to put it on; just as every schoolboy also knows that Thomas Cromwell, on the eve of his execution, was created Earl of Essex. But he does not expect to be accused of ignorance by sectarians and pedants if he still refers to them, in the customary manner, as Bishop Fisher and Thomas Cromwell.

Secondly, the meaning of the word "recusant." On this subject, since my family were recusants for two hundred years while Mr. Waugh's Catholicism is, I think, still rather crude and green, I may perhaps claim a finer sense than he. At all events, on the basis of my reading, I ventured to suggest that *before* 1570 – i.e., before the meaning became specialised through the papal Bull of Excommunication – the word was used of those who refused the oath of Supremacy. With a triumphant flourish Mr. Waugh now quotes from the *Oxford English Dictionary* the specialised meaning which, *after* 1570, I of course allow. What he prudently conceals from your readers is the fact that, with one exception, every instance of that meaning given by the Dictionary is *after* 1570, and therefore, of course, quite irrelevant to my remarks. Further, the one exception (from an Act of Parliament of 1553) proves, on closer examination, to have been erroneously included under that heading. Reference to the original Statute (7 Edward VI c.4) shows that in fact the term is there used to describe, not abstainers from the Protestant church, but clergy who refuse to pay their tenths and firstfruits. Thus the evidence of the Dictionary is in no way inconsistent with my suggestion. Further, those who have studied the matter less superficially than Mr. Waugh seem to agree with me. Thus the Roman Catholic scholar Fr. Godfrey Anstruther, in his family-history *Vaux of Harrowden*, writes: "A recusant is one who refuses. The word first appears in the Statutes as early as 1548, when it meant an incumbent who refused to pay tenths to the King. *Early in Elizabeth's reign it meant one who refused the oath of Supremacy*. It was *later* used to designate a Papist who refused to resort to divine worship in Protestant churches ..." This is exactly my conclusion.

Mr. Waugh has presumed to tell me what is "the only honourable course" for me to adopt. Perhaps he will now consider what is the least dishonourable course left to those who, in order to gain debating points, are convicted of falsifying documents, concealing relevant evidence and relying on abuse.

Finally Mr. Waugh asks, "If we (the English Roman Catholics) are empty, what does Christendom contain?" Less parochial in my observation than Mr. Waugh, I have noticed other Christians besides Roman Catholics, and other Roman Catholics besides that minority of Englishmen whom Mr. Waugh (doubtless to their embarrassment) so loudly claims to represent.

H. R. TREVOR-ROPER

TO THE EDITOR OF THE NEW STATESMAN   Piers Court.
11 January 1954

Sir, – Pray rest assured that this is the last letter I shall address to you on this subject. Any comment Mr Roper cares to make, I will read with barely flagging interest but leave unanswered. I write now only because Mr Roper suffers from a delusion which I find personally annoying.

On December 5 he wrote: "Follow me, says Mr Waugh ... and join the old English recusants." This week he writes of "That minority of Englishmen whom Mr Waugh ... so loudly claims to represent."

Believe me, Sir, I have never, loudly or quietly or in the silence of my heart, claimed or aspired to represent or lead any one of my fellow Catholics. Mr Roper does not know me but he claims acquaintance with a variety of other Catholics. He should thereby realise that the suggestion is preposterous.

Having said this, may I try to leave a clean plate of the pedantries? Mr Roper admits that he was wrong about the date of St John Fisher's execution. He now tacitly, I take it, admits he was wrong when he called it "the first" case of recusancy. There remain then under discussion only the title of Cardinal and the proper use of "recusant."

(1) A Cardinal holds a purely papal appointment. No other ruler can confer the rank or remove it. No consecration is required. A man is a Cardinal from the moment the Pope declares him so, not from his reception of the hat. In the last month of his life St John Fisher's position resembled that of Cardinal Stepinac today. It would have been injudicious to have referred to him as "His Eminence" before Henry VIII, but Mr Roper need not fear to do so. St John enjoyed the same rank and suffered the same local disability as Cardinal Wiseman. Mr Roper appeals to popular usage and quotes Thomas Cromwell, Earl of Essex, as a parallel. A simple test is to consult the Encyclopaedia Britannica where he will find four Earls entered under Essex, none of them Cromwell. If he looks up St John he will find "Fisher, John, Cardinal."

(2) Recusant. I took Mr Roper to task because in an historical essay he used a term which has borne a "limited and valuable" meaning for at least 250 years in a loose and misleading way. He retorts that it did not bear this precise meaning before 1570. What has that to do with it? "Recusant" before and after 1570 could be used generally to qualify anyone who refused anything. Wordsworth used it with poetic licence of boys who refused to do their lessons. But for at least a century before him the technical meaning was a man who refused to attend church. (I do not know why Mr Roper attaches such importance to the year 1570. Compulsory attendance at Protestant worship under pain of fines was prescribed in 1558.)

May I make the point clearer? A cavalier poet might well have written: "Bid me to live and I will die, Thy Recusant to be." If I were told that Mr Roper had never met a Protestant, I should be incredulous. If I were further told that my informant happened to feel like a cavalier that day and that by "Protestant" he meant "one who protested his devotion," I should think the statement plausible but the expression fantastic.

I cannot accept the theory that because Mr Roper's family apostasised more recently than mine, he has inherited a superior insight into the proper use of language.

EVELYN WAUGH

(Mr. Trevor-Roper writes: "May I recommend to Mr. Waugh a period of silent reading? In particular, he might glance at (1) The Catholic Who's Who and Yearbook, published by Burns, Oates and Washbourne, publishers to the Holy See. There he will find, in "The Kalendar" (I quote from the 1938 edition, which is before me) that the date 9 July has been declared the official saints-day of SS. John Fisher, Bishop, and Thomas More Martyrs? There is no mention of "Cardinal." (2) My own article, in which he will find that I made the necessary qualifications about my application of the word "recusant" to More: an application which Mr. Waugh ignorantly challenged and which I have now proved correct. He will also find other matter which he will do well to digest." – Ed., N.S. & N.)

Appendix of Names

Acton, Daphne (1911–   ). Daughter of Lord Rayleigh, married Lord Acton in 1931 and had five sons and five daughters. A close friend of Ronald Knox, who once threw her lipstick into the Mediterranean. Lived with her husband in Rhodesia until UDI was declared; then fervently religious in Australia.

Acton, Sir Harold (1904–   ). Writer. With a mother from Chicago, a home in Florence, a collection of poems with a publisher and a reputation already earned at Eton, Acton was the dominating aesthete of his Oxford generation. He opposed not only the beer-drinking 'Georgian' poets but also the tired imitations of the styles of the nineties: 'Plus ça change, plus c'est la même pose', as his friend and sometimes rival Brian Howard observed. He wished to replace them with admirers of the new, in particular Ronald Firbank, T.S. Eliot and the Sitwells. 'Early Victoriana was so unfashionable that a taste for it was also novel so "Back to Mahogany" was my battle-cry.'

Acton became a close friend to Waugh, who wrote in *A Little Learning*: 'What, I think, we had in common was *gusto* in the English use of the word; a zest for the variety and absurdity of the life opening to us, a veneration for (not the same) artists, a scorn for the bogus. He was always the leader; I, not always, the follower.' The better characteristics of Anthony Blanche in *Brideshead Revisited* and most of Ambrose Silk in *Put Out More Flags* are drawn from Acton. He has lived mainly in Italy and 1933–9 in Peking. Publications include *Memoirs of an Aesthete* (1948), *The Bourbons of Naples* (1956) and *Nancy Mitford: a memoir* (1975).

Asquith, Katharine (1885–1977). Daughter of Sir John Horner, married in 1907 Raymond Asquith, who was killed in action in 1916 before his father, the Prime Minister, accepted an earldom. A Roman Catholic convert, she inherited the Manor House at Mells in Somerset, and Monsignor Ronald Knox came to live there in 1949. With Christopher Hollis and later Anthony Powell near the same village, it became a centre of Waugh's friends. He was somewhat nervous, though respectful, of her opinion of his books.

Avon, Countess of (1920–   ). Clarissa Churchill, niece of Sir Winston and so cousin of Randolph. Married in 1952 Anthony Eden, who became Prime Minister in 1955 and Earl of Avon in 1961.

Baldwin of Bewdley, 3rd Earl (1904–78). Succeeded in 1958. Son of the Prime Minister, he was called Frisky, which derived from the jingle 'you have whisky to make you frisky', or, more widely, Bloggs. Made friends with Waugh as they pursued Teresa Jungman without success. Wrote: 'He [Waugh] was always wonderfully unrude to me and my wife; I can't think why; and I've always been grateful.' Publications include *My Father: the True Story* (1956) and *A Flying Start* (autobiography) (1967).

Balfour, Patrick, see Lord Kinross.

Beerbohm, Sir Max (1872–1956). Essayist and carica-turist. Waugh described him as 'an idol of my adolescence to whom every year deepened my devotion'. He was an extreme example of the sort of meticulous, unpretentious talent of which Waugh approved. Publications include *Zuleika Dobson* (1911) and *Rossetti and his Circle* (1922).

Betjeman, Sir John (1906–   ). Poet. A friend at Oxford, where neither of them was seen as a distinguished writer of the future. Married Penelope Chetwode in 1933. Resisted Waugh's aggressive attempts to convert him to Roman Catholicism in 1947–8. Knighted in 1969. Poet Laureate 1972. His many books of poetry and on English churches and architecture include *Summoned by Bells* (autobiography) (1960) and *English Churches* (1964).

Betjeman, Penelope (1910–   ). Daughter of Field Marshal Lord Chetwode, Commander-in-Chief in India 1930–5. Married John Betjeman in 1933, became a Catholic in 1948. Waugh drew on her and her love of horses for *Helena*. Moti, her Arab pony, used to come into Lord Berners's drawing room at Faringdon and remain for tea. Publications include *Two Middle-aged Ladies in Andalusia* (1963) and 'Recollections' in *Evelyn Waugh and his World* (1973).

Bowra, Sir Maurice (1898–1971). Oxford don, Warden of Wadham College from 1938. Encouraged such undergraduates as Kenneth Clark and John Betjeman to enjoy themselves. Waugh's uneasy relationship with him faltered when he wrote in *A Little Learning:* 'He [Cyril Connolly] and Maurice Bowra were both acquaintances who became friends after I attracted some attention as a novelist'. He explains in a letter (p.625) that this was not an accusation of lion-hunting; it still reads like one. In some respects the model for Mr Samgrass in *Brideshead Revisited.* Knighted 1951. Among his publications are *The Greek Experience* (1957) and *Memories 1898–1939* (1966).

Bradwell, Lord. See Driberg.

Carew, Dudley (1903–). Published the first of six novels in 1924 and worked on the *London Mercury* under J.C.Squire, whose powerful literary set, known as 'the squirearchy', opposed obscure new writers such as T.S.Eliot. Carew joined *The Times* in 1926 and during the next thirty-seven years reckons that he wrote nine million words, for the most part anonymously. 'I [Waugh] fascinated and dominated a boy in another House ...', *A Little Learning*, p.129. Publications include *A Fragment of Friendship* (1974), a reminiscence of Waugh at school.

Churchill, Randolph (1911–68). Journalist, son of Sir Winston Churchill. Married Pamela Digby 1939–46 and June Osborne 1948–61. In his autobiography, *Twenty-One Years* (1965), he says that he enjoyed 'a warm friendship interrupted from time to time' with Waugh from 1929. They were both godparents of Jonathan Guinness.

Connolly, Cyril (1903–74). Critic and author. Created his own persona of a brilliant youth, who failed to live up to expectations, in *Enemies of Promise* (1938). When he was elected to 'Pop' at Eton, Hubert Duggan asked: 'Is that the tug [Colleger] who's been kicked in the face by a mule' (*Infants of the Spring*, p.120, by Anthony Powell). In the war 'his face was round, plump and pale, his shoulders sloped from a short thick neck and dark hair was fluffed thickly out behind the ears that seemed no longer to protrude. He had a short snub Irish nose and under shaggy Irish brows, his eyes, set far apart, looked both hooded and alert,' J.Maclaren-Ross in *Memoirs of the Forties*, p.62. An Oxford acquaintance of Waugh's and a lasting if much teased friend. One of the founders and editor of *Horizon* 1939–50 and then chief reviewer of the *Sunday Times.* There is a General Connolly in *Black Mischief* and some evacuees called Connolly in *Put Out More Flags* have been said to show his vices of lust, gluttony and sloth. In *Sword of Honour*, Everard Spruce, editor of *Survival*, is in spite of Waugh's assurances to the contrary, drawn in part from Connolly. Each minded criticism from the other. Waugh worried over the phrase 'benign lethargy' bestowed by Connolly in a review of *Officers and Gentlemen.* Connolly was bitterly hurt when, after Waugh's death, he came by chance on the contemptuous annotations scribbled in Waugh's copy of *The Unquiet Grave* (1944). He married three times: Jean Bakewell, Barbara Skelton and Deirdre Craig.

Cooper, Lady Diana (1892–). Indestructible beauty. Daughter of the Duke of Rutland, married in 1919 Duff Cooper, who was created Viscount Norwich in 1952. Met Waugh, whom she called Mr Wu, when she was acting the Madonna in *The Miracle* and he kept her company while she toured the provinces. Perhaps the most deep and enduring of all his friendships. Ambassadress in Paris 1944–7. The most direct portrait to appear in Waugh's work, she is Mrs Stitch in *Scoop* and *Sword of Honour.* Publications consist of an autobiography in three volumes: *The Rainbow Comes and Goes* (1958), *The Light of Common Day* (1959) and *Trumpets from the Steep* (1960).

Driberg, Tom (1905–76). Created Lord Bradwell in 1975. Journalist, politician and homosexual. Educated at Lancing and Christ Church, Oxford. *Daily Express* 1928–43 partly as its gossip columnist William Hickey. Labour MP 1942–55, and 1959–74. Chairman of Labour Party 1957–8. Publications include: *Beaverbrook: A Study in Power and Frustration* (1956) and *Ruling Passions* (autobiography) (1977).

Duggan family. Grace Hinds, an American, married in 1902 Alfred Duggan, who was a Roman Catholic of Irish descent with estates in the Argentine. He worked at the Argentinian embassy in London and after his death, in 1915, she married Lord Curzon, then Leader of the House of Lords. So her Duggan children, Alfred (1903–64), Hubert (1904–43) and Marcella, born 1906, had a splendid background. Waugh met the boys at Oxford where he found Hubert 'a delicate dandy of the Regency' and his brother 'a full-blooded rake of the Restoration ... we were often drunk, Alfred almost always'. *A Little Learning*, p.202. Hubert was a Conservative MP 1931–43. His deathbed scene inspired that of Lord Marchmain in *Brideshead Revisited.* Alfred reformed in middle-age; he controlled his drinking, and, his money spent, wrote a series of historical novels which Waugh praised and encouraged.

Fielding, Daphne. See Vivian.

Fleming, Ann (1913–). Ann Charteris, granddaughter of the Earl of Wemyss, married in 1932 Baron O'Neill, who was killed in 1944; 1945–52 Viscount Rothermere; and in 1952 Ian Fleming, who created James Bond the next year and died in 1964. Though a cousin of Laura Waugh's and an acquaintance as Lady

Rothermere the political hostess, she became a close friend of Waugh's at the time she married Ian Fleming and he stayed with them in Jamaica. Stylish and witty, she was not in the least afraid of Waugh and when he used his large ear-trumpet more than seemed necessary she struck it with a spoon: 'The noise, Evelyn told me later, was that of a gun being fired an inch away'. *Evelyn Waugh* by Christopher Sykes, p. 374.

Green, Henry. See Yorke.

Greene, Graham (1904–   ). Novelist. A contemporary at Oxford but not then a friend. Described at the age of thirty-four by J.Maclaren-Ross in *Memoirs of the Forties*: '. . . his lean face was unlined then, but the skin was rough and a little worn; though his cheeks were carefully shaven, there was still a suggestion of stubble. He smiled a lot and the set of his mouth was amiable rather than severe as in the photographs.' Often bracketed with Waugh as a Roman Catholic convert successful in the same profession. Their friendship survived religious arguments, opposed political opinions and Greene's frequent absences, partly because they admired one another's books. Publications include *England Made Me* (1935), *Brighton Rock* (1938), *The Power and the Glory* (1940), *The Heart of the Matter* (1948), *The Comedians* (1970), plays, stories, essays and children's books.

Herbert family. Aubrey Herbert (1880–1923), the second son of the 4th Earl of Carnarvon and a Conservative MP who was offered the throne of Albania, married in 1910 Mary Vesey, daughter of Viscount de Vesci, and had four children: Gabriel (1911–   ), who married Alexander (Alick) Dru in 1943; Bridget (1914–   ), who married Captain Allister Edward Grant in 1935; Laura (1916–73), who married Evelyn Waugh in 1937; and Auberon (1922–74).

Heygate, John (1903–76). Writer. Succeeded as 4th baronet in 1940. Dim at Eton, where his father was a master, and Oxford where he was a contemporary of Waugh's. He resigned as Editor of the News when cited in Waugh's divorce case, because it was known that the BBC would not allow him to continue. Married to Evelyn Gardner 1930–6. Publications include *Decent Fellows*, a realistic novel of Eton life.

Kinross, Baron (1904–77). Writer. Patrick Balfour until he succeeded to the title in 1939. Married 1938–42 to Angela Culme-Seymour. An acquaintance at Oxford, on Waugh's last night he lowered him from a Balliol window on a rope. They became friends as fellow-journalists, particularly in Ethiopia where they were war correspondents. Kinross was Mr Gossip in the *Daily Sketch* and was in the R.A.F. during World War II. Waugh may have drawn on him for the Earl of Balcairn in *Vile Bodies*

and Lord Kilbannock in *Sword of Honour*. Nicknamed 'Pauper'. Publications include *Society Racket* (1933) and *Ataturk: The Rebirth of a Nation* (1964).

Lygon family. The children of the 7th Earl Beauchamp (1872–1938). Waugh knew Viscount Elmley, later Earl Beauchamp (1903–79) and his brother Hugh Lygon (1904–36) at Oxford. In 1931 he met the sisters: Lady Lettice Cotterell (1906–73), Lady Sibell Rowley (1907–   ) and his two great friends Lady Mary Lygon (1910–   ), who married 1939–56 H.H. Prince Vsevelode Joannovitch of Russia, and Lady Dorothy Lygon (1912–   ). Lady Mary was known to all as 'Maimie' and to Waugh as 'Blondy', Lady Dorothy as 'Coote' and to Waugh as 'Poll' or 'Pollen'. Richard Lygon (1916–70) lived with his mother after his father went into exile. Lady Mary was Waugh's main confidante in the 1930s. Laura Waugh, in a letter to her husband, described Lady Dorothy as 'the nicest of all your friends'.

McDougall, John (1903–76). Publisher. Contemporary, but not an acquaintance, at Oxford, where Waugh describes him as a member of 'the literary élite who formed a gentle, close set'. In 1946 joined Chapman & Hall, who published all Waugh's fiction, and became a friend for life.

Mitford, Diana (1910–   ). Married 1929–34 to Bryan Guinness, who succeeded as Baron Moyne in 1944; and to Sir Oswald Mosley, founder of the British Union of Fascists, from 1936. Both Mosleys were interned during World War II; since 1951 they have lived in France. A deep friendship with Waugh in the early 1930s lasted, though they rarely saw each other. Her only book is an unapologetic autobiography, *A Life of Contrasts* (1977).

Mitford, Nancy (1904–73). Novelist. Met Waugh through his first wife and was their lodger in Canonbury Square in 1929. Married 1933–58 Peter Rodd. Waugh knew her brother and sisters, in particular Diana, who became Lady Mosley, and 'Debo', who became Duchess of Devonshire. 'Her clear smooth skin and clear quizzical eyes under a high forehead with chestnut hair like a wavy turban above it would have been portrayed to perfection by Sir Joshua Reynolds. She appeared much younger than her age and her humour had the gaiety of girlhood.' Harold Acton in *Nancy Mitford*. After the war she moved to France and, as a result, became Waugh's main correspondent. An article in *Encounter* in 1955 with an answer from Waugh formed the basis of *Noblesse Oblige*, which started a vogue for the expressions 'U' and 'non-U' for social classification. She received much and ignored some advice on how to write; showed courage and remained witty and gay in her last illness. Publications include *The Pursuit of Love* (1945), *Love in a Cold Climate* (1949), *The Blessing* (1951) and *The Sun King* (1966).

Peters, Augustus Detlof (1892–1973). Married to Helen MacGregor. Set up his own literary agency in 1924, adding W.N.Roughead in 1927, Margaret Stephens in 1929. It still handles the Waugh estate. 'Easy to like, difficult to know,' Arthur Koestler has said. Alec Waugh found him 'reserved. He found it difficult to be encouraging.' But Evelyn Waugh was by no means the only one to whom he lent money.

Powell, Anthony (1905–). Novelist. Married 1934 Lady Violet Pakenham. An acquaintance of Waugh's at Oxford; 1927–35 worked for Duckworths, where he introduced Waugh, with the result that they published his first book *Rossetti: His Life and Works* (1928). Lifelong friend. Publications include 'The Music of Time' series of twelve novels 1951–75, and three volumes of memoirs: *To Keep the Ball Rolling*.

Rothermere, Lady. See Fleming.

Roughead, William Nicol (1905–75). A rugger blue at Oxford, 'Roughie' played for Scotland fourteen times, as captain on four of them. He was also an expert fly fisherman. Joined A.D.Peters in 1927 and on rejoining after the war became a partner.

Sykes, Christopher (1907–). Biographer of Waugh among others and novelist. A Roman Catholic, at Oxford after Waugh. In the Foreign Office 1928–31 and the Features Department of the BBC 1949–68. Publications include *Four Studies in Loyalty* (1946), *A Song of a Shirt* (1953) and *Evelyn Waugh* (1975).

Vivian, Daphne (1904–). Writer. Married 1926–53 to Viscount Weymouth, later Marquess of Bath; 1953–78 to Major Alexander Fielding. Publications include *Mercury Presides* (autobiography) (1954) and *The Duchess of Jermyn Street* (1964) a biography of Rosa Lewis.

Waugh, Alec (1898–). Writer and traveller. Married 1919–21 Barbara Jacobs, daughter of the writer W.W.Jacobs; 1932–69 Joan Chirnside, an Australian; and in 1969 Virginia Sorensen, an American writer of children's books. He published *The Loom of Youth* in 1917, when he was nineteen; it became a bestseller and by 1962 it had never been out of print, but had earned him less than £1000. As a result of this precocious success and his father's position, he entered the world of literature and journalism of the 1920s. In a projected second volume of autobiography, to be called *A Little Hope*, Evelyn wrote of this time: 'I have seldom shared his tastes either in friends or in women. My heart sinks when

a new acquaintance introduces himself as a friend of Alec's. But in the years of my poverty and obscurity I was constantly at his table.' Other publications include *Island in the Sun* (1956), *My Brother Evelyn and Other Portraits* (1961), *The Early Years of Alec Waugh* (1962) and *The Best Wine Last* (more autobiography) (1978).

Waugh, Arthur (1866–1943). Married Catherine Raban in 1893. Competent in most literary spheres, an excellent publisher. Alan Pryce-Jones in *Evelyn Waugh and his World* writes: 'A pessimist, an asthmatic, a rather shy man, as I remember him, who offset these disadvantages by extreme joviality. He was a play-actor by nature, taking up one part after another: the martyr, the businessman, the man of instant decision, the amateur comedy star. He excelled at paper-games, and fancied himself as a lyric writer after the school of W.S.Gilbert.' He retired as Director of Chapman & Hall in 1929. Publications include *One Man's Road* (1931), an autobiography in which he does not mention *Decline and Fall* or *Vile Bodies*.

Waugh, Catherine (Raban). Born in India, brought up by maiden aunts in Somerset. In *A Little Learning* Evelyn writes: 'My mother was small, neat, reticent and, until her last decade, very active. She had no special literary interests, but read a book a fortnight, always a good one ... I associate her less with lilies than with earthy wash-leather gloves and baskets of globe artichokes and black and red currants.' Evelyn tried to be patient with her after his father's death, but did not always succeed.

Waugh family. Evelyn Waugh (1903–66) married Laura Herbert in 1937 and had seven children: Teresa (1938–) married Professor John D'Arms in 1961; Auberon (1939–) married Lady Teresa Onslow in 1961; Mary born and died 1940; Margaret (1942–) married Giles FitzHerbert 1962; Harriet (1944–); James (1946–) married Rachel Green in 1976; and Septimus (1950–) married Nicola Worcester in 1976.

Yorke, Henry (1905–73). Novelist under the pseudonym Henry Green 'His movements like his voice were indolent, one had the impression that he should have been eating grapes, but at the same time his half-closed eyes missed nothing.' J.Maclaren-Ross in *Memoirs of the Forties*. In the 1920s he and Waugh admired one another's writing greatly, but Waugh's admiration waned. Yorke spent the war in the ranks of the Auxiliary Fire Service. Managing Director of H.Pontifex & Co., an engineering company in Birmingham, he published nothing after 1952. Publications include *Living* (1929), *Party Going* (1939) and *Loving* (1945).

Index